CONTRACT LAW

AUSTRALIA
Law Book Co.
Sydney

CANADA and USA
Carswell
Toronto

HONG KONG
Sweet & Maxwell Asia

NEW ZEALAND
Brookers
Wellington

SINGAPORE and MALAYSIA
Sweet & Maxwell Asia
Singapore and Kuala Lumpur

CONTRACT LAW

Sweet & Maxwell's Textbook Series

1st edition

Robert Duxbury, LL.B (Hons), Barrister
*Principal Lecturer in Law, Nottingham Law School,
Nottingham Trent University*

THOMSON

SWEET & MAXWELL

First edition 2008
by Robert Duxbury

Published in 2008 by
Sweet & Maxwell Limited of
100 Avenue Road, London NW3 3PF
(http://www.sweetandmaxwell.co.uk)
Typeset by Servis Filmsetting Ltd, Stockport, Cheshire
Printed in Great Britain by
Ashford Colour Press, Gosport, Hants

No natural forests were destroyed to make the product;
only farmed timber was used and replanted

A C.I.P. catalogue
record for this book
is available from
the British Library

ISBN: 9781847031273

CONTENTS

PREFACE

The writing of this book stems from a desire on my part to write a text based upon many years of experience teaching the law of contract at degree level. I do so fully conscious of the fact that there are already many excellent books on the topic, some of them being of great authority. But some of these works are, in my view, too detailed for the needs of the typical undergraduate or conversion course student who will be looking for a text that covers the fundamentals of the subject in a straightforward way, and which is not excessively technical or theoretical. At the same time, they will require a work that approaches the law in a critical manner with an eye to its future development.

I have placed some emphasis on a discussion of the case law in contract. Not only is this a rich source of learning on the subject but it enables the novice student to acquire a grasp of the case law method that is one of the basic tools of the lawyer. The statutory and regulatory law that is becoming increasingly prominent in contract is also analysed in depth. Given that readers are likely to be new to the law, whether law students or, for example, business students, I have included a glossary of some of the more commonly encountered technical (and not so technical) legal terms in contract. At the end of each chapter, I have indicated further reading which I hope readers may find beneficial and of interest.

With regard to the coverage of the book, I have tried to concentrate on those topics which are common to the majority of degree courses on contract and those which, from my own experience, I know students find challenging. The familiar contours of the subject have changed in recent years not only because of the growing significance of European Union law but also as a result of a number of important decisions of the Court of Appeal and House of Lords. I have attempted to give due prominence to these developments. In dealing with case law in this book, for the sake of consistency I use the term "claimant" to refer to the party bringing proceedings whether the case was decided before or after the introduction of the Civil Procedure Rules. As readers may be aware, the rules substituted the expression "claimant" for "plaintiff".

I would like to express my thanks to the many people who have helped me in one way or another in the preparation of this book, especially the publishing team at Sweet and Maxwell. Writing a book is a deeply anti-social activity and the greatest debt of gratitude is owed to my wife, Jenny, who has endured this (and other publishing ventures) with much greater tolerance and understanding than I have any right to expect! I would like to dedicate the book to my father, John M Duxbury, who was recently commended by the Solicitors' Regulation Authority for being admitted to the roll of solicitors for over 70 years.

Robert Duxbury, Nottingham Law School, January 2008

GLOSSARY

Anticipatory breach A breach of contract occurring before performance is due where one party indicates to the other that they do not intend to perform their obligations under the contract. In such circumstances the innocent party has the right to "accept" the breach and sue for damages immediately or await the date of performance and hold the other party to the contract.

Appellant A party who appeals to a superior court with jurisdiction to hear appeals such as the Court of Appeal or House of Lords.

Bailment The transfer of possession, but not ownership, of goods from the owner (the "bailor") to another party (the "bailee") for a specific purpose, such as in a contract of hire or where goods are delivered for repair. Bailment may be contractual (a "bailment for reward") or purely gratuitous such as where goods are lent to a friend.

Bill of exchange A bill of exchange is a form of "negotiable instrument" (see below). Such bills are defined by the Bills of Exchange Act 1882, s.3 as "an unconditional order in writing, addressed by one person [the 'drawer'] to another [the 'drawee'], signed by the person giving it, requiring the person to whom it is addressed to pay on demand or at a fixed and determinable future time a sum certain in money to or to the order of a specified person [the 'payee'], or to bearer." Bills of exchange facilitate the transfer of an enforceable right to a sum of money from one person to another; they are also "negotiable" in that where the bill is transferred to a party who takes in good faith and for value (a "holder in due course") they take free of any defect in title of the transferor. A cheque is a bill of exchange drawn on a bank.

Bill of lading A document effecting the transfer of title of goods shipped by sea, under which the master of the ship undertakes to deliver the goods of the shipper ("consignor") to a party named in it (usually the "consignee"), on payment of freight. A bill of lading also embodies the terms of the contract of carriage and acts as a receipt for the goods from the master to the consignor. Although transferable by endorsement and delivery, a bill of lading is not a negotiable instrument, so that the transferee receives no better title than the transferor. The relevant law is contained in the Carriage of Goods by Sea Acts.

Charterparty A written contract for the hire of a ship by the hirer (the "charterer") from the shipowner. The hiring may either be for a particular voyage (a "voyage charter") or for a specified period of time (a "time charter") and the usual purpose of the hire is for the carriage of goods. Normally the shipowner retains possession and control of the ship subject to the charterer's instruction but in a "charterparty by way of demise" the contract operates as a lease with the charterer becoming for the time being shipowner.

c.i.f. ("Cost, insurance, freight") A type of contract for the sale of goods overseas where the seller takes responsibility for shipment by entering into a contract of carriage by sea. The seller must ensure delivery of the goods at the port of destination and insure the goods whilst in transit for the benefit of the buyer. The seller must deliver up an invoice, the bill of lading (see above) and the insurance policy. The buyer must accept the documents and pay the price on delivery. The goods are usually at the buyer's risk as from shipment. (Cf "f.o.b." below).

Claimant, plaintiff The party bringing civil proceedings, e.g. for breach of contract.

Constructive notice Knowledge that is imputed to a person even if they are ignorant of the actual facts, where the circumstances are such that a person of ordinary prudence would have discovered the facts.

Contra proferentem A rule of construction that any ambiguities in a document are construed narrowly against the drafter, commonly applied in the construction of exclusion and limitation clauses.

Conversion The tort of wrongfully dealing with another person's goods, i.e. in a manner inconsistent with the rights of the owner.

Counterclaim A claim in civil proceedings raised by a defendant against a claimant in response to that party's claim.

Damages A sum of money awarded by a court to compensate the claimant for loss or damage, e.g. as a result of a breach of contract. As a general rule, damages in contract are designed to put the innocent party in the position they would be in had the contract been properly performed.

Defendant The party against whom civil (or criminal) proceedings are brought.

Del credere agent An agent instructed to sell goods on behalf of a principal who guarantees that the principal will receive all moneys due from the buyer, usually in return for a higher commission.

Demurrage A liquidated sum payable to the charterer where a ship is detained in port beyond the number of days specified in the charterparty ("lay days").

Estoppel A rule of evidence that prevents a person from denying the truth of a statement they have made and upon which another has relied. It is usually a requirement that the person relying on the statement has altered their position on the faith of the statement.

f.o.b ("Free on board") A type of contract for the sale of goods overseas where, in the classic case, it is the seller's duty is to see that the goods are on loaded on board ship, whereas it is the buyer's responsibility to arrange for the shipping of the goods and to insure them. The risk normally passes to the buyer when the goods are loaded on board ship. (Cf "c.i.f. above).

Injunction An order of the court either prohibiting a party from doing an act (a "prohibitory" injunction) or ordering a party to carry out an act (a "mandatory" injunction). As an equitable remedy, an injunction will only be granted at the discretion of the court and will not be granted if damages would be an adequate remedy. An "interim" injunction is one granted temporarily in an amergency.

Laches Unreasonable delay or neglect in bringing proceedings to enforce a right. It may operate to debar a claim. Where there is a statutory limitation period, however, a claim can be brought at any time up to the expiry of that period.

Licence In relation to land, a permission to enter or occupy land but which, unlike a lease, does not usually confer any estate or interest in the land or any right of exclusive possession. A licence may be contractual or gratuitous.

Lien A right to retain possession of the property of another person as security for the performance of an obligation by that other person. Thus a repairer of goods may retain them until paid by the owner and, in some circumstances, an unpaid seller of goods has a lien over them.

Negotiable instrument A document containing an obligation to pay a sum of money which upon delivery to another person gives that person the right to sue upon it in their own name. Providing the transferee takes bona fide and for value, they receive a good title, free of any defects affecting the transferor's title. It is this quality that is referred to as "negotiability". Negotiable instruments include bills of exchange and promissory notes.

Promissory note A signed document containing an unconditional promise by one person to pay a sum of money to (or to the order of) a specified person or the bearer (Bills of Exchange Act 1882, s.83). The note is either payable on demand or at some fixed or determinable future time. Promissory notes are negotiable instruments (see above). A bank note is effectively a promissory note issued by a bank promising to pay the bearer the sum of money specified on the note.

Quantum meruit An action on a quantum meruit ("as much as he deserves") may be brought to recover reasonable remuneration for work done and materials provided.

Repudiation An indication by words or conduct that a party does not intend to be bound by a contract.

Rescission The setting aside of a contract either by the court (or by one of the parties) e.g. for misrepresentation. The aim of rescission is to put the parties back in the position they were in before the contract.

Respondent The party against whom an appeal is brought in an appellate court.

Restitution A legal process whereby money or property is restored to the person entitled to possession of it, with the aim of preventing unjust enrichment.

Set-off The right to deduct money already owed from a claim. Thus if A owes B £1,000 and B brings an action to recover that sum, A may "set-off" an existing debt whereby B owes A £500, so that B recovers only £500.

Specific performance An order of the court compelling the performance of a contract. The remedy is something of an exception and will not be ordered where damages are an adequate remedy; it is an equitable remedy and at the discretion of the court.

Strict liability Liability without fault. Contractual liability is said to be strict in the sense that contract-breaker is liable for breach even though there may be no fault or negligence on his part.

Tort A civil wrong entitling the victim to redress, e.g. damages or an injunction, other than a wrong that is purely a breach of contract. The most commonly encountered tort is negligence.

Ultra vires ("Beyond the powers") An ultra vires act is one outside the powers conferred upon the body exercising it, and therefore invalid. An example is a contract entered into by a local authority in excess of its statutory powers.

Vitiating factor A factor affecting the validity of a contract, such as misrepresentation; mistake; duress and undue influence; and illegality.

Void contract A contract that is void has no legal effect at all, for example where it is entered into under an operative mistake. The transaction is null and void from the beginning ("ab initio").

Voidable contract A voidable contract does have legal effect, but one party may have the right to avoid it, for example, where they are the victim of an actionable misrepresentation by the other party. Thus the contract is valid until avoided.

TABLE OF CASES

TABLE OF STATUTES

TABLE OF STATUTORY INSTRUMENTS

Chapter 1

INTRODUCTION TO THE LAW OF CONTRACT

What is a contract?

It is quite likely that the first question that students new to the law of contract are asked by their tutor is: "What is a contract?" Many will answer by saying that a contract is a legally binding agreement. This is, of course, correct. But when a further question is asked, namely, "what do we mean by 'legally binding?'", some misconceptions may be revealed. It may be suggested that a contract, to be binding, should be in writing or that it must be signed by the parties. These things are certainly true of some transactions, the formation of which is regulated by statute (see para.5–003), but as we shall see, they are not general requirements.

When we say that a contract is a legally binding agreement, we mean that it generates rights and obligations that can be enforced by legal action in the courts. The usual way of enforcing the agreement is by an action for monetary compensation ("damages") and it is only in particular types of transaction that the courts will compel actual performance. The breach of a contract for the sale of land is an example. Here the remedy of specific performance may be ordered, on the basis that each piece of land is regarded as unique. But in the usual case the contract is "enforced" by the contract-breaking party compensating the innocent party, so far as money will do it, for the losses caused by breaching the contract.

Having the right to sue for breach of contract is one thing, but actually bringing legal action is quite another. For example, the breach might be trivial and easily resolved—legal action might needlessly antagonise the other party, a party upon whom one's business might be commercially dependent. And of course, litigation may be risky, expensive and time-consuming. In some cases, the possession of the right to sue for breach of contract may be sufficient to persuade the other party into compliance. A retail contract for the sale of goods is an example, where the Sale of Goods Act 1979 places "implied terms" into the contract to the effect that the goods shall be of satisfactory quality and fit for purpose, and these rights cannot be contracted out of as against a consumer. It will often be possible to resolve such disputes without recourse to litigation.

Contracts are ubiquitous. In order to live, people must daily enter into contracts to acquire goods and services. On any given day, most citizens will enter into a number of contracts—they may take a train or bus to work and buy food and drink or other goods. They will no doubt be subject to longer term transactions: at work they will be under a contract of employment; they may be occupying their home under a lease or buying it on a mortgage; they may be buying a car under a loan agreement and they will, of course, have entered into transactions for utilities at their place of residence for such essentials as gas, electricity and water supplies. And they may be students paying for tuition and accommodation at university. The concept of contract is

1–001

1–002

therefore not merely essential for the smooth functioning of business and commerce but it underpins society itself. The prevalence of contract illustrates another fundamental point—as a legal subject, contract is of great significance. It lies at the heart of many other legal topics including the law of property, commercial law, consumer law and the law of employment; and it is very closely related to another great common law subject, the law of torts.

The "law of contract" may be described, therefore, as a body of rules relating to the enforceability of agreements between members of society, and the remedies available for the failure to fulfil those agreements.

The classical doctrine: "freedom of contract"

1–003   Many of the principles of modern English contract law were developed by the courts in the eighteenth and nineteenth centuries under the prevailing "classical" doctrine of freedom (or sanctity) of contract. Under this theory, the parties are free to enter into whatever transactions they wish with a minimum of interference by the state or the courts. Once they have entered their agreement, however, they are strictly bound even if the contract proves to be disadvantageous to one of the parties. It is not seen to be the function of the law to protect the parties to a contract from the consequences of a "bad" bargain. The parties are considered to be the best judges of what is in their interests and regulation by the courts should only occur where, for example, there is serious wrongdoing such as fraud or illegality. This doctrine owed much to the philosophy known as "laissez-faire" with its emphasis on the freedom of the individual.

Although the theory of freedom of contract may be acceptable between, for example, experienced business people bargaining on equal terms, it breaks down where there is inequality of bargaining power. Many people enter contracts from a position of relative weakness or vulnerability—tenants, employees and consumers are obvious examples—and it has now become accepted that the law must play its part in protecting their interests. This has been achieved, in the twentieth century, by a progressive intervention into certain types of contractual relationships both by the courts, in judicial decisions, and by Parliament, through legislation. The position of what we nowadays refer to as the "consumer" in sales of goods contracts is a good illustration of this process.

As far back as 1893 (in the Sale of Goods Act) the law placed implied terms into contracts for the sale of goods made in the course of a business to the effect that the goods should be of merchantable quality and fit for their intended purpose. However, businesses exercised their rights of freedom of contract to exclude those liabilities in non-negotiated "standard form" contracts. These are contracts drawn up in advance by the stronger party—often containing many paragraphs of small print—which the consumer has no realistic opportunity but to accept. It is a case of "take it or leave it" and the problem is compounded by the fact that suppliers across an industry may adopt substantially the same terms; there is, therefore, little real freedom of choice. The courts developed various doctrines to counter such standardised exemptions in individual cases but it was not until the 1970s that legislation was introduced to render invalid attempts to exclude liability, as against a consumer, for the quality and fitness of the goods sold. Similar protection was extended to consumers entering into other types of contract, including hire-purchase transactions and contracts for the supply of goods and services. The relevant provisions are now contained in the Unfair Contract Terms Act 1977, a measure which regulates and restricts the use of exclusion clauses not only as against consumers but also between businesses. The Act of 1977 treats some types of exclusion clause as being of no effect whilst others must, in order to be valid, satisfy a requirement of reasonableness; that is, the clause must be a fair and reasonable one to be included in the circumstances.

Despite these interventions, it would be wrong to suppose that the classical theory of freedom of contract does not exert a considerable influence over the law of contract even today. Many of its fundamental principles continue to survive. It has been observed that:

> "The principle of sanctity of contract is a thread which runs through contract from beginning to end, enjoining the courts to be ever-vigilant in ensuring that established and new doctrines do not become an easy exit from bad bargains".[1]

Contemporary influences on contract law

There are influences upon English contract law deriving from international sources. The United Kingdom's membership of the European Union has had a significant impact on the development of the law, especially in the area of consumer transactions. **1–004**

The principal European measure to be transposed into domestic contract law to date is the Directive on Unfair Terms in Consumer Contracts.[2] The Directive was initially implemented in 1994 by a set of government regulations, the Unfair Terms in Consumer Contracts Regulations, but these regulations were updated in 1999.[3] The provisions seek to regulate unfair terms in standard form contracts between sellers or suppliers on the one hand and consumers on the other. An unfair term will not be binding on the consumer—the test of unfairness is linked to the European civil law concept of "good faith", a notion that has hitherto only played a minor role in English contract law. Another European measure that has been implemented in national law is Directive 97/7/EC for the protection of consumers purchasing at a distance, such as by telephone, email or the internet.[4]

In addition to the adoption of these piecemeal measures, there have been moves to harmonise contract law in the member states of the European Union. As part of this movement, the Lando Commission has published a set of *Principles of European Contract Law* which seek to resolve some of the differences of approach between English common law and European civil law.[5] These principles do not have the force of law but they might point the way towards a European "Contract Code" which could be binding in member states at some time in the future, subject to agreement between member states.[6]

Another potential influence on domestic contract law is the European Convention on Human Rights (ECHR). The Human Rights Act 1998, which came into force on October 2, 2000, incorporates the provisions of the E.C.H.R. into the domestic law of the United Kingdom. Under the Act of 1998, the rights and fundamental freedoms set out in the Convention and its protocols are defined as "Convention rights", and so far as it is possible to do so, primary and subordinate legislation must be read and given effect in a way which is compatible with

---

[1] Adams and Brownsword, *Understanding Contract Law* 5th edn, (Oxford, Clarendon Press, 1979) p.197.

[2] (93/113/EC).

[3] SI 1999/2083, coming onto force on October 1, 1999. The regulations are discussed at para.7–064.

[4] The relevant provisions are contained in the Consumer Protection (Distance Selling) Regulations 2000 (SI 2000/2334), as amended. The regulations are considered at para.5–005. Further, Directive 2000/31/EC on electronic contracts has been implemented by Electronic Commerce (EC Directive) Regulations 2002 (SI 2002/2013) – see para.2–051.

[5] See Lando and Beale, *Principles of European Contract Law* Parts 1 and II, (2000) Kluwer Law International; and Lando, *Principles of European Contract Law* Part III, (2003) Kluwer Law International.

[6] See Staudenmayer, *A More Coherent European Contract Law – the European Commission's Action Plan on Contract Law* (2003) 100 L.S.G. 28.

Convention rights (s.3(1)). This provision does not give the courts a power to strike down primary legislation that is incompatible with the rights of the Convention but they may make a "declaration of incompatibility" where legislation is in conflict with Convention rights (s.4(2)). In *Wilson v Secretary of State for Trade and Industry*,[7] the Court of Appeal declared that s.127(3) of the Consumer Credit Act 1974 was incompatible, so far as the creditor's rights were concerned, with Art.6(1) and Art.1 of the First Protocol of the ECHR. These provisions respectively guarantee the right to a fair trial in determining a person's civil rights and obligations, and entitle every natural or legal person to the peaceful enjoyment of their possessions. The House of Lords did not agree as the events and cause of action had arisen before the Act of 1998 came into force. Although their Lordships did not consider that the relevant provision was incompatible, the case signals that similar challenges may be mounted in the future.[8]

1–005   There are wider international influences on contract law. These include the International Institution for the Unification of Private Law (UNIDROIT) which in 1994 produced a set of uniform principles of contract law, the *Principles of International Commercial Contracts*. The principles may be adopted by the parties in any jurisdiction but, as with the *Principles of European Contract Law* (to which reference was made above), the principles do not have the force of law. Nevertheless, they are likely to inform the future development of the law.

It should be noted that the law of contract of this country has been followed in other common law jurisdictions, in parts of the English-speaking world and in Commonwealth countries. This may mean that where there is no English authority on a particular legal problem, reference is sometimes made to persuasive precedents of, for example, the courts of the United States or Australia. As we shall see, this process has occurred in particular when dealing with the formation of contracts.

Classification of contracts

1–006   One way of classifying contracts is to distinguish between promises which are contained in a deed and agreements that are "simple contracts".

Deeds

1–007   The concept of a deed is of ancient origin and it signifies an obligation that is binding merely because of the form in which it is made – its binding effect does not rest on agreement at all.[9] Historically, a deed had to be "signed, sealed and delivered" but in modern times the sealing and delivery were loosely interpreted by the courts and sealing is no longer necessary where the deed is executed by an individual. It is now the requirement in such cases that the deed should be signed, witnessed and delivered. "Delivery" now means little more than that the person executing the document evinces an intention to be bound by it – it does not necessarily involve any physical transfer. Deeds do not require to be supported by "consideration" which, as we shall see, is one of the essential elements of a binding simple contract (para.4–001). Certain types of transaction must be effected by deed, the most common example being the transfer of the legal estate in land, although any transaction can be put into the form of a deed if the parties so wish.[10]

---

[7] The case is more fully discussed at para.5–004.
[8] See also *Shanshal v Al-Kishtaini [2001]* EWCA Civ 264.
[9] *Hall v Palmer* (1844) 3 Hare. 532.
[10] See the discussion at para.5–002.

Simple contracts

Agreements not contained in a deed but which nevertheless are legally binding (according to the criteria to be discussed in Chapters 2–4 of this book) are known as "simple contracts". A simple contract does not need any formalities in order to be binding—it can be made in writing or be purely oral or it can be implied from conduct. Indeed, a great many everyday transactions take place with the minimum of formalities or even communication. A person buying a newspaper from a news vendor's stand is an example. The customer may pick up the paper and hand over the correct money, nothing at all may be said and there will probably be no receipt given. But, viewed objectively, it is perfectly obvious that a binding contract for the sale of goods is taking place. The purchase of goods from a coin-operated automatic machine is another example. Of course, there will be situations where, from the standpoint of proof or evidence, it is desirable that the contract should be recorded in writing and there are some contracts where this is a legal requirement (see para.5–003) but writing is not a general requirement for a simple contract.

1–008

There are certain essential elements which must be in place for a valid and binding simple contract to come in to existence. First, the parties must have reached agreement. Whether they have done so is ascertained objectively and the usual formula for establishing this is "offer and acceptance"—this involves asking whether one party made an offer to the other which that other has unequivocally accepted.[11] Secondly, for the agreement to be valid, its terms must be expressed with a reasonable degree of certainty. If the terms are too vague or ambiguous and there are no criteria upon which the court can infer the terms of the agreement, the contract may fail. Thirdly, the parties must intend to enter into legal relations. In commercial transactions, for example, there is a strong but rebuttable presumption that the parties intend to be contractually bound, but in the social and domestic sphere, the presumption is the other way. The law recognises that some agreements are not intended by the parties to be attended by legal consequences—a social invitation is an example.[12] Finally, a promise, to be binding as a contract, must be supported by consideration. A purely gratuitous promise made by one party in the other party's favour is not binding—the other party must have given (or promised) something of value in return. Thus a contract in English law is a *bargain*. In the example of the sale of a newspaper given above, both parties provide consideration, the seller delivers the goods and the buyer pays the price.[13]

Another way of categorising contracts is according to whether they are "unilateral" or "bilateral". The distinction is of particular relevance in the formation of contracts.

Unilateral contracts

In what is often referred to as a "unilateral contract", one party promises to do something in return for an act by the other party, e.g. where A issues an advertisement promising a reward of £100 to anyone who will find his lost dog. The essence of the transaction is that only one party, A, is obliged to do anything. No one is bound to search for the lost animal, but if B, having seen the offer, finds the dog and returns it, B is entitled to the reward. As Diplock L.J. observed in *United Dominions Trust (Commercial) Ltd v Eagle Aircraft Services Ltd*,[14]

1–009

[11] Offer and acceptance is examined in Chapter 2.
[12] Certainty and intention are considered in Chapter 3.
[13] For consideration, see Chapter 4.
[14] [1968] 1 W.L.R. 74.

"a unilateral contract of itself never gives rise to any obligation upon the promisee to do or refrain from doing anything."

Unilateral contracts often involve offers made to the world at large, as in the famous case of *Carlill v Carbolic Smoke Ball Company* (discussed at para.2–007 below) where the company offered a reward to anyone who caught influenza after using their medical preparation, the "Carbolic Smoke Ball". The company was held to be bound to pay the promised reward. But a unilateral offer may be made to an individual or to a specific group of persons. Thus if A says to B, "I will pay you £20 if you wash my car tomorrow", A has made a promise, the fulfilment of which is conditional on the performance of an act by B, and the contract might well be categorised as unilateral. But if B were to reply to A's offer by saying, "OK" or "Yes, I will" the contract will probably not be unilateral but fall into the bilateral category, as explained below.

Bilateral contracts

1–010   In a bilateral contract[15] a promise by one party is exchanged for a promise by the other. The exchange of the promises is sufficient to render them both enforceable; thus in a contract for the sale of goods, the buyer promises to pay the price and the seller promises to deliver the goods. Once they have reached agreement, both parties are contractually bound with each party being simultaneously a promisor and a promisee.

Introduction to the law of contract: conclusion

1–011   This chapter will be concluded by briefly outlining the format of this book.

Up to a point, we follow the life of a contract from inception to determination, beginning with the formation of the contract—how it is brought into existence and what elements it must contain in order to be legally binding (Chapters 2–5). The terms of the contract, with particular reference to clauses excluding or restricting liability will be examined in Chapters 6 and 7. The position of third parties under the doctrine of Privity of Contract is discussed in Chapter 8.

The way in which contracts are brought to an end—the "discharge" of contracts—is then considered (in Chapters 9 and 10) followed by five chapters dealing with so-called "vitiating factors". These are factors which may affect the validity of a contract: misrepresentation; mistake; duress and undue influence; and illegality (Chapters 11–14). Contracts in restraint of trade are considered separately in Chapter 15.

The book is concluded by two chapters examining remedies. Remedies I (Chapter 16) considers damages for breach of contract. Remedies II (Chapter 17) addresses further remedies including equitable remedies and restitution. The limitation of actions is discussed at the end of this chapter.

Further reading

Adams and Brownsword, *The Ideologies of Contract* (1987) 7 L.S. 205.
Atiyah, *The Rise and Fall of Freedom of Contract* (Oxford: Clarendon Press, 1979).

---

[15] In *Hong Kong Fir Shipping Co Ltd v Kawasaki Kisen Kaisha* [1962] 2 Q.B. 26, Diplock L.J. preferred the term "synallagmatic" to bilateral. This is in recognition of the fact that such a contract may have more than two parties.

Chapter 2

OFFER AND ACCEPTANCE

As already observed in the preceding chapter, a simple contract will only be enforceable if the parties have reached agreement. How does the law ascertain whether the parties have reached agreement? The usual formula for determining the issue is to ask whether one party has made an offer to enter into a binding contract which the other has unequivocally accepted, thus *offer* plus *acceptance* equals *agreement*. Before considering the rules of offer and acceptance, it is necessary to examine the so-called "objective test".

2–001

The objective test

The test of whether the parties have reached agreement is said to be objective. This objective principle involves asking whether a reasonable person, observing what has been said, done or written by the parties would infer that they have reached agreement. The parties' real intentions, that is, their actual subjective state of mind, is of no relevance. Thus in *Smith v Hughes*[1] Blackburn J. famously asserted:

2–002

> "If, *whatever a man's real intention may be*, he so conducts himself that a reasonable man would believe that he was assenting to the terms proposed by the other party, and that other party upon that belief enters into the contract with him, the man thus conducting himself would be equally bound as if he had intended to agree to the other party's terms [Author's italics]."

In more modern times Lord Denning M.R., in *Storer v Manchester City Council*,[2] has expressed the principle thus:

> "In contracts you do not look into the actual intent in a man's mind. You look at what he said and did. A contract is formed where there is, to all outward appearances, a contract. A man cannot get out of a contract by saying: 'I did not intend to contract', if by his words he has done so."

This emphasis on objectivity has not always prevailed. Historically, the courts required true consent, so that there would be no contract unless the minds of the two parties were

---

[1] (1871) LR 6 QB 597. The case itself is discussed at para.12–025.
[2] [1974] 3 All E.R. 824.

as one. This requirement of a "meeting of the minds", which is elegantly termed in legal Latin as a *consensus ad idem*, is an essentially subjective approach. Towards the end of the nineteenth century, the objective principle assumed ascendancy in cases relating to the formation of contract although *consensus* theory is clearly evident in a case on formation of contract where there was a mistake as to identity, *Cundy v Lindsay*[3] decided by the House of Lords in 1878.

There are variations in the judicial approach to objectivity. In some cases the reasonable person is the detached third party observer, the "fly on the wall"—this is perhaps what most people would understand by an objective test. In other cases, the assessment of intention is either made from the standpoint of the reasonable offeror or from that of the reasonable offeree.[4] In *Smith v Hughes*, for example, the court seems to have adopted the latter approach, as the above-mentioned quotation of Blackburn J indicates (the case itself is discussed at para.12–025). Subjectivity is not entirely excluded by the courts, however. Where the offeror makes a mistake as to the terms of the proposed contract, for example, as to the way the goods in a contract of sale are priced, the offeree may not validly accept the offer if they *actually knew* or ought reasonably to have known that the offeror was mistaken.[5] Of course, in many cases, the parties will be in agreement both objectively *and* subjectively in the sense that they are effectively of one mind as far as their intentions are concerned. But this subjective element has long ceased to be a general requirement for a binding contract.

2–003   The main advantage of the objective test is certainty. It is obviously a lot easier to ascertain the outward appearance of a person's conduct than their inward mental intent at the particular time of entering an alleged agreement. Indeed, to ascertain reliably the latter is impossible, particularly since when the matter comes before a court, the parties will be in dispute and may be tempted to tailor their recollections to suit their own interests. But the objective principle can operate harshly. For example, the courts have laid down a strict rule that a person who signs a contractual document is bound by its terms whether or not they have understood the document, or whether or not they have even read it.[6] The rule was applied in *Galbraith v Mitchenall Estates Ltd.*[7] Without reading the document, the claimant signed a contract with the defendants in the mistaken belief that it was a hire-purchase agreement under which he would ultimately acquire ownership of a caravan. It was in fact a contract of hire for a term of five years but the defendants had not misrepresented the effect of the document nor acted improperly in any other way. The claimant fell into arrears with the rental payments and, relying on the terms of the contract, the defendants repossessed the caravan and retained the initial payment of £550. The value of the caravan was approximately £800. The claimant sought to recover the initial payment. The action failed—it was held by Sachs J. that the claimant was bound by the agreement despite, as the court acknowledged, the undue harshness of its terms.

---

[3] (1878) 3 App Cas 459; the case is discussed at para.12–030.
[4] For an analysis, see Howarth (1984) 100 L.Q.R. 265. The terminology used refers to "detached objectivity"; "promisor objectivity"; and "promisee objectivity".
[5] *Hartog v Colin & Shields* [1939] 3 All E.R. 566 (the case is discussed at para.12–024). Cf *Centrovincial Estates Plc v Merchant Investors Assurance Co Ltd* [1983] Com LR 158, also discussed at para.12–024. The latter case is a good illustration of the objective approach. See further the cases involving agreements to abandon arbitration clauses: *Paal Wilson & Co A/S v Partenreederei Hannah Blumenthal, The Hannah Blumenthal* [1983] 1 A.C. 854; and *Allied Marine Transport Ltd v Vale do Rio doce Navegacao SA, The Leonidas D* [1985] 1 W.L.R. 925.
[6] *L'Estrange v Graucob* [1934] 2 K.B. 394. The case is discussed at para.7–004.
[7] [1965] 2 Q.B. 473.

Judicial approaches to agreement

The analysis of agreement in terms of offer and acceptance, objectively ascertained, has the   **2–004**
merit of certainty and predictability. But it has been seen as inflexible, and in some cases the
rules of offer and acceptance, if applied mechanically, can produce a questionable result. Under
the rules there may appear in a particular case to be no concluded contract but common sense
may suggest otherwise. Therefore the courts on occasion feel required to "find" an offer and
acceptance in cases where there is undoubtedly agreement but the facts are difficult to support
in terms of that analysis. This was recognised by Lord Wilberforce in *New Zealand Shipping Co
Ltd v A M Satterthwaite & Co Ltd, The Eurymedon*[8] when he said:

> "English law, having committed itself to a rather technical and schematic doctrine of con-
> tract, in application takes a practical approach, often at the cost of forcing the facts to fit
> uneasily into the marked slots of offer, acceptance and consideration."

Relying on this statement, Lord Denning M.R. in *Butler Machine Tool Co Ltd v Ex-Cell-O
Corp*[9] favoured an expansive approach whereby all the correspondence and documents passing
between the parties should be examined so as to glean from them, or from the conduct of the
parties, whether agreement has been reached on all the material terms. His Lordship was to
repeat these sentiments in forceful terms in the Court of Appeal in the case of *Gibson v
Manchester City Council*.[10] The case was concerned with the issue of whether the council had
made an offer capable of acceptance to Mr Gibson for the sale of a council house. Lord
Denning M.R. said:

> "You should look at the correspondence as a whole and at the conduct of the parties and
> see therefrom whether the parties have come to an agreement on everything that was mate-
> rial. If by their correspondence and their conduct you can see an agreement on all the
> material terms – which was intended thenceforward to be binding – then there is a binding
> contract in law even though all the formalities have not been gone through."

This approach did not find favour on appeal to the House of Lords. The case involved an   **2–005**
exchange of correspondence between the parties (the facts are discussed at para.2–021) where
the successive communications were, other than the first, in reply to one another. Lord Diplock
considered that, although there may be exceptional cases which do not fit easily into the normal
analysis of offer and acceptance, the transaction which was before the court was not one of
them. His Lordship continued:

> "I can see no reason in the instant case for departing from the conventional approach of
> looking at the handful of documents relied upon as constituting the contract sued upon
> and seeing whether upon their true construction there is to be found in them a contractual
> offer by the corporation to sell the house to Mr Gibson and an acceptance of that offer by
> Mr Gibson. I venture to think that it was by departing from this conventional approach
> that the Court of Appeal was led into error."

[8] [1975] A.C. 154. The case is discussed at para.7–035.
[9] [1979] 1 All E.R. 965. The case is discussed at para.2–028.
[10] [1978] 1 W.L.R. 520.

An alternative approach was once again canvassed by the Court of Appeal in *G Percy Trentham Ltd v Archital Luxfer Ltd*.[11] Here the claimants T were main contractors employed to design and build some industrial units; and the defendants A were manufacturers and installers of aluminium screens and windows. As subcontractors, A carried out work for T installing these products and were paid. The parties had entered into negotiations to draw up a contract but no finally agreed contractual document was ever concluded. A dispute arose between whereby T alleged that A were in breach of contract but A denied the existence of a binding contract. At first instance the trial judge found that there was a binding contact in that A, by carrying out the works, had accepted T's offer. In effect, A had accepted by conduct (see para.2–037). The Court of Appeal agreed with the conclusion but not the reasoning of the court below.

Steyn L.J. (with whom the other members of the court agreed) considered that four matters were of importance in addressing the issue of contract formation in the case. First, the general approach to contract formation in English law is objective and the law "ignores the subjective expectations and unexpressed mental reservations of the parties." The criterion therefore was the reasonable expectations of honest men – in this case of sensible businessmen. Secondly, his Lordship considered that in the vast majority of cases the mechanism of contract formation will be the coincidence of offer and acceptance; this was particularly so in the case of a contract allegedly made by an exchange of correspondence. But it will not necessarily be the case in a contract alleged to have come into existence "during and as a result of performance". For this proposition Steyn L.J. cited, inter alia, the case *Brogden v Metropolitan Railway Co* (the case is discussed at para.2–037). Thirdly, the fact that a contract has been executed (i.e. the performance of the contract has been carried out) rather than executory was of primary importance as it will make it difficult to argue successfully that there was no intention to create legal relations or that the contract was void for uncertainty. His Lordship's fourth point was that if a contract only comes into existence during and as a result of performance of the transaction, it will frequently be possible to hold that the contract impliedly and retrospectively covers pre-contractual performance.[12]

2–006   Applying these principles to the case, the Court of Appeal held that there was a binding contract. Steyn L.J. said:

> "The judge analysed the matter in terms of offer and acceptance. I agree with his conclusion. But I am, in any event satisfied that in this fully executed transaction a contract came into existence during performance even if it cannot be precisely analysed in terms of offer and acceptance, and it does not matter that a contract came into existence after part of the work had been carried out and paid for. The conclusion must be that when the contract came into existence it impliedly governed pre-contractual performance."

His Lordship was satisfied that the parties intended to enter into legal relations and it was not a case where there was an understanding that a contract would only come into being if a written contract was concluded. The contemporary exchanges, and the carrying out of what was agreed in those exchanges, supported the view that there was a course of dealing between the parties. On T's side there was a right to performance of the work by A, and on A's side there was a right to be paid on the agreed basis.

---

[11] [1993] 1 Lloyd's Rep. 25.

[12] Steyn L.J. cited for this proposition the case of *Trollope & Colls Ltd v Atomic Power Construction Ltd* [1963] 1 W.L.R. 333.

Although Steyn L.J. acknowledged that the formation of the "vast majority" of contracts will continue to be tested by the existence of offer and acceptance, his approach to agreement in this case is similar to the judgment of Lord Denning M.R. in *Gibson v Manchester City Council* (discussed above) with its emphasis on the "correspondence as a whole" and the "conduct of the parties". But this formulation of Lord Denning was decisively rejected by the House of Lords in *Gibson*. It is doubtful therefore that *Trentham v Archital Luxfer* opens up an alternative "flexible" approach to contract formation, although it does perhaps clarify matters with regard to executed or partially executed transactions. But even here the notion that earlier actions can be governed retrospectively by a later contract could prove problematical in practice. The judge at first instance had found a contract through offer and acceptance and it is likely that many contracts that come into being through performance can be analysed on the basis that an acceptance takes place by conduct. This was certainly the case in *Brogden v Metropolitan Railway Co* (the facts are given at para.2-037), a case relied in by Steyn L.J. as involving a contract coming into being through performance.

We are now in a position to examine the classical rules of offer and acceptance.

THE OFFER

An "offer" may be defined as a statement of willingness to contract on specified terms made with the intention that, if accepted, it shall become a binding contract. The offer is made on the basis that, if accepted by the offeree, the offeror will be contractually bound and no further negotiation is envisaged.   **2–007**

An offer may take many forms—it may be express, such as where it is made orally or in writing, or it may be implied from conduct. An example of the latter is the past practice in some areas of coal merchants who would simply leave a bag of coal outside peoples' homes. If the householder took the coal inside, this was understood to amount to the acceptance of an offer and the merchant would return for payment. Similarly, it seems that when a bus travels along its route it is making an offer of carriage to passengers which is accepted when the passenger, by conduct, places himself either on the platform or inside the bus.[13]

An offer may be addressed to one particular person, to a group of persons or indeed to the world at large. This is what happened in the leading case of *Carlill v Carbolic Smoke Ball Company*.[14] In that case, the company, proprietors of a medical preparation, the "Carbolic Smoke Ball", issued advertisements in which they promised to pay a reward of £100 to any person who, having used one of their balls in the prescribed manner (inhalation three times a day for two weeks), contracted influenza. The company also stated in their advertisement that £1,000 had been deposited in the Alliance Bank, Regent Street, showing their sincerity in the matter. The claimant, Mrs Carlill, purchased such a ball and used it as prescribed but nevertheless contracted influenza. Hawkins J. upheld her claim for the reward and the company appealed.

Before the Court of Appeal, the defendant company raised a number of defences. Thus, it was said that the advertisement was advertisers' puff or "mere puff" meaning nothing at all—in modern parlance, a promotional gimmick designed to promote sales. However the Court considered that the deposit of the money in the bank negatived the suggestion that there was

---

[13] *Wilkie v London Passenger Transport Board* [1947] 1 All E.R. 258, obiter, per Lord Greene M.R.
[14] [1893] 1 Q.B. 256.

no intention to be legally bound. It was also contended that the promise of the reward was not binding because there had been no offer to a specific person and that it was not possible to contract with the whole world. Addressing this argument, Lindley L.J. said:

> "Now that point is common to the words of this advertisement and to the words of all other advertisements offering rewards. They are offers to anybody who performs the conditions named in the advertisement, and anybody who does perform the condition accepts the offer."

2–008   In other words, the contract thus concluded was of the "unilateral" type.[15] The defendants further suggested that there was no contract because Mrs Carlill had not communicated her acceptance to the company. Rejecting the argument, Bowen L.J. said that in advertisement cases, the inference is that the acceptor is not to notify his acceptance before he performs the condition, but if he performs the condition, notification is dispensed with. Thus in the unilateral contract, the offeror impliedly waives the need to communicate acceptance and acceptance occurs on the performance of the condition in the offer. Thus having used the smoke ball as prescribed, and having contracted influenza, Mrs Carlill was entitled to the reward.[16]

The *Carbolic Smoke Ball* case was relied on by the Court of Appeal in *Bowerman v Association of British Travel Agents Ltd*.[17] The Court held that the association had made a unilateral offer to prospective customers to provide protection in the event of the financial failure of one of its members. The offer was based on a notice published by ABTA and displayed in tour operators' offices. The offer was accepted by booking a holiday with an association member.[18]

Offer and invitation to treat

2–009   A genuine offer, as we have defined it above, must be distinguished from what the law refers to as an "invitation to treat". An invitation to treat is a statement that is, at most, inviting people to come forward and make an offer. The parties are still in negotiation—unlike the offer, there is no final intention to be bound, leaving the offeree with the choice of either acceptance or rejection. The distinction is not always easy and, as with many issues in the law of contract, it turns on the intentions of the parties, objectively ascertained. The use of the word "offer" or expressions such as "offer for sale" will not be decisive in determining the position.

The distinction between an offer and an invitation to treat has arisen in a number of areas which will be considered below.

Advertisements

2–010   We have seen, in the discussion of the *Carbolic Smoke Ball* case above, that an advertisement can amount to an offer. In that case a promise was made to the world at large that persons fulfilling

---

[15] Unilateral contracts are explained at para.1–009 above.

[16] The Court of Appeal also rejected the argument that the transaction was too vague or uncertain to be enforceable as a contract and that there was no consideration; see para.3–002 and para.4–001 below. For a fascinating account of the history and background of the case, see Simpson (1985) 14 J Legal Studies 345.

[17] [1996] C.L.C. 451.

[18] Hirst L.J., dissenting, considered that the ABTA notice was not worded sufficiently clearly enough to be promissory in nature. He considered that its intention was only to reassure the public.

certain conditions would be entitled to a reward. The offers contained in such advertisements lead to contracts that are unilateral in nature. The position would be the same where a reward was offered for the return of a lost dog or for information leading to the conviction of an offender.

What is the position, however, where a person simply advertises goods for sale in a newspaper or magazine? Such advertisements would, if the parties reach agreement, lead to bilateral contracts. These advertisements are normally construed as invitations to treat rather than offers.

In *Partridge v Crittenden*[19] the appellant placed an advertisement in the publication *Cage and Aviary Birds* stating, "Bramblefinch cocks, bramblefinch hens, 25s each." The advertisement was placed under the "classified" column and there was no direct use of the words "offer for sale". A reader, having seen the advertisement, wrote for a hen which the appellant sent to him. The appellant was charged with a criminal offence in that he had unlawfully offered for sale a wild bird contrary to s.6(1) of the Protection of Birds Act 1954. He was convicted by the justices. On appeal, his conviction was quashed by the Divisional Court on the ground that he had not offered the goods for sale because his advertisement was merely an invitation to treat.[20]

Equating the situation with the display of goods in a shop,[21] the court concluded that the insertion of such an advertisement in the form adopted under the title "Classified Advertisements" was simply an invitation to treat. Lord Parker C.J. said that when one was dealing with advertisements and circulars, there was business sense in their being construed as invitations to treat. He based this on what is sometimes called the "quantity argument". In *Grainger & Son v Gough (Surveyor of Taxes)*[22] agents for a French wine merchant circulated price lists on the merchant's behalf. The question was whether this distribution amounted to an offer or an invitation to treat. Lord Herschell said:

> "The transmission of such a list does not amount to an offer to supply an unlimited quantity of the wine described at the price named, so that as soon as an order is given there is a binding contract to supply that quantity. If it were so, the merchant might find himself involved in any number of contractual obligations to supply wine of a particular description which he would be quite unable to carry out, his stock of wine of that description being necessarily limited."

It is possible, however, that an advertisement of goods for sale might go further than merely stating that the goods are for sale. Suppose that a shopkeeper issues an advertisement stating, "Widgets for sale. Will be sold at 90 per cent discount to the first five customers who notify us of their intention to purchase." Such a statement could be construed as an offer of a potentially unilateral contract as it specifies a condition which, if fulfilled, would mean that the shopkeeper would be bound to sell on the terms promised. There is an American authority which supports such a view; the case of *Lefkowitz v Great Minneapolis Surplus Stores*.[23] Here the defendants issued an advertisement stating, "Saturday 9 am sharp; 3 Brand new fur coats, worth to $100. First come first served, $1 each." Although the plaintiff was one of the first three customers in accordance with the advertisement, the defendants refused to sell him a fur coat. They claimed

2–011

---

[19] [1968] 2 All E.R. 421.
[20] The appellant could, under s.6 of the Act of 1954, have been charged with selling the bird or having it in possession for the purposes of sale. As Ashworth J. wryly remarked, "For some reason which counsel for the respondent has been unable to explain, those responsible for the prosecution in this case chose, out of the trio of possible offences, the one which could not succeed."
[21] See para.2–012.
[22] [1896] A.C. 325.
[23] (1957) 86 N.W. 2d 689.

that, under the house rules, the offer was open only to women. However, the court held that the advertisement constituted an offer which the plaintiff had duly accepted.

Display of goods

2–012   If one were to ask a non-lawyer whether the display of merchandise in a shop, with the price attached, was in law an offer to sell those goods, it is quite likely that they would think it was.[24] However, in the law of contract, the display of goods in shops is regarded as an invitation to treat, thus it is the customer who makes the offer to buy which the shopkeeper is free to accept or reject. Moreover this would seem to be the case even where words such as "offer" or "special offer" are applied to the goods.

The position regarding goods displayed on shelves in self-service stores was considered in *Pharmaceutical Society of Great Britain v Boots Cash Chemists (Southern) Ltd*,[25] a case decided when the self-service system in this country was in its infancy. Under the Pharmacy and Poisons Act 1933, s.18(1), certain drugs could only be sold under the supervision of a registered pharmacist. The defendants had converted one of their branches to the self-service system; customers entered the shop and placed the drugs they wished to buy in a wire basket and took them to the cash desk, where the cashier stated the price and received payment. The transaction at the cash desk was supervised by a registered pharmacist who was authorised to prevent the removal of any drug from the premises. The Pharmaceutical Society brought an action alleging an infringement of the Act of 1933. The Society argued that the display of goods on the shelves was an offer which the customer accepted by placing the goods in the basket—the sale was therefore completed at that point and so was unsupervised. The Court of Appeal held that the Act had not been infringed—the self-service system did not amount to an offer to sell but rather an invitation to the customer to offer to buy. The offer was made by the customer at the cash desk and this where the sale took place. The sale was therefore supervised.

The main ground for the Court of Appeal's decision was the proposition that, if the Society's analysis of the transaction had been correct, once the customer had placed an article in the basket, they would be bound to buy it and could not put it back on the shelf and replace it with another article. Somervell L.J. put the matter thus:

> "Is a contract to be regarded as being completed when the article is put into the receptacle, or is this to be regarded as a more organised way of doing what is done already in many types of shops – and a bookseller is perhaps the best example – namely, enabling customers to have free access to what is in the shop, to look at the different articles, and then, ultimately, having got the ones which they wish to buy, to come up to the assistant saying, 'I want this'? The assistant 999 times out of 1,000 says 'That is all right,' and the money passes and the transaction is completed."

2–013   A few years after the *Boots* case, the Divisional Court arrived at a similar decision relating to goods displayed in a shop window. In *Fisher v Bell*[26] the defendant shopkeeper displayed a flick

---

[24] In *Fisher v Bell* (1961) 1 Q.B. 394, Lord Parker C.J. said, "I confess that I think most lay people and, indeed I myself when I first read the papers [in the case], would be inclined to the view that to say that if a knife was displayed in a window like that with a price attached to it was not offering it for sale was just nonsense."
[25] [1953] 1 Q.B. 401.
[26] [1961] 1 Q.B. 394.

knife in his shop window, with the label, "Ejector knife – 4s." Under the Restriction of Offensive Weapons Act 1959, s.1(1), it was an offence to "offer for sale" such a knife. The shopkeeper was charged with the offence but the Divisional Court upheld the decision of the justices that no offence had been committed. Given the absence of an extended definition in the Act of 1959 of the words "offer for sale" the expression had to be given its ordinary meaning in the law of contract. Under that law, the display of goods in a shop window with a price ticket attached is no more than an invitation to treat—the shopkeeper had therefore not offered the goods for sale.

Lord Parker C.J. said that at first sight it seemed absurd that (under the Act of 1959) such knives could not be manufactured, sold, hired, lent or given but they could be displayed in shop windows. Even if this was a *casus omissus*,[27] and his Lordship by no means said it was, it was not for the court to supply the omission.

The consequence of these decisions is that a customer cannot demand to buy a particular item on display, thus the shopkeeper has the right to pick and choose his customers (subject to legislation rendering discrimination unlawful). A refusal to serve a customer may, of course, be perfectly justified where the customer or potential sale is undesirable, thus the proprietor of an off-licence may not wish to serve with alcohol someone who is obviously drunk. It also follows that the shopkeeper is not bound to sell at the price indicated, for example where the shopkeeper mistakenly labels a television set worth £1,000 as being for sale at £10. This sits uneasily with the fact that the shopkeeper in these circumstances may be committing a criminal offence under s.20 of the Consumer Protection Act 1987. Under that provision an offence will be committed where a person, in the course of any business of his, gives an indication to consumers which is misleading as to the price at which any goods or other services are available. Under s.21 of the Act an indication will be "misleading" if, inter alia, it leads the consumer to think that the price is less than in fact it is.

The reasoning behind the general rule relating to the display of goods in shops is not entirely convincing. First, it has been said that "[a] shop is a place for bargaining, not for compulsory sales".[28] There may be some types of shops or transactions where bargaining is still appropriate but is this really true of much modern retailing with its automated checkouts? Secondly, it is said that, if the display of goods were an offer, the shopkeeper might be exposed to actions for breach of contract if more customers accepted than his stock could satisfy.[29] But there is nothing to prevent the shopkeeper from making his offer subject to a condition that the offer will lapse when his stock is exhausted—indeed such a stipulation might well be implied. Thirdly, the notion that if the display was an offer, the placing the goods in the basket would constitute acceptance (as relied on in the *Boots* case) is questionable. A better analysis would be to say that the offer is accepted when the goods are presented at the checkout. This would allow customers to change their mind and return items to the shelf before proceeding to the checkout.[30]

2–014

Where goods are displayed on an automatic vending machine, it would seem that the position is different to that established by the *Boots* case and *Fisher v Bell*. As Lord Denning M.R. noted in *Thornton v Shoe Lane Parking Ltd* [31] one cannot negotiate with a machine. The case concerned the issue of whether a reference to terms displayed inside a car park on a ticket issued

---

[27] A matter which should have been, but has not been, provided for in a statute.

[28] Winfield (1939) 55 L.Q.R. 499.

[29] The "quantity argument", relied on in relation to advertisements of goods for sale in *Partridge v Crittenden* [1968] 2 All E.R. 421, discussed at para.2–010. See Unger (1953) 16 M.L.R. 369.

[30] In the United States it has been held that acceptance does not occur until goods are presented at the checkout; *Lasky v Economy Grocery Stores* (1946) 5 N.E. 2d 305.

[31] [1971] 1 All E.R. 686.

by an automatic machine was sufficient to incorporate those terms into the contract.[32] Analysing the transaction, Lord Denning M.R. said:

> "The customer pays his money and gets a ticket. He cannot refuse it. He cannot get his money back. He may protest at the machine, even swear at it, but it will remain unmoved. He is committed beyond recall. He was committed at the very moment when he put his money in the machine; the contract was concluded at that time. It can be translated into offer and acceptance in this way. The offer is made when the proprietor of the machine holds it out as being ready to receive the money. The acceptance takes place when the customer puts his money into the slot."

It follows from this that the display of goods on an automatic machine is an offer. The same is presumably true of an unattended display of goods where customers take the item and leave their money in a receptacle. In more honest times this was a method of selling newspapers.

Auction sales

2–015 What is the position where an auctioneer requests bids at an auction sale?

In *Payne v Cave*[33] Cave withdrew his bid at an auction before the fall of the hammer. It was held that he was entitled to do so because the bid was the offer and the auctioneer, by requesting bids, had merely invited offers. Cave's offer had not therefore been accepted by the fall of the auctioneer's hammer. This meant that Cave's offer could be withdrawn at any time before acceptance.[34]

The rule appears in statutory form in s.57(2) of the Sale of Goods Act 1979 which states:

> "A sale by auction is complete when the auctioneer announces its completion by the fall of the hammer, or in other customary manner; and until the announcement is made any bidder may retract his bid."

What is the status of an advertisement that states that certain goods will be sold by auction on a certain day? In *Harris v Nickerson*[35] an auctioneer advertised that brewing materials, plant and office furniture would be sold at Bury St Edmunds on a certain day. Harris went to the sale but the office furniture in which he was interested had been withdrawn from sale. He sued the auctioneer for the loss of his time and expenses in going to the sale. It was held that the claimant's action failed. The advertisement of the sale was a mere declaration of intention and not an offer. If the sale was not held or lots were withdrawn before the bidding commenced the auctioneer was not bound to indemnify those persons who attended.

2–016 Of the claimant's argument that the advertisement amounted to an offer to all who should act upon it by attending the sale, Blackburn J. said:

> "This is certainly a startling proposition, and would be excessively inconvenient if carried out. It amounts to saying that anyone who advertises a sale by publishing an advertisement

---

[32] The case is discussed more fully at para.7–012.
[33] (1789) 3 Term Rep. 148.
[34] As to the effect of revocation, see para.2–054.
[35] (1873) LR 8 Q.B. 286.

becomes responsible to everybody who attends the sale for his cab hire or travelling expenses."

However, the position may be different where an auction sale is held "without reserve". A "reserve" is a price determined in advance—if the bidding does not reach the reserve, the goods will be withdrawn from sale. In *Warlow v Harrison*[36] the defendant put up a horse for sale "without reserve" and the claimant's bid was the highest bid apart from a bid from the owner himself who then instructed the horse to be withdrawn from sale. The Court of Exchequer Chamber held that on the pleadings as entered the claimant could not recover; but a majority of the court were of the view, obiter, that if the claimant had argued that the highest bona fide bidder at an auction may sue the auctioneer on his promise that the sale would be without reserve, he would have succeeded. In other words, the auctioneer who conducts a sale that is promised to be "without reserve" makes a unilateral offer to all those attending that the highest bidder shall be the buyer; it is accepted by the highest bidder when he bids and it binds the auctioneer not to put on a reserve. If he does so, the auctioneer will be liable in damages to the highest bidder. This offer, however, only arises if the bidding commences. If the advertised "without reserve" sale is cancelled or the particular lot is withdrawn in advance, there will be no liability on the part of the auctioneer because of *Harris v Nickerson*.

The approach of *Warlow v Harrison* was followed by the Court of Appeal in *Barry v Davies*[37] where it was affirmed that, in a sale without reserve, there was a collateral contract[38] between the auctioneer and the highest bidder. There was consideration[39] both in the form of detriment to the bidder, since his bid could be accepted, and benefit to the auctioneer, as the bidding was driven up. It is now therefore confirmed that the auctioneer in such circumstances who refuses to sell to the highest bidder will be in breach of contract. However, there will be no contract of sale between the vendor owner of the property and the highest bidder, who will not be entitled to the goods. The fact that damages may more than adequately compensate the bidder in such cases is illustrated by *Barry v Davies*. Here the claimant's bid, of £200 each for two machines, was not accepted by the auctioneer because he considered it to be too low and the goods were withdrawn. The claimant recovered against the auctioneer damages of £27,600 representing the difference between the contract price and the market price of the goods.

Tenders

Some potential contracts are put out to tender, i.e. a party invites "tenders" or bids to be sub- **2–017** mitted quoting the terms on which goods or services may be supplied.

Thus if, say, a university wishes to engage a firm to supply its catering services, it will invite tenders from firms. The tenders will usually have to be submitted within a certain time limit and they will normally be confidential in the sense that firms will be unaware of the prices that their competitors are quoting. Generally, the invitation to tender in such circumstances is regarded as an invitation to treat—the tenders are offers which the party inviting the tenders is free to accept or reject.

[36] (1859) 29 L.J.Q.B. 14.
[37] [2000] 1 W.L.R. 1962. See Scott (2001) L.M.C.L.Q. 334.
[38] See para.6–015.
[39] See generally Chapter 4.

In *Spencer v Harding*[40] the defendants issued a circular stating that they were "instructed to offer to the wholesale trade for sale by tender the stock-in-trade of Messrs G. Eilbeck & Co . . . which will be sold at a discount in one lot. Payment to be made in cash. The stock may be viewed on the premises . . . up to Thursday, the 20th instant, on which day, at 12 o'clock, noon precisely, the tenders will be received and opened at our offices." The claimants submitted a tender which proved to be the highest submitted but the defendants refused to sell to them. The claimants argued that, on the analogy of the reward cases, the circular amounted to a promise to sell to the highest bidder. Willes J. rejected this contention. He said:

> "If the circular had gone on, 'and we undertake to sell to the highest bidder' the reward cases would have applied, and there would have been a good contract in respect of the persons. But the question is, whether there is here any offer to enter into any contract at all, or whether the circular amounts to anything more than a mere proclamation that the defendants are ready to chaffer for the sale of goods, and to receive offers for the purchase of them . . . Here there is a total absence of any words to intimate that the highest bidder is to be the purchaser. It is a mere attempt to ascertain whether an offer can be obtained within such a margin as the sellers are willing to accept."

The contention that an invitation to tender may amount to a unilateral offer, as recognised obiter in *Spencer v Harding*, came before the House of Lords in *Harvela Investments Ltd v Royal Trust Company of Canada (CI) Ltd*.[41] In this case, the first defendants invited the claimants and the second defendants to make sealed competitive bids for a parcel of shares, stating; "We confirm that if the offer (i.e. tender) submitted by you is the highest offer received by us we bind ourselves to accept such offer." The claimants bid $2,175,000 and the second defendants bid $2,100,000 or $101,000 "in excess of any other offer". The first defendants thought they were bound to accept the bid of the second defendants, as being the higher bid.

Such bids are called "referential bids". Their Lordships considered that, in the circumstances of the case, the referential bid was invalid—it was inconsistent with what was, in effect, a fixed bidding sale. It was therefore held that the first defendants were obliged to sell to the claimants. The invitation to tender amounted to a unilateral offer to accept the highest bid—the offer was accepted by the submission of the highest bid.

2–018   In the later case of *Blackpool and Fylde Aero Club Ltd v Blackpool Borough Council*[42] the court was presented with a different problem—are there any circumstances in which the party inviting tenders is under a contractual obligation to *consider* all the tenders received? Here, the defendant council, who owned an airport at Squires Gate, Blackpool, granted a concession to operate pleasure flights from the airport. On the expiry of the then current concession, the council invited the claimant club and six other parties to submit tenders for the concession. Under a clearly laid down procedure, tenders had to be submitted by noon on March 17 in order to be considered. The claimant's tender was posted by hand in the town hall letter box one hour before the time limit expired. Owing to an administrative error on the part of the council, the claimant's tender was wrongly recorded as being late and so was not considered.

Plainly, there had been no promise on the part of the defendants to accept the highest bid; however, the claimants argued that the council should have considered all the tenders submitted

---

[40] (1870) LR 5 C.P. 561.
[41] [1986] A.C. 207.
[42] [1990] 3 All E.R. 25. See also Adams and Brownsword (1991) 54 M.L.R. 281.

in accordance with the council's own rules for the conduct of the sale. If such an argument were to succeed, it would depend upon the court finding that a unilateral contract could be implied from the circumstances. The Court of Appeal found such a contract and held that the council was liable in damages. Readily accepting that contracts should not lightly be implied, Bingham LJ said that where, as in the present case:

">. . . tenders are solicited from selected parties all of them known to the invitor, and where a local authority's invitation prescribes a clear, orderly and familiar procedure . . . the invitee is in my judgment protected at least to this extent: if he submits a conforming tender before the deadline he is entitled, not as a matter of mere expectation but of contractual right, to be sure that his tender will after the deadline be opened and considered in conjunction with all other conforming tenders or at least that his tender will be considered if others are."

Agreeing with Bingham L.J., Stocker L.J. considered that the format of the invitation to tender document itself suggested that a legal obligation to consider a tender applied to any operator who complied with its terms and conditions. Of course, this would not preclude or inhibit the council from deciding not to accept any tender or to award the contract, providing they acted in good faith, to any tenderer.[43]

The *Blackpool and Fylde* decision does not, it would seem, lay down a general rule that when-   **2–019**
ever tenders are invited a contractual obligation to consider all the bids arises. Although Bingham L.J. indicates certain circumstances in which such an obligation may arise, the scope of the duty remains unclear.

In our discussion of tenders thus far we have seen that, in the normal case, as established by *Spencer v Harding*, an invitation to tender is usually, but not invariably, an invitation to treat. In such a case the tender constitutes an offer, however, the "acceptance" of a tender does not always result in an immediate contract. It seems that there are two possibilities:

First, if a party invites tenders for the supply of a specific or ascertainable quantity of goods to be delivered at a specified time or over a specified period, then acceptance of the tender results in a binding contract to deliver the goods. Thus, if a restaurant invited tenders from wine merchants asking them to quote prices at which they would supply 10 cases of a named brand of vintage of champagne for immediate delivery, acceptance of a tender sent in response would result in a binding contract to deliver what the restaurant has asked for. The position would be no different if the restaurant had invited tenders requesting prices at which merchants could deliver, for example "all available supplies" of the specified wine over the coming year. The basis of this is that the transactions are sufficiently certain to be enforceable as contracts.

The second possibility is that the proposed transaction may be less certain and the tenders   **2–020**
will be what are called "standing offers". Suppose that the restaurant invites tenders requiring the supply of the wine in such quantity as may be ordered from time to time, or as and when, or if and when, required. Here "acceptance" of the tender does not at that stage conclude a contract. Any tender submitted is a standing offer which is only accepted in the legal sense when an order is placed for a quantity of wine and there will result a binding contract confined to

---

[43] It should be noted that the *Blackpool and Fylde* case was distinguished on the facts in *Fairclough Building Ltd v Borough Council of Port Talbot* (1993) 62 Build L.R. 82—a local authority may be justified in not considering a tender where there is a conflict of interest.

that quantity.[44] The standing offer, which is in the nature of a unilateral offer, may be revoked at any time although the tenderer may be bound to deliver orders already made.

The leading case on standing offers is *Great Northern Railway Co v Witham*.[45] Here the company invited tenders for the supply of certain goods at fixed prices over 12 months "in such quantities . . . as the company's storekeeper may order from time to time." The defendant's tender was accepted and he made several deliveries of the goods, but, before the year was out the defendant refused to make further deliveries. The company argued that the defendant had, in his tender, made a standing offer. The Court of Common Pleas accepted the argument—it was held that the defendant had to honour the orders already placed but was entitled to withdraw his standing offer for the future.

Statements of minimum price

2–021   A statement of the minimum price at which a party may be willing to sell may not amount to an offer.

The issue has often arisen in transactions involving land – these tend to be relatively complex transactions in which the courts seem to require greater evidence than usual that an offer as opposed to an invitation to treat has been made. Thus in *Harvey v Facey*[46] the claimants cabled the defendants, "Will you sell us Bumper Hall Pen [a piece of land]? Telegraph lowest cash price." The defendants replied by telegraph, "Lowest cash price for Bumper Hall Pen, £900." The claimants then cabled the defendants, "We agree to buy Bumper Hall Pen for the £900 asked by you." The Judicial Committee of the Privy Council held that there was no contract— the second telegram did not constitute an offer.

In more recent times, a similar situation came before the House of Lords in the case of *Gibson v Manchester City Council*.[47] Manchester City Council had adopted a policy of selling council houses to tenants. The council wrote to the claimant in the following terms; "The corporation may be prepared to sell the house to you at the purchase price of [£2,180]" and went on to say "if you would like to make a formal application to buy your council house, please complete the enclosed application form and return it to me as soon as possible." On March 5 the claimant returned the completed form with an accompanying letter seeking to purchase at a lower price. This was refused. On March 18 the claimant wrote asking the council to "carry on with the purchase as per my application." However, before contracts could be exchanged, political control of the council passed from Conservative to Labour and, owing to a change of policy, the council refused to sell the house to the claimant. The claimant sought specific performance of the transaction, claiming that the council had made an offer which had been accepted by him in correspondence on March 5 and 18. The House of Lords held that there was no contract because no offer capable of acceptance had been made by the council. The use of the words by the council, "may be prepared to sell" and inviting the claimant "to make a formal application to buy" was not language consistent with offer but with invitation to treat. Lord Diplock considered that these words:

> ". . . make it quite impossible to construe this letter as a contractual offer capable of being
> converted into a legally enforceable open contract for the sale of land by Mr Gibson's

---

[44] *Percival v LCC Asylums and Mental Deficiency Committee* (1918) 87 L.J.K.B. 677.
[45] (1873) L.R. 9 C.P. 16.
[46] [1893] A.C. 552. See also *Clifton v Palumbo* [1944] 2 All E.R. 497.
[47] [1979] 1 All E.R. 972. See, by way of comparison, *Storer v Manchester City Council* [1974] 1 W.L.R. 1403.

written acceptance of it. The words, 'may be prepared to sell' are fatal to this; so is the invitation, not, be it noted, to accept the offer, but 'to make formal application to buy' upon the enclosed application form. It is . . . a letter setting out the financial terms on which it may be the council will be prepared to consider a sale and purchase in due course."

The House of Lords in *Gibson* relied on the conventional approach to contract formation, i.e. looking at the documents to see whether, on their true construction, there is to be found in them an offer and an acceptance.   **2–022**

That the application of the conventional approach may not always be predictable in its outcome is illustrated by *Bigg v Boyd Gibbins*.[48] The case concerned negotiations for the sale of a property, Shortgrove Hall, Newport. The claimant wrote to the defendant: "As you are aware that I paid £25,000 for this property, your offer of £20,000 would appear to be a little optimistic. For a quick sale I would accept £26,000 so that my expenses may be covered." The defendant replied stating, "I accept your offer", and asked the claimant to contact the defendant's solicitors. The claimant's final letter said: "I am putting the matter in the hands of my solicitors. . . My wife and I are both pleased that you are purchasing the property." The Court of Appeal acknowledged that agreement as to the price of land does not necessarily mean agreement on sale and purchase; and the word "offer" may relate to a particular term with a view to negotiation continuing. Nevertheless the court was satisfied that a contract existed in this case—Russell L.J. said; "I cannot escape the view that the parties would regard themselves at the end of the correspondence, quite correctly, as having struck a bargain for the sale and purchase of the property." The court considered that the claimant's first letter constituted an offer to which the defendant had signified acceptance and no further negotiation was envisaged.

One should be wary of treating cases such as *Harvey v Facey*, discussed above, as laying down any general rule regarding statements of minimum price. The case itself concerned a sale of land but one could imagine a similar sequence of events concerning other types of property leading to a different outcome. Suppose that A, while admiring a painting on B's living room wall says, "How much do you want for it?" In reply, B says, "£2,000", to which A says, "Done!" It would be difficult to argue, applying the objective test, that there is not a concluded offer and acceptance here. After all, it would have been open to B to reply that his painting was not for sale.

THE ACCEPTANCE

Thus far we have defined what is meant by an offer in the law of contract and distinguished it from an invitation to treat. The "acceptance" of an offer may take many forms but in essence it amounts to an unqualified and unconditional assent, communicated by the offeree to the offeror, to all the terms of the offer, made with the intention of accepting. Whether an acceptance has taken place may be gathered from the words spoken or the correspondence between the parties or it may be inferred from their conduct. The fact of acceptance is ascertained objectively.   **2–023**

It should not be assumed, however, that discerning an offer and an acceptance is necessarily a simple or straightforward matter. In some cases it may be so, but often negotiations between

[48] [1971] 2 All E.R. 183.

parties are protracted and complex and it may be difficult to say at what point agreement has been reached or indeed upon which party's terms. Moreover the rules of offer and acceptance that have been laid down by the courts are really only presumptions based on common sense and business practice. As has memorably been said:

> "It must . . . be emphasised that the phrase 'offer and acceptance', though hallowed by a century and a half of judicial usage, is not to be applied as a talisman revealing, by a species of esoteric art, the presence of a contract. It would be ludicrous to suppose that business-men couch their communications in the form of a catechism . . ."[49]

The extensive case law on the issue of acceptance covers a number of principles. These will be considered below.

Acceptance must be unqualified

2–024   An acceptance is a final indication of assent leaving no further room for negotiation. To put it another way, the offeree's indication of assent must match exactly the terms of the offer. This sometimes referred to, perhaps slightly imprecisely, as the "mirror image rule".[50]

Counter-offer

2–025   If the offeree, whilst purporting to accept the offer, introduces some new term not previously mentioned, this will not be an acceptance but amount to a "counter-offer". A counter-offer has the effect of destroying the original offer rendering it no longer capable of acceptance. The proposition is illustrated by the well-known case of *Hyde v Wrench*.[51] Here the defendant offered to sell a farm to the claimant for £1,000. In reply, the claimant offered £950—this was rejected by the defendant. Later, the claimant purported to accept the original offer of £1,000. The claimant sought specific performance. In the Rolls Court, Lord Langdale M.R. thought there was no binding contract between the parties for the sale of the farm. The defendant had offered to sell it for a stipulated price and if that had at once been unconditionally accepted there would have been a binding contract. He said that instead of that, the claimant made an offer of his own, to purchase the property for £950, and he thereby rejected the offer previously made to the defendant. Lord Langdale thought that "it was not afterwards competent for him to revive the proposal of the defendant, by tendering an acceptance of it . . ."

The rule in *Hyde v Wrench* means that in a course of negotiations, it is only the most recent offer which may be accepted. The logic of the rule is that a counter-offer operates as a rejection, regardless of the fact that the offeree who counters an offer with a lower price might still be interested in paying the original price quoted by the offeror. The rule has been defended on the basis that, were it otherwise, offerees would unfairly advantaged—they could pitch their first counter-offer low but still have in reserve the option of accepting the original offer.[52] It also promotes certainty in that, as the counter-offer negates the original offer, once the counter-offer

[49] Cheshire, Fifoot and Furmston, *Law of Contract*, 15th edn, (Oxford: Oxford University Press, 2006) p. 47.
[50] A mirror image is reversed.
[51] (1840) 3 Beav. 334.
[52] Atiyah, *Introduction to the Law of Contract*, 6th edn, (Oxford: Oxford University Press, 2006) p. 48.

has been made the original offeror knows that he may safely contract with another person if he wishes. The original offer is no longer capable of being accepted by the offeree.

It should not be forgotten that the counter-offer is, of course, itself an offer and may be accepted or expressly rejected by the offeree. The latter may continue to negotiate by making a counter-counter-offer and that process could continue indefinitely until one party accepts. This process has implications for the question of on which party's terms the contract is made—this issue, the "battle of the forms" will be considered shortly.

Request for information

A counter-offer must be distinguished from a mere "request for information". It should not be assumed that at every stage of a negotiation where some new issue is raised there is necessarily a counter-offer. The offeree may be seeking to clarify some point regarding the offer or might be trying to discover whether the offeror would be willing to amend the offer in some way. Such requests for information are not regarded as counter-offers with the consequence that they do not destroy the original offer. In *Stevenson, Jacques & Co v McLean*[53] the defendant offered to sell the claimant iron for "40s, net cash, open till Monday." On Monday morning the claimants telegraphed to the defendants, "Please wire whether you would accept forty for delivery over two months, or if not, the longest limit you would give." The defendant received the claimant's telegram; the defendant did not reply but sold the iron to a third party. On Monday afternoon at 1.25 pm the defendant telegraphed the claimant saying that he had sold the iron. At 1.34 pm on the Monday the claimant telegraphed an acceptance. At 1.46 pm the defendants' telegram arrived. The claimants sued for breach of contract and the defendants argued that the telegram sent by the claimants on Monday morning amounted to a rejection.

Distinguishing *Hyde v Wrench*, the court of the Queen's Bench Division held that the claimant's telegram of Monday morning was a mere request for information and not a counter-offer. Since the defendants' purported revocation was ineffective,[54] it was held that there was a binding contract between claimant and defendant.

2–026

"Battle of the forms"

The "offer/acceptance/counter-offer" analysis discussed above has particular relevance to a phenomenon known as the "battle of the forms". Most businesses today contract on a standard set of terms and conditions which are usually printed on company documents, such as order forms and delivery notes. The use of such standard terms avoids having to enter into specific negotiations each time a contract is entered into.

In the battle of the forms scenario, one party A makes an offer in a document containing his own standard terms; the other party B purports to accept in a document containing his own standard terms. If, as is usually the case, the terms conflict, the question arises as to whether there is a contract. Applying the principles in the cases discussed above the answer to this question would be in the negative. B's "acceptance" would amount to a counter-offer. However, a

2–027

---

[53] (1880) 5 Q.B.D. 246.
[54] Revocation is ineffective unless communicated - the rules regarding revocation of offers are discussed at para.2–054.

contract might arise if B's counter-offer was accepted by conduct on the part of A, such as the delivery of goods. In such a case it is said that B would have fired the "last shot" in the battle of the forms. B would have won the battle

In *British Road Services Ltd v Arthur Crutchley & Co Ltd*[55] the claimants delivered, under a long established course of dealing between the parties, a cargo of whiskey to the defendants for storage at the defendants' warehouse. The claimants' driver handed the defendants a delivery note purporting to incorporate the claimants' conditions of carriage. The note was stamped by the defendants as "received" under the [defendants'] conditions. Thus, the delivery note was transformed into a receipt and handed back to the claimants' driver. It was argued that this amounted to a counter-offer which the claimants accepted by conduct in handing over the goods. The Court of Appeal agreed and held that the defendants' conditions prevailed—they had got in the last shot in the battle of the forms. The fact that the parties had had previous dealings was relevant. Had it been otherwise, it could have been argued that the claimants' driver may not have had authority to act on the defendants' contractual document.

2–028   The leading case on the battle of the forms—*Butler Machine Tool Co Ltd v Ex-Cell-O Corporation (England) Ltd*[56] is inconclusive. The facts were that the claimant sellers offered to sell a Butler Double Column Plane-Miller machine tool to the defendant buyers. The offer was made in a document containing certain terms, including a price variation clause, which were to "prevail over any terms and conditions in the buyer's order." The defendants placed an order and their letter had conflicting conditions, and especially had no price variation clause. At the bottom of the order form was a tear-off slip which was expressly stated to be subject to the buyers terms, which the claimants completed and returned with an accompanying letter stating that the defendants' order had been entered into in accordance with the claimants' original offer. When the machine tool was delivered the claimants sought an additional sum of money under the price variation clause. The Court of Appeal held that the claimants had contracted on the buyers' terms—the tear-off slip was an acceptance of the buyers' counter-offer. The accompanying letter was interpreted as doing no more than identifying the subject matter of the contract; it was not a counter-offer. The judge at first instance, Thesiger J., had found the additional sum to be recoverable on the basis that the parties had reached agreement subject to the emphatic stipulation that the sellers' terms were to prevail—he had taken a broad approach to the question of agreement.

In the Court of Appeal the majority of the judges favoured the traditional approach set out by Lord Langdale M.R. in *Hyde v Wrench* and affirmed in more recent times by Megaw J. in *Trollope & Colls Ltd v Atomic Power Constructions Ltd*[57], where that judge had described the effect of a counter-offer as "to kill the original offer." Lawton L.J. in *Butler Machine Tool* said:

"The modern commercial practice of making quotations and placing orders with conditions attached, usually in small print, is indeed likely, as in this case, to produce a battle of forms. The problem is how that battle should be conducted? The view taken by Thesiger J [at first instance] was that the battle should extend over a wide area and the court should do its best to look into the minds of the parties and make certain assumptions. In my judgment, the battle has to be conducted in accordance with set rules. It is a battle more on

[55] [1968] 1 All E.R. 811.
[56] [1979] 1 All E.R. 965. See Adams (1979) 95 L.Q.R. 481. See also *Pickfords Ltd v Celestica Ltd* [2003] EWCA Civ 1741. The case is discussed at para.2–056.
[57] [1962] 1 All E.R. 1035.

classical 18th century lines when convention decided who had the right to open fire first rather than in accordance with the modern concept of attrition."

Lord Denning M.R., although arriving at the same decision as the other judges regarding the outcome of the appeal, preferred a more radical analysis. Expressing sympathy with the approach of the judge at first instance, Lord Denning considered that the traditional analysis of offer, counter-offer, rejection, acceptance and so forth to be out of date. Acknowledging that Lord Wilberforce had said as much in *New Zealand Shipping Co Ltd v A M Satterthwaite & Co Ltd*,[58] Lord Denning stated that the better way was to look at the totality of the documents passing between the parties and attempt to glean from them, or from the parties' conduct, whether agreement had been reached on the material points, even though there may be differences in the forms and the printed conditions.[59] Lord Denning said:

> ". . . in most cases when there is a 'battle of forms', there is a contract as soon as the last of the forms is sent and received without objection being taken to it . . . In some cases, however, the battle is won by the man who gets the blow in first. If he offers to sell at a named price on the terms and conditions stated on the back and the buyer orders the goods purporting to accept the offer on an order form with his own terms and conditions on the back, then, if the difference is so material that it would affect the price, the buyer ought not to be allowed to take advantage of the difference unless he draws it specifically to the attention of the seller. There are yet other cases where the battle depends on the shots fired on both sides. There is a concluded contract but the forms vary. The terms and conditions of both parties are to be construed together. If they can be reconciled so as to give a harmonious result, all well and good. If the differences are irreconcilable, so that they are mutually contradictory, then the conflicting terms may have to be scrapped and replaced by a reasonable implication."

Considering the documents as a whole, and as a matter of construction, Lord Denning considered that the claimants' acknowledgement by tear-off slip was the decisive document. It made it clear that the contract was on the buyers' terms, not the sellers'.

There is something to be said for Lord Denning's approach—it seeks to avoid the confrontational aspect of contract formation by treating it as a two-stage process. First, have the parties reached agreement? Secondly, if so, what are the terms? Such an approach may well accord with the expectations of business people since they will often rely on their belief that there is an agreement by incurring expenditure. This was the case in *Butler Machine Tool* because the claimants manufactured an expensive machine to the defendants' specification and the defendants did not seek an alternative source to meet their requirements. The traditional approach, favoured by the majority of the court in *Butler Machine Tool*, treats the existence of contract and the terms to which the agreement is subject as a single process to be determined once and for all by the rules of offer and acceptance. This may mean that when the shooting is over in the battle of forms the contract may be entirely on one party's terms, or, what may be worse for both parties, there may be no contract at all. It is said that the traditional analysis provides greater certainty and predictability than Lord Denning's more flexible and discretionary

2–029

2–030

---

[58] [1975] A.C. 154. See para.2–004 above.
[59] Lord Denning relied on a statement of Lord Cairns in *Brogden v Metropolitan Railway Co* [1877] 2 App. Cas. 666, where he said: " . . . there may be a *consensus* between the parties far short of a complete mode of expressing it, and that *consensus* may be discovered from letters or from other documents of an imperfect and incomplete description . . ."

approach. But is this really the case? After all, as the cases show, fitting the often tortuous ins and outs of correspondence and negotiation into the slots of "offer", "counter-offer" and "acceptance" can be far from easy.

Acceptance must be unconditional

2–031   A conditional acceptance is not a valid acceptance. Thus no contract will be concluded where party purports to accept an offer but makes their acceptance conditional upon some event, such as receiving advice from a third party.

A classic illustration of the above-stated principle is the use of the formula "subject to contract" in transactions involving land. This means that the vendor and purchaser will not be bound until a formal contract has been drawn up and executed by the parties.[60] Such an arrangement allows the purchaser a period within which to have the property surveyed, obtain a mortgage and carry out searches and so forth. Of course, neither party is bound by the original "agreement" and no contract may ever result. Note however, that in very exceptional cases, the normal meaning of the words "subject to contract" can be displaced.[61]

Where language other than "subject to contract" is used, it is a question of construction whether agreement is negated. In *Branca v Cobarro*[62] the vendor agreed to sell the lease and goodwill of a mushroom farm on terms that: "This agreement is a provisional agreement until a fully legalised agreement drawn up by a solicitor and embodying all the conditions herewith stated is signed." At first instance, Denning J. considered that the word "provisional" meant "tentative" and so the parties were not bound by the agreement. The Court of Appeal disagreed. Lord Greene M.R. felt that both parties were determined to be bound from the outset. They realised that a formal document would be desirable but their intention was that there should be no escape for either of them in the interim period between the provisional agreement and the formal agreement. He said: " . . . the word 'until' is certainly not the right word to import a condition or a stipulation as to the event referred to."

2–032   In *Tomlin v Standard Telephones and Cables Ltd*[63] the words "without prejudice" were in issue. The claimant was injured at work and claimed compensation from the defendants, his employers. The claimant's solicitors and the defendants' insurers negotiated a settlement that liability would be accepted on a 50 per cent basis. The defendants argued that they were not bound by this agreement because the correspondence relating to it was headed "without prejudice". The Court of Appeal held that on a proper construction of the letters sent by the defendants' insurers there was a binding contract to pay half the damages. Danckwerts L.J. relied on the well-known judgment of Lindley L.J. in *Walker v Wilsher*[64] where he said:

> "What is the meaning of the words "without prejudice" ? I think they mean without prejudice to the position of the writer of the letter if the terms he proposes are not accepted. If the terms proposed in the letter are accepted a complete contract is established and the letter, although written without prejudice, operates to alter the old state of things and to establish a new one."

---

[60] *Winn v Bull* (1877) 2 Ch. D. 29.
[61] See *Alpenstow Ltd v Regalian Properties Plc* [1985] 2 All E.R. 545.
[62] [1947] K.B. 854.
[63] [1969] 3 All E.R. 201.
[64] (1889) 23 Q.B.D. 335.

Danckwerts L.J. considered that this statement applied exactly to the case if in fact there was a binding agreement, or an agreement intended to be binding, reached between the parties.

What is the position where offerees purport to accept the offer in one document but attach a covering letter stating that they will not be in a position to incur the liability under the agreement? This is what happened in *Society of Lloyds v Twinn*[65] but the Court of Appeal held that acceptance was sufficiently unconditional; the covering letter sought an indulgence but it was separate and collateral to the concluded contract rather than a condition of acceptance. It seems that the question of whether there has been an unconditional acceptance will depend on the facts of the case and the issue must be judged objectively from the language used and the surrounding circumstances.

The general rule: acceptance must be communicated

Once the fact of acceptance has been established the general rule is that, for a contract to come into existence, acceptance must be communicated to the offeror by the offeree or by someone with the offeree's authority.[66] What constitutes "communication" for the purposes of the rule?   **2–033**

Acceptance will be communicated when it is actually brought to the notice of the offeror. In *Entores Ltd v Miles Far East Corporation*[67] Denning L.J. explained what this means:

> "Suppose, for instance, that I shout an offer to a man across a river or a courtyard but I do not hear his reply because it is drowned by an aircraft flying overhead. There is no contract at that moment. If he wishes to make a contract, he must wait till the aircraft is gone and then shout back his acceptance so that I can hear what he says. Not until I have his answer am I bound."

In the case of the making of a contract over the telephone, Denning L.J. explained that a similar situation would occur if the line goes "dead" at the crucial moment and the offeror does not receive the words of acceptance. The offeree will in general be aware of this, so that if they wish to make a contract, they must get through again so as to make sure that the offeror hears. There are a number of exceptions and qualifications to this general rule.

Unilateral contracts

In unilateral contracts, the need to communicate acceptance is impliedly waived. It may be recalled that in the case of *Carlill v Carbolic Smoke Ball Company*[68] the company's argument that the claimant should have notified the company of her acceptance of the offer was emphatically rejected by the Court of Appeal. In a unilateral contract, it is the performance of the stipulated act that constitutes the acceptance. The offeror will be bound when the offeree has fulfilled the conditions specified in the offer. This is not to say that there may not be cases where   **2–034**

---

[65] (2000) *The Times*, April 4.
[66] An uncommunicated mental assent will not suffice—in *The Leonidas D* [1985] 1 W.L.R. 925, Goff L.J. said that it is "axiomatic that acceptance of an offer cannot be inferred from silence save in the most exceptional circumstances". See also *Powell v Lee* (1908) 99 L.T. 284.
[67] [1955] 2 Q.B. 327.
[68] [1893] 1 Q.B. 256; see para.2–007.

the condition specified by the offeror is actual communication to the offeror, for example if a supplier issued an advertisement stating, "MP3 players to be sold at half price to customers who notify us of their intention to purchase by the end of the week." In such a case notification to the offeror in accordance with the terms of the offer would bind the offeror. Whether silence can amount to acceptance in bilateral contracts is considered at para.2–038.

Acceptance by post

2–035   In general, under the "postal rule", where the post is an appropriate method of acceptance, the contract is concluded at the moment of posting even if the letter does not actually reach the offeror. Clearly this is a fundamental exception to the general rule regarding acceptance—the postal rule will be considered in detail later in this chapter at para.2–042.

Conduct of offeror

2–036   There will be cases where it is the conduct of the offeror that prevents the offeree's acceptance being communicated. In *Entores Ltd v Miles Far East Corporation*, to which reference was made above in discussing the general rule regarding communication, Denning L.J. considered (obiter) the situation of the offeree who does not know his message did not get home but who thinks it has. This can occur if, e.g. the offeror on the telephone does not catch the words of acceptance but nevertheless does not trouble to ask for them to be repeated, so that the offeree reasonably believes that his message has got through. Denning L.J. said:

> "The offeror in such circumstances is clearly bound, because he will be estopped from saying that he did not receive the message of acceptance. It his own fault that he did not get it. But if there should be a case where the offeror without any fault on his part does not receive the message of acceptance – yet the sender of it reasonably believes it has got home when it has not – then I think there is no contract."

It should be noted that the Court of Appeal in the *Entores* case was dealing with the effect of an instantaneous communication of acceptance by telex—the court ruled that the contract came into being when and where acceptance was received. In a later case, however, the House of Lords[69] observed that communication by telex was not always instantaneous and therefore no universal rule could cover the situations that could arise. These issues will be considered in more detail later in this chapter.[70]

Acceptance by conduct

2–037   In potentially bilateral contracts, it is possible for acceptance to be signified by the parties' conduct. Thus in *Brogden v Metropolitan Railway Co*[71] Brogden had supplied the railway

---

[69]   *Brinkibon v Stahag Stahl GmbH* [1983] 2 A.C. 34.
[70]   See para.2–049.
[71]   (1877) 2 App. Cas. 666.

company with coal for some years without a formal agreement. They decided to formalise their arrangements and so the company sent Brogden a draft contract. Brogden entered certain details, including the name of an arbitrator, signed it, wrote "approved" on it and returned it to the company whose manager put it in a desk drawer. Nothing further was done to execute this document. However, for some time coal was supplied and paid for. A dispute arose and Brogden argued that there was no binding contract between the parties. Clearly, the insertion of the name of an arbitrator by Brogden amounted to a counter-offer. Had it been accepted by the company? The House of Lords held that it had—there was a binding contract between the parties upon the terms of the uncompleted draft contract in the company's drawer.

Lord Cairns L.C. thought that there was a consensus between the parties embodied in the document signed by Brogden subject only to the approval of the additional term relating to name of the arbitrator; that approval was given when the company commenced a course of dealing referable to the contractual document, in that coal was ordered and delivered. This constituted acceptance by conduct of Brogden's counter-offer.[72]

Silence as acceptance

As we have seen, in unilateral contracts acceptance is denoted by the conduct of the offeree in fulfilling the stipulated conditions of the offer; and in bilateral contracts an acceptance by conduct may occur where, as in the *Brogden* case discussed above, performance is referable to a draft contract which embodies the agreement between the parties. These principles are well-established.

2–038

Can acceptance, in a potentially bilateral contract, be inferred from silence on the part of the offeree? In general terms the answer must be no, since as we have seen, the rule is that acceptance must be communicated. If it were otherwise, there might be the danger that a contract could be imposed on an unwilling offeree by the offeror, deeming that silence shall constitute acceptance. This is perhaps implicit in the case of *Felthouse v Bindley*.[73] Here, after some negotiations, the claimant offered to buy a horse belonging to his nephew John. The claimant wrote to John saying, "If I hear no more about him, I consider the horse mine at £30.15s." John did not reply but ordered the horse to be withdrawn from an auction sale of his assets due to be held in six weeks time. Bindley, the defendant auctioneer, mistakenly sold the horse at auction and the claimant sued him in the tort of conversion for the value of the horse. Success in this claim depended upon the claimant having entered into a binding contract with his nephew John to buy the horse.

The Court of Common Pleas held that the claimant's action must fail. Willes J. said:

> "It is . . . clear that the uncle had no right to impose upon the nephew a sale of his horse for £30.15s. unless he chose to comply with the condition of writing to repudiate the offer. . . . The horse in question being catalogued with the rest of the stock, the auctioneer (the defendant) was told that it was already sold. It is clear therefore that the nephew in his own mind intended the uncle to have the horse at the price which he (the uncle) had named, £30. 15s: but he had not communicated such an intention to his uncle, or done anything to bind himself."

---

[72] In *Jayaar Impex Ltd v Toaken Group Ltd* [1996] 2 Lloyd's Rep. 437 *Brogden* was distinguished—acceptance by conduct must be referable to a specific contract and it must be clear what that contract is.
[73] (1862) 11 C.B., N.S. 869.

2–039   The decision has been criticised.[74] As acknowledged by Willes J. in the quotation above, there doesn't seem to be any doubt that the nephew intended to accept the offer and therefore it is arguable that his conduct in instructing the auctioneer not to sell the horse is consistent enough with such intention as to amount to acceptance. It is not surprising that the nephew did not communicate his intention since that is the very thing that he had been told he need not do by his uncle. Moreover, commentators have queried whether the result would have been the same if the action had been brought by the nephew against the uncle, had the uncle refused to be bound by the transaction.[75] Whatever the reservations there may be concerning the actual decision on the facts in *Felthouse v Bindley*, insofar as the case embodies the principle that a contract cannot be imposed on an unwilling offeree, the decision is sound.

Nevertheless, it is suggested that, even in a bilateral contract, the offeror may expressly or impliedly waive the need for communication of acceptance by the offeree. Assuming the offeree is willing to accept, acceptance in such a case could be denoted by some conduct on the part of the offeree that is sufficiently unequivocal as to amount to an indication of assent. Here the contract is based on a "pre-agreed silence". In *Weatherby v Banham*[76] unrequested periodicals were sent to the defendant by the claimant. The latter had stipulated that if the periodicals were not returned by a certain date, he would assume that the defendant had purchased them. It was held that there was a contract as the defendant had accepted by implication in keeping the periodicals.

The retailing method employed in *Weatherby v Banham* came to be known as "inertia selling". There is no problem if the recipient wishes to buy the goods; by using them they will be contractually bound to purchase. But what if the recipient does not want them? They are either saddled with having to pay for goods they do not want or are put to the trouble and expense of having to return them. The practice of inertia selling, which became common in the 1960s, was brought under legislative control by the Unsolicited Goods and Services Acts of 1971 and 1975. Under these provisions the recipient of unsolicited goods may, under certain circumstances, treat the goods as an unconditional gift. However, so far as goods sent to consumers are concerned, the provisions have been replaced by reg.24 of the Consumer Protection (Distance Selling) Regulations 2000.[77] This applies where (a) unsolicited goods are sent to a recipient with a view to their acquiring them; (b) the recipient has no reasonable cause to believe that they were sent with a view to their being acquired for the purposes of a business; and (c) the recipient has neither agreed to acquire nor agreed to return them. Under these circumstances, the recipient may, as between the recipient and the sender, use, deal with or dispose of the goods as if they were an unconditional gift; and the rights of the sender to the goods are extinguished.

Where a method of acceptance is prescribed

2–040   The offeror may prescribe that the offeree should accept by a particular method, for example by return of post or by email or by responding to the offer at a particular place. What is the

---

[74] See Miller 35 M.L.R. 489.

[75] See, e.g. Atiyah, *Introduction to the Law of Contract*, 6th edn, p.52. Insofar as such an argument rests upon estoppel, there is the problem that estoppel cannot generally be raised as a cause of action: see *Fairline Shipping Corp v Adamson* [1975] Q.B. 180.

[76] (1832) 5 C. & P. 228. See also *Taylor v Allon* (1966) 1 Q.B. 304 where Lord Parker C.J. considered , obiter, that an offer to insure a motor vehicle might be accepted by conduct where the driver took the vehicle out on the road without communicating that fact to the insurers.

[77] SI 2000/2334.

position if the offeror uses a different method of acceptance—is the acceptance invalid so that there is no contract?

The matter came before the Supreme Court of the United States in *Eliason v Henshaw*.[78] Eliason offered to buy flour from Henshaw requesting that an answer should be sent to him at Harper's Ferry by the wagon which brought the offer. Henshaw sent a reply accepting the offer by post to Georgetown, thinking that his reply would reach Eliason more speedily. He was mistaken about this because his letter arrived some time after Eliason's wagoner had returned empty handed. Assuming that Henshaw was not interested, Eliason bought flour elsewhere. It was held that there was no contract—Eliason had specified a mode of acceptance with which Henshaw had failed to comply. Would the outcome have been different if the letter of acceptance had been sent to Harper's Ferry and had arrived before the wagon? The court appear to suggest that it would, since the place to which the acceptance was to be sent was an essential part of the offer, the means of conveyance apparently was not.

Later cases have introduced an important qualification; that if the offeror wishes to make a particular method of acceptance mandatory (such that no contract will result if a different method is adopted) then very clear words must be used. It may be necessary for the offeror to make it clear that no other method would do. Thus in *Yates Building Co Ltd v Pulleyn & Sons (York) Ltd*[79] a stipulation to reply to an offer by registered or recorded delivery post was held to be merely directory, not mandatory, and acceptance by ordinary post was sufficient.

If a method of acceptance is prescribed without it being made clear that no other method will suffice, it seems that an equally advantageous method will do; in *Tinn v Hoffmann*[80] it was said that if the offeree was requested to reply by "return of post" then any method which would arrive no later than return of post would suffice. It should be noted, however, that it is open to the offeror, having prescribed a method of acceptance, to waive the right to insist on that method.

2–041

In some cases it is the offeree who prescribes a method of acceptance and does so for the offeree's own benefit. In *Manchester Diocesan Council for Education v Commercial and General Investments Ltd*[81] the claimants invited tenders, requesting the tenderers to supply an address to which acceptances should be sent. The defendants' tender was accepted but the acceptance was sent to an address different to the one given by the tenderers; it was sent to the defendants' surveyor. Buckley J. held this to be a good acceptance—the claimants had introduced the prescribed method for their own protection and it could be waived by the claimants providing the defendants were not prejudiced.

The postal rule of acceptance

A further exception to the rule that acceptance must be communicated is where acceptance is effected by post. The rule is that where acceptance by post has been requested, or where it is an appropriate and reasonable means of communication between the parties, acceptance is effective immediately the letter of acceptance is posted, even if the letter is delayed, destroyed or lost

2–042

---

[78] (1819) 4 Wheat. 225.
[79] (1975) 119 Sol. Jo. 370.
[80] (1873) 29 L.T. 271.
[81] [1970] 1 W.L.R. 241.

in the post so that it never reaches the offeror.[82] The ambit of the rule was indicated by Lord Herschell in *Henthorn v Fraser*[83] where he said:

> "Where the circumstances are such that it must have been within the contemplation of the parties that, according to the ordinary usages of mankind, the post might used as a means of communicating the acceptance of an offer, the acceptance is complete as soon as it is posted."

The origin of the rule is to be found in the case of *Adams v Lindsell*.[84] The defendants wrote to the claimants offering to sell wool and requested a reply "in course of post". The letter containing the offer was wrongly addressed; because of this the letter of acceptance was posted and received two days later than the defendants would have reasonably expected. The day before receiving the letter of acceptance, the defendants sold the wool to a third party, but the letter of acceptance had been posted before the day on which the wool had been sold. The claimants' action for breach of contract succeeded—the contract was concluded when the letter of acceptance was posted. The court said that, if it were otherwise, no contract would ever be concluded by post. If no contract comes into existence until the letter of acceptance is received, the offerees should not to be treated as bound until they are notified that the offerors had received their acceptance; and so it might go on *ad infinitum*.

On the other hand, if acceptance is effective on posting, as soon as the letter of acceptance is posted the offeree may assume that a contract had been concluded and may act on that basis.[85] The rule therefore favours the offeree since the offeror might likewise act on the non-receipt of the acceptance by entering into a contract relating to the same subject matter with a third party. It is essentially a rule of covenience and has been justified on the basis that if the offeror chooses the post as a means of effecting a contract, they must accept the inherent risks. This justification is not entirely convincing since, as we shall see, the rule may apply where the offeree chooses the post as a method of acceptance.

2–043   The postal rule was applied by the House of Lords in *Dunlop v Higgins*.[86] In 1879 the rule was extended to a letter of acceptance that did not arrive in the case of *Household Fire and Carriage Accident Co v Grant*.[87] The acceptance of Grant's offer to buy shares in the claimant company was posted to him but he never received it. When the company was wound up Grant refused to pay for the shares. The Court of Appeal held that the contract was concluded on posting and Grant had therefore become a shareholder.

The postal rule is not of universal application to postal acceptances; there are some situations where the rule may not apply.

Letter of acceptance not properly posted

2–044   The postal rule may not apply where the letter of acceptance has not been properly posted. In *Re London and Northern Bank, Ex p. Jones*[88] a letter of acceptance was handed to a postman

---

[82] The postal rule is confined to letters of acceptance sent via the Post Office and to communications of acceptance via telegram/telemessage. The rule has not, as yet, been applied to private postal services.
[83] [1892] 2 Ch. 27.
[84] (1818) 1 B. & Ald. 681.
[85] See Evans (1966) 15 I.C.L.Q. 533; and Gardner (1992) 12 O.J.L.S. 170.
[86] (1848) 1 H.L. Cas. 381.
[87] (1879) 4 Ex. D. 216.
[88] [1900] 1 Ch. 220.

only authorised to deliver. This was contrary to the rules of the Post Office which provided that town postmen were not allowed to take charge of letters for the post.

Letter of acceptance misaddressed

It seems that the rule may likewise not apply if the letter of acceptance is wrongly addressed. **2–045** The analogous case of *Getreide-Import- Gesellschaft MBH v Contimar SA Compania Industrial Commercial y Maritima*[89] supports the view that the rule may not apply in these circumstances. The case involved a procedure providing for an appeal against the award of an arbitrator. Under the rules there was a rule similar to the postal rule in contract, i.e. that notice of appeal was deemed to have arrived within 24 hours of it being posted. The rule was held not to apply to a misaddressed notice which was posted but arrived outside the time limit for appealing.

A hard and fast rule on misaddressed acceptances might operate unjustly where, for example, the offeror gives the offeree the wrong address. Accordingly, Treitel suggests that the better rule would be to say that a misdirected acceptance takes effect, if at all at, at the time least favourable to the party responsible for misdirection.[90]

Exclusion of postal rule by offeror

The possibility that the offeror may by the terms of the offer exclude the operation of the postal **2–046** rule has long been recognised. In *Household Fire and Carriage Accident Insurance v Grant*, Bramwell L.J., in a dissenting judgment, spoke of the difficulties he saw in the application of the postal rule as being obviated only when the rule was "made nugatory by every prudent man saying, 'your answer by post is only to bind if it reaches me'."

The issue has come before the Court of Appeal in much more recent times. In *Holwell Securities Ltd v Hughes*,[91] the defendant granted the claimants an option to purchase a property, the option to be exercised "by notice in writing to [the defendant] at any time within six months from the date hereof." The claimants posted a letter exercising the option which was sent by ordinary post. It never arrived. Templeman J. dismissed the claimants' action for specific performance or damages.

The Court of Appeal held that the option had not been validly exercised. Lawton L.J. confirmed that the postal rule does not apply in all cases where the parties expected the post to be used as a means of acceptance. First, it does not apply where the express terms of the offer specify that acceptance must reach the offeror. The words "notice in writing" to the intending vendor clearly have that effect. After all, as the court observed, a notice is a means of making something known and so a notice that never arrives makes nothing known. It is probably the case that any words on the part of the offeror that indicate that they wish to receive the acceptance would suffice to oust the postal rule, for example if the offeror were to say, as part of the offer, "let me have your reply . . ." or "let me know your answer . . .". Secondly, Lawton L.J. considered that the postal rule probably does not operate if its application "would produce manifest inconvenience and absurdity." He saw these factors of inconvenience and absurdity as

---

[89] [1953] 2 All E.R. 223.
[90] Treitel, *Law of Contract*, 12th edn, (London: Sweet & Maxwell, 2007) p.30. In *Korbetis v Transgrain Shipping BV* [2005] EWHC 1345, which concerned a misdirected fax, Toulson J., obiter, endorsed this general approach.
[91] [1974] 1 W.L.R. 155.

part of a wider principle that the postal rule will not apply if, having regard to all the circumstances including the nature of the subject-matter, the parties cannot have intended that there should be a contract until the offeree has actually communicated acceptance.

The post must be a reasonable method of acceptance

2–047　It is a corollary of the above-mentioned dictum of Lawton L.J. that, for the postal rule to apply, the post must be a reasonable and appropriate method of acceptance in the circumstances. Where the offer is communicated by post it would obviously be reasonable to accept by post. It may also be reasonable to accept by post where the offer is not made in that way—this was recognised by the Court of Appeal in *Henthorn v Fraser*.[92] Here the claimant was handed a note containing an offer at the defendants' office in Liverpool. The claimant took the note with him to his home in Birkenhead and the following day posted a letter of acceptance to the defendants. It was held that the postal rule applied—as the claimant resided in another town it must have been within the contemplation of the defendants "according to the ordinary usages of mankind" (per Lord Herschell) that if he accepted it would be by post. But where the offer is made by instantaneous means such telephone or telex it may not be reasonable to accept by post.[93]

Retraction of postal acceptance

2–048　How far is it possible for the offeree, having posted a letter of acceptance, to recall that acceptance by a quicker method of communication, such as telephone or telex? To permit such retraction might allow the offeree to speculate at the offeror's expense, for example, where the market falls after the letter of acceptance is posted. It could be argued that if the postal rule provides that the contract is concluded on posting, no such retraction would be possible.

　　The authorities are uncertain on the point. There is no English decision but a Scottish case, *Dunmore (Countess) v Alexander*[94] has been cited as an authority supporting retraction. The case is an unreliable basis for such a proposition as it is not entirely clear whether the letter which was overtaken was regarded as an offer or an acceptance—the majority of the court seem to have regarded it as the former. A New Zealand case suggesting that retraction is not possible is *Wenckheim v Arndt*[95] where the defendant, a young lady, received an offer of marriage from the claimant. The defendant posted a letter of acceptance but before the acceptance arrived, the defendant's mother sent a telegram purporting to cancel the agreement. However, the actual decision seems to turn on agency, i.e. the mother's lack of authority to countermand the daughter's acceptance.

Instantaneous modes of communication

2–049　The postal rule of acceptance is clearly an exception to the general rule that acceptance must be communicated but the courts have not extended the postal rule beyond acceptances by post

---

[92] (1892) 2 Ch. 27.
[93] *Quenerduaine v Cole* (1883) 32 W.R. 185—held not reasonable to accept by post to an offer made by telegram.
[94] (1830) 9 S. 190. See Hudson (1966) 82 L.Q.R. 169.
[95] 1 JR 73 (1873). See also *A to Z Bazaars (Pty) Ltd v Minister of Agriculture* 1974 (4) SA 392 (South Africa).

and via cable. There are now methods of communication which did not exist at the time the postal rule was established—these include telephone and telex. These methods are seen, when working properly, as either instantaneous or virtually instantaneous; the parties are treated as if they were dealing face to face.

That the postal rule has no application to acceptances by instantaneous modes such as telex or telephone has been established by both the Court of Appeal and the House of Lords. In *Entores v Miles Far East Corporation*[96] the claimants had offices in London and the defendants in Amsterdam. The two offices were linked by teleprinters so that a message typed on one machine was automatically typed out on the other. The claimants made an offer by telex and the defendants' acceptance was received by the claimants on their machine in London. Subsequently, there was a dispute between the parties and the question arose, for the purpose of commencing legal proceedings, as to where the contract had been made—in London or Amsterdam? The Court of Appeal held that the contract had been concluded in London where the acceptance was received. The general principles as set out by Denning L.J. in this case regarding communication of acceptance have been discussed at para.2–033 above.

The decision of the Court of Appeal in the *Entores* case with regard to acceptance by telex was confirmed by the House of Lords in *Brinkibon Ltd v Stahag Stahl GmbH*.[97] The *Entores* case established where acceptance was received but not necessarily when it was received. Where a telexed acceptance is sent during normal business hours and read as soon as it is printed out in the offeror's office there is no problem. In such a case the communication is instantaneous; in the *Brinkibon* case Lord Fraser said of this situation that, once the message has been received on the offeror's telex machine, it is not unreasonable to treat it "as delivered to the principal offeror, because it is his responsibility to arrange for the prompt handling of messages within his own office."

But what is the position where communication is not instantaneous? For example, the telex message may be sent out of working hours so that it is not read until a later time or there may be some fault at the recipient's end which prevents receipt at the time contemplated by the sender. In such circumstances, when can the message be said to have been communicated? Is it when the message arrives, or within a reasonable time thereafter, or when it is actually read? In the *Brinkibon* case, Lord Wilberforce said (obiter) that:

> "No universal rule can cover such cases; they must be resolved by reference to the intentions of the parties, by sound business practice and in some cases by a judgment where the risks should lie."

Each case therefore must fall to be decided on its own facts. What this dictum of Lord Wilberforce probably means in practice is that acceptance in such cases will take effect at the time the offeree would reasonably expect the acceptance to have been read.[98] Thus those who conduct their business by telex should read their incoming messages and if they fail to do so it may be at their own risk.

2–050

---

[96] [1955] 2 Q.B. 327.

[97] [1983] 2 A.C. 34. In *Apple Corps Ltd v Apple Computer Inc* [2004] EWHC 768 a transatlantic telephone conversation, the content of which was disputed, could not be a basis for deciding in which jurisdiction the contract was made.

[98] See *Mondial Shipping and Chartering BV v Astarte Shipping Ltd* [1995] C.L.C. 1011 which involved a telexed notice of withdrawal from a charter sent outside office hours. Gatehouse J. held that the notice was effective at the start of the next working day. Cf *The Brimnes* [1975] Q.B. 929 where the notice was sent during office hours and was held to be effective when received even though not read until the following Monday.

It seems that the principles regarding instantaneous modes of communication developed in the telex cases discussed above also apply to communications by fax.[99] What is the position where an offer is accepted by email? Communications by email bear some resemblance to postal communications in that the message is sent via an online server and may not be immediately received. If the postal rule applied, the contract would come into being at the moment the offeree clicked on the "send" button. However, since the sender will generally know if his message has not been sent, it seems preferable to apply the rule relating to instantaneous modes, i.e. that the contract will not come into being until the acceptance has been received. Thus acceptance should be effective when received on the offeror's computer, or within a reasonable time thereafter. The place where the offer is accepted could be significant as it could determine the jurisdiction in which the contract was made, as with the telex cases discussed above.[100]

Internet transactions

2–051   Many people nowadays are familiar with buying goods and services online via websites. There would seem to be little doubt that when products are put up for sale on a website, this amounts to an invitation to treat and not an offer. If it were an offer the same problem of multiple acceptances would arise as we saw with newspaper advertisements, price-lists and circulars—the "quantity argument" discussed above at para.2–010. There could be—as has happened in practice on a number of occasions—thousands of customers purporting to accept, at the click of a button, offers to sell goods that are wrongly priced. Of course, there is nothing to prevent an offer on a website amounting to a unilateral offer promising to sell goods at a specified price if certain conditions were complied with.

In a typical online transaction, the customer will browse the site and having made their selection, will click on a checkout icon. The seller may at this point confirm that the goods are in stock and the customer will then be asked to submit credit or debit card details. It is only when the card has been accepted that the seller will confirm details of what has been ordered and ask the buyer whether they wish to continue with the transaction. If the buyer does indicate that they wish to continue a screen will come up to confirm receipt of the order. This is usually followed by a confirmatory email to the buyer. The Electronic Commerce (EC Directive) Regulations 2002[101] are of relevance, although the regulations are not drafted in the language of "offer" and "acceptance".

Regulation 11(1) of the regulations provides that unless agreed otherwise by parties who are not consumers, where the buyer places their order through technological means, the seller shall [para.(a)] acknowledge receipt of the order without undue delay and by electronic means. For this purpose reg.11(2) [para.(b)] states that the order and the acknowledgment of receipt will be deemed to be received when the parties to whom they are addressed are able to access them. On this basis, it is arguable that the contract will come into being when the customer receives, on their computer, the acknowledgment of the order, as once received it is accessible by the recipient.

---

[99]   *JSC Zestafoni Nikoldze Ferroalloy Plant v Ronly Holdings Ltd* [2004] 2 Lloyd's Rep. 335.
[100]   In *Initial Electronic Security Systems Ltd v Avdic* [2005] I.C.R. 1598 the Employment Appeal Tribunal accepted that, in relation to the lodging of a claim form by email, the reasonable expectation of the sender of the email is that it would arrive within a very short time thereafter.
[101]   SI 2002/2013.

Acceptance in ignorance of the offer

Is it possible for a person to "accept" an offer that they are unaware of? Suppose that the police **2–052** issue an advertisement offering a reward for information leading to the arrest and conviction of the perpetrator of a crime. X has that information but, in ignorance of the offer contained in the advertisement, provides the information to the police. If X subsequently sees the advertisement may he claim the reward? It might be thought perfectly just that X should receive the reward; after all, the police have obtained the information they sought and the public have benefited from that.[102] But this is not the law.

In the American case of *Fitch v Snedaker*[103] the plaintiff gave the police information which led to the apprehension and conviction of a murderer. At the time of giving the information he was ignorant of the fact that the sheriff had offered a reward of $200 for such information. The Court of Appeals of the State of New York held that his action to recover the reward must fail. Woodruff J. said:

> "The motive inducing consent may be immaterial, but the consent is vital. Without that there is no contract. How can there be consent or assent to that of which the party has never heard?"

On the face of it, the later English decision of *Gibbons v Proctor*[104] appears to be contrary to the proposition stated by Woodruff J. in *Fitch v Snedaker*. In *Gibbons v Proctor* the claimant, a policeman, gave information concerning a criminal to a fellow officer some nine hours before instructions were given to issue an advertisement offering a reward. However, the information was received by the superintendent after the advertisement had been issued. It was held that the claimant was entitled to the reward. The decision can be supported on the basis that the condition contained in the offer—informing the superintendent—was fulfilled after the publication of the advertisement. The decision of the High Court of Australia in *R v Clarke*[105] would seem to extend the principle in *Fitch v Snedaker* to the case of a person who had once known of the offer but at the time of the purported acceptance it had passed out of their mind. As Higgins J. said in *Clarke*, ". . . ignorance of the offer is the same thing, whether it is due to never hearing of it or to forgetting it after hearing."

Providing the acceptor is aware of the offer, their motive in accepting is not relevant; in *Williams v Carwardine*[106] it was held that the claimant was entitled to a reward for information leading to the conviction of a murderer. It mattered not that she confessed that she gave the information to ease her conscience.

A similar problem to the cases discussed above is that of "identical cross-offers", i.e. where X offers to sell and Y offers to buy the same goods on the same terms, each offer being made in ignorance of the other and the offers crossing in the post. It is thought that, unless one party subsequently accepts the offer of the other, no contract would come into being on these facts as there is no true offer and acceptance—this was the obiter view of the majority of the court in *Tinn v Hoffmann & Co.*[107] It is submitted that this is the correct approach since although

---

[102] See Hudson (1968) 84 L.Q.R. 503.
[103] (1868) 38 N.Y. 248
[104] (1891) 64 L.T. 594.
[105] (1927) 40 C.L.R. 227.
[106] (1833) 5 C. & P. 566.
[107] (1873) 29 L.T. 271.

subjectively the parties might be said to be "in agreement" in this situation, objectively they are not.

TERMINATION OF OFFER

2–053   Unless accepted, an offer has no legal effect. An offer may be terminated, before acceptance, in a number of ways which are discussed below.

Revocation

2–054   The offeror may revoke the offer at any time until acceptance. It makes no difference that the offeror has promised to keep the offer open—the general rule is illustrated by *Routledge v Grant*[108] where the defendant offered to buy the claimant's house, saying that he would give him six weeks to think the offer over. Before that time was up, the defendant revoked his offer; shortly after the claimant purported to accept. It was held that there was no contract. A promise to keep the offer open will be ineffective unless the offeree provides some consideration to make the promise to keep the offer open binding, such a process is known as "purchasing an option". The rule has attracted some criticism since the offeree may incur liability in reliance on the offeror's promise, for example where the offerors are subcontractors and the offeree relies on their quotes when tendering for a contract.[109]

Revocation must be communicated

2–055   Revocation is ineffective unless it has been communicated to the offeree and is effective, if communicated by post, when it arrives. Thus the postal rule of acceptance has no application to revocations. This may mean that a postal acceptance may take effect after the revocation has been posted but before it arrives. In *Byrne & Co v Van Tienhoven & Co*[110] on October 1 the defendants in Cardiff wrote to the claimants in New York offering to sell 1,000 boxes of tinplate at a fixed price. On October 8 the defendants wrote a further letter revoking their offer. On October 11 the claimants received the offer and immediately telegraphed their acceptance, confirming by post on October 15. On October 20 the defendants' revocation reached the claimants. It was held that the contract came into being on October 11 (it may be recalled that the postal rule also applies to acceptance by telegram). The ruling of the court in this case is a classic example of the objective approach since the parties at no time were subjectively in agreement—there was no meeting of the minds. Nevertheless the principle is sound and Lindley L.J. considered that any other conclusion would produce extreme injustice and inconvenience. He said:

---

[108] (1828) 4 Bing. 653. The rule was established in *Payne v Cave* (1789) 3 Term. Rep. 148.

[109] As far back as 1937 the Law Revision Committee recommended that promises to keep an offer open should be binding despite the absence of consideration. (Sixth Interim Report, Cmd 5449 (1937)). More recently, the Law Commission made a similar recommendation in the case of firm offers made in the course of business; Law Commission Working Paper No 60 (1975).

[110] (1880) 5 C.P.D. 344.

"If the defendants' contention were to prevail no person who had received an offer by post and had accepted it would know his position until he had waited such a time as to be quite sure that a letter withdrawing the offer had not been posted before his acceptance of it."

Although revocation must, as a general rule, be communicated, the offeror need not personally inform the offeree of the revocation—this can be done via a reliable third party. Thus in *Dickinson v Dodds*,[111] Dodds offered in writing to sell some property to Dickinson, the offer to be left open until Friday. Dickinson decided to buy the property, but before he could accept he heard on Thursday from a third party, Berry, that Dodds had sold the property to Allan. Dickinson immediately accepted the original offer and later sought specific performance of the sale on the ground that Dodds had not himself expressly revoked the offer, thus leaving it open for him to accept. The Court of Appeal held that there was no contract between Dickinson and Dodds. That the decision is influenced by *consensus ad idem* theory is made plain by the following words of James L.J.:

"It is to my mind quite clear that before there was any attempt at acceptance by the [claimant], he was perfectly well aware that Dodds had changed his mind, and that he had agreed to sell the property to Allan. It is impossible, therefore, to say that there was ever that existence of the same mind between the two parties which is essential in point of law to the making of an agreement."

The difficulty with this ruling is that it leaves it to the offeree to decide whether the information is coming from a reliable source or not. There may also be difficulties in establishing precisely when the offer is supposed to have been revoked. Perhaps a better rule, as Treitel has suggested, would be to say that the offer may only be revoked by the offeror, or by someone acting with the offeror's authority.[112]   **2–056**

A subsequent offer may have the effect of revoking a previous offer—the issue may arise in the context of the "battle of the forms" (discussed at para.2–027 above). The possibility of such revocation is illustrated by the case of *Pickfords Ltd v Celestica Ltd*.[113] For this to happen there may have to be a substantial difference between the two offers. The facts were that on September 13 Pickfords offered to carry out a removal of Celestica's workshop and office equipment to a new location, specifying their charges and stating that the cost would not exceed £100,000. On September 27 Pickfords sent a further communication providing more details and offering to carry out the work at a fixed price of £98,760. Then on October 15 Celestica sent a fax purporting to accept the offer that Pickfords had made on September 13. The Court of Appeal held that the second offer of September 27 revoked the first offer of September 13 and this meant that the fax of October 15 purported to accept an offer which had been revoked. It followed therefore that the fax amounted to a counter-offer which had been accepted by conduct when Pickfords carried out the removal work. The contract was on the terms of the first offer.

Revocation and unilateral contracts

Offers of potentially unilateral contracts pose some problems in relation to revocation. As the acceptance in such contracts is denoted by the performance of some stipulated act, the question   **2–057**

---

[111] (1876) 2 Ch. D. 463.
[112] Treitel, *Law of Contract*, 12th edn, p.44.
[113] [2003] EWCA Civ 1741.

arises as to when acceptance is effective so as to prevent revocation. Is it possible for the offeror to revoke the offer once the offeree has begun to accept?

For example, suppose that X offers £100 to the first person to swim across the River Trent on New Year's Day. Y, having seen the offer, dives in and starts to swim across. When Y is just a few metres from the other bank of the river, X shouts to Y, "Sorry, the offer is withdrawn!" If the general rule as to acceptance in unilateral contracts were applied, acceptance would not be complete until the act was fully performed, leaving the offeror free to revoke at any time until the act was completed. This state of affairs has been condemned as unjust—one solution that has been put forward is the so-called "two contract theory".[114] Under this theory the offer is accompanied by another implied offer not to revoke providing the offeree begins the task within a reasonable time. Once the task is commenced there comes into existence a secondary contract which consists of an obligation not to revoke until the offeree has had the opportunity to complete the task.

The courts in England have approached the problem pragmatically. In *Errington v Errington and Woods*[115] a father invited his son and daughter-in-law to live in a house which he had purchased for £750, £500 being borrowed from a building society. The house was in the father's name and he promised the couple that if they paid off the remaining mortgage instalments, the house would become theirs. Although the couple did not contractually promise to do so, they did in fact pay the mortgage instalments as they fell due. The father died before the whole debt had been paid off and the father's widow sought possession of the house. The Court of Appeal held that as long as the instalments were paid, the father's promise could not be revoked. Denning L.J. said:

> "The father's promise was a unilateral contract – a promise of the house in return for their act of paying the instalments. It could not be revoked by him once the couple entered on performance of the act but it would cease to bind him if they left it incomplete and unperformed, which they have not done."

2–058   It is difficult to see the theoretical basis for this decision. On what does the obligation not to revoke rest? Perhaps it owes something to the "two contract theory" to which reference was made above. It has been suggested that the decision is based on estoppel—if so, one would have expected this to made more explicit by a court that included Denning L.J. Whether the case lays down a general principle relating to unilateral contracts is open to question. Nevertheless, the approach of Denning L.J. was supported in *Daulia v Four Millbank Nominees Ltd*[116] where Goff L.J. said, obiter:

> "There must be an implied obligation on the part of the offeror not to prevent the condition becoming satisfied, which obligation it seems to me must arise as soon as the offeree starts to perform. Until then the offeror can revoke the whole thing, but once the offeree has embarked on performance it is too late for the offeror to revoke his offer."

Another problem in relation to the revocation of unilateral offers is that of communication. The general rule is, as we have seen, that revocation of an offer must be communicated. Suppose

---

[114] McGovney, 27 Harvard Law Review 644.
[115] [1952] 1 K.B. 290.
[116] [1978] 2 All E.R. 557. See also *Luxor (Eastbourne) Ltd v Cooper* [1941] A.C. 108 where the House of Lords considered that, in the circumstances of the case, the unilateral offer was freely revocable and refused to imply a promise not to revoke.

that a unilateral offer has been made to the world at large, e.g. by an advertisement published in the press and other media. The offeror then wishes to revoke the offer—how is this to be done? Plainly, it is not possible to communicate with all those persons who may have seen the original advertisements. A common sense solution would be to say that the offeror should issue advertisements giving the same degree of publicity to the revocation of the offer as was given to the original offer. Not all the potential offerees will see the notice of revocation but at least the offeror will have done all that is reasonable to achieve the desired outcome. There is no English decision on the point but a decision of the US Supreme Court in a reward case, *Shuey v United States*[117] adopts this approach, i.e. that the same notoriety should be given to the revocation as was given to the offer (per Strong J.).

Other methods of termination of the offer

Rejection

An offer will be terminated if it is expressly rejected by the offeree—we have already seen this process with the counter-offer, which is discussed at para.2–025 above. Providing the rejection is unequivocal and communicated to the offeror, the offeree will not be able to subsequently change their mind and purport to accept without the offeror's assent.   **2–059**

Lapse of time

An offer will lapse where the offeror indicates that it will only be open for a fixed period of time, such as where the offeror makes an offer to the offeree and says, "let me have your answer by 5.30pm on Friday." Even where no fixed period has been stipulated the offer will lapse after a reasonable length of time. What is reasonable is a question of fact in each case—it may depend on the nature of the subject matter. Offers to sell perishable goods or commodities that fluctuate in value may only be open for a relatively short period of time.[118]   **2–060**

Effect of death

It would seem that the offeree cannot accept after he has had notice of the offeror's death.[119] However, if the offeree is ignorant of the offeror's death, the offeree may only validly accept if it is the kind of contract that is capable of performance after death, i.e. not a contract involving the personal services of the offeror. Where it the offeree who dies after an offer being made, it would seem that the offer terminates automatically, although there is no direct authority on the point.[120]   **2–061**

---

[117] 92 U.S. 73 (1875).
[118] In *Ramsgate Victoria Hotel Co Ltd v Montefiore* (1866) L.R. 1 Ex. 109 an offer to buy shares could not be accepted after the expiry of five months—it was held to have lapsed. An offer may also lapse if it is subject to some condition, express or implied, which then fails. In *Financings Ltd v Stimson* [1962] 3 All E.R. 386 an offer to sell a car on hire-purchase was held to be subject to an implied condition that the car remained undamaged until the moment of acceptance. As this condition had been broken there was no contract.
[119] *Bradbury v Morgan* (1862) 1 H. & C. 249.
[120] There is an obiter statement to that effect in *Reynolds v Atherton* (1921) 125 L.T. 690, per Warrington L.J.

Offer and acceptance: conclusion

2–062 We observed at the beginning of this chapter (para.2–004) that offer and acceptance, although the usual formula for determining whether the parties have reached agreement, is not a universal one.

Inevitably, there will be cases where, although it is clear that the parties have reached agreement, it is not possible to analyse the transaction in terms of offer and acceptance. An example of this phenomenon in the case of *Clarke v Dunraven, The Satanita*[121] where the owners of two yachts, *The Satanita* and *The Valkyrie* entered them for a race organised by the Mudhook Yacht Club. In letters to the secretary of the club, each entrant undertook to obey the rules of the club, which included an obligation to pay "all damages" caused by fouling. At the start of the race, Clarke's vessel *The Satanita* fouled and sank Dunraven's yacht *The Valkyrie*. Under the Merchant Shipping Amendment Act 1862 liability in such circumstances was limited to £8 per ton of the registered tonnage, unless there was an agreement to the contrary. Clarke sought to rely on the statute but Dunraven contended that the rules of the club were the basis of a contract between the parties and he could therefore recover all damages. The question that arose, therefore, was whether there was a contract between the parties—obviously, there was no direct offer and acceptance between them.

The House of Lords held that there was a contract between Clarke and Dunraven. The agreement had come into existence, either when they entered their vessels for the race, or when their vessels actually sailed. The decision is impossible to support on the basis of offer and acceptance and is best viewed as embodying a special rule for the conclusion of multi-party agreements.

Further reading

Howarth, *The Meaning of Objectivity in Contract* (1984) 100 L.Q.R. 205.
Unger, *Self-service Shops and the Law of Contract* (1953) 16 M.L.R. 369.
Miller, *Felthouse v Bindley Revisited* (1972) 35 M.L.R. 489.
Evans, *The Anglo-American Mailing Rule* (1966) 15 I.C.L.Q. 553.
Hudson, *Retraction of Letters of Acceptance* (1966) 82 L.Q.R. 169.

---

[121] [1897] A.C. 59.

Chapter 3

CERTAINTY AND INTENTION

In the first part of this chapter we will examine the necessity that, for a contract to be binding, the parties must have expressed themselves with a reasonable degree of clarity on the essential terms—the requirement of certainty. The issue of contractual intention will then be considered. Not all agreements are binding contracts—even if the other essential elements of a contract are present the transaction may fail because the parties do not have the necessary intention to create legal relations. This may be because of the relationship between the parties or it may arise from the nature of the transaction itself. **3–001**

CERTAINTY

Even though the parties have complied with the rules of offer and acceptance, there may still be no contract because the terms upon which they have apparently contracted are too vague or uncertain or they have left important issues for further agreement. Business people often enter into arrangements that they believe to be binding contracts but leave the details—the dotting of the "i's" and the crossing of the "t's", as they would see it, to be sorted out later. **3–002**

This is an area of contract law that presents some difficulties for the courts—on the one hand they cannot be expected to enforce irredeemably inchoate transactions, but on the other they have a role in giving effect to the reasonable expectations of business people. Whereas the courts will be reluctant to create or construct a contract for the parties, they will endeavour to salvage an incomplete agreement if there is some objective criteria which will enable them to fill the gaps. One factor of relevance here is whether, and to what extent, the agreement has been performed.

Contracts void for uncertainty

Where the parties have not embarked on performance, a transaction may be declared void where, despite the existence of offer and acceptance, the terms are not reasonably certain. For example, in *Scammell & Nephew Ltd v Ouston*[1] the claimants agreed to buy a van on a part exchange deal from the defendants and the agreement included the words, "This order is given on the understanding that the balance of the purchase price can be had on hire-purchase terms **3–003**

---

[1] [1941] A.C. 251. See also *McNicholas Construction (Holdings) Ltd v Endemol UK Plc* [2003] EWHC 2472 (Ch).

over a period of two years." Before any hire-purchase terms could be agreed, the defendants withdrew from the transaction and argued that there was no contract on the grounds of uncertainty. The House of Lords agreed. The agreement to adopt "hire-purchase terms" was too vague to be enforceable as a contract. Viscount Maugham said that hire-purchase contracts could take many forms and some of the variations in those forms were of the most important character, "for example, those which relate to termination of the agreement, warranty of fitness, duties as to repair, interest, and so forth." Thus without such details being finalised the parties had never got beyond the negotiating process and so had never reached agreement at all.

Similarly, in *King's Motors (Oxford) Ltd v* Lax[2] a lease contained an option that, providing certain conditions were satisfied, the landlords would grant a further term "at such rental as may be agreed upon between the parties hereto in writing". It was held that the contract giving the option was void for uncertainty—the rent was a necessary term and it had not been agreed upon.

Just as an agreement to agree is too uncertain to be enforced, so too is a contract to negotiate. In *Courtney & Fairbairn Ltd v Tolaini,*[3] Lord Denning M.R. in the Court of Appeal rejected the proposition that a contract to negotiate could be enforceable. He said:

> "[I]t is too uncertain to have any binding force. No court could estimate the damages because no one can tell whether the negotiations would be successful or would fall through: or if successful, what the result would be. It seems to me that a contract to negotiate . . . is not a contract known to the law."

3–004 Some years later the status of an agreement to negotiate came before the House of Lords in the case of *Walford v Miles.*[4] In this case, the defendants, who were owners of a photographic business, entered into negotiations to sell the business to the claimants. The parties agreed that if the claimants would provide a letter of comfort[5] from their bankers to the effect that they would finance the purchase, the defendants would promise not to negotiate with anyone else. Later, however, the defendants sold the business to a third party. The claimants sued alleging the breach of an enforceable agreement not to negotiate with anyone else which, they argued, was subject to an implied term to negotiate in good faith with them. Their action failed.

The House of Lords confirmed the principle laid down by Lord Denning in *Courtney & Fairbairn Ltd v Tolaini* that an agreement to negotiate (termed a "lock in") was unenforceable as it lacked certainty. Moreover, the implication of a duty to negotiate in good faith was, in the view of the court, inconsistent with the nature of negotiations where each party is entitled to act in their own interests and withdraw from them if appropriate.[6] Nevertheless, the court recognised that an agreement not to negotiate with others (a "lock out") could be enforceable if it was for a specified period but in this case the agreement did not specify how long it was to last for. It was therefore unenforceable.

Subsequently, a lock out agreement between a vendor and a purchaser of land for a limited period of two weeks was upheld by the Court of Appeal in the case of *Pitt v PHH Asset Management Ltd.*[7]

---

[2] (1970) 21 P. & C.R. 507.
[3] [1975] 1 W.L.R. 297.
[4] [1992] 2 A.C. 128.
[5] As to "letters of comfort", see para.3–022 below.
[6] This aspect of the decision has prompted some debate—see e.g. Neill (1992) 108 L.Q.R. 405; and Buckley (1993) J.C.L. 58.
[7] [1994] 1 W.L.R. 327.

Incomplete contracts

A contract may be incomplete because the parties are agreed in principle but have left some details for further decision. Such a state of affairs is quite common in practice and, in purely business terms, may be quite sensible. The problem is, as the cases discussed above show, in theory there ought to be no binding contract in these circumstances. However the courts will generally strive to enforce a bargain which is silent on some matters or leaves issues for further resolution if they possibly can, for example, by implying terms into the transaction. Inevitably, much will depend on the circumstances of the particular case, but through the decided cases a number of criteria have been identified to which the court may have resort. Nevertheless, it should be borne in mind that the courts are anxious to avoid any appearance of "making a contract" for the parties. The factors to which they may have regard include the following:

3–005

Previous dealings between the parties

In *Hillas & Co Ltd v Arcos* Ltd[8] the claimants agreed to purchase from the defendants "22,000 standards of softwood goods of fair specification over the season 1930." The contract contained a clause giving the claimants the option of buying 100,000 standards for delivery during 1931 but did not describe the goods to be sold. The parties traded on the terms of the agreement during 1930 but in November of that year the defendants sold their 1931 output to a third party. The claimants then purported to exercise their option. The defendants argued that the option was an unenforceable agreement but the House of Lords disagreed, holding that it was binding. The option clause was part of a wider contract and it was possible by a process of implication to fill the apparent gaps in the 1931 option by reference to the previous dealings of the parties over 1930. The process was assisted by admitting as evidence the customs of the timber trade. Lord Wright said:

3–006

> "The [contractual document of 1930] cannot be regarded as other than inartistic, and may appear repellent to the trained sense of an equity draftsman. But it is clear that the parties both intended to make a contract and thought they had done so. Business men often record the most important agreements in crude and summary fashion; modes of expression sufficient and clear to them in the course of their business may appear to those unfamiliar with the business far from complete or precise. It is accordingly the duty of the court to construe such documents fairly and broadly, without being too astute or subtle in finding defects . . . [This] does not mean that the court is to make a contract for the parties, or to go outside the words they have used, except in so far as there are appropriate implications of law."

The differences between *Hillas v Arcos* and *Scammell v Ouston* are that in the former case there had been contractual performance when the dispute arose and there were terms available to the court which could be implied—in the latter the whole transaction was, as it were, in the future and there were no usual hire-purchase terms which could be implied into the contract.

---

[8] (1932) 147 L.T. 503. See also *Grow With Us v Green Thumb (UK) Ltd* [2006] EWCA Civ 1201 where the Court of Appeal held that an option to extend a contract was unenforceable as an important term had not been agreed.

Machinery for resolving uncertainty

3–007   In some cases, the contract itself contains a mechanism which can be used for resolving the uncertainty. For example, where the price of land is to be fixed by valuers appointed by the parties, the courts may be prepared to uphold the agreement. Thus in *Sudbrook Trading Estate Ltd v Eggleton*[9] the claimants were tenants of four adjoining premises leased to them by the defendants. A clause in the leases gave the claimants an option to purchase the freehold reversion at a price to be agreed by two valuers, one to be nominated by each party. If no agreement was reached between the two valuers, they were to appoint an umpire. When the claimants sought to exercise the option, the defendants argued that the option clauses were void for uncertainty and refused to appoint a valuer. The defendants claimed that the option clauses were merely agreements to agree in the future.

The House of Lords found for the claimants and ordered the options to be specifically enforced. The machinery for ascertaining the value of the properties was subsidiary and non-essential to the main purpose of the clause, which was to fix a fair price. The fact that the machinery had broken down did not prevent the court from substituting its own machinery which it did by ordering an inquiry into the fair value of the premises. The *Sudbrook* case was distinguished in *Gillatt v Sky Television Ltd*[10] where the contract provided that the claimant was entitled to a percentage of the open market value of certain shares as determined by an independent chartered accountant. The Court of Appeal held that the appointment of an accountant was not merely machinery, but an essential condition precedent to the existence of any entitlement under the contract. As the parties had not bothered to appoint the valuer, as stipulated by the contract, the court was not prepared to substitute its own machinery.

Another possibility is that the contract contains an appropriately drafted arbitration clause. This was the position in *Foley v Classique Coaches Ltd*[11] where the claimant owned a petrol station and the land adjacent. The defendants operated a coach company and the claimants entered into an agreement to sell them the adjacent land, on condition that they entered into an agreement to buy petrol "at a price to be agreed by the parties in writing and from time to time." There was a further clause which provided that any dispute arising on the subject matter or construction of the agreement should be submitted to arbitration. The agreement was acted upon for some three years before the defendants argued that the contract was void for uncertainty as to price. It might be thought, at first sight, that this was another "agreement to agree" but the Court of Appeal found a contract.

3–008   The court held that a term should be implied into the agreement that the petrol supplied should be of reasonable quality and be supplied at a reasonable price. If any dispute arose as to what was a reasonable price the matter could be referred to and determined by arbitration. Moreover, the agreement had been acted on for three years, i.e. there had been performance, and it formed part of a larger transaction being linked to a conveyance of land.

The relevance of performance

3–009   As the decisions in *Hillas v Arcos* and *Foley v Classique Coaches* show, performance is a highly significant factor in influencing the court to uphold a contract. This is not surprising. It would

[9] [1982] 3 All E.R. 1.
[10] [2000] 1 All E.R. Comm. 461.
[11] [1934] 2 K.B. 1.

be illogical if the court concluded there was "no contract" after the parties had acted upon an apparent agreement for some time without any difficulties. It is also unquestionably the case that the fact that the transaction has been performed makes the process of implying terms into the agreement much easier.

Performance, however, will not inevitably mean that the contract is enforceable. In some cases the parties may substantially perform an apparent agreement and yet there is still no binding contract because essential terms are yet to be agreed. This is what happened in *British Steel Corporation v Cleveland Bridge and Engineering Co Ltd.*[12] The defendants requested the claimants to manufacture steel nodes for a major construction project with discussion about the precise specification continuing. It was confidently expected that an agreement would be reached. Work was then begun although matters such as specification, price, delivery and liability had yet to be resolved. All the nodes bar one were delivered and that one was delayed owing to an industrial dispute at the claimants' works. The claimants sought a reasonable sum for work done on a quantum meruit basis[13] contending that no agreement had been reached between the parties. The defendants counter-claimed for breach of contract. Robert Goff J. held that as there had been no final agreement on essential terms, there was no contract between the parties. Nevertheless, the claimants recovered a reasonable sum for work done on a quantum meruit basis.

Statutory provision

In some cases the gaps in an incomplete agreement may be filled by the court resorting to relevant legislative provisions. For example s.8 of the Sale of Goods Act 1979 (headed "Ascertainment of Price") provides: **3–010**

"(1) The price in a contract of sale may be fixed by the contract, or may be left to be fixed in a manner agreed by the contract, or may be determined by the course of dealing between the parties.
(2) Where the price is not determined as mentioned in subsection (1) above the buyer must pay a reasonable price.
(3) What is a reasonable price is a question of fact dependent on the circumstances of each particular case."

There is a parallel provision in s.15 of the Supply of Goods and Services Act 1982 with regard to the payment of a reasonable charge for a service.

In *May and Butcher Ltd v R*[14] there was an agreement for the sale of surplus government tentage which provided that the price to be paid "shall be agreed upon from time to time" between the parties. The House of Lords held that the transaction was void for uncertainty. Their Lordships refused to resort to the Sale of Goods Act in order to imply a term that the price should be a reasonable price. Viscount Dunedin said, " . . . the Sale of Goods Act provides for silence on the point and here there is no silence." In other words, a reasonable price will only

---

[12] [1984] 1 All E.R. 504.
[13] As to quantum meruit, see para.17–024 below.
[14] [1934] 2 K.B. 17n. See also *Rafsanjan Pistachio Producers Co-operative v Kauffmans Ltd*, Independent, January 12, 1998, where an agreement which failed to determine the price was held to be void, applying *May and Butcher v R*.

be implied where the contract is silent as to price—this is a rather restrictive interpretation of the provision. The agreement also contained an arbitration clause which provided that all disputes arising out of the agreement should be submitted to arbitration. Whereas, as we have seen, an arbitration clause can provide a mechanism for resolving uncertainty, in this case it did not. As Lord Buckmaster said:

> "The clause refers 'disputes with reference to or arising out of this agreement' to arbitration, but until the price has been fixed, the agreement is not there."

The arbitration clause in *Foley v Classique Coaches*, where as we have seen the contract was held enforceable, was differently worded, referring to disputes as to the subject matter of the agreement.

Meaningless phrases

3–011   In the case of *Nicolene Ltd v Simmonds*[15] the contract contained a term: ". . . I assume that we are in agreement that the usual conditions of acceptance apply." In fact there were no usual conditions of acceptance and so the words were meaningless. As they were superfluous, the court was prepared to sever them and enforce the contract. Denning L.J. said:

> "A clause which is meaningless can often be ignored, whilst leaving the contract good; whereas a clause which has yet to be agreed may mean that there is no contract at all, because the parties have not agreed on all the essential terms."

Denning L.J. was concerned that, if it were otherwise, parties could escape from their obligations by inserting meaningless exceptions—"You would find defaulters all scanning their contracts to find some meaningless clause on which to ride free."

INTENTION TO CREATE LEGAL RELATIONS

3–012   We have seen thus far that, for a binding contract to arise, the parties must have reached agreement on terms that are reasonably certain. Even where there is agreement, there may be no contract because the parties do not intend to create legal relations—thus the intention to be bound is a separate requirement of a contract.[16] There is a further requirement for simple contracts, i.e. the existence of consideration and this will be considered in the following chapter.

The law relating to contractual intention has traditionally operated by applying certain presumptions. Thus in the domestic and social sphere there is a rebuttable presumption that the parties do not intend to be legally bound. Broadly speaking this is a sensible approach—it reflects the desire of the courts to restrict contract law as far as possible to the commercial sphere. It would be absurd if a couple's agreement that one would babysit while the other went

---

[15] [1963] 1 Q.B. 543.

[16] This proposition has been questioned. See, e.g. Hepple (1970) 20 C.L.J. 122 who argues that as a contract is a bargain, offer, acceptance and consideration will suffice and the additional test of intention is superfluous and artificial. This is not the position in law, however, as the cases discussed in this chapter demonstrate.

to the pub, or a friend's failure to keep a dinner date, were brought before the courts. By contrast, in the case of agreements in the world of business, there is a strong but rebuttable presumption that the parties do intend to be legally bound. Whether there is an intention to create legal relations or not is a matter for the court to acertain objectively by reference to what the parties said, did or wrote.

The law in this area may be classified under five heads: domestic agreements; social agreements; commercial agreements; advertisements; and collective agreements.

Domestic agreements

Husband and wife

The leading case on domestic agreements is *Balfour v Balfour* and it involved an agreement between a husband and a wife.[17] The defendant was a civil servant who was posted to Ceylon and he left his wife, the claimant, in England. The claimant's health was not good enough for her to accompany her husband. Before leaving, the defendant promised to pay the claimant an allowance of £30 per month whilst they were apart. Some months later the defendant wrote to the claimant suggesting that they should remain apart. The claimant sought to enforce the promise to pay her £30 per month. At first instance, Sargant J. found for the claimant on the basis that the defendant was obliged to support the claimant and the consent of the claimant to the arrangement was sufficient consideration. The defendant appealed to the Court of Appeal.

3–013

It was held that the appeal would be allowed. The agreement was not legally enforceable because there was no intention to create legal relations—there was a presumption that such domestic agreements are not intended to be legally binding and the claimant wife had failed to rebut the presumption. Lord Atkin said:

> "Agreements such as these are outside the realm of contracts altogether. The common law does not regulate the form of agreements between spouses. Their promises are not sealed with seals and sealing wax. The consideration that really obtains for them is that natural love and affection which counts for so little in these cold courts."

Lord Atkin expressed concern that if such agreements were enforceable:

> "... the small Courts of this country would have to be multiplied one hundredfold if these arrangements were held to result in legal obligations."

It may be inferred from these statements of Lord Atkin that although the decision in *Balfour v Balfour* is expressed in terms of contractual intention, there may be an underlying policy consideration that the courts should not get involved in family relationships and that if they did, the floodgates of litigation would open. The "floodgates" argument is perhaps a little exaggerated since it is unlikely that most parties in a domestic situation would desire litigation over such disputes. It should also be emphasised that agreements between husband and wife of a non-domestic nature may have the necessary contractual intention, for example the wife may be the

3–014

---

[17] [1919] 2 K.B. 571. See Hedley (1985) 5 O.J.L.S. 391.

husband's tenant, or vice versa, or they may be business partners. However, *Balfour v Balfour* is itself very much a borderline case. This was acknowledged by the House of Lords in *Pettitt v Pettitt*,[18] a case where a spouse carried out improvements to the matrimonial home which was in the name of the other spouse. Here Lord Diplock drew a distinction between domestic agreements between husband and wife that are executory and those where the promises are executed. In the case of the latter proprietary rights may arise. He said:

> "If spouses do perform their mutual promises the fact that they could not have been compelled to do so while they were executory cannot deprive the acts done by them of all legal consequences upon proprietary rights; for these are within the field of the law of property rather than of the law of contract. It would, in my view, be erroneous to extend the presumption accepted in *Balfour v Balfour* that mutual promises between man and wife in relation to their domestic arrangements are prima facie not intended to be legally enforceable to a presumption of a common intention of both spouses that *no* legal consequences should flow from acts done by them in peformance of mutual promises with respect to the acquisition, improvement or addition to real or personal property . . . for this would be to intend what is impossible in law."

3–015   In *Balfour v Balfour*, although the couple did eventually separate, it was particularly significant that at the time of making their agreement the couple were not separated. The position may be very different where the parties are not living together in amity at the time of the agreement. This was the state of affairs in *Merritt v Merritt*[19] where a married couple had separated. They later met and agreed that if the husband paid off the outstanding mortgage payments on the matrimonial home, the house would be hers. At the insistence of the wife, the husband recorded in writing: "In consideration of the fact that you will pay all charges in connection with the house . . . [when] the mortgage repayment has been completed . . . I will agree to transfer the property into your sole ownership." In reliance on the agreement the wife paid off the mortgage but the husband refused to transfer the house to her. The Court of Appeal held that there was an intention to create legal relations and the husband was compelled to convey the house. Lord Denning M.R. did not think that *Balfour v Balfour* had any application. He said:

> "It is altogether different when the parties are not living in amity but are separated, or are about to separate. They then bargain keenly. They do not rely on honourable understandings. They want everything cut and dried. It may safely be presumed that they intend to create legal relations."

The fact that the terms of the agreement in *Merritt v Merritt* were recorded in a written document was important because it provided the degree of certainty that sometimes such agreements may lack. Thus in *Gould v Gould*[20] a married couple had separated and the husband promised to pay the wife £12 a week "so long as I can manage it". It was held that the words used introduced such an element of uncertainty that there was no intention to create legal relations.

---

[18] [1970] A.C. 777.
[19] [1970] 1 W.L.R. 1211.
[20] [1970] 1 Q.B. 275.

Parent and child

The presumption against the intention to create legal relations also applies to agreements **3–016** between parent and child. In *Jones v Padavatton*[21] the claimant mother, in 1962, persuaded the defendant daughter to move from the USA to England to read for the Bar examinations. The claimant lived in Trinidad and she hoped the daughter would practise law there when she had qualified. The claimant promised to pay the defendant $200 a month by way of maintenance. In 1964 there was a further arrangement whereby the claimant purchased a house in London for her daughter to live in along with paying tenants. By 1967 the defendant had not yet passed all of Part I of the Bar examinations. The claimant and defendant then fell out and the claimant sought possession of the house.

The Court of Appeal, by a majority, held that the agreement was not intended to create legal relations and it was far too vague and uncertain to be enforceable as a contract. The claimant, therefore, was entitled to possession. However, Danckwerts L.J. found the action "deplorable"— the differences between the two sides appeared comparatively small, and he found it distressing that they could not settle their differences amicably and avoid the bitterness and expense of litigation. This statement suggests that the underlying basis of the decision is really one of policy. Danckwerts L.J. went on to say:

> "The present case is one of those family arrangements which depend on the good faith of the promises which are made and are not intended to be rigid, binding agreements. *Balfour v Balfour* was a case of husband and wife, but there is no doubt the same principles apply to dealings between other relations, such as father and son and daughter and mother."

Salmon L.J. agreed with the decision of the majority but he arrived at it by a different route. He **3–017** thought that the original agreement had been intended by the parties to be legally binding as the daughter had relied on it by giving up her job and moving to England. However, a term should be implied that the agreement was to last for a reasonable length of time which his Lordship considered to be five years. This would have enabled her either to pass the examinations and be called to the Bar or give up her unequal struggle against the examiners. As this period of time had elapsed the agreement was no longer valid. With regard to the further arrangement relating to the house, Salmon L.J. considered this to be very vague and lacking in contractual intent. It is suggested that the approach of Salmon L.J. to this case is to be preferred.

Other domestic agreements

Where members of a household who are other than husband and wife or parent and child enter **3–018** into domestic agreements, the presumption against contractual relations is still there. However, there is evidence that the courts are prepared to have regard to the seriousness of the transaction for the lives of the parties involved, and the extent to which one party may have relied on the agreement.

These factors can be seen at work in the decision in *Parker v Clark*.[22] The defendants, the Clarks, were an elderly couple who lived in a large house in Torquay, and the claimants were a

---

[21] [1969] 1 W.L.R. 328.
[22] [1960] 1 W.L.R. 286.

younger couple who had a cottage in Sussex. Mrs Parker was the niece of Mrs Clark. The Parkers visited the Clarks often and eventually the Clarks invited the other couple to come and live with them. The household expenses were to be shared and the Clarks would leave the house in Torquay and its contents to Mrs Parker, her sister and daughter. The younger couple then sold their cottage and moved in with the older couple. After a while relations between the couples deteriorated and after much unpleasantness the Parkers were told to leave and find alternative accommodation. The Parkers sued for breach of contract and succeeded; they were awarded damages to cover the cost of moving and the third share of the Clarks' house which was to be left to Mrs Parker and her relatives. There was ample evidence that the parties intended legal relations. Devlin J. said:

"A proposal between relatives to share a house and a promise to make a bequest of it may very well amount to no more than a family arrangement of the type considered in *Balfour v Balfour* which the courts will not enforce. But there is equally no doubt that arrangements of this sort, and in particular a proposal to leave property in a will, can be the subject of a binding contract . . . The question must, of course, depend on the intention of the parties to be inferred from the language which they use and from the circumstances in which they use it."

It should not be assumed that all agreements entered into by members of a household who are not related are necessarily unenforceable. Some agreements may not be purely domestic or social in nature—in such cases the court will examine all the circumstances having regard to the factors referred to above by Devlin J. For example, in *Simpkins v Pays*[23] the members of the household consisted of the defendant, the defendant's grand-daughter Esme, and the claimant, who was a lodger. The trio were in the habit of entering a fashion competition organised by Sunday newspaper. The entries were submitted in the defendant's name and all contributed equally to the competition although there was no regular arrangement regarding expenses. One week Esme's entry was successful and the prize of £750 was paid to the defendant. The claimant brought an action for a one-third share. Sellers J. held that the claimant was so entitled—it was a joint enterprise in which each participant expected to share any winnings. The judge found a mutuality in the arrangement between the parties which signified a binding contract.

Social agreements

3–019   As mentioned at the beginning of this chapter, it is recognised that there is a sphere of social relations where contractual relations are not intended—"To offer a friend a meal is not to invite litigation."[24] The notion was accepted judicially by Atkin L.J. in *Balfour v Balfour* where he said that it was necessary to remember that there were agreements which did not result in a contract within the meaning of the law:

"The ordinary example is where two people agree to take a walk together, or where there is an offer and acceptance of hospitality. Nobody would suggest in ordinary circumstances that those agreements result in what we know as a contract."

[23] [1955] 3 All E.R. 10.
[24] Cheshire, Fifoot and Furmston, *Law of Contract*, 15th edn, (Oxford: Oxford University Press, 2006) p.142.

This presumption against contractual relations has been applied by the courts to a variety of situations including a golf competition[25] and to an arrangement for sharing petrol costs where a person is given a lift to work.[26]

Commercial agreements

In commercial agreements, there is a strong presumption that the parties intend to be legally bound. The presumption can be rebutted by clear express words as is illustrated by *Rose and Frank Co v J R Crompton & Bros*[27] where the appellants were an American company who dealt in carbon copy materials. The respondents were an English firm and the parties signed a document appointing the appellants sole agents of the respondents for the sale of their carbonising tissue in the USA and Canada. The arrangement was to last for three years and the document contained an "honourable pledge clause" which provided: "This arrangement is not entered into, nor is this memorandum written, as a formal or legal agreement, and shall not be subject to legal jurisdiction in the Law Courts . . . but . . . is only a definite expression and record of the purpose and intention of the . . . parties concerned, to which they each honourably pledge themselves . . ." Later, the respondents purported to terminate the arrangement and failed to give notice as required by the document—they also refused to fulfil orders already received by them prior to their decision to terminate the arrangement. The appellants brought an action for breach of contract and for non-delivery of the goods which had been ordered.

The Court of Appeal held that the agency agreement did not constitute a binding contract and therefore no action could lie upon it, and a majority of that court (Atkin L.J. dissenting) held that there was no liability for non-delivery of goods ordered. On appeal to the House of Lords, their Lordships were in agreement that there was no binding contract because of the honourable pledge clause, but held that where orders had been accepted, there was a legal obligation to deliver. Lord Phillimore, who thought the clause "remarkable", said:

> "According to the course of business between the parties which is narrated in the unenforceable agreement, goods were ordered from time to time, shipped, received and paid for, under an established system: but the agreement being unenforceable there was no obligation on the American company to order goods or upon the English companies to accept an order. Any actual transaction between the parties, however, gave rise to the ordinary legal rights; for the fact that it was not of obligation to do the transaction did not divest the transaction when done of its ordinary legal significance. This . . . will . . . be plain if we begin with the latter end of each transaction. Goods were ordered, shipped and received. Was there no legal liability to pay for them? One stage further back. Goods were ordered, shipped and invoiced. Was there no legal liability to take delivery? I apprehend that in each of these cases the American company would be bound."

The House of Lords therefore decided that, without reference to the arrangement contained in the original document, each time an order was accepted, a binding contract came into existence

3–020

3–021

---

[25] *Lens v Devonshire Club* (1914) Times, December 4.

[26] *Coward v Motor Insurers' Bureau* [1963] 1 Q.B. 259; *Buckpitt v Oates* [1968] 1 All E.R. 1145. However, see now the Road Traffic Act 1988, ss145 and 149.

[27] [1923] 2 K.B. 261, Court of Appeal; [1925] A.C. 445, House of Lords.

based upon the parties' conduct. This is a perfectly just and sensible solution to the problem of executed transactions within an unenforceable agreement. But what of the decision that the agreement itself is devoid of contractual force? It may be asked, why is the honourable pledge clause binding on the parties if there is no binding contract as stated by the clause itself? Although it seems illogical that the clause should be binding, perhaps the answer lies in the pragmatic readiness of the courts to give effect to the clear intentions of the parties. In the Court of Appeal's decision in *Rose and Frank v Crompton* Atkin L.J. said:

> "I find myself driven to the conclusion that the clause in question expresses in clear terms the mutual intention of the parties not to enter into legal obligations in respect to the matters upon which they are recording their agreement. I have never seen such a clause before, but I see nothing necessarily absurd in business men seeking to regulate their business relations by mutual promises which fall short of legal obligations, and rest on obligations of either honour or self-interest, or perhaps both."

In fact, honour clauses have for many years been used by football pool companies in their coupons. Thus in *Jones v Vernon's Pools Ltd*[28] the claimant alleged that he had posted a coupon to the defendants' football pool but the defendants denied receiving it. It was a condition of entry to the competition that ". . . all arrangements, agreements and transactions [relating to the football pool] should be binding in honour only." It was held that the claimant had no legal claim arising from the coupon. There is therefore no obligation on the pools companies to pay out winnings. In *Jones v Vernon's Pools* Atkinson J. considered that, if it were otherwise, large numbers of people might allege and call evidence that they had sent in the winning coupon—the pools company would be faced with the prospect of fighting cases to decide whether those coupons had been sent in and received. He did not think the business could be carried on for a day on such terms. It could only be carried on on a basis of trust and, if things did go wrong, it was at the entrant's risk.

The onus of rebutting contractual intent in commercial agreements is a heavy one and it seems that very clear words are required to achieve this effect. This is aptly illustrated by the case of *Edwards v Skyways Ltd.*[29] The board of directors of an airline company agreed with representatives of the British Airline Pilots Association (BALPA) that pilots made redundant by the company would be given an "ex gratia" payment equivalent to the company's contributions to the pension fund. They would be entitled to a refund of their own contributions to the fund. The claimant, a pilot employed by the company, was made redundant and left the company. He informed the company that he had decided to take the refund and the ex gratia payment; the company, however, refused to make the payment.

3–022   The claimant's action to recover the ex gratia payment succeeded. Megaw J. held that where an agreement was reached in the course of a business, there was a heavy onus on the party alleging that it was not intended to give rise to legal obligations. The use of the words "ex gratia" in this case did not discharge that burden. The judge said:

> "[T]he words 'ex gratia', in my judgment, do not carry a necessary, or even a probable, implication that the agreement is to be without legal effect. It is, I think, common experience amongst practitioners of the law that litigation or threatened litigation is frequently

[28] [1938] 2 All E.R. 626.
[29] [1964] 1 W.L.R. 349.

compromised on terms that one party shall make the other a payment described in express terms as 'ex gratia' . . . [n]o one would imagine that a settlement, so made, is unenforceable at law."

The issue of contractual intent in commercial agreements has arisen in the context of "letters of comfort". In the case of *Kleinwort Benson Ltd v Malaysia Mining Corporation Bhd*[30] the claimant merchant bank agreed with the defendants to make a loan of £10 million available to a wholly–owned subsidiary of the defendants, M, which traded in tin. As part of this arrangement, the defendants provided the claimants with two letters of comfort which stated that it was their policy to ensure that the business of M was at all times in a position to meet its liabilities under the loan arrangement. Subsequently, the world market in tin collapsed but the full amount owed by M to the claimant was still outstanding. M went into liquidation and the claimant sought from the defendants the whole amount. The judge at first instance, Hirst J., followed *Edwards v Skyways* in holding that the words used were insufficient to rebut the presumption of contractual intent in a commercial agreement. The Court of Appeal approached the question differently—it was necessary first to construe the wording of the letters to see whether a contractual promise had been made. The court concluded that the words in question were intended as a statement of existing fact and not as a contractual promise. *Edward v Skyways* was therefore distinguished—that case concerned a contractual promise supported by consideration.

An interesting case in the area of commercial agreements is *Edmonds v Lawson*.[31] Here a pupil barrister contended that pupillage constituted a "contract of employment" under s.54(3)(a) of the National Minimum Wage Act 1998. Although pupils are generally unpaid, the Court of Appeal held that there was an intention to create legal relations. However, pupillage was not a contract of apprenticeship and the claimant was not a "worker" within the meaning of the 1998 Act—there was therefore no entitlement to receive the national minimum wage. Rather than applying a presumption, the court examined all the circumstances in order to ascertain objectively the parties' intentions.

It is not always easy to categorise an agreement as either commercial or social. It is possible that some agreements fall between an obviously commercial transaction and a purely social exchange. This difficulty faced the court in *Sadler v Reynolds*[32] where the claimant, an experienced journalist and professional ghostwriter claimed damages for breach of contract from the defendant businessman in relation to an alleged oral agreement to ghostwrite the defendant's autobiography. The claimant's case was based on a number of meetings between the parties including one that was of a social nature as the parties' wives were present. As a result of the discussions that took place between claimant and defendant, the former believed that an agreement had been entered into whereby the claimant would procure a publishing deal for writing the book and share any proceeds 50:50. The parties were offered an advance by a reputable publishing house at which point the defendant entered into an agreement with another writer to produce the autobiography.

It was held by Elizabeth Slade Q.C., sitting as deputy judge, that the facts of the case placed the agreement somewhere between the commercial and the social. The onus was on the claimant to prove an intention to create legal relations, although the onus was less heavy than that which

3–023

---

[30] [1989] 1 All E.R. 785.
[31] [2000] Q.B. 501
[32] [2005] EWHC 309.

would be required if the agreement was purely social in nature. The judge held that the claimant had discharged the necessary burden and therefore the defendant was liable in damages for breach of contract when he entered into a publishing contract for his autobiography to be written by another author.

Advertisements

3–024 Everyone nowadays will be familiar with the claims made by advertisers—indeed the public is bombarded with advertisements in almost all communications media. Advertisements are designed to attract custom, not legal liability, and are often deliberately vague and exaggerated—such statements are traditionally referred to as "advertisers' puff" or "mere puff".

The law has always held that mere puff is not intended to be legally binding—it is too vague to be legally enforceable. It should be noted, however, that even a precise statement will not be binding if it is clear that it was not seriously intended. In *Weeks v Tybald*[33] the defendant entered a tavern and, after drinks had been consumed, offered £100 to the man who would marry his daughter Polly, with his consent. The offer was accepted by the claimant but later the defendant refused to pay. The court held that the defendant was not bound—his words were simply "general words spoken to excite suitors".

It should not be assumed, however, that advertisements cannot have contractual force. It may be recalled that in the case of *Carlill v Carbolic Smokeball Company*[34] one of the company's defences was that there was no intention to be legally bound but the Court of Appeal rejected this argument on the ground that the company had deposited £1,000 in a bank as proof of their sincerity. The advertisement constituted an offer to the world at large which was accepted when a person fulfilled the condition contained in the offer.

3–025 The issue of contractual intention arose in an advertising context in the case of *Esso Petroleum Co Ltd v Customs and Excise Commissioners*[35] where, as a sales promotion scheme, Esso produced millions of free "World Cup coins". Each coin bore a likeness of members of the England squad for the 1970 World Cup. They advertised that they would give away a coin with the purchase of four gallons of petrol. The main issue in the case was whether the coins were produced for sale, and therefore subject to purchase tax. The House of Lords held (Lord Fraser dissenting) that, even if there was a contract, there was no sale as such. A "sale" involved, under the relevant legislation, a contract for which the consideration was a money price. In this case, the consideration for the coin was the entry by the motorist into another contract to buy the petrol. This resulted in a unilateral contract under which the petrol station proprietor bound himself to provide a coin to anyone purchasing four gallons of petrol.

On the issue of contractual intention the majority of the court was evenly divided. Lords Simon and Wilberforce considered that the circumstances were commercial in nature. Lord Simon said:

"Esso and the garage proprietors put the material out for their commercial advantage, and designed it to attract the custom of motorists. The whole transaction took place in a setting of business relations . . . It seems to me in general undesirable to allow a commercial

[33] (1605) Noy. 11.
[34] See para.2–007 above.
[35] [1976] 1 W.L.R. 1.

promoter to claim that what he has done is mere puff, not intended to create legal relations. . . The coins may have been themselves of little intrinsic value; but all the evidence suggest that Esso contemplated that they would be attractive to motorists and that there would be a large commercial advantage to themselves from the scheme, an advantage to which the garage proprietors would also share."

Viscount Dilhorne and Lord Russell considered that there was no intention to create legal relations because of the very small value of the coins, and also because of the language used which intimated that the coins were a free gift.

Collective agreements

A collective agreement is an agreement between a trade union and an employer regulating rates of pay and conditions of work. If the terms of such an agreement are incorporated into an individual employee's contract of service, they will be legally binding.[36]   **3–026**

With regard to the agreement itself, the position at common law was that collective agreements were not intended to be legally binding between union and employer. In *Ford Motor Company Ltd v Amalgamated Union of Engineering and Foundry Workers* [1969][37] Fords, with the purpose of ending a strike, brought an action against the union to enforce the terms of a collective agreement entered into by the company and the union. The company sought injunctions, however evidence was adduced that the general climate of opinion in the industry was that collective bargaining agreements of the type sought to be enforced were not intended to be legally binding. After referring to industrial, trade union and academic opinion, Geoffrey Lane J. held that the injunctions should be discharged—although such agreements were made in a commercial setting, their wording and the background against which they were made, i.e. adverse to enforcement, showed that the parties did not intend them to be binding contracts.

The position at common law has been affirmed by statute—under s.179(1) and (2) of the Trade Union and Labour Relations (Consolidation) Act 1992, a collective agreement is conclusively presumed not to have been intended by the parties to be a legally enforceable contract unless it is in writing and expressly provides to the contrary.

Certainty and intention: conclusion

We have seen that although a contract may be struck down on the grounds of vagueness or uncertainty, the courts may prepared to enforce a bargain which is incomplete and will fill the gaps by implying terms. They may have regard to previous dealings between the parties, any machinery within the contract or outside it (such as statutory provision) for resolving the uncertainty. Whether or not there has been performance under the contract is particularly significant. At the same time it may be possible to sever meaningless but superfluous terms from the contract to permit enforcement.   **3–027**

Intention to create legal relations is, as the authorities establish, an essential element of a binding contract. However, it does not have to be proved in every case as the law operates by

---

[36] *National Coal Board v Galley* [1958] 1 All E.R. 91.
[37] [1969] 2 Q.B. 303.

applying presumptions. In domestic and social agreements, the law presumes that there is no contractual intention and this may reflect an unwillingness on the part of the courts to become involved in disputes within families and amongst friends. It is also recognised that vague statements by advertisers, ("mere puff") are not intended to be legally binding. Commercial agreements, on the other hand, are presumed to be legally binding and it is a presumption not easily displaced. It would be surprising if it were otherwise.

We are now in a position to consider the requirement of consideration as a necessary element of a binding simple contract. This will be discussed in the next chapter.

Further reading

Buckley, R *Walford v Miles: a False Certainty about Uncertainty – an Australian Perspective* (1993) JCL 58.

Neill, P *A Key to Lock-out Agreements?* (1992) 108 L.Q.R. 405.

Hedley, S *Keeping Contract in its Place: Balfour v Balfour and the Enforceability of Informal Agreements* (1985) 5 O.J.L.S. 391.

Hepple, B *Intention to Create Legal Relations* (1970) 20 C.L.J. 122.

Chapter 4

CONSIDERATION AND ESTOPPEL

In addition to agreement (usually arrived at through offer and acceptance) and intention to create legal relations, a third requirement, "consideration" is an essential element in the formation of a simple contract. It is not, however, a requirement of a contract contained in a deed.[1] To the student approaching contract law for the first time, the concept of consideration is not perhaps as readily understandable as the need for agreement and the necessity of contractual intent. The first point to grasp is that in the formation of simple contracts English law enforces *bargains* as opposed to *promises*.

4–001

By way of example, suppose that one party, A (the "promisor") promises B (the "promisee") that A will paint the exterior of B's house. At this stage A has made a "bare" or gratuitous promise. A's promise will only become enforceable by B as a contract if B provides some consideration. The consideration from B might take the form of a payment of money but could consist of some other service to which A might agree—indeed it could involve an undertaking by B *not* to do something he otherwise might have done. Thus, the promisee must give something in return for the promise of the promisor in order to convert a bare promise made in his favour into a binding simple contract.

Moreover, the promise of a money payment or the rendering of a service *in the future* may be just a sufficient consideration as the actual payment itself or the actual rendering of the service. In this situation the consideration is referred to as being "executory"—thus a binding bilateral contract would be formed where X & Co agree with Y & Co that the former will deliver a consignment of widgets to the latter's premises the following Friday afternoon, payment to be made on delivery. The whole transaction, at the moment of offer and acceptance, is in the future. On the other hand, consideration will be classed as "executed" where it has been performed by a party—this is most likely to arise in the case of the unilateral contract where, e.g. a person offers a reward to anyone who provides certain information. It is only when the information has been provided that the promisor becomes liable on the promise. Both these types of consideration, executed and executory, must be distinguished from "past" consideration, which will be discussed below.

It follows that the law requires a simple contract to be a bargain and this aspect is stressed in the definition of consideration provided by Sir Charles Pollock, which was approved by Lord Dunedin in the case of *Dunlop Pneumatic Tyre Co Ltd v Selfridge Co Ltd*[2]:

4–002

---

[1] The distinction between deeds and simple contracts is discussed at para.1–006.
[2] [1915] A.C. 847. The quotation is taken from *Pollock on Contracts*, 8th edn., p.175.

"An act or forbearance of one party, or the promise thereof, is the price for which the promise of the other is bought, and the promise thus given for value is enforceable."

This definition emphasises the notion of exchange, i.e. that which is done, not done or promised by one party is given in return for the promise of the other.

Another well-known definition—and one that has attracted some criticism—was given by Lush J. in *Currie v Misa*[3]:

"A valuable consideration in the sense of the law, may consist either in some right, interest, profit or *benefit* accruing to the one party, or some forbearance, *detriment*, loss or responsibility given, suffered or undertaken by the other." [Author's italics]

Thus consideration may consist in a benefit to the promisor or a detriment to the promisee. Taken literally, this definition of Mr Justice Lush ignores the possibility that valuable consideration may be, as we have seen, purely executory. It also speaks of benefit and detriment as alternatives, "either/or". Whereas this is certainly correct—it is not necessary to have both—it might be more precise to say that whilst consideration may consist of a benefit to the promisor, in practical terms it must always consist of a detriment to the promisee because of the rule (discussed at para.4–009. below) that consideration must move from the promisee.

4–003   It should be noted that the words "benefit" and "detriment" do not refer to whether or not the bargain is an advantageous one—they are used in a legal as opposed to a factual sense. A person who, in return for a promise of a payment of money, promises to abstain from smoking will legally incur a detriment and provide consideration even though the promise is beneficial to the promisee's health. Despite the criticisms that have been made of the benefit/detriment dichotomy, it is suggested that it remains a useful test of whether there is consideration[4] although, as will be seen, it will not explain all of the decisions of the courts.

As we shall see in the discussion of estoppel later in this chapter, some promises may be binding even in the absence of consideration, that is where they have been relied on by the promisee.

Consideration is not so much a doctrine as a series of rules. The rules are: (i) consideration must not be past; (ii) consideration must move from the promisee; (iii) consideration need not be adequate but must be sufficient; and (iv) consideration must not consist of a duty already owed. These principles will now be considered.

Consideration must not be past

4–004   Consideration is said to be "past" when it consists of some benefit or service previously rendered to the promisor. Unlike executory or executed consideration, to which reference was made above, past consideration is not good or valid consideration. Suppose that, without being asked, a neighbour decides to weed my garden and mow my lawns. When he has finished, I promise him a case of wine. Am I contractually bound to deliver the wine? The answer is no, because the consideration from the neighbour was past consideration.

---

[3] (1875) L.R. 10 Ex. 153. See also *Thomas v Thomas* (1842) 2 Q.B. 851 where Patteson J. said: "Consideration means something which is of value in the eye of the law, moving from the plaintiff: it may be some detriment to the plaintiff or some benefit to the defendant."

[4] The benefit/detriment analysis played a significant role in the decision of the Court of Appeal in *Williams v Roffey Bros and Nicholls Ltd* [1991] 1 Q.B. 1 – see para.4–024.

In a nineteenth century decision, *Roscorla v Thomas*[5] Lord Denman C.J. stated that the promise must be "coextensive" with the consideration. In the case itself, the claimant had purchased the defendant's horse for £30. After the sale had been completed, the defendant promised that the creature was "sound and free from vice". In fact the horse turned out to be vicious. The claimant's action for breach of contract failed as the consideration for the promise, i.e. the sale, was past.

A more modern authority which embodies the same principle is the case of *Re McArdle , Decd.*[6] Here, the estate of a testator was held on trust for his five children (of whom Monty McArdle was one), in equal shares subject to the prior life interest of the testator's widow. Monty and his wife Marjorie lived in a bungalow forming part of the estate. Marjorie spent the sum of £488 carrying out improvements and alterations to the bungalow which were completed in 1944. In 1945 the McArdle children signed a document in the following terms:

> "To Mrs Marjorie McArdle . . .In consideration of your carrying out certain alterations improvements to the property . . . at present occupied by you. We the beneficiaries under the will hereby agree that the executors . . . shall repay to you from the said estate when so distributed the sum of £488 in settlement of the amount spent on such improvements."

The testator's widow later died and Marjorie sought payment of the £488 but the McArdle children, other than Monty, instructed the executors not to pay her. It was held by the Court of Appeal that since all the works had been completed before the execution of the document of 1945, the consideration for the promise to pay was wholly past—the promise was therefore purely gratuitous and unenforceable as a contract. In other words there was no exchange; nothing had been given in return for the promise. It made no difference that the promise was embodied in a signed document having all the appearance of a "contract". The outcome, however, seems rather unjust—one solution that might be open to the courts would be to imply a request to carry out the work. In commercial transactions it seems that there is a greater readiness to do this as may be seen from the cases considered below relating to the exception to the rule regarding past consideration—i.e. where performance is requested.   **4–005**

Requested performance exception

The courts may be prepared to find a consideration where the past service is preceded by the defendant's request. In *Lampleigh v Brathwait*[7] Brathwait had committed murder and he asked Lampleigh to obtain a pardon from the King. Accordingly, Lampleigh rode to and from London, Royston and Newmarket at his own expense and managed to get the pardon. Brathwait then promised Lampleigh the sum of £100 for his trouble but he later failed to pay. It was held that Brathwait was bound to pay the sum. The report of the case records: **4–006**

> "A mere voluntary courtesie will not have consideration to uphold an assumpsit [agreement]. But if that courtesie were moved by a suit or request of the party that gives the assumpsit, [ie the defendant] it will bind, for the promise, though it follows, yet it is not naked, but couples itself with the suit before."

[5] (1842) 3 Q.B. 234. See also *Eastwood v Kenyon* (1840) 11 A. & E. 238.
[6] [1951] Ch. 669.
[7] (1615) Hob. 105, Common Bench.

In other, more modern language, if A asks B to perform a service, B then performs it and sub-sequently A promises to pay B for the service or render some other service in return, A's promise is supported by consideration. There is the element of exchange which was lacking from the cases involving purely past consideration discussed in the previous section. In *Lampleigh v Brathwait* the contract-making process is a more protracted affair in which the request, the service and the payment are part of the same transaction. Indeed the promise to pay for the service is merely seen as fixing the amount. It may have been the case that Brathwait's request carried with it an implied promise that, if the pardon was obtained, Lampleigh would be rewarded in some way. This interpretation was suggested by Erle C.J. in *Kennedy v Broun*[8] where, in speaking of the *Lampleigh v Brathwait*, he said:

> "Probably . . . such service on such request would have raised an implication to pay what it was worth; and the subsequent promise of a sum certain would have been evidence for the jury to fix the amount."

4–007   For the exception to apply, it seems that the parties must have assumed throughout that the service would be paid for or rewarded in some way. This is more likely to be the case in a com-mercial context. A leading authority on the point is *Re Casey's Patents, Stewart v Casey*[9] where the claimant and partner registered certain patents for methods of storing hazardous liquids. They then approached the defendant with a view to exploiting commercially the patents, which he did. The claimant and partner later wrote to him in the following terms, "We now have pleasure in stating that in consideration of your services as practical manager in working both our patents . . .we hereby agree to give you one third share of the patents . . . . " The defendant later filed a claim to a one third share in the patents. In an action to have that claim removed from the register of patents, the Court of Appeal held that the defendant had a good claim. In addressing the argument that the defendant's consideration was past, Bowen L.J. said:

> "Now, the fact of a past service raises an implication that at the time it was rendered it was to be paid for, and, if it was a service which was to be paid for, when you get in the subse-quent document a promise to pay, that promise may be treated as an admission which evidences or as a positive bargain which fixes the amount of that reasonable remuneration on the faith of which the service was originally rendered. So that here for past services there is ample justification for the promise to give the one third share."

Whether there is an assumption that the requested service will be paid for depends on the context. In the commercial sphere the assumption is likely to be present because there is an expectation of payment. If my car breaks down and I phone the local garage to come and rescue me and fix the car, no-one would imagine that this service will provided for free. The position may be different if I were to phone a friend with the same request.

In *Pao On v Lau Yiu Long*[10] Lord Scarman summarised the position as follows:

> "An act done before the giving of a promise to make payment or to confer some other benefit can sometimes be consideration for a promise."

---

[8] (1863) 13 C.B. (NS) 677.
[9] [1892] 1 Ch. 104.
[10] [1979] 3 All E.R. 65.

Lord Scarman went on to identify three essentials:

(i)   the act must have been done at the promisor's request;

(ii) the parties must have understood that the act was to be remunerated either by payment or the conferment of some other benefit; and

(iii) payment, or the conferment of a benefit, must have been legally enforceable had it been promised in advance.

Statutory exceptions

Two statutory exceptions to the rule that past consideration is not good consideration should be noted. **4–008**

First, under the Bills of Exchange Act 1882, s.27(1)(b) an antecedent debt or liability is valuable consideration to support a bill of exchange. This means that past consideration will support a cheque, for example where a bank honours a cheque on an overdrawn account.

Secondly, s.29(5) of the Limitation Act 1980 provides that acknowledgment of a debt accrues from the date of the acknowledgment and not before. The effect of the provision, where it applies, will be to extend the normal statutory limitation period for the recovery of a debt. In the case of an action founded on a simple contract, that period is one of six years from the date on which the cause of action accrued.[11] Thus, if the debtor acknowledges the debt in the form of a promise within the original six year limitation period, the limitation period begins to run afresh—however the acknowledgment must be in writing and signed by the person making it.[12] In such cases, the only consideration for the acknowledgment of the debt is the pre-exiting debt, i.e. a past consideration.

Consideration must move from the promisee

It is a general rule that only a person who has provided consideration in return for a promise may enforce that promise as a contract. Thus in *Price v Easton*[13] Price was indebted to the claimant in the sum of £13. Price agreed to work for the defendant who promised to pay Price's wages to the claimant in order to settle the debt. Although Price duly worked for the defendant, the latter did not pay his wages to the claimant. It was held that the claimant could not recover the money from the defendant—no consideration had moved from claimant to defendant. **4–009**

At common law, the rule that consideration must move from the promisee may cause some hardship where, say, A enters into a contract with B that A and B will confer a benefit on C. Thus in *Tweddle v Atkinson*[14] Guy agreed with John Tweddle that they would each pay a sum of money to Tweddle's son William, who was Guy's prospective son-in-law. William's action against Guy's executors failed as no consideration had moved from him. This was so even though the purpose of the transaction was to benefit William in view of his forthcoming marriage to the daughter of Guy. Crompton J. said:

[11] Limitation Act 1980, s.5. Limitation of actions is discussed at para.17–027.
[12] Limitation Act, s.30(1).
[13] (1833) 4 B. & Ad. 433.
[14] (1861) 1 B. & S. 393. This decision was endorsed by the House of Lords in *Dunlop Pneumatic Tyre Co Ltd v Selfridge Co Ltd* [1915] A.C. 847, which is discussed at para.8–003.

> "The modern cases . . . show that the consideration must move from the party entitled to sue upon the contract. It would be a monstrous proposition to say that a person was a party to a contract for the purpose of suing upon it for his own advantage, and not a party to it for the purpose of being sued."

These references of Crompton J. to the parties to the contract are indicative of the fact that the rule that "consideration must move from the promisee" is closely related to another rule, the rule of "privity". Under the rule of privity, at common law, a person who was not a party to a contract (i.e. not "privy" to it) could not maintain an action under it. Similarly, a person who was not privy to a contract could not be bound by it. The rule of privity, insofar as it prevented a third party from enforcing a contract made for his benefit, has been substantially modified by the Contracts (Rights of Third Parties) Act 1999 which will be considered in Chapter 8. Inevitably, the reforms made by the Act have had an impact on the rule that consideration must move from the promisee with the result that third parties who have provided no consideration in cases such as *Tweddle v Atkinson* may now be able to succeed.

Although consideration must move *from* the promisee, it does not need to move *to* the promisor. This is illustrated by *Tweddle v Atkinson* itself since there was an enforceable contract between Guy and John Tweddle in which consideration had moved from John, although John would not benefit from the transaction, at least not in the practical sense.

Consideration need not be adequate but must be sufficient

4–010   Providing some consideration, as recognised by the law, is given in exchange for a promise, the courts are not concerned with whether the consideration is adequate in the circumstances—a contract is a bargain freely entered into and the courts are unconcerned with the relative value of the consideration given by either party. A contract that may be a bad bargain for one party will still be a valid contract. Thus, if in the absence of fraud or other legal wrong, A agrees to sell his Bentley Continental car worth £65,000 to B for £10, this is a perfectly good contract—each party has got what they bargained for even though for A it is an extremely bad bargain. Similarly, a rent of £1 per annum (a "peppercorn" rent) would be good consideration for the grant of a lease of a property with a market value of many millions providing, again, that the transaction was entered into freely.

Although consideration need not be adequate, it is said that to amount to good or valuable consideration to support a contract, it must be "sufficient". For consideration to be sufficient it must have some value in the eyes of the law. The meaning of these labels is far from obvious—a useful starting point in examining what is meant is the case of *Thomas v Thomas*.[15] Before his death, the claimant's husband had expressed the wish that the claimant should, after his death, live in his cottage for as long as she desired. After the husband had died, the claimant entered into a written agreement with her deceased husband's executors (the defendants) "in consideration" of the deceased's wish. The terms of the agreement were that the executors would convey the cottage to the widow for life on certain conditions, provided she paid the executors £1 per annum rental and kept the property in good repair. Later, however, the executors refused to convey the property to the claimant and turned her out of the cottage.

It was held by the Court of the Queen's Bench that there was a binding contract and so the

[15]   (1842) 2 Q.B. 851.

widow was allowed to remain in the cottage. The deceased's wish did not amount to good consideration, even though described as such in the agreement, as it did not move from the claimant. This was simply the motive for the promise. Sufficient consideration, however, was found in the promises to pay £1 a year towards the ground rent and in the undertaking to keep the property in good repair. It made no difference that £1 was not a full market rent for the property—consideration does not need to be adequate.

Trivial but sufficient consideration

A decision of the House of Lords—*Chappell & Co Ltd v Nestle Co Ltd*[16]—illustrates the point   **4–011** that consideration may consist of something apparently quite trivial. Nestle Co contracted with Hardy Co, manufacturers of gramophone records, to buy, for 4d a copy, records of a dance tune called "Rockin' Shoes". Chappell & Co owned the copyright in this tune. Nestle Co advertised the records for sale to the public at 1s 6d each plus three wrappers from their sixpenny milk chocolate bars. The wrappers, which were intrinsically worthless, were simply thrown away when received. The appellants, Chappell & Co, brought an action against the respondents, Nestle, claiming an injunction for breach of copyright. Now, s.8 of the Copyright Act 1956 permitted the making of records for retail sale provided that, from the retail sale of records, the copyright owner was paid a royalty of six and a quarter per cent of the "ordinary retail selling price". The question therefore arose as to whether the sale was a retail sale, where the only consideration is money, or were the wrappers part of the consideration? The House of Lords held, with Viscount Simonds and Lord Keith dissenting, that the wrappers were part of the consideration for the sale of the records. As the sale was therefore outside s.8 of the Act of 1956, there was a breach of copyright. In the majority, Lord Somervell said:

> "[The wrappers] are, in my view, part of the consideration. It is said that, when received, the wrappers are of no value to Nestle's. This I would have thought irrelevant. A contracting party can stipulate for whatever consideration he chooses. A peppercorn does not cease to be good consideration if it is established that the promisee does not like pepper and will throw away the corn. As the whole object of selling the record, if it was a sale, was to increase the sales of chocolate, it seems wrong not to treat the stipulated evidence of such sales as part of the consideration."

Lord Reid stressed the benefit to the respondents when he said:

> "The requirement that wrappers should be sent was of great importance to the Nestle Co.; there would have been no point in their simply offering records for 1s 6d each. It seems to me quite unrealistic to divorce the buying of the chocolate from the supplying of the records. It is a perfectly good contract if a person accepts an offer to supply goods if he (a) does something of value to the supplier and (b) pays money: the consideration is both (a) and (b)."

Lord Keith, dissenting, thought that the production of the wrappers was merely a qualification   **4–012** for purchasing the record. Both Lord Keith and Viscount Simonds were undoubtedly influenced

---

[16] [1960] A.C. 87.

in their minority view that the wrappers did not form part of the consideration by the fact that the wrappers were valueless and thrown away.

Consideration can therefore be relatively trivial but nevertheless sufficient. Another example of such consideration is the temporary and apparently purposeless deprivation of a chattel in the case of *Bainbridge v Firmstone*.[17] For reasons known only to himself, the defendant wanted to weigh two boilers belonging to the claimant. The claimant gave him permission to do so and the defendant promised that he would "within a reasonable time . . . leave and give up the boilers in as perfect and complete a condition" as when they were borrowed. The defendant weighed the boilers but left them in a "detached and divided" condition, i.e. in bits and pieces. When sued for breach of contract, the defendant argued that there was no consideration to support the contract in that there had been no detriment to the claimant nor benefit to himself. The Court of the Queen's Bench held that there was sufficient consideration—the transaction was not gratuitous. Patteson J. thought that the consideration was that the claimant, at the defendant's request, had consented to allow the defendant to weigh the boilers. He said:

"I suppose the defendant thought he had some benefit; at any rate, there is a detriment to the [claimant] from his parting with possession for even so short a time."

Compromise of claims and forbearance to sue

4–013   It is a well established principle that if, in civil proceedings, a person with a valid legal claim against another, for example in contract or tort, promises to forbear from enforcing it, this will constitute good consideration for a promise to settle the claim made by the other. This is the basis of "out of court" settlements. It seems that the position will be the same where there is no actual promise to forbear but the party with the claim actually forbears. In *Alliance Bank Ltd v Broom*[18] the defendant borrowed £22,000 from the claimant bank at which point the claimant asked for security and the defendant promised to give the claimant a charge over goods the defendant was due to receive from a third party. In return, the claimant made no express promise not sue the defendant. However, the defendant failed to complete the necessary documentation and the claimant sought to enforce the charge by obtaining the documents of title to the goods. The issue was whether the claimant had given any consideration in return for the defendant's promise. It was held that the claimant had provided consideration in its actual forbearance from suing, even in the absence of an express promise. Kindersley V.C. considered that although there was no promise on the part of the claimants to abstain from suing, the effect was that:

". . . the [claimant] did in effect give, and the defendant received, the benefit of some degree of forbearance; not indeed, for any definite time but, at all events, some extent of forbearance."

It is difficult to see how actual forbearance in these circumstances could be regarded as a detriment suffered by the claimant or a benefit to the defendant since the claimant would be free at any time to enforce the security. Perhaps the decision is best explained as an example of the

---

[17] (1838) 8 Ad. & E. 743.
[18] (1865) 34 L.J. Ch. 256.

court's readiness to find a consideration where it considers the transaction ought to be binding, in the interests of justice, policy or commercial practice.

The courts have further held that a promise not to pursue an invalid claim, i.e. one that would fail at law, may constitute sufficient consideration to settle an action. In *Callisher v Bischoffsheim*[19] the claimant believed that money was owed to him by the Government of Honduras. He was about to commence proceedings to enforce payment when the defendant promised to deliver to him certain securities if the claimant would forbear from suing the Honduras Government. In fact the claim was unfounded. It was held that the defendant was bound as the fact that the action would have failed did not invalidate the consideration. Cockburn C.J. said:

> "The authorities clearly establish that if an agreement is made to compromise a disputed claim, forbearance to sue in respect of that claim is a good consideration; and whether proceedings to enforce the disputed claim have or have not been instituted makes no difference. If the defendant's contention were adopted, it would result that in no case of a doubtful claim could a compromise be enforced. Every day a compromise is effected on the ground that the party making it has a chance of succeeding in it, and *if he bona fide believes he has a fair chance of success*, he has a reasonable ground for suing, and his forbearance to sue will constitute a good consideration. [Author's italics]"[20]

If the claimant, however, knows that they have no valid cause of action they will not give good consideration. In *Wade v Simeon*[21] the claimant was aware that he had no valid claim and the agreement to stay proceedings was not enforceable.

Finding a consideration

The courts can, on occasion, be fairly imaginative in "finding" a consideration in the interests of justice. Put simply, if the court considers that the promise ought to be legally enforceable, it may find something of value given in exchange for the promise. One such example is the decision in *Ward v Byham*[22] which is discussed below at para.4–020 and another is the case of *De la Bere v Pearson*.[23] In this case the defendants, proprietors of a newspaper called MAP, advertised in the paper that their city editor would give free financial advice to readers. The claimant wrote to the city editor asking for the name of a "good stockbroker". The editor recommended a broker who was an undischarged bankrupt. Although this fact was unknown to the editor, he could easily have discovered the broker's financial position, had he made inquiries. The claimant, in reliance on the editor's recommendation, sent sums of money to the broker who misappropriated them. The Court of Appeal held that there was a contract between the claimant and the defendants. The defendants' advertisement constituted an offer which the claimant had accepted when he wrote in for advice. Vaughan Williams L.J. found consideration in the fact that:

4–014

---

[19] (1870) L.R. 5 Q.B. 449.
[20] See also *Horton v Horton (No 2)* [1961] 1 Q.B. 215. In addition to having a bona fide belief in the success of the claim, it seems that the potential claimant must make full and honest disclosure to the potential defendant of matters which might affect the validity of the claim; *Miles v New Zealand Alford Estate Co* (1886).
[21] (1846) 2 C.B. 548.
[22] [1956] 1 W.L.R 496. See also *Shadwell v Shadwell* (1860) 9 C.B. N.S. 169, discussed below at para.4–026.
[23] [1908] 1 K.B. 280.

"The questions and answers were, if the defendants chose, to be inserted in their paper as published; such publication might obviously have a tendency to increase the sale of the defendants' paper. I think that this offer, [in the advertisement] when accepted, resulted in a contract for good consideration."

Vaughan Williams L.J. provided no further illumination on the question of consideration and the other members of the court assumed the existence of contract—consideration was not therefore an issue in the case. Nevertheless, the notion that the claimant provided consideration is open to criticism. One possible explanation may lie in the fact that the claimant purchased a copy of the paper. But it is difficult to see how the claimant could be said to have given something of value in exchange for the promise if all he did was to buy a copy of the paper. The other possibility, and the one put forward by Vaughan Williams L.J., i.e. that the publication of the letter might increase the paper's circulation seems rather artificial. The reality is that, unless a contract could be found, the claimant would have gone without a remedy. This is because the case pre-dated the recognition by the courts—in *Hedley Byrne & Co Ltd v Heller & Partners*[24]— that negligent misstatement causing economic loss could render the giver of advice liable in negligence. Were the facts to arise today, it is likely that a remedy would be found in the tort of negligence.

Illusory consideration

4–015   We have seen that, in order to be sufficient, consideration must have some value, however trivial or slight. There are, however, limits. If the consideration is empty or illusory, or concerned with feelings or sentiment, the courts have tended to regard it as insufficient. This principle is sometimes expressed by saying that consideration must have some "economic" value, although, as we have seen, this economic value could be vestigial.

In *White v Bluett*[25] the defendant became indebted to his father and he gave the father a promissory note. The defendant then complained bitterly to his father that the father had treated him less well than his siblings. The father then agreed with the defendant that, in consideration of the defendant ceasing to complain and also out of natural love and affection for his son, his father would release him from liability on the debt. On the father's death, the claimant, who was the executor of the father's estate, brought an action to recover the loan. The action succeeded. The court held that no consideration had been furnished by the defendant—the son's promise not to bore the father with his complaints was considered to have no economic value.

Moral obligation not consideration

4–016   *Eastwood v Kenyon*[26] supports the notion that a promise is not rendered enforceable by the existence of a moral obligation. In that case the claimant was the guardian of a minor, Sarah Sutcliffe. He borrowed £140 from a third party in order to manage and improve her property

---

[24] [1964] A.C. 465. See para.11–023.
[25] (1853) 23 L.J. Ex. 36.
[26] (1840) 11 Ad. & E. 438.

and to pay for her education. When Sarah came of age, she promised to reimburse the claimant. The defendant, whom she later married, made the same promise but later, the defendant refused to pay. The claimant's action to recover payment failed because the pre-existing moral obligation was insufficient consideration.[27] The case is also an example of "past" consideration.[28]

Consideration must not consist of a duty already owed

Another group of cases where consideration has been held to be insufficient is where it consists of a promise to perform, or the performance of, some existing duty owed by the promisee to the promisor, either as a result of some public duty or under an existing contract with the promisor.

4–017

Existing public duty

Collins v Godefroy[29] is the traditional authority for the proposition that the performance of an existing public duty (or the promise to perform it) is not a sufficient consideration. In that case, the defendant promised to pay the claimant a sum of money for giving evidence in a court action in which the claimant had been served with a subpoena. As the claimant was under a legal duty to attend the trial, it was held that he had not furnished consideration. Although witnesses are now entitled, under changes brought about by statute, to receive expenses and in some cases compensation, the principle in the case is still a good one.

4–018

There are, however, suggestions in some cases (e.g. *Morgan v Palmer*[30]) that the real reason for the law refusing to enforce promises to perform an existing public duty is not of lack of consideration, but public policy.

Where the promisee exceeds their existing public duty, they thereby provide good consideration. They are doing more than they are already bound to do. The issue has arisen in connection with payments to the police for providing services going beyond their ordinary run of duty.

In *Glasbrook Bros Ltd v Glamorgan County Council*[31] the defendants owned collieries in Glamorganshire. In 1921 a settlement of the national miners' strike was reached but workers in the defendants' mines remained on strike. When the "safety men" whose job it was to keep the mines clear of water felt unable to work for fear of reprisals, the defendants approached the police to ask for protection for the men. The police considered that a mobile guard, which could be deployed swiftly if trouble occurred, would be sufficient. The defendants, however, insisted on having officers billeted at the mines and the police only agreed to this request if the defendants agreed to pay them for the service. Eventually, the strike was resolved peacefully but the defendants refused to pay the sum of £2,200 11s. 6d. requested by the police authority. The defendants argued that the police, in providing protection, had done no more than their existing duty by law.

---

[27] The court rejected Lord Mansfield's doctrine that, "Where a man is under a moral obligation . . . the honesty and rectitude of the thing is consideration . . . The ties of conscience upon an upright mind are sufficient consideration." (*Hawkes v Saunders* (1782) 1 Cowp. 289).

[28] For a discussion of past consideration, see para.4–004.

[29] (1831) 1 B. & Ad. 950.

[30] (1825) 2 B. & C. 729.

[31] [1925] A.C. 270.

4–019 The House of Lords held that the police were entitled to recover, as their duty only required them to provide such protection as was, in their opinion, reasonably necessary. In providing a stationary guard they had exceeded that duty and were entitled to payment. The basis of the decision in this case was explained by Viscount Finlay:

> "There is no doubt that it is the duty of the police to give adequate protection to all persons and to their property. In discharging this duty, those in control of the police must exercise their judgment as to the manner in which that protection should be afforded. If a particular person desires protection of a special sort and the police can give this without interfering with the discharge of their duties elsewhere, it is difficult to see on what ground of public policy it should be illegal that a charge should be made in respect of special protection."

Ultimately, cases of this nature must be governed by considerations of public policy rather than the rules of consideration. Any suggestion that the promise to pay has been obtained by corrupt means, e.g. extortion, will mean that the transaction would be unenforceable on public policy grounds.

The common law principle established in *Glasbrook v Glamorgan* was placed on a statutory basis by s.15(1) of the Police Act 1964. Under this provision the police could claim payment for "special police services" rendered at the request of persons requiring the services. The provision was in issue in *Harris v Sheffield United Football Club*.[32] When football matches were being played at Sheffield United's ground police officers were in attendance. The club formed the view that the chief constable was obliged to provide police attendance in order to fulfil his existing duty to maintain law and order and protect life and property. The club accordingly refused to make payments to the police authority who then brought an action to recover payment on the ground that their attendances constituted "special police services". The club argued that the attendances did not constitute such services as the police, in attending the matches, were doing no more than fulfilling their existing duty. The club also denied that it had "requested" such services.

The Court of Appeal held that the provision of police officers at the ground to guard against the possibility of violence did constitute special police services for which a charge could be made. Since a police presence was required in order for matches to take place it followed that a request for their attendance by the club was implied.

4–020 *Harris v Sheffield United FC* was distinguished by the Court of Appeal in *Reading Festival Ltd v West Yorkshire Police Authority*.[33] In this case the claimant police authority sought to recover payment for special police services, under the Police Act 1996, s.25(1) which, in identical terms, replaced s.15(1) of the Police Act 1964. For some years the defendants, promoters of a music festival, had requested and paid the claimants for special police services at their annual festival. The defendants then wished to move their festival to a different venue but the claimants opposed their application for a public entertainments licence. As a result the parties did not come to an agreement as to how the police were to be deployed. Following the grant of the entertainment licence, there was a change of police strategy at the new venue, in that there would be a small number of plain clothes officers on site but a greater number of officers in the surrounding area. The defendants had therefore hired private security staff to make up for the

---

[32] [1987] 2 All E.R. 838.
[33] [2006] 1 W.L.R. 2005.

lack of police presence on the festival site itself. The defendants argued (1) that they had made no request for special police services; and (2) the services provided by the police were not special police services within the meaning of the Act of 1996. The basis of the latter contention was that if there were no police presence on site they were not liable to pay for other services—officers deployed off site were providing ordinary police services and not special police services.

Reversing a decision of Grenfell J., the Court of Appeal found for the defendants. On the facts there had been no request for special police services, nor were the services themselves "special police services". Scott Baker L.J. said:

"[T]he fact that the services were not on private property in this case is an important factor. In many, perhaps most, cases whether the services are provided on private property or in a public place is likely to be a very strong factor in determining whether they are 'special police services'. There is a strong argument that where promoters put on a function such as a music festival or sporting event which is attended by large numbers of the public the police should be able to recover the additional cost they are put to for policing the event and the local community affected by it. That however is not the law."

The court came to a unanimous conclusion that the claimants did not, on balance, provide special police services.

The issue of whether existing public duty constitutes consideration has arisen in the area of family relationships. In *Ward v Byham*[34] a man and a woman lived together unmarried during which time a daughter was born. Later, the father turned the mother out and put the child into the care of a neighbour. Subsequently, the mother found work as a housekeeper and asked for her daughter to come and live with her. The father wrote to the mother in the following terms, "I am prepared to let you have [the child] and pay you up to £1 per week allowance providing you can prove that she will be well looked after and happy and also that she is allowed to decide for herself whether or not she wishes to come and live with you." The mother agreed and looked after the child on these terms. The father kept up the payments but later stopped paying when the mother married another man. The mother sued the father for the allowance and the father claimed that the mother had not provided any consideration, in that the mother, in looking after the child, was only doing what she was legally bound to do. The basis of this claim was that, as the mother of an illegitimate child she was already required by statute, under s.42 of the National Assistance Act 1948, to "maintain" the child.

The Court of Appeal found for the mother. The majority of the court (Morris and Parker L.JJ.) held that the mother had exceeded her statutory duty in promising to keep the child well looked after and happy and by allowing her to choose with whom she lived. It could be argued that keeping a child "well looked after" and "happy" is part and parcel of maintaining it and so in finding as they did the majority have stretched the limits of legal benefit and detriment in order to arrive at a just result. The majority decision is also difficult to reconcile with the principle that consideration must have some economic value and should not be concerned with feelings and sentiment and suchlike.[35]

Lord Denning L.J. agreed that there was consideration but on a quite different and more radical basis. He said:

4–021

---

[34] [1956] 1 W.L.R. 496.
[35] See para.4–015.

"I approach the case, . . . on the footing that the mother, in looking after the child, is only doing what she is legally bound to do. Even so, I think that there was sufficient consideration to support the promise. I have always thought that a promise to perform an existing duty, or the performance of it, should be regarded as good consideration, because it is a benefit to the person to whom it is given. Take this very case. It is as much a benefit for the father to have the child looked after by the mother as by a neighbour. If he gets the benefit for which he stipulated, he ought to honour his promise; and he ought not to avoid it by saying that the mother was herself under a duty to maintain the child."

Denning L.J. was prepared to recognise a factual benefit as constituting consideration. He was later to repeat this proposition in *Williams v Williams*[36] adding the proviso that there should be nothing in the transaction that is contrary to the public interest.

Existing contractual duty

4–022   The traditional rule here is that the performance of an existing contractual duty owed to the promisor, or the promise thereof, is not a sufficient consideration. The promisee provides no consideration for a fresh promise made by the promisor in simply doing, or promising to do, something the promisee is already contractually bound to the promisor to do. The promisee incurs no detriment by repeating an existing obligation, nor does the promisor enjoy a benefit.

Authority for the principle is to be found in the case of *Stilk v Myrick*.[37] Here, on a voyage from London to the Baltic and back, two seamen deserted at a port of call. The captain was unable to find replacements at Cronstadt and so offered the remaining eight crew members the deserters' wages divided equally between them if they would work the ship short-handed back to London. The crew did this but the captain did not honour his promise. It was held by the Court of the King's Bench that the captain's promise was not binding.

The reports of the case reveal two alternative bases for the decision; (i) that the crew had not provided any consideration; and (ii) that the promise could not be enforced as it was contrary to public policy. With regard to the first ground, the principle is that the seamen had, by sailing the ship home, simply performed an existing contractual duty. Lord Ellenborough said:

"[T]he agreement is void for want of consideration. There was no consideration for the ulterior pay promised to the mariners who remained with the ship. Before they sailed from London they had undertaken to do all that they could under all emergencies of the voyage. . . . the desertion of a part of the crew is to be considered an emergency of the voyage as much as their death; and those who remain are bound by the terms of their original contract to exert themselves to the utmost to bring the ship in safety to her destined port."

4–023   This basis for the decision, i.e. that the agreement lacked consideration, has been supported in more modern times in *Swain v West (Butchers) Ltd*[38] and *North Ocean Shipping Co Ltd v*

---

[36] [1957] 1 W.L.R 148.
[37] (1809) 2 Camp. 317; and (1809) 6 Esp. 129.
[38] [1936] 3 All E.R. 261.

Hyundai Construction Co Ltd, The Atlantic Baron.[39] The other reported basis for the decision—and the one considered less authoritative—is that of public policy. This derived from another seamens' wages case, *Harris v Watson*[40] where a seaman claimed that the captain had promised a sum over and above his ordinary wages if he would assist in navigating the ship when the ship was in danger. The claim failed, Lord Kenyon C.J. saying:

> "If this action were to be supported, it would materially affect the navigation of this kingdom . . . if sailors were in all events to have their wages, and in times of danger entitled to insist on an extra charge on such a promise as this, they would in many cases suffer a ship to sink, unless the captain would pay the extravagant demand they might think proper to make."

The decision reflected a concern that the law should not encourage a situation that might lead to extortion or even mutiny on the part of sailors. However, there was no suggestion of any such thing on the facts in *Harris v Watson* or *Stilk v Myrick*. The more authoritative report of *Stilk v Myrick* has Lord Ellenborough saying that *Harris v Watson* was rightly decided but that he doubted whether public policy was the true ground on which the claimants' action in *Stilk v Myrick* failed—as we have seen he preferred to base it on want of consideration.

As with existing public duty, discussed above, it seems that where the existing contractual duty is exceeded, consideration will be provided. In *Hartley v Ponsonby*[41] the ship *Mobile* left England with a crew of 36. At Port Philip 17 sailors deserted and of the 19 remaining on board, only four or five were able seamen. Being unable to sign on any hands, the defendant (the ship's captain) promised to pay the remaining able seamen (including the claimant) an extra £40 each if they would work the ship to Bombay. They agreed and the ship arrived safely at Bombay. Later the defendant refused to pay the extra wages; however, the claimant's action against him for the extra pay succeeded. Consideration had been provided because the multiple desertion had left the ship so short handed that the voyage had become dangerous. Lord Campbell C.J. explained the decision on the basis that the claimant and the remaining crew were not bound under their original contract to proceed on the voyage and so were free to enter into a fresh bargain—nowadays this would be treated as a case of discharge of a contract by "frustration".[42]

The rule in *Stilk v Myrick* came in for some re-evaluation by the Court of Appeal in *Williams v Roffey Bros. & Nicholls (Contractors) Ltd.*[43] The claimant was a carpenter who contracted with the defendants to carry out carpentry work for the agreed sum of £20,000. The defendants were the main contractors in refurbishing a block of 27 flats; this contract contained a time penalty clause. The transaction proved to be unprofitable for the claimant and he got into financial difficulty. Concerned that the claimant would not complete the carpentry work on time, the defendants promised the claimant the additional sum of £10,300 (at £575 per completed flat) if he would carry out the work on time. The claimant substantially completed eight

4–024

---

[39] [1979] Q.B. 705. The case is discussed at para.13–004. In *Compagnie Noga D'Importation et D'Exportation SA v Abacha (No 4)* [2003] 2 All E.R. (Comm) 915 the Court of Appeal distinguished *Stilk v Myrick*—it has no application where an earlier agreement is discharged by agreement and replaced by later one. In such a case, consideration is provided by the mutual release of the executory promises under the earlier agreement as well as the provision of fresh consideration under the later agreement.

[40] (1791) Peake. 102.

[41] (1857) 7 El. & Bl. 872.

[42] See Chapter 10.

[43] [1991] 1 Q.B.1. See also Coote (1990) 3 J.C.L. 23 and Halson (1990) 106 L.Q.R. 183.

more flats but was not paid the amount promised. The claimant stopped work and brought an action against the defendants for the additional sum promised by them.

It is worth pausing at this moment to note that, on these facts, it would appear that the claimant has done no more than promise to perform an existing contractual duty. Legally, he has incurred no additional detriment nor has he conferred a benefit on the defendants. Nevertheless the court held that the promise to pay the claimant the extra money was contractually binding, i.e. there was sufficient consideration. The court identified certain practical benefits that the defendants admitted they hoped to secure from the agreement, i.e. ensuring that the claimant continued with the work; avoiding the penalty for delay; avoiding the trouble and expense of engaging another carpenter to complete the work; and replacing a haphazard method of payment by a more formal scheme involving the payment of a specified sum on the completion of each flat. As the transaction had been freely entered into and served the interests of both parties, why should these not be capable of amounting to consideration to support a variation of the contract? Purchas L.J. said that prima facie, the case appeared to be a classic *Stilk v Myrick* one. However, he continued :

> "With some hesitation . . . I consider the modern approach to the question of consideration would be that where there were benefits derived by each party to a contract of variation even though one party did not suffer a detriment this would not be fatal to the establishing of sufficient consideration to support the agreement. If both parties benefit from an agreement it is not necessary that each also suffers a detriment."

In a similar vein, Russell L.J. said that he did not believe that "the rigid approach to the concept of consideration to be found in *Stilk v Myrick* is either necessary or desirable." Glidewell L.J. expressed the principle being laid down more precisely than the other members of the court. The "Glidewell criteria" are as follows:

> "If A has entered into a contract with B to do work for, or to supply goods and services to, B in return for payment by B; and (ii) at some stage before A has completely performed his obligations under the contract, B has reason to doubt whether A will, or will be able to, complete his side of the bargain; and (iii) B thereupon promises A an additional payment in return for A's promise to perform his contractual obligations on time; and (iv) as a result of giving his promise, B obtains in practice a benefit, or obviates a disbenefit; and (v) B's promise is not given as a result of economic duress or fraud on the part of A; then (vi) the benefit to B is capable of being consideration for B's promise, so that the promise will be legally binding."

4–025   Glidewell L.J. found support for these propositions in the approach of the majority in *Ward v Byham* (see para.4–018) and in the rule that the performance of, or the promise to perform, an existing contractual duty owed to a third party constitutes good consideration. This is an established exception to the rule in *Stilk v Myrick* and was affirmed in the cases of *New Zealand Shipping Co Ltd v A M Satterthwaite & Co Ltd*[44] and *Pao On v Lau Yiu Long*[45] which are discussed at paras 7–033 and 13–010 respectively.

Glidewell L.J. did not consider that the propositions being put forward in *Williams v Roffey*

[44] [1975] A.C. 154.
[45] [1980] A.C. 614.

Bros contravened the principle in *Stilk v Myrick,* instead he thought they refined and limited the application of the principle. The principle itself he saw as being unscathed and applying, for example, where the promisor secures no benefit by his promise. But, as the captain of the ship in *Stilk v Myrick* surely did receive practical or factual benefits from his promise to pay the extra money, it is difficult to see the precise basis upon which *Stilk v Myrick* was being distinguished in *Williams v Roffey Bros.* One possible distinction is that in *Williams v Roffey Bros* the public policy element identified in one of the reports of *Stilk v Myrick* was lacking, i.e. there was no evidence in the former case that duress or improper pressure was brought to bear by the claimant Williams on the defendants Roffey Bros. Thus, in the course of his judgment, Purchas J., in referring to *Harris v Watson* and *Stilk v Myrick,* said:

> "There were strong public policy grounds at that time to protect the master and owners of a ship from being held to ransom by disaffected crews . . . the decision that the promise to pay extra wages even in the circumstances established in those cases, was not supported by consideration is readily understandable."

The principle established in *Williams v Roffey Bros* is also open to criticism on the basis that it appears to ignore the rule, discussed above at para.4–009, that consideration must move from the promisee, i.e. the benefits potentially enjoyed by the defendants did not arise from anything done by the promisee Williams in exchange for the promise. The factual benefits identified in the case derived from the promise to pay extra money so that the work would be completed on time.[46]

Whatever the reservations concerning *Williams v Roffey Bros*[47] there can be no doubt that the decision marks a move away from reliance on technical rules of consideration towards a climate where the courts will be more willing to enforce contractual renegotiations freely entered into by parties of not unequal bargaining power. The safeguard against abuse of this freedom lies in the developing doctrine of economic duress.[48]

Existing contractual duty owed to third party

Suppose that A makes a promise to B in return for B performing, or promising to perform a duty which B already owes to C under an existing contract with C. Does B provide consideration? Given what has already been said about existing duties not amounting to consideration, it might be thought that no consideration is furnished in this situation, but this is not the law.   **4–026**

The first case to be considered is *Shadwell v Shadwell.*[49] Charles Shadwell wrote to his nephew Lancey, after the latter had engaged to marry Ellen Nichol, in the following terms, "I am glad to hear of your intended marriage with Ellen Nichol, and, as I promised to assist you at starting,

---

[46] In *South Carribean Trading v Trafigura Beheer BV* [2005] 1 Lloyd's Rep. 128 Colman J. obiter, strenuously criticised the reasoning on which the decision in *Williams v Roffey Bros* was based—he considered that the decision was "inconsistent" with the rule that consideration, being the price of the promise sued upon, must move from the promisee.

[47] The approach of the Court of Appeal in *Williams v Roffey Bros* has been applied in *Anangel Atlas Compania Naviera SA v Ishikawajima Heavy Industries Co Ltd (No 2)* [1990] 2 Lloyds Rep. 526; *Lee v GEC Plessey Telecommunications* [1993] I.R.L.R. 383; and *Simon Container Machinery Ltd v Emba Machinery AB* [1998] 2 Lloyd's Rep. 429.

[48] For a discussion of economic duress, see Chapter 13.

[49] (1860) 9 C.B. N.S. 159. See also *Chichester v Cobb* (1866) 14 L.T. 433 where the court arrived at the same conclusion as *Shadwell v Shadwell* on similar facts.

I am happy to tell you that I will pay you £150 yearly during my life, and until your annual income derived from your profession as a Chancery barrister shall amount to 600 gns . . . ". Lancey married Ellen but the uncle did not pay all the instalments. On the uncle's death, Lancey brought an action to recover the arrears from the uncle's executors. The defendant executors argued that the claimant Lancey had given no consideration for the uncle's promise as, when the uncle made his promise, the claimant was already contractually bound to marry Ellen (such engagement being a contractually binding commitment at the time). The court found a consideration and held that the uncle's promise was binding. The claimant, in the view of Erle C.J. (with whom Keating J. agreed), had suffered a detriment because he may well have incurred financial liabilities on the strength of the promise. The marriage was a benefit to the uncle because it was "an object of interest" with a near relative. Byles J., dissenting, considered that the promise was no more than a gift conditional on marriage. The decision has come in for some criticism—it is difficult to see how the nephew incurred any additional detriment in reliance on the uncle's promise; and the benefit identified by the majority of the court seems to be concerned with sentiment rather than having some economic value. It is also doubtful, given the family nature of the arrangement, whether there was any intention to create legal relations.

A more reliable authority and one concerning a commercial transaction is *Scotson v Pegg*.[50] Here the claimants entered into a contract with X to deliver a cargo of coal to X "or to X's order" (i.e. to whomsoever X should order it to be delivered). X directed the claimants to deliver it to the defendant, who promised to unload it at the rate of 49 tons a day, but this undertaking was not observed. The claimants argued that the delivery of the coal to the defendant was consideration for the defendants' promise. It was the defendant's contention that, in delivering the coal, the claimants provided no consideration as they were already contractually bound to X to deliver it; they had incurred no detriment. The claimants' action succeeded. Martin B considered that the defendant obtained a benefit by the delivery of the coals to him and "it is immaterial that the [claimants] had previously contracted with third parties to deliver their order." Wilde B found a detriment suffered by the claimant in that it might have suited him to breach the contract with X and compensate X, and by delivering the coal to defendant this possibility was extinguished.

4–027   In these cases we see the courts content to uphold a contract on the basis of an existing contractual duty owed to a third party, but using considerable imagination in order to justify the decisions on the basis of benefit and detriment. One explanation for the rule could be that, where B promises A that B will perform an existing contractual duty owed to C, consideration has moved from B as he has made himself liable to an additional party, A. The detriment suffered by B lies in the fact that he could be sued by A as well as the third party C. But perhaps the principle is best explained on the basis that in this situation the promise is binding even though no additional detriment is incurred by B; in other words it is simply an exception to the rule in *Stilk v Myrick* regarding existing contractual duty owed to the promisor. Such an exception can be justified on the basis that the "public policy" element in *Stilk v Myrick* is lacking— the risk that promises could be obtained by extortion or duress where three parties are involved is not as great.

Whatever doubts there may be concerning the earlier cases, modern authority has affirmed the principle in them. In *New Zealand Shipping Co Ltd v A M Satterthwaite & Co Ltd*[51] Lord Wilberforce stated:

---

[50] (1861) 3 L.T. 753.
[51] [1975] A.C. 154. The case is discussed further at para.7–XX.

"An agreement to do an act which the promisor is under an existing obligation to a third party to do, may quite well amount to valid consideration . . . the promisee obtains the benefit of a direct obligation which he can enforce. This proposition is illustrated and supported by *Scotson v Pegg* . . . which their Lordships consider to be good law."

In the case itself, the defendants, stevedores, unloaded a cargo from a ship, this being something they were already contractually bound to do in a contract with a third party. The performance of this act was held to be sufficient consideration for the claimant's promise to exempt the defendants from liability for damaging the goods.

Lord Scarman was to confirm Lord Wilberforce's statement in *N Z Shipping v Satterthwaite* in a later case—*Pao On v Lau Yiu Long*[52]—and with equal certainty.

PART PAYMENT OF DEBTS

The discharge of debts gives rise to certain problems with regard to consideration. Suppose that A owes £100 to B. B accepts £50 in full satisfaction of the debt. Can B later claim the balance of £50 from A? Whether B can do so will depend on whether A has provided any consideration for the promise to accept part payment.   **4–028**

Part payment: the common law rule

The traditional rule was laid down in *Pinnel's Case* (1602).[53] P sued C for a debt of £8 10s which was due to be paid on November 11. C argued that P had requested him, on October 1, to pay £5 2s 6d and that P had accepted this in full satisfaction. P succeeded on a technicality. However, the Court of Common Pleas made it clear that, but for this, judgment would have been in favour of C because he had tendered part payment, at the request of P, at a date earlier than required under the contract. In modern terms, he had provided what would now be regarded as consideration for the promise to accept part payment.   **4–029**

The court, through Lord Coke, laid down the general rule at common law with regard to the part payment of debts (although it is strictly obiter):

"Payment of a lesser sum on the day [it is due to be paid] cannot be any satisfaction for the whole, because it appears to the judges that by no possibility a lesser sum can be satisfaction to the [claimant] for a greater sum."

However the court considered that satisfaction would be provided (so as to discharge the debt) if, at the creditor's request, (i) part payment was tendered at an earlier date than the due date (as in the case itself); (ii) goods were tendered instead of money (a "horse, a hawk or a robe"); or (iii) part payment was accepted at a different place.

The rule about part payment was affirmed, with some reluctance, by the House of Lords in *Foakes v Beer*.[54] Dr Foakes was indebted to Mrs Beer in the sum of £2,090. 19s for which she

---

[52] [1980] A.C. 614.
[53] (1602) 5 Co. Rep. 117a.
[54] (1854) 9 App. Cas. 605. The principle in *Foakes v Beer* was applied in *Ferguson v Davies* [1997] 1 All E.R. 315.

went to court and obtained judgment against him. Mrs Beer was prepared to allow the debtor time to pay and they agreed in writing that if he would pay off the debt by instalments she would "not take any proceedings whatever on the said judgment". Dr Foakes duly paid off the debt. Mrs Beer then realised that she had not charged the interest of 4% that, by statute, was always due on a judgment debt. When Dr Foakes refused to pay the additional sum, she applied for leave to sue for it and contended that Dr Foakes had given no consideration for the agreement. The House of Lords held that the claimant was entitled to the interest.

On the construction of the agreement their Lordships were divided; however there was no disagreement that the defendant had not provided any consideration for the claimant's promise to forgive the interest. The Earl of Selborne V.C. said:

> "The question . . . nakedly raised by this appeal, whether your Lordships are now prepared to overrule, as contrary to law, the doctrine . . . laid down by all the judges of the Common Pleas in *Pinnel's Case*. . . The doctrine itself . . . may have been criticised, as questionable in principle, by some persons whose opinions are entitled to respect, but it has never been judicially overruled . . . I cannot think that your lordships would do right, if you were now to reverse, as erroneous, a judgment of the Court of Appeal, proceeding upon a doctrine which has been accepted as part of the law of England for 280 years."

Lord Blackburn, in a famous speech, assented to the decision of the court, albeit with reluctance. He stressed the commercial realities when he said:

> "[A]ll men of business . . . do everyday recognise and act on the ground that prompt payment of part of their demand may be more beneficial to them than it would be to insist on their rights and enforce payment of the whole. Even where the debtor is perfectly solvent, and sure to pay at last, this is often so. Where the credit of the debtor is doubtful it must be more so."

4–030   Not only has the common law rule about part payment been criticised as commercially unrealistic, it has also been seen as operating harshly where part payment is accepted "in full settlement" and the debtor has relied on that. When coupled with the rule that "consideration need not be adequate" the principle is potentially absurd given that the goods or services requested by the creditor in lieu of part payment could have a very slight economic value in relation to the outstanding debt. The rule, however, has produced just results where improper pressure is brought to bear by the debtor to compel the creditor to accept part payment.[55]

The rule in *Pinnel's Case* and *Foakes v Beer* was considered in *Re Selectmove Ltd.*[56] A company owed the Inland Revenue £20,000 taxes under PAYE and the company offered, through its managing director, to pay the arrears by monthly instalments of £1,000 each. The collector of taxes said that he would have to obtain the approval of his superiors for such an arrangement but that he would come back to the company if the offer was unacceptable. He never did so and so the company commenced paying the instalments—they had made seven such payments when the Revenue brought proceedings to wind up the company on account of the remaining arrears. The company argued, inter alia, that the payment of the instalments constituted a "practical benefit" to the Revenue, and therefore there was good consideration.

---

[55] See, e.g. *D & C Builders Ltd v Rees* [1966] 2 QB 617, discussed at para.4–043.
[56] [1995] 1 W.L.R. 474.

This contention was based on the decision of the Court of Appeal in *Williams v Roffey Bros* (which was discussed at para.4–024).

The Court of Appeal held there were no grounds upon which the winding up could be opposed. The offer to pay by instalments had not been accepted but even if the offer had been accepted, there was insufficient consideration. Dealing with the proposition that *Foakes v Beer* might need reconsideration in the light of *Williams v Roffey Bros,* Peter Gibson L.J. said:

"I see the force of the argument, but the difficulty I feel with it is that if the principle of the *Williams* case is to be extended to an obligation to make payment, it would in effect leave the principle in *Foakes v Beer* without any application. When a creditor and a debtor who are at arm's length reach agreement on the payment of the debt by instalments to accommodate the debtor, the creditor will no doubt always see a practical benefit to himself in so doing. In the absence of authority, there would be much to be said for the enforceability of such a contract. But that was a matter expressly considered in *Foakes v Beer* yet held not to constitute good consideration in law. *Foakes v Beer* was not even referred to in the *Williams* case, and it is in my judgment impossible, consistently with the doctrine of precedent, for this court to extend the principle of the *Williams* case to any circumstances governed by the principle in *Foakes v Beer*. If that extension is to be made, it must be by the House of Lords or, perhaps even more appropriately, by Parliament after consideration by the Law Commission."

Given the doctrine of precedent, the court could have arrived at no other conclusion. However, the distinction the court was compelled to make between obligations to pay money on the one hand and obligations to deliver goods and services on the other is untenable and difficult to justify on rational grounds.

Part payment: exceptions to the common law rule

The rule about part payment is subject to certain exceptions at common law: **4–031**

Composition with creditors

A composition occurs where a debtor owes money to a number of creditors and the creditors   **4–032** jointly agree with the debtor that they will accept a percentage of the money owed to them by the debtor in full settlement, e.g. a part payment of 50p in the pound. Although the rule in *Pinnel's Case* would suggest that such arrangements would not be binding they have long been upheld as valid.

The most commonly accepted reason for such arrangements being binding is that if an individual creditor "broke ranks" and sued the debtor for the balance, this would amount to a fraud on the other creditors.[57] This analysis has the advantage of making it unnecessary to find a consideration on the part of the debtor. It is also consistent with the position established regarding part payment by a third party which is discussed below.

[57] This approach is supported by *Wood v Robarts* (1818) 2 Stark. 417; and *Cook v Lister* (1863) 13 C.B. N.S. 543.

Part payment of a debt by a third party

4–033   It seems that if part payment offered by a third party is accepted by the creditor in full settlement, this will afford a good defence to a later action by the creditor against the debtor for the balance. Thus in *Welby v Drake*[58] the defendant owed the claimant the sum of £18 on a bill of exchange and the claimant accepted £9 from the defendant's father in full satisfaction. The claimant's action against the defendant failed because by suing the son he was committing a fraud on the father.

This principle has been followed in a modern case, *Bracken v Billinghurst*.[59] A dispute as to liability for building works led to an adjudicators'award in favour of the claimants of over £43,000. Following the award, the claimants offered to settle the dispute if they were paid £6,000 by the defendant. This was met by a counter-offer of £5,000 from a third party enclosing a cheque for that sum offered in full and final settlement. The claimants banked the cheque but later purported to withdraw the offer of settlement and indicated that they would pursue the amount originally owed. Wilcox J held that there had been a valid agreement to compromise the claim. The third party's counter-offer had been accepted by the claimants when they presented the cheque to their bank.

Part payment by negotiable instrument

4–034   We have seen that, under the rule in *Pinnel's Case,* although part payment is not good consideration, satisfaction may be provided by payment in kind, e.g. a chattel instead of money, and the value of the chattel is irrelevant since consideration need not be adequate.

In *Sibree v Tripp*[60] it was held that part payment by a promissory note was sufficient consideration to settle a debt. In this case a debt of £1,000 was discharged by the creditor agreeing to give the creditor promissory notes for £300 in full satisfaction. Alderson B. said:

> "If for money you give a negotiable security, you pay it in a different way. The security may be worth more or less: it is of uncertain value."

The principle was extended to part payment by cheque in *Goddard v O'Brien*.[61] But this case was overruled in 1965 by the Court of Appeal in *D & C Builders Ltd v Rees*[62] where Lord Denning M.R. said:

> "No sensible distinction can be taken between payment of a lesser sum by cash and payment of it by cheque. The cheque, when given, is conditional payment. When honoured, it is actual payment. It is then just the same as cash. If a creditor is not bound when he receives payment by cash, he should not be bound when he receives payment by cheque."

The case of *Sibree v Tripp* was, however, distinguished by the court on the basis that the promissory notes in that case were accepted in absolute discharge of the debt.

---

[58] (1825) 1 C. & P. 557. See also *Hirachand Punamchand v Temple* [1911] 2 K.B. 330.
[59] [2003] EWHC 333 (TCC).
[60] (1846) 15 M. & W. 23.
[61] (1882) 9 Q.B.D. 37.
[62] [1966] 2 Q.B. 617.

Part payment in equity

A possible way round the common law rule on the part payment of debts has been opened up with the development of the equitable doctrine of "promissory estoppel". This is discussed below.   4–035

PROMISSORY ESTOPPEL

"Estoppel" is a concept that evades precise definition.   4–036

Estoppel takes several different forms but, in essence, an estoppel may arise where, for example, A makes a statement to B, intending that B should act in reliance on it and B does in fact rely on it. A cannot then turn round and act inconsistently with what he has said. A is "estopped" (i.e. prevented or barred) from going back on his statement.

If this principle were applied to the part payment of debts it could provide a means of evading the rule in *Foakes v Beer*. Suppose a creditor promises the debtor that the creditor will accept part payment of the debt in full satisfaction. This promise is made by the creditor with the intention that the debtor should rely on the promise and the debtor does rely on it. If the creditor later sues for the balance, the debtor may be able to raise the defence of estoppel and the creditor's action will fail. The important thing to note is that the debtor *has not given any consideration*.

Central London Property Trust Ltd v High Trees House Ltd

The possibility of invoking estoppel to mitigate the effects of *Foakes v Beer* was recognised, obiter, by Denning J. in *Central London Property Trust Ltd v High Trees House Ltd*[63] (the "High Trees case"). In 1937 the claimants let a block of flats in London to the defendants at a rental of £2,500 a year under a 99-year lease. It was the defendants' intention to sub-let the flats. The outbreak of war, and particularly the bombing of the capital, caused very few of the flats to be sub-let, and the claimants promised to reduce the rent to £1,250 a year, effective from the beginning of the lease. No consideration was given for this promise. By 1945 all the flats were sub-let and so the claimants contended that the full rent of £2,500 a year was once again payable. They brought an action for that full rent for the last two quarters of 1945 in a test case.   4–037

Denning J. held that the claimants should succeed because the circumstances that had given rise to the agreement of 1940 no longer applied. The wartime conditions had ended. He went on to say, obiter, that had the claimants sought to recover the full rent that had fallen due from 1940 to 1945, they would have been prevented in equity from succeeding.

The first hurdle that Denning J. faced in promulgating this doctrine was a decision of the House of Lords in 1854, *Jorden v Money*.[64] This was a case of common law estoppel or "estoppel by representation." In this case, Money owed Mrs Jorden the sum of £1,200 but she often told Money that she did not intend to enforce the debt. Encouraged by these assurances, Money got married and then sought a declaration that his debt to Mrs Jorden had been abandoned. He argued that he had relied on Mrs Jorden's representations and therefore she was estopped

---

[63] [1947] K.B. 130.
[64] (1854) 5 H.L. Cas. 185.

from going back on her word and insisting on payment. The House of Lords dismissed Money's action—estoppel by representation operated only to cover a false representation of existing fact, not a representation of future intention, such as a promise not to enforce a debt. However, the landlords' promise in *High Trees*—to accept a reduction in the rent for the future—was also a statement of future intention. Accordingly, Denning J. distinguished *Jorden v Money* on the basis that, in *Jorden v Money* the promisor did not intend to be legally bound, whereas in *High Trees*, the promisor did.

Denning J. considered that "the law has not been standing still" since *Jorden v Money*—there had been developments in equity whereby promises made with the intention that they be acted upon and in fact acted upon had to be honoured notwithstanding the absence of consideration. Although there was no cause of action in damages for the breach of such promises, the courts had not allowed the parties making such promises to act inconsistently with them. It was in this sense only that such promises gave rise to an estoppel. He said:

"The logical consequence, no doubt, is that a promise to accept a smaller sum, if acted upon, is binding notwithstanding the absence of consideration: and if the fusion of law and equity lead to this result, so much the better. That aspect was not considered in *Foakes v Beer* . . . At this time of day, however, when law and equity have been joined together for over seventy years, principles must be considered in the light of their combined effect."

4–038   Denning J. placed reliance on the decision of the House of Lords in *Hughes v Metropolitan Railway Co*[65] where a landlord gave a tenant six months notice to repair. As the tenant had undertaken to repair in the lease, he could be ejected for failure to repair. After a month the landlord opened negotiations with the tenant for the sale of the freehold and, because of this, the tenant did nothing about the repairs. After a further two months, the negotiations broke down. At the end of the original six months, the landlord sought to eject the tenant. The House of Lords held that he could not do so and the six months notice had to run from the breakdown of negotiations. The opening of negotiations by the landlord amounted to a promise that, as long as they continued, he would not enforce the notice. The tenant had relied on this promise by not carrying out any repairs and was entitled in equity to relief against forfeiture of the lease. Lord Cairns L.C. explained the position in equity as follows:

"It is the first principle upon which all courts of equity proceed, that if parties who have entered into definite and distinct terms involving certain legal results . . . afterwards by their own act . . . enter upon a course of negotiations which has the effect of leading one of the parties to suppose that the strict rights arising under the contract will not be enforced, or will be kept in suspense, or held in abeyance, the person who otherwise might have enforced those rights will not be allowed to enforce them where it would be inequitable having regard to the dealings which have thus taken place between the parties."

Viewed from the strict perspective of the doctrine of precedent, Denning J.'s reliance on *Hughes* in *High Trees* is open to criticism. First, the factual situations in the cases are significantly different. In *Hughes* the landlord was effectively saying, "while we are in negotiation I will not treat

---

[65] (1877) 2 App. Cas. 439. The principle in *Hughes v Metropolitan Rwy* was applied by the Court of Appeal in *Birmingham & District Land Co v London & North Western Railway Co* (1888) 40 Ch. D. 268; and *Salisbury v Gilmore* [1942] 2 K.B. 38. Both these cases were referred to by Denning J. in *High Trees* as supporting the doctrine put forward.

your failure to repair as a breach of contract entitling forfeiture of the lease"; in *High Trees* the landlords, having promised to accept a reduction in the rent contractually due under the lease, were seeking to recover the full rent. The landlords were not alleging that the tenants were in breach of contract. Secondly, and this point is closely related to the first, the decision in *Hughes* merely suspended the landlord's rights whereas *High Trees* goes further and says that the landlord's contractual right to receive the full rent could be extinguished. This latter point is perhaps the most controversial aspect of the doctrine. Thirdly, some commentators have expressed surprise that the *Hughes* case was not considered in *Foakes v Beer*, decided by the House of Lords seven years later and having two judges, Lord Blackburn and the Earl of Selborne, in common. Given Lord Blackburn's acknowledged antipathy to *Pinnel's Case*, the answer to this point may be that that neither he nor the other judges considered *Hughes* to be relevant.

Nevertheless, whatever objections may be made to Denning J.'s reasoning in the *High Trees* case, the principle of promissory estoppel has become firmly established, if in a more restricted form than that advanced by Denning J. in 1947. The exact nature and scope of the doctrine continues to be a matter of debate—this was acknowledged by Lord Hailsham L.C. when he said in *Woodhouse A C Israel Cocoa Ltd SA v Nigerian Produce Marketing Co Ltd*[66]:

> "[A]s is common with an expanding doctrine [the cases] do raise problems of coherent exposition which have never been fully explored."

Requirements for the application of promissory estoppel

We are now in a position to examine the requirements that must be in place if the doctrine of promissory estoppel is to apply. Some of these elements are relatively clear cut, whereas others are not yet fully resolved. **4–039**

Existing legal relationship

There must be some existing legal relationship between the parties before the doctrine can apply—this will usually be a contractual relationship. As we have seen, in *High Trees* the parties were in a landlord and tenant relationship and the landlords' promise, which Denning J. considered would be binding in equity, was a variation of their existing contract. It seems that the pre-existing legal relationship need not necessarily be contractual providing it is one which could in certain circumstances give rise to liabilities and penalties.[67] **4–040**

Clear and unambiguous statement

There must be a clear and unambiguous statement by the promisor that strict rights will not be enforced, however *Hughes v Metropolitan Railway* shows that the statement can be implied from conduct. **4–041**

---

[66] [1972] A.C. 741.
[67] *Durham Fancy Goods Ltd v Michael Jackson (Fancy Goods) Ltd* [1968] 2 Q.B. 839. See also *Brikom Investments Ltd v Carr* [1979] Q.B. 467, where Lord Denning M.R. was of the view that the doctrine could apply to promises made by parties in negotiation for a contract, i.e. who are not yet in any legal relationship with each other. Such an extension of the doctrine is difficult to reconcile with the law relating to pre-contractual representations, see para.6–008.

Reliance

4–042 Traditionally, estoppel by representation required that the promisee should have acted in reliance on the promise to their detriment, i.e. the promisee would be placed in a worse position if the promise were revoked than if the promise had never been made. So far as promissory estoppel is concerned, in the *High Trees* case Denning J. did not specifically state how it was that the tenant relied on the landlord's promise, although the fact that the tenant did rely on the promise is implicit in the judgment. The reliance seems to consist in the fact that the tenant conducted his affairs on the basis of the rent reduction. There may therefore be cases where no positive act as such is required on the part of the promisee.

In *W J Alan & Co Ltd v El Nasr Export and Import Co*[68] Lord Denning M.R. could find no support in the authorities for the requirement of detriment. He said the promisee must have "conducted his affairs on the basis of the promise" so that "it would now be inequitable to deprive him of its benefit." Some cases speak of the requirement that the promisee must have "altered his position"[69] but Lord Denning considered this to mean that the promisee "must have been led to act differently to what he otherwise would have done."

In *Societe Italo-Belge pour le Commerce et l'Industrie SA v Palm & Vegetable Oils (Malaysia) Sdn Bhd, The Post Chaser*[70] Robert Goff J related the issue to whether or not it is inequitable for the promisor to revert to his strict legal rights. He said:

> "The fundamental principle is that stated by Lord Cairns LC [in *Hughes v Metropolitan Railway*] viz that the representor will not be allowed to enforce his rights 'where it would be inequitable having regard to the dealings which have thus taken place between the parties'. To establish such inequity, it is not necessary to show detriment; indeed, the representee may have benefited from the representation, and yet it may be inequitable, at least without reasonable notice, for the representor to enforce his legal rights . . . But it does not follow that in every case in which the representee has acted, or failed to act, in reliance on the representation, it will be inequitable for the representor to enforce his rights for the nature of the action or inaction may be insufficient to give rise to the equity."

Thus the requirement of reliance is inextricably linked with the next requirement which is discussed below.

Reversion to strict legal rights must be inequitable

4–043 It must be inequitable for the promisor to go back on their word and insist on a reversion to the promisor's strict legal rights. Whether reversion is or is not inequitable is a matter for judicial discretion based on the circumstances of the case.

This process is illustrated by *D & C Builders v Rees*.[71] The claimants were jobbing builders who had done some work at the defendant's shop for an agreed price, of which just over £480 remained outstanding. For some months the claimants pressed for payment. Eventually the defendant's wife, knowing that the claimants were in serious financial difficulties, offered them

---

[68] [1972] 2 Q.B. 189.
[69] See, *Ajayi v Briscoe (RT) (Nigeria)* [1964] 1 W.L.R. 1326, per Lord Hodson.
[70] [1982] 1 All E.R. 19.
[71] [1966] 2 Q.B. 617.

a cheque for £300 in full settlement. The claimants felt they had no choice but to accept, but later brought an action claiming the balance. The Court of Appeal found for the claimants—all the judges (including Lord Denning M.R.) based their decision on the common law rule in *Pinnel's Case* and *Foakes v Beer*.

Lord Denning, however, went on to consider whether the defendant could have raised the defence of promissory estoppel. He observed that, in his view, the principle could be applied, "not only so as to suspend strict legal rights, but also so as to preclude the enforcement of them." In applying the principle, there was a qualification, i.e. that the creditor would be precluded from enforcing their strict legal rights where it would be inequitable to insist on them. He considered that Mrs Rees had acted inequitably. He said:

> "The debtor's wife held the creditor to ransom . . . When she said: "We will pay you nothing unless you pay £300 in full settlement," she was putting undue pressure on the creditor. She was making a threat to break the contract (by paying nothing) and she was doing it so as to compel the creditor to do what he was unwilling to do (to accept a £300 settlement): and she succeeded. . . . No person can insist on a settlement procured by intimidation."

We see in this case the much vilified rule in *Pinnel's Case* producing a just result, whereas in *Foakes v Beer* the outcome was unfair to the debtor. In fact today it is likely that the agreement in *D & C Builders v Rees*, even if consideration could be found, would be regarded as voidable on the grounds of economic duress (see para.13–004).

Promissory estoppel does not found a cause of action

The orthodox view of promissory estoppel, and currently the position in English law, is that it **4–044** operates as a defence rather than a self-standing cause of action—a "shield and not a sword." The consequences of it being other than a defence were spelt out by the Court of Appeal in *Combe v Combe*.[72] A married couple separated and the wife obtained a decree nisi of divorce. The husband promised to make the wife an allowance of £100 per annum free of income tax. The decree was then made absolute. For some years she received nothing from her ex-husband but then the wife brought an action against him for the arrears of maintenance. In the High Court, Byrne J. found for the wife. He held that the wife had not provided any consideration for the husband's promise—although she had not applied to the divorce court for maintenance, this was not at the husband's request, and she would have been free so to apply had she wished. Nevertheless the judge held that the husband's promise was binding under the principle enunciated in the *High Trees* case—it was a promise intended to be acted upon and in fact acted upon.

This extension of the promissory estoppel doctrine went too far for the Court of Appeal, and the decision of the court below was reversed. As Denning L.J. explained:

> "Much as I am inclined to favour the principle applied in the *High Trees* case . . . it is important that it should not be stretched too far, lest it be endangered. That principle does not create new causes of action where none existed before. It only prevents a party from insisting upon his strict legal rights, when it would be unjust to allow him to enforce them, having

---

[72] [1951] 2 K.B. 215.

regard to the dealings which have taken place between the parties . . . That, I think, is its true function. It may be part of a cause of action, but not a cause of action in itself."

Having confirmed the essentially defensive nature of the doctrine Denning L.J. expressed the reason for this restriction on its scope as follows:

"Seeing that the principle never stands alone as giving a cause of action in itself, it can never do away with the necessity of consideration when that is an essential part of the cause of action. The doctrine of consideration is too firmly fixed to be overthrown by a sidewind . . . it still remains a cardinal necessity of the formation of a contract, though not of its modification or discharge."

Thus the Court of Appeal was not prepared to countenance the possibility of a contract coming into being where a party has relied on a promise, as opposed to them providing consideration in exchange for the promise. It would "do away with" consideration in the formation of contracts.

It is interesting to compare the position with other forms of estoppel. "Proprietary estoppel", for example, can found a cause of action. This may arise where a landowner encourages a party to believe that they will enjoy rights over the land and that party relies on the promise to their detriment. Such a promise is enforceable by the promisee.[73] It is also the case that other common law jurisdictions have been prepared to recognise that promissory estoppel can, in certain circumstances, found a cause of action—this is what was decided by the High Court of Australia in *Waltons Stores (Interstate) Ltd v Maher*.[74]

The time may come when we see such a development in English law, although such a change could only be instigated by the House of Lords.[75]

Promissory estoppel: extinctive or merely suspensory?

4–045   The generally accepted view is that promissory estoppel suspends rights rather than extinguishes them, i.e. the promisor can, by giving reasonable notice (which need not be formal) revert to their strict legal rights. If this is correct, then it places a considerable limitation on the scope of doctrine as expressed by Denning J. in *High Trees*.

The leading authority is *Tool Metal Manufacturing Co Ltd v Tungsten Electric Co Ltd*.[76] In 1938 the appellant company granted the respondent company a licence to deal in metal alloys of which the appellants owned the patent. Under the agreement, the appellants were to be paid a royalty based on the amount of material used, and "compensation" if the respondents used more than a specified amount per month. The compensation was paid until the outbreak of

---

[73] See *Crabb v Arun District Council* [1976] Ch. 179; and *Gillett v Holt* [2000] 3 W.L.R. 815. It is as yet unclear whether "estoppel by convention" may found a cause of action. In this situation, both parties to a contract are under a common mistake as to the meaning or effect of the transaction and they proceed on the basis of that mistaken assumption. The parties will be subsequently estopped from denying the assumed state of affairs where it would be unconscionable. Thus the original contract is replaced by the conventional one: *Amalgamated Investment and Property Co Ltd (in liquidation) v Texas Commerce International Bank Ltd* [1982] Q.B. 84.

[74] (1988) 76 A.L.R. 513.

[75] See *Baird Textile Holdings Ltd v Marks & Spencer plc* [2001] C.L.C. 999 where the Court of Appeal considered that neither estoppel by convention nor promissory estoppel founded causes of action—the state of the authorities was such that the position could only be corrected by the House of Lords.

[76] [1955] 2 All E.R. 657.

war in 1939 when the appellants agreed to suspend the payments—there was an understanding that a new agreement would be entered into when the war was over. In 1944 the parties began to negotiate a new agreement but negotiations broke down. The following year the respondents brought an action against the respondents for breach of contract and the appellants counter-claimed for the payment of compensation from June 1, 1945. In the Court of Appeal it was held that, although the agreement of 1939 was to suspend and not terminate the compensation pay-ments, the counterclaim failed. The appellants had not given reasonable notice of their inten-tion to resume the compensation payments. The appellants subsequently brought a second action, claiming compensation as from January 1, 1947. The House of Lords held that this action succeeded—the appellants' counterclaim in the first action constituted reasonable notice of their intention to resume strict legal rights.

This decision was important because it established that the promisor's right to future pay-ments could be restored on giving reasonable notice. So promissory estoppel is suspensory as to the future. But it says nothing about whether the appellants could have recovered compensa-tion for past payments falling due during the period of suspension because the appellants were not claiming these. The approach of the House of Lords was endorsed by the Judicial Committee of the Privy Council in *E A Ajayi v R T Briscoe (Nigeria) Ltd*[77] and the court pro-vided some further clarification. Lord Hodson considered that the equity raised in the promisee by promissory estoppel was subject to three qualifications:

(1)   that the promisee has altered their position;
(2)   that the promisor can resile from the promise on giving reasonable notice, which need not be formal notice; and
(3)   the promise only becomes final and irrevocable if the promisee, having altered their posi-tion, cannot resume their original position.

The proposition at point (3) is that promissory estoppel can extinguish rights but only where the promisee has altered their position in reliance on the promise detrimentally, possibly by entering into burdensome commitments, with the result that they cannot be restored to their original position.   **4–046**

The case law, however, still leaves the position unclear particularly with regard to the part payment of debts. There are two distinct situations; there are contracts involving a simple lump sum debt and those involving continuing periodic payments.

(i) Suppose that A owes B £1,000 to be repaid as a lump sum. B agrees to accept £500 in full settlement. Denning J. in *High Trees* and later (as Lord Denning M.R.) in *D & C Builders v Rees* suggested, obiter, that providing the equity could be raised in the promisee's favour, the credi-tor's right to recover the balance could be permanently extinguished. This view is not supported by any authority and is arguably irreconcilable with the decision of the House of Lords in *Foakes v Beer*. But if, in this simple debt scenario, the promisor's rights are only suspended, then promissory estoppel will only serve to give the debtor further time to pay the full original amount. Such a postponement may in itself be a valuable right, but it falls well short of the claims made for the doctrine made by Denning J. in the *High Trees* case.

(ii) Periodic payments. Where the contractual obligation is, for example, to pay sums by instalments (such as rent under a lease, compensation under a patent etc) it has been argued that although the estoppel is suspensory as to the future, existing rights may be extinguished.

[77] [1964] 1 W.L.R. 1326.

Thus suppose that A rents a boat to B for 12 months at a rental of £12,000 to be paid in monthly instalments of £1,000 and suspends payments at the outset. If A later serves reasonable notice to revive existing rights after six instalments have been unpaid, A will only be able to recover from B £6,000. But even this view is controversial and it may be that when rights are revived, a debtor making periodic payments is not only liable for future payments, but they must pay those falling due during the period of suspension. Severe as this may seem, it at least has the merit of consistency with the position outlined at (i) above. It is hard to justify the lump sum payer being in a worse position than the periodic payer.

Consideration and estoppel: conclusion

4–047   By way of conclusion, we may ask the question—does the English law of contract actually need the concept of consideration?

If two parties enter into an agreement of which the essential terms are certain and both intend to be legally bound, why must the law impose a further obligation in the shape of consideration? When one sees that consideration may consist of a peppercorn, and a peppercorn is sufficient to make the transaction binding (even if the parties do not like pepper and will throw away the corn), the concept becomes difficult to defend from a charge of absurdity. At the same time, moral obligations and the ties of love and affection—in the minds of many people the most real considerations of all—have been shunned by the courts as having insufficient value. As a result, in cases involving family arrangements, the courts have found artificial considerations in order to do justice, for example in *Ward v Byham*.[78] As we have seen, the rule that part-payment of a debt is not good consideration for a promise to forgo the balance has been applied by the courts, even in the nineteenth century, only with reluctance.[79] Indeed, Lord Jessel M.R. famously attacked the principle in the following terms:

> "A creditor may accept anything in satisfaction of his debt except a lesser amount of money. He might take a horse, or a canary or a tom-tit if he chose . . . but by a most extraordinary peculiarity of English common law, he could not take [part payment of the sum due]."[80]

The reason for these inconsistencies may lie in the history of consideration. As Atiyah has argued,[81] consideration was originally understood as a good reason (*causa* in Roman law) for enforcing or not enforcing promises but in the nineteenth century it became formalised into a firmer set of rules, such as the need to identify benefit and detriment. But these rules were never rigidly applied by the courts. Rather, the courts used consideration to identify those types of arrangements for which enforcement would be inappropriate and those which were deserving of enforcement. Examples of the former include promises that are contrary to public policy; promises made in the social and domestic sphere; and bargains procured by duress or extortion.

What has been done by the courts to modify consideration so as to mitigate its acknowledged defects? Clearly promissory estoppel has been a major development, although for the reasons

---

[78] See para.4–020.
[79] See para.4–029.
[80] In *Couldery v Bartrum* (1881) 19 Ch. D. 394.
[81] See, generally, Atiyah, *Essays on Contract*, (Oxford; Clarendon Press, 1986); see also Atiyah, *Introduction to the Law of Contract*, 6th edn, pp. 108–109.

explained above[82] its impact has been on the discharge and variation of contracts—it cannot as yet in English law found a cause of action. Nevertheless, there remains uncertainty as to its scope and it has still not been determined that it could be applied so as to extinguish the right to recover the balance of a lump sum debt (as Denning J. in 1947 argued it could). The re-definition, or relaxation, of consideration in *Williams v Roffey Bros*[83] so as to embrace practical benefits has been another major departure. According to the Court of Appeal in that case, this has been made possible by the evolution of the doctrine of economic duress in recent years. The expansion of the same doctrine may remove the only surviving justification for the rule in *Pinnel's Case*, i.e. that it protects the creditor against intimidation by the debtor.

Williams v Roffey Bros, however, has not met with universal approval, either judicially or academically, and the failure to extend the decision so as to cover part payment of debts in *Re Selectmove*, admittedly on the grounds of precedent, is unsatisfactory. It has produced an anomaly as significant as any that has existed with consideration in the past.[84]

It is too early to assess the impact of *Williams v Roffey Bros*. It extends enforceability to transactions that would formerly have been regarded as unenforceable but its scope is yet to be delineated. For example, it may encroach upon cases traditionally dealt with under the doctrine of promissory estoppel. Suppose that a party promises not to insist on their strict legal rights and the promisee relies on that promise by doing something that amounts to a practical benefit for the promisor. It is suggested that this is a possibility because, under *Williams v Roffey Bros*, the practical benefit to the promisor does not need to arise from anything done by the promisee in exchange for the promise. If such could be regarded as consideration, would the promisor be able to revert to their strict legal rights on reasonable notice?

4–048

Should consideration be abolished? As far back as 1937 the Law Revision Committee[85] recommended reforms to the doctrine which, if implemented, would have swept away most of the rules that we have discussed in this chapter, e.g. the rules concerning past consideration and performance of existing duties. But wholesale abolition would leave a gap in the law in that there needs to be a test for the enforceability of promises. This is currently performed, not always satisfactorily, by consideration. Abolition of consideration would throw the emphasis onto the requirement that there should be an intention to create legal relations.

In the case of commercial agreements the existing strong, but rebuttable, presumption that contractual relations are intended is entirely viable even in the absence of consideration. The difficulty is likely to arise in relation to arrangements of a non-commercial character, such as domestic agreements. We have already observed that the line between domestic agreements which are intended to be binding and those which are not can be difficult to draw—a good illustration is the case of *Parker v Clark*[86] where the court had regard to the surrounding circumstances including the extent to which the agreement had been relied on. If these matters were to become the sole test of enforceability a "doctrine" could develop which might be no less technical and problematic than consideration has proved.

Another possible test of enforceability is reliance. Atiyah has supported detrimental reliance as a more reliable test of enforceability than consideration.[87] This would involve a move away

4–049

---

[82] See para.4–044.
[83] See para.4–024.
[84] See para.4–030.
[85] The Sixth Interim Report (Cmnd. 5449.).
[86] See para.3–018 above.
[87] See Atiyah, *Essays on Contract*, 1986, chap.2; see also Atiyah, *Introduction to the Law of Contract*, 6th edn, pp. 128–130.

from the concept of contract as "bargain" and exchange of "promises" towards a solution centred on estoppel. This has already happened to some extent with the development of promissory estoppel and we have noted that the legal systems of other common law jurisdictions have been prepared to countenance estoppel as a cause of action, e.g. where detrimental reliance would produce an unconscionable result.[88] Reliance also formed part of the recommendations of the Law Revision Committee in 1937 which recommended that a promise should be binding where the promisor knows, or should reasonably know, that it will be relied upon by the promisee.

How useful is reliance as a test of enforceability? First, as the cases concerning reliance for the purposes of promissory estoppel show, what constitutes reliance in some cases is far from clear cut and involves an analysis of conduct that could be equivocal and open to differing interpretation. Moreover, there is still some tension in the case law as to what is the actual test of reliance for promissory estoppel.[89] These sorts of difficulties would not make the task of the courts in discovering an enforceable contract any easier.

Secondly, the concept of reliance is arguably less certain than consideration. One of the virtues of consideration is that it recognises the enforceability of an executory promise, i.e. a promise to do something in the future. This makes it possible to say at the time a transaction is entered into whether or not a promise will result in a binding contract. One can see whether the three ingredients for a binding contract are in place; offer and acceptance, intention and consideration. In many cases the same will be true of reliance—each party's detrimental action in reliance will be contemporaneous with the agreement. The sale of goods in a shop is an example. But there will be cases in which the action in reliance on the promise may not occur until later— here it will not be known at the time when the promise is made whether or not it will give rise to an enforceable obligation. This will not promote commercial certainty.

4–050   Thirdly, it is by no means clear that a contract based on reliance will afford the same remedies as one supported by consideration. The usual remedy for breach of contract is to award damages based on "loss of expectation", i.e. the loss of the benefits that the innocent party expected to receive under the contract. The alternative basis, and one that is applied only in a minority of cases, is "reliance loss". Here compensation is awarded in a much more limited way so as to compensate for expenditure wasted as a result of reliance on the contract.[90] The matter has been subject to some debate but it is possible that reliance loss is the appropriate remedy in contracts binding as a result of estoppel.[91] If this is the case, then only a promise supported by consideration will give rise to the full range of remedies for breach of contract afforded to the innocent party.

Consideration should be retained, at least for the time being, as a test of the enforceability of a promise. There is no telling how the changes brought about by *Williams v Roffey Bros* will develop—in one sense the case appears to affirm the need for consideration but the tone of the judgments seems to view consideration as essentially a negative factor inhibiting mutually advantageous renegotiations. There is no real objection to a more expansive role for estoppel but the doctrine needs to be made more coherent if it is effectively to fulfil that role.

There is, however, one quite straightforward way in which a promise unsupported by consideration can be made binding. This is, as we observed at the beginning of this chapter, to place it in a deed.

---

[88] See para.4–044.
[89] See para.4–042.
[90] The issues of expectation and reliance loss are covered below, at paras 16–003 and 16–004.
[91] See the Australian case of *Commonwealth of Australia v Verwayen* (1990) 170 C.L.R. 394; Cf *Giumelli v Giumelli* (1990) 196 C.L.R. 101. See also Cooke (1997) 17 L.S. 258 and Robertson (1998) 18 L.S. 360.

Further reading

Coote, *Consideration and Benefit in Fact and in Law* (1990) 3 J.C.L. 23.

Atiyah, Consideration: a Restatement in *Essays on Contract* (1986) Clarendon Press.

Treitel, Agreements to Vary Contracts *Some Landmarks of 20th Century Contract Law* (Oxford: Clarendon Press, 2002).

Cooke, *Estoppel and the Protection of Expectations* (1997) 17 L.S. 258.

Robertson, *Reliance and Expectation in Estoppel Remedies* (1998) 18 L.S. 360.

Chapter 5

FORMALITIES AND CAPACITY

THE REQUIREMENT OF FORM

As we have seen from the preceding chapters, providing that the essential elements of a valid **5–001** simple contract are in place, i.e. offer and acceptance, intention and consideration, the contract will be binding and enforceable. The law does not, as a general rule, require any further formalities—thus a contract does not need to be in writing. It can be purely oral or take place entirely by conduct and many contracts take this form. Of course, the parties are free to draw up a written contract if they wish and one very obvious reason for doing this is evidential. Should it come to a dispute, resolution of the dispute may be easier if there is written evidence. There are other reasons why a written contract is advisable, for example it could be one of the factors in a domestic or social agreement that rebuts the presumption that the contract lacks legal intention.[1]

It goes without saying that it is highly advisable in the commercial sphere that transactions should be committed to writing. The contract may be very large and complex and/or considerable sums of money may be involved.

To the general rule that a contract does not require any formalities, there are some exceptions. These are: contracts which must be made by deed; contracts which must be in writing; and contracts which must be evidenced in writing. Each of these shall be examined in turn.

Contracts which must be made by deed

The nature of a deed was briefly outlined at para.1–007 above, and it is necessary to say a little more **5–002** about the formal requirements for a deed and for what types of transactions they are required.

The requirement that an instrument should be sealed when executed as a deed by an individual was abolished by the Law of Property (Miscellaneous Provisions) Act 1989.[2] Thereafter, an instrument shall not be a deed unless it makes clear on its face that it is intended to be a deed by the party making it and is validly executed as a deed by that party.[3] As to execution, the Act of 1989, s.1(3) provides:

---

[1] See para.3–015.
[2] s.1(1)(b). For companies incorporated under the Companies Acts, the necessity for the corporate seal was removed by s.36(A)(3) of the Companies Act 1985, as inserted by s.130(2) of the Companies Act 1989.
[3] Law of Property (Miscellaneous Provisions) Act 1989, s.1(2), as amended by the Regulatory Reform (Execution of Deeds and Documents) order 2005 (SI 2005/1906).

"An instrument is validly executed as a deed by an individual if, and only if –
(a) it is signed –
(i) by him in the presence of a witness who attests the signature; or
(ii) at his direction and in his presence and the presence of two witnesses who each attest the signature; and
(iii) it is delivered as a deed by him or a person authorised to do so on his behalf."

The most common transaction requiring a deed, as house buyers will be aware, is a conveyance of the legal estate in land.[4] However, anyone can execute by deed for any type of transaction if they so wish.

A contract contained in a deed does not require any consideration in order to be binding, thus the deed can be used to make binding "gratuitous" promises, such as gifts. Covenants, whereby donors undertake to make gifts to charities, are made binding by the execution of a deed. There is a longer limitation period for a deed—an action for the breach of an obligation in a deed must be brought within 12 years from when the cause of action accrued. The limitation period for simple contracts is only six years.[5] For this reason, it is not uncommon for long running contracts in the construction and engineering industries to be contained in deeds.

Contracts which must be in writing

5–003   Contracts falling within this category are required to be in writing in order to be enforceable. This formal requirement is in addition to the need for offer and acceptance, intention and consideration. We shall consider a number of examples.

Consumer credit legislation

5–004   An example of statutory formalities, and one widely encountered by consumers wishing to obtain finance for their purchases, is the consumer credit legislation. The Consumer Credit Act 1974, as amended by the Consumer Credit Act 2006, requires agreements regulated under the Act, such as hire purchase and credit sales agreements, to be in a prescribed form. The requirements include the provision of certain information and a statutory "cooling off" period within which the consumer debtor may cancel the agreement. The contract must be signed by both parties, and the consumer must be supplied with a copy. Non-compliance with the requirements will not necessarily invalidate the agreement, but an agreement that is not properly executed in accordance with the Act can only be enforced against the consumer on an order of the court. No such order can be made if the consumer did not sign the agreement; or receive a copy of it; or notification of the right to cancel.

The compatibility of the formal requirements of the Consumer Credit Act 1974 with the European Convention on Human Rights (ECHR) arose in the case of *Wilson v Secretary for Trade and Industry*.[6] In January 1999 Mrs Wilson borrowed £5,000 from pawnbrokers First County Trust Ltd (FCT) putting up her BMW car as security. Mrs Wilson was charged a

---

[4] Law of Property Act 1925, s.52(1).
[5] Limitation Act 1980, s.5 [simple contract] and s.8(1) [deed, or "specialty" as deeds are referred to in the legislation.]. See para.17–028.
[6] [2004] 1 A.C. 816, *sub nom Wilson v First County Trust Ltd (No 2)*.

"document fee" of £250 and this was added to the amount of the loan which was stated in the agreement as £5,250. When she failed to repay the loan FCT sought repayment. Mrs Wilson commenced proceedings arguing that the agreement was invalid as it was not in the form prescribed by the Act of 1974 and so by s.127(3) of the Act was unenforceable. The Court of Appeal agreed, holding that the additional fee added to the loan was not "credit" and so the agreement did not contain all the prescribed terms. This meant that Mrs Wilson was not required to repay the loan or interest and could recover her car.

The Court of Appeal took the opportunity to declare that s.127(3) was incompatible with Article 6(1) and Article 1 of the First Protocol of the ECHR. Article 6(1) guarantees the right to a fair trial in the determination of a person's civil rights and obligations; and Article 1 of the First Protocol entitles every natural or legal person to the peaceful enjoyment of their possessions. On appeal to the House of Lords it was held that the Court of Appeal had been wrong to declare as it did because the events and cause of action arose before the Human Rights Act 1998 came into force. In any event their Lordships held that the relevant provisions were not incompatible with Convention rights.

Distance selling contracts

Another example of legislation prescribing statutory formalities is to be found in the Consumer Protection (Distance Selling) Regulations 2000[7] implementing Directive 97/7/EC. The regulations apply to "distance contracts", that is: **5–005**

> "Any contract concerning goods or services concluded between a seller and a consumer under an organised distance sales or service provision scheme run by the supplier who, for the purposes of the contract, makes exclusive use of one or more means of distance communication up to and including the moment when the contract is concluded."[8]

Schedule 1 to the regulations contains a list of methods of distance communication to which the regulations apply, including: letter; press advertising with order forms; catalogue; telephone; radio; videophone; email; fax; internet; and teleshopping.

The regulations, in reg.7(1), require certain information to be given to the consumer prior to the conclusion of the contract, including the identity of the supplier; a description of the goods and services; the price; delivery costs; and the existence of a right of cancellation. By reg.7(2) the supplier must ensure that this information is given in a form that is appropriate to the form of distance communication used. The regulations, in reg.8, require the supplier to confirm in writing, or another durable medium (e.g. email) the information already given and also some additional information on the right to cancel.

The provisions as to the right to cancel are contained in regs.10—12. The "cooling off" period (i.e. right to cancel) is, in the case of services, seven working days from the day after the date of the contract; or in the case of goods, from the day after the date of delivery of the goods.[9] In the case of services, the supplier is obliged to inform the consumer as to how the right to cancel

---

[7] SI 2000/2334, as amended by the Consumer Protection (Distance Selling) (Amendment) Regulations 2005 (SI 2005/689).

[8] Distance Selling Regulations 2000, reg.3(1).

[9] It should be noted that there are some exceptions to the right to cancel contained in reg.13 of the regulations.

may be affected if the consumer agrees to begin performance before the seven working days is up. Where the supplier provides the information required by reg.8 before performance begins and the consumer agrees to performance beginning before the end of the cooling off period, there is no right to cancel. Where the supplier fails to comply with the information requirement at all, the cooling off period is extended by three months.

Under reg.5 certain contracts are excluded from the regulations, including: sales of land and construction agreements (other than rental agreements); financial services; contracts concluded by automated machines, via public pay phones and at auction.

Contracts for the sale or other disposition of an interest in land

5–006   These contracts are governed by the Law of Property (Miscellaneous Provisions) Act 1989. In order to understand the current position, it is necessary to examine something of the historical background which can be traced back to the seventeenth century.

In 1677, the Statute of Frauds was passed to prevent perjured testimony being given by witnesses as, under the then rules of procedure, the parties to an action could not themselves give evidence. The statute laid down that a number of specified contracts could only be enforced where written evidence existed of the contract between the parties—the contract had to be "evidenced in writing". Changes in court procedure and improving standards of morality meant that the reason for the existence of the statute largely disappeared and so most sections of the statute were repealed.

By 1989 there were only two types of contract that were still required to be evidenced in writing; these were:

(i)   Contracts for the sale or other disposition of an interest in land (which by now was governed by s.40 of the Law of Property Act 1925); and
(ii)   Contracts of guarantee (under s.4 of the Statute of Frauds 1677).

So far as contracts of guarantee are concerned, s.4 is still in force and these contracts are discussed at para.5–011 below.

Under s.40, no action could be brought upon any contract for the sale or other disposition of land unless the agreement or some memorandum or note of it was in writing and signed by the party to be charged (i.e. made liable) or by their duly authorised agent. The "memorandum or note" of the contract need not have been made when the contract was made but had to be in existence before the action was brought to enforce the contract and it had to contain all the material terms of the contract, i.e. a description of the parties; a description of the subject matter and the consideration. The memorandum had to contain the signature of the party to be charged, however it did not need to be contained in one document—it could be contained in a number of connected documents provided there was sufficient reference in the signed document to the others. There had to be a sufficiently complete memorandum formed by the two or more documents when read together.

The most controversial aspect of s.40 was that the memorandum, provided it contained all the material terms, did not need to have been deliberately prepared as a memorandum and could have been provided by the party to be charged quite inadvertently. If a contract within s.40 was not evidenced in writing by a sufficient memorandum as outlined above, it was unenforceable at common law but could become enforceable in equity under the doctrine of part-performance.

Under this doctrine specific performance might have been granted on the basis of some behaviour which was referable to the alleged oral contract, e.g. going into possession.

The Law of Property (Miscellaneous Provisions) Act 1989, which came into force on **5–007** September 27, 1989 brought major reform. The new Act repealed s.40 of the Act of 1925 and set out new rules governing formalities which are required for all contracts for the sale or other disposition of an interest in land entered into after that date. From then on such contracts no longer had to be "evidenced in" writing but be "made in" writing. The equitable doctrine of part-performance disappeared.

The relevant provisions of s.2 of the Act of 1989 provide as follows:

(1) A contract for the sale or other disposition of an interest in land can only be made in writing and only by incorporating all the terms which the parties have expressly agreed in one document or, where contracts are exchanged, in each.
(2) The terms may be incorporated in one document either by being set out in it or by reference to some other document.
(3) The document incorporating the terms or, where contracts are exchanged, one of the documents incorporating them (but not necessarily the same one) must be signed by, or on behalf of, each party to the contract.

Excluded from the new rules by virtue of s.2(5) of the Act are: (i) contracts for the grant of leases for a term of three years or less; (ii) contracts made in the course of a public auction; and (iii) contracts regulated under the financial services legislation. The sub-section further provides that nothing in s.2 affects the creation or operation of resulting, implied or constructive trusts.

The most obvious difference between the old s.40 and the new s.2 is that s.2 requires the signatures of each party to the contract. Under s.40 only the signature of the party to be charged was required with the result that a party who had not signed a s.40 memorandum could, once they had received the memorandum, enforce it against the other party. The non-signatory party, however, could not themselves be made liable on the contract.

It can be seen that s.2(2) (above) provides that the terms of the contract can be set out in one document or they may be incorporated by reference to another document. To satisfy s.2(2) it seems that the contract which the parties have signed must refer to and identify the other document which is sought to be incorporated. Nevertheless, a collateral contract may be used to avoid the requirements of s.2.[10] This solution was adopted by the court in *Record v Bell*.[11] The day before exchange of contracts for the sale of a house, the vendor had not received Land Registry documents confirming title. The purchaser was concerned about undisclosed entries on the register and so the vendor gave a warranty as to title to the purchaser. On the basis of this the parties exchanged contracts and their oral agreement was confirmed by an exchange of correspondence. The title to the house was exactly as warranted by the vendor but the purchaser subsequently refused to complete the transaction, arguing non-compliance with s.2 because all the material terms were not incorporated in either the contracts as exchanged or the exchange of correspondence. The vendor sought specific performance. It was held that the vendor was entitled to succeed. The warranty as to title was a separate contract collateral to the main contract and it was not caught by s.2 of the Act.

Where there is more than one document, the document that must be signed by each party is **5–009** the principal document. Thus in *Firstpost Homes Ltd v Johnson*[12] the principal document, a

[10] For a discussion of collateral contracts, see para.6–015.
[11] [1991] 1 W.L.R. 853.
[12] [1995] 4 All E.R. 355.

letter which the vendor signed, referred to an attached plan and also had the purchaser's name typed on it as addressee. The purchaser signed only the plan. The Court of Appeal held that s.2 had not been complied with—the principal document should have been signed, not the plan. The court also refused to apply the interpretation under s.40 as to what constitutes a signature, where a typed or printed name might well have sufficed.

Where contracts are exchanged, s.2(3) (above) indicates that a binding contract will come into being when each party has signed their copy. In other words, in these circumstances, it need not be the same document which contains each party's signature. There must, however, be an exchange of contracts in the established sense, an exchange of correspondence will not satisfy s.2.[13]

The issue of whether the exercise of an option to purchase land was caught by s.2 arose in *Spiro v Glencrown Properties Ltd*.[14] The claimant granted the first defendants an option to purchase a property—this grant complied with s.2 as it was signed by both parties. The defendants gave notice to exercise the option in a document which was signed only by the purchaser but they then failed to complete the purchase. The claimant sued and the first defendants (and their guarantors, the second defendants) argued that the requirements of s.2 had not been met since the notice exercising the option had been signed only by one party. It was held that the claimant should succeed as the notice was not caught by s.2 of the 1989 Act.

A contract for the sale or other disposition of an interest in land that fails to comply with the s.2 requirements is of no effect. Thus the position that pertained under s.40—that an oral contract was "unenforceable" at common law but could be enforced in equity by part-performance—has gone.

Contracts which must be evidenced in writing

5–010   With the repeal of s.40 of the Law of Property Act 1925 (discussed at para.5–006 above) the only remaining class of contract that is required to be evidenced in writing is the contract of guarantee under s.4 of the Statute of Frauds 1677. The requirement of written evidence is similar to s.40[15] and means that there must be some written memorandum or note of the contract in existence before the contract is sought to be enforced. The memorandum must be signed by the party to be charged (i.e. made liable) or by some person lawfully authorised[16] and it must contain the material terms of the contract. Unlike s.40, however, it seems that the doctrine of part- performance has no application to guarantees. If a contract of guarantee is not evidenced in writing as required by s.4 it will be unenforceable.

Definition of contract of guarantee

5–011   A contract of guarantee is defined by s.4 of the Statute of Frauds 1677 as "any . . . promise to answer for the debt, default or miscarriage of another person".

---

[13] *Commission for the New Towns v Cooper (Great Britain) Ltd* [1995] 2 All E.R. 929.

[14] [1991] 2 W.L.R. 931.

[15] See para.5–006 above. In *Actionstrength Ltd v International Glass Engineering* [2003] 2 A.C. 541 the House of Lords held that to permit an estoppel to avoid the application of the Statute of Frauds to an oral contract of guarantee would be inconsistent with the terms of the statute.

[16] The contract may be enforceable where the person authorised signs in an agency capacity; it makes no difference whether the agent signs the memorandum as agent or on their own behalf: *Elpis Maritime Co v Marti Chartering Co, The Maria D* [1991] 3 W.L.R. 330.

The words "debt" and "default" refer to contractual obligations but the word "miscarriage" in s.4 has been taken to refer to financial liability arising out of a tortious act.[17] In a contract of guarantee properly so-called there are three parties, the principal debtor, the creditor and the guarantor. For example, suppose that A (the principal debtor) owes money under a contract to B (the creditor) and a third party C (the guarantor) promises B that C will pay the debt *if A fails to pay*, there is a contract of guarantee which must be evidenced in writing in order to be enforceable. If, however, C makes the promise to the principal debtor A, the transaction will not be a contract of guarantee. Thus in *Eastwood v Kenyon*[18] the claimant was liable to a third party on a promissory note. The defendant's promise to the claimant that he would pay and discharge the note was held not to be a guarantee under the statute.

Guarantee and indemnity distinguished

It is important to distinguish between a contract of guarantee and a contract of indemnity, as the latter is not caught by s.4. In a contract of indemnity C *takes over* the liability of the debtor A and A is discharged; thus in *Goodman v Chase*[19] the defendant's son, having failed to satisfy a judgment debt, was arrested. The defendant obtained his release by promising to satisfy the judgment debt. This was not a contract of guarantee as the release of the son had discharged the son's debt and the defendant had assumed primary liability.

5–012

In *Birkmyr v Darnell*[20] the distinction between a guarantee and an indemnity was illustrated by reference to a transaction in a shop. Thus suppose that two people enter a shop. One buys and the other says to the shopkeeper, "If he does not pay you, I will" this is a guarantee. However, if the other says, "Let him have the goods. I will pay you"; or "I will see you get paid" this is an indemnity—the person who utters these words is the very buyer. This is a helpful illustration but caution should be exercised as the words used are no more than indicators of a party's intention and cannot be divorced from the circumstances in which they are used. Ultimately, it is a question of intention whether the promisor is giving a guarantee or an indemnity.

Where there has never been a debt, a third party's promise cannot be in the nature of a guarantee. In *Mountstephen v Lakeman*[21] a local board intended to connect the drains of certain houses to the main sewer and the board's chairman Lakeman told the claimant Mountstephen to do the work. When Mountstephen asked how he was to be paid, Lakeman said; "Go on, Mountstephen, and do the work, and I will see you paid." Lakeman argued that the promise was the guarantee of the debt of another and so unenforceable as not evidenced in writing. The House of Lords held that as Mountstephen had never been authorised to do the work by the board, there was no primary liability which could be guaranteed by Lakeman. The contract fell outside the statute—Lakeman was liable as the only debtor.

---

[17] In *Kirkham v Marter* (1819) 2 B. & Ald. 613, A wrongfully rode B's horse and killed it (a tortious act). C promised to pay B a sum of money as compensation if B would refrain from suing A in tort. C's promise was held to be a promise to answer for the "miscarriage" of another and so it fell within s.4 and was required to be evidenced in writing.

[18] (1840) 11 Ad. & El. 438.

[19] (1818) B. & Ald. 297. See also *Guild v Conrad* (1894) 2 Q.B. 885.

[20] (1704) 1 Salk. 27.

[21] (1874) L.R. 7 H.L. 17.

There are certain guarantees which fall outside the statute and therefore need not be evidenced in writing. The first is where the guarantee forms part of a larger transaction and the second is where the guarantee is given in order to release property from liability. These will be considered below.

Where the guarantee forms part of a larger transaction

5–013   To fall within the statute, it seems that the guarantee must stand alone and not form part of some larger contract. One example is the position of so-called "del credere agents". This is an agent who guarantees that his principal will receive all moneys due from clients whom the agent introduces to the principal and with whom the agent contracts as agent.[22] For this undertaking, which is clearly a guarantee, the agent usually earns a higher commission. Given the greater responsibility that such an agent assumes, the courts do not regard the guarantee as the main object of the transaction and it falls outside the statute.[23] A similar example is to be seen in the case of *Sutton & Co v Grey*[24] where S, stockbrokers, orally agreed with G that, in respect of clients introduced by G, G should have half the commission earned as a result of the introductions and G would pay S any loss sustained in respect of them. The Court of Appeal held that although the latter obligation was essentially a guarantee it was part of a larger transaction and therefore outside s.4 of the Statute of Frauds.

Guarantee given to release property from liability

5–014   Where the guarantor gives his promise in order to secure the release of a claim of another person which affects the guarantor's property rights, the transaction may fall outside the statute. In *Fitzgerald v Dressler*[25] B sold linseed to A, who resold at a higher price to C. B remained in possession of the goods under a lien (an unpaid seller's security) until he received payment from A. In order to obtain immediate possession of the goods, C undertook to guarantee A's debt to B. It was held that C was bound even in the absence of a sufficient memorandum.

Subsequently, in such cases the courts have established that, for the contract to fall outside the statute, the guarantor must be the substantial owner of the property for the protection of which the guarantee is given. In *Harburg India Rubber Comb Co v Martin*[26] there was an oral promise by a shareholder in a company to guarantee the company's debts in order to prevent seizure of goods by judgment creditors. The Court of Appeal refused to treat the case as falling within one of the recognised exceptions, thus it would have to have been evidenced in writing to be enforceable. The shareholder had no property in the goods upon which it was sought to levy execution—his interest was personal rather than proprietary.

---

[22] See *Morris v Cleasby* (1816) 4 M. & S. 566.
[23] See *Couturier v Hastie* (1852) 8 Exch. 40.
[24] [1894] 1 Q.B. 285.
[25] (1859) 7 C.B. N.S. 374.
[26] [1902] 1 K.B. 778.

CAPACITY

Minors

"Minors" in law are persons under 18 years of age. Originally the age of majority was 21 and persons below that age were traditionally referred to as "infants", however the Family Law Reform Act 1969 reduced the age of majority to 18. The law regarding minors' contracts is more complex than one might expect; historically it was governed by common law as supplemented by the Infants Relief Act 1874. The provisions of that Act were not well-designed and gave rise to some difficulties in practice and in 1987 the Act of 1874 was repealed by the Minors' Contracts Act.

5–015

The fundamental position at common law is that contracts are not binding on minors—the assumption is that they are in need of protection from adults some of whom may be unscrupulous. However, contracts by which minors acquire "necessaries" and also beneficial contracts of service are binding on them and in a further class of contracts, the transaction is treated as "voidable". We will examine the position relating to these three exceptional contracts before returning to the underlying position.

Contracts for necessaries

It is a long established principle that minors will be bound to pay for necessary goods and services delivered or supplied. So far as necessary goods are concerned, the position at common law is in general affirmed by s.3 of the Sale of Goods Act 1979 which states:

5–016

"(2) Where necessaries are sold and delivered to a minor . . . he must pay a reasonable price for them.
(3) In subsection (2) above "necessaries" means goods suitable to the condition in life of the minor . . . and to his actual requirements at the time of the sale and delivery."

"Necessaries" are not the same thing as the "necessities" of life and regard may be had to the minor's wealth and social background.

In *Chapple v Cooper*[27] the defendant minor was held liable for the cost of her late husband's funeral—it was a necessary service for which she was bound to pay the undertaker. Alderson B. said:

"Things necessary are those without which an individual cannot reasonably exist . . . it must first be made out that . . . the things furnished are essential to the existence and reasonable advantage and comfort of the infant contractor. Thus articles of mere luxury are always excluded, though luxurious items of utility are in some cases allowed."

As indicated by Alderson B., the first thing that the claimant must persuade the court of is whether the goods or services are capable in law of being necessaries. The next question is whether they are in fact necessaries as far as the particular minor is concerned—this will depend

[27] (1844) 13 M. & W. 252.

on the minor's standard of living.[28] The court will also have regard to whether the minor is not already adequately supplied with the particular goods (or services) at the time of delivery. This may be a difficult matter for the claimant to prove.

In the well-known case of *Nash v Inman*[29] the defendant was an undergraduate of Trinity Hall, Cambridge and, whilst under the then age of majority 21, purchased clothing from the claimant, a Savile Row tailor. The items purchased included 11 fancy waistcoats at 2 gns each and the claimant brought proceedings to recover the cost of the goods supplied. The court heard evidence to the effect that the defendant was already adequately supplied with clothing fit for his station in life. On this basis, the Court of Appeal held that the goods were not necessaries and the claimant's action failed.

5–017   It seems that, certainly as far as necessary goods are concerned, the minor will only be liable on an executed contract, i.e. the goods must have been sold and delivered to the minor and he is only liable to pay a reasonable sum. The wording of s.3 of the Sale of Goods Act (above) suggests that the liability is not truly contractual, and this would rule out liability on an executory contract. Nevertheless a partially executory contract for a necessary service was upheld in *Roberts v Gray*.[30] Here the defendant, a minor, was a professional billiard player and he contracted with the claimant Roberts, a top professional billiard player, to go on a world tour and play matches with Roberts. The defendant was to learn from Roberts how to play the game at a higher level. In making arrangements for the tour, the claimant incurred expenditure. The defendant repudiated the contract over a dispute about which type of billiard balls should be used and the claimant brought an action for damages for beach of contract claiming £1,500. The Court of Appeal found for the claimant, treating the contract as one for necessaries as the defendant would benefit from the teaching and experience of the senior professional. It made no difference that the contract was still largely executory. Hamilton L.J. emphatically asserted that if "the contract is binding at all, it must be binding for all such remedies as are appropriate to the breach of it." Unless the case creates a separate category of contracts for necessary education, it is very difficult to reconcile with the received wisdom regarding contracts for necessary goods.

Even where it is established that the contract is for necessaries, the minor may not be liable where it contains an onerous term. In *Fawcett v Smethurst*[31] a minor hired a car (a necessary service) but was held not liable for damaging the car. The contract contained a term that the hirer should be absolutely liable for all damage whether or not the hirer was at fault. The contract was held to be void—it was not substantially for the minor's benefit.

Beneficial contracts of service

5–018   The common law has long upheld contracts of service entered into by minors for education, apprenticeship or employment providing the contract is, on the whole, for the minor's benefit.

A contract of service can be substantially for the minor's benefit even though it contains some onerous provisions. In *Clements v London & North Western Railway Co*[32] the claimant, a minor,

---

[28] See *Ryder v Wombwell* (1868) L.R. 4 Ex. 32 where the court set aside the jury's verdict that a pair of jewelled cufflinks worth £25 and an antique goblet, bought as a present for a friend by the son of a baronet, were necessaries.
[29] [1908] 2 K.B. 1.
[30] [1913] 1 K.B. 520.
[31] (1914) L.J. K.B. 473.
[32] [1894] 2 Q.B. 482.

was employed by the defendant railway company as a porter. His contract of employment deprived him of the right to sue the defendants for personal injury under the Employers' Liability Act 1880 in return for membership of an insurance scheme. The scheme provided for payments lower than those payable under the Act but compensation under the scheme was not dependent on proving negligence. The claimant was injured in the course of his employment and brought an action under the Act of 1880. The Court of Appeal held that the claim failed. The claimant was bound by his contract of service because, taken as a whole, it was beneficial to him.

The case of *De Francesco v Barnum*[33] affords a vivid comparison. The minor in question was a young girl who wished to learn stage dancing. She and her mother entered into a contract under seal with the claimant, Signor De Francesco, for the girl to be apprenticed to him for seven years to learn to dance. During that time, the girl agreed that she would not marry; would not accept professional engagements without the claimant's consent; and would not be maintained or paid unless actually employed by the claimant, which he was not bound to do. If paid, the rates of pay were extremely low. The claimant could terminate the contract without notice if, after a fair trial, the girl proved unsuited for stage dancing. When she broke the terms of the agreement by accepting a contract to dance for the defendant, the claimant sued. The action failed as the terms of the deed the claimant sought to enforce were unreasonably harsh and one-sided. The contract was not beneficial to the minor.

In more recent years the courts have been prepared to uphold contracts that are analogous to contracts of service. In *Doyle v White City Stadium Ltd*[34] Doyle, a minor, was a professional boxer who entered into a contract with the British Boxing Board of Control to secure a licence—essential if he was to earn a living as a professional boxer. One of the rules of the licence was that if a boxer was disqualified for foul play he would lose his "purse", i.e. fee. Doyle took part in a fight at the White City in which he was disqualified for hitting below the belt and the purse of £3,000 was withheld. The claimant's action to recover the money failed, the contract was closely analogous to a contract of service and was binding on the minor. Looked at as a whole it was for his benefit. This decision was relied upon by the Court of Appeal in a later case which further widened the concept of beneficial contract of service. In *Chaplin v Leslie Frewin (Publishers) Ltd*[35] a contract to produce an autobiography of Charlie Chaplin's son, a minor, was upheld. Publication of the book (which was to be called, "I Couldn't Smoke the Grass on my Father's Lawn") would have benefited the minor as it would have helped him begin a career as an author and would have earned him money rather than relying on social security.

There are limits to the concept of beneficial contracts of service in that trading contracts **5–019** entered into by minors have never been regarded as binding on minors, however beneficial. Thus in *Cowern v Nield*[36] the defendant, a minor, ran a business as hay and straw dealer. The claimant ordered goods from the defendant and sent a cheque, but the goods were never delivered. The claimant's action to recover the amount paid failed. The contract was a trading contract, and whether or not it was for the minor's benefit, it could not be enforced against the minor.

---

[33] (1890) 45 Ch. D. 430.
[34] [1935] 1 K.B. 110.
[35] [1966] Ch. 71. In *Proform Sports Management Ltd v Proactive Sports Management Ltd* [2006] EWHC 2903 a football agency agreement between a young player (Wayne Rooney) and a company was held not to be analogous to a contract of service—it did not in any way contribute to his ability to earn a living (nor was it a contract for necessaries).
[36] [1912] 2 K.B. 419.

Voidable contracts

5–020   There is a further category of contract, referred to as "voidable contracts" which are binding on both parties unless repudiated by the minor either during minority or within a reasonable time after attaining majority.[37]

The category comprises specific types of contract—these are transactions where the minor acquires an interest in the subject matter involving continuing or recurring obligations. The relevant contracts include: marriage settlements; partnership agreements; liabilities in relation to shareholding; and contracts relating to an interest in land.

If the minor repudiates a voidable contract, what is the effect of repudiation? Clearly, the minor will no longer be liable under the contract as to the future, but will the minor be continue to be liable for obligations that have already arisen at the date of repudiation? The law is inconclusive on the issue—it depends upon whether repudiation is correctly seen as the equivalent of rescission and therefore operates retrospectively.[38]

The courts have also addressed the issue of whether a minor can recover moneys paid under the contract before repudiation. In *Corpe v Overton*[39] the claimant, a minor, entered into an agreement with the defendant to form a partnership the following January. The claimant paid a £100 deposit, the balance to be paid on execution of the partnership deed. On attaining majority, the claimant repudiated the agreement and sued to recover the £100. The Court of Common Pleas upheld his claim—there had been a total failure of consideration. At the time of repudiation he had received nothing in return for what he had paid. The case of *Steinberg v Scala (Leeds) Ltd*[40] affords a comparison. Here, a minor applied for and was allocated shares in a company. She paid the amount due when the shares were allotted and on first call. Some eighteen months later she repudiated the contract and brought an action to recover what she had paid. The Court of Appeal held that her action failed—there had been no total failure of consideration as she had received what she had bargained for under the contract and what she received was something of tangible value.

Other contracts

5–021   At common law, contracts made by minors which do not fall into one of the categories discussed above are not binding on the minor. It was held in *Bruce v Warwick*[41] that the minor may enforce the contract against the other party should the minor choose to do so, but the remedy of specific performance may not be available to the minor.[42] The minor may ratify such a contract upon attaining majority, a right restored to the minor by the Minors' Contracts Act 1987, repealing s.2 of the Infants Relief Act 1874. Money or property transferred by the minor under such a contract may only be recovered where there has been a total failure of consideration.[43]

---

[37] *Edwards v Carter* [1893] A.C. 360.
[38] See *North Western Railway Co v M'Michael* (1850) 5 Ex. 114; cf *Blake v Concannon* (1870) I.R. 4 C.L. 323.
[39] (1833) 10 Bing. 252.
[40] [1923] 2 Ch. 452.
[41] (1815) 6 Taunt. 118.
[42] *Flight v Boland* (1824) 4 Russ. 298. The reason is lack of mutuality—see para.17–010. If, however, the minor has completely performed their part of the contract, specific performance may be granted.
[43] *Valentini v Canali* (1889) 24 Q.B.D. 166.

Liability in tort

Minors can be held liable in tort, but not where such liability would be an indirect means of enforcing an unenforceable contract against the minor. Thus in *Leslie (R) Ltd v Sheill*[44] the defendant lied about his age to the claimant moneylenders and obtained a loan of £400. The claimants were precluded from suing the minor under the contract so they brought an action in the tort of deceit. The Court of Appeal disallowed the claim as it would be tantamount to enforcing a void contract.

    It is not always easy to decide whether holding the minor liable in tort will be an indirect way of enforcing the contract. It seems to depend on how closely the tortious act is linked with the contract—two contrasting cases illustrate the point. In *Jennings v Rundall*[45] the defendant, a minor, hired a mare from the claimant on the understanding that she would be moderately ridden. The defendant rode the animal in an "immoderate, excessive and improper" manner so that she was considerably damaged. It was held that the claimant's action in tort failed as it was too closely linked to the unenforceable contract. However, in *Burnard v Haggis*[46] the defendant minor hired a mare from the claimant on condition that she was not to be jumped or ridden by anyone other than the defendant. The defendant allowed her to be ridden by a friend and the mare died in an unsuccessful attempt at jumping. Willes J. said:

> "The act of riding the mare into the place where she received her death-wound was as much a trespass . . . as if, without any hiring at all, the defendant had gone into a field and taken the mare out and hunted her and killed her. It was a bare trespass."

In this case, then, the actions of the defendant went beyond those expressly contemplated by the contract and he was therefore held liable in tort.[47]

5–022

Restitution

Equity has come to the assistance of the other party where the minor has obtained property by fraud, e.g. by misrepresenting their age. We have seen from *Leslie (R) Ltd v Sheill* (above) that in such circumstances the adult party may not bring an action in tort, nevertheless the court may make an order of restitution against the minor whereby property must be restored to the other party. In *Lempriere v Lange*[48] the defendant, a minor, impliedly represented that he was of adult age and obtained the tenancy of a furnished house belonging to the claimant, who had relied on the representation. The claimant brought an action to recover possession of the house and succeeded under the equitable doctrine of restitution.

    There are limits to the remedy. First, it seems that restitution will not be granted if the minor, having obtained property by fraud, no longer has possession of it. In *Leslie (R) Ltd v Sheill*, Lawrence J. said:

> "[I]f when the action is brought, the property and the proceeds are gone, I can see no ground upon which a court of equity could have founded its jurisdiction."

5–023

---

[44] [1914] 3 K.B. 607.
[45] (1799) 8 Term. Rep. 335.
[46] (1863) 14 C.B. N.S. 45.
[47] See also *Fawcett v Smethurst* (1914) 84 L.J. K.B. 473; and *Ballet v Mingay* [1943] K.B. 281.
[48] (1879) 12 Ch. D. 675.

An apparently contrary decision had been arrived at by Lush J. in *Stocks v Wilson*[49] shortly before the decision in *Leslie (R) Ltd v Sheill*. In *Stocks v Wilson*, the defendant minor, having obtained goods from the claimant by fraud, disposed of them to a third party. It was held that the minor was liable in equity to account to the claimant in the sum of £130, the amount received for the goods. However, the basis of this decision was criticised by the Court of Appeal in the later decision of *Leslie (R) Ltd v Sheill*.

The second limitation is that a minor who obtains a loan of money by fraud will not be bound to repay the value (unless he has the actual banknotes and coins in his possession). To compel repayment of the value would effectively involve enforcing the contract, rather than ordering restitution.

Minors' Contracts Act 1987, s.3

5–024   An alternative statutory remedy of restitution is provided by s.3 of the Minors' Contracts Act 1987 which provides:

"(1) Where-
(a) a person ("the plaintiff") has after the commencement of this Act entered into a contract with another ("the defendant"), and
(b) the contract is unenforceable against the defendant (or he repudiates it) because he was a minor when the contract was made, the court may, if it is just and equitable to do so, require the defendant to transfer to the plaintiff any property acquired by the defendant under the contract, or any property representing it.
(2) Nothing in this section shall be taken to prejudice any other remedy available to the plaintiff."

This remedy, which is at the discretion of the court, has some advantages over restitution in equity, which is preserved by s.3(2). There is no requirement of fraud under the statute and the remedy applies not just to the property acquired but to "property representing" that acquired under the contract. It is doubtful whether the remedy would be available where the property has been consumed by the minor or dissipated in some other way, however the concept of property under the Act may extend to money.[50]

Guarantees

5–025   Under the Infants Relief Act 1874 loans to minors were "absolutely void" and it was thought that guarantees of such loans were similarly void.[51] The Act of 1874 has now been repealed; in its place s.2 of the Minors' Contracts Act 1987 provides that such a guarantee shall not be enforceable merely on the ground of the minority of the principal debtor.

---

[49]   [1913] 2 K.B. 235.
[50]   See Treitel, *Law of Contract*, 12th edn, p.582.
[51]   See *Coutts & Co v Browne-Lecky* [1947] K.B. 104.

Mental disability and drunkenness

Mental disability

Some persons may be suffering from such a degree of mental disability that their affairs come under the protection of the court under the Mental Capacity Act 2005. Any contracts made by such persons are under the control of the court and if such a person purports to make a contract personally, it will be unenforceable against them.

5–026

Where a person's affairs are not under the control of the court but they are nevertheless suffering from mental disability, any contracts they make will be valid unless the person is, at the time of the contract, incapable of understanding the nature of the transaction and the other party is aware of this.[52] In such circumstances, the contract is voidable at the option of the person suffering from the mental disability. In *Hart v O'Connor*[53] the Privy Council declined to set aside a sale of land where, unknown to the purchaser, the vendor was of unsound mind when the contract was signed. The court considered that where the sane party is unaware of the other's disability, the contract should be judged by the same standards as if the contract were between two persons of sound mind. Thus the transaction would only be set aside if unconscionable.[54]

Contracts for "necessaries" are binding on the party suffering from mental disability.[55] The Mental Capacity Act 2005, s7 provides that (i) if necessary goods or services are supplied to a person who lacks capacity for the supply, they must pay a reasonable price for them; and (ii) and "necessary" means suitable to a person's condition in life and to their actual requirements at the time of supply.

Drunkenness

It seems that drunkenness is treated similarly to mental disability, i.e. the contract will be voidable where a party is so drunk as to be incapable of understanding what they are doing and the other party is aware of that fact.[56] Such a transaction may be ratified by the drunk on regaining sobriety.[57] But if by reason of drunkenness a person is incompetent to contract, they must pay a reasonable price for "necessaries" sold and delivered to them.[58]

5–027

Corporations

A corporation is a legal entity in its own right as distinct from is members. One way of classifying corporations is according to the manner in which they are created, i.e. as registered, statutory or chartered corporations.

5–028

---

[52] *Molton v Camroux* (1849) 18 L.J. Ex. 68. The burden of proof is on the party mentally disabled.
[53] [1985] 2 All E.R. 880.
[54] See para.13–319.
[55] See para.5–016 above as to the meaning of "necessaries" in relation to minors.
[56] Gore v Gibson (1843) 13 M. & W. 625.
[57] *Matthews v Baxter* (1873) L.R. 8 Ex. 132.
[58] Sale of Goods Act 1979, s.3(2). As with minors, "necessaries" means goods suitable to the condition in life of the drunken person and their actual requirements at the time of sale and delivery.

Companies registered under the Companies Acts

5–029   Companies registered under the Companies Acts had capacity to enter into any contract that was within the limits of the "objects" clause of the company's memorandum of association. At common law, a company that acted outside these limits acted ultra vires ("outside the powers") and any transaction entered into was void.[59] The rule worked to the benefit of shareholders and creditors of the company but to the disadvantage of third parties who dealt with the company in good faith, who might enter into a contract with the company unaware that it was ultra vires.

The common law position was modified by statute—the Companies Act 1985, s.35 (as amended by the Companies Act 1989) provided that an ultra vires contract could be enforceable against a company by a person dealing with the company in good faith. The ultra vires rule was therefore effectively abolished with regard to innocent third parties dealing with the company in such a way. The Companies Act 2006, s.39(1), now provides that the validity of an act done by a company cannot be called into question on the ground of a lack of capacity by reason of anything in the company's constitution.

Statutory corporations

5–030   Many public bodies, including for example local authorities, are statutory corporations. These are corporations created by Act of Parliament. The contractual capacity of such corporations is to be found in the incorporating statute; any contract entered into outside the powers contained in the statute is ultra vires and void.

Chartered corporations

5–031   Chartered corporations are set up by Royal Charter and include charitable associations and some universities. Such bodies possess the same contractual capacity as natural persons of full age and capacity.

Formalities and capacity: conclusion

5–032   Now that we have considered the requirement of form and the law of contractual capacity, the discussion of the way contracts are brought into existence is concluded. We turn, in the next chapter, to the contents of the contract itself—contractual terms.

Further reading

Howell, *Informal Conveyances and Section 2 of the Law of Property (Miscellaneous Provisions) Act 1989 (1990)* Conveyancer and Property Lawyer 441.
Dumbill, *Spiro*: The Easy Option (1991) 141 N.L.J. 124.
Hudson, *Mental Incapacity Revisited* (1986) Conveyancer and Property Lawyer 178.

---

[59]   *Ashbury Railway Carriage and Iron Co v Riche* (1875) L.R. 7 H.L. 653.

Chapter 6

CONTRACTUAL TERMS

Contracts consist of various statements, promises and stipulations which are referred to as the **6–001** "terms" of the contract. The terms may be express or implied—it is the terms of the contract that determine the extent of each party's contractual rights and duties. The remedies available if the terms are breached are determined by the relative importance of the terms.

We will consider first the express terms of the contract.

EXPRESS TERMS

Express terms are terms that are specifically agreed between the parties. The contract may be **6–002** purely oral and here it is a matter for the court to establish what the parties actually said. This may be difficult but it is essentially a matter of proof. Conversely, the contract may be contained entirely in a written document and it will be a question of construction for the court to establish the meaning of the words used by the parties. There will be many cases, however, where the parties make a contract that is partly written and partly oral—in this situation the so-called "parol evidence rule" may come into play.

The parol evidence rule

The rule provides that where a contract is embodied in a written document, then extrinsic evi- **6–003** dence is not admissible to add to, vary, subtract from or contradict the terms of the written document.[1] The use of the term "parol" is slightly misleading as, under the rule, extrinsic evidence is not confined to oral statements but can extend to written matter such as draft contracts and correspondence. The rule can be supported on the basis that it reflects the parties' presumed intentions—if they have gone to the trouble of negotiating a contract and reducing it to a written document they must have intended that document to contain the complete contract; anything excluded from it cannot have been intended to be part of the contract. Seen in this light, the rule serves the interests of commercial certainty in that all interested parties can rely on the written contract, secure in the knowledge that additional terms will not be unexpectedly

---

[1] *Jacobs v Batavia and General Plantations Trust* [1924] 1 Ch. 287.

imported. On the other hand the rule, if applied strictly, smacks of rigidity and could be productive of inconvenience and injustice.

The reality is, however, that the rule has rarely been applied strictly in the sense that the courts have been prepared to recognise numerous exceptions to the rule. Indeed, it has been judicially acknowledged that the "rule" is no more than a presumption.[2] The established exceptions to the rule include the following:

Contract partly written and partly oral

6–004   The parol evidence rule does not apply to a contract *intended* to be partly written and partly oral. Extrinsic evidence may be introduced in order to establish whether the contract was intended to be in writing only—this "exception" turns the rule inside out and has been described as rendering the rule no more than a "self-evident tautology".[3] In *Walker Property Investments (Brighton) Ltd v Walker*[4] the defendant negotiated to take the lease of a flat from the claimants. The defendant orally stipulated that if he took the flat, he would be able to use the basement for storage and use the garden. The claimants agreed but the subsequent formal lease omitted these undertakings. The Court of Appeal held that the oral and written elements together formed one contract.

A similar process can be seen at work in *Couchman v Hill*[5] where the claimant bought a heifer belonging to the defendant at an auction which the auction catalogue described as "unserved". The catalogue also stated that the sale would be subject to the auctioneer's usual conditions. These were exhibited and included a condition to the effect that the lots were sold "with all faults, imperfections and errors of description". Before bidding, the claimant asked both the defendant and the auctioneer to confirm that the heifer was unserved and this they did. The claimant bid for the heifer and it was knocked down to him. The heifer was found to be in calf (i.e. not unserved) and died some eight weeks later as a result of carrying a calf at too young an age. The Court of Appeal considered that the oral statements that the animal was unserved had to be considered alongside the written conditions. It was held that the claimant was entitled to damages.

It may be possible to avoid the argument that the contract is partly written and partly oral by the insertion of an "entire agreement clause" in the written contract. Such a clause states that the written document is intended and agreed to contain the entirety of the contract, each party acknowledging that they have not relied on any representation or statement outside the written contract.

Collateral contract

6–005   Extrinsic evidence of a collateral contract is admissible. Where a party enters into a written contract on the faith of an oral promise by the other, they may provide consideration for a

---

[2] *Gillespie Bros & Co v Cheney, Eggar & Co* [1896] 2 Q.B. 59, per Lord Russell.
[3] See Wedderburn [1959] C.L.J. 58. In 1976 the Law Commission (Law. Com. W.P. 70) recommended abolition of the parol evidence rule; ten years later the Commission (Law. Com. W.P. 154) thought abolition unnecessary as the rule effectively no longer existed.
[4] (1947) 177 L.T. 204.
[5] [1947] K.B. 544. See also *Harling v Eddy* [1951] 2 K.B. 739; *SS Ardennes (Cargo Owners) v Ardennes (Owners)* [1950] 2 All E.R. 517; *Birch v Paramount Estates Ltd* (1956) 16 E.G. 396; and *J Evans & Sons (Portsmouth) Ltd v Andrea Merzario Ltd* [1976] 2 All E.R. 930.

secondary or "collateral" contract which circumvents the parol evidence rule. The consideration consists in entering into the main written contract in reliance on the oral promise.

Collateral contracts will be discussed more fully later in this chapter (see para.6–015) but for present purposes the case of *City of Westminster Properties (1934) Ltd v Mudd*[6] is instructive. The defendant rented a shop from the claimants who knew that the defendant often slept there. When a new lease came up for negotiation, the claimants told the defendant that he could still sleep on the premises after signing the lease. There was a clause in the written document restricting the use of the premises to "showrooms, workrooms and offices only". In reliance on the oral assurance, the defendant signed the lease. The defendant continued to live there and the claimants brought an action for forfeiture of the lease alleging a breach of covenant not to use the premises for other than business purposes. Although the defendant was in breach of contract, Harman J. held that the defendant could plead a collateral contract as a defence—by entering the new lease the defendant had provided consideration for a promise not to enforce the strict terms of the lease against him. The judge rejected the notion that the case raised the issue of estoppel.[7] He said:

> "This is not a case of a representation made after contractual relations existed between the parties to the effect that one of the parties would not rely on his rights. . . [I]t is case of a promise made to [the defendant] before the execution of a lease that if he would execute it in the form put before him, the landlord would not enforce against him personally the covenant . . .there was a clear contract acted upon by the defendant to his detriment and from which the [claimants] cannot be allowed to resile."

It seems that the insertion of an entire agreement clause may prevent a party from setting up a collateral contract as a defence to an action for breach of contract.[8]   **6–006**

Other exceptions to the parol evidence rule

Further exceptions to the rule include: **6–007**

Custom; evidence of the customs of a locality or trade usage may be admissible to show that a term could be implied by custom. Thus in *Smith v Wilson*[9] the written contract referred to "1,000 rabbits". Oral evidence was admitted to show that by a local custom of Suffolk, 1,000 rabbits meant 1,200 rabbits.

Operation of the contract; extrinsic evidence is permissible to show that the contract has not yet come into operation or has ceased to operate. Thus in *Pym v Cambell*[10] there was a written agreement for the sale of a share in a patent but the parties orally agreed that the contract was not to operate until a third party approved the invention. Evidence of the oral agreement was admitted.

Validity; extrinsic evidence is permissible to show that the written contract lacks validity, e.g. for want of consideration, incapacity, misrepresentation or mistake.

---

[6] [1959] Ch. 129.
[7] See para.4–036 above.
[8] *Deepak Fertilisers & Petrochemical Corporation v Davy McKee (London) Ltd* [1999] 1 Lloyd's Rep. 387; and *Inntrepreneur Pub Co v East Crown Ltd* [2000] 2 Lloyd's Rep. 611.
[9] (1832) 3 B. & Ad. 728.
[10] (1856) 6 E. & B. 370.

Representations and terms

6–008   In the course of negotiations leading up to a contract, the parties may make many statements and it may be a matter of some difficulty to establish their legal effect. Not all such statements will form part of the contract itself. Pre-contractual statements fall into three categories. First, some statements may be so vague or exaggerated as to amount to no more than "mere puff" creating no legal liability at all. Secondly, some statements may be classed as "representations"—these are statements of fact made during the course of negotiations that may have the effect of inducing the other party to enter the contract but they do not form part of the contract itself. Finally, it is possible that a statement is a term of the contract.

The essential distinction between a representation and a term is that the former is merely a statement of fact which may be true or false. A term, on the other hand, constitutes a binding promise by which a party commits to fulfilling an obligation. The most obvious difference between the two types of statement lies in the remedies available. If a representation proves false and falls within the definition of an "actionable misrepresentation"[11] the innocent party may have the right to rescind (set aside) the contract and may be able to claim damages for misrepresentation. If a term of the contract is broken, the remedy lies in an action for breach of contract.

These remedies are very different. In many respects the victim of a breach of contract is in a better position than a misrepresentee. The award of damages for misrepresentation depends on establishing degrees of fault, i.e. that the misrepresentor was fraudulent or negligent. If the misrepresentation is innocent, damages cannot be claimed as such but may be awarded at the court's discretion. On the other hand, where a contract has been breached, the innocent party has a right to claim damages if it is proved that a term has been broken. There are differences, too, in the measure of damages awarded. For misrepresentation, the award of damages is on the tortious basis designed to put the party into the position they would have been in had the contract never been entered into. In contract, however, damages are usually based on "expectation loss" which will put the injured party in the position they would have been in had the contract been properly performed, i.e. if the statement embodied in the term had been true.

6–009   The distinction between terms and representations is no longer quite as crucial as it once was. The reason is that before 1964 all misrepresentations were classed as either fraudulent or innocent and damages were not available for innocent misrepresentations. The only possibility, therefore, of recovering damages for a non- fraudulent statement lay in establishing that it was a term of the contract. The decision of the House of Lords in *Hedley Byrne & Co Ltd v Heller Partners and Partners Ltd*[12] in 1964 introduced the possibility of claiming damages for economic loss for negligent misstatement and the Misrepresentation Act 1967 introduced a statutory claim for damages for negligent misrepresentation. Cases decided before these developments taking place in the mid-1960s need to be viewed against this background.

Whether a statement is a term or representation is primarily a question of intention, and this is a matter that is ascertained objectively. This is illustrated by the decision of the House of Lords in *Heilbut, Symons & Co v Buckleton*.[13]

In this case, the claimant telephoned the manager of a firm of rubber merchants (the defendants) and said, "I understand you are bringing out a rubber company" and he was told that they

[11] For misrepresentation, see Chapter 11.
[12] [1964] A.C. 465.
[13] [1913] A.C. 30.

were. The claimant then asked if the company was all right and the manager said, "We are bringing it out." The claimant then said that that was good enough for him and agreed to buy 5,000 shares which were allotted to him. The company was not described in the letter of allotment, merely named. The shares slumped in value and the claimant brought an action alleging that it was a term of the contract that the company was a rubber company. Reversing the decision of the Court of Appeal, the House of Lords held that, although the company could not properly be described as a rubber company, there was no contractual promise to that effect. The court found that the claimant was not too concerned with whether it was a rubber company—the main inducement was that the defendants were bringing out a company. There was no evidence of an intention by the parties that the defendants' manager's statement should give rise to contractual liability. Lord Moulton considered that the question of whether an affirmation made by a vendor at the time of sale constitutes a term, as opposed to a representation, depends on the intention of the parties to be deduced from the whole of the evidence.

It is not an easy matter to deduce the parties' intentions and the courts have developed, through the cases, a number of indicators as to whether the parties intend a statement to be a contractual term or mere representation. None of these indicators should be regarded as decisive because the court must have regard to the totality of the evidence but they may be helpful in guiding the court to a decision.

Manner and timing of statement

The manner in which a statement is made may give a clue as to the parties' intentions. Thus, a statement is not likely to be a term if the person making the statement suggests the other party should check or verify it. This is illustrated by the case of *Ecay v Godfrey*.[14] In the course of negotiations for the sale of a boat, the seller stated that he believed the boat was sound but suggested that the buyer should have her surveyed. The buyer did not have her surveyed because he was in a hurry to buy. The vessel turned out to be in a poor condition but Lord Goddard C.J. refused to treat the statement that the boat was sound as a term of the contract.   **6–010**

Conversely, if a statement is made with the intention of preventing the other party from finding a defect, and succeeds in this, the court may consider it to be a term. In *Schawel v Reade*[15] the claimant went to the defendant's stables to look for a horse for stud purposes. While the claimant was examining a horse called "Mallow Man", the defendant said: "You need not look for anything: the horse is perfectly sound. If there was anything the matter with the horse, I would tell you." The claimant stopped the inspection and the price was agreed a few days later; the contract was completed three weeks later. The animal turned to be unfit for stud purposes because of an eye disease. The House of Lords unanimously held that the statement that the horse was sound was a term. Lord Macnaghten considered that the words used were about as plain a warranty (i.e. contractual term) as to the soundness of the horse as could be given.

It seems that where there is a distinct interval between the making of the statement and the conclusion of the contract, this may indicate that the statement is intended to be only a representation. The case of *Routledge v McKay*[16] affords a good illustration. The defendant was

---

[14] (1947) 80 Lloyds L. Rep. 286.

[15] [1913] 2 I. R. 81. Cf *Hopkins v Tanqueray* (1854) 15 C.B. 130, where on very similar facts the court held the statement to be a representation even though the interval between the making of the statement and the conclusion of the contract was just one day.

[16] [1954] 1 All E.R. 855.

selling a motor bike combination and told the claimant that it was a 1942 model. Seven days later a written contract was drawn up which made no reference to the date of the machine, but it was discovered later that it was first registered in 1930. The Court of Appeal held that the claimant could not recover damages from the defendant as the statement was not a term of the contract. Since the statement was made some time before the contract was concluded it was only a representation. This decision may be compared with *Schawel v Reade* where clearly the court regarded the contract as having been made over a prolonged period. Nevertheless, in more recent times it has been judicially stated that the longer the interval between the statement and the conclusion of the contract, "the greater the presumption must be that the parties did not intend the statement to have contractual effect."[17]

Importance of statement

6–011   A statement is likely to be a term if it is such that the injured party indicates that they would not have entered the contract had the statement not been made; thus the importance they attach to the truth of the statement is made clear.

In *Bannerman v White*[18] the defendants wished to buy hops for brewing purposes. Brewers were concerned at the time that the cultivation of hops with sulphur affected the quality of the beer. Before negotiations began with the claimants for the sale of hops the defendants had made it known that they did not wish to buy hops to which sulphur had been applied. The defendants were shown a sample of hops by the claimants and the defendants asked whether sulphur had been used and said that if it had, they would "not even trouble to ask the price". A contract for the sale of 300 acres of hops was agreed but the buyer later discovered that sulphur had been used on five acres and then all the hops had been mixed together. The defendants argued that they were not bound by the contract because a term had been broken. It was held that the pre-liminary negotiations were part of the contract and the defendants were entitled to repudiate the transaction. The importance of the statement regarding the non-use of sulphur had been clear to both parties and they had contracted on that footing.

In both *Schawel v Reade* and *Bannerman v White* the statements that were held to be contractual terms were made by parties who obviously had superior knowledge of the subject matter than did the purchasers. Later cases have stressed this factor as relevant in deciding upon the nature of the particular statement.

Special knowledge and skill

6–012   One party may possess superior skill and knowledge relating to the subject matter of the contract than the other party and therefore statements made by the party in the stronger position are more likely to be regarded as terms. The point may illustrated by comparing two well-known cases.

In *Dick Bentley Productions Ltd v Harold Smith (Motors) Ltd*[19] the claimant, Dick Bentley, told the defendant car dealer that he wished to buy a "well-vetted" Bentley car, that is, one of which the history is known. Later, the defendant showed the claimant a car which he said had

---

[17]   *Inntrepreneur Pub Co (GL) v East Crown Ltd* [2000] 2 Lloyd's Rep. 611, per Lightman J.
[18]   (1861) 10 C.B. N.S. 844.
[19]   [1965] 1 W.L.R. 623.

done 20,000 miles since being fitted with a replacement engine and gearbox. The speedometer on the car showed only 20,000 miles. The claimant bought the car but it proved disappointing and gave the claimant a lot of trouble and so he brought an action for damages for breach of contract. The defendant's statements about the mileage of the vehicle were untrue. The real history of the car showed that it must have done over 100,000 miles. The Court of Appeal found for the claimant and held that the statement as to the mileage was a term of the contract. In holding the statement to be a term, Lord Denning M.R. said:

> "Here we have a dealer . . . who was in a position to know, or at least to find out, the history of the car. He could get it by writing to the makers. He did not do so . . . When the history of the car was examined, his statement turned out to be quite wrong. He ought to have known better."

In arriving at this conclusion the Court of Appeal distinguished an earlier decision, *Oscar Chess Ltd v Williams*.[20] Here, in a part-exchange deal the defendant sold to the claimants, motor dealers, a second hand Morris saloon car. The defendant honestly believed that the vehicle was a 1948 model and he showed the claimants the registration book which confirmed that 1948 was the year of first registration. There was no interval between the making of the statement and the conclusion of the contract. Some eight months after the contract had been concluded the claimants discovered that the car was a 1939 model—the outward appearance of the particular model had not changed between 1939 and 1948. The registration book had presumably been altered by a previous owner. The Court of Appeal, applying *Heilbut, Symons v Buckleton* and *Routledge v McKay*, held that the defendant's confirmation of the age of the car was a representation and not a term of the contract. The claimants, being dealers, had the special knowledge. Denning L.J. said:

> "It must have been obvious to both [parties] that the seller had himself no personal knowledge of the year when the car was made. He only became owner after a great number of changes. He must have been relying on the registration book. It is unlikely that such a person would warrant the year of manufacture. . . . In these circumstances the intelligent bystander would, I suggest, say that the seller did not intend to bind himself so as to warrant that it was a 1948 model."

In *Dick Bentley v Harold Smith* Lord Denning appears to distinguish *Oscar Chess v Williams* on the basis that in that case the maker of the statement was not at fault in relying on the registration book, whereas the dealer in *Dick Bentley v Harold Smith* was negligent in not checking the mileage. Whereas this is clearly, on the facts, a difference between the two cases, the presence or absence of negligence should not be a decisive issue in determining whether a statement is a term or a representation. The true distinction between the two cases surely lies in the relative degree of expertise between the maker of the statement and the party relying on the statement in each case.   **6–013**

Statement excluded from written contract

An oral statement made during negotiations may be followed by the parties recording their agreement in a written document. If the statement is excluded from the written terms, the   **6–014**

---

[20]   [1957] 1 W.L.R. 370.

inference is that the parties cannot have intended it to be a term of their contract but a representation only. But this is only an inference and as we saw in the discussion of the parol evidence rule (see para.6–004), the parties may well have intended the contract to be partly written and partly oral. Another possibility is that the oral statement gives rise to a collateral contract and this will be considered below.

Collateral contracts

6–015   Where a contract is entered into on the faith of a statement made by one of the parties, the court may decide that it founds a collateral contract. We have already seen how the collateral contract device forms an exception to the parol evidence rule (see para.6–005). In *Heilbut, Symons & Co v Buckleton*[21] Lord Moulton considered that the courts should be slow to find a collateral contract although this must be seen in the light of the refusal of the courts at that time to award damages for non-fraudulent misrepresentation. He explained the basis of the device as follows:

> "It is evident, both on principle and on authority, that there may be a contract the consideration for which is the making of some other contract. 'If you will make such and such a contract I will give you one hundred pounds,' is in every sense of the word a complete legal contract. It is collateral to the main contract, but each has an independent existence, and they do not differ in respect of their possessing to the full the character and status of a contract."

A good illustration of the use of a collateral contract is the case of *De Lassalle v Guildford*.[22] Here the defendant was negotiating the lease of a house to the claimant, who refused to complete unless the defendant orally assured him that the drains were in order. The defendant gave such an assurance but no term to that effect was inserted into the lease document. The drains were not in order and the claimant sued for damages not upon the lease, which did not refer to the drains, but on a collateral contract based on the defendant's oral assurance. The consideration to enforce this promise as a separate contract was the claimant's execution of the lease, i.e. his entering into the main contract.

A number of points should be noted in connection with collateral contracts. First, although the collateral contract arises from a process of judicial implication, in theory the court should not find such a contract unless the elements of a separate valid contract are in existence. Thus the promise that founds the collateral contract must be made with the intention that it be acted upon and supported by consideration. The consideration usually consists of the act of entering the main contract.

6–016   Secondly, a collateral contract may be valid even though it conflicts with a term in the main contract. We saw in *City of Westminster Properties v Mudd* (see para.6–005 above) that an oral assurance by a landlord that a tenant could continue to reside on the premises overrode a covenant in the lease that the property should only be used for business. The oral assurance formed the basis of a collateral contract which could be raised as a defence in an action for breach of covenant by the landlord. It was previously thought that the parol evidence rule could only be

---

[21] [1913] A.C. 30. The case is discussed at para.6–009 above.
[22] [1901] 2 K.B. 215.

circumvented by a collateral contract where the statement in question added to, rather than varied or contradicted, the written document.[23]

Thirdly, not only may the collateral contract device be used to side-step the parol evidence rule, but it has been used in certain other contexts, for example, to evade an exclusion clause[24] or to avoid the effects of an illegal contract.[25] In *Shanklin Pier Ltd v Detel Products Ltd*[26] the device was used to get round the difficulties caused, at common law, by the rule of privity of contract (the case is discussed at para.8–021). The decision in *Record v Bell*[27] shows that the collateral contract can be relied upon in certain circumstances to get round s.2 of the Law of Property (Miscellaneous Provisions) Act 1989. In that case it was held that although the correspondence did not satisfy the formality requirement in s.2, a letter by the vendor offering a warranty as to title, intended to induce the purchaser to exchange, amounted to an enforceable collateral contract when accepted by the exchange of contracts.

The concept of the collateral contract proved useful in circumventing the rule that damages were not available for non-fraudulent misrepresentation even where the misrepresentor had been negligent. Since damages can now be claimed for negligent misrepresentation and negligent misstatement (see para.11–022), this particular role of the collateral contract has lost some of its significance. Many of the cases of this type refer to the oral statement giving rise to liability as a "collateral warranty" without always making it clear whether what is being referred to is a warranty in a separate collateral contract or in the main contract.

6–017 Even after the introduction of remedies in damages for negligent statements, the courts have shown a readiness to find a collateral contract or warranty. This may be where the statement is in the form of an opinion or promise as to the future which may not give rise to liability in misrepresentation under the Misrepresentation Act 1967. An example is *Esso Petroleum Co Ltd v Mardon*[28] where the claimants wished to build a petrol filling station at Southport and identified a suitable site. They carried out a survey and concluded that a filling station on the site would be likely to sell approximately 200,000 gallons of petrol a year by the second year of operation. The claimants obtained planning permission from the local authority who imposed a condition that the petrol pumps should be at the back of the premises, i.e. screened from the road. The site was developed according to this plan and it was completed in 1963; the claimants did not, however, revise their estimated annual throughput of petrol. The claimants entered into negotiations with the defendant who was interested in taking a tenancy. The claimants' experienced representative informed the defendant that he estimated that the site would have an annual throughput of 200,000 gallons. On the basis of that figure, the defendant took a tenancy of the station but the sales never amounted to half the gallonage predicted by the claimants. The defendant could not run the station at a profit and ultimately the claimants sought possession of the site and the defendant counterclaimed for damages for negligence.

6–018 The Court of Appeal held that when the claimants, through their representative, made their forecast as to the potential throughput of the site, they made a collateral warranty that they had used reasonable care and skill in making their forecast. This was based on the claimants' superior skill and knowledge of the petrol trade which meant that their statement, although in

---

[23] See Wedderburn (1959) C.L.J. 58.
[24] *Webster v Higgin* [1948] 2 All E.R. 127.
[25] *Strongman (1945) Ltd v Sincock* [1955] 2 Q.B. 525. See para.14–035.
[26] [1951] 2 K.B. 854.
[27] [1991] 2 W.L.R. 931. See para.5–007.
[28] [1976] Q.B. 801.

the form of an opinion, was intended to induce the defendant to enter the contract. As the claimants were in breach of this promise, they were liable in damages. The court also held that the statement constituted a negligent misstatement.[29]

In *Evans (J) & Sons (Portsmouth) Ltd v Andrea Merzario Ltd*[30] an oral assurance that goods would be carried in the hold of a ship was held to override a written contract that permitted carriage on deck. The defendants were held liable in damages when the claimant's container was swept overboard. The majority of the Court of Appeal (Roskill and Geoffrey Lane L.JJ.) held that the oral assurance was a term of a contract partly written and partly oral. Lord Denning M.R. relied on the collateral contract device. The two concepts, though clearly different, were treated in this case as interchangeable.

IMPLIED TERMS

6–019   Thus far we have been considering terms which are expressly agreed between the parties to the contract. However, even where terms are not expressed they may, in certain circumstances, be implied into the contract.

In some cases the parties may contract against a background of trade custom and usage and matters upon which the contract is silent may be implied into the contract according to the customs of a particular trade, business or locality.

Another possibility is that the parties may not have considered every eventuality that may arise under the contract once it has been executed or they may consider that some matters are too obvious to be the subject matter of an express term. In such cases, the courts may be prepared to imply terms into the contract upon matters for which the contract does not expressly provide.

Finally, the provisions of a statute may imply terms into a contract—the most well-known example is the Sale of Goods Act 1979 which implies various terms into contracts for the sale of goods. Thus it is an implied term of such a contract that, inter alia, the seller shall be the owner and where the sale is in the course of a business that the goods supplied must be of satisfactory quality.

There are three ways in which terms may be implied into a contract; (i) by custom; (ii) by the courts (where terms may be implied in fact or in law); and (iii) by the provisions of a statute.

Terms implied by custom

6–020   A term may be implied into a contract according to local custom. In *Hutton v Warren*[31] the lease of a farm was lawfully determined by the landlord and the tenant sought a reasonable sum in respect of tillage, sowing and cultivation (i.e. for the crops that had been sown but not harvested). Although the lease was silent on these matters agricultural custom required such a payment. The court held that the custom would be implied into the lease and found for the tenant.

---

[29] See para.11–023.
[30] [1976] 2 All E.R. 930.
[31] (1836) 2 Gale. 71.

A custom will not, however, be implied if it is contrary to the express terms of the contract. In the case of *Affreteurs Reunis SA, Les v Leopold Walford (London) Ltd*[32] a charterparty contained a clause that commission was to be paid to the broker of the charterers "on signing the charter". The owners, who were sued by the broker for his commission, argued a custom of the trade that commission was payable only when the hire had been earned. The House of Lords held that commission was payable on signing the charter—the custom was incompatible with the clear wording of the clause in the contract.

Terms implied by the courts

Apart from the implication of terms by custom, there are two distinct processes whereby a court may imply a term into a contract—these are terms "implied in fact" and terms "implied in law".   **6–021**

Terms implied in fact

A term will be implied in fact where the court is satisfied that the parties, having omitted to insert a provision in their contract to deal with a particular eventuality, must have intended it as a matter of fact to be part of their agreement. Thus the court does not see itself as rewriting the contract for the parties but rather giving effect to what the parties had agreed and would have explicitly stated had they thought about the matter.   **6–022**

It is said that the term to be implied must be necessary in order to give the contract "business efficacy". Some idea of what these words mean is provided by one of the leading cases in this area of the law, *The Moorcock*.[33] The facts were that the defendants agreed to let the claimants use their wharf and jetty, which extended into the River Thames, to discharge and store cargo from their steamship, *The Moorcock*. The ship would be moored alongside the jetty where it would be grounded at low tide. However, the ship having moored, when low tide came, she was damaged owing to a ridge of hard ground beneath the mud. The defendants had done nothing to ascertain whether the river bed adjacent to their jetty was a safe place for mooring and there was no express term as to its suitability for such a purpose. The claimants sought damages from the defendants who denied liability.

The Court of Appeal held that the defendants were liable. A warranty must be implied into the contract that the defendants had taken reasonable care to ensure that the vessel could safely moor as this must have been the intention of the parties. The court could imply the term as it was necessary to make the contract commercially workable, i.e. to give it business efficacy. As Bowen L.J. explained:

> "In business transactions such as this, what the law desires to effect by the implication is to give such business efficacy as must have been intended by both parties who are business men."

---

[32] [1919] A.C. 801. In *Exxonmobil Sales and Supply Corpn v Texaco Ltd* [2002] EWHC 1964 (Comm) an entire agreement clause (see para.6–004) which stated that there was no "usage" affecting the agreement was effective to exclude implied terms based on usage or custom.
[33] (1889) 14 P.D. 64.

The test established in this case is a narrow and restrictive one based on "necessity". It is not enough to show that the implied term would better reflect the parties' intentions or that the implication of the term would be reasonable. In *Liverpool City Council v Irwin*[34] the House of Lords rejected an attempt by Lord Denning M.R. in the court below to suggest that the courts could imply a term where it would be reasonable to do so. Their lordships confirmed that the test is one of necessity.

6–023   In the years since *The Moorcock* was decided there have been a number of cases which have attempted to formulate a test for implying terms. Perhaps the best-known is the case of *Shirlaw v Southern Foundries (1926) Ltd.*[35] Here, MacKinnon L.J. put forward what has come to be known as the "officious bystander" test. He said:

> "Prima facie that which in any contract is left to be implied and need not be expressed is *something so obvious that it goes without saying*; so that, if while the parties were making their bargain, an officious bystander were to suggest some express provision for it in their agreement, they would testily suppress him with a common 'Oh, of course!' [Author's italics]"

Expressing some confidence in this test, MacKinnon L.J. added:

> "At least it is true . . . that, if a term were never implied by a judge unless it could pass that test, he could not be held to be wrong."

The test has been applied many times by the courts, usually in conjunction with the business efficacy test of *The Moorcock*. It is not, however, without its limitations. It may be difficult to apply in highly complex transactions involving technical issues where the eavesdropping bystander might struggle to find a question the answer to which is so obvious that it goes without saying.

The officious bystander test cannot be successfully applied where both parties do not share the knowledge of the matter to be implied. This is illustrated by *Spring v National Amalgamated Stevedores and Dockers Society*[36] where it was held that the "Bridlington Agreement" (a Trades Union Congress agreement relating to the transfer of members from one union to another) could not be implied into a contract of employment because the average employee would never have heard of it. Sir Leonard Stone V.C. explained the basis of the decision as follows:

> "If [the officious bystander] test were to be applied to the facts of the present case and the bystander had asked the [claimant] at the time he paid his five shillings and signed the acceptance form, 'Won't you put into it some reference to the Bridlington Agreement?', I think (indeed, I have no doubt) the [claimant] would have answered 'What's that?'"

Further, if there are doubts as to whether one of the parties would have agreed to the bystander's suggestion, the term cannot be implied. Two cases demonstrate this point.

6–024   In *Luxor (Eastbourne) Ltd v Cooper*[37] the appellants employed the respondent, an estate agent, to sell some property. The respondent, by the terms of the contract, was to be paid a

---

[34] [1977] A.C. 239.
[35] [1939] 2 K.B. 206.
[36] [1956] 1 W.L.R. 585.
[37] [1941] A.C. 108.

considerable sum by way of commission on completion of sale. He found a buyer ready, willing and able to purchase at the asking price but the appellants refused to proceed with the transaction—they had found a buyer themselves. The appellants refused to pay the commission but the respondent argued that a term should be implied that the appellants should not, without good reason, refuse to sell the property to persons introduced by the respondent. The House of Lords held that no such term could be implied because both parties would not have agreed to it at the time of the agreement. It was doubtful that the appellants would have assented to the term. Their lordships considered that no necessity existed for the term to be implied; the officious bystander test was not specifically mentioned in the case but it is a clear illustration of its application.

In *Shell UK Ltd v Lostock Garage Ltd*[38] the defendants, who operated a small country garage, had an exclusive dealing agreement (a "solus" tie[39]) with the claimants, Shell UK, under which the defendants agreed to buy all their petrol from the claimants. The defendants were in competition with four local garages, two of which were also tied to the claimants. Following the energy crisis of 1974, the demand for petrol slumped and there took place a price war between garages. The four local competitors were selling petrol at 70p per gallon but the defendants, being bound by the solus tie, had to sell at 75p per gallon. The two local garages that were free from ties were able to purchase petrol cheaply from independent suppliers; whereas the two which were tied to the claimants benefited from a price support scheme operated by the claimants which kept the price at 70p. The defendants' garage was too small to benefit from this scheme. In order to stay in business, the defendants switched to a cheaper supplier thereby breaching the tie. The claimants brought an action seeking an injunction and damages—the defendants argued that the claimants were in breach of an implied obligation in the solus agreement that the claimants would not abnormally discriminate against them.

A majority of the Court of Appeal held that no such term could be implied. As Lord Denning M.R. explained: **6–025**

> "If the Shell company had been asked at the beginning: 'Will you agree not to discriminate abnormally against the buyer?' I think they would have declined. It might be a reasonable term, but it is not a necessary term."

Lord Denning added an additional reason why the term could not be implied, that is that it could not "be formulated with sufficient precision." Thus attempts to imply terms may fail because the proposed term is insufficiently certain to be enforceable. Another possibility is that there are several different versions of the implied term and the court is reluctant to say which one the parties must have intended. In some cases where the parties have negotiated a detailed written contract the court may conclude that the omission of the term sought to be implied is deliberate on their part. The parties cannot therefore have intended it to have been included.[40]

The basis upon which a term could be implied in fact came before the House of Lords a few years ago in *Equitable Life Assurance Society v Hyman*.[41] Under article 65 of the claimant society's articles of association the amount of any bonus awarded to policyholders was within the

---

[38] [1976] 1 W.L.R. 1187.
[39] Solus agreements are discussed at para.15–016.
[40] See *Trollope & Colls v North West Metropolitan Regional Hospital Board* [1973] 1 W.L.R. 601.
[41] [2002] 1 A.C. 408.

absolute discretion of the directors. The defendant represented the interests of policyholders who held retirement with-profits policies with the society containing a guaranteed annuity rate. This guaranteed rate was higher than the then current interest rates. The claimants wished to award the same bonus to all their policyholders, whether or not they held a policy with a guaranteed rate. The consequence was that the policyholders represented by the defendant received lower bonuses than would have been the case for such a class of policyholder in the past. The claimants sought a declaration that such a course of action was legitimate under article 65 and the terms of the defendant's policy. Sir Richard Scott V.C. upheld the legitimacy of the society's action but a majority of the Court of Appeal reversed that decision. The claimants appealed to the House of Lords.

The House of Lords held that it was necessary to imply a term into the society's articles that the directors would not exercise their discretion under article 65 in such a way as to defeat the reasonable expectations of the guaranteed annuity rate policyholders. The commercial objective of the guaranteed rate was to protect the policyholder from a fall in market rates—the availability of the guaranteed rate had been a good selling point and would have attracted purchasers. Lord Steyn confirmed that a term could be implied in fact only according to a test of strict necessity—it was a stringent test but it had been satisfied in this case. Although the court used the language of necessity, the term actually implied appears to owe more to the court's view of the parties' reasonable expectations rather than to their presumed intentions. Would both parties have agreed to the inclusion of the term if suggested at the time of the contract? Whether the case signals a more liberal approach to the implication of terms that that indicated by *The Moorcock* and the officious bystander test remains to be seen.

Terms implied in law

6–026 Whereas terms implied in fact are essentially gap–fillers in an individual contract, terms implied in law are terms attached to particular types of contract by the law itself. In *Shell v Lostock Garage*, discussed above, Lord Denning M.R. considered that terms implied in law comprehend relationships of common occurrence, such as buyer and seller, master and servant, landlord and tenant. In these relationships the law has imposed obligations on one or other of the parties which are not based upon the actual or presumed intentions of the parties but on more general considerations. The parties can expressly exclude or modify these obligations, but unless they do so, the obligation is a legal incident of the relationship. It seems that it is attached by the law itself and not by reason of the implication of a term.

The leading modern case is the decision of the House of Lords in *Liverpool City Council v Irwin*.[42] The defendant in this case was the tenant of a maisonette on the ninth and tenth floors of a block of flats in Everton owned by the landlord, the claimant city council. There was a one-sided tenancy agreement which contained a list of the obligations of the tenant under the agreement but there were none imposed on the landlord. Owing to vandalism and alleged non-co-operation by the tenants, the block was in an appalling condition. The staircases were not properly lit, the lifts rarely functioned and the refuse disposal chutes were frequently blocked. The tenants went on a "rent strike" and the claimant brought possession proceedings. The tenants counterclaimed, arguing, inter alia, that the claimants were in breach of an implied term to keep the common parts in repair.

---

[42] [1977] A.C. 239.

The House of Lords held that a term must be implied that the claimants should take reasonable care to keep the common parts in a reasonable state of repair. However, there was no evidence that the claimants had breached this obligation; indeed, their endeavours had been frustrated by vandals—they had spent more on repairs than they had received in rents.

A term will be implied in law (i) where the contract is one of common occurrence; and **6–027** (ii) where it would be necessary to imply the term. In *Liverpool CC v Irwin*, Lord Wilberforce stressed that the test was one of necessity—he thought that the obligation should be read into the contract as the contract itself implicitly required, no more and no less. Lord Salmon said:

> "I find it difficult to think of any term which it would be more necessary to imply than one without which the whole transaction would become futile, inefficacious and absurd as it would do if in a 15 storey block of flats . . . the landlords were under no legal duty to take reasonable care to keep the lifts in working order and the staircases lit."

Lord Cross, however, appeared to adopt a test of reasonableness in relation to implying terms in law when he said that the test was whether "in the general run of such cases the term in question would be one which it would be reasonable to insert." This formulation is perhaps nearer the mark in defining what the courts are actually doing in such cases.[43] Nevertheless, later decisions have articulated the test as being one of necessity as indicated by Lord Wilberforce in *Liverpool CC v Irwin*.

In *Scally v Southern Health and Social Services Board*[44] the claimant was a doctor employed by the defendant in Northern Ireland. A change in the health authority regulations gave employees the right to buy in extra years on their pension on favourable terms but the right had to be exercised within 12 months from a certain date. No publicity was given to this amended regulation and employees were not informed of it. As a result the claimant was unable to take advantage of the right. It was argued that a term should be implied in his contract of employment that the employer should take reasonable steps to notify employees of their rights. The House of Lords held that such a term should be implied. Lord Bridge considered that it was necessary to imply a term where: (1) the terms of the contract have not been negotiated with the individual employee but result from negotiation with a representative body or are otherwise incorporated by reference; (2) a particular term of the contract makes available to the employee a valuable right contingent upon action being taken by him to avail himself of its benefit; (3) the employee cannot, in all the circumstances, reasonably be expected to be aware of the term.

Lord Bridge said:

> "I fully appreciate that the criterion to justify an implication of this kind is necessity, not reasonableness. But I take the view that it is not merely reasonable, but necessary, in the circumstances postulated, to imply an obligation on the employer to bring the term of the contract in question to the employee's attention."

Despite the judicial insistence on the test being one of "necessity" this case is surely an example of a term being implied because it is a reasonable one to be implied in the circumstances for

---

[43] See Peden (2001) 117 L.Q.R. 459.
[44] [1992] 1 A.C. 294.

this particular type of contract. It is difficult to see in what sense the term could be considered necessary.[45]

Terms implied by statute

6–028   Various Acts of Parliament and statutory instruments have, over the years implied terms into particular types of contract. Where this is done, it has nothing to do with the intentions of the contracting parties; indeed, the terms are imposed regardless of their wishes. This process is a significant instance of legislative intervention in contract making and part of the long march away from the classical theory of freedom of contract.

The most commonly encountered instances of implied terms in the law of contract are those contained in the Sale of Goods Act 1979. The terms are concerned primarily with the seller's title and the quality of the goods sold. The implied terms as to quality originally appeared in the Sale of Goods Act 1893 and they were introduced so that businessmen could better regulate their affairs—it was possible to exclude the terms and such exclusion was frequent before the 1970s. In those years, however, the implied terms as to quality came to be seen as an important measure of consumer protection and the Unfair Contract Terms Act 1977 rendered void any attempt to exclude the terms by a business as against a consumer. Exclusion of the terms between businesses was made subject to a requirement of reasonableness.

In 1979 a revised version of the Sale of Goods Act was enacted—the implied terms that we are concerned with are to be found in ss.12–15. That Act was amended by the Sale and Supply of Goods Act 1994 which implied a condition that the goods must be of satisfactory quality instead of merchantable quality, the standard that had applied since 1893. Further reform came with the implementation of the Sale and Supply of Goods to Consumers Regulations 2002.[46] These regulations enhance the remedies available to consumers where the goods do not conform to the express or implied terms of the contract—the new remedies are repair; replacement; reduction in price and rescission.

The Consumer Credit Act 1974, as amended by the Consumer Credit Act 2006, implies terms analogous to those in the Sale of Goods Act into hire-purchase or other credit sale agreements; and similar terms are implied into contracts for the supply of goods by the Supply of Goods and Services Act 1982.[47] We now turn to an examination of the terms implied under the Sale of Goods Act.

Sale of Goods Act: implied terms

6–029   The sale of goods implied terms cover matters of seller's title, correspondence with description, satisfactory quality, fitness for a particular purpose and sales by sample. The terms are classified as either "conditions" or "warranties"—for the purposes of the present discussion a condition is a major term the breach of which will give the innocent party a right to treat himself as discharged from the contract as well as a right to recover damages. A warranty is a lesser term giving only a right to claim damages. A fuller discussion of the meaning of these expressions is given later in this chapter.[48]

---

[45] See Phang [1998] J.B.L. 1.
[46] SI 2002/3045.
[47] The changes introduced by the Sale and Supply of Goods to Consumers Regulations 2002 also apply here.
[48] See para.6–042.

Title: s.12

There is an implied condition in a contract for the sale of goods that in the case of a sale, the seller has a right to sell the goods, and in the case of an agreement to sell, he will have such a right at the time the property is to pass (s.12(1)). "Right to sell" refers to title, i.e. ownership.   **6–030**

In *Rowland v Divall*[49] the claimant bought a car from the defendant and used it for several months. It then came to light that the defendant had never had title to the car and the claimant was required to restore it to its true owner. The claimant brought an action for breach of contract to recover the full purchase price he had paid. The Court of Appeal held that the implied term that the seller has the right to sell was breached and that this constituted a total failure of consideration. This meant that he could recover the full price even though he had used the car for some months and it had depreciated in value. What he had paid for was ownership of the car and he had not received that.

In addition to the above implied condition, there are also, in s.12, implied warranties that the buyer will have quiet possession and the goods will be free from encumbrances (s.12(2)).

Description: s.13

Where there is a contract for the sale of goods by description, there is an implied condition that the goods will correspond with the description (s.13 (1)).   **6–031**

In *Varley v Whipp*[50] the defendant agreed to buy a reaping machine from the claimant which the claimant said had been new the previous year and had only cut 50 or 60 acres. The defendant had never seen the machine until it was delivered. It turned to be an old machine that had been mended at some stage and was of no use to the defendant and so he returned it. The claimant brought an action to recover the price but failed—it was a sale by description and the goods did not correspond with the description. This breach of condition entitled the defendant to treat the contract as repudiated.

In fact, most sales of goods will be sales by description. The Act (s.13(3)) makes it clear that a sale of goods is not prevented from being a sale by description "by reason only that, being exposed for sale or hire, they are selected by the buyer." This is referring to a self-service transaction where the buyer relies on some description of the goods on the packaging or labelling.

The fact that the label may amount to a description is illustrated by the case of *Beale v Taylor*[51] where the defendant advertised his car for sale as a "[Triumph] Herald convertible, white, 1961." The claimant inspected the car and saw on the rear of the vehicle a metallic 1200cc badge. He did not test-drive the car because he had no insurance. When he took delivery of the vehicle the claimant found that the steering pulled dangerously to one side. On inspection, it was discovered that the car was in fact two cars that had been welded together. The front part was an earlier model Herald 998cc and the rear was a 1961 1200cc. The Court of Appeal held that the advertisement and badge on the back of the car constituted a description and therefore there was a breach of the condition implied by s.13.

If it can be shown that the buyer did not rely on the description there may be no liability   **6–032**

---

[49] [1923] 2 K.B. 500.
[50] [1900] 1 Q.B. 513.
[51] [1967] 1 W.L.R. 1193.

under s.13. *Harlingdon & Leinster Enterprises Ltd v Christopher Hull Fine Art Ltd*[52] concerned the sale of a painting for £6,000 described in the seller's catalogue as being by Munter, a German expressionist. Both the buyers and the sellers were art dealers. The painting turned out to be a fake and worth no more than £100 but it was held that the seller was not liable for a breach of s.13. On the facts it was found that the buyers had relied on their own judgment on the question of attribution, rather than the description in the catalogue.

The implied term in s.13 applies to private transactions as well as to those in the course of a business.

Satisfactory quality: s.14(2)

6–033   Where goods are sold in the course of a business, there is an implied condition that the goods supplied under the contract are of satisfactory quality.

Under the original provisions of the Sale of Goods Act, the standard that the goods had to meet under the implied term was "merchantable quality". However, the Sale and Supply of Goods Act 1994 substituted the term "satisfactory quality" for the term "merchantable quality". The two concepts are similar but not identical and so not all of the older cases dealing with merchantable quality will continue to be relevant on the issue of what constitutes satisfactory quality.

The term under s.14(2) (and also under s.14(3)—discussed below) will only be implied where the sale is "in the course of a business". In many cases, there will be little doubt whether or not a transaction is made in the course of a business. Thus the sale of goods in a supermarket will obviously fall into this category, whereas the purely private sale of, say, a family car by a member of the public will clearly not. But what is the position where goods are sold by a business but the sale is merely incidental to the organisation's business? This issue was considered in the case of *Stevenson v Rogers*.[53] Here the defendant was a fisherman who in 1983 purchased a fishing boat, the *Jelle*. He carried on his business with that vessel until he sold her to the claimant in 1988 for £600,000. Subsequently, the defendant purchased the *Marilyn Jane* which he thereafter used for his fishing business. After reviewing the authorities and the legislative history, the Court of Appeal concluded that the sale was made in the course of a business. The condition implied by s14(2) was not dependent on the seller being a dealer in the category of goods sold—the court would not introduce an implied qualification to that effect into the words of the section. It followed that the sale by the fisherman of the *Jelle* was made in the course of a business. It mattered not that he was not in the business of regularly selling fishing boats. In arriving at this conclusion, the court rejected the narrower meaning of the expression "in the course of a business" which the courts have adopted under the Unfair Contract Terms Act 1977.[54]

6–034   For the purposes of the Act, goods will be of satisfactory quality if they would meet the standard that a reasonable person would regard as satisfactory, taking into account any description of the goods, the price (if relevant) and all other relevant circumstances (s14(2A)). Further guidance is provided by s14(2B) which provides:

" . . . the quality of goods includes their state and condition and the following (among others) are in appropriate cases aspects of the quality of goods –

[52] [1990] 1 All E.R. 737.
[53] [1999] Q.B. 1028.
[54] See para.7–043.

(a) fitness for all the purposes for which goods of the kind in question are commonly supplied,

(b) appearance and finish,

(c) freedom from minor defects,

(d) safety, and

(e) durability."

An example of a case where the implied condition as to quality was breached is *Grant v Australian Knitting Mills*.[55] The claimant purchased two pairs of woollen underpants which were packed in a sealed transparent bag. When he began to wear the garments he developed a rash which developed into acute dermatitis—this was caused by the presence of sulphites in the material owing to a negligent manufacturing process. The claimant sought damages against the retailers on the basis, inter alia, that the goods were not of merchantable quality under an Australian statutory provision identical to the Sale of Goods Act 1893, s.14(2). The Privy Council held that the retailers were liable—the goods were not of merchantable quality. It is likely that the same result would reached under the test of "satisfactory quality" in the amended Sale of Goods Act 1979. For good measure, the retailers were also held liable for breach of the implied term that the goods were not fit for their purpose impliedly made known (see below) and the manufacturers were additionally held liable in negligence.

The reference in s.14(2) to goods "supplied" under the contract means that all the materials supplied to the purchaser under the contract will be covered by s.14(2). In *Wilson v Rickett Cockerell & Co Ltd*[56] the claimant purchased a bag of "Coalite" (a manufactured smokeless fuel). When she put the Coalite on the fire there ensued an explosion which caused damage to the claimant's dining room, although the claimant herself was uninjured. The cause of the explosion was the presence in the bag of a piece of coal containing an explosive which had got mixed in with the Coalite, probably in transit. Counsel for the defendant coal merchants argued that there was no liability because the Coalite itself was not defective. The Court of Appeal found for the claimant—the presence of the explosive made the whole consignment defective.

The goods supplied under the contract will not breach s.14(2) where defects have been specifically brought to the buyers attention before the contract is made (s.14 (2C)(a)). Similarly, there will be no liability where the buyer examines the goods before the contract is made, and the defects are such that the examination ought to have revealed them (s.14(2C)(b)). In *Bramhill v Edwards*[57] there was no breach of s.14(2) where an imported American motor-home exceeded the maximum width permitted by United Kingdom construction and use regulations. The purchasers, who were aware of the regulations, had had ample opportunity to measure the vehicle before purchase had they wished to do so.

6–035

The scope of the test of satisfactory quality in consumer contracts has been extended significantly by an amendment made by the Sale and Supply of Goods to Consumers Regulations 2002.[58] Where the buyer deals as consumer, the relevant circumstances for deciding whether goods are of satisfactory quality (in s.14(2A))– see above) now include any public statements on the "specific characteristics of the goods made about them by the seller, the producer or his representative, particularly in advertising or on labelling" (s.14(2D)). Thus account may be

---

[55] [1936] A.C. 85.
[56] [1954] 1 Q.B. 598.
[57] [2004] EWCA Civ 403.
[58] SI 2002/3045.

made of statements made, e.g. by manufacturers in advertising about the characteristics of goods on sale. However, this provision may not apply if the seller can show that, at the time of the contract, (a) he was not aware of the statement; (b) the statement had been withdrawn or corrected; or (c) the statement could not have influenced the buyer (s.14(2E)).

Fitness for a particular purpose: s14(3)

6–036   This sub-section applies where there is a sale in the course of a business and the buyer, expressly or impliedly, makes known to the seller a particular purpose for which the goods are being bought. In such a case, there is an implied condition that the goods supplied under the contract are reasonably fit for that purpose, whether or not that is a purpose for which such goods are commonly supplied, unless the circumstances show that the buyer does not rely, or that it is unreasonable for him to rely on the seller's skill and judgment.

In *Baldry v Marshall*[59] the claimant wished to buy a car and applied to the defendant dealers telling them that he wanted a comfortable car suitable for touring purposes. The defendants said that a "Bugatti" car would meet those requirements, and showed the claimant such a car. The claimant, who knew nothing about the marque, ordered an eight cylinder Bugatti which was delivered to him but it proved uncomfortable and unsuited to touring. The Court of Appeal held that the defendant was in breach of the implied term that the goods should be reasonably fit for the purpose made known. By contrast, in *Griffiths v Peter Conway*[60] the claimant, who had unusually sensitive skin, contracted dermatitis as a result of wearing a Harris Tweed coat that she had bought. Her action for breach of the implied term of fitness for purpose failed as the seller was not made aware of the circumstances of her skin condition. Where the goods have only one normal use the purpose will be impliedly made known; thus in *Priest v Last*[61] the claimant asked to buy a hot water bottle which subsequently burst in use and his wife was badly scalded. By requesting a hot water bottle the claimant was intimating that he wished to buy goods fit for the purpose of filling with hot water and warming the bed without bursting. It was held that there was a breach of the implied term as to fitness for purpose.

Sale by sample: s.15

6–037   Under the Act, where there is a sale by sample there is an implied condition that the bulk shall correspond with the sample in quality (s.15(2)(a)); and an implied condition that the goods will be free from defects rendering their quality unsatisfactory which would not be apparent on a reasonable examination of the sample (s.15(2)(c)).

In *Godley v Perry*[62] a boy of six bought a plastic catapult from a shopkeeper. The shopkeeper had ordered a quantity from a wholesaler after testing a sample of the toy brought to the shop by the wholesaler's representative. The boy was injured and lost his eye when properly firing a stone from the catapult—the handle, being of brittle plastic construction, fractured. The shop-keeper was held liable in damages to the boy under s.14 of the Act and claimed an indemnity from the wholesaler. Edmund Davies J. held that the sale by the wholesaler to the shopkeeper

[59] [1925] 1 K.B. 260.
[60] [1939] 1 All E.R. 685.
[61] [1903] K.B. 148.
[62] [1960] 1 W.L.R. 9.

was a sale by sample and was subject to the implied term in s.15(2)(c) of the Act. The term had been breached because the bulk of the catapults were of defective quality and the defect was not apparent on a reasonable examination of the sample.

Supply of Goods and Services Act: implied terms

The Supply of Goods and Services 1982 implies certain terms into contracts for the supply of goods and services.

6–038

Supply of goods

In a contract for the supply of goods, ownership of the goods is transferred under a contract which is not a sale of goods, a hire-purchase agreement or one of a number of other specified transactions (s.1(1) and (2)). The provisions of the Act apply to such a transfer of ownership whether or not services are also provided under the contract (s.1(3)). A typical example of a contract for the supply of goods would be a contract for work and materials such as where a car is taken to be serviced. As part of the service the garage will change the oil, the filters and the spark plugs and so forth and these goods thereby become the property of the car owner.[63]

6–039

The Act of 1982 implies terms equivalent to those in ss.12–15 of the Sale of Goods Act (discussed above) into contracts for the supply of goods. The implied terms cover title (s.2); correspondence with description (s.3); satisfactory quality and fitness for purpose (s.4); and transfer by sample (s.5). The Act also implies equivalent terms into contracts for the hire of goods in ss.7–10.

Supply of services

The 1982 Act implies certain terms into contracts of service, other than contracts of employment or apprenticeship (s.12(1) and (2)). The provisions of the Act apply whether or not goods are transferred or hired under the contract (s.12(3)).

6–040

Under s.13 it is provided that:

> "In a contract for the supply of a service where the supplier is acting in the course of a business, there is an implied term that the supplier will carry out the service with reasonable care and skill."

Under s.14(1), where the supplier is acting in the course of a business, there is an implied term that the supplier will carry out the service within a reasonable time, unless the time is fixed by the contract, ascertainable from the contract or determined by a course of dealing. What is a reasonable time is a question of fact (s.14(2)). Finally, where the parties have not fixed a price

---

[63] The distinction between contracts for the sale of goods and contracts for work and materials has been a difficult one to draw. Compare *Lockett v Charles Ltd* [1938] 4 All E.R. 170 (restaurant meal held to be a sale of goods) with *Robinson v Graves* [1935] 1 K.B. 579 (contract to paint a portrait held to be one of work and materials). However, so far as the implied terms as to quality, fitness etc are concerned the distinction makes no difference as the equivalent terms are implied by statute in each case.

for the supply of a service, under s.15(1) there is an implied term that the party contracting with the supplier will pay a reasonable price. The term will not be implied where the price is determined by the contract, ascertainable from the contract or by reference to a course of dealing. As with the issue of time, what is a reasonable price is a question of fact (s.15(2)).

Exclusion or restriction of liability

6–041　The exclusion or restriction of liability for breach of the statutory implied terms in ss.12–15 of the Sale of Goods Act 1979 (and for the corresponding provisions in contracts of hire-purchase and the supply of goods and services) is regulated by the Unfair Contracts Terms Act 1977 (see para.7–047).

CONDITIONS, WARRANTIES AND INNOMINATE TERMS

6–042　Unless terms are implied in one of the ways we have discussed above, it is for the parties themselves to decide what express obligations are to be included in their contract. The parties may be fairly sure what terms they wish to see in their agreement but they may not give much thought to what the consequences will be if a particular term is breached. They will certainly expect redress if the other party breaks the terms of the contract, but what will that redress be? Will the breach be so serious that the contract ought to be brought to an end or will it be one where compensation is the appropriate remedy but the contract nevertheless continues to subsist. Clearly, not all the terms of the contract will be of equal importance.

The law has traditionally categorised contractual terms as being divided into two types, conditions and warranties, the former being terms more important than the latter. More recently a third type of term, the innominate (or intermediate) term has emerged. When the words "condition" and "warranty" are used to denote different types of contractual term, they are being used in a technical sense. The words have other meanings in the law of contract and it is useful to identify some of the more common of these.

The word "condition" is used in its everyday sense where an offer to contract is made subject to the fulfilment of some contingency or other by the party accepting the offer. It may be recalled from the discussion of unilateral contracts in Chapter 2 above[64] that in *Carlill v Carbolic Smokeball Company*, by the terms of the offer the company was only bound to pay the reward if the claimant had fulfilled the stipulation of using the smokeball as prescribed and catching influenza. Here, liability is contingent on the fulfilment of a condition.

6–043　The law also recognises the concept of the "condition precedent" – here the parties identify an event which must come about before the contract comes into existence; an illustration is the case of *Pym v Cambell* (the facts are given at para.6–007). The condition precedent must be distinguished from the "condition subsequent". In this case, the contract comes into being but there is provision for it to terminate on the occurrence (or non-occurrence) of some event. Thus in *Head v Tattersall*[65] the claimant bought a horse from the defendant who guaranteed that the horse had hunted with the Bicester hounds, adding that if it had not, the claimant could return

---

[64] See para.2–007.
[65] (1871) L.R. 7 Ex. 7.

it up until the following Wednesday. Otherwise, the claimant would be obliged to keep the horse with all faults. When it transpired that the horse had not been hunting as described, it was held that the claimant was entitled to return it within the time limit and recover the price paid. The option to return the goods was a condition subsequent.

The word warranty is used in more than one sense. As Denning L.J. explained in *Oscar Chess Ltd v Williams* (the case is discussed at para.6–012) in its ordinary English meaning the word "warranty" is used to denote a binding promise and this is the meaning it has borne in English law for over 300 years. Confusingly, when used in this sense, the word is used to refer to a term of the contract whether or not it is a condition or a warranty in the technical sense.

Conditions and warranties

Turning now to the technical meaning of "condition" and "warranty", a condition is regarded as an important or fundamental term which is said to "go to the root of the contract". The breach of a condition entitles the injured party to repudiate the contract as well as the right to claim damages for loss suffered. A warranty, on the other hand, is a term of lesser importance, the breach of which entitles the injured party to claim damages only and not to enjoy a right to repudiate the contract. These definitions are essentially based on those provided by s.11(1) (b) of the original Sale of Goods Act 1893. That Act, by s.62, also stated that a warranty was "collateral to the main purpose of the contract."

6–044

Whether a term is a condition or a warranty depends on the intention of the parties at the time of contracting.[66] In deciding whether a term is a condition or a warranty, the courts are not supposed to have regard to the *actual* breach of contract, although the court will of course be aware of it. Rather, the court must attempt to assess the status of the term by construing the contract with reference to the possible or potential or breaches of contract.

On the other hand, if an innominate term is breached the injured party will always be able to claim damages and may be able to repudiate the contract if the effects of the actual breach are sufficiently serious. In other words, the court examines the actual consequences of the breach. More will be said about the circumstances in which terms may be classed as innominate later in this chapter (see para.6–048).

Where a court classifies a term as a condition then the injured party will have a right to repudiate the contract even where the effects of the breach are trivial or where they have some ulterior motive for termination, such as an adverse change in market conditions. This is illustrated by *Arcos v Ronaasen*[67] where timber staves described as being half an inch in thickness were purchased for making into cement storage barrels. The timber actually supplied was one sixteenth of an inch thicker than as decribed but this made no difference to the usefulness of the wood for making the barrels. This was a breach of the condition implied by s.13 of the Sale of Goods Act (see para.6–031) and so the buyer was entitled to reject the entire consignment. It made no difference that the buyer's real reason for rejection was a fall in the market value of the goods below the contract price. This and other similar cases were criticised by Lord Wilberforce in *Reardon-Smith Line Ltd v Hansen Tangen*[68] as being overly rigid and inconsistent with the modern development of the innominate term. He thought them due for

6–045

---

[66] *The Mihalis Angelos* [1971] 1 Q.B. 164.
[67] [1933] A.C. 470. See also *Re Moore & Co v Landauer & Co* [1921] 2 K.B. 519.
[68] [1976] 3 All E.R. 570.

fresh examination by the courts. Although these decisions have not been specifically overruled by the courts, a measure of reform has come through a statutory modification to the Sale of Goods Act 1979. The Sale and Supply of Goods Act 1994 added a new s.15A to the Act of 1979 which provides that where the breach of the terms implied by ss.13, 14 or 15 is so slight that it would be unreasonable for the buyer to reject the goods, then if the buyer *does not deal as consumer*, the breach is not to be treated as a breach of condition but as a breach of warranty. Thus where the buyer does deal as consumer they retain the right to reject the goods on account of some trivial or technical breach. This can be justified on the basis that the consumer will usually be dealing with a party of superior bargaining strength.

Two cases that have traditionally been used to demonstrate the difference between a condition and a warranty are *Poussard v Spiers and Pond*[69] and *Bettini v Gye*.[70] They also illustrate the difficulty of the distinction. In the former case, the claimant entered into a contract with the defendants to take the female lead in a new operetta for a three month season at the defendants' theatre. The claimant fell ill and missed the final rehearsals and the performances on the first four nights and as a result the defendants had to engage a substitute. When the claimant turned up for the fifth performance, the defendants refused her services and purported to terminate the contract. The claimant sued the defendants arguing that she had been wrongfully dismissed. Her action failed, the court holding that her promise to perform from the opening night amounted to a condition, the breach of which permitted the defendants to repudiate. It was important that the operetta started well and the claimant's absence was the breach of a term going to the root of the contract.

6–046   In *Bettini v Gye* the claimant was contracted to the defendant to sing at various theatres over a whole season. He agreed to be in London for rehearsals six days before the start of the season. Owing to ill-health he arrived in London only two days before the first performance and the defendants repudiated the contract. In an action by the claimant for breach of contract it was held that missing a few days of rehearsals was not the breach of an obligation which went to the root of the contract and there was no right to repudiate. Damages for breach of warranty was the only remedy which would have been available to the promoters. When viewed comparatively, one can see why the breach in *Bettini v Gye* was perceived by the court as being less serious than the breach in the other case. But is the breach in *Bettini v Gye* really just a minor one? One can imagine that from the point of view of the promoters of concerts, who may have invested heavily in them, the failure to attend rehearsals could be regarded as serious and indeed was so regarded by the defendants in this case.

Since the objective of the court in classifying a term is to establish the intention of the parties, it might be thought that if a term was specifically labelled as a "condition" in the contract, this would be conclusive. However, this does not seem to be the case. In *Schuler AG v Wickman Machine Tool Sales Ltd*[71] the claimants, a German company, entered into an agreement with the defendants giving the defendants sole selling rights of the claimants' products in the United Kingdom. In order to promote sales, Clause 7 of the written contract stated that it was "a condition of this agreement" that the defendants should make 1,400 visits to six named car companies over a four and a half year period. Clause 11 set out a procedure whereby the contract could be terminated upon a "material breach". The defendants failed to carry out all of the visits specified by Clause 7. The claimants argued that since the term in question was labelled

---

[69] (1876) 1 Q.B.D. 410.
[70] (1876) 1 Q.B.D. 183.
[71] [1974] A.C. 235.

as a condition, any breach (e.g. the failure to make just one visit) would justify termination. By a majority, the House of Lords (Lord Wilberforce dissenting) disagreed with the claimants' contention.

The House considered that the parties had not intended to use the word "condition" in its technical sense—they could not have intended the word to be used in this sense where it would have produced such an unreasonable result. It would not have been reasonable to allow termination of the contract where just one visit was missed. The majority concluded that the word "condition" in Clause 7 could not have the meaning contended for by the claimants as this would not be consistent with the procedure for material breaches laid down in Clause 11. This decision was arrived by construing the whole contract rather than looking at the term in isolation. In the minority, Lord Wilberforce felt that "condition" was being used in its technical sense. He thought that to introduce as a test of the validity of the clause the "reasonable man" was to assume, contrary to the evidence, that both parties to the contract had adopted an easygoing, tolerant standard rather than one of "aggressive, insistent punctuality and efficiency."

Although not concerned with the meaning of "condition", an approach to construction similar to that adopted in *Schuler v Wickman Machine Tools* is to be seen in the case of *Rice v Yarmouth Borough Council*.[72] Here there was a clause in a long term leisure management agreement that "if the contractor committed a breach of any of its obligations under the contract . . . the Council . . . may terminate [the contract]." The Court of Appeal held that the clause could not have been intended by the parties to apply to minor breaches, but only those giving rise to a right to terminate the contract.

6–047

If the labelling of a term as a condition is not conclusive as to its status, the best advice to parties wishing to make a term of fundamental importance is that they should specifically state that the consequence of the breach of a particular term is that it will entitle the other party to repudiate the contract. This approach worked in *Lombard North Central Plc v Butterworth*[73] because the clause was sufficiently explicit—in *Rice v Yarmouth Borough Council* the clause was too wide, referring to the breach of any obligation under the contract.

Innominate terms

Where a term is classed as innominate the right of the innocent party to repudiate the contract (in addition to claiming damages) will depend on the nature and consequences of the actual breach of contract. The more serious the effects of the breach, the more likely it is that there will be a right to repudiate—the less serious the effects the less likely that there will be such a right.

6–048

Innominate terms were not unknown to the law in the past particularly before the passing of the original Sale of Goods Act in 1893, however the concept owes its significance in the modern law to the decision of the Court of Appeal in *Hong Kong Fir Shipping Co Ltd v Kawasaki Kisen Kaisha Ltd*.[74] The facts were that the defendants chartered a ship from the claimant owners for a period of two years from February 1957, there being a term of the contract that the ship should be "in every way fitted for ordinary cargo service". In fact the

---

[72] [2001] 3 L.G.L.R. 4.
[73] [1987] 1 All E.R. 267. Cf *Financings Ltd v Baldock* [1963] 2 QB 104.
[74] [1962] 2 Q.B. 26.

engines were old and the engine room crew were incompetent with the result that repairs were needed which took five out of the first six months of the charter period. The defendants repudiated the charter in June, although the ship would have been seaworthy by September. The claimants sought damages for wrongful repudiation. The Court of Appeal held that the claimants' breach did not entitle the defendant to repudiate the contract and the claimant therefore succeeded. Diplock L.J. did not consider that the problem in the case could be solved by debating whether the owner's obligation to provide a seaworthy ship was a condition or a warranty. He said:

> "There are . . . many contractual undertakings of a more complex character which cannot be categorised as being 'conditions' or 'warranties' . . . of such undertakings all that can be predicated is that some breaches will and others will not give rise to an event which will deprive the party not in default of substantially the whole benefit which it was intended that he should obtain from the contract; and the legal consequences of a breach of such an undertaking, unless provided for in the contract, depend on the nature of the event to which the breach gives rise and do not follow automatically from a prior classification of the term as a 'condition' or 'warranty'."

6–049   Thus where the term is categorised as innominate, the test of whether the injured party has a right to repudiate in addition to claiming damages involves asking whether they have been substantially deprived of the whole benefit which it was intended they should obtain from the contract. In *Hong Kong Fir* this test was not satisfied in the view of the court as the ship had been made seaworthy and there were still 17 months left under the charter; an award of damages was therefore the appropriate remedy. But why was the obligation to provide a seaworthy ship considered to be innominate? As Upjohn L.J. explained:

> "[The term is innominate] for the simple reason that the seaworthiness clause is breached by the slightest failure to be fitted 'in every way for service'. Thus . . . if a nail is missing from one of the timbers of a wooden vessel or if proper medical supplies or two anchors are not on board at the time of sailing, the owners are in breach of the seaworthiness stipulation. It is contrary to common sense to suppose that in such circumstances the parties contemplated that the charterer should at once be entitled to treat the contract as at an end for such trifling breaches."

It was therefore recognised that where a term contains a bundle of obligations and the breach of the term could give rise to very serious consequences or relatively trivial consequences, then unless the legal consequences are provided for in the contract, it may be appropriate to treat the term as innominate. The advantage of the innominate approach is flexibility but it is achieved at the expense of certainty because the parties will not know their position in relation to a particular breach until the issue is brought before a court. For this reason, i.e. commercial certainty, the courts have not been reluctant post-*Hong Kong Fir* to classify terms as conditions or warranties in the traditional sense where they felt the circumstances so required.[75]

This is illustrated by the case of *Maredelanto Compania Naviera SA v Bergbau-Handel GmbH, The Mihalis Angelos*.[76] The defendants chartered the ship *Mihalis Angelos* from the

---

[75] See Weir [1976] C.L.J. 33.
[76] [1971] 1 Q.B. 164.

claimant owners, the charterparty including a clause that the vessel was "expected ready to load under this charter about 1 July 1965" at Haiphong. It was not possible for the ship to be at Haiphong at that time and the claimants knew this when they entered into the contract. The defendants repudiated the charter on July 17, 1965 and the claimants sued for breach of contract. The issue was whether the breach of the expected readiness to load clause gave the defendants a right to repudiate the contract, i.e. was the clause a condition of the contract? The Court of Appeal declined to follow the approach laid down in its previous decision in the *Hong Kong Fir* case. It was held that the clause was a condition in the technical sense which gave the defendants a right to repudiate the contract. Clauses similar to the one in this case had been held to be conditions in the past and to apply the *Hong Kong Fir* approach to the present case would create uncertainty. Megaw L.J. said:

"Such a term in a charterparty ought to be regarded as being a condition of the contract, in the old sense of the word 'condition' . . . One of the most important elements in the law is predictability. At any rate in commercial law, there are obvious and substantial advantages in having, where possible, a firm and definite rule for a particular class of legal relationship: for example, as here, the legal categorisation of a particular, definable type of contractual clause in common use. It is surely much better, both for shipowners and charterers (and, incidentally, for their advisers), when a contractual obligation of this nature is under consideration . . . to be able to say categorically: 'If a breach is proved, then the charterer can put an end to the contract.'"

Some twenty years after the decision in *The Mihalis Angelos* the House of Lords arrived at a similar decision in relation to an expected readiness to load clause in *Bunge Corporation v Tradax SA*.[77] It was held that the clause was a condition. Lord Wilberforce stated: **6–050**

"I do not doubt that in suitable cases, the courts should not be reluctant, if the intentions of the parties as shown by the contract so indicate, to hold that an obligation has the force of a condition, and that indeed they should usually do so in the case of time clauses in mercantile contracts. To such cases the gravity of the breach approach approach of *Hong Kong Fir* would be unsuitable."

When *The Mihalis Angelos* was decided at the beginning of the1970s there was a reaction in some quarters that the case could not be reconciled with *Hong Kong Fir* and that a decision of the House of Lords (or even legislation) was required to clarify the law. In fact, despite the tension between the two approaches, they have co-existed relatively harmoniously in subsequent years and the innominate approach has been applied in suitable cases. It has even been applied to a contract governed by the Sale of Goods Act even though, as we have seen, that Act refers only to conditions and warranties.

In *Cehave NV v Bremer Handelsgesellschaft GmbH, The Hansa Nord*[78] citrus pulp pellets worth over £100,000 were sold. It was a term of the contract that they be shipped "in good condition". On arrival, it was discovered that some of the pellets had been damaged by overheating—they were not therefore in good condition. The buyer rejected the whole consignment. The goods were then sold to a third party and they were eventually purchased by the original

---

[77] [1981] 1 W.L.R. 711.
[78] [1976] Q.B. 44.

buyer for £30,000, a price much lower than the contract price. The market value of citrus pulp had fallen since the date of the contract. The original buyer was able to use them as originally intended in the manufacture of animal feed, but in slightly reduced proportions. The question that arose was whether the buyer had been justified in refusing to take delivery for a breach of the term that they would be shipped in good condition.

6–051   The Court of Appeal held that the term was not a condition but was an intermediate (innominate) term. However, the consequences of the breach were not sufficiently serious so as to justify termination although the buyers were entitled to damages for the difference in value between damaged goods and sound goods on arrival. In a case such as this the innominate approach prevents the innocent party from terminating the contract where the breach is trivial but the innocent party has an ulterior motive for repudiation. This often occurs where there has been a collapse in the market so that the transaction is no longer profitable for the innocent party. A similar process, and a similar result, can be observed in the decision of the House of Lords in *Reardon Smith Line Ltd v Hansen-Tangen*.[79]

Advantages and disadvantages of the two approaches

6–052   As Megaw L.J. observed in *the Mihalis Angelos,* the chief merit of classifying a term as a condition in the technical sense is certainty. The parties know where they stand from the outset—any breach of the term will justify repudiation by the innocent party. In a commercial context this is important because once a breach of condition occurs, the innocent party can act immediately by terminating the contract and looking for, without delay, an alternative contractor. The innocent party can act safely in the knowledge that what they have done is, under the terms of the contract, lawful. Similarly, where a term is classified as a warranty, no breach of it, however serious the consequences, can give rise to termination. The remedy of the innocent party will be limited to damages.

The labelling of terms as conditions or warranties is not only beneficial to commercial parties, it is also advantageous to the consumer. The need for certainty and predictability here is just as great because the consumer will normally be dealing with a party of superior bargaining power. The implied conditions as to description, quality and fitness in the Sale of Goods Act (see para.6–029 above) provide the consumer with enforceable and clearly defined rights. The consumer who buys goods that are defective has the right immediately to return them and reclaim from the supplier the money they have paid. A flexible approach here, depending on the consequences of the breach, would not work to the advantage of the consumer.

As we saw from *Arcos v Ronaasen* (see para.6–045) the disadvantage of classifying terms as conditions is that the innocent party is able to terminate the contract for a trivial breach, even where they have an ulterior motive, although this has to some extent been mitigated by s.15A of the Sale of Goods Act in non-consumer cases. Classifying terms as innominate avoids this difficulty as the court is better able to arrive at a just result by examining the consequences of the breach. This flexibility, however, is bought at the price of uncertainty since the consequences of the breach may not be fully known until some time later. There may therefore be considerable delay before the dispute can be resolved. It is the innocent party who must decide whether the breach is sufficiently serious so as to give a right to terminate and if they are wrong about that they may themselves be in breach of contract for wrongful repudiation. Nevertheless, as

---

[79] [1976] 3 All E.R. 570.

the *Hong Kong Fir* case shows, the innominate approach lends itself to clauses containing multiple obligations, the breach of which might have differing degrees of seriousness.

Contractual terms: conclusion

In the wake of the decision of the Court of Appeal in *Hong Kong Fir* it came to be accepted   **6–053** that there were three types of contractual term, conditions, warranties and innominate terms. A warranty may be classified as such by statute and it is always open to the parties to specify that a term is a warranty (although this is probably quite rare these days). Where this is the intention of the parties the term will be regarded as a warranty in the technical sense and the actual effects of the breach will be ignored and the innocent party will only be entitled to damages. But what is the position where a term (that is not a condition) is not designated either by statute or the parties as a warranty? There would seem to be good sense in treating such terms as innominate, that is, regard may be had to the actual consequences of the breach in deciding what will be the rights of the innocent party. Given the continued existence of statutorily implied warranties, it is probably going too far to suggest that there are now only two types of term, conditions and innominate terms, but this quite possibly represents the approach of the courts today.

A useful guide as to when a term will and will not be classified as a condition was provided by the Court of Appeal in *B S & N Ltd (BVI) v Micado Shipping Ltd (Malta), The Seaflower*.[80] This was a case in which a clause in a charterparty requiring the approval of a ship by the major oil companies was held to be a condition and not an intermediate term of the contract. Waller L.J. adopted the following set of conclusions:

"A term of a contract will be held to be a condition:
(i) if it is expressly so provided by statute;
(ii) if it has been so categorised as the result of previous judicial decision (although it has been said that some of the decisions on this matter are excessively technical and are open to re-examination by the House of Lords);
(iii) if it is so designated in the contract or if the consequences of its breach, that is, the right of the innocent party to treat himself as discharged, are provided for expressly in the contract; or
(iv) if the nature or the subject-matter or the circumstances of the case lead to the conclusion that the parties must, by necessary implication, have intended that the innocent party would be discharged from further performance of his obligations in the event that the term was not fully and precisely complied with.
Otherwise a term of the contract will be considered to be an intermediate term. Failure to perform such a term will ordinarily entitle the party not in default to treat himself as discharged only if the effect of the breach of the term deprives him substantially of the whole benefit which it was intended that he should obtain from the contract."

Having examined in this chapter the law relating to the terms of the contract we now turn, in the next chapter, to the position where a term of the contract purports to exclude or limit the liability of one of the parties.

---

[80] [2001] 1 All E.R. (Comm) 240.

Further reading

Wedderburn, *Collateral Contracts* [1976] C.L.J. 58.

Peden, *Policy Concerns Behind Implication of Terms in Law* (2001) 117 L.Q.R. 459.

Phang, *Implied Terms, Business Efficacy and the Officious Bystander – A Modern History* [1998] J.B.L. 1.

Weir, *The Buyer's Right to Reject Defective Goods* [1976] C.L.J. 33.

Chapter 7

EXCLUSION AND LIMITATION CLAUSES

It is an inevitable corollary of the concept of freedom of contract that one party may insert a **7–001** term into a contract that purports to exclude (or financially limit) their liability for breach of contract, negligence or misrepresentation. In other words, an exclusion clause, where it is valid, will allow the party relying on the clause to breach the contract (or commit other legal wrongs in connection with it) with impunity, leaving the other party with no redress.

Such clauses are ubiquitous. Few can have failed to notice signs in public places such as cinemas, superstores or car parks saying, for example, "The proprietors do not accept liability for loss or damage to customers' property" or "All cars parked at owner's risk". Similarly, when a person enters into everyday transactions such as booking a holiday, taking out insurance or having the car serviced the contract will be subject to terms and conditions which will include clauses excluding or limiting liability—often contained in "small print" paragraphs. Such clauses will also, of course, be found in commercial transactions entered into between businesses.

Generally speaking, when a contract is negotiated between two business concerns they will negotiate from a position of equality—they are said to have "equality of bargaining power". Each party will be able to look after themselves and will be expected to understand the implications of the contractual provisions into which they enter. Freedom of contract in this situation is much more acceptable than in the case where a private person, dealing as consumer, contracts with a business organisation. Here there may be little or no negotiation and the terms will be contained in a document in standard form; in other words, the terms are effectively dictated by the stronger party. If the consumer objects to the terms, they may be told that they can take it or leave it. In such situations there is *inequality* of bargaining power.

How does the law address these problems? Our starting point must be the common law **7–002** because under the doctrine of freedom of contract an exclusion or limitation clause will be just as valid as any other term of the contract. The judges have no inherent power at common law to strike down such a clause because it unfair or unreasonable.[1] Nevertheless, the courts have been concerned about the abuse of such clauses and therefore developed certain doctrines which placed obstacles in the way of those seeking to rely on them, which we will refer to as the "common law rules." These rules were developed largely in the nineteenth and early to mid-twentieth century.

---

[1] In *Levison v Patent Steam Carpet Cleaning Co Ltd* [1977] 3 All E.R. 498, Lord Denning M.R. asserted such a power but the case immediately preceded the passing of the Unfair Contract Terms Act 1977 which introduced a statutory requirement of reasonableness in certain cases.

More recently Parliament has intervened most notably with the Unfair Contract Terms Act 1977—the Act, amongst other things, declares certain types of exclusion or restriction of liability invalid and others it subjects to a requirement of reasonableness. In addition, the EC Directive on Unfair Contract Terms (93/13 EEC) has been implemented in English Law by the Unfair Terms in Consumer Contracts Regulations 1994.[2] These were then replaced by regulations introduced in 1999.[3] The regulations provide protection for the consumer against unfair terms generally, not merely exclusion and limitation clauses. These statutory and regulatory controls will be fully considered later in this chapter.

It is important to appreciate that the statutory controls do not replace the common law rules, rather they provide an additional body of law by which the validity of exclusion and limitation clauses must be judged. The significance of the common law rules has diminished now the legislative controls are in place; nevertheless in any case where the validity of such a clause in issue, the common law rules should be applied, and they should be considered first, i.e. before considering the statutory position.

From now on in this narrative, the expression "exclusion clause" will be used so as to embrace both exclusion and limitation clauses unless it is specifically stated that different rules apply to one or other type of clause.

The common law rules that will be discussed are (i) incorporation; (ii) construction; and (iii) further limitations at common law on exclusion clauses.

INCORPORATION

7–003   A party will only be bound by an exclusion clause if it has been incorporated into the contract—that is, it is part of the contract into which they have entered. The same rule applies to contractual terms generally but in case law the problem has most often arisen in relation to exclusion clauses and therefore this is the most appropriate context in which to study the rule.

There are three ways in which a clause may be incorporated—by signature, by notice or by a course of dealing.

Signature

7–004   A person who signs a contractual document is bound by its terms whether or not they have read the document and if, having read it, whether or not they have understood it. The principle is known as "the rule in *L'Estrange v Graucob*" (a case decided in 1934) although the rule is of much earlier vintage.

In *L'Estrange v F Graucob Ltd*[4] the claimant, who owned a café in Llandudno, purchased from the defendants an automatic cigarette vending machine. She was persuaded by the defendants' salesmen to sign a "Sales Agreement" which was printed on brown paper in small print although it was quite legible. The claimant did not read the contract and was unaware of its terms. One of the clauses stated that "any express or implied condition, statement, or warranty,

---

[2]   SI 1994/3159.
[3]   Unfair Terms in Consumer Contract Regulations 1999 (SI 1999/2083).
[4]   [1934] 2 K.B. 394.

statutory or otherwise not stated herein is hereby excluded". When the machine was delivered, it failed to work properly and after a few days it jammed and became unusable. The claimant sued but it was held in the Divisional Court that her action must fail—she was bound by the clause as she had signed the contract. Scrutton L.J. said that the claimant:

> ". . . having put her signature to the document and not having been induced to do so by any fraud or misrepresentation, cannot be heard to say that she is not bound by the terms of the document because she has not read them."

The decision seems harsh, particularly since the defendants had no doubt deliberately made the document difficult to read and also in view of the inequality of bargaining power between the parties. Moreover, the circumstances were such that the defendants' representatives knew that the claimant had not read the contract.[5] Nevertheless, it can be justified on the ground of commercial certainty—a person cannot be compelled to sign a document, but if they do, they arc deemed to agree to the terms. Arguments about whether enough was done to bring the terms to the notice of the signer are avoided, and third parties can rely on the document as being valid without having to investigate the circumstances in which it was signed.

As Scrutton L.J. indicated in *L'Estrange v Graucob* even a signed document can be rendered wholly or partly ineffective by a misrepresentation as to its effect. In *Curtis v Chemical Cleaning and Dyeing Co*[6] the claimant took her white satin wedding dress to the defendants' establishment to be cleaned. The defendants' assistant asked the claimant to sign a document headed "Receipt" which included a clause stating that the cleaners accepted no liability for any damage howsoever arising. Before signing, the claimant had asked why her signature was required and the assistant had said (words to the effect that) the document only excluded liability for certain risks including damage to the beads and sequins on the dress. The claimant signed but when the dress was returned it was stained. The Court of Appeal held that defendants could not rely on the clause because of the innocent misrepresentation as to its effect. It seems that the clause would, however, have protected the defendants in the event of damage to beads and sequins but that was not what had happened.

The strictness of the rule in *L'Estrange v Graucob* has been mitigated by statute in the case of clauses excluding or restricting liability. If the case were being decided today, despite the fact that the contractual document had been signed, the clause would not be binding on the signer if it failed to meet the criteria for validity laid down by ss.6 and 11 of the Unfair Contract Terms Act 1977; see para.7–047.

7–005

Notice

Where the document is unsigned but merely delivered to the other party, then reasonable and sufficient notice of the existence of the exclusion clause must be given by the party purporting to rely on the clause. The test is an objective one and what constitutes reasonable notice will vary according to the circumstances. It should be noted that it is only the existence of the clause that must be communicated, not necessarily its actual content.

7–006

[5] See Spencer [1973] C.L.J. 104. See also *Tilden Rent-a-Car Co v Clendenning* (1978) 83 D.L.R. (3d) 400 where the Court of Appeal of Ontario distinguished *L'Estrange v Graucob* in circumstances where the other party cannot reasonably have believed that the signer had agreed to the clause.
[6] [1951] 1 All E.R. 631.

The rule emerged from the so-called "ticket cases" in the nineteenth century where railway companies sought to impose conditions on passengers. The leading case is *Parker v South Eastern Railway Co.*[7] The claimant deposited his bag in the defendants' cloakroom, paid 2d and received a ticket on the front of which were the words, "See back". On the back was a notice containing a condition that limited the company's liability to packages the value of which did not exceed £10. There was also a notice in the cloakroom displaying the same condition. The claimant's bag was lost and he claimed its full value of £24 10s from the railway company; the company pleaded the limitation in their condition. The claimant argued that he had not seen the notice or read what was printed on the ticket—he thought the ticket was merely a receipt for 2d or an acknowledgment that the bag was in the company's possession.

The Court of Appeal ordered a retrial as the judge at first instance had misdirected the jury on the issue of incorporation. In essence, the higher court said that if it could be shown that a party knew that there were conditions they would be bound; likewise they would be bound if reasonable steps had been taken to bring the conditions to their attention. On the facts it was clear that this test had been satisfied and the limitation clause was incorporated.

7–007   The rule laid down in *Parker v South Eastern Railway Co* has a number of aspects which have been elaborated upon in subsequent cases and which will now be considered.

Clause must be contained in a contractual document

7–008   To be binding on a party, the exclusion clause must be contained in a "contractual document", that is, a document which the reasonable person would expect to contain contractual terms.

In *Chapelton v Barry Urban District Council*[8] the claimant wished to hire two deck chairs on Cold Knap beach, Barry. Adjacent to a pile of deckchairs operated by the defendant council was a notice which said that hirers should obtain tickets from chair attendants, price 2d per session of three hours. This notice did not refer to any exclusion of liability. The claimant obtained two chairs and received tickets which he put into his pocket without reading. The tickets contained a clause excluding liability for accident or damage arising out of the hire of the chair. The deck chair collapsed as the claimant sat on it—the canvas came away from the top of the chair and he was injured. When the claimant sought damages the defendants purported to rely on the exclusion clause printed on the ticket. The Court of Appeal held that they could not rely on the clause. The reasonable person would assume that the ticket was merely a receipt for payment and not a document containing contractual terms and so the exclusion clause was not incorporated.

The court considered that the object of giving the ticket was to provide the hirer with evidence that they had paid for the hire of the chair and it was quite different from, for example, a railway ticket which contained on it the terms upon which the railway company agreed to carry the passenger.

The principle that a clause, to be valid, must be contained in a contractual document has been applied to a signed document thus placing a further limitation on the principle in *L'Estrange v Graucob*, discussed above. In *Grogan v Robin Meredith Plant Hire Ltd*[9] the Court of Appeal held that the signing of a time sheet containing an indemnity clause was ineffective

---

[7] [1877] L.R. 2 C.P.D. 416.
[8] [1940] 1 K.B. 532.
[9] [1996] C.L.C. 1127.

so as to incorporate the term as the document was not one which the reasonable person would expect to contain terms.

The word "document" should not be taken too literally in the context of the rule under examination because a notice or sign containing a clause which is visible at the time of entry into the contract may be sufficient notice. Thus in *Thornton v Shoe Lane Parking Ltd*[10] a sign displayed at the entry to a car park giving the parking charges and stating, "All cars parked at owner's risk" was incorporated and would have been effective to exclude the proprietors' liability for damage to the claimant's car or its contents. The claim, however, in this case was for personal injury and terms displayed inside the car park relating to this form of liability were not incorporated. That aspect of the case is discussed at para.7–012 below.   **7–009**

Where a sign is used, it must obviously be sufficiently large and prominently located and the exempting conditions must not be buried in acres of small print. In *McCutcheon v David MacBrayne Ltd*[11] exclusion clauses were contained in noticeboards both inside and outside the defendants' offices containing over 4,000 words in 27 paragraphs of small print. They were also to be found in a risk note which had not been signed by the claimant. It was held that the terms were not incorporated.

Timing of notice

The existence of the clause must be brought to the claimant's attention before or at the time of the contract. Once the contract has come into being through offer and acceptance, no further notice of terms can affect the claimant's rights. The classic illustration of this rule is the case of *Olley v Marlborough Court Hotel*.[12]   **7–010**

The facts were that the claimant Mrs Olley and her husband arrived at the defendants' hotel and, at the reception desk, paid for a week's accommodation in advance. They then went to their room and later went out, leaving the room key at reception. Through the negligence of the defendants, a thief took the key and stole from the room jewellery and other valuables belonging to Mrs Olley. A notice on the wall of the bedroom stated: "The proprietors will not hold themselves responsible for articles lost or stolen, unless handed to the manageress for safe custody." The claimant sued the defendants who pleaded the exclusion clause in the notice. The Court of Appeal held that this notice came too late to be incorporated into the contract—the contract had been concluded at the reception desk and no further notice could affect the claimant's rights.

The defendants might have been more successful in their argument that the clause was incorporated had they displayed a prominent sign at the reception desk containing the clause, or if they had required Mrs Olley to sign a document in which the term was included, but she could not be bound by a notice that she had no opportunity of seeing at the time of entering the contract.

What is reasonable notice?

What constitutes reasonable notice is a question of fact, and is objectively ascertained. It is not a question of whether a party actually read or understood the exempting conditions. Rather it   **7–011**

[10] [1971] 1 All E.R. 686.
[11] [1964] 1 All E.R. 430.
[12] [1949] 1 K.B. 532.

is a question of whether the party relying on the clause did what was reasonable to bring the existence of the terms to the claimant's attention. In assessing whether there has been reasonable notice, the court will have regard to all the circumstances of the case and the situation of the parties—it may depend on the category or class of person to whom the claimant belongs.

In *Thompson v London, Midland and Scottish Railway Co*[13] the claimant, who was illiterate, sent her niece to obtain an excursion train ticket for her from the railway station. On the face of the ticket was printed, "For conditions see back" and on the reverse side of the ticket was statement that excursion tickets were issued subject to conditions in the company's timetables. A copy of the timetables could have been purchased for 6d (about 20 per cent of the price of a ticket). One of the conditions stated that the company was not liable to excursion ticket holders for personal injury howsoever caused; this appeared on page 552 of the document. The claimant, who had not ascertained the conditions, was injured through the negligence of the company and sought damages.

The Court of Appeal had to consider whether the defendant company had taken reasonable steps to bring the condition to the claimant's notice. The court concluded that reasonable notice had been given of the clause—it was sufficient that the company should do what was reasonable to communicate it to the ordinary passenger, who could be presumed, in a well-educated society, to be literate. Once the passenger had been made aware, by the ticket, that there were conditions, they were put on notice and could check them out before deciding whether to travel. It made no difference that a circuitous route had to be followed before one was in a position to read the condition. Nevertheless, despite the decision in this case, where a contracting party is aware of some disability suffered by the other, it may be that a greater degree of notice would be regarded as reasonable. An example might be where a railway company entered into a contract whereby it organised a special train for a party of visually impaired people.

7–012   The decision in *Thompson* at the extreme of what could be regarded as reasonable notice and is a manifestation of a strict "freedom of contract" approach. It is questionable whether in today's more consumer oriented society the steps taken by the company would be considered to be reasonable and sufficient. In commenting on *Thompson v London, Midland and Scottish Railway Co* and other so-called ticket cases in a later case[14] Lord Denning M.R. had this to say:

> "These cases were based on the theory that the customer, on being handed the ticket, could refuse it and decline to enter into a contract on those terms. He could ask for his money back. That theory was, of course, a fiction. No customer in a thousand ever read the conditions. If he had stopped to do so, he would have missed the train."

Fiction or not, the *Thompson* case remains an authority on the general question of reasonable notice. As a general rule, all that is required is reasonable notice of the existence of the clause and in this respect it may be sufficient that the document or sign refers to some other document where the conditions may be found. The contractual document need not itself contain the exempting conditions. From later cases has emerged a principle that a greater degree of notice should be accorded to unusual or onerous terms. This is sometimes referred to as the "red hand rule". In *Spurling v Bradshaw*[15] Denning L.J. said:

---

[13] [1930] 1 K.B. 41.
[14] *Thornton v Shoe Lane Parking Ltd* [1971] 1 All E.R. 686.
[15] [1956] 1 W.L.R. 461.

"The more unreasonable a clause is, the greater degree of notice which must be given of it. Some clauses which I have seen would need to be printed in red ink on the face of the document with a red hand pointing to it before the notice could be held to be sufficient."

The Court of Appeal applied this principle in *Thornton v Shoe Lane Parking Ltd.*[16] In this case, the claimant drove into a multi-storey car park which he had never used before and an automatic machine at the entrance issued a ticket which he took. The claimant noticed the time of entry which was printed on the ticket but he did not read the other printed words on the ticket. The words said, "This ticket is issued subject to conditions of issue as displayed on the premises." On a pillar inside the car park was a notice listing a number of conditions, one of which exempted the defendant car park proprietors for injury to the customer howsoever caused. On his return to the car park a few hours later the claimant was seriously injured owing to the negligence of the defendants. In an action for damages for personal injury, the defendants purported to rely on the exclusion clause.

The Court of Appeal held that the condition displayed inside the car park was not incorporated. Lord Denning M.R. was of the view that the clause in question was so wide and destructive of rights that "the court should not hold a man bound by it unless it is drawn to his attention in the most explicit way". He considered that the offer made by the car park was accepted when the claimant drove up to the entrance and the car came to a halt. The ticket then thrust at the claimant came too late in the transaction to incorporate the unusual terms displayed inside the premises. Lord Denning thought that the ticket cases (such as *Thompson v London, Midland and Scottish Railway Co*) had no application to the situation where a ticket was issued by an automatic machine:

> "The customer pays his money and gets a ticket. He cannot refuse it. He cannot get his money back. He may protest at the machine, even swear at it. But it will remain unmoved. He is committed beyond recall."

The other members of the court (Megaw L.J. and Sir Gordon Willmer) did not find it necessary to say precisely when the contract was concluded. However, they did not consider that the defendants had done what was reasonable to communicate to the claimant the existence of such an unusual and onerous clause. Megaw L.J. did not think that customers had been given a fair opportunity of discovering the conditions by which they were to be bound—he considered that the practical difficulty of the chosen method of attempted incorporation was relevant. He said:

> "As a matter of hard reality it would have been practically impossible for [the claimant] to withdraw from his intended entry upon the premises for the purpose of leaving his car there. It does not take much imagination to picture the indignation of the defendants if their potential customers, having taken their tickets and observed the reference therein to contractual conditions . . . were one after the other to get out of their cars, leaving the cars blocking the entrance to the garage, in order to search for, find and peruse the notices."

7–013

[16] [1971] 1 All E.R. 686.

The red hand rule was applied by the Court of Appeal to a case not involving an exclusion clause in *Interfoto Picture Library Ltd v Stiletto Visual Programmes Ltd*.[17] The claimants ran a library of photographic transparencies and the defendants were an advertising agency. In response to an enquiry by the defendants, the claimants despatched 47 transparencies to the defendants with a delivery note containing nine printed conditions, one of which specified that a holding fee of £5 plus VAT per day would be charged for each transparency retained after 14 days. The defendants, who had not dealt with the claimants before, did not read the conditions and returned the transparencies four weeks later. In accordance with the condition, the claimants invoiced the defendants for the sum of £3,783.50. The Court of Appeal considered the clause to be onerous and unusual and, as it had not been specifically drawn to the defendants' attention, was not incorporated. The claimants were held to be entitled only to a reasonable sum for the use by the defendants of the transparencies. The decision is remarkable because it was not a consumer transaction; both parties were businesses, which meant that the defendants might be thought well able to look after themselves by reading the relevant conditions which were not disguised or concealed in any way. However, the clause was of an extortionate nature and Bingham L.J. felt that the rules of reasonable sufficiency of notice were appropriate to regulate such terms, given the lack of an overriding doctrine of good faith in English law.

7–014   The *Interfoto Picture Library* case was applied by the Court of Appeal to a consumer contract in *O'Brien v MGN Ltd* (Mirror Group Newspapers).[18] The claimant purchased a Sunday newspaper containing a "scratchcard" game, relating to a competition which was to be printed in the *Daily Mirror*, a title published by the defendants, one week later. The claimant's card revealed two sums of £50,000 . One week later the claimant bought another copy of the *Mirror* and, as indicated in the newspaper, telephoned a "hotline" and was informed that the prize for that day was £50,000 so he believed he had won that amount. Although there was only supposed to be one or two £50,000 prizes per week, owing to an error on the part of the organisers, 1,472 other people were led to believe they had won £50,000. The claimant alleged a breach of contract. The defendants sought to rely on Rule 5 of the competition rules which provided that "should more prizes be claimed than are available in any prize category for any reason, a simple draw will take place for the prize". In due course a draw of all the "winning" cardholders was held but the claimant was not successful in winning the £50,000 and received only £33. 99p. The card that the claimant had received with his Sunday paper had stated: "Full rules and how to claim— see *Daily Mirror*". The paper containing the hotline number stated "Normal Mirror Group rules apply." The competition rules were published in several of the defendants' newspapers but were not printed in every edition. The issue therefore was whether the rules of the competition were incorporated into the contract.

At first instance, Judge Hegarty Q.C. held that the claimant's telephone call constituted the acceptance of an offer made in the *Mirror* of that day. The judge thought it highly likely that the claimant, as a regular purchaser of the papers with an interest in the game, had seen the rules or was aware that there were rules, although he may have paid little attention to them. Despite expressing sympathy for the cruel disappointment the claimant had suffered, he held that the claimant was bound by Rule 5. The claimant appealed, arguing that the effect of Rule 5 was to "turn winners into losers" and that the defendants had failed to draw it sufficiently to the claimant's attention. The Court of Appeal agreed with the decision of the trial judge and found for the

---

[17] [1989] Q.B. 433. See further *AEG (UK) Ltd v Logic Resource Ltd* [1996] C.L.C. 265; *Ocean Chemical Transport Inc v Exnor Craggs Ltd* [2000] 1 All E.R. (Comm) 519; and Bradgate (1997) 60 M.L.R. 582.
[18] [2002] C.L.C. 33.

defendants. Hale L.J., in the majority, considered that, although Rule 5 did turn an apparent winner into a loser, it could not "by any normal use of language be called 'onerous' or 'outlandish'." She thought it could be distinguished from the clause in *Interfoto Picture Library*, which imposed an extra burden on the claimant, or the one in *Thornton v Shoe Lane Parking Ltd* which sought to exclude liability for personal injury, negligently caused. In addition, there was no evidence that Rule 5 was an "unusual" term in competitions of this sort. Her Ladyship said:

> "[Rule 5] merely deprives the claimant of a windfall for which he has done very little in return. . . .He bought two newspapers . . . He made a call to a premium rate number, which will have cost him some money . . . but only a matter of pennies, not pounds."

Evans L.J. agreed that the appeal should be dismissed but only on the basis that the court should not interfere with the findings of fact of the judge in the court below. He thought the clause to be sufficiently unusual as to require greater prominence and that it was only a matter of chance as to whether the reader could find out what were the rules.   **7–015**

Now that exclusion clauses and other unfair terms are controlled by statutory means (under the Unfair Contract Terms Act and the Unfair Terms in Consumer Contracts Regulations) the use of the red hand rule to regulate such terms seems unecessary, especially in transactions between businesses, where it is not likely to promote certainty. The use of a rule of incorporation to strike at unreasonable and unfair contractual terms does not sit easily with the statutory regimes. The rule ought to be confined to those contracts not regulated by legislation.

Course of dealing

Even where there has been insufficient notice on the occasion in question, a clause may be incorporated on the basis of a previous course of dealing between the parties. Thus in *Olley v Marlborough Court Hotel*, which was discussed above in connection with the timing of notice, the claimant might well have been bound by the clause had she regularly stayed at the hotel in the past, even if she had never read the terms on the wall in the room.   **7–016**

In *Spurling Ltd v Bradshaw*[19] the claimants were warehousemen and the defendant had stored goods at their warehouse over a number of years in the past. The claimants accepted eight 60 gallon casks of orange juice from the defendant for storage and a few days later the defendant received a document containing an exclusion clause. When the defendant went to collect the barrels they were found to be empty and he refused to pay the storage charges. The claimants brought an action to recover the charges and the defendant argued that the clause was ineffective as it had been received by him after the formation of the contract. The Court of Appeal held that the claimant was bound by the clause—he had received the document containing the clause on many occasions in the past and it made no difference that he had not troubled to read the document. A previous course of dealing had been established.

The rule is qualified by two factors; first, the previous dealings must have been consistent, and secondly, there must have been an element of frequency or regularity about the dealings.

The issue of consistency arose in *McCutcheon v David MacBrayne Ltd.*[20] The claimant took   **7–017**

---

[19] [1956] 1 W.L.R. 461. See also *Hardwick Game Farm v Suffolk Agricultural and Poultry Producers Association Ltd* [1969] 2 A.C. 31.
[20] [1964] 1 All E.R. 430.

his car on the defendants' ferry which was sailing between the Scottish mainland and Islay. Owing to the negligence of the defendants, the vessel sank after striking a rock and the car was lost. On previous occasions when the defendant had taken his car on the defendants' ferry he had been asked to sign a "risk note" containing 4,000 words and including a clause exempting the defendants from liability. On this occasion, the car had been shipped by a Mr McSporran, the claimant's brother-in-law, and he had not been required to sign a risk note. After he had paid the fare, Mr McSporran had been given a receipt stating that goods were carried subject to conditions set out in the risk note and on noticeboards at the defendants' offices. Neither the defendant nor Mr McSporran had ever read those conditions although both had on previous occasions usually been asked to sign risk notes. The claimant sued the defendants who purported to rely on the exclusion clause.

The House of Lords held that the clause was not incorporated and the defendants were liable. Their Lordships found that the receipt had been given only after the contract had been concluded and the defendants had effectively made an oral contract with the claimant's agent, Mr McSporran, where there was no contractual document. The basis of the decision is best explained in the speech of Lord Reid:

> "There had been no constant course of dealing, sometimes he [Mr McSporran] was asked to sign [the risk note] and sometimes he was not. . . . This time he was offered an oral contract without reference to conditions, and he accepted the offer in good faith."

The approach of the court to incorporation by course of dealing was indicated by Lord Reid thus (adopting Gloag on Contract, 1927, a Scottish text):

> "The judicial task is not to discover the actual intentions of each party; it is to decide what each was reasonably entitled to conclude from the attitude of the other."

In addition to consistency, the previous dealings must have been regular, i.e. the terms have been used with such frequency that it can be inferred that the parties intended to contract on that basis on the occasion in question. This is illustrated by the case of *Petrotrade Inc v Texaco Ltd*[21] where the parties had orally agreed the sale of a cargo by telephone. Later the claimants sent a telex to the defendants confirming the transaction which included an additional clause providing for payment in full without deduction or set-off. The claimants contended that this provision was incorporated on the basis of a course of dealing consisting of five transactions on the same terms including the clause in issue over the previous thirteen months. The Court of Appeal concluded that the parties had made their agreement on the basis that the contract would be subject to the same terms as before. The approach indicated by Lord Reid in *McCutcheon v David MacBrayne*, to which reference was made above, was applied.

7–018   There are grounds for thinking that, as against a party who is a consumer as opposed to a business, a greater number of past transactions may be required to establish a course of dealing. In *Hollier v Rambler Motors (AMC) Ltd,*[22] the claimant had had his car repaired at the defendants' garage on three or four occasions over a period of five years. Each time he had signed an invoice containing conditions but he had not read them. It was held that there was no sufficient course of dealing so as to incorporate an exclusion clause. It was, perhaps, a significant factor

---

[21] [2000] C.L.C. 1341.
[22] [1972] 2 Q.B. 71.

that the claimant was dealing as a consumer not a business and there was therefore an inequality of bargaining power between the parties.

In some cases, there may have been no previous dealings at all between the parties, but the clause is nevertheless held to be incorporated on the basis of trade custom or usage. In *British Crane Hire Corporation Ltd v Ipswich Plant Hire Ltd*[23] both parties were in the business of hiring out heavy excavating machinery. The defendants urgently required a dragline crane in connection with some drainage work they were carrying out, and they orally agreed to hire one from the claimants. No reference was made in the conversation between the parties about any conditions of hire, however the defendants printed conditions of hire, which were standard in the trade, were forwarded later. One of these conditions provided that hirers were liable to indemnify the owners in certain circumstances and the issue was whether, at the time of the contract, the condition was incorporated. Lord Denning said:

> "The parties were both in the trade and were of equal bargaining power. Each was a firm of plant hirers who hired out plant. The defendants themselves knew that firms in the plant hiring trade always imposed conditions in regard to the hiring of plant; and that their conditions were on much the same lines. . . . It seems to me that, in view of the relationship of the parties . . . the [claimants] were entitled to conclude that the defendants were accepting [the crane] on the terms of the claimants own printed conditions."

The Court of Appeal accordingly held that the conditions were incorporated.

CONSTRUCTION

Once it is established that an exclusion clause is incorporated into the contract, the contract will be construed, i.e. interpreted, to see whether the wording of the exclusion clause covers the breach which has occurred. Before looking at the approach of the courts to the construction of exclusion clauses, it is necessary to consider the principles upon which the courts construe contracts generally. The construction of exclusion clauses in commercial transactions must take these principles into account.   **7–019**

General approach to construction

Historically, the courts were concerned to ascertain the intention of the parties from the literal meaning of the words used in the contractual document. They were not supposed to go outside the contract or consider the commercial context in which the agreement was made, although they were aided by certain legal rules of construction. In *Prenn v Simmonds*[24] in 1971 Lord Wilberforce in the House of Lords rejected this literal approach in favour of a contextual approach examining, if necessary, the matrix of facts forming the background to the agreement—this may involve evidence of the "genesis" and the objective "aim" of the transaction. However, what was said by the parties in the negotiations leading up to the formation of the   **7–020**

---

[23] [1975] Q.B. 303.
[24] [1971] 1 W.L.R. 1381.

contract must be disregarded. Lord Wilberforce considered such evidence to be unhelpful—he said:

> "By the nature of things, where negotiations are difficult, the parties' positions, with each passing letter, are changing and until the final agreement, though converging, still divergent. It is only the final document which records a consensus. If the previous documents use different expressions, how does construction of those expressions, itself a doubtful process, help on the construction of the contractual words?"

A more complete statement of the modern approach was provided by Lord Hoffmann in a later case, *Investors Compensation Scheme Ltd v West Bromwich Building Society.*[25] He referred to the fundamental change that had overtaken the law particularly as a result of the speeches of Lord Wilberforce in *Prenn v Simmonds* and also *Reardon Smith Line Ltd v Hansen-Tangen.*[26] He said that almost all "the old intellectual baggage of 'legal' interpretation" had been discarded so as to assimilate the way in which contractual documents are construed by the courts to "the common sense principles by which any serious utterance would be interpreted in ordinary life."

He summarised the principles of interpretation as follows:

> "(1) Interpretation is the ascertainment of the meaning which the document would convey to the reasonable person having all the background knowledge which would reasonably have been available to the parties in the situation in which they were in at the time of the contract.
>
> (2) The background was famously referred to by Lord Wilberforce as the 'matrix of fact', but this phrase is, if anything, an understated description of what the background may include. Subject to the requirement that it should have been reasonably available to the parties and to the exception to be mentioned next, it includes absolutely anything which would have affected the way in which the language of the document would have been understood by the reasonable man.
>
> (3) The law excludes from the admissible background the previous negotiations of the parties and their declarations of subjective intent. They are only admissible in an action for rectification [an action to rectify a written contractual document on the grounds of mistake]. The law makes this distinction for reasons of practical policy and, in this respect only, legal interpretation differs from the way we would interpret utterances in ordinary life. . . .
>
> (4) The meaning which a document (or any other utterance) would convey to a reasonable man is not the same thing as the meaning of the words. The meaning of words is a matter of dictionaries and grammars; the meaning of the document is what the parties using those words against the relevant background would reasonably have been understood to mean. The background may not merely enable the reasonable man to choose between the possible meanings of words which are ambiguous but even (as occasionally happens in ordinary life) to conclude that the parties must, for whatever reason, have used the wrong words or syntax (see *Mannai Investment Co Ltd v Eagle Star Life Assurance Co Ltd* [1997] CLC 1124; [1997] AC 749).

[25] [1998] 1 All E.R. 98.
[26] [1976] 1 W.L.R. 989.

(5) The 'rule' that words should be given their 'natural and ordinary meaning' reflects the common sense proposition that we do not easily accept that people have made linguistic mistakes, particularly in formal documents. On the other hand, if one would nevertheless conclude from the background that something must have gone wrong with the language, the law does not require judges to attribute to the parties an intention which they plainly could not have had. Lord Diplock made this point more vigorously when he said in *Antaios Compania Naviera SA v Salen Rederierna AB* [1985] A.C. 191 at p. 201: "if detailed semantic and syntactical analysis of words in a commercial document is going to lead to a conclusion that flouts business commonsense, it must be made to yield to business commonsense".

There is undoubtedly considerable merit in having principles of interpretation based on business "common sense" and on examining the context and background of the contract. However, these principles are, by their very nature, difficult to apply. The problem is that the principles are inevitably rather vague and therefore invite wide- ranging legal argument, to say nothing of differences of judicial opinion. The literal approach at least had the virtue of providing a measure of certainty and predictability—these are important factors in commercial litigation.[27] On the other hand, the old approach did not always produce a fair result or meet the reasonable expectations of the parties.

7–021

The case of *Bank of Credit and Commerce International SA v Ali (No 1)*[28] involved an application of the principles laid down in the *West Bromwich* case. An employee of the Bank of Credit and Commerce, N, was made redundant by the bank in 1990. As part of the redundancy package, N signed a release which was expressed to be "in full and final settlement of all or any claims . . . of whatsoever nature that exist or may exist" against the bank. The following year the bank went into insolvent liquidation and it was discovered that the bank had been conducting its business in a corrupt and illegal manner, something which received widespread publicity. Subsequently, some former employees of the bank who had found difficulty in obtaining alternative employment recovered compensation in court for the "stigma" of having worked for the bank.[29] This was a type of claim which the law had not previously recognised. N wished to make such a claim but the liquidators argued that the release signed by N precluded such a claim. In the High Court, Lightman J. so held but the Court of Appeal allowed the appeal. On appeal by the bank to the House of Lords it was held by the majority that N was not precluded from pursuing a stigma claim by the terms of the release. Applying the dicta of Lord Hoffmann in the *West Bromwich* case, the majority construed the terms of the release and concluded that neither party could have intended that the release could operate to prevent a subsequent stigma claim by N. Neither could have contemplated the possibility of such a claim being successful. This conclusion was arrived at by examining all the surrounding circumstances, i.e. the context in which the agreement was made. Lord Bingham said:

"On a fair construction of this document I cannot conclude that the parties intended to provide for the release of rights and the surrender of claims which they could never have had in contemplation at all. If the parties had sought to achieve so extravagant a result they should in my opinion have used language which left no room for doubt and

[27] See Staughton [1999] C.L.J. 303.
[28] [2001] W.L.R. 735.
[29] In *Malik v Bank of Credit and Commerce International SA* [198] A.C. 20.

which might at least have alerted [N] to the true effect of what (on that hypothesis) he was agreeing."

Although applying the rules of construction that he had put forward in the *West Bromwich* case, Lord Hoffmann dissented from the majority on the construction of the release. Referring to the second of the *West Bromwich* principles (see above), his Lordship had this to say:

"When . . . I said that the admissible background included 'absolutely anything which would have affected the way in which the language of the document would have been understood by the reasonable man', I did not think it necessary to emphasise that I meant anything which a reasonable man would have regarded as *relevant*. I was merely saying that there is no conceptual limit to what can be regarded as background."

The decision illustrates the difficulty with the contextual approach, that is, judges applying the same principles of construction can arrive at quite different conclusions.

Construction of exclusion clauses

7–022   The rules applied by the courts to the construction of exclusion clauses are applicable to contract terms generally but, historically, the rules have been applied with considerable rigour to clauses of exclusion. The reason is that, before the enactment of the Unfair Contract Terms Act, construction (along with incorporation) was a major weapon used by the judges to counter the abuse of exclusion clauses. Now that such clauses are regulated by statute, there is no longer any need for "hostile" or strained construction by the courts and it has, thankfully, been discarded. This is clear from certain judicial statements to which reference will be made below.

First we begin with a general rule of construction that ambiguity in the wording of a document will be construed against the drafter of the document.

Contra proferentem rule

7–023   Under the *contra proferentem* rule, any ambiguity in the wording of a clause will be construed narrowly against the party who has inserted the clause into the contract and is purporting to rely on it (the *proferens*). The strict, not to say strained, application of this rule to exclusion clauses can be illustrated by some of the older cases.

In *Beck & Co Ltd v Szymanowski & Co Ltd*[30] the defendants sold 2,000 gross of reels of sewing cotton to the claimants, the length of cotton on each reel was stipulated as being 200 yards. Clause 5 of the contract provided that the goods delivered were deemed to conform with the contract specification unless the defendants were informed otherwise within 14 days of delivery of the goods. Some 18 months later, the claimants discovered that each reel contained on average only 188 yards of cotton. The House of Lords held that the defendants could not rely on the clause. Lord Shaw stated that the damages were claimed "not in respect of the goods delivered but in respect of goods which were not delivered." Thus the clause was construed as referring to the quality of the goods, not the shortfall in quantity.

[30]   [1924] A.C. 43.

Similar word games can be seen at play in the case of *Andrews Bros (Bournemouth) Ltd v Singer & Co Ltd*[31] in which the claimant car dealers contracted to buy from the defendants several "new Singer cars". Under the terms of the agreement a clause provided that "all conditions, warranties and liabilities implied by statute, common law or otherwise are excluded." One of the vehicles delivered by the defendants had been driven over 550 miles to be shown to a potential customer and therefore strictly speaking was a used car. The Court of Appeal held that the defendants could not rely on the clause as it applied only to implied terms—the description of the car as "new" was an express term.

Liability for negligence

It seems that particularly clear words are required where it is sought to exclude liability for   **7–024**
negligence. This is based on the seriousness of the liability being excluded; in *Gillespie Brothers & Co Ltd v Roy Bowles Transport* Ltd[32] Buckley L.J. said that it was "inherently improbable that one party to the contract should intend to absolve the other party from the consequences of the latter's own negligence".

In *Canada Steamship Lines Ltd v The King*[33] Lord Morton in the Privy Council laid down a three stage test for determining whether liability in negligence is effectively evaded in a particular case. The principles, which have been adopted in a number of subsequent cases,[34] may be summarised as follows:

(1)   If the clause contains an express reference to "negligence" it will be effective.
(2)   If there is no express reference to negligence, are the words wide enough, in their ordinary meaning, to cover negligence? If there is any doubt, the clause is construed *contra proferentem*.
(3)   Even if the words are wide enough to cover negligence, could the party in breach be liable on some ground other than negligence? If they could, and the other ground is not so fanciful or remote that the party in breach cannot be supposed to have desired protection against it, the words are likely to be taken to refer to the non-negligent liability only.

Stage (1) is relatively straightforward. Calling a spade a spade will do the trick. The problem is that an express reference to non-liability for "negligence" could conceivably frighten off some potential contractors—the draftsman might therefore prefer to achieve the same result in a less explicit fashion. This may be possible because, as the House of Lords confirmed in *Smith v South Wales Switchgear Co Ltd*,[35] some synonym for negligence may suffice, such as, for example, an exclusion of liability "for breach of the common law duty of care".

The case of *Monarch Airlines Ltd v London Luton Airport Ltd*[36] affords an illustration. The claimant airline sued Luton Airport for damages in negligence after one of the claimants'

---

[31] [1934] 1 K.B. 17. See also *Houghton v Trafalgar Insurance* [1954] 1 Q.B. 247—a clause in an insurance policy excluding liability where an excess "load" was being carried did not apply where the car was carrying six passengers rather than the five for which it was constructed.
[32] [1973] Q.B. 400.
[33] [1952] A.C. 192.
[34] See, for example, *Monarch Airlines Ltd v London Luton Airport Ltd* [1997] C.L.C. 698.
[35] [1978] 1 W.L.R. 165. The case concerned the construction of an indemnity clause.
[36] [1997] C.L.C. 698.

aircraft was damaged by loose paving blocks on the airport runway whilst preparing to take off. There was a clause in the contract between the parties which purported to exclude liability for loss or damage to the aircraft arising from any "act, omission, neglect, or default" on the part of the airport company. Clarke J. held that the words "neglect or default" were synonymous with negligence and the parties must therefore have intended the clause to cover negligence.

7–025   Stage (2) refers to the situation where general words of exclusion are used. A clause referring to the exclusion of liability for loss or damage "howsoever caused" has been held to include negligence.[37] Similar expressions likely to produce the same effect are: "arising from any cause whatsoever"; at the customer's "sole risk"; and "shall incur no liability whatsoever". In *Lamport & Holt Lines Ltd v Coubro and Scrutton Ltd, The Raphael*[38] during a refit of the claimants' ship and due to the defendants' negligence, a derrick collapsed. The Court of Appeal held that an exclusion clause referring to damage arising from "any act or omission" was sufficiently wide to embrace negligence.

Stage (2) is qualified by stage (3). Thus, even if the words are wide enough to cover negligence, they will be ineffective if there is some other liability to which the words could apply. The words will be taken to refer to the non-negligent liability only. At this point it is necessary to explain that liability for breach of contract is a form of what is termed "strict" liability in which a party is liable even if they have acted reasonably and could not have avoided breaking the contract. However, a party's failure properly to perform the contract can involve both a breach of strict contractual liability and also liability in negligence for the damage caused. It is this situation to which stage (3) of the *Canada Steamship* guidelines refers.

Stage (3) can be illustrated by comparing two well-known cases, *White v John Warwick & Co Ltd*[39] and *Alderslade v Hendon Laundry Ltd*.[40]

In the former case, the claimant was injured whilst riding a cycle hired from the defendants—the saddle tilted forwards and the claimant fell off. The locknut for clamping the saddle to the seat post was rusted and could not be tightened. A generally worded clause in the contract stated that "nothing in this agreement shall render the owners liable for any personal injuries". In supplying a defective cycle the defendants could have been liable for (i) breach of the strict contractual liability to supply a machine fit for purpose; and (ii) negligence, owing to the failure to take reasonable care to ensure the cycle was in a safe condition. The Court of Appeal held that the clause was ambiguous and was effective to exclude only the contractual liability of the defendants—this meant that the claimant's action in negligence succeeded. In *Alderslade v Hendon Laundry* the claimant sent articles for laundering which were then lost as a result of the defendants' negligence. A limitation clause in the contract referred to lost articles and stated that the maximum allowance for such articles was 20 times the laundering charge. It was found that the laundry's only liability in relation to the laundered items was in negligence, i.e. they were under an obligation to take reasonable care of the goods but this liability was not strict. The Court of Appeal held that the clause must apply to negligence since if it did not apply to negligence it would be redundant.

7–026   It is instructive to compare *Alderslade v Hendon Laundry* with a later case, *Hollier v Rambler Motors (AMC) Ltd*.[41] In *Hollier* the claimant took his car to the defendants' garage to be repaired where it was damaged by a fire caused by the defendants' negligence. A clause in the contract stated, "the Company is not responsible for damage caused by fire caused to customers'

---

[37] *Joseph Travers & Sons Ltd v Cooper* [1915] 1 K.B. 73.
[38] [1982] Lloyd's Rep. 42.
[39] [1953] 1 W.L.R. 1285.
[40] [1945] K.B. 189.
[41] [1972] 2 Q.B. 71.

cars on the premises." There was therefore no express reference to negligence but the garage owners' only liability in relation to damage caused by fire was in negligence. The clause was not incorporated into the contract since there had been insufficient notice but, in any event, the Court of Appeal considered that the clause could not have been relied on by the defendants.

The court approached the clause from the viewpoint of the ordinary customer in the position of the claimant. Salmon L.J. felt that such a person would not think the garage was excluding liability for its own negligence, rather they would assume the clause was referring to non-negligently cause fire. Such fires could occur in many ways, for example where vandals enter the premises unlawfully and intentionally create a conflagration. The clause, therefore, in the view of the court, operated as no more than a warning that the defendants were not to be liable for non-negligently caused fire. *Alderslade v Hendon Laundry* was distinguished on the basis that the ordinary customer reading the conditions would have understood that liability for the negligence of the laundry was limited.

Hollier v Rambler has been subjected to some criticism.[42] It is arguable that it would be obvious to the reasonable person that the garage would not be liable in the absence of negligence and therefore the clause must necessarily have been referring to negligence. The outcome could be justified on the basis that it was a consumer case, not a contract between businesses, in which the court felt that the defendants should have used much more explicit language to get their meaning across.

Before leaving the question of negligence it should be pointed out that the Unfair Contract Terms Act 1977 has had a considerable impact on the exclusion of liability for this form of liability. These matters will be discussed more fully later in this chapter (see para.7–040) but for present purposes it should be noted that, after the Act, liability for death or personal injury caused by negligence cannot lawfully be excluded; and liability for other loss or damage can only be excluded insofar as the term in question satisfies a requirement of reasonableness. Indeed, the special protection afforded to consumers in the post-1977 Act regime may mean that such clauses may not be regarded as reasonable as against consumers. They may also be found to fall foul of the fairness test in the Unfair Terms in Consumer Contracts Regulations 1999.

Less strict approach to construction

It is clear that, since the passing of the Unfair Contract Terms Act, the courts no longer need to resort to artificial or "strained" construction to restrict the operation of exclusion clauses. There has been a number of judicial statements to this effect, perhaps the most unequivocal being that of Lord Diplock in *Photo Production Ltd v Securicor Transport Ltd*[43] where he said: **7–027**

"[T]he reports are full of cases in which what would appear to be very strained constructions have been placed on exclusion clauses . . . [mainly as against the consumer and in standard form contracts] . . . any need for this kind of judicial distortion of the English language has been banished by Parliament having made these kind of contracts subject to the Unfair Contract Terms Act, 1977."

---

[42] See Barendt (1972) 35 M.L.R. 644.
[43] [1980] A.C. 827.

This means that many of the older cases should be viewed with caution on the issue of construction. Construction must now also have regard to the principles laid down in the *West Bromwich* case (see para.7–020) where the court may take into consideration admissible background and the commercial context. As a result, the nature of the judicial approach to exclusion clauses is, at present, difficult to state with precision. If the courts should not resort to strained construction, then it seems reasonable to suggest that the *contra proferentem* rule should be reserved for cases where there is genuine, not artificial, ambiguity.

On one issue the judges have spoken with a measure of certainty, that is that clauses limiting liability (limitation clauses) should be construed less strictly than clauses totally excluding liability (exclusion clauses). In *Ailsa Craig Fishing Co Ltd v Malvern Fishing Co Ltd*[44] Lord Fraser considered that the *Canada Steamship* principles (see para.7–024) should not be applied in their full rigour when considering the effect of limitation clauses. His lordship said:

> "[Limitation] clauses will of course be read *contra proferentem* and must be clearly expressed, but there is no reason why they should be judged by the specially exacting standards which are applied to exclusion . . . clauses."

7–028 The main reason for this distinction appears to be the "inherent improbability" that a party to a contract would intend that the party relying on the clause should be released from all liability under the contract. It is not, however, according to Lord Fraser, quite as improbable that a party would agree to a limitation clause, particularly where the potential liability in damages greatly exceeds the cost of the services for which a charge is made. Lord Wilberforce considered that limitation clauses should not be regarded with the same hostility as exclusion clauses because:

> "[T]hey must be related to other contractual terms, in particular to the risks to which the defending party may be exposed, the remuneration which he receives, and possibly also the opportunity of the other party to insure."

The logic is not compelling—the difficulty with the analysis is that some limitation clauses limit liability to a sum so small that they amount to a virtual exclusion of liability; it follows therefore that the same considerations could be applied to exclusion clauses (as is illustrated by the case of *Photo Production Ltd v Securicor Transport Ltd*, discussed at para.7–031).

Fundamental breach

7–029 In the 1950s and 1960s there developed a doctrine that no exclusion clause could protect a party from liability for a very serious or fundamental breach of contract. The "doctrine of fundamental breach" was, before being re-assessed by the House of Lords (see para.7–031) and the enactment of the Act of 1977, a major weapon deployed by the courts in dealing with the perceived abuses of exclusion clauses.

The doctrine was applied to two situations. The first of these was total non- performance, such as where a party contracts to buy peas and the other sends him beans[45]—no exclusion

---

[44] [1983] 1 W.L.R. 983. The approach was also affirmed by the House of Lords in *George Mitchell (Chesterhall) Ltd v Finney Lock Seeds Ltd* [1983] 2 A.C. 803. The case is discussed at para.7–058.

[45] *Chanter v Hopkins* (1838) 4 M. & W. 399.

clause can apply because a fundamental term has been breached. In the second type of situation the breach itself was seen as being so grave that it destroyed the whole basis of the contract; once again, the party in breach was not allowed to shelter behind a clause excluding liability. On the face of it, this sounds perfectly reasonable. The difficulty was that the doctrine was applied as if it were a rule of substantive law, i.e. that if there was a fundamental breach, no exclusion clause, however well-drafted, could cover the breach. As such it was too blunt an instrument to deal with the complexities of exclusion clauses.

The case of *Karsales (Harrow) Ltd v Wallis*,[46] decided by the Court of Appeal in the 1950s affords an apt illustration of this phase of fundamental breach. The defendant acquired a Buick car on hire purchase. The contract contained a widely drawn exclusion clause stating that "no condition or warranty that the vehicle is roadworthy or as to its age, condition or fitness for any purpose is given by the owner or implied herein." The vehicle in question was towed around to the defendant's house at night—the cylinder head was broken off, the valves were burnt out and two pistons were broken. The "automobile" was incapable of independent propulsion. The defendant repudiated the hire-purchase contract, the finance company assigned its rights to the claimant dealers who sued, relying on the clause.

The Court of Appeal held that the exclusion clause did not apply. The claimants could not be permitted, through an exclusion clause, to evade their fundamental obligation to deliver a "car", that is a machine capable, when in the hands of a driver, of self-propulsion.   **7–030**

In *Suisse Atlantique Societe d'Armement Maritime SA v NV Rotterdamsche Kolen Centrale*[47] the House of Lords sought to assert the correct legal basis of fundamental breach. It was perhaps unfortunate that the facts of the case were not typical, involving a "demurrage" clause in a charterparty which their Lordships concluded was an agreed damages clause (see para.16–043), not an exclusion clause. This meant that the observations of the House regarding fundamental breach were strictly obiter; nevertheless, their Lordships considered that whether an exclusion clause can protect a party who is in breach of a fundamental obligation is a matter of construction of the contract. There was a presumption that an exclusion clause was not intended by the parties to extend to a fundamental breach; and to be effective, such a clause had to be expressed in clear and unambiguous language so that the parties plainly meant it to apply to such a breach, and such clauses should be construed *contra proferentem*. Rejecting the "rule of law" approach, Viscount Dilhorne said:

> "[I]t is not right to say that the law prohibits and nullifies a clause exempting or limiting liability for fundamental breach . . . Such a rule of law would involve a restriction on freedom of contract and in the older cases I can find no trace of it."

One of the objections to the doctrine being a rule of law was that it treated all cases in the same way, whether at one end of the spectrum it was a large concern imposing standard terms on a consumer, or, at the other extreme, businesses bargaining on equal terms where a widely drawn exclusion clause is freely accepted. As Lord Reid explained:

> "[The] rule appears to treat all cases alike. There is no indication in the . . . cases that the courts are to consider whether the exemption is fair in all the circumstances or is harsh and unconscionable or whether it was freely agreed by the customer. . . . It does not seem to me

[46] [1956] 1 W.L.R. 936.
[47] [1967] 1 A.C. 361.

satisfactory that the decision must always go one way if, eg defects in a car or other goods are just sufficient to make the breach of contract a fundamental breach, but must always go the other way if the defects fall just short of that."

7–031   In other words, the validity of exclusion clauses was a complex problem. Lord Reid considered that the solution should be left to Parliament.

One might have though that *Suisse Atlantique* would have heralded the demise of fundamental breach as a rule of law. The rule of law approach was, however, revived in the 1970s by the Court of Appeal, led by Lord Denning M.R., in *Harbutt's Plasticine Ltd v Wayne Tank and Pump Co Ltd*.[48] This was a case in which the claimants contracted with the defendants for the installation of equipment at the claimants' plasticine factory. The plant in question was for the storage and dispensing of stearine (a component of plasticine) at temperatures of up to 160 degrees F. The defendants installed a type of plastic piping which was quite unsuitable and when the molten liquid was forced through the pipes it caused a fire which destroyed the premises. The claimants sued for the replacement cost of the factory but the defendants purported to rely on a clause in the contract limiting the defendants' liability to the sum of £2,300. The Court of Appeal held that the consequences of the breach were so serious as to amount to a fundamental breach of the contract. This breach, in the view of the court, automatically brought an end to the contract, including the limitation clause, which could not be relied on. This reasoning was rejected by the House of Lords in a case decided in 1980, *Photo Production Ltd v Securicor Transport Ltd*[49] and *Harbutt's Plasticine* was overruled.

In *Photo Production v Securicor* the claimants employed the defendants to protect their Christmas card factory by a visiting patrol. The contract contained a widely drawn exclusion clause providing that under "no circumstances shall the Company (Securicor) be responsible for any injurious act or default by any employee of the Company". One night, one of the defendants' security guards entered the building and lit a fire which got out of control and destroyed the premises at a cost of £615,000. The Court of Appeal held that the conduct of the defendants, through their guard, amounted to a fundamental breach of contract and the defendants could not rely on the exclusion clause. On appeal, the House of Lords disagreed with this conclusion as it could not stand with their Lordships' earlier ruling in *Suisse Atlantique* where the House had made it clear that whether an exclusion clause could cover a fundamental breach was a question of the proper construction of the contract, and could not be determined by a rule of law. There were no exceptions to this and, in particular, the doctrine that an exclusion clause could be destroyed by breach was considered to be without foundation. The principle that a breach does not have this effect was subsequently enacted in statutory form in s.9 of the Unfair Contract Terms Act 1977 (see para.7–049) although it is, in any event, a long-standing principle of the common law. Nevertheless, their Lordships acknowledged that the more fundamental or serious the liability sought to be excluded, the clearer the wording required to achieve that objective.

7–032   The House of Lords concluded that the clause in question, on its true construction, covered the breach which had occurred and therefore could be relied on by the defendants. The contract in this case was entered into before the Unfair Contract Terms Act came into force and therefore the exclusion clause was not subject to the statutory requirement of reasonableness in that Act. In referring to the position after the Act, Lord Wilberforce said:

---

[48]   [1970] 1 Q.B. 477.
[49]   [1980] A.C. 827.

"[I]n commercial matters generally, when the parties are not of unequal bargaining power, and when the risks are normally borne by insurance, not only is the case for judicial intervention undemonstrated, but there is everything to be said, and this seems to have been Parliament's intention, for leaving the parties free to apportion the risks as they think fit and for respecting their decisions."

These principles can be seen at work in the case itself. The relative bargaining strength of the two (business) parties was equal and the defendants were providing a service involving periodical visits for a modest sum. The claimants were the party who would be aware of the value of their premises and the effectiveness of their fire precautions—they were therefore the party who could appropriately take out fire insurance. Assuming the defendants had been able to obtain insurance, the expense of the premiums may have increased the fee they charged customers for their services. The parties had therefore allocated the risk of fire between themselves as they thought fit, the greater burden falling on the claimants.

There can be little doubt that *Photo Production v Securicor* represented a robust re- assertion of "freedom of contract" in business to business transactions. The current status of fundamental breach is that it is now of much more limited significance than formerly—it is really little more than a guide to construction that clear and unambiguous words will be required to cover such a breach. Providing such words are used, if the clause is one to which the requirement of reasonableness under the Unfair Contract Terms Act applies, the clause will be valid if the court considers that it satisfies that test.

FURTHER LIMITATIONS ON EXCLUSION CLAUSES

The common law has imposed restrictions on exclusion clauses in ways other than applying the rules of incorporation and construction. Historically, a third party to the contract could not claim the protection of an exclusion clause contained in it and in some cases, the clause has been effectively overridden by a warranty given by the party purporting to rely on the clause. These matters will be considered in turn.   **7–033**

The position of third parties

Under the doctrine of privity of contract (which is discussed more fully in Chapter 8 below) the traditional rule at common law was that a third party, i.e. a stranger to the contract, could neither sue nor be sued on that contract. The rule has always been subject to exceptions and has been substantially modified by the Contracts (Rights of Third Parties) Act 1999.   **7–034**

As applied to exclusion clauses, the rule of privity traditionally meant that an employee would not be able to take the protection of an exclusion clause in a contract made between their employer and another party. Thus in *Adler v Dickson*[50] the claimant, Mrs Adler, suffered injury whilst boarding the P & O Lines steamship *Himalaya* to go on a Mediterranean cruise. Owing to the negligence of the captain and boatswain of the ship the gangway collapsed and the claimant fell 16 feet onto the dock below. A clause in the claimant's contract with the shipping line

---

[50] [1955] 1 Q.B. 158.

provided, "the Company will not be responsible for any injury whatsoever to the person of any passenger arising from or occasioned by the negligence of the Company's servants." This clause on its wording clearly protected the Company and so the claimant sued the captain and boatswain for negligence. The action succeeded—the Court of Appeal held that as members of the crew the defendants could not rely on the clause because they were not parties to the contract between the claimant and their employers. A majority of the court considered, obiter, that the outcome would have been no different if the clause had expressly purported to extend to the liability of the servants. Denning LJ, although in agreement with the result, dissented on this point.

The decision in *Adler v Dickson* was confirmed by the House of Lords in *Scruttons Ltd v Midland Silicones Ltd*.[51] Here there was a contract for the carriage by sea of a drum of chemicals from the United States to England which contained a clause limiting the liability of the "carriers" to $500. The drum was damaged through the negligence of a firm of stevedores whom the carriers had employed to unload the ship. It was held that the stevedores could not rely on the clause as it was contained in a contract to which they were not a party—that contract was between the owners of the drum and the carriers. The phrase in the contract referring to "the carriers" did not extend to the stevedores—the orthodox rule of privity was therefore upheld. Nevertheless the House was prepared to recognise a possible exception where it could be shown that a contracting party was acting as agent for a third party involved in the performance of the contract. Lord Reid indicated the circumstances in which such an agency could arise. These were:

(i)   the contract of carriage must make it clear that the stevedore is intended to be protected by the exclusion clause;

(ii) the contract of carriage must make it clear that the carrier is contracting both on his own behalf and as agent for the stevedore;

(iii) the stevedore must have authorised the carrier to contract in this way; and

(iv) the stevedore must have provided consideration for the promise to exclude liability.

7–035   These criteria were subsequently applied by the Privy Council in the case of *New Zealand Shipping Ltd v A M Satterthwaite & Co Ltd, The Eurymedon*.[52] A drilling machine was shipped from England to New Zealand under a contract of carriage entered into between the consignors of the cargo and the carriers. The defendant stevedores agreed with the carriers that the goods would be unloaded on arrival in Wellington, New Zealand. The defendants negligently damaged the machine during unloading, although by this time, the consignor's rights under the contract had been transferred to the claimant consignees. In an action for damages brought by the claimants, the defendants purported to rely on an exclusion clause in the contract of carriage which provided, inter alia, that the carrier was to be regarded as acting as agent for any independent contractors involved in the transaction and that such parties would enjoy the benefit of the exclusion clause. The Privy Council held that the defendants were protected by the clause.

The decision is founded upon a judicially constructed unilateral contract. Under this contract, the owners had promised to confer the benefit of the clause upon the stevedore if they would unload the ship. This offer had been made to the stevedore through their agent, the carrier, and the stevedore had provided consideration by unloading the ship. By so doing, the stevedore was performing an existing contractual duty owed to a third party. This, it may be recalled from the discussion of cases such as *Scotson v Pegg* (see para.4–026), constitutes good

[51] [1962] A.C. 446.
[52] [1975] A.C. 154.

consideration. The principle established in *New Zealand Shipping v Satterthwaite* was followed by the Privy Council in *Port Jackson Stevedoring Pty Ltd v Salmond & Spraggon (Australia) Pty Ltd, The New York Star*.[53] The difficulty with the principle is that it is highly artificial and depends on a complex and particular set of circumstances and relations between the parties. It did not establish a general rule that a third party may take the benefit of an exclusion clause. This outcome required legislation—this is discussed below.

Another inroad into the position established by *Scruttons v Midland Silicones* can be seen in cases such as *Norwich City Council v Harvey*.[54] Here, the exclusion clause was construed as restricting the duty of care in negligence. Building owners employed the main contractors to construct an extension to a swimming pool. A clause in the standard form contract provided that the risk of fire damage should be upon the owners and required them to maintain adequate insurance. The contractors sub-contracted certain roofing work; the agreement bound the sub-contractors to "the same terms and conditions as those in the main contract". The defendant, an employee of the sub-contractors, negligently damaged the building by fire. An action by the claimant owners against the defendant failed on the basis that no duty was owed to the owners who were taken to have assumed the risk of damage.

The Contracts (Rights of Third Parties) Act 1999 has made it possible for a third party to claim the benefit of an exclusion clause in a much more straightforward way than has been possible under case law. The test of enforceability in s.1 of the Act is discussed in detail at para.8–007. Of particular importance is s.1(6) of the Act which provides: **7–036**

> "Where a term of a contract excludes or limits liability in relation to any matter references in this Act to the third party enforcing the term shall be construed as references to his availing himself of the exclusion or limitation."

This means that providing the clause is enforceable under the Act, the third party may shelter behind the clause. The wording of the contractual provision will be important because it will need to specifically refer to the third parties whether they be servants, agents or independent contractors. Where the test of enforceability under the Act is not satisfied, the common law principles will continue to apply.

Inconsistent oral promise

We have already seen that an exclusion clause can be rendered wholly or partly ineffective by an inconsistent oral statement as to the effect of the clause by the party purporting to rely on it. This was the position in *Curtis v Chemical Cleaning and Dyeing Co*, discussed at para.7–005 above. In that case, the clause was contained in a signed document but the principle applies equally to clauses contained in documents which are merely delivered to the other party. In *Mendelssohn v Normand*[55] an oral statement by a garage attendant that the claimant should leave his car unlocked was held to override an exclusion clause excluding liability for goods **7–037**

---

[53] [1981] 1 W.L.R. 138. In *The Mahkutai* [1995] A.C. 650 the Privy Council refused to apply the principle to an exclusive jurisdiction clause on the basis that such a clause is designed for the mutual benefit of both parties, unlike an exclusion clause which is inserted for the benefit of one party only.

[54] [1989] 1 W.L.R. 828. See also *Southern Water Authority v Carey* [1985] 2 All E.R. 1077.

[55] [1970] 1 Q.B. 177. An oral assurance was also held to override an exclusion clause in *J Evans & Son (Portsmouth) Ltd v Andrea Merzario Ltd*. [1976] 1 W.L.R. 1078.

stolen. The defendant garage was held not to be protected by the clause when valuables were stolen from the claimant's car.

In some cases, the court has treated the inconsistent oral promise as forming the basis of a collateral contract. Thus, in *Webster v Higgin*[56] an oral promise by a dealer that a car was in good condition was held to be enforceable as a collateral contract despite the fact that the hire-purchase contract (the main contract) contained an exclusion clause.

UNFAIR CONTRACT TERMS ACT 1977 (UCTA)

7–038   The statutory control of exclusion clauses was not a new phenomenon when UCTA was enacted in 1977. It has been introduced in a piecemeal fashion. Thus the Road Traffic Act 1960, s.151 rendered void any attempt to negate or restrict liability for death or personal injury where passengers travelled in public service vehicles. However, the first major attempt to control exclusion clauses in contracts generally came with s.3 of the Misrepresentation Act 1967 (now replaced in an amended version by s.8 of UCTA), followed by the Supply of Goods (Implied Terms) Act 1973 (similar provisions are now to be found in s.6 of UCTA). These measures permitted the exclusion or restriction of liability for misrepresentation and breach of the statutory implied terms respectively but only insofar as it was fair and reasonable to allow reliance on the clause.

The legislative scheme introduced by UCTA is more comprehensive. The basic purpose of the Act is to restrict the extent to which liability can be excluded or restricted for breach of contract or negligence—this is achieved largely by a requirement of reasonableness and in some cases by a specific prohibition. The Act generally provides greater protection to those dealing as consumer than it does to those dealing in the course of a business. The title of UCTA, however, is slightly misleading—the Act is concerned mainly with terms and notices which exclude or restrict liability rather than with unfair terms generally; and it applies not only to contractual terms and notices but to non-contractual notices which purport to exclude or restrict liability in tort.

Scope of UCTA

7–039   Save for an exception in s.6(4) relating to implied terms in sales of goods contracts (see para.7–047), the Act in general only applies to what is termed "business liability". Under s.1(3) business liability is defined as liability arising from things done by a person in the course of a business; or from the occupation of business premises for business purposes. "Business" is interpreted in s.14 as including a profession and the activities of any government department or local or public authority. It follows that transactions of a purely private nature are outside the scope of the Act—any restrictions of liability will be governed by common law principles.

In addition, Schedule 1 provides that the Act does not apply to certain types of contract including insurance contracts; contracts concerning the creation or transfer of interests in land, intellectual property rights or securities; and contracts relating to the formation or dissolution etc of companies.

---

[56] [1948] 2 All E.R. 127. For collateral contracts, see para.6–015.

Negligence liability

For the purposes of the Act, "negligence" is widely defined by s.1(1) so as to include: (a) the **7–040** contractual duty to take reasonable care or exercise reasonable skill in the performance of a contract; (b) the duty of care arising in tort; and (c) the common duty of care under the Occupiers' Liability Act 1957.

One of the key provisions of the Act is to be found in s.2(1)—it provides that liability for death or personal injury cannot be excluded or restricted by any contract term or notice. Any provision purporting to have this effect is invalid. This means that if cases such as *Thornton v Shoe Lane Parking* or *White v John Warwick* (see paras.7–012 and 7–025 above respectively) were to arise today, the exclusion clauses would be ineffective without the need for any reference to common law principles of incorporation and construction.

So far as other loss or damage caused by negligence are concerned (i.e. damage to property or pure economic loss), s.2(2) provides that liability can be excluded or restricted but only so far as the term or notice satisfies the test of reasonableness in s.11 UCTA (as to which, see para.7–054 below).

In s.2(3) it is provided that where a contract term or notice purports to exclude or restrict liability for negligence a person's agreement to or awareness of it is not of itself to be taken as indicating their voluntary acceptance of any risk.

Contractual liability

In s.3 the Act provides that where one party deals as consumer or on the other party's written **7–041** standard terms of business then the other party cannot exclude or restrict their liability for breach of contract, except subject to the requirement of reasonableness (s.3(2)(a)). (The requirement of reasonableness is considered at para.7–054 below).

In s.3(2)(b) the reasonableness requirement is also extended to terms purporting to entitle the other party to render:

(i)   performance substantially different from that reasonably expected; or
(ii) in respect of the whole or any part of the contractual obligation, no performance at all.

The provisions contained in s.3(2)(b) (i) and (ii) above are aimed at disguised exclusion clauses. These are often skillfully drafted terms which are worded in such a way as to define a party's obligation rather than to exclude liability for a particular breach. For example in *Sze Hai Tong Bank Ltd v Rambler Cycle Co*[57] goods were shipped under a clause providing that the responsibility of the carrier should cease absolutely after the goods had been discharged from the ship. It was held that the clause must be construed so as to prevent reliance where the goods were knowingly delivered to a party not entitled to receive them, since this would defeat the main purpose of the contract.

Examples of such obligation defining clauses have been common in the tourist industry where operators may include terms reserving the right of the operator to change travel arrangements, hotels and even destinations. In *Anglo-Continental Holidays Ltd v Typaldos Lines (London)*

---

[57] [1959] A.C. 351.

Ltd[58] the claimants were travel agents who booked accommodation for clients on a luxury cruise liner with an itinerary involving two days in Haifa. This was important for their clients who wished to spend some time seeing Israel. The clients were, at short notice, booked on a different ship—one that was small and old and docked only for a few hours in Haifa. The claimants sued for breach. The defendant shipping line purported to rely on a small print clause in the contract which stated, "Steamers, Sailing Dates, Rates and Itineraries are subject to change without prior notice". Finding for the claimants, the Court of Appeal held that the clause could not be used in such a way that effect could not be given to the substance or "main object" of the contract. The case was decided on common law principles before UCTA came into effect but such a case would surely now fall within the ambit of s.3(2)(b) and be subject to the reasonableness requirement.

7–042　　More recently, in *Paragon Finance plc v Nash*[59] the Court of Appeal held that a clause permitting mortgage providers to vary interest rates was not caught by s.3(2)(b)—by fixing interest rates the lenders were not altering any performance required of them under the contract. Rather, they were altering the performance required of the borrowers.

Unlike s.2, s.3 is limited to the situation where one party *deals as consumer* or on the other party's *written standard terms of business*. The italicised expressions in the preceding sentence are important and must now be considered.

Deals as consumer

7–043　　UCTA s.12(1) provides that a party "deals as consumer" in relation to another party if:

> "(a) he neither makes the contract in the course of a business nor holds himself out as doing so; and
> (b) the other party does make the contract in the course of a business; and
> (c) in the case of a contract governed by the law of sales of goods or hire purchase, or by s.7 of this Act, the goods passing under or in pursuance of the contract are of a type ordinarily supplied for private use and consumption.
> [(1A) But if the first party mentioned in subsection (1) is an individual paragraph (c) of that section must be ignored.]"

Under s.12 it may be necessary to decide whether a particular transaction is made "in the course of a business"; it seems that the fact that a party is a business will not prevent it from "dealing as consumer".

The case of *R & B Customs Brokers Co Ltd v United Dominions Trust Ltd*[60] was decided under s.6(2) of UCTA (see para.7–047) but the court's interpretation of s.12 is equally applicable to s.3. The claimant company was in the business of freight forwarding and shipping and was owned and controlled by a married couple, who were the company directors. The company purchased a second-hand car from the defendants under a conditional sale agreement and the vehicle was to be used both for the business and personal use of its directors. The claimant company had made only two or three such purchases in the past. It was discovered that the car was defective—the roof had an incurable leak that rendered the upholstery sodden with water

---

[58] [1967] 2 Lloyds Rep. 61. See further *Timeload Plc v British Telecommunications Plc* [1995] E.M.L.R. 459.
[59] [2002] 1 W.L.R. 685.
[60] [1988] 1 W.L.R. 321.

so that it became "mouldy and evil smelling". The contract contained a clause excluding the defendants' liability unless the buyer was dealing as consumer. The Court of Appeal held that the defendants were liable because the claimant company had not made the purchase in the course of a business but had dealt as consumer.

Placing reliance on case law decided under Trade Descriptions legislation the court concluded that a transaction would only be "in the course of a business" for the purposes of s.12 where it was (i) integral to the business itself, or (ii) where there was a regularity of such dealings. Clearly, the acquisition of a car was only incidental to the freight forwarding business run by the claimants and there had not been a regularity of such transactions. The test in the case is difficult to apply and has been criticised. It is unduly narrow. One may ask, to what type of businesses would the purchase (and/or sale) of cars be integral or regular transactions? This would certainly be true of car dealers and, probably, those businesses which own and operate fleets of hire cars, but beyond that few such transactions are likely to be regarded as being made in the course of a business under the *R & B Customs Brokers* test.

The decision in the case would have been no different had the car been intended solely for business use. The *R & B Customs Brokers* approach might be justified on the ground that small businesses, when dealing with larger organisations on the basis of standard terms, may be in no better position than private consumers—bargaining power is not equal. But it is clear that the test does not depend on relative bargaining strength.

In *Stevenson v Rogers* (the facts are given at para.6–033) the Court of Appeal declined to follow the *R & B Customs Brokers* approach in interpreting the meaning of "in the course of a business" under s.14 of the Sale of Gods Act 1979 and an incidental transaction was held to be in the course of a business. Some have argued that the *Stevenson v Rogers* approach would be appropriate to cases under UCTA.[61] Whatever the merit of such an argument may be, the Court of Appeal preferred to follow *R & B Customs Brokers* in the case of *Feldaroll Foundry Plc v Hermes Leasing (London) Ltd.*[62] The facts were that the claimant foundry company acquired a Lamborghini car from the defendants for their managing director for £64,995 on hire purchase terms. The agreement, which was signed by the managing director on behalf of the company stated that the goods "will be used for the purpose of my/our business." The agreement also contained a clause excluding liability for the quality, merchantability, fitness or correspondence with description of the goods. After delivery, the car proved to have serious defects and the defendants sought to rely on the exclusion clause. In the Court of Appeal the issue was whether the claimant had entered into the agreement dealing as consumer. If so, the defendants would be unable to exclude liability under the terms of s.6(2) of UCTA (see para.7–047).

Following the approach taken in *R & B Customs Brokers*, the Court of Appeal held that the claimant company dealt as consumer. The transaction was not integral to the claimant's business, it was merely incidental. It made no difference that the claimant was a public company as opposed to a small private company, as was the case in *R & B Customs Brokers*. Moreover, the statement in the agreement that the car was to be used for business purposes dealt only with the use to which the car was intended to put and not the capacity in which the claimant was dealing—it said nothing about whether the purchase of the car was integral to the foundry business.

It should be noted that the Law Commission has produced proposals for a unified regime for consumer contracts under which only individuals will be consumers, although there will be some

7–044

7–045

[61] See Macdonald (1999) 3 Web J.C.L. 1.
[62] [2004] EWCA Civ 747.

protection for small businesses.[63] In contracts for the sale of goods, hire-purchase or those governed by s.7 of UCTA (see para.7–048), a business will only be dealing as consumer (under s.12(1)(c) above) where the goods are of a type ordinarily supplied for private use and consumption. Thus in *R & B Customs Brokers* and *Feldaroll Foundry v Hermes* the goods in question were cars and so s.12(1)(c) was fulfilled. The position is different where goods are supplied to an individual as there has been an amendment to s.12 UCTA made by the Sale and Supply of Goods to Consumers Regulations 2002[64] which introduced a new ss.1A (see above, at para.7–043, in square brackets). The effect of this reform is that liability for breach of statutory implied terms cannot be excluded as against a consumer who is an individual regardless of the type of goods supplied.

With regard to the burden of proof, it is for those claiming that a party does not deal as consumer to show that they do not (s.12(3) UCTA).

Written standard terms of business

7–046   We have seen that s.3 UCTA applies where one party deals as consumer or on the other party's written standard terms of business. There is no definition in the Act of the term "written standard terms of business". So far as the courts are concerned it does not seem to be necessary that the contract as a whole is in standard from—nor will it matter if one of the non-material clauses has been varied.[65] In *Pegler Ltd v Wang (UK) Ltd*[66] the only clauses in the contract that were in standard form were the exclusion and limitation clauses themselves. It was established that these clauses were, from point of view of the defendant, not negotiable. Judge Bowsher Q.C. held that the defendant had contracted on the defendant's "written standard terms of business" and therefore s.3 UCTA applied.[67]

Sale of goods and hire purchase

7–047   UCTA s.6 governs the exclusion or restriction of the implied terms in the Sale of Goods Act 1979 (SGA) (see para.6–029) and the equivalent implied terms in contracts of hire purchase by the Supply of Goods (Implied Terms) Act 1973 (SG(IT)A). The section may be summarised as follows:

(i)   Liability for breach of the implied terms relating to title (in s.12 SGA and s.8 SG(IT)A) *cannot* be excluded or restricted by reference to any contract term (s.6(1) UCTA). This prohibition reflects the importance attached to the seller's obligation to convey a good title to the purchaser.

(ii)   As against a person *dealing as consumer* liability for breach of the implied terms relating to correspondence with description, quality, fitness for purpose and sales by sample (in ss.13, 14 and 15 SGA and s. 9, 10 and 11 SG(IT)A) *cannot* be excluded or restricted by

---

[63]   Law Com No 292, Cm 6464. Proposals for reform are discussed at para.7–074.

[64]   SI 2002/3045. UCTA s.12 is also amended by the regulations so as to provide that the buyer is not in any circumstances to be regarded as dealing as consumer (a) if he is an individual and the goods are second hand goods sold at public auction at which individuals have the opportunity of attending the sale in person; or (b) if he is not an individual and the goods are sold by auction or by competitive tender. (s.12(2)(a) and (b)).

[65]   *St Albans & City District Council v International Computers Ltd* [1996] 4 All E.R. 481; and *Watford Electronics Ltd v Sanderson CFL Ltd* [2000] 2 All E.R. (Comm) 984, per Thornton J. at first instance.

[66]   [2000] B.L.R. 218.

[67]   See also *British Fermentation Products Ltd v Compare Reavell Ltd* [1999] B.L.R. 352.

reference to any contract term (s.6(2) UCTA). The definition of "consumer" in s.12 UCTA is discussed at para.7–043.

(iii) As against a person dealing *otherwise than as consumer*, the liabilities specified in (ii) above can be excluded or restricted by reference to a contract term, but only in so far as the term satisfies the requirement of reasonableness (discussed at para.7–054).

It should be noted that, under s.6(4), s.6 applies to all liabilities, whereas the Act in general is concerned only with business liability. It follows that s.6 applies to contracts of sale of goods and hire purchase between private individuals, although the significance of this is reduced by the fact that the implied terms as to quality and fitness in SGA and SG(IT)A only arise in any event where the transaction is made in the course of a business.

Other contracts under which goods pass

UCTA, s.7 applies to contracts (other than sale of goods or hire purchase) where the possession or   **7–048** ownership of goods passes, i.e. contracts of hire and contracts for work and materials. Such contracts are governed by the Supply of Goods and Services Act 1982 (which is discussed at para.6–038).

Essentially, s.7 applies the same regime as in s.6 above to terms excluding or restricting liability for breaches of the statutory implied terms in the contracts covered by s.7. There is a difference with regard to the implied terms as to title in that under s.7(3A) the implied terms as to title cannot be excluded in a contract for work and materials, whereas in contracts of hire, the right to transfer possession of goods can be excluded, but only in so far as the clause satisfies the requirement of reasonableness.

Effect of breach and affirmation

Notwithstanding that a contract has been terminated by breach or by a party electing to treat   **7–049** it as repudiated, a term which is required to meet the requirement of reasonableness under s.11 UCTA may nevertheless be found to do so and given effect to (s.9(1)). It would seem that this provision was introduced to confirm the position established by the House of Lords in *Photo Production Ltd v Securicor Transport Ltd* (see para.7–031) with regard to the effect of a breach on an exclusion clause. Conversely, where, on breach, the contract is nevertheless affirmed by a party entitled to treat it as repudiated, this does not of itself exclude the requirement of reasonableness in relation to any contract term (s.9(2)).

Meaning of "exclude or restrict" liability

The Act of 1977 in general regulates clauses which "exclude or restrict" liability. UCTA, s.13(1),   **7–050** extends the meaning of these words so as to include:

(a) making the liability or its enforcement subject to restrictive or onerous conditions;
(b) excluding or restricting any right or remedy in respect of the liability, or subjecting a person to any prejudice in consequence of him pursuing any right or remedy;

(c)   excluding or restricting the rules of evidence or procedure or (in ss.2 and 5 – 7 UCTA) excluding or restricting the relevant obligation or duty.[68]

The above provisions were introduced to inhibit avoidance of UCTA. Often, exclusion clauses are dressed up in different clothing by the use of skilful drafting— under the provisions of s.13(1) such clauses will be caught by the Act providing they have the effect of excluding or restricting liability. For example, a tour operator who inserts a term in the contract with the holidaymaker that, should any claim or complaint arise, 10 copies of the claim or complaint must be submitted to the tour company's head office within 48 hours of the claim arising, may well fall foul of paragraph (a) above.

Disclaimers may fall under these provisions. Thus in *Smith v Eric S Bush*[69] a building society valuation was undertaken on terms that the valuer's report would be supplied "without any acceptance of responsibility" on the part of the valuer. The House of Lords held that the clause fell within paragraph (c) above—a clause which prevented any duty of care from arising operated to "exclude or restrict the relevant obligation or duty" (under s. 13(1)(c) UCTA). Similarly, a clause which indicates that the buyer is bound to pay for goods which are defective or not in conformity with the contract description may amount to an exclusion clause. In *Stewart Gill Ltd v Horatio Myer & Co Ltd*[70] the defendants purchased an overhead conveyor system from the claimants. The price was payable in instalments and the defendants claimed to be entitled to withhold the final 10 per cent because of certain breaches of contract by the claimants. A clause in the contract provided that "the Customer shall not be entitled to withhold payment of any amount due to the Company under the Contract by reason of any . . . set-off [or] counterclaim . . .". The Court of Appeal held that the clause fell within s.13(1)(b) as excluding a right or remedy which the customer would otherwise have enjoyed (see paragraph (b) above).

Under s.13(2) of UCTA a written agreement to submit disputes to arbitration is not regarded for the purposes of the Act as excluding or restricting liability.

Further provisions of UCTA

7–051   There are some further sections of UCTA which deal with specific issues in relation to unfair contract terms. These include s.4 (indemnity clauses); and s.5 (guarantees of consumer goods).

Indemnity clauses

7–052   Under an indemnity clause, a party to the contract agrees to indemnify (i.e. reimburse) a person for any loss arising from negligence or breach of contract. A typical example is where a person hires a car and the contract with the hire company contains a term providing that the hirer shall indemnify the company against any claims arising from the use of the car.

UCTA s.4(1) provides that where a party deals as consumer such a term will be ineffective except in so far as it satisfies the requirement of reasonableness (see para.7–054). This will be

---

[68]   Clauses that define one party's obligation under s.3 are controlled by s.3(2)(b)—see para.7–041 above. The reference to clauses excluding or restricting the relevant obligation or duty has no application to s.4 UCTA—indemnity clauses (see para.7–052).

[69]   [1990] 1 A.C. 831.

[70]   [1992] 1 Q.B. 600.

the case whether the person to be indemnified is a party to the contract or not. Further, the section applies whether the liability is directly that of the person to be indemnified or is incurred by them vicariously; or whether the liability is to the person dealing as consumer or to someone else (s.4(2)(a) and (b)).[71]

Guarantees of consumer goods

UCTA s.5 relates to guarantees given by manufacturers of consumer goods. The section provides as follows: **7–053**

> "(1) In the case of goods of a type ordinarily supplied for private use and or consumption, where loss or damage –
> (a) arises from the goods proving defective while in consumer use; and
> (b) results from the negligence of a person concerned in the manufacture or distribution of the goods, liability for the loss or damage cannot be excluded or restricted by reference to any contract term or notice contained in or operating by reference to a guarantee of the goods.
> (2) For these purposes –
> (a) goods are to be regarded as 'in consumer use' where a person is using them, or has them in possession for use, otherwise than exclusively for the purpose of a business; and
> (b) anything in writing is a guarantee if it contains or purports to contain some promise or assurance (however worded or presented) that defects will be made good by complete or partial replacement, or by repair, monetary compensation or otherwise.
> (3) This section does not apply as between the parties to a contract under or in pursuance of which possession or ownership of the goods passed."

This provision seeks to nullify the type of guarantee which promises the consumer that defective goods will be, for example, replaced or repaired but the manufacturer abandons any greater liability in tort. It should be noted that the section applies to goods "in consumer use"—this is a different concept from the situation where a party "deals as consumer" as used elsewhere in the Act. Moreover, as is made clear by s.5(3), the section has no application where the guarantee is given by a party who sells or hires goods directly to the consumer. Such cases will fall under ss.6 and 7 of UCTA.

The requirement of reasonableness

Where a clause must satisfy the requirement of reasonableness, s.11(1) of UCTA provides that   **7–054**
the test is:

> ". . . that the term shall have been a fair and reasonable one to be included having regard to the circumstances which were, or ought reasonably to have been, known to or in the contemplation of the parties when the contract was made."

---

[71] For cases involving indemnity clauses where neither party deals as consumer, see *Thompson v T Lohan (Plant Hire) Ltd* [1987] 1 W.L.R. 649; and *Phillips Products Ltd v Hyland Ltd* [1987] 2 All E.R. 631.

This is a very general test which leaves a great deal of room for judicial decision making—this makes it difficult for those drafting contracts to predict the validity or otherwise of a particular clause. What is made clear, however, is that the clause must be a fair and reasonable one to be included at the time of entering the contract and this means that subsequent events, such as the actual breach which has occurred, should be left out of account. Further, where a clause contains an exclusion or restriction of liability which fails to satisfy the reasonableness test, it is the whole clause that is invalid. The severance of unreasonable parts of a clause so as to allow reliance on reasonable parts is not permitted.[72] With regard to the burden of proof, it is for those who claim that a contract term or notice satisfies the reasonableness test to show that it does (s.11(5)).

Where the reasonableness requirement is required to be met in the case of a limitation clause, the court's attention is drawn to (a) the resources available on the part of the party relying on the clause to meet the liability; and (b) the extent to which insurance cover was open to the party purporting to limit the liability (s.11(4)). Consideration of these matters is not confined to limitation clauses since the availability and cost of insurance may be relevant to the reasonableness of an exclusion clause; and they are not the only matters governing the reasonableness of limitation clauses. In the context of limitation clauses, however, (a) and (b) above may be inter-related; thus a party may be unable to obtain insurance (or obtain cover at an acceptable cost) against certain liabilities because the potential level of damages awarded may be high. Given that such awards may severely strain the financial resources of the party relying on the clause, some limitation of liability may be fair and reasonable in the circumstances.

7–055   No further guidance as to reasonableness is provided by the Act, except that in relation to clauses excluding or restricting liability for breach of the implied terms as to quality, etc in contracts for the sale, hire-purchase and supply of goods (i.e. those governed by ss.6 and 7 of the Act) certain guidelines are laid down in Schedule 2 to the Act. The courts are prepared to look at these guidelines in other types of contract in addition to those under ss.6 and 7 and this approach has been judicially confirmed.[73]

Schedule 2 guidelines

7–056   The guidelines, so far as appear to the court to be relevant, are as follows:

> "(a) The strength of the bargaining positions of the parties relative to each other, taking into account (among other things) alternative means by which the customer's requirements could have been met."

Clearly, inequality of bargaining power, where a stronger party imposes terms on a weaker party, is a fundamental issue in assessing reasonableness. The second part of guideline (a) is related to the question of whether the supplier has a monopoly, or could the customer have obtained the goods or services elsewhere.

> "(b) Whether the customer received an inducement to agree to the term, or in accepting it had an opportunity of entering into a similar contract with other persons, but without having to accept a similar term."

[72] *Stewart Gill Ltd v Horatio Myer & Co Ltd* [1992] 1 Q.B. 600.
[73] *Overseas Medical Supplies Ltd v Orient Transport Services Ltd* [1999] 2 Lloyd's Rep. 273.

It may be a relevant factor that a customer is offered a discount or a special cheap rate or has a choice of suppliers, not all using the same terms. In some cases goods or services are offered more cheaply with an exclusion clause but more expensively without, what has been called a "two-tier price system". Thus in *R W Green Ltd v Cade Bros Farms*[74] a contract for the sale of seed potatoes was made subject to the standard terms of a trade association—a limitation clause relating to uncertified seed was upheld as the purchaser could have bought certified seed at a higher price.

> "(c) Whether the customer knew or ought reasonably to have known the existence and extent of the term (having regard, among other things, to any custom of the trade and any previous course of dealing between the parties)."

This guideline, it is suggested, is referring not to the common law test of incorporation but to the notion that the more familiar a clause is to a party, the more fair and reasonable it may be to uphold the clause. Thus it would be a relevant factor in determining reasonableness that a business party has contracted with another business many times in the past on the basis of the same terms, and has done so without objection.

> "(d) Where the term excludes or restricts any relevant liability if some condition is not complied with, whether it was reasonable at the time of the contract to expect that compliance with that condition would be practicable."

In *R W Green Ltd v Cade Bros Farms* (mentioned above) there was another clause which pro-   **7–057**
vided that seed potatoes were delivered on terms that any notice of rejection or complaint must be made within three days after delivery. The clause was held by Griffiths J. to be unreasonable in relation to a defect (a virus) not discoverable on inspection at the time of delivery. It was a defect that might not manifest itself until up to some nine months later.

> "(e) Whether the goods were manufactured, processed or adapted to the special order of the customer."

It is probably reasonable in such cases for the manufacturer to exclude most obligations other than conformity with specification.

The guidelines in Schedule 2 of UCTA are just that; they are only guidelines and the reliance to be placed on them (if at all) is a matter for the court. They are not exhaustive—the court may take into account other factors as considered appropriate.

Judicial approaches to the requirement of reasonableness

A number of decisions of the courts have, over the years, given some indication of the factors   **7–058**
that may be relevant in determining whether a clause satisfies the requirement of reasonableness. Case law in this area should be approached with caution because, as recognised by the Court of Appeal in *Phillips Products Ltd v Hyland*,[75] such decisions are of limited value as precedents.

---

[74] [1978] 1 Lloyd's Rep. 602.
[75] [1987] 2 All E.R. 631.

Each case turns on its own particular circumstances and so just because a particular type of clause has been held to be unreasonable in one case, it cannot automatically assumed that it will be struck down in all other circumstances.

That the judges have considerable scope is made plain by a statement of Lord Bridge in *George Mitchell (Chesterhall) Ltd v Finney Lock Seeds Ltd*[76] where, in explaining the proper approach to what is "fair and reasonable", he said:

> "[T]he court must entertain a whole range of considerations, put them in the scales on one side or the other, and decide at the end of the day on which side the balance comes down. There will sometimes be room for a legitimate difference of judicial opinion as to what the answer should be, where it will be impossible to say that one view is demonstrably wrong or the other demonstrably right . . . the appellate court should treat the original decision [of the trial judge] with the utmost respect and refrain from interference with it unless satisfied that it proceeded upon some erroneous principle or was plainly and obviously wrong."

The balancing exercise referred to by Lord Bridge can be seen in operation in the case of *George Mitchell v Finney Lock* itself, one of the two leading House of Lords decisions on the requirement of reasonableness.

7–059   The facts were that the respondents, who were farmers, ordered a quantity of Dutch winter white cabbage seeds for £201 from the appellants, a firm of seed merchants. The appellants supplied very inferior autumn cabbage seed which the respondents planted but the crop failed causing a loss of over £61,000. The respondents brought an action against the appellants who relied on a clause in their standard conditions of sale limiting liability to the replacement of the defective seeds or refunding the contract price. The clause was subject to the test of reasonableness contained (by the date of the judgment) in s.55(4) of the Sale of Goods Act 1979, a transitional provision which has been superseded by s.11 of UCTA. This test was whether it was fair and reasonable to allow reliance on the clause. A majority of the Court of Appeal held, applying common law principles, that as a matter of construction the clause did not apply. That court was, however, unanimous that the clause was unreasonable under the statutory test.

On appeal to the House of Lords, their Lordships found the clause to be sufficiently clear and unambiguous to cover the breach. On the issue of reasonableness Lord Bridge turned to the guidelines as to reasonableness in s.55(5) of the Sale of Goods Act which are now contained in Schedule 2 to UCTA (see above at para.7–056). The analysis of Lord Bridge is instructive and worth examining in detail.

The fact that the respondents knew of the condition from previous dealings (guideline (c)) and the magnitude of the damages in relation to the purchase price of the seeds weighted the scales in the appellants' favour. Two factors weighted the scales in the respondents' favour— first, the supply of the wrong type of seeds was due to negligence, and the seeds supplied could not be grown commercially; secondly, the seedsmen could have insured against the risk of crop failure without significantly increasing the price of the seeds. The relative bargaining power of the parties (guideline (a)) and the possibility of buying seeds without the limitation clause (guideline (b)) were related. Similar clauses had been incorporated in contracts between seedsmen and farmers for many years but the limitation clause had never been negotiated; nor had

---

[76] [1983] A.C. 803.

it been objected to by the farmers' representative body. In the view of Lord Bridge, these factors, viewed in isolation, were equivocal. He considered that the decisive factor was an admission by the seed company that they had in the past negotiated payments in excess of the value of the seeds if they thought the claim was genuine and justified. This concession showed that the seedsmen did not themselves think that the clause was fair and reasonable. Accordingly, the House of Lords held that the limitation clause was unreasonable. In addition to the statutory guidelines we see other factors being brought into account in this case—i.e. that the seedsmen made ex gratia payments instead of relying on the clause; that the breach was as a result of negligence; and the insurance position.

The other decision of the House of Lords addressing the requirement of reasonableness is **7–060** *Smith v Eric S Bush*.[77] The claimant, when buying a house, paid for the building society to carry out a mortgage valuation. The building society instructed the defendant firm to carry out a survey—their surveyor failed to inspect the loft. Had he done so, he would have seen that the chimney breasts had been cut away and the brickwork was unsupported. Eighteen months after the purchase, the chimneys came crashing down through the house. The House of Lords held that the defendants were liable in tort for negligence and were unable to rely on an unreasonable disclaimer.

Lord Griffiths laid down that there were four questions which should always be considered in deciding the issue of reasonableness (in italics):

(1) *Were the parties of equal bargaining power?* Clearly the buyer in this type of case lacks the bargaining power to object to the disclaimer.

(2) *In the case of advice, would it have been reasonably practical to obtain the advice from an alternative source taking into account considerations of cost and time?* In the case of properties at the bottom end of the housing market, buyers are likely to rely on the surveyor's report to the building society and this is a fact of which surveyors are aware. Such buyers will usually be under financial pressure and it is therefore less reasonable to expect the purchaser to go to the expense of arranging a second structural survey.

(3) *How difficult is the task being undertaken for which liability is being excluded?* In the case of difficult or dangerous undertakings it may be more reasonable to exclude liability. This was not the case with a house valuation which was work at the lower end of the surveyor's field of professional expertise.

(4) *What are the practical consequences of the decision on the question of reasonableness?* On this question, Lord Griffiths said:

"This must involve the sums of money potentially at stake and the ability of the parties to bear the loss involved, which in turn, raises the question of insurance . . . everyone knows that all prudent, professional men carry insurance, and the availability and cost of insurance must be a relevant factor when deciding which of two parties should be required to bear the risk of a loss. We are dealing in this case with a loss which will be limited to the value of a modest house and against which it can be expected that the surveyor will be insured."

His Lordship considered that requiring the surveying profession to bear the loss would not **7–061** cause significant hardship to the profession but could be financially disastrous for the purchaser. He continued:

[77] [1990] 1 A.C. 831.

"The result of denying a surveyor, in the circumstances of this case, the right to exclude liability will result in distributing the risk of negligence among all house purchasers through an increase in fees to cover insurance, rather than allowing the whole of the risk to fall on one unfortunate purchaser."

Of course the position may be very different where, say, a business concern purchases large commercial premises and on such transactions the House of Lords expressly reserved its position. In *Smith v Eric S Bush* we see the judges conducting a balancing exercise but one of a rather different type to the one in *George Mitchell v Finney Lock*. The effect of the ruling in the former case is to lay down a general principle as to the acceptability of a certain type of exclusion in a very common consumer transaction involving a particular type of purchaser. In this respect it is one of the most significant cases decided under UCTA.[78]

In general, at the level of the Court of Appeal there has been a disinclination to upset the decision taken by the trial judge on the question of reasonableness, thus following the dictum to that effect of Lord Bridge in *George Mitchell v Finney Lock*. In transactions involving businesses dealing on standard terms the courts have displayed a considerable reluctance to hold that terms are not fair and reasonable.

7–062   A good illustration of this, and a case where the decision of the trial judge was overturned, is the decision in *Granville Oil & Chemicals Ltd v Davies Turner & Co Ltd*.[79] The appellants were an international freight forwarding company and the respondents manufactured and exported paint products. The appellants agreed with the respondents to carry a return consignment of paint from Kuwait to the respondents' warehouse near Rotherham. The contract was subject to the standard conditions of the British International Freight Association (BIFA) of which clause 30A required any claim to be made in writing within 14 days and clause 30B required any legal action to be brought within nine months of the event giving rise to the alleged cause of action. The appellants agreed to arrange insurance of the consignment against all risks in transit. The paint was packed and shipped from Kuwait but when the paint was received by the respondents it was found to have been damaged in transit. Accordingly, the respondents made a claim against the appellants which was submitted within the 14 day time limit prescribed by clause 30A. The appellants then made an insurance claim on the respondents' behalf but the underwriters rejected the claim. The appellants did not inform the respondents of this until one day before the nine month period in clause 30B expired. Legal proceedings were not commenced by the respondents until some three months after the time limit had expired. They alleged breach of contract for the damage to the goods and for the failure to insure. The judge at first instance held on a preliminary issue that clause 30B did not satisfy the test of reasonableness in s.11 UCTA as it might be used in a situation where fraud was involved in that facts giving rise to a claim were concealed.

The Court of Appeal disagreed that the clause could be interpreted so as to cover fraud and held that the clause was fair and reasonable at the time the contract was made. The parties were of equal bargaining power and this was a commercial contract between business parties where the respondents may have been able to contract on other than BIFA conditions or make their own insurance arrangements. The respondents ought reasonably to have known of the time bar which had been sufficiently brought to their attention. The court considered that nine months

---

[78] For an interesting case where the approach of Lord Griffiths in *Smith v Eric S Bush* was applied to the reasonableness of a limitation clause in a contract between a local authority and a software supplier, see *St Albans City & District Council v International Computers Ltd* [1996] 4 All E.R. 481.

[79] [2003] EWCA Civ 570.

was a reasonable time limit as the loss or damage could be ascertained on delivery and there would be ample time to decide whether to bring proceedings. Freight forwarders needed a nine month time limit to enable them to make a claim against the carrier before that claim became time-barred which was usually after 12 months. With regard to the failure to insure, the court considered that it was in the circumstances fair and reasonable to fix the same time limit for a claim based on failure to insure as for the claim for damage to the goods. As the appellants had acted as agents of the respondents in pursuing the insurance claim, the appellants' failure to inform the respondents that there was no insurance cover was a breach of duty. As they were in continuing breach of this duty until the appellants were informed, under clause 30B the respondents would have had nine months in which to make a claim but unfortunately had not done so.[80] Tuckey L.J. (with whom Potter L.J. and Hart J. agreed) said:

> "[UCTA 1977] obviously plays a very important role in protecting vulnerable consumers from the effects of draconian contract terms. But I am less enthusiastic about its intrusion into contracts between commercial parties of equal bargaining strength, who should generally be considered capable of being able to make contracts of their choosing and expect to be bound by their terms."

Another case where the Court of Appeal differed from the decision of the trial judge on the reasonableness issue is *Watford Electronics Ltd v Sanderson CFL Ltd*.[81] In this case the claimants (W) sought damages from the defendants (S) for breach of an agreement to supply computer hardware and software. The contract contained (a) an entire agreement clause (see para.6–004); (b) a clause excluding liability for direct and consequential losses; and (c) a clause limiting liability to the price paid by W under the contract, which was £104,600. The system installed failed to perform satisfactorily and W sought damages of £5.5 million in respect of losses and other costs.   **7–063**

At first instance Judge Thornton Q.C. held that clauses (b) and (c) were unreasonable in their entirety and fell foul of s.11 of UCTA. The Court of Appeal found that the judge had erred in his approach as clauses (b) and (c) consisted of two distinct terms, in relation to each of which it was necessary to consider whether the reasonableness requirement was satisfied. Accordingly the judge's decision was reversed and the clauses upheld as reasonable. The court rejected the judge's finding that clause (b) covered liability for misrepresentation. The entire agreement clause prevented that liability from arising.

The Court of Appeal stressed that the contract had been negotiated between experienced businessmen of equal bargaining power. Unless it was clear that one party had taken unfair advantage of the other, or that a term was so unreasonable that it could not have been properly understood or considered, the court should not interfere. Gibson L.J., adopting a dictum of Judge T Forbes in *Salvage Association v CAP Financial Services Ltd*[81a] said:

> "Generally speaking, where a party well able to look after itself enters into a commercial contract and, with full knowledge of all relevant circumstances, willingly accepts the terms

---

[80] For other cases concerning BIFA conditions, see *Schenkers v Overland Shoes Ltd* [1998] 1 Lloyd's Rep. 498 where clause 23(A) (a no set-off clause) was held to be reasonable; and *Overseas Medical Supplies Ltd v Orient Transport Services Ltd* v Orient Services Ltd [1999] 2 Lloyds Rep. 273 where a limitation in clause 29(A) was held to be unreasonable. In both cases the decision of the judge at first instance was upheld by the Court of Appeal.

[81] [2001] EWCA Civ 317.

[81a] [1995] F.S.R. 654.

of the contract which provides for the apportionment of the financial risks of that transaction, I think that it is very likely that those terms will be held to be fair and reasonable."

Sentiments such as this and those of Tuckey L.J. in *Granville Oil & Chemicals Ltd v Davis Turner,* mentioned above, appear to cast UCTA as essentially a consumer protection measure since the scope for clauses in commercial contracts negotiated on terms of equality to be struck down would appear to be extremely limited.

UNFAIR TERMS IN CONSUMER CONTRACT REGULATIONS 1999 (UTCCR)

7–064   The EC Directive on Unfair Terms in Consumer Contracts (Directive 93/13) was originally transposed into domestic legislation by the Unfair Terms in Consumer Contracts Regulations 1994, which came into force on July 1, 1995. These regulations have now been replaced by the 1999 regulations[82] which came into operation on October 1, 1999. The purpose of the Directive was to harmonise the rules in member states relating to unfair terms in consumer contracts. To some extent the regulations overlap with UCTA but they are significantly broader in that they regulate unfair terms generally and not merely clauses which exclude or restrict liability, or have like effect. In other respects they are narrower as they apply only to consumers, as defined in the regulations.

When faced with the need to transpose the Directive in the early 1990s, the government opted to implement it by a set of regulations in the form of a self-standing statutory instrument, leaving UCTA unamended. With hindsight, it would have been better to repeal UCTA and enact a single domestic statute assimilating the provisions of the Directive and the matters controlled by UCTA. That the government did not do so has meant that two parallel but different legislative regimes have co-existed side by side. The result has been that the law has been rendered unnecessarily complex and confusing, particularly where both sets of rules (i.e. UCTA and UTCCR) apply. In fact, the Law Commission has now recommended the unification of the two regimes and has published a draft Bill (see para.7–074).

Scope of UTCCR

7–065   The regulations apply to unfair terms in contracts concluded between a seller or supplier and a consumer (reg.4(1)). The meaning of "unfair term" will be considered shortly; however the definition of "consumer" is fundamental to the application of the regulations. A consumer is "any natural person who . . . is acting for purposes which are outside his trade, business or profession" (reg.3). A consumer for the purposes of the regulations is therefore a human consumer. As to the other party to the contract, the "seller or supplier", this is defined as "any natural or legal person who . . . is acting for purposes relating to his trade, business or profession, whether publicly owned or privately owned" (reg.3).

The definition of consumer in UCTA, s.12 is in rather different terms to the one in UTCCR and, as we have seen, has been interpreted to apply to businesses acting outside their normal business (see para.7–043).

[82] SI 1999/2083.

The regulations are concerned with unfair terms in standard form consumer contracts, that is, terms which have not been individually negotiated. Under the regulations, a term "shall always be regarded as not having been individually negotiated where it has been drafted in advance and the consumer has not therefore been able to influence the substance of the term" (reg. 5(1)). The burden of proving that a term has been individually negotiated lies on the seller or supplier (reg.5(4)). Nevertheless, even where a term (or aspects of it) has been individually negotiated, this will not prevent the regulations applying to the rest of the contract if, overall, it is a pre-formulated standard form contract (reg. 5(3)). For example, a person entering a consumer credit agreement might well negotiate such matters as the period of repayment but this will not prevent the regulations applying to the other non-negotiated terms.

The regulations do not apply to terms which are incorporated to reflect the statutory or regulatory requirements of UK or Community law, or the provisions or principles of international conventions to which the Member States or the Community itself are a party (reg. 4(2) (a) and (b)).

Unfair terms

The regulations provide that an unfair term in a contract to which the regulations apply "shall not be binding on the consumer"; however the contract shall continue to bind the parties if capable of subsisting without the unfair term (reg. 8(1) and (2)).   **7–066**

When will a term be unfair? The test of unfairness in reg. 5(1) states:

> "A contractual term which has not been individually negotiated shall be regarded as unfair if, contrary to the requirement of good faith, it causes a significant imbalance in the parties' rights and obligations arising under the contract, to the detriment of the consumer."

The underlying concept in this rather convoluted test is that of "good faith"—not an entirely unfamiliar notion in English law but one that is more established in European jurisprudence, especially German law. This element of the test is considered at para.7–071. It is worth noting that Schedule 2 to the previous regulations of 1994 stated that in making an assessment of good faith, regard should be had to the following matters:

> "(a) the strength of the bargaining position of the parties;
> (b) whether the consumer had an inducement to agree to the term;
> (c) whether the goods or services were sold or supplied to the special order of the consumer; and
> (d) the extent to which the seller or supplier has dealt fairly or equitably with the consumer."

The first three of these guidelines, paragraphs (a)–(c) are very similar to some of the matters referred to in Schedule 2 of UCTA which are relevant to establishing the reasonableness of an exclusion clause (see para.7–056). Paragraph (d) is rather more general in scope. The guidelines derive from recital 16 of the Directive but were omitted from the revised UTCCR of 1999. In practice, however, they are clearly relevant matters in establishing good faith.

In addition, reg.6 provides that, in assessing whether a term is unfair, the following matters must be taken into account: (i) the nature of the goods or services for which the contract was concluded; (ii) all the circumstances attending the conclusion of the contract; and (iii) all the other terms of the contract or of another contract on which it is dependent.

7–067   Schedule 2 to the regulations contains an "indicative and non-exhaustive list" of some seventeen terms which may (but not necessarily must) be regarded as unfair. It is a "grey list" not a blacklist. By way of illustration, the examples in the list include the following:

> "(a) excluding or limiting the legal liability of a seller or supplier in the event of the death of a consumer or personal injury to the latter resulting from an act or omission of that seller or supplier . . .
> (c) making the agreement binding on the consumer whereas provision of services by the seller or supplier is subject to a condition whose realisation depends on his will alone . . .
> (e) requiring any consumer who fails to fulfil his obligation to pay a disproportionately high sum in compensation . . .
> (i) irrevocably binding the consumer to terms with which he had no real opportunity of becoming acquainted before the conclusion of the contract . . .
>
> (o) obliging the consumer to fulfil all his obligations where the seller or supplier does not perform his."

It is important to stress that the list is not exhaustive and terms of a type not listed in the Schedule may be found to be unfair. Some of the examples are of terms which are controlled by UCTA, see for example paragraph (a) above; and paragraph (i) above echoes the common law rules of incorporation. The examples in the list generally reflect the "significant imbalance" to which reference is made in the test of unfairness in reg.5(1).

Core provisions

7–068   Regulation 6(2) provides as follows with regard to "core provisions":

> "In so far as it is in plain, intelligible language, the assessment of fairness of a term shall not relate –
> (a) to the definition of the main subject matter of the contract, or
> (b) to the adequacy of the price or remuneration, as against the goods or services supplied in exchange."

This provision (subject to the plain intelligible language proviso) seeks to preserve the underlying caveat emptor position in not protecting a party from the consequences of a bad bargain even if the seller or supplier has not acted in good faith. Paragraph (b) above is relatively straightforward—the courts are not concerned with the fairness of the price that the consumer has to pay for the goods or services. The courts are not valuers and the rule reflects the common law principle that they should not be concerned with the adequacy of consideration. Paragraph (b), which is closely related to (a), is aimed at terms which go to the "core of the contract" or the "substance of the bargain".

Whether a term was a "core" was in issue in the first case to come before the courts on the interpretation of UTCCR (the 1994 version), *Director General of Fair Trading v First National*

Bank Plc.[83] The case concerned a term in the Bank's standard form consumer loan agreement. The term provided that, where the borrower was in default and the Bank had obtained a court judgment for the amount due, interest at the contract rate continued to be payable until the judgment was discharged. This was so despite the fact that the debtor had paid all the instalments due under the judgment. There was the possibility that borrowers who thought they had discharged their obligations by paying the instalments under the judgment would discover that they owed further sums of interest at the contract rate. The Director General sought an injunction to restrain the use of the standard term on the ground that it was unfair under the regulations. The Bank contended that the term was not a "core term" under reg.3(2) of the 1994 regulations (now reg.6(2) of the 1999 regulations) but that, in any event, the term was not unfair. The Court of Appeal held that the term was not a core term (and therefore the regulations did apply) but considered it to be unfair in view of the unpleasant shock or surprise it might give to consumers.

On appeal to the House of Lords, Lord Bingham (with whom the other members of the House were in agreement) had this to say about the core provision argument in this case:

> "[T]here is an important "distinction between the term or terms which express the substance of the bargain and 'incidental' (if important) terms which surround them" [adopting *Chitty on Contracts*, 28th edn, 1999, p 747]. The object of the regulations and the directive is to protect consumers against unfair and prejudicial terms in standard form contracts into which they enter, and that object would plainly be frustrated if regulation 3(2)(b) [now reg. 6(2) of the 1999 regulations] were so broadly interpreted as to cover any terms other than those falling squarely within it. In my opinion, the term, as part of a provision prescribing the consequences of default, plainly does not fall within it. It does not concern the adequacy of the interest earned by the bank as its remuneration but is designed to ensure that the bank's entitlement to interest does not come to an end on the entry of judgment."

Accordingly the House of Lords held that the regulations applied to the term in question but held that it was not unfair as it did not cause a significant imbalance in the parties' rights and obligations to the detriment of the consumer in a manner contrary to the requirement of good faith. It was legitimate because it had been sufficiently drawn to the attention of the consumer who would understand that the borrower must pay the principal and interest in return for the advance of the loan. The term was designed to ensure that the entry of judgment in favour of the Bank would not affect this position. The conclusion of the House of Lords that reg.6(2) should be interpreted restrictively was followed in *Bairstow Eves London Central v Smith*,[84] a case concerning the basis on which an estate agent's commission was charged.

7–069

Plain intelligible language

The regulations provide that the seller or supplier is to ensure that any written term of a contract is expressed in plain intelligible language, and if there is any doubt about the meaning of a written term, the interpretation which is most favourable to the consumer shall prevail (reg.7(1) and (2)).

7–070

---

[83] [2002] 1 A.C. 481. See s.17 of the Consumer Credit Act 2006 inserting a new s.130A into the Consumer Credit Act 1974. In the circumstances of the *First National Bank* case, the creditor must now notify the debtor of an intention to recover post-judgment interest. Where the creditor fails to provide such notice, the debtor will not be liable to pay interest.

[84] [2004] EWHC 263 (QB). See further *Bankers Insurance Co Ltd v South* [2003] EWHC 380 (QB).

Presumably it is intended that provisions which fail to satisfy this regulation will not be binding although the regulation does not specifically state this. Perhaps the intention is that terms which are not expressed with sufficient clarity will be regarded as unfair and the fact that core provisions (see above) may be struck down if not in plain language lends support to this interpretation.

Although one may applaud the sentiment behind this requirement, the problem is that contract terms, if they are to be unambiguous, may have to be couched in "legal jargon" to render them sufficiently certain to be enforceable. (See the discussion of the *contra proferentem* rule at para.7–023).

"Significant imbalance" and "good faith"

7–071   It will be recalled that, under the regulations, a term will be unfair if, contrary to the requirement of good faith, it causes a significant imbalance in the parties' rights and obligations arising under the contract, to the detriment of the consumer (reg.5(1)).

We have seen that in *Director General of Fair Trading v First National Bank* the House of Lords rejected the Court of Appeal's conclusion that the term in question was unfair. In approaching the test of unfairness (in what is now reg.5(1)) Lord Bingham, with whom the other members of the House agreed, had this to say regarding the requirement of "significant imbalance":

> "The requirement of significant imbalance is met if a term is so weighted in favour of the supplier as to tilt the parties' rights and obligations under the contract significantly in his favour. This may be by the granting to the supplier of a beneficial option or discretion or power, or by the imposing on the consumer of a disadvantageous burden or risk or duty."

Lord Bingham considered that the indicative list of terms which may be regarded as unfair in (what is now) Schedule 2 to the regulations (see para.7–066) were very good examples of unfair terms; whether a given term was unfair depended on whether it caused a significant imbalance—this involved looking at the contract as a whole. As to "good faith" his Lordship continued:

> "The requirement of good faith in this context is one of fair and open dealing. Openness requires that terms should be expressed fully, clearly and legibly, containing no pitfalls or traps. Appropriate prominence should be given to terms which might operate disadvantageously to the customer. Fair dealing requires that a supplier should not, whether deliberately or unconsciously, take advantage of the consumer's necessity, indigence, lack of experience, unfamiliarity with the subject matter of the contract, weak bargaining position or any other factor listed in or analogous to those listed in Schedule 2 of the Regulations ...Regulation [5(1)] lays down a composite test, covering both the making and substance of the contract."

7–072   Lord Bingham's reference to a "composite test" indicates that he considered that the test is concerned with both procedural and substantive unfairness. Lord Steyn felt that the argument that good faith was largely concerned with defects in negotiating procedures was not sustainable. He said that any "purely procedural or even predominantly procedural interpretation of the requirement of good faith must be rejected."

The test of unfairness under the regulations was applied by the Court of Appeal in *Bryen & Langley Ltd v Martin.*[85] One of the issues here was whether the adjudication provisions of the Joint Contracts Tribunal (JCT) standard form, which were found to be incorporated into a building contract, satisfied the test of fairness in the UTCCR. The court held that in deciding whether the terms were unfair under regulation 5(1) it was necessary to consider whether terms had been imposed on the consumer in such a way that the supplier had fallen short of the requirements of fair dealing. However, here the consumer had not had the terms imposed on him by the supplier (a building contractor) but by the consumer's agent (a quantity surveyor) who imposed them on the supplier in the invitation to tender. The supplier had therefore been asked to tender on the very terms of which the consumer alleged were unfair. Rhimer J. said:

> "The situation at which Regulation 5(1) is directed is one in which the supplier, who will normally be assumed to be in the stronger bargaining position, has imposed a standard form contract on the consumer containing terms which are . . . loaded unfairly in favour of the supplier."

Accordingly, there was no lack of openness, fair dealing or good faith in the manner in which the contract was made and therefore the consumer's case under the regulations failed.[86]

Supervision and enforcement

The UTCCR have an important supervisory and enforcement function; in other words, legal action is not the only means of attacking unfair terms in consumer contracts.   7–073

The Office of Fair Trading (OFT) must consider any complaint made to it about the fairness of any contract term drawn up for general use and may seek an injunction restraining the use of such a term (reg.10). These powers may also be exercised by certain qualifying bodies listed in Schedule 1 to the regulations, they must however notify the OFT of their intention (regs.11 and 12). The qualifying bodies include statutory regulators and the trading standards departments of local authorities. The OFT and the qualifying bodies also have powers to require traders to produce copies of their standard form contracts and give information about their use so as to facilitate investigation and compliance (reg.13). The OFT has the power to publish information and advice about the operation of the UTCCR and provide details of any relevant compliance measures (reg.15).

Exclusion and limitation clauses: conclusion

The relationship between the common law and statutory rules on exclusion clauses is in a state of transition—the role of the common law, especially the rules of construction, is likely to diminish in future, although the *contra proferentem* rule may continue to apply to cases of genuine ambiguity. In cases where the exclusion clause is clearly void under UCTA, for example the exclusion of liability for death or personal injury or for the quality and fitness of goods sold to a consumer, one might as well go straight to the statute. In other cases, it is appropriate to consider   7–074

---

[85] [2005] EWCA Civ 973.
[86] See also *Westminster Building Co Ltd v Beckingham* [2004] EWHC 138 (TCC); and *Lovell Projects Ltd v Legg* [2003] 1 B.L.R. 452. Cf *Picardi v Cuniberti* [2002] EWHC 2923.

first whether the clause has been incorporated into the contract and whether on its true construction it covers the liability in question, before applying the statutory controls.[87]

The greatest difficulty at present with the law on exclusion clauses is the confusing and uneasy co-existence of two sets of partly overlapping statutory controls, UCTA and UTCCR. As mentioned earlier in this chapter, the Law Commission has produced proposals for reform of the law in this area including a draft Bill.[88] The impetus for reform came from the government who saw the need for a more accessible unified statutory regime and for greater protection for small businesses which in many cases are in no better position than consumers in dealing with large organisations. In 2006 the government accepted the proposals and indicated that it would legislate them when a suitable opportunity arose.

The main recommendations of the Law Commission are given below. A single "Unfair Contract Terms Act" will replace both UCTA and UTCCR. The proposals relating to unfair contract terms include those relating to (i) consumer contracts; (ii) business contracts; and (iii) small business contracts.

Consumer contracts

7–075   The definition of "consumer" should only apply to natural persons acting for purposes unrelated to their business. This would put an end to the difficult case law on "dealing as consumer" under s.12 of UCTA (see para.7–043).

Clauses which are ineffective under UCTA (such as exclusions of liability for death and personal injury) will be likewise void under the new legislation. However, s.5 of UCTA (dealing with guarantees of consumer goods) would not be replicated. Further, in general *any* term in a consumer contract, whether individually negotiated or in standard form, will be subject to the "fair and reasonable" test (as to which, see below). The exception for "core provisions" will continue but subject to a proviso that such terms must be transparent (i.e. clearly presented in plain language) and substantially the same as the consumer reasonably expected.

Where terms are not automatically void under the legislation, the general test to be applied to the validity of contract terms is that they be "fair and reasonable"—there is no longer to be any express reference to "good faith". Whether a term is fair and reasonable is to be determined by taking into account (a) the extent to which the term is transparent; and (b) the substance and effect of the term, and all the circumstances existing when the contract was made. There are to be substantive guidelines for the application of the test included in the Act. There is to be a replacement for the Indicative List of terms which may regarded as unfair—it will be reformulated in more accessible language. The burden of proving that a term in a consumer contract is fair and reasonable is to rest on the business party.

Business contracts

7–076   In business to business transactions, certain provisions of UCTA are to be preserved. Thus liability for death or personal injury cannot be excluded at all and the exclusion of liability for

---

[87] This is certainly the case for students of the law of contract attempting examination questions on exclusion clauses. For a modern case decided solely on construction, see *University of Keele v Price Waterhouse* [2004] EWCA Civ 583.

[88] Law. Com. No 292 (2005) *Unfair Terms in Contracts*. See Beale and Goriely (2005) N.L.J. 318.

other loss or damage caused by negligence will be subject to the fair and reasonable test. The effect of s.3 of UCTA is also to be retained in that exclusion clauses in business contracts where a party is dealing on the other party's written standard terms of business will be subject to the fair and reasonable test. However, ss.6(3) and 7(3) and (4) of UCTA will not be replicated in the new legislation; this means that the test of reasonableness in business to business contracts where liability is excluded for the breach of the statutory implied terms as to description, quality etc disappears. The exclusion of such liability would fall under the successor to s.3 of UCTA.

Small business contracts

One of the main innovations of the new regime will be the control over small business con-   **7–077**
tracts—the aim is to provide a measure of protection for small businesses in their dealings with other businesses, regardless of size. A "small business" is to be defined as a business with nine or fewer employees, however there are to be exemptions from the regime for small businesses associated with larger ones. The control is not to extend to small business contracts with a value of more than £500,000. Any terms of a small business contract, other than core provisions, must satisfy the fair and reasonable test although the burden of establishing unfairness will fall on the small business.

Further reading

Spencer, Signature, Consent and the Rule in *L'Estrange v Graucob* [1973] C.L.J. 104.
Staughton, *How do the Courts Interpret Commercial Contracts?* [1999] C.L.J. 303.
Barendt, *Exclusion Clauses: Incorporation and Interpretation* (1972) 35 M.L.R. 644.
Macdonald, *In the Course of a Business – a Fresh Examination* (1999) 3 Web J.C.L. 1.
Bradgate, *Unreasonable Standard Terms* (1997) 60 M.L.R. 582.
Collins, *Good Faith in European Contract Law* (1994) 14 O.J.L.S. 229.

Chapter 8

PRIVITY OF CONTRACT

The rule of "privity of contract" is a long established principle in English law. It provides that **8–001** a person who is not privy to a contract, that is, a third party, can neither sue nor be sued on the contract. In other words, the rule treats a contract as an essentially private affair between two parties under which third parties acquire neither liabilities nor rights, even though they might well have some interest which would be served by the performance of the contract.

Where the rule prevents a contract imposing a *burden* on a third party, the rule is, in most situations, perfectly sensible and just. Thus if A enters into a contract with B stipulating that a third party C will swim across the Channel on New Year's Day, C cannot be compelled to do so against his wishes. The contract cannot be enforced against the third party.

The rule of privity is less easy to justify where a contract between A and B confers a *benefit* on a third party C. Under the traditional doctrine, C has no rights under the contract, even if it was intended to benefit him. We encountered this principle when considering the rule that "consideration must move from the promisee" in Chapter 4, where in *Tweddle v Atkinson*[1] the claimant's father and prospective father-in-law entered into a contract that they would each pay the claimant a sum of money. The claimant could not enforce the contract as he had provided no consideration under it, even though the contract purported to give the claimant full power to sue the parties. However, he was not a party to the contract and would have failed on this ground alone because of the doctrine of privity.

Legislative reform to allow the third party to sue in circumstances such as those that arose in **8–002** *Tweddle v Atkinson* and similar cases was mooted over 70 years ago by the Law Revision Committee. In 1996 the Law Commission put forward draft legislation which ultimately became the Contracts (Rights of Third Parties) Act 1999 (C(ROTP)A). Where certain conditions are satisfied, the Act allows a third party to enforce a contract made for their benefit. The provisions of the Act will be considered in detail later in this chapter.

It is important to note that C(ROTP)A does not do away with the fundamental rule of privity regarding the enforcement of the benefit of a contract by a third party, but it does create a substantial exception to the rule. The basic rule should be retained because there will be cases where the parties to a contract simply do not intend the third party to enforce the contract. Indeed if there was a general right given to third parties to enforce the benefit of a contract, it might become arguable that the right should extend to an indeterminate number of unintended or incidental beneficiaries. So far as the rule of privity prevents the burden of a contract being imposed on a third party, C(ROTP)A does not impact on this principle.

[1] (1861) 1 B. & S. 393. See para.4–009 for a fuller discussion of the case.

Dissatisfaction with the rule of privity has led to a number of exceptions to the rule being carved out over the years in common law, equity and statute. These matters will be discussed later in the chapter but we begin by looking at the development of the doctrine.

DEVELOPMENT OF THE DOCTRINE OF PRIVITY

Common law

8–003   The modern common law doctrine of privity is generally regarded as being derived from *Tweddle v Atkinson* in the mid-nineteenth century. In the case, Wightman J., repudiating earlier authority said:

> "Some of the old decisions appear to support the proposition that a stranger to the . . . contract may maintain an action upon it . . . But there is no modern case in which the proposition has been supported. On the contrary, it is now established that no stranger to the consideration can take advantage of a contract, although made for his benefit."

The privity rule became more firmly established as a rule related to, but distinct from, the rule that consideration must move from the promise, by the decision of the House of Lords in *Dunlop Pneumatic Tyre Co Ltd v Selfridge & Co Ltd*.[2]

The facts of the case were that that the claimants, tyre manufacturers, sold tyres to Dew & Co, wholesale distributors, on terms that Dew & Co would obtain an undertaking from retailers that they would not sell below the claimant's list price. Dew & Co sold some of the tyres to the defendants, who agreed to the minimum resale price term. The defendants, however, retailed them below list price and the claimants sought an injunction and damages. The House of Lords held that the action should fail—although there was a contract between Dew & Co and the defendants, the claimants were not a party to it; and further, the claimants had not provided any consideration for the defendants' undertaking not to sell below list price. It followed that the obligation that the claimants sought to impose on the defendants was unenforceable. In the course of his speech Viscount Haldane L.C. laid down an authoritative ruling:

> "My Lords, in the law of England, certain principles are fundamental. One is that only a person who is a party to a contract can sue on it. Our law knows nothing of a *jus quaesitum tertio* [third party right] arising by way of contract. Such a right might be conferred by way of property, as, for example, under a trust, but it cannot be conferred on a stranger to a contract as a right to enforce the contract *in personam*. A second principle is that if a person with whom a contract not under seal has been made is to be able to enforce it consideration must have been given by him to the promisor or to some other person at the promisor's request."

8–004   The requirement, which is clearly laid down by the House of Lords in *Dunlop v Selfridge*, that, in order to be able to enforce a contract, the claimant must both be a party to the contract

---

[2] [1915] A.C. 847.

and have provided consideration under it has led to some elaborate devices being judicially constructed in order to avoid the rule of privity.[3] As we shall see, where the third party has an enforceable right to the benefit of the contract under the provisions of C(ROTP)A, there is no requirement that the third party should have provided consideration, providing of course that the promisee has under the contract supplied consideration.

Since *Dunlop v Selfridge* in 1915, a number of challenges to the rule of privity were mounted but the traditional rule was confirmed once again by the House of Lords in 1962 in *Scruttons Ltd v Midland Silicones Ltd*[4] (the case is discussed at para.7–034) where their Lordships denied the benefit of an exclusion clause to a third party to a contract. The House did, however, accept the possibility that the doctrine could be evaded by means of agency in circumstances where the third party had provided consideration although the conditions were not present in the case itself.[5]

A few years later a determined assault was made by the Court of Appeal on the privity rule in the case of *Beswick v Beswick*.[6] An attempt was made to rely on s.56(1) of the Law of Property Act 1925 which provides that a person may acquire an interest in land or other property, or the benefit of a covenant relating to land or other property, although not actually named as a party in the conveyance or other document. Further, s.205(1) provides that, unless the context otherwise requires, the word "property" means any interest in real or personal property. Liberally interpreted, these provisions could present a means of evading the doctrine of privity, particularly if the reference to "other property" could embrace contractual rights. In *Beswick v Beswick*, a nephew agreed to a buy coal merchant's business belonging to his uncle, and in return the nephew agreed to pay a weekly sum to his uncle, and after the uncle's death, a weekly sum would be paid to the uncle's widow. After the uncle died, the nephew refused to make the payments and the widow brought an action for arrears of the weekly sum and for specific performance of the agreement. She sued (i) as adminstratrix of her deceased husband's estate, and (ii) in her personal capacity, relying on s.56(1).

The Court of Appeal unanimously held that the widow was entitled as adminitratrix to an order of specific performance; a majority of the court (Lord Denning M.R. and Danckwerts L.J.) found that she could also succeed in her personal capacity by virtue of s.56(1). On appeal to the House of Lords, their Lordships upheld her claim as adminitratrix and awarded specific performance of the agreement—her personal claim, however, should fail as s.56(1) was limited to transactions involving realty. There was a presumption that the Law of Property Act 1925, being a consolidating Act, did not fundamentally alter the common law by a "sidewind". Lord Hodson said:

8–005

> "I am unable to believe that such an enormous change in the law has been made by s.56 as to establish that an agreement by A with B to pay money to C gives C a right to sue on the contract."

Although the House was able to achieve what was undoubtedly a just result by upholding the widow's claim on other grounds, the doctrine of privity was once again re-affirmed.

---

[3] See, for example, *New Zealand Shipping Co Ltd v A M Satterthwaite & Co Ltd, The Eurymedon* [1975] A.C. 154, discussed at para.7–035.
[4] [1962] A.C. 466.
[5] But see the *New Zealand Shipping* case at para.7–035.
[6] House of Lords: [1968] A.C. 58; Court of Appeal: [1966] 3 W.L.R. 396.

Since that time there have been forceful judicial criticisms of the doctrine, most notably in *Darlington Borough Council v Wiltshier Northern Ltd*[7] where Steyn J. stated:

"The case for recognising a contract for the benefit of a third party is simple and straightforward. The autonomy of the will of the parties should be respected. The law of contract should give effect to the reasonable expectations of contracting parties. Principle certainly requires that a burden should not be imposed on a third party without his consent. But there is no doctrinal, logical or policy reason why the law should deny effectiveness to a contract for the benefit of a third party where that is the expressed intention of the parties."

Ultimately, the impetus for reform came from the Law Commisssion, and C(ROTP)A was largely based on the Commission's report, *Privity of Contract: Contracts for the Benefit of Third Parties* published in 1996.[8] The Commission did not favour wholesale abolition of the common law rule of privity in so far as it prevented the benefit of a contract being enforced by a third party. Such a reform would be likely to create uncertainty and open the floodgates to claims by unintended and incidental beneficiaries. Instead, it favoured creating a statutory exception to the rule giving third parties the right to enforce the benefit of a contract where it is the intention of the contracting parties that the third party should have such a right. The legislation should not therefore affect any of the other established exceptions to privity (to be discussed later in this chapter) and if the third party can successfully base their claim on one of these they are not disentitled from so doing.

Contracts (Rights of Third Parties) Act 1999 (C(ROTP)A)

8–006   The Act came into force on November 11, 1999, but does not apply in relation to a contract entered into before May 11, 2000 (s.10(2) of the Act). The Act also applies to contracts made during the six months on or after November 11, 1999, if the contract expressly provides that the Act will apply (s.10(3)). In this discussion the "promisor" means the party to the contract against whom the contract is enforceable by the third party; and the "promisee" means the party to the contract by whom the term is enforceable by the third party (s.1(7)).

Enforcement of third party right – s.1 C(ROTP)A

8–007   The fundamental modification to the common law brought about by the Act is to be found in s. 1(1) and (2). C(ROTP)A, s.1(1) states:

"Subject to the provisions of this Act, a person who is not a party to the contract (a "third party") may in his own right enforce a term of the contract if –
(a) the contract expressly provides that he may, or
(b) subject to subsection (2), the term purports to confer a benefit on him."

---

[7]   [1995] 1 W.L.R. 68. See also *Woodar Investment Development Ltd v Wimpey Construction (UK) Ltd* [1980] 1 All E.R. 571, at p 591. Lord Scarman said: "If the opportunity arises, I hope the House will reconsider *Tweddle v Atkinson* and the other cases which stand guard over this unjust rule."

[8]   Law. Com. No. 242, Cmnd. 3329.

However, 1(2) provides that s.1(1)(b) above will "not apply if on a proper construction of the contract it appears that the parties did not intend the term to be enforceable by the third party." Thus, in accordance with s.1(1)(a), parties wishing to be absolutely sure that the third party will be able to enforce the benefit should say so explicitly in the contract. A slightly less certain route to achieving the same objective is provided by subsections 1(1)(b) and (2) which seem to establish a rebuttable presumption in favour of an enforceable third party right where a term purports to confer a benefit on a third party—this may be displaced by an objective construction of the contract as a whole. This second test of enforceability may assist those parties who do not have the benefit of sound legal advice. In the first reported case under the Act, *Nisshin Shipping Co Ltd v Cleaves & Co Ltd*,[9] the High Court held that the effect of s.1(2) was to provide that s.1(1)(b) was disapplied if on a proper construction it appeared that the parties did not intend third party enforcement—if the contract was neutral on the question, s.1(2) did not disapply s.1(1)(b). Of course, it follows that parties who do not wish the third party to have an enforceable right can specifically say so in their contract, and the decision in *Nisshin Shipping v Cleaves* underlines the fact that they should do so in clear and unambiguous terms. The interpretation adopted by the court in *Nisshin Shipping v Cleaves* was confirmed by the Court of Appeal in *Laemthong International Lines Co Ltd v Artis, The Laemthong Glory (No 2)*.[10]

The Act provides that the third party must be expressly identified in the contract "by name, as a member of a class or as answering a particular description but need not be in existence when the contract is entered into" (s.1(3)). This provision restricts the range of beneficiaries yet it does confer rights on children yet to be born, spouses yet to marry or incorporated bodies not yet formed. It seems that the rights must be conferred by contract and not, for example by a will, as in *White v Jones*.[11] C(ROTP)A, s.1(3) was considered by the Court of Appeal in *Avraamides v Colwill*[12] Here, the contract in question failed to identify any third party or class of third parties. Waller L.J. said that s.1(3), "by the use of the word 'express' simply does not allow a process of construction or implication." The Act therefore did not apply.

8–008 The rights which are conferred on the third party "are subject to and in accordance with any other relevant terms of the contract" (s.1(4)), thus the rights conferred on the third party might be limited by other express terms of the contract. Once it is established that a third party has an enforceable right, the Act makes available to them any remedy that would have been available to them in an action for breach of contract, e.g. damages, injunction or specific performance (s.1(5)); likewise they may take the benefit of an exclusion or limitation clause(s.1(6)).

The common law rule that "consideration must move from the promisee" has not been abolished by the Act but it does not apply where a third party has an enforceable right under s.1 C(ROTP)A.

Variation and rescission of the contract—s.2 C(ROTP)A

8–009 At common law the parties to a contract are free to vary or rescind the terms of a contract as they wish. This could mean that where A contracts with B to confer a benefit on C at some time in the future, there is nothing to prevent A and B, the day after their contract and without C's

---

[9] [2003] EWHC 2602. See Burrows [2000] L.M.C.L.Q. 540.
[10] [2005] 1 Lloyds Rep. 688.
[11] [1995] 2 A.C. 207.
[12] [2006] EWCA Civ 1533.

consent, agreeing to reduce or even cancel C's benefit altogether. A completely unfettered right to do this at any time might make it too easy to defeat the object of the rights granted by s.1; on the other hand, to disallow rescission or variation in all circumstances would probably be unduly restrictive. Accordingly, the Law Commission recommended a compromise which is to be found in s.2 of the Act.

Section 2, to some extent, preserves the underlying freedom of contract position as s.2(3) provides that the parties may include an express term to the effect that the contract may be rescinded or varied without the third party's consent; or they may include a term which provides for different provisions for consent from those laid down in the Act. If the parties do not include such a clause, the provisions of s.2(1)(a)–(c) come into play which provide that the parties to the agreement may not rescind or vary the beneficial term to the detriment of the third party if:

(a) the third party has communicated to the promisor, by words or conduct, his assent to the relevant term (s.2 (1)(a)). The "postal rule" of acceptance (see para.2–042 above) does not apply in this situation (s.2(2));

(b) the promisor is aware that the third party has relied on the relevant term (s.2(1)(b)); or

(c) the promisor can reasonably be expected to have foreseen that the third party would rely on the relevant term and the third party has in fact relied on it (s.2(1)(c).

Thus once an enforceable third party right arises under s.1, s.2(1) imposes restrictions on the freedom of the parties subsequently to cancel or vary the agreement, unless the contract otherwise provides under s.2(3). Where the third party has relied on the term, there is no requirement that they should have done so to their detriment—the reliance could be beneficial to the third party. All that is required is that the promisor is aware of the reliance, or that the third party has relied on the term and the promisor could reasonably be expected to have foreseen that there would be such reliance.

The court (or arbitral tribunal) has the power to dispense with third party consent if the third party's whereabouts cannot reasonably be ascertained or if they are mentally incapable of giving consent (s.2(4); or if it cannot reasonably be ascertained whether or not the third party has in fact relied on the term (s.2(5). The court (or arbitral tribunal), where it dispenses with third party consent, may impose such conditions as it thinks fit, including a condition requiring compensation to be paid to the third party (s.2(6)).

Defences—s.3 C(ROTP)A

8–010   Section 3(2) of the Act provides that the promisor may, unless the contract otherwise provides (s.3(5)), raise against the third party any defence or set-off that could have been raised by the promisee. In other words, so far as the enforceability of the beneficial term is concerned, under the Act, the third party is in the same position as the promisee would have been. The Explanatory Notes to the Act[13] state that "a third party can no more enforce a void, discharged or unenforceable contract than the promisee could" and give the following example of the operation of s.3(2):

"P1 (the promisor) and P2 (the promisee) contract that P2 will sell goods to P1, who will

---

[13] The Notes are prepared by the Lord Chancellor's Department as a guide to understanding the Act. They are not part of the Act and have not been endorsed by Parliament.

pay the contract price to P3 (the third party). In breach of contract, P2 delivers goods that are not of the standard contracted for. In an action for the price by P3 (just as in an action for the price by P2) P1 is entitled to reduce or extinguish the price by reason of the damages for breach of contract."

The above example concerns breach of contract but no doubt the remedies available to the third party against the promisor would be similarly diminished or extinguished where the promisee has induced a contract by some vitiating factor such as fraud, misrepresentation or duress.

Under s.3(3) defences or set-offs arising from a wholly unrelated transaction between the promisor and the promisee may be raised by the promisor against the third party where there is an express term in the contract to that effect. The Explanatory Notes give an illustration of where this situation may arise:

"P1 [the promisor] and P2 [the promisee] contract that P1 will pay P3 [the third party] if P2 transfers his car to P1. P2 owes P1 money under a wholly unrelated contract. P1 and P2 agree to an express term in the contract which provides that P1 can raise against a claim by P3 any matter which would have given P1 a defence or set-off to a claim by P2."

Further, s.3(4) provides that the promisor, unless the parties have agreed otherwise (s.3(5)), may rely on any defences, set-offs or counterclaims against the third party which do not arise from the contract itself but from previous dealings. Thus, for example[14]:   **8–011**

"P1 [the promisor] contracts with P2 [the promisee] to pay P3 [the third party] £1,000. P3 already owes P1 £600. P1 has a set-off to P3's claim so that P1 is only bound to pay P3 £400."

Under s.3(6), where an action is brought *against* the third party and they seek to rely on a term of the contract under s.1, they may not do so if they could not have done, had they been a party to the contract. This will be particularly relevant to an exclusion or limitation clause—thus if such a clause is invalid as between the promisor and promisee, it cannot be relied upon by the third party.

Right of promisee to enforce the contract—s.4 C(ROTP)A

The right of the promisee to enforce the contract against the promisor is preserved by s.4 which provides that s.1 "does not affect any right of the promisee to enforce any term of the contract."   **8–012**

Protection of promisor from double liability—s.5 C(ROTP)A

The fact that s.4 (above) expressly preserves the promisee's rights could open up the possibility that the promisor is exposed to double liability in that they might have to compensate both the promisee and the third party in respect of the same loss. This undesirable prospect is addressed   **8–013**

---

[14] Explanatory Notes, para.18.

by s.5. Where the promisee has recovered substantial damages in respect of the third party's loss, and the third party has an enforceable right under s.1, this will be taken into account in any proceedings brought by the third party. Thus any award to the third party may be reduced by the court (or arbitral tribunal) to the extent considered appropriate.[15]

Exempted contracts—s. 6 C(ROTP)A

8–014   There are some categories of contract which are exempted from the operation of the Act. Thus no rights are conferred on a third party in the case of contracts on a bill of exchange, promissory note or other negotiable instrument (s.6(1)). No rights are conferred on a third party in the case of any contract binding on a company and its members under s.14 of the Companies Act 1985 (s.6(2)); or in the case of the incorporation document of a limited liability partnership or any limited liability partnership agreement as defined in the Limited Liability Partnership Regulations 2001 (s.6(2A). Enforcement of the terms of an employment contract, as against the employee by a third party, are excluded (s.6(3)(a)).

Further, the Act does not create any enforceable third party rights in the case of a contract for the carriage of goods by sea; a contract for the carriage of goods by rail or road; or for the carriage of cargo by air which is subject to the rules of the appropriate international transport convention (s.6(5)). There is an exception, however, in that a third party may in reliance on s.1 C(ROTP)A avail themselves of an exclusion or limitation clause in such contracts. This means that a third party may rely on an exclusion or limitation clause in a contract of carriage without having to rely on the agency device in *New Zealand Shipping Co Ltd v A M Satterthwaite & Co Ltd*.[16]

Further provisions

8–015   C(ROTP)A, s.7(1) states that the Act "does not affect any right or remedy of a third party that exists or is available apart from this Act." Established judicial exceptions to privity will, therefore, continue to exist as will, of course, the various statutory exceptions to the rule.

Under s.7(2), a third party may not rely on s.2(2) of the Unfair Contract Terms Act 1977 in order to challenge the validity of an exclusion or limitation clause which restricts the promisor's liability for loss or damage caused by negligence. It may be recalled that UCTA, s.2(2) requires that clauses excluding or restricting liability for loss or damage caused by negligence, other than for death or personal injury, must satisfy a requirement of reasonableness (see para.7–054). Thus the promisor may rely on the clause even where the clause would otherwise be regarded as invalid under UCTA, if it does not satisfy the test of reasonableness under s.11 UCTA. A clause restricting liability for death or personal injury would, of course, be void in any event under s.2(1) of UCTA.

Before considering the established exceptions to privity, it is necessary to examine the position at common law where the promisee brings an action to enforce a term of the contract which benefits a third party. This possibility pre-dates C(ROTP)A and is unaffected by the new Act.

---

[15] The Act does not provide for the converse situation but presumably any substantial damages awarded to the third party will be taken into account in awarding damages to the promisee, although in most cases the promisee's loss may only be nominal.

[16] [1975] A.C. 154. See para.7–035.

Action brought by promisee

Where A enters into a contract with B, under which A promises B that A will confer a benefit **8–016** on C, we have seen that at common law C has no rights because of privity, although since 1999 C(ROTP)A has introduced a major exception to the fundamental rule. It should not be forgotten, however, that A and B are parties to a contract and therefore there is nothing to prevent the promisee B suing the promisor A for breach of contract where A has failed to deliver the agreed benefit to C. This possibility pre-dates C(ROTP)A and the new Act does not remove the promisee's right to attempt to enforce the contract in this way.

The problem here is that in many cases, damages will be the usual remedy, unless specific performance can be ordered. In strict theory the damages will only be nominal since the claimant B, as a contracting party, will have suffered no direct loss; and, as a general rule, the promisee will be unable to recover damages for the loss suffered by the third party. Nevertheless the Court of Appeal was prepared to award such damages in *Jackson v Horizon Holidays Ltd.*[17]

In this case, the claimant booked a package holiday with the defendants in Ceylon (now Sri Lanka) for himself, his wife and twin sons aged three. The hotel accommodation was described in glowing terms in the defendants' brochure but it turned out to be of an unacceptably poor standard, far below what had been promised. The problems included fungus on the walls of the children's bedroom, unclean WC, dirty bed linen, unpalatable catering and many of the promised facilities, such as a golf course, were lacking. The family holiday was ruined. The claimant sued the defendants for breach of contract—the defendants admitted liability but sought to challenge the amount of damages (£1,100) awarded by the trial judge. This sum was slightly less than the cost of the holiday. The Court of Appeal dismissed the appeal, holding that the damages were not excessive. The claimant had purchased a family holiday and although only he could sue for damages for breach of the contract, he could be awarded damages not only for his own distress and disappointment but also for that of his wife and children. As Lord Denning M.R. explained:

> "In this case it was a husband making a contract for the benefit of himself, his wife and children. Other cases readily come to mind. A host makes a contract with a restaurant for a dinner for himself and his friends. The vicar makes a contract for a coach trip for the choir. In all these cases there is only one person who makes the contract . . . It would be a fiction to say that the contract was made by all the family, or all the guests, or all the choir . . . the real truth is that in each instance, the father, the host or the vicar, was making a contract himself for the benefit of the whole party. In short, a contract by one for the benefit of third persons."

Lord Denning thought that in such cases the contracting party could recover damages not only **8–017** for their own loss but also for the other members of the group. He relied on a dictum in *Lloyd's v Harper*[18] where Lush L.J. said:

> "I consider it to be an established rule of law that where a contract is made with A for the benefit of B, A can sue on the contract for the benefit of B and recover all that B could have recovered if the contract had been made with B himself."

---

[17] [1975] 1 W.L.R. 1468. For an unusual case where the promisee was able to obtain the benefit for the third party through a stay of proceedings, see *Snelling v John G Snelling Ltd* [1973] Q.B. 87.
[18] (1880) 16 Ch. D. 290.

Rejecting the view that Lush L.J. was referring to a contract where A was trustee for B, Lord Denning thought the dictum was correct, as long as the law disallowed the third parties from suing for damages. He saw it as the only way in which a just result could be achieved. Lord Denning was therefore putting forward a general principle which was difficult to reconcile with *Beswick v Beswick* (see para.8–004). James L.J., however, in a brief judgment seems to have quantified the figure awarded to the claimant as consisting of his own disappointment and his additional disappointment caused by the distress of his wife and children.[19]

It was not long before the issue of damages awarded to cover the third party's loss came before the House of Lords. In *Woodar Investment Development Ltd v Wimpey (UK) Construction Ltd*[20] the claimants Woodar agreed to sell land at Cobham, Surrey to the defendants Wimpey for £850,000. It was a condition of the agreement that, on completion, the defendants should pay £150,000 of the contract price to a third party, Transworld Trade Ltd. The contract provided (clause E(a)(iii)) that the defendants could withdraw from the transaction if before completion a statutory body "shall have commenced" compulsory acquisition of the land. Both parties were aware that a draft compulsory purchase order had already been made at the time of the contract and, on this basis the defendants purported to repudiate the contract. The claimants sought damages for wrongful repudiation, including the loss sustained by the third party, Transworld. The House of Lords, by a majority, held that even though the defendants were in error (clause E(a)(iii) only applied to compulsory acquisition launched after the date of the contract) there had not been a wrongful repudiation—they had merely relied on a term of the contract and had not manifested an intention to abandon it. The House considered, obiter, the question of damages in the light of *Jackson v Horizon Holidays Ltd*.

8–018   The views of Lord Denning M.R. in *Jackson* were disapproved as being too wide—Lord Wilberforce stated:

> "I am not prepared to dissent from the actual decision in [*Jackson v Horizon Holidays Ltd*]. It may be supported either as a broad decision on the measure of damages (per James LJ) or possibly as an example of a type of contract – examples of which are persons contracting for family holidays, ordering meals in restaurants, hiring a taxi for a group – calling for special treatment . . . there are many situations in daily life which do not fit neatly into conceptual analysis, but which require some flexibility in the law of contract. *Jackson's* case may well be one."

Their Lordships refuted Lord Denning's reliance on the judgment of Lush L.J. in *Lloyds v Harper*—the case rested on principles of agency. Their Lordships confirmed that where a contract provided for a sum of money to be paid to a third party, a promisee who has himself suffered no loss cannot recover substantial damages for non-payment of that sum unless it could be shown that the promisee was acting as agent or trustee for the third party.

Another exception to the general rule that the promisee cannot recover substantial damages on behalf of a third party was allowed by the House of Lords in *Linden Gardens Trust Ltd v Lanesta Sludge Disposals Ltd, St Martins Property Corporation Ltd v Sir Robert McAlpine &*

---

[19] Note that the Package Travel, Package Holidays and Package Tours Regulations 1992 (SI 1992/3288) which regulate such holidays as that in *Jackson v Horizon Holidays Ltd* provide that a consumer of a package holiday includes "the principal contractor" and any persons on whose behalf the principal contractor agrees to purchase the package holiday—the "principal beneficiaries" (reg. 2(2). Such parties acquire direct contractual rights against the tour provider.

[20] [1980] 1 W.L.R. 277.

Sons Ltd.[21] Under a building contract A employed B to carry out work on his land, in circumstances where it was understood that A was likely to transfer the property to C. The property was later transferred to C. However, the work done by B was defective and in breach of contract and C incurred expenditure in remedying the defects. C could not sue since the assignment of contractual rights was contractually excluded. In an action brought by A for breach of contract, B argued that the damages should only be nominal as the loss had been suffered by a third party. The House of Lords did not accept the argument and held that this was a situation in which substantial damages could be recovered.

Lord Browne-Wilkinson (with whom Lords Ackner, Bridge and Keith agreed) relied on an exception developed in shipping law.[22] He said:

> "The contract was for a large development of property which, to the knowledge of both [A] and [B], was going to be occupied, and possibly purchased, by third parties and not by [A] itself. Therefore it could be foreseen that damage caused by breach would cause loss to a later owner and not merely to the original contracting party, [A] . . . In such a case, it seems to me proper, as in the case of carriage of goods by land, to treat the parties as having entered into the contract on the footing that [A] would be able to enforce contractual rights for the benefit of those who suffered from defective performance but who, under the terms of the contract, could not acquire any right to hold [B] liable for the breach . . . the rule provides 'a remedy where no other would be available to a person sustaining loss which under a rational legal system ought to be compensated by the person who has caused it'."

Lord Griffiths expressed the principle on a broader ground than Lord Browne-Wilkinson. His Lordship could not accept that in a contract for labour and materials (such as the present case) the recovery of substantial damages was dependent upon the claimant having a proprietary interest in the subject matter of the contract at the date of the breach. This view seems to be based on the theory that A suffers a loss because they did not receive what they had bargained for—this is their loss. Lord Bridge and Keith expressed some sympathy for this approach. **8–019**

In *Darlington Borough Council v Wiltshier Northern Ltd*[23] the Court of Appeal applied the *Linden Gardens* principle (as expressed by Lord Browne-Wilkinson in that case) to a situation where A never owned the land affected by the breach—it was owned by the third party C from the outset. This "conservative and limited" extension of the principle was justified by Steyn L.J. on the "need to avoid a demonstrable unfairness which no rational legal system should tolerate". If it were otherwise, the liability of B would fall into a "legal black hole" which would result from a strict application of the rule of privity, debarring the third party C from suing on the contract and limiting the promisee B to the recovery of nominal damages. However, the *Linden Gardens* decision was distinguished by the House of Lords in the case of *Alfred McAlpine Construction Ltd v Panatown Ltd*.[24] The facts were similar to the *Darlington* case in that A had never owned the land in question but there was a difference in that the third party C had also entered into a direct contractual obligation with B (a "duty of care deed") which required B to use reasonable care and skill in carrying out the works. A majority of the House of Lords (3-2) held that, where the work carried out by B was defective, A could not recover substantial damages. Where C had a direct right to sue the contractor, there was no necessity

---

[21] [1994] 1 A.C. 85.
[22] In *Albacruz (Cargo Owners) v Albazero (Owners), The Albazero* [1977] A.C. 774, per Lord Diplock, p. 847, explaining the decision in *Dunlop v Lambert* (1839) 6 Cl. & F. 600.
[23] [1994] C.L.C. 691.
[24] [2001] 1 A.C. 518.

to depart from the general rule that substantial damages cannot be recovered by the promisee. There was, in other words, no "legal black hole" in this case.[25] A minority of the House in *Panatown* (Lords Goff and Millett) would have allowed the claim either on the "narrow ground" of Lord Browne-Wilkinson in *Linden Gardens* or on the "broader ground" expressed by Lord Griffiths in that case—the views of the minority, however, may yet prove to be influential in the further development of the law on this issue.

Having considered the development of privity and examined the position of both the promisee and third party at common law and in statute, we will now consider the established exceptions to privity. We will take into consideration the possible impact of C(ROTP)A on such exceptions, before concluding with an assessment of the impact of the legislation on the doctrine of privity as a whole.

ESTABLISHED EXCEPTIONS TO THE DOCTRINE OF PRIVITY

8–020   There are some exceptions to privity created judicially at common law and in equity allowing a third party to take the benefit of a contract to which they are a stranger. Some exceptions exist by virtue of statute. There are also exceptional cases where it is possible for a contract to impose a restriction on a third party.

Collateral contract

8–021   A collateral contract is a contract secondary to a main contract whereby, usually, A offers an inducement to B if the latter will enter into the main contract. The promised inducement becomes enforceable as a separate "collateral" contract as, by entering the main contract, B provides consideration (collateral contracts are discussed more fully at para.6–015). The device has proved useful in circumventing certain rules such as the parol evidence rule. The previous examples of collateral contracts that we have looked at involved two parties but where there are three parties the device provides a means of evading the doctrine of privity.

In *Shanklin Pier v Detel Products Ltd*[26] the claimants were the owners of Shanklin Pier in the Isle of Wight. They employed contractors to repaint their pier and specified that the defendants', i.e. Detel's, paint (known as DMU) was to be used. The defendants had previously represented to the claimants that the paint would last from seven to ten years. The defendants sold the paint to the contractors and it was used but it only lasted for three months. Although the claimants could not sue the defendants on the contract for the sale of the paint, to which they were not a party, Mc Nair J. held that the claimants could sue the defendants on a collateral contract arising from their promise as to the longevity of the paint. The claimants' consideration to enforce this promise consisted of their causing the contractors to enter into a contract to buy paint from the defendants. The judge explained the principle in the case as follows:

> "Counsel for the defendants submitted that in law a warranty could give rise to no enforceable cause of action except between the same parties as the parties to the main

---

[25] See further Unberath (1999) 115 L.Q.R. 535.

[26] [1951] 2 K.B. 854. See also *Charnock v Liverpool Corporation* [1968] 1 W.L.R. 1498. In strict theory, the collateral contract is not really an *exception* to privity since there is a binding contract between the parties to the collateral contract. It is best seen as a means available to the courts of circumventing the doctrine.

contract in relation to which the warranty was given. In principle, this submission seems to me to be unsound. If, as is elementary, the consideration for the warranty in the usual case is the entering into of the main contract in which the warranty is given, I see no reason why there may not be an enforceable warranty between A and B supported by the consideration that B should cause C to enter into a contract with A or that B should do some other act for the benefit of A."

In *Wells (Merstham) Ltd v Buckland Sand and Silica Ltd*[27] the principle was extended, perhaps questionably, to a situation where at the time of the warranty there was no specific main contract in view. Edmund Davies J. held that it was sufficient that there was *animus contrahendi*, i.e. that it was within the parties' contemplation that a main contract based on the warranty would be entered into in the near future. Presumably, the courts will be less willing to find the existence of a collateral contract now that C(ROTP)A provides for an enforceable third party rights.

Trust of a promise

The concept of the trust was developed in equity. Thus if A conveys property to B (the trustee) to hold on trust for C (the beneficiary) a trust will arise whereby, in equity, the trustee must have regard to the interests of the beneficiary. The beneficiary has an equitable interest in the property and has rights that can be enforced against the trustee. The trust device offers a means of evading the privity rule, thus if A contracts with B to confer a benefit on C, if B can be regarded as holding their contractual rights on trust for C, C may be able to ask B to sue as trustee; in the event of a refusal, C may bring proceedings joining the trustee as co-defendant. The third party is provided with a remedy denied at common law owing to the doctrine of privity.

8–022

The trust device[28] in this context can be traced to *Gregory and Parker v Williams*[28] in 1817 and had become firmly established by the time of *Les Affreteurs Reunis SA v Leopold Walford (London) Ltd.*[29] In this case, Walford, a broker, arranged a charterparty between shipowners and charterers. The charterparty contained a term by which the shipowners promised to pay Walford three per cent commission on the value of the hire. Although Walford was not a party to the contract between the charterers and shipowners, the House of Lords held that the charterers were to be regarded as trustees for the broker, and they could therefore enforce payment of the commission against the shipowners. It will be noticed that in this case, the trust was not of property, but of a contractual obligation in the form of a promise to pay money.

Liberally applied, therefore, the trust offered the potential of driving a coach and horses through the doctrine of privity. The difficulty, however, is that to create a trust there must be an intention to create a trust and "an intention to provide benefits for someone else and pay for them does not of itself give rise to a trusteeship".[30] In fact, contracting parties in many cases are unlikely to *intend* to create a trust since a trust, once established is generally regarded as irrevocable[31] and, unlike a contract, cannot be varied or rescinded by the parties as this would interfere with the beneficiary's rights under the trust.[32] A further requirement is that, for a trust

---

[27] 2 W.L.R. 453.
[28] (1817) 3 Mer. 582.
[29] [1919] A.C. 801.
[30] *Green v Russell* [1959] 2 Q.B. 226, per Romer L.J.
[31] *Re Sinclair's Life Policy* [1938] 1 Ch. 799.
[32] Although, under C(ROTP)A, unless otherwise agreed, there are restrictions on the variation or rescission of the third party's rights—see para.8–009 above.

to arise, there must be a positive intention to benefit the third party. If it can be shown that the real intention of the contract was to benefit the promisee, as in *Vandepitte v Preferred Accident Insurance Corporation of New York*,[33] there will be no trust.

8–023   In truth, the device depends largely on the readiness of the court to construe a trust and many of the decided cases are inconsistent. The judicial tide seems to have turned against the device in the case of *Re Schebsman*.[34] The facts were that, for many years, S was employed by a Swiss company and its English subsidiary. On termination of his employment, an agreement was entered into whereby the companies would pay him £2,000 immediately and a further £5,500 in six annual instalments or, in the event of his death, to his widow and daughter. Neither of these women was a party to the contract and therefore, under the doctrine of privity, had no rights under it. S was later adjudicated bankrupt and he died while the instalments were being paid. S's trustee in bankruptcy claimed the sums payable to S's widow and daughter under the agreement as forming part of the debtor's S's estate. The Court of Appeal held that there was no trust in favour of the widow and daughter and they therefore had no legal right to the money that could be enforced. But the companies had performed the contract by choosing to make payments under it and neither S, during his lifetime, nor his trustee in bankruptcy could therefore intercept the money. In a well-known judicial statement Du Parcq L.J. said:

> "It is true that, by the use possibly of unguarded language, a person may create a trust, as Monsieur Jourdain talked prose, without knowing it, but unless the intention to create a trust is clearly to be collected from the language used and the circumstances of the case, I think the Court ought not to be astute to discover indications of such an intention. I have little doubt that in the present case both parties (and certainly the debtor) intended to keep alive their common law right to vary consensually the terms of the obligation undertaken by the company, and if circumstances had changed in the debtor's lifetme injustice might have been done by holding that a trust had been created and that those terms were accordingly unalterable."

It is noteworthy that in *Beswick v Beswick* (the facts are given at para.8–004) all three judges of the Court of Appeal were of the view that no trust could be inferred in favour of the third party and the matter was not canvassed before the House of Lords. The possibility of finding a trust where a contract purports to confer a benefit on a third party still exists but because of the narrow constraints imposed by the courts the likelihood is that such a ruling will be rare.[35] After 1999, in most cases C(ROTP)A will provide a simpler way of securing benefits for a third party although it clearly creates rights which are more limited than a trust.

Agency

8–024   A contract of agency arises where one person (the "principal") appoints an agent to enter contracts on their behalf with third parties. Once the contract has been made with third party, the

---

[33] [1933] A.C. 70.
[34] [1944] Ch. 83. Compare this case with *Re Flavell* (1884) 25 Ch. D. 89, where in 1883, on very similar facts, the Court of Appeal found a trust.
[35] The trust argument was unsuccessfully raised in *Rolls Royce Power Engineering plc v Ricardo Consulting Engineers Ltd* [2003] EWHC 2871 (TCC).

agent drops out of the transaction. As a general rule, the principal, even if undisclosed (ie the third party is unaware of the principal's existence at the time of the contract) may sue and be sued by the third party. Agency is possibly only a genuine exception to privity when the principal is undisclosed since in the normal case, the principal and agent are, in law, one and the same person.

The courts are generally unwilling to infer an agency relationship solely in order to evade the privity rule although an example of where agency was used to circumvent privity is the case *New Zealand Shipping Co Ltd v A M Satterthwaite & Co Ltd*[36] in the context of whether a third party could rely on an exclusion clause (see para.7–035). Agency arises where the agent has authority to bring about a change in the principal's legal position. This authority may be acquired in a number of ways: there may be actual authority—this may be express or implied; or there may be apparent (or "ostensible" authority); and there may be a separate category of authority termed "usual" authority.[37]

Actual authority is the most straightforward and is based upon agreement between the principal and agent, i.e. where the parties agree that the agent should have such authority. The third party is a stranger to this agreement and, as we have noted above, may be unaware of the existence of any authority on the agent's part. Actual authority is said to be "express" when created in words either orally or in writing; it is said to be "implied" when it is inferred from the conduct of the parties and the circumstances of the case, such as where the board of directors of a company appoint one of their members to be managing director.

Whereas actual authority arises from agreement between principal and agent, apparent authority arises from the state of affairs *as it appears* to the third party. This may occur where the principal has made a representation to the third party that a person has authority to act as agent—having made such a representation, the principal may be estopped from denying it. The representation may take a variety of forms of which the most common is a representation by conduct and, in general, the representation that gives rise to such authority must come from the principal, not the agent. Apparent authority is illustrated by *Freeman & Lockyer v Buckhurst Park Properties (Mangal) Ltd*[38] where a company was formed to carry out the development of a large estate. The company's articles contained the power to appoint a managing director but none was appointed. However, the board permitted a director, K, to act as if he had been so appointed and he instructed FL, architects, to submit a planning application. When the architects had done the work, the company refused to pay them on the basis that K had not been appointed as managing director and therefore had no authority. It was held that the company were bound by the contract which K had made as it was within the scope of his apparent authority. The company had effectively represented that K had authority to bind the company and FL had relied on that by entering the contract.

8–025

Ratification

The principal will bound by a contract made by an agent clothed with any of the types of authority discussed above, providing the contract falls within the scope of that authority.

8–026

---

[36] [1975] A.C. 154.
[37] See the case of *Watteau v Fenwick* [1893] 1 Q.B. 346. Agency may also arise by operation of law and by subsequent ratification by the principal.
[38] [1964] 2 Q.B. 480.

However, even where an agent acts without authority or in excess of authority, the principal may subsequently ratify the transaction that the agent has entered into and become liable upon it. For ratification to be effective, the principal must be in existence at the time the agent enters into the transaction[39] and the agent must purport to act as agent for a named or ascertainable principal.[40] Ratification will not be possible where the agent enters into a contract which the principal, at the time, was incapable of making. Thus a contract of fire insurance was held not to be ratifiable where the property in question was destroyed by fire at the time of the purported ratification.[41] Where it occurs, ratification operates retrospectively, that is to say, the contract will be regarded as binding on the principal and third party from the date the contract was made by the agent. That this can operate harshly as far as the third party is concerned is demonstrated by *Bolton & Partners v Lambert*[42] where on December 8 L made an offer to a director of the claimant company to take a lease of certain factory premises. The offer was accepted although the director concerned had no authority in that regard. On January 13 L withdrew the offer, but the company later purported to ratify the contract and claimed specific performance of the agreement. The Court of Appeal held that the ratification related back to the time of the original contract, thus the purported revocation was ineffective. The effect of the ruling is perhaps tempered by the principle that ratification must take place within a reasonable time.

Doctrine of the undisclosed principal

8–027   As we have already observed, where the principal is undisclosed in that the third party does not know that the agent is acting for a principal, the position is governed by "the doctrine of the undisclosed principal". The doctrine, which is peculiar to English law, provides that despite the fact the principal is undisclosed, the third party will find themselves contractually bound to, and have rights against, a person of whom they had no knowledge at the time of the contract.

The doctrine cannot really be reconciled with privity of contract and has been accepted as an anomalous doctrine which can be justified on the grounds of commercial expediency. In *Keighley Maxsted & Co v Durant & Co*[43] Lord Lindley explained the rationale of the doctrine as follows:

> "[T]here is an anomaly in holding one person bound to another of whom he knows nothing and with whom he did not, in fact, intend to contract. But middlemen, through whom contracts are made, are common and useful in business transactions, and in the great mass of contracts it is a matter of indifference to either party whether there is an undisclosed principal or not. If he exists, it is, to say the least, extremely convenient that he should be able to sue and be sued as principal, and he is only allowed to do so on terms which exclude injustice."

It is submitted that this reasoning holds just as good today as it did at the turn of the twentieth century when the case was decided. There is, however, an important qualification—the doctrine

---

[39] *Kelner v Baxter* (1866) L.R. 2 C.P. 175.
[40] *Keighley Maxsted & Co v Durant & Co* [1901] A.C. 240.
[41] *Grover & Grover Ltd v Matthews* [1910] 2 K.B. 401.
[42] (1889) 41 Ch. D. 295. The decision was confirmed by the Court of Appeal in 1993 in *Presentaciones Musicales SA v Secunda* [1994] Ch. 271.
[43] [1901] A.C. 240. In the case, the House of Lords refused to permit an undisclosed principal to ratify.

will not apply where the agent does not have authority at the time of the contract. But even where the agent does have authority, there are certain situations where the courts have ruled that the undisclosed principal cannot sue on the contract. First, the undisclosed agency must be consistent with the terms of the contract. Thus if the agent signs a contract in his own name and describes himself as "owner" of the property the subject matter of the contract, evidence will not be admissible to show that another person was the owner and that the agent was merely acting as such. The undisclosed principal will be unable to sue or be sued on the contract.[44] Secondly, where the character or personality of the agent is of importance to the third party, the undisclosed principal may not be allowed to intervene.[45] It was accepted by the Privy Council in *Siu Yin Kwan v Eastern Insurance Co Ltd*[46] that this argument may prevail where the contract is one requiring personal skills. In that case, Lord Lloyd stated:

> "[T]here is a class of personal contract where the burden cannot be performed vicariously. The example often given is a contract to paint a portrait. Such a contract cannot be enforced by an undisclosed principal since . . . his intervention in such a case would be a breach of the very contract in which he seeks to intervene."

As long as the principal remains undisclosed, the agent remains personally liable to the third party on the contract. Once the existence of the undisclosed principal has been revealed, the third party may sue either the principal or the agent. However, once the third party, with knowledge of all the facts, unequivocally elects that he is going to sue the one and not the other, he is stuck with that choice.[47] **8–028**

Breach of warranty of authority

An agent who purports to act for a principal but who has no authority to do so, or who exceeds their existing authority, may be liable for "breach of warranty of authority". Such a warranty may be express or implied and it must be relied on by the third party, e.g. by entering into the contract with the principal. **8–029**

In *Collen v Wright*[48] A professed to act on behalf of P and leased P's farm to the claimant. It was held that A's personal representatives were liable to the claimant as A had impliedly warranted that he had the authority to enter into the lease. Liability for breach of warranty of authority is strict[49] and it seems that the third party cannot sue the agent if he knew or ought to have known that the agent was not warranting their authority. Similarly, the agent will not be liable if the contract excluded their liability.[50]

Liability for breach of warranty of authority may extend widely. This is illustrated by *Penn v Bristol and West Building Society*[51] where it was held by the Court of Appeal that the third

---

[44] *Humble v Hunter* (1848) 12 Q.B. 310. This case was distinguished in *Fred Drughorn Ltd v Rederiaktiebolaget Transatlantic* [1919] A.C. 203 where the evidence that a party had contracted as agent for an undisclosed principal did not vary the terms of the contract.
[45] *Greer v Downs Supply Co* [1927] 2 K.B. 28.
[46] [1994] 1 Lloyd's Rep. 616. See also *Said v Butt* [1920] 3 K.B. 497.
[47] See *Clarkson Booker Ltd v Andjel* [1964] 2 Q.B. 775 where, on the facts, it was held that no election had been made.
[48] (1857) 8 E. & B. 647.
[49] *Yonge v Toynbee* [1910] 1 K.B. 215.
[50] *Lilly Watson & Co v Smales Eeles & Co* [1892] 1 Q.B. 456.
[51] [1997] 3 All E.R. 470.

party could hold the agent liable for breach of warranty where the loss resulted from the third party contracting with some party other than the principal. A solicitor erroneously believed that he had authority to act for both a husband and wife as joint owners of a house but he had no such authority to act for the wife. In the course of negotiations, the solicitor warranted to the purchaser's solicitors that he was acting for husband and wife jointly. Relying on this, the building society and their solicitors arranged for the purchaser to execute a charge over the house. The contract of sale was declared null and void at the instigation of the wife. The Court of Appeal allowed the building society's claim for breach of warranty of authority and ordered the solicitor to pay the building society's costs.

The level of compensation for breach of warranty of authority is arrived at by considering the difference in the position that the third party (or other person relying on the warranty) would have been in had the representation been true and the position they are actually in as a result of it being untrue.[52]

Assignment

8–030   The possibility of assigning contractual rights is a significant exception to the rule of privity.

Thus if, under a contract, A owes B a sum of money, the creditor B may assign his contractual right to receive that sum of money to a third party C. C thereby acquires B's rights and B no longer has any rights against the debtor A—C can recover the debt from A. The consent of the debtor A to an assignment is not required, although they should normally be notified of the transaction. The assignee takes over the assignor's rights "subject to equities", meaning that the debtor A will be able to raise against the assignee C any defence which could have been raised against the assignor B.

There are some restrictions on assignment, for example where personal performance is required such as where a writer is contractually obliged to write a book for a publisher, the publisher may not assign. Here the prohibition on assignment is usually implied but, in any type of contract, the parties to the contract can expressly provide that assignment is prohibited, or that it is prohibited without consent. Assignment may take place either under the Law of Property Act 1925, s.136 or under equitable rules.

Statutory exceptions

8–031   Over the years, a number of specific statutory exceptions to the privity rule have been introduced, usually on grounds of commercial convenience. Thus under the Married Women's Property Act 1882, s.11, as amended, a spouse may obtain the benefit of a contract of life assurance which is made for the benefit of the other spouse; under the Bills of Exchange Act 1882, s.29, a third party may sue on a bill of exchange or cheque; and under the Road Traffic Act 1988, s.148(7) an injured third party may proceed directly against the motorist's insurance company even though they are not a party to the contract.

None of the established statutory exceptions are affected by C(ROTP)A. To the list of statutory exceptions to privity must now be added, of course, the enforceable third party rights made possible by C(ROTP)A itself.

---

[52] Per Lord Esher M.R. in *Firbanks Executors v Humphreys* (1886) 18 Q.B.D. 54, at p.60.

Restrictive covenants and the Strathcona case

We are concerned here with the situation where a contract between A and B attempts to impose **8–032** a burden on the third party C—under the rule of privity at common law, such an imposition on C is unenforceable by the parties to the contract. In transactions involving land, however, such restrictions may be enforceable in equity. Suppose that A buys a plot of land from B and A promises B that he will not build on the land. As between A and B there is privity of contract and the promise is enforceable by B, but what if A later sells the land to C? Is C bound by the restriction, and if so, under what circumstances?

In the famous case of *Tulk v Moxhay*[53] T owned several properties in Leicester Square, London. T sold the gardens in the centre of the square to E who covenanted that he would maintain the gardens in their present condition and allow the residents of the square to use them. E later sold the land to M and although the conveyance to M did not contain a similar covenant, M was aware of the restriction on the use of the land. T, who still owned properties in the square, heard that M was intending to build on the gardens and he sought an injunction to restrain him from doing so. The Court of Chancery granted the injunction. The restriction was enforceable because M was aware of the existence of the covenant—he had notice of it at the time of the purchase. In later cases, however, the courts emphasised that for such a covenant to be enforceable against the subsequent purchaser, the vendor must have retained a proprietary interest, i.e. land (usually adjacent) capable of benefiting from the restriction. Thus mere notice is, by itself, insufficient to render the covenant enforceable. Providing certain requirements are satisfied, therefore, restrictive covenants may "run with the land" and be binding upon subsequent purchasers.

The question has arisen as to whether the restrictive covenant doctrine can be used to impose on third parties restrictions upon the use of goods. If so, this would constitute a significant exception to the rule of privity.

In *Lord Strathcona Steamship Co Ltd v Dominion Coal Co Ltd*[54] the respondents chartered **8–033** the ship SS *Lord Strathcona* for use on the St Lawrence River for several summer seasons. During the period of the charterparty, the ship was sold to the appellants who took with notice of the charterparty but the appellants subsequently refused to permit the respondents to use the ship in accordance with the contract. The Privy Council granted an injunction to restrain the appellants from using the ship in a manner inconsistent with the charterparty. The Committee placed reliance on a dictum of Knight Bruce L.J. in an earlier case, *De Mattos v Gibson*[55] where he said:

> "[A]s a general rule, where a man, by gift or purchase, acquires property from another, with knowledge of a previous contract, lawfully and for valuable consideration made by him with a third person, to use and employ the property for a particular purpose in a specified manner, the acquirer shall not, to the material damage of the third person, in opposition to the contract and inconsistently with it, use and employ the property not allowable to the giver or seller."

In applying this principle in the *Strathcona* case, the Privy Council seems to have viewed *Tulk v Moxhay* as equally applicable to restrictions relating to chattels. The difficulty with this is that, in the years following *Tulk v Moxhay*, the doctrine of restrictive covenants on land had

---

[53] (1848) 2 Ph. 744.
[54] [1926] A.C. 108.
[55] (1859) 4 D. & J. 276.

developed further so that such covenants could only be enforced where the vendor had a proprietary interest capable of benefiting from the restriction, such as the retention of adjoining land. This requirement is not easy to translate to moveable property but in any event it is well-established that the charterer of a ship does not have a proprietary interest in the ship. In *Strathcona*, the Privy Council accepted that an injunction could only be granted where the applicant has a continuing interest in the property but seemed to regard a bare contractual right (i.e. the right to have the contract performed) as sufficient for the purpose.

8-034   In *Clore v Theatrical Properties Ltd*[56] the Court of Appeal considered that the *Strathcona* decision should be limited to the special and particular case of the charterparty of a ship. In *Port Line Ltd v Ben Line Steamers Ltd*[57] Diplock J. went further and considered that *Strathcona* was wrongly decided and declined to follow it. In the case itself, P had chartered a ship from S, S then sold the vessel to B but subject to an immediate recharter by B to S. Under the terms of the charterparty between P and S, the requisitioning of the vessel did not determine the charter; under the charterparty between B and S it did have that effect. In 1956 the ship was requisitioned and P claimed from B the whole or part of the compensation received by B from the Crown for the requisition. It was held that the action should fail. Even if *Strathcona* was correctly decided, P's claim did not come within its principles as, (i) B had no actual knowledge at the time of the purchase of P's rights under the charter; constructive notice will not suffice; (ii) B was in no breach of duty to P as the unavailability of the vessel was due to an act of the Crown; and (iii) P was not entitled to any remedy against B except a right to restrain B from using the ship inconsistently with the charter.

In fact, despite the doubts expressed by the court in *Port Line v Ben Line*, the *Strathcona* case met with the approval of Browne-Wilkinson J. in more recent times in *Swiss Bank Corporation v Lloyds Bank Ltd*.[58] He thought that the principle expressed by Knight Bruce L.J. in *De Mattos v Gibson* (on which the Privy Council in *Strathcona* relied) was good law and represented "the counterpart in equity of the tort of knowing interference with contractual rights". A claim in tort may lie against a person who knowingly and intentionally interferes with contractual relations of two other parties[59] and Diplock J. in *Port Line v Ben Line* indicated that the decision in *De Mattos v Gibson* could have been arrived at on that basis. Whatever the relationship between *Strathcona* and the tort of knowingly interfering with contractual relations may be, (it seems to be regarded as distinct from the tortious action) it remains a difficult authority and the precise ambit of its operation has yet to be clarified by the courts. *Strathcona* was considered by Hoffmann J. in *Law Debenture Trust Corporation v Ural Caspian Oil Corporation Ltd*[60]—the judge confirmed that the principle could only be used as a basis for injunctive relief to ensure compliance with a restrictive covenant; it cannot be used to secure compliance with a positive covenant or to found a claim for damages. Hoffmann J. considered it beyond doubt that the principle "does not provide a panacea for outflanking the doctrine of privity of contract."

Privity of contract: conclusion

8-035   There is no doubt that C(ROTP)A will improve the position of third parties who, under the traditional doctrine of privity, have been denied the right to enforce a contract made for their

[56] [1936] 3 All E.R. 483.
[57] [1958] 2 Q.B. 146.
[58] [1979] 3 W.L.R. 210.
[59] See *Lumley v Gye* (1853) 2 E. & B. 216; and *British Motor Trade Association v Salvadori* [1949] Ch. 556.
[60] [1993] 1 W.L.R. 138; reversed by the Court of Appeal on other grounds at [1994] 3 W.L.R. 1221.

benefit. It is instructive to consider how some of the old cases would now be decided under the new Act.

In *Tweddle v Atkinson* (the facts are given at para.4–009) it was specifically agreed between the promisor and the promisee that "the said [third party] has full power to sue the said parties [to the contract] in any court of law or equity". Clearly, therefore, the contract would today be seen as expressly providing that the third party could in his own right enforce the beneficial term under s.1(1)(a) of C(ROTP)A and the outcome the case would now be different. In *Beswick v Beswick* (see para.8–004) the fact that Mrs Beswick was named in the contract satisfies the requirements of s.1(3) but it is not, by itself, sufficient to enable her to enforce the contract. The widow would have to bring herself within s.1(1)(b) and s.1(2), i.e. that the term purports to confer a benefit on her, unless on a proper construction of the contract the parties did not intend the term to be enforceable by the third party. It would seem that the term in question did confer an enforceable benefit on the widow and therefore she would presumably now succeed in her personal capacity without having to rely on the fact that she happened to be adminstratrix of her deceased husband's estate. A similar result, that is, allowing the third party to enforce the contract would be quite likely in the case of *Woodar Investment Development v Wimpey* (see para.8–017) and presumably, families in cases similar to *Jackson v Horizon Holidays* (see para.8–016), assuming the holiday falls outside the Package Travel, Package Holidays and Package Tour Regulations 1992, would now be able to recover full compensation in a more straightforward way.

The Act is likely to prove most helpful to those contractors who *intend* to benefit a third party; providing they make their intention clear in the contract, the third party will have a remedy. The difficulties, if any, are likely to arise under s.1(1)(b) of the Act where a term which "purports to confer a benefit" on a third party might well be found to extend to unintended beneficiaries. However, the ease with which the provisions of the Act may be excluded may mean that lawyers drafting contracts for commercial concerns will take care to eliminate the possibility of unintended third parties acquiring enforceable rights.

Finally, there is another "exception" to privity which must be mentioned. A third party to a contract may well have enforceable rights in tort, particularly in the tort of negligence. This will depend on the third party establishing that the promisor owed them a duty of care and also that they were negligent in that they breached that duty of care. Thus in *Donoghue v Stevenson*[61] the claimant and her friend entered a café and the friend ordered for her a bottle of ginger beer which came in an opaque stone bottle. The claimant consumed some of the drink but when the remainder was poured, out came the remains of what was apparently a decomposed snail and the claimant became ill. She could not sue the café proprietor for breach of contract as she was not a party to the contract for the sale of the drink—it had been brought by her friend. Instead, she sued the manufacturer, contending that he owed the claimant a duty of care. A majority of the House of Lords held that manufacturers of products owe a duty of care in negligence to see that the ultimate consumers of their products do not suffer injury owing to the defective nature of the products. Thus the injured party was not dependent upon her friend bringing an action for breach of contract but was able to proceed directly against the manufacturer.[62]

Donoghue v Stevenson concerned physical injury—a third party to a contract is more likely to be the victim of economic loss but the courts have traditionally shown a marked reluctance

8–036

---

[61] [1932] A.C. 562.
[62] Were the facts to arise today, the manufacturer would probably be liable under the Consumer Protection Act 1987 (Part 1–Product Liability) without the need to establish fault.

to allow recovery for pure economic loss caused by negligence. There must normally be some physical injury or damage to property. However, in *Junior Books Ltd v Veitchi Ltd*[63] the House of Lords were prepared to award damages for economic loss in a negligence action in favour of a third party.

8–037   J employed a building firm to construct a factory for them. On the instructions of J's architect, the laying of the factory floor was subcontracted out to V, specialist flooring contractors. Two years after the work had been completed, the floor developed cracks as it had been defectively laid by V. J sued V in negligence to recover the cost of replacing the floor and consequential economic losses—there was, of course, no privity of contract between them. In the normal case, J would have sued the main contractors who, in turn, would recover from V. The House of Lords held that V owed J a duty of care and that they could be liable in damages to J. J could therefore be placed in the position they would have been in had the contract between between V and the main contractors been properly performed, i.e. damages could be recovered on a contractual rather than a tortious basis. The decision was based on the very close proximity between the parties—V were specialist contractors who had been nominated on the instructions of J and J had relied upon V's skill and experience. Lord Roskill considered that the relationship of the parties "was as close as it could be short of actual privity of contract." Subsequent decisions, however, have sought to confine the case to its facts; in *D & F Estates Ltd v Church Commissioners for England*[64] the facts of *Junior Books* were described as "unique". It is perhaps best viewed as an anomalous decision.

Further reading

Smith, *Contracts for the Benefit of Third Parties: in Defence of the Third Party Rule* (1997) 17 O.J.L.S. 643.
Burrows, *The Contracts (Rights of Third Parties) Act and its Implications for Commercial Contracts* [2000] L.M.C.L.Q. 540.
Stevens, *The Contracts (Rights of Third Parties) Act 1999* (2004) 120 L.Q.R. 292.
Unberath, *Third Party Losses and Black Holes: Another View* (1999) 15 L.Q.R. 535.

---

[63] [1983] 1 A.C. 520. See also the decision of the House of Lords in *White v Jones* [1995] 2 A.C. 207.
[64] [1989] A.C. 177.

Chapter 9

DISCHARGE BY PERFORMANCE, BREACH AND AGREEMENT

9–001

In previous chapters we have looked at the way contracts come into existence and examined the content of contracts. In this chapter we are concerned with three ways in which contracts may be discharged so that the parties have no further obligations under them. These are discharge by performance; by breach; and by agreement. A fourth way in which contracts may be discharged, by frustration, is discussed in the following chapter.

DISCHARGE BY PERFORMANCE

9–002

If both parties perform their obligations under the contract, the contract is discharged. This raises the question, what amounts to performance?

The general rule at common law holds that performance must be precise and exact. In *Cutter v Powell*[1] Cutter agreed to serve as second mate on a ship sailing from Jamaica to Liverpool for the sum of 30 guineas. Cutter began the voyage and did his duty as second mate but died when the ship was 19 days short of Liverpool. Cutter's widow claimed a proportion of the deceased's wages in respect of the time in which he had acted as second mate. The Court of King's Bench held that her action failed—on the express wording of the contract, there was no liability to pay the wages until the voyage was completed. In other words the contractual obligation was "entire". Whether an obligation is entire depends upon the intention of the parties, ascertained objectively having regard to all the circumstances.

The decision in *Cutter v Powell* seems harsh but it should be noted that the sum agreed was nearly four times the ordinary rate—Lord Kenyon C.J. saw it as "a kind of insurance" that the voyage would be completed. Cutter's death was not, of course, a breach of contract and for this reason the case would today be dealt with as a case of discharge by frustration (see Chapter 10 below). The case was decided some time before that doctrine developed.

The rule that performance must be precise and exact has been applied very strictly in cases under s.13 of the Sale of Goods Act 1893 (now s.13 of the 1979 Act). The section implies an obligation that where there is a sale by description, the goods shall correspond with the description. In *Re Moore & Co and Landauer & Co*[2] the defendants agreed to buy from the claimants

[1] (1795) 6 T.R. 320.
[2] [1921] 2 K.B. 519.

3,000 tins of canned fruit to be packed in cases containing 30 tins. Some of the consignment was packed in cases containing 24 tins and because of this it was held that the defendants were entitled to reject the whole consignment. There had not been satisfactory performance. This and other similar cases were criticised by the House of Lords in *Reardon Smith Line Ltd v Hansen-Tangen*[3] and indeed in non-consumer sales, s.15A of the Sale of Goods Act 1979 (as inserted by s.4(1) of the Sale and Supply of Goods Act 1994) prevents the purchaser from unreasonably rejecting gods which are only slightly different from the contract description. (The provision is discussed more fully at para.6–045). The hardship of the general rule regarding performance is mitigated by various exceptions which will be discussed below.

Divisible contracts and obligations

9–003   Although it is always open to the parties to stipulate for entirety in their contract, entire contracts or obligations tend to be the exception rather than the rule. Many contracts are "divisible" in the sense that the contract is divided into stages and once a particular stage has been satisfactorily completed by a party, they are entitled to payment. This is usually the position in large scale construction contracts and there are many other commercial transaction which provide for payment in a similar manner. A further example is contracts of employment which may provide for employees to be paid weekly or monthly. They are entitled to payment on the completion of each week or month of work (even if the salary is quoted on an annual basis). In *Cutter v Powell* the conclusion might well have been different had the contract stipulated for Cutter to be paid a certain amount per week.

There is another sense in which contracts, or more correctly, obligations, can be said to be divisible. This is where obligations in the contract (but not necessarily all of them) may be enforced independently of performance by the other party. Whether this is the case will be a question of construction of the contract. For example, in *Roberts v Havelock*[4] a ship was damaged en route from Cardiff to Alexandria and had to be docked at Milford Haven for essential repairs. The claimant carried out the repairs, but before he had completed the contract he requested payment for work carried out thus far. His action to recover payment succeeded as the contract did not require him to complete all the repairs before making a demand for payment.

Substantial performance

9–004   There is authority to the effect that a party who performs their contractual obligations *substantially*, though not precisely, may be able to enforce the contract.[5] However, the substantial performer may be liable to compensate the other party for his imprecise performance. Two cases illustrate the operation of the doctrine. In *Dakin (H) & Co Ltd v Lee*[6] the claimant builders agreed to carry out repairs at the defendant's house for £1,500. The defendant refused to pay the outstanding balance because of certain defects. The concrete underpinning of a wall was only two feet thick instead of four as specified in the contract; columns of solid iron four inches in diameter had been used instead of hollow iron of five inches diameter; and steel joists over

---

[3] [1976] 3 All E.R. 570.
[4] (1832) 3 B. & Ad. 404.
[5] The origin of the principle seems to be *Boone v Eyre* (1779) 1 H. Bl. 273 n., per Lord Mansfield.
[6] [1916] 1 K.B. 566.

a bay window had not been bolted as agreed. The Court of Appeal held that the claimants could recover the outstanding balance, less the cost of remedying the defects, which amounted to £80. Sankey J. explained the principle as follows:

> "Where a builder has supplied work and labour for the erection or repair of a house under a lump sum contract, but has departed from the terms of the contract, he is entitled to recover for his services, unless (1) the work that he has done is of no benefit to the owner; (2) the work that he has done is entirely different from the work he has contracted to do; or (3) he has abandoned the work and left it unfinished."

The case was one of negligence and bad workmanship and not a case where items in the specification had been omitted or the job abandoned. The result therefore seems entirely sensible and just. A similar conclusion was reached in *Hoenig v Isaacs*[7] where the claimant agreed to redecorate and refurnish the defendant's flat at a cost of £750. After the claimant said that he had completed the work, the defendant alleged that there was faulty design and bad workmanship, and the defendant paid only £400. The claimant sued for the balance. It was held that the only defects were in the furniture which could be corrected at a cost of £55 and as the claimant had substantially performed the contract, he was entitled to the balance less £55.

In *Bolton v Mahadeva*[8] the Court of Appeal ruled that a claim for substantial performance failed. The claimant agreed to instal a central heating system in the defendant's house for a lump sum of £560. The system he installed was defective in that the house was on average 10 per cent less warm than it should have been and, because of a defective flue, the system gave off fumes. The cost of remedying the defects was £174. As the system as a whole was ineffective for its intended purpose, the claimant could recover nothing. Thus the defendant obtained a benefit whilst the claimant received nothing for the work done. You might consider this just given the quality of the work, however this case was criticised by the Law Commission on the basis that the claimant should receive some payment in such cases.[9] One of the members of the Commission, Brian Davenport Q.C., entered a dissent. He pointed out that in small domestic building contracts, the householder's only effective security that the job will be completed satisfactorily is the power to withhold payment. Since almost all larger scale building contracts provide for staged payments (i.e. the obligations are divisible not entire), the entire contracts rule served a useful purpose in cases such as *Bolton v Mahadeva*. The proposals of the Commission have not been implemented.

Voluntary acceptance of partial performance

Where performance by one party is only partial, the other party may elect to accept the partial performance. In *Christy v Row*[10] the claimant was contracted to ship the defendant's coal from Shields to Hamburg. The ship was unable to reach that destination and, at the request of the consignee, the master of the ship delivered some of the cargo at a different port. The claimant's action for freight succeeded—although he had not completely performed the contract, his partial performance had been accepted.

9–005

---

[7] [1952] 2 All E.R. 176.
[8] [1972] 1 W.L.R. 1009. On the issue of substantial performance, this case was followed in *Williams v Roffey Bros & Nicholls (Contractors) Ltd* [1991] 1 Q.B. 1 (the facts are given at para.4–024).
[9] Law Com No 121 (1983) *Pecuniary Restitution on Breach of Contract*. See Burrows (1984) 47 M.L.R. 76.
[10] (1808) 1 Taunt. 300.

Where a partial performance is accepted, the partial performer will be discharged from further performance and have a claim on a quantum meruit basis in respect of work done. The other party, however, must have genuine choice whether or not to accept the partial performance. In *Sumpter v Hedges*[11] the claimant builder agreed to erect buildings on the defendant's land for £565. The claimant did part of the work to the value of about £333 and then abandoned the project. The defendant himself finished the work using the materials which the claimant had left on the land. The Court of Appeal held that the claimant could recover nothing for the work that he had done as the defendant had no real choice but to accept the partial performance—the circumstances must be such that the defendant has the option of taking the benefit of the work done. Here he did not, but the claimant was allowed to recover for the materials used as the defendant did have a choice whether or not to use them in the completion of the buildings.

The rule concerning acceptance of partial performance is recognised by the Sale of Goods Act 1979, s.30(1):

> "Where the seller delivers to the buyer a quantity of goods less than he contracted to sell, the buyer may reject them, but if the buyer accepts the goods so delivered he must pay for them at the contract rate."

Prevention of performance

9–006 A party to a contract that provides for payment on completion may be wrongfully prevented by the other party from completing performance. The position in such circumstances was explained by Alderson B. in *De Bernardy v Harding*[12] as follows:

> "Where one party has absolutely refused to perform, or has rendered himself incapable of performing, his part of the contract, he puts it in the power of the other party either to sue for breach of it or rescind the contract and sue on a *quantum meruit* for the work actually done."

In *Planche v Colburn*[13] the claimant agreed to write a book on costume and ancient armour which was to appear in series published by the defendants called "The Juvenile Library". He was to receive £100 on completion of the book to which end he carried out research and wrote part of the book but the defendants then abandoned the series. It was held that the claimant was entitled to recover 50 guineas on a quantum meruit basis.

TENDER OF PERFORMANCE

9–007 Where one party is unable to complete performance without the collaboration of the other party, they may make an offer or "tender" of performance. If this is rejected by the other party, the party tendering performance will be discharged from further liability. Thus it is said that a tender of performance is equivalent to performance.

---

[11] [1898] 1 Q.B. 673. See also *Foreman & Co Ltd v The Ship "Liddesdale"* [1900] A.C. 190.
[12] (1835) 8 Exch. 822.
[13] [1831] 8 Bing. 14.

The principle is illustrated by *Startup v Macdonald*[14] where the claimants agreed to sell 10 tons of linseed oil to the defendant and to deliver it within the last 14 days of March. The claimants attempted to deliver at 8.30pm on Saturday March 31 but the defendant refused to take delivery or pay for the goods because of the lateness of the hour. It was held that this tender of performance was as good as performance and the claimants were entitled to recover damages for non-acceptance. The claimants had tendered the goods before the end of March with sufficient time for the defendant to examine the goods to ensure that they were in compliance with the contract. It should be noted, however, that s.29(5) of the Sale of Goods Act 1979 now provides that:

> "Demand or tender of delivery may be treated as ineffectual unless made at a reasonable hour; and what is a reasonable hour is a question of fact."

Where a party is under a contractual obligation to pay a sum of money, a tender of money by the debtor, if refused, will not discharge the debtor from liability. If sued, the tenderer may pay the sum of money into court and if the action is proceeded with, the other party may be ordered to pay costs. The debtor must tender the exact amount of money due to the creditor in "legal tender" i.e. bank notes and particular types of coinage up to certain amounts as determined by statute[15].

STIPULATIONS AS TO TIME

Where the contract does not fix a time for performance, as a general rule performance must be effected within a reasonable time. This is given statutory effect by s.29(3) of the Sale of Goods Act 1979 in relation to the obligation to deliver goods under a contract of sale.   **9–008**

At common law, where time was fixed for performance of one party's obligations under the contract, time was "of the essence" unless the parties had otherwise agreed. The failure to perform by the due date was a breach entitling the innocent party to repudiate the contract. Nevertheless, equity would grant specific performance despite a failure to comply with a stipulation as to time, and s.41 of the Law of Property Act 1925 (re-enacting s.25 of the Judicature Act 1873) effectively provides that the equitable principle shall prevail. The result is that as a general rule time in a contract is not of the essence except in the three situations where time was regarded in equity as being of the essence, i.e. where:

(1) the parties expressly stipulate that conditions as to time must be strictly complied with; or
(2) the nature of the subject matter of the contract or the surrounding circumstances show that time should be considered to be of the essence; or
(3) a party who has been subjected to unreasonable delay gives notice to the party in default making time of the essence.

The House of Lords confirmed this statement of the law to be correct in *United Scientific Holdings Ltd v Burnley Borough Council*.[16] The situation envisaged in paragraph (3) above is

---

[14] (1843) 6 Man. & G. 593.
[15] Currency and Bank Notes Act 1954, s.1; Coinage Act 1971, s.1.
[16] [1978] AC 904. In *Bunge Corporation v Tradax SA* [1981] 1 W.L.R. 711. the House, whilst endorsing the statement once again, also indicated that "broadly speaking" time will be considered to be of the essence in mercantile contracts.

illustrated by the case of *Charles Rickards Ltd v Oppenheim*.[17] The defendant placed an order with the claimants for building a new body on a Rolls Royce chassis and it was agreed that it should be completed within six, or at most, seven months. When the body was not ready within this period, the defendant extended the time limit by three months. This period elapsed but it was still incomplete. The defendant therefore issued an ultimatum—he would cancel the order unless the job were finished within four weeks. The car was not delivered within that period. Three months later the claimant tendered the car. The Court of Appeal held that the defendant was entitled to refuse delivery. Although the defendant had waived the original time limit when he agreed to the three month extension, at the end of that period he had given reasonable notice making time of the essence. The claimant's action for the price failed.

9–009   In *British & Commonwealth Holdings Plc v Quadrex Holdings Inc*[18] the question arose as to the type of notice required to make time of the essence in a contract where it was not originally of the essence and no date for performance was specified. Lord Browne-Wilkinson V.C. considered that the party who had not completed on time ". . . has to have been guilty of unreasonable delay before a notice to complete can be served." In another case, *Behzadi v Shaftesbury Hotels Ltd*[19] it was held that where a contract specified a date for performance, without making time of the essence, the innocent party could serve notice making time of the essence as soon as the date for performance had passed. The innocent party in such circumstances would be justified in serving an immediate notice making time of the essence. The court did not feel bound by the previous ruling and took a different view of the authorities.

Where time is of the essence in a contract, it is clear that any delay, however slight, will afford a ground for repudiation. In *Union Eagle Ltd v Golden Achievement Ltd*[20] there was a written agreement for the sale of a flat which provided that the completion date was to be September 31, 1991 before 5pm. The purchaser paid a deposit of 10 per cent and the contract stated that time was to be of the essence and that non-compliance with any terms would give the vendor the right to rescind the contract and forfeit the deposit. In fact, the purchaser tendered the purchase price at 5.10pm on the day of completion. The vendor therefore rescinded the contract and forfeited the deposit. By a majority decision of the Court of Appeal of Hong Kong the purchaser's action for specific performance failed. On appeal to the Privy Council it was held that the failure to complete on time was a repudiatory breach of contract entitling the vendor to rescind the contract and forfeit the deposit—there had been a breach of an essential condition of the contract.

Where time is not of the essence, the failure to perform by the stipulated time is still nevertheless a breach of contract entitling the injured party to damages, as confirmed by the House of Lords in *Raineri v Miles*.[21]

DISCHARGE BY BREACH

9–010   A breach of contract will occur where one party fails to fulfil, or states that they do not intend to fulfil, their obligations under the contract. The consequences of the breach of particular types of term has already been considered (see para.6–042). It may be recalled that a breach of

---

[17] [1950] 1 K.B. 616.
[18] [1989] Q.B. 842.
[19] [1992] Ch. 1.
[20] [1997] A.C. 514.
[21] [1981] A.C. 1050.

warranty—a less important term—entitles the innocent party to sue for damages only. Breaches of major terms, i.e. conditions, will entitle the innocent party, in addition to claiming damages, to treat themselves as discharged from the contract. The position will also be the same where there has been the breach of an innominate term giving rise to serious consequences. Where the breach gives rise to a right to a right to terminate in this way, it is generally described as a "repudiatory breach". A repudiatory breach may also occur where a party simply abandons the contract and intimates that they do not intend to continue with it. This could occur expressly or it might be implied from conduct that renders performance impossible.

The important point to grasp is that termination of the contract does not arise automatically upon a repudiatory breach. After such a breach, the innocent party has an election—they may decide to "accept" the breach as a repudiation of the contract or they may decide to affirm the contract ("reject" the breach). Thus innocent parties are not bound to discharge themselves from the contract after a breach. In reality, however, in many cases they will have little choice but to accept the breach as they may be unable to continue performance of the contract without the co-operation of the other party. A contract of employment is a good example.[22]

Anticipatory breach

It is quite common that a repudiatory breach is "anticipatory" in nature. An anticipatory breach is one that occurs before performance is due such as where a party, in advance, indicates to the other party that they do not intend to perform their part of the contract. It must be clear beyond reasonable doubt that they are renouncing the contract, otherwise there will be no repudiation.   **9–011**

Anticipatory breach may be explicit, as in *Hochster v De La Tour*[23] where the defendant agreed in April to employ the claimant as a courier commencing in June. In May, the defendant informed the claimant that he would not require his services. The claimant's action for damages in May succeeded. Alternatively, it may be implicit, where the defendant by conduct disables himself from performance, as in *Frost v Knight*.[24] Here, the defendant, having agreed to marry the claimant on his father's death, broke off the engagement and married another person during his father's lifetime. It was held that, at that point, the claimant was entitled to sue for damages.

Whatever the type of anticipatory breach, the innocent party has an immediate right of action; they may accept the repudiation and sue for breach of contract at once, or they may await the date of performance and hold the other party to the contract. The possible controversial consequences of this with regard to a claim for compensation by the innocent party are illustrated by the case of *White & Carter (Councils) Ltd v McGregor* (see para.16–037). Allowing innocent parties to sue at once for damages is sensible—it permits them to mitigate their losses and move on.

Affirmation

If the innocent party elects to affirm the contract, the contract remains in being for the future on both sides. In *Howard v Pickford Tool Co*[25] Asquith L.J. memorably stated: **9–012**

---

[22] See, e.g. *Soares v Beazer Investments Ltd* [2004] EWCA Civ 482.
[23] (1853) 2 E. & B. 678.
[24] (1872) L.R. 7 Ex. 111.
[25] [1951] 1 K.B. 417.

"An unaccepted repudiation is a thing writ in water and of no value to anybody; it affords no legal rights of any sort or kind."

The possible dangers of not accepting a repudiation are illustrated by *Averay v Bowden.*[26] The defendant chartered the claimant's ship, agreeing to load her with a cargo at Odessa within 45 days. The ship berthed at Odessa but the defendant was unable to get a cargo and told the claimant that he could not fulfil his part of the contract and advised the claimant to sail away. Instead, the claimant waited at Odessa hoping a cargo would be found. Before the 45 days was up the Crimean War broke out between England and Russia. Performance of the contract would have been illegal as Odessa became an enemy port (i.e. the contract was "frustrated"—see Chapter 10). The defendant's failure to provide a cargo was an anticipatory breach and the claimant could have sued immediately; however, he elected not to do so and the contract remained on foot. Frustration intervened with the result that both parties were discharged from the contract and therefore it was held that the claimant's action for damages failed. Had the repudiation been accepted, damages would have been recoverable.

Another possible outcome of affirmation is illustrated by *Fercometal SARL v Mediterranean Shipping Co SA, The Simona.*[27] It seems that a party who has affirmed the contract following an anticipatory breach may not be allowed to rely on that breach to justify their own failure to perform the contract. In this case, the charterparty of a ship provided that the charterers were entitled to cancel if the ship was not ready to load on or before July 9. On July 2, the owners requested an extension of the loading date to 13–16 July—such a request is not a repudiation. The charterers responded by purporting to cancel the contract which constituted an anticipatory breach. The owners did not accept this repudiation and on July 5 told the charterers that the ship would after all be ready to load on July 8. However, the owners were not ready to load on that date and so the charterers exercised their option to cancel. The owners brought an action for deadfreight. The Court of Appeal held that the charterers' wrongful repudiation, which had not been accepted by the owners, did not preclude the charterers from cancelling the contract for the owners' failure to fulfil the obligations of the contract.

9–013   The House of Lords upheld the decision of the Court of Appeal that the cancellation was valid—the contract had survived intact with its right of cancellation unaffected. As Lord Ackner explained:

"When A wrongfully repudiates his contractual obligations in anticipation of the time for their performance, he presents the innocent party B with two choices. He may either affirm the contract by treating it as still in force or he may treat it as finally and conclusively discharged. There is no third choice, as a sort of *via media*, to affirm the contract and yet be absolved from tendering further performance unless and until A gives reasonable notice that he is once again able and willing to perform."

Thus the contract is kept alive for the benefit of both parties.

Acceptance of repudiation

9–014   Where the innocent party elects to accept the breach as a repudiation of the contract, this must, as a general rule, be communicated to the other party in a clear and unequivocal way. The issue

---

[26]   (1855) 5 E. & B. 714.
[27]   [1988] 3 W.L.R. 200.

of what constitutes adequate communication in such circumstances came before the House of Lords in *Vitol SA v Norelf Ltd, The Santa Clara*.[28]

The facts of the case were that Vitol agreed to purchase a cargo of propane from Norelf to be shipped from the United States and loaded on board ship at Houston between 1–7 March. Loading was not completed on March 8 and Vitol sent Norelf a telex repudiating the contract as loading would not be completed by March 9. The telex was found to amount to an anticipatory breach which, if accepted, would bring an immediate end to the contract. The loading was completed by March 9 and Norelf informed Vitol that this had been done on the March 11 but took no further steps to perform the contract. On March 15 Norelf managed to sell the propane to a third party at a price which was less than half the contract price. On August 9 Norelf sent a letter to Vitol claiming the difference between the contract price and the resale price. The dispute was referred to arbitration where an award was made in favour of Norelf. The arbitrator found that Vitol's wrongful repudiation had been accepted by Norelf as it had, to the knowledge of Vitol, not taken any further steps to perform the contract. This was sufficient communication of acceptance.

In the High Court, Phillips J. upheld the finding of the arbitrator. The Court of Appeal disagreed, holding that the innocent party's ability to elect between accepting the repudiation and affirming the contract made it necessary for the innocent party's choice to be clear and unequivocal. Although silence and inaction were in the generality of cases equally consistent with affirmation, they could not constitute acceptance of repudiation. The court considered that the innocent party's failure to perform was equivocal in that it was equally consistent with a misunderstanding by the innocent party as to their position, or with indecision or even inadvertence.

The House of Lords reversed the decision of the Court of Appeal and the decision of the arbitrator was reinstated. Lord Steyn stated the following principles as representing established law:

9–015

> "(1) Where a party has repudiated a contract the aggrieved party has an election to accept the repudiation or to affirm the contract . . . (2) an act of acceptance of a repudiation requires no particular form: a communication does not have to be couched in the language of acceptance. It is sufficient that the communication or conduct clearly and unequivocally conveys to the repudiating party that that aggrieved party is treating the contract as at an end. (3) . . . the aggrieved party need not personally, or by an agent, notify the repudiating party of his election to treat the contract as at an end. It is sufficient that the fact of the election comes to the repudiating party's attention, for example notification by an unauthorised broker or other intermediary may be sufficient."

The House of Lords considered that non-performance of an obligation was, as a matter of law, capable of constituting an act of acceptance of repudiation. Whether it did so depends on the particular contractual relationship and the particular circumstances. Ultimately the issue of whether, in *Vitol SA v Norelf*, the innocent party had accepted the repudiation was a matter of fact within the exclusive jurisdiction of the arbitrator.

There will be occasions when a party treats some action by the other party as repudiatory when subsequently it turns out not to be so, by the decision of a court. In such a situation the

---

[28] [1996] A.C. 800.

erstwhile "innocent" party finds itself in breach of contract for its response to the alleged repudiation. The case of *Hong Kong Fir Shipping v Kawasaki Kaisen Kaisha*, which was discussed at para.6–048, affords a good illustration of this state of affairs. Similarly, in *Federal Commerce and Navigation Ltd v Molena Alpha Inc, The Nanfri*[29] under the charterparty of a ship, the charterers deducted certain sums from their hire payments. The shipowners disputed the charterers' right to do this and withdrew their authority to sign bills of lading; the result was that the charterers could not work the ship if such bills were not issued. The shipowners honestly believed that they were entitled to act as they did—the charterers claimed that the shipowners' actions amounted to a repudiatory breach. The House of Lords agreed with the charterers. Doubts were cast by the majority of the House of Lords in a later case as to the validity of this conclusion.

9–016   In *Woodar Investment Development Ltd v Wimpey Construction Ltd*[30] (the case is discussed more fully at para.8–017) a party purported to exercise a right of rescission provided for by the contract although the circumstances giving rise to this right were not present. They honestly believed they had a right to rescind. Even though the actual motive for rescission was to escape an uneconomic transaction, it was held that there had not been a repudiatory breach. Lord Wilberforce considered that a party who in good faith relies on an express provision in contract in order to rescind or terminate the contract should not be treated a having repudiated if it turns out they were mistaken as to their rights. His Lordship thought that repudiation was a "drastic conclusion" which should only arise where a party was clearly refusing to perform their contractual obligations, in a matter going to the root of the contract. This approach was subsequently applied by the Privy Council in *Vaswani v Italian Motors (Sales and Services) Ltd*.[31]

Once acceptance of the breach is communicated to the party committing a repudiatory breach, the contract is terminated for the future. The party in breach will be liable for the breach leading to the termination of the contract, and also for any earlier breaches, but they will be excused further performance. In some of the cases we have discussed thus far, there are references to a party "rescinding" the contract for breach. That this terminology is not technically correct in the circumstances in which it is used was confirmed by the House of Lords in *Johnson v Agnew*[32] where Lord Wilberforce said:

> "[T]his so-called 'rescission' is quite different from rescisson *ab initio*, such as may arise for example in cases of mistake, fraud or lack of consent. In those cases, the contract is treated as never having come into existence . . . In the case of an accepted repudiatory breach the contract has come into existence but has been put to an end or discharged. Whatever contrary indications may be disinterred from old authorities, it is now quite clear, under the general law of contract, that acceptance of a repudiatory breach does not bring about 'rescission *ab initio*.'"

Rescission ab intio is discussed at para.11–029 in the context of rescission for misrepresentation.

---

[29] [1979] A.C. 757.
[30] [1980] 1 W.L.R. 277.
[31] (1996) 1 W.L.R. 270.
[32] [1980] A.C. 367.

DISCHARGE BY AGREEMENT

Just as contract must be created by agreement so it must be discharged by agreement. It follows that as consideration is required for the formation of contract, as a general rule it is required for the dissolution of a contract. In some cases, formalities may be required.

9–017

Consideration and formalities

Discharge by agreement may be "bilateral" or "unilateral".

9–018

Bilateral discharge

Where a simple contract is executory on both sides, an agreement to discharge the contract provides its own consideration; each party agrees to release the other from their outstanding respective obligations under the contract.

9–019

Unilateral discharge

Where a simple contract is executed on one side, a deed will be effective to release the other party from their obligations under the contract. In the absence of a deed, the other party must provide fresh consideration. This termed an "accord and satisfaction". This was explained by Scrutton L.J. in *British Russian Gazette and Trade Outlook Ltd v Associated Newspapers Ltd*[33] as follows:

9–020

> "Accord and satisfaction is the purchase of a release from an obligation, whether arising under contract or tort by means of any valuable consideration, not being the actual performance of the obligation itself. The accord is the agreement by which the obligation is discharged. The satisfaction is the consideration which makes the agreement operative."

What might constitute "satisfaction" is illustrated by *Pinnel's Case* which concerned the part-payment of a debt (the case is discussed at para.4–029). That case envisaged executed satisfaction but it seems that an executory promise may suffice. In *Elton Cop Dyeing Co v Broadbent & Son Ltd*[34] a purchaser of defective machinery reached a compromise with the seller that he would withdraw an action for breach of contract if the seller would promise to repair the machinery, sharing the cost. The seller's executory promise to repair was effective to discharge the buyer's cause of action.

The satisfaction must not consist of a lesser obligation than was owed under the original contract (see para.4–029). But even in the absence of valid satisfaction a promise to discharge a party from liability may be binding under the doctrine of promissory estoppel although it should not be forgotten that there are doubts as to whether the doctrine extends to a promise to extinguish rights (see paras. 4–036 and 4–045).

---

[33] [1933] 2 K.B. 616. It should be noted that no satisfaction is required for the discharge of a bill of exchange or a promissory note: Bills of Exchange Act 1882, s.62.

[34] (1919) 89 L.J.K.B. 186.

Formalities

9–021   There are two special cases:

(1) Contracts required to be evidenced in writing. Where the contract is one that is required to be evidenced in writing in order to be enforceable (see para.5–XX above) it may be discharged by an oral agreement with no requirement of written evidence. Although the oral words will suffice to discharge the original agreement, any new agreement substituted in its place will be required to be evidenced in writing.[35]

(2) Contracts contained in a deed. At common law, a contract contained in a deed could only be discharged in the form in which it was made. However, in equity (which now prevails) such a contract may be discharged or by an oral or written simple contract. This was confirmed in *Berry v Berry*.[36]

Variation and waiver

9–022   Thus far we have been considering the situation where a contract is discharged by agreement. This must be distinguished from the situation where the contract remains in being but the parties wish to alter or vary the terms. Such a variation of a simple contract will require consideration to be enforceable. What constitutes consideration in such circumstances is discussed at paras. 4–017 to 4–026.

Since variation requires consideration, and in some cases formalities, the common law developed the doctrine of "waiver", principally as a means of evading the requirements of the Statute of Frauds (see para.5–006). Whereas a variation involves an alteration in the terms of a contract, a waiver is an indulgence voluntarily given by one party to the other that the former will not insist on the precise mode of performance laid down by the contract. The important point to note is that a waiver may take effect without consideration and without the formalities that may be required for certain types of variation. In other words, a purely gratuitous promise is regarded as binding, something which in strict theory, ought not to be the case. A common example is where a buyer of goods allows the seller to make late delivery.

At common law, the waiver is binding on the party who grants it[37] and the party seeking the indulgence is not permitted to repudiate the waiver and set up the original terms of the contract.[38] In *Charles Rickards Ltd v Oppenheim*[39] (the facts are given at para.9–008) the original time limit for performance was postponed and although that waiver was binding on party who granted it, by giving reasonable notice he was able to make time of the essence again by warning that he would cancel the contract unless the goods were delivered by a stipulated date. Thus, as a general rule, the party granting the waiver may be able to revert to their strict legal rights by giving reasonable notice.

It is clear that the common law doctrine of waiver is closely akin to the equitable doctrine of promissory estoppel which was discussed in Chapter 4. Indeed in *Charles Rickards Ltd v*

[35] *Morris v Baron & Co* [1918] A.C. 1.
[36] [1929] 2 K.B. 316.
[37] *Hartley v Hymans* [1920] 3 K.B. 475.
[38] *Levey & Co v Goldberg* [1922] 1 K.B. 688.
[39] [1950] 1 K.B. 616.

Oppenheim, Denning L.J. made the following observation concerning the defendant's agreement to postpone the time limit for performance:

"Whether it be called waiver or forbearance on his part, or an agreed variation or substituted performance, does not matter. It is a kind of estoppel. By his conduct he evinced an intention to affect their legal relations. He made, in effect, a promise not to insist on his strict legal rights. That promise was intended to be acted on, and was in fact acted on. He cannot afterwards go back on it."

It is probably not a strict requirement of waiver that the party who is granted the indulgence has relied on it, but in cases where the time for performance has been postponed this will have happened in any event.

Discharge by performance, breach and agreement: conclusion

We have examined discharge by performance and discharge by breach under separate headings but it should be noted that performance and breach are closely interconnected.   **9–023**

A very common type of contractual dispute may involve both aspects. For example, suppose a householder, A, contracts with B, a builder, to construct a small extension to A's house for an agreed price of £10,000. B carries out the work and feels that he has performed all that he was obliged to do under the contract, i.e. that he is discharged from further obligation and claims the contract price. A, however, may feel that B's performance is defective in that the work is sub-standard and therefore he, A, is discharged from his obligation to pay the contract price. Alternatively, A may feel that B should at least remedy the defects or deduct a sum from the contract price representing the cost of remedying them. B may counter this by arguing that the work is not in fact defective.

If B's workmanship is defective so that he has breached the contract, A's rights will depend upon the terms of the contract. If there has been a breach of what amounts to a condition or a very serious breach of an innominate term, A may be justified in regarding himself as discharged from his obligation to make payment under the contract. Otherwise he will not.

Further reading

Burrows, *Law Commission Report on Pecuniary Restitution on Breach of Contract* (1984) M.L.R. 47.
Treitel, *Affirmation After Repudiatory Breach* (1998) 114 L.Q.R. 22.
Dugdale and Yates, *Variation, Waiver and Estoppel – A Reappraisal* (1976) 38 M.L.R. 680.

Chapter 10

FRUSTRATION

A contract may be discharged under the doctrine of frustration.

10–001

Discharge by performance and breach, which were considered in the previous chapter, were concerned with the situation where one party, or possibly both parties, are at fault in some way in relation to the performance of the contract. We saw that a party will be discharged from the contract by a failure by the other party substantially to perform the contract or the commission by the other of a repudiatory breach of contract. Even here, the innocent party may elect either to accept or reject the breach as terminating the contract.

Frustration, however, is concerned with a different situation. Suppose that, during the currency of a contract, the objective that the parties had in view becomes impossible to achieve owing to a fundamental change of circumstances that is outside their control. The result is that the parties would have to perform a contract radically different from that originally undertaken. Where this occurs the law may treat the contract as having become frustrated in which case the contract will be discharged and the parties excused further performance. Frustration is sometimes termed "subsequent" or "supervening" impossibility so as to distinguish it from "initial" impossibility or common mistake (see para.12–005). Common mistake, which if operative, renders the contract void, may arise from similar factual circumstances—the difference is that the particular event occurs before the parties reach agreement. The doctrine of frustration will not apply where the parties have themselves expressly provided in the contract where the loss will lie on the occurrence of particular eventualities. Such provisions are termed force majeure clauses and they are very common in commercial contracts.

Origins and theoretical basis of the doctrine

The old rule at common law was the rule as to "absolute contracts" which provided that where a person undertook a contractual obligation, they were absolutely bound to deliver it even if prevented by circumstances beyond their control. In *Paradine v Jane*[1] a tenant was sued for arrears of rent and pleaded in his defence that he had been evicted from the land by Prince Rupert, an enemy alien with a hostile army. As a result, he was unable to take the benefit of the lease because of events not of his making. The Court of King's Bench held that this was no excuse and the tenant was liable for the rent. This seems harsh; it was justified by the court on the basis that the parties were free to make provision for a particular event in their contract. But

10–002

[1] (1647) Aleyn 26.

this possibility, which continues to be the case today as noted above, is hardly sufficient to mitigate the potential injustice of the absolute contracts rule.

The judges in the nineteenth century recognised this and in *Taylor v Caldwell*[2] found a way of creating an exception where a contract, without the fault of either party, becomes impossible of performance through some event beyond the parties' control. This case paved the way for the development of the modern doctrine of frustration.

In *Taylor v Caldwell* the defendant agreed to give the claimant the use of the "Surrey Gardens and Music Hall" for a series of concerts on certain specified days. Without the fault of either party, a week before the date of the first concert the music hall was destroyed by fire. The claimant's action for damages for breach of contract failed, the court holding that since the contract could not be carried out, the parties were excused further performance. Giving the judgment of the court, Blackburn J. found that the agreement was subject to an implied term that the music hall would continue to exist at the time when the contract was to be fulfilled. Although there was no express term to this effect, this must have been the intention of the parties who, had they thought about it at the time of the contract, would have readily agreed to such an insertion.

10–003   As to the theoretical premise upon which the doctrine of frustration is based, many theories have been identified although two leading ones have emerged. The first is the "implied term" theory which, as we have seen, stems from *Taylor v Caldwell* and it has been followed in many subsequent cases. In *F A Tamplin Steamship Co Ltd v Anglo-Mexican Petroleum Products Co Ltd*,[3] Lord Loreburn endorsed the approach in the following terms:

> "A court can and ought to examine the contract . . . in order to see whether or not from the nature of it the parties must have made their bargain on the footing that a particular thing or state of things would continue to exist. And if they must have done so, then a term to that effect will be implied, though it be not expressed in the contract . . . no court has an absolving power, but it can infer from the nature of the contract and the surrounding circumstances that a condition which is not expressed was a foundation on which the parties contracted."

The notion that frustration rests on an implied term doubtless proved attractive to the courts in the earlier cases as it was not inconsistent with freedom of contract under which the rights and liabilities of the parties are determined at the time of the contract according to their actual or presumed intentions. It may be recalled, however, (see para.6–022) that terms can only be implied in fact (as opposed to terms implied in law) where they concern facts which are within the knowledge of both parties—something "so obvious it goes without saying".

Accordingly, the implied term theory has been called into question in later cases on the basis that it rests on a fiction—in *Davis Contractors Ltd v Fareham Urban District Council*[4] Lord Radcliffe found a logical difficulty "in seeing how the parties could even have impliedly provided for something which, *ex hypothesi*, they neither expected nor foresaw". Lord Radcliffe went on to expound what he saw as the true basis of the intervention of the courts in cases of frustration. He said:

> "Frustration occurs whenever the law recognises that without the default of either party a contractual obligation has become incapable of being performed because the circum-

---

[2] (1863) 3 B. & S. 826.
[3] [1916] 2 A.C. 397.
[4] [1956] A.C. 696.

stances in which performance is called for would render a thing radically different from that which was undertaken by the contract. *Non haec in foedera veni*. It was not this that I promised to do."

This approach has been termed the "construction" theory in that it involves construing the contract in the light of its nature and surrounding circumstances in order to establish the parties' obligations. If what has occurred subsequently would require the parties to perform something fundamentally or radically different from that which was originally undertaken, the contract will be discharged by operation of law. This approach was preferred by the House of Lords in *National Carriers Ltd v Panalpina (Northern) Ltd*[5] and has been approved (obiter) more recently by the Court of Appeal in *Great Peace Shipping Ltd v Tsavliris Salvage (International) Ltd*.[6] In essence, the two theories are not that different from each other but the "construction" formula provides a more certain basis for frustration as it is the more objective of the two formulations. In reality, both are probably no more than attempts to describe the basis on which justice requires a departure from the absolute contracts rule and enables the court to impose a solution in the form of dissolving the contract.[7] Nevertheless, the construction theory is the one currently in favour.

10–004

It may be useful at this point to recap. A contract will become frustrated where something occurs which: (a) is not due to the actions of either party; (b) brings about a radical change in the obligation originally undertaken by the parties; and (c) is not an event for which the risk of occurrence is provided for by the contract. In the case of (c) not being satisfied, the legal position between the parties to the contract is governed by the terms of the contract and the law of frustration is excluded.

Frustrating events

The situations in which a contract might become frustrated cannot be exhaustively listed but it will be convenient to categorise some of the decided cases under a number of discrete headings. These are (i) impossibility; (ii) illegality; (iii) non-occurrence of an event; and (iv) leaseholds.

10–005

Impossibility

A contract may become frustrated through impossibility where the subject matter is destroyed. The case of *Taylor v Caldwell*, discussed above, affords a classic example. Similarly, frustration may occur where the subject matter becomes, through some extraneous cause, unavailable as in *Nickoll & Knight v Ashton Eldridge & Co*[8] where a ship required for the performance of the contract became stranded.

10–006

The unavailability of a particular person required for the performance of a contract may have the effect of frustrating the contract. As with any case of unavailability, the position may

---

[5] [1981] A.C. 675.
[6] [2003] Q.B. 678.
[7] See, for example, the comments of Lord Sumner in *Hirji Mulji v Cheong Yue Steamship Co Ltd* [1926] A.C. 497 at p. 510.
[8] [1901] 2 KB 126. See also *Jackson v Union Marine Insurance Co Ltd* (1874) L.R. 10 C.P. 125, where a ship under charter ran aground and the interruption was held to be of sufficient duration for the contract to be frustrated.

depend on the length of the period of time for which the person is, or is likely to be, unavailable. Such unavailability may occur through death, illness, internment or other circumstances.

In *Morgan v Manser*[9] the defendant was the comedian "Cheerful" Charlie Chester and in 1938 he engaged the claimant as his manager for a period of 10 years. Under the terms of the contract, the defendant was not to undertake any professional engagements without the claimant's consent. In 1940 the claimant was conscripted and after the war he sought damages for breach of contract from the defendant as he had undertaken engagements without the claimant's permission. It was held that the contract was frustrated as the claimant's military service might have lasted for the duration of the war which may have endured for a substantial part of the 10 year period. In *Condor v The Barron Knights Ltd*[10] a talented drummer was contracted with a pop group to play seven nights a week for them for five years but, shortly after the contract was entered into, he suffered a minor nervous breakdown. He was medically advised that he should only work four nights a week if he was to avoid a more serious breakdown. The group dismissed him but his action for wrongful dismissal failed. The contract had become frustrated—there was a real possibility that serious illness would result if the drummer tried to go on and it was impossible to tell when, if ever, he would fully recover.

10–007 Where the period of unavailability is, or is likely to be, short, the contract may not be frustrated. Thus on the outbreak of World War I a long term agency contract was held not to be frustrated where the agent was interned. As the agent was an Alsatian of French extraction and had anti-German sympathies the internment was not likely to last for very long.[11]

Illegality

10–008 A contract may become frustrated where, owing to a change in the law, further performance becomes illegal. One such example may occur on the outbreak of hostilities where a declaration of war may render further performance of a trading contract illegal as trading with the enemy. Thus in *Fibrosa SA v Fairbairn Lawson Combe Barbour Ltd*[12] a contract whereby an English company agreed to sell machinery to a company in Poland was frustrated after the invasion of Poland by Germany led to a declaration of war.

The requisitioning of property by the government can lead to frustration. In *Metropolitan Water Board v Dick, Kerr & Co*[13] the respondents agreed in July 1914 to construct an extensive reservoir system for the appellants, to be completed within six years. The agreement contained a term that if work should be "unduly delayed or impeded", an extension of time would be granted. In August 1914, World War I broke out and in February 1916 the Minister of Munitions ordered the work to stop and the plant to be sold. This order was made under emergency regulations and was still in force in November 1917. The respondents claimed that the order had frustrated the contract but the appellants contended that the contract should continue with an extension of time. The House of Lords held that the contract had been frustrated—the undue delay envisaged by the parties did not include the interruption that had in fact occurred. This stoppage was of such a character and duration that the contract, if resumed,

---

[9] [1948] 1 K.B. 184.
[10] [1966] 1 W.L.R. 87.
[11] *Nordman v Rayner & Sturgess* (1916) 33 T.L.R. 87. The period of internment lasted for one month.
[12] [1943] A.C. 32. See also *Avery v Bowden* (1855) 5 E. & B. 714, discussed at para.9–012 above.
[13] [1918] A.C. 119. See further *Denny, Mott & Dickson Ltd v Fraser & Co Ltd* [1944] A.C. 265.

would be of an essentially different nature from the one that had been compulsorily suspended. The opposite conclusion was arrived by a majority of the House of Lords in *F A Tamplin Steamship Co v Anglo-Mexican Petroleum Products Ltd*[14] where a ship was requisitioned by the government for use as a troopship in February 1915. The respondents had chartered the vessel from the appellants for a period of five years from December 1912. The appellants, wishing to receive compensation from the government, argued that the requisitioning had the effect of discharging the contract. The court disagreed, holding that the contract was not frustrated. The interference was insufficiently serious as there might have been many months during which the ship would have been commercially available before the five years had expired.

Non-occurrence of an event

There may be cases where a contract is entered into in contemplation of the happening of some event. If the event does not take place, the question may arise as to whether the contract is frustrated. It is a feature of such cases that performance may be technically or literally possible but the contract may be rendered futile by the non-occurrence of the particular event. The predicament arose in relation to the postponement, owing to illness, of the coronation of Edward VII in a number of so-called "coronation cases". Two well-known such cases that are difficult to reconcile are *Krell v Henry*[15] and *Herne Bay Steam Boat Co v Hutton*.[16]

10–009

In the former case, the defendant Henry agreed in writing to hire from the claimant Krell an apartment overlooking Pall Mall for the two days planned for the coronation processions of Edward VII. The contract contained no express reference to the coronation processions although the rooms were advertised by the claimant as being suitable for viewing the processions. The contract provided that the defendant was to have the use of the rooms during the daytime only. The defendant paid a deposit as agreed but when the coronation was cancelled he refused to pay the balance and the claimant sued him for it. The Court of Appeal held that the claimant was not entitled to recover the balance as the contract was frustrated. Drawing necessary inferences from the surrounding circumstances, the court concluded that the coronation processions were regarded by both parties as the "foundation" of the contract and their non-occurrence discharged the contract. As Vaughan-Williams L.J. explained:

> "The use of the rooms was let and taken for the purpose of seeing the Royal procession. It was not a demise of the rooms, or even an agreement to let and take the rooms. It is a licence to use the rooms for a particular purpose and none other . . . the taking place of those processions on the days proclaimed along the proclaimed route, which passed 56A Pall Mall, was regarded by both parties as the foundation of the contract."

In the *Herne Bay* case the Court of Appeal (made up of the same judges as *Krell v Henry*) came to a different conclusion on the question of frustration. Here the defendant chartered the vessel *SS Cynthia* from the claimant for the two days of Edward VII's coronation festivities. The defendant wished to take fare paying passengers to see the naval review by the King at Spithead where the fleet was anchored. The written contract provided that the purpose of the charter was

---

[14] [1916] 2 A.C. 397.
[15] [1903] 2 K.B. 740.
[16] [1903] 2 K.B. 683.

"viewing the naval review and for a day's cruise round the fleet." Owing to the King's illness, the review was cancelled although the fleet remained anchored at Spithead. The claimant successfully sued the defendant for the balance of the hire charge, the court holding that the contract was not frustrated.

10–010   At first sight the decisions in the two cases are hard to reconcile—however the Court of Appeal in the *Herne Bay* case seem to have concluded that it was still possible, as a commercial venture, for the defendant to take fare-paying passengers for a cruise round the fleet. Vaughan-Williams L.J. considered that the defendant, in hiring the vessel had two objects in view, i.e. first, taking passengers to see the naval review; and secondly, taking them round the fleet. It could not be inferred, merely because those were the defendant's purposes, that the happening of the naval review was the basis and foundation of the contract. Romer L.J. saw the contract as one merely for the hire of a ship and the fact that the defendant, as hirer, had a special object in view was a matter with which the defendant alone was concerned. He said:

> "The ship (as a ship) had nothing particular to do with the review or the fleet except as a convenient carrier of passengers to see it: any other ship suitable for carrying passengers would have done equally as well. Just as in the case of the hire of a cab or other vehicle, although the object of the hirer may be stated, that statement would not make the object any less a matter for the hirer alone, and would not directly affect the person who was letting out the vehicle for hire."

The distinction drawn in these cases is an extremely fine one but it is submitted that the distinction is correctly drawn—the very special and unusual facts in *Krell v Henry* meant that both parties must have regarded the coronation processions as the foundation and object of the contract. The contract was to provide a view of a particular procession, it was not merely for the hire of a room in Pall Mall. Nevertheless *Krell v Henry* has been criticised as taking the doctrine of frustration a step too far in that it potentially allows parties to escape from transactions which have become less profitable owing to changed circumstances.

Leaseholds

10–011   At one time there was uncertainty as to whether the doctrine of frustration could apply to a lease of land. It was considered by many that the doctrine could not apply to leaseholds because the grant of a lease creates a legal estate in the land—it is more than merely a contract for the use of the land for a particular purpose. It is clear from the decision in *Krell v Henry*, however, that a contractual licence to use land for a special purpose can be frustrated and in *Amalgamated Investment and Property Co Ltd v John Walker & Sons Ltd*[17] the Court of Appeal seem to have assumed that a contract for the sale of land can be frustrated. It seems illogical, especially where premises are let for commercial purposes, to say that a leasehold could not also be discharged by impossibility

In 1945 the matter was left open by the House of Lords in *Cricklewood Property and Investment Trust Ltd v Leighton's Investment Trust Ltd*.[18] The facts were that the defendants took a 99-year building lease from the claimants in 1936, the defendants covenanting to build

---

[17] [1976] 3 All E.R. 509. For a discussion of the case, see para.12–051.
[18] [1945] A.C. 221.

a shopping centre on the land to serve a residential area. Before building could begin, World War II broke out and government regulations were introduced which prevented the shops from being built. The defendants stopped paying rent and contended that the lease had been frustrated. The House of Lords held that the defendants were not excused from paying rent. Their Lordships were unanimous that, even if a lease could be frustrated, it could not be frustrated on these particular facts. Over 90 years were left to run on the lease and the prohibition on building would not be in force for anything like that period of time. On the theoretical issue of whether a lease could be frustrated Viscount Simon L.C. considered that, given the right circumstances, the doctrine could apply. Lord Wright, who was in agreement with Lord Simon on this point stressed that frustration might occur but only in "rare and exceptional cases." He gave the example of a 99-year building lease subjected by a public body to an indefinite prohibition on building, the end of which, if it ever came, could not be foreseen. Lords Russell and Goddard, however, considered that a lease could not be frustrated and Lord Porter expressed no opinion on the matter.

The judicial uncertainty on the issue was resolved by a later decision of the House of Lords, **10–012**
National Carriers Ltd v Panalpina (Northern) Ltd.[19] In January 1974 the defendants leased a warehouse from the claimants for a period of 10 years. In May 1979 the street where the warehouse was situated was closed to traffic owing to the dangerous condition of another warehouse nearby. The street was the only vehicular access to the demised premises and the closure was likely to last for some eighteen months. The defendants claimed that the lease had been frustrated but the House of Lords found that there had been no frustration—after the interruption, three years of the lease would still be left to run. Four of their Lordships held that frustration could, as a matter of principle, apply to a lease (Lord Russell expressed doubts) although it would only do so rarely. A lease for a long term of years is unlikely to be frustrated as the period of interruption will in many cases represent a small proportion of the demised term. Frustration is more likely to occur where land is leased for a short term for a particular purpose which then, owing to some supervening event outside the parties' control, becomes impossible to fulfil. In practice, many leases contain express covenants dealing with particular eventualities, should they occur.

Limits to the doctrine of frustration

We have already looked at cases where the courts have held that a particular contract is not **10–013**
frustrated because the change of events has not brought about a fundamental change in the contractual obligation or that a particular event is not, for both parties, the foundation of the contract. Over the years the courts have developed some more specific limitations on frustration which at this point require examination.

Contract merely more onerous

A contract will not be frustrated where a change of circumstances makes it more onerous or **10–014**
expensive to perform but does not bring about a radical change in the obligation originally entered into by the parties.

[19] [1981] A.C. 675.

In *Davis Contractors Ltd v Fareham Urban District Council*[20] the claimant contractors entered into a building contract to build 78 council houses for the defendant local authority for a specified sum within eight months. Owing to labour shortages (a circumstance outside the parties' control) the work took some 22 months. The contract therefore proved unprofitable for the claimants as their costs exceeded the agreed price. They argued that the contract had been frustrated by delay and that they were therefore entitled to a sum in excess of the contract price on a quantum meruit basis. The House of Lords held that the contract had not been frustrated—it was true that the claimant's obligations had become more onerous than they had expected but this was not a ground for relieving them of their contractual obligations. The possibility of insufficient labour being available was a risk which the claimants must be taken to have been aware and it could have been provided for in the contract. In a well-known dictum Lord Radcliffe said:

> "[I]t is not hardship or inconvenience or material loss itself which calls the principle of frustration into play. There must be as well such a change in the significance of the obligation that the thing undertaken would, if performed, be a different thing from that contracted for."

The principle that a contract will not be discharged by frustration where it becomes more expensive to perform was illustrated in litigation arising out of the closure of the Suez Canal during the international crisis of 1956. In *Tsakiroglou & Co Ltd v Noblee & Thorl GmbH*[21] the appellants, in October 1956, agreed to sell 300 tons of Sudanese groundnuts to the respondents and to ship them to Hamburg from Sudan in November or December 1956. The normal route for shipment was via Suez and the price of the nuts had been assessed on that basis although the contract did not stipulate it as the exclusive route. In the wake of military action the Suez Canal was closed to shipping on November 2, 1956 until April 1957 and the appellants failed to deliver the goods. In an action by the respondents for damages, the appellants claimed that the contract was frustrated because shipment would have to made via the Cape of Good Hope. This voyage was more than twice as long as via Suez and much more costly. The House of Lords held that the contract was not frustrated—the voyage via the Cape was not commercially or fundamentally different from shipment via the Canal, merely more expensive.

Self-induced frustration

10–015   We have already observed that frustration will only occur where the event is not due to the actions of either party. This principle is often expressed by saying that the alleged frustration should not be "self-induced". Obviously, where one party is in breach of contract, that party cannot rely on frustration and the other party will be entitled to damages and may be entitled to repudiate the contract. But the law goes further than this and provides that frustration cannot apply where the alleged frustrating event arises from a deliberate act or choice of one party.

In *Maritime National Fish Ltd v Ocean Trawlers Ltd*[22] the appellants chartered a steam trawler, the *St Cuthbert*, from the respondents which was fitted with an otter trawl. Both parties

---

[20] [1956] A.C. 696.
[21] [1962] A.C. 93. See also *Ocean Tramp Tankers Corporation v V/0 Sovfracht, The Eugenia* [1964] 2 Q.B. 226.
[22] [1935] A.C. 524.

were aware that, under the Canadian Fisheries Act, it was an offence to use an otter trawl without a licence from the Canadian government. The appellants applied for five licences but only obtained three. They elected to use the three licences for their own vessels and not the *St Cuthbert* with the result that the ship could not be used. The respondents brought an action for the hire charges and the appellants sought to repudiate the charterparty on the grounds of frustration. The Privy Council held that the contract was not frustrated as the alleged frustration was due to the election of the appellants who remained liable for the hire. As the decision was based on this ground, the Judicial Committee did not consider it necessary to rule on another argument raised, namely that the contract could not be frustrated by an event which the parties must have contemplated when the contract was made. They were aware of the need for a licence and the appellants might be deemed to have taken the risk that one would not be granted, but they had inserted no provision in the contract for that eventuality.

The principle in the *Martime National Fish* case was applied controversially by the Court of Appeal in *J Lauritzen AS v Wijsmuller BV, The Super Servant Two*.[23] In this case, the defendants contracted with the claimants to transport a large drilling rig belonging to the claimants from a Japanese shipyard to Rotterdam. Under the terms of the contract, the rig was to be transported by either the vessel *Super Servant One* or *Super Servant Two* at the defendants' option. The defendants allocated the *Super Servant Two* to perform the contract and allocated her sister ship *Super Servant One* to other contracts with third parties. Prior to performance, *Super Servant Two* sank whilst being used on another job in the Zaire River. Since *Super Servant One* was engaged on other duties, the defendants informed the claimants that they would not be performing the contract. It was held that the claimants could not rely on frustration.

The court took the view that the defendants did have a choice—they could have applied *Super Servant One* to the contract with the claimants but had chosen not to do so. The fact that this would have placed them in breach of contract with third parties made no difference. Thus frustration is something that discharges the contract automatically and cannot depend on a decision of one of the parties, however reasonable and commercially sound that decision may be, and even if they have been neither negligent nor in breach of contract.

10–016

The decision in the case of *The Super Servant Two* has attracted considerable criticism. Thus it has been argued that the defendants did not have any real choice—they could not allocate the *Super Servant One* to all the contracts they had concluded and so the sinking of the *Super Servant Two* compelled them to make the decision they did.[24] The decision is therefore seen as harsh, placing all the risk on the defendant even where the circumstances which give rise to the non-performance of the contract are effectively beyond their control. On the other hand, it may not be just to place all the risk on the claimant where the defendant has perhaps unwisely entered into over-extensive commitments. It is, of course, open to the defendant to obtain some protection by negotiating a force majeure clause and indeed this was the case in *The Super Servant Two* as the contract did contain such a clause. The court held that the clause could be relied on provided the sinking of *Super Servant Two* occurred without any negligence on the part of the defendants or their employees.

The cases discussed so far on the issue of self-induced frustration concerned parties exercising a choice so as to bring about the allegedly frustrating event. What is the position where a party commits a negligent act so as bring about the particular event which it is claimed frustrates the contract? In general terms the answer must be that the frustration would be regarded

---

[23] [1990] 1 Lloyd's Rep. 1.
[24] See, e.g. McKendrick [1990] L.M.C.L.Q. 153.

as self-induced—in *Taylor v Caldwell* (see para.10–002) Blackburn J. considered that where the fire which brought about the destruction of the concert hall had been caused by the negligence of the owners, the contract would not have been frustrated.

It seems that the burden of proving self-induced frustration lies on the party making the allegation.[25]

Supervening event foreseeable

10–017   As a general rule a contract will not be frustrated by events which were foreseen, or should have been foreseen, by both parties, on the basis that they could have provided for it in their contract.

There are many dicta to this effect the cases. For example, in *Cricklewood Property and Investment Trust Ltd v Leighton's Investment Trust Ltd* (the facts are given at para 10–001) Viscount Simon L.C. in the House of Lords referred to frustration as being an intervening event "entirely beyond what was contemplated by the parties when they entered into the agreement." And in *Davis Contractors Ltd v Fareham Urban District Council* (the case is discussed at para.110–014), where it was held that a building contract was not frustrated by labour shortages, Lord Radcliffe (with whom the other members of the House agreed) explicitly held that frustration did not apply because, first, the delay was not due to any new state of affairs which the parties could not have reasonably foreseen; and secondly, the possibility of insufficient resources was within the parties' contemplation but was not made the subject of special provision in the contract.

The cases are not quite all one way. It has been recognised that the parties may foresee a particular event but are unable to agree as to what provision to place in the contract to provide for it. This is what happened in *Ocean Tramp Tankers Corporation v VIO Sovfracht, The Eugenia*[26] where the Court of Appeal found that although the parties had contemplated the possibility of the closure of the Suez Canal, this did not mean that the charterparty could not be frustrated by that event. On the issue of forseeability Lord Denning M.R. said:

> "It has frequently been said that the doctrine of frustration only applies where the new situation is 'unforeseen' or 'unexpected' or 'uncontemplated' as if that were an essential feature. But it is not so. The only thing that is essential is that the parties should have made no provision for it in the contract. The only relevance of it being 'unforeseen' is this: if the parties did not foresee anything of the kind happening, you can readily infer they have made no provision for it: whereas if they did foresee it, you would expect them to make provision for it."

Lord Denning made reference to the case of *W J Tatem Ltd v Gamboa*[27] where Goddard J. held that the charterparty of a ship carrying refugees during the Spanish Civil War was not frustrated when the ship was seized by a Nationalist cruiser, even though this was foreseeable. The decision is usually explained on the ground that it was not foreseeable that the ship would be seized for such a lengthy period of time, nevertheless Goddard J. stated that the contract would have been frustrated even if this eventuality had been foreseen. These dicta of Lord Denning and Goddard J. suggest that a high degree of forseeability is required to exclude frustration.

---

[25] *Joseph Constantine Steamship Line Ltd v Imperial Smelting Corporation ltd* [1942] A.C. 154.
[26] [1964] 2 Q.B. 226.
[27] [1939] 1 K.B. 132.

There is one clear exception to the principle that a contract cannot be frustrated where the **10–018** supervening event has been foreseen by both parties, and that is where the declaration of war renders a contract illegal as amounting to trading with the enemy. It makes no difference that the outbreak of war was foreseeable.

What is the position where the particular event is foreseen by one party but not the other? In *Walton Harvey v Walker & Homfrays Ltd*[28] the defendants granted the claimants the right to display an electric advertising sign on the defendants' hotel premises for a period of seven years. The defendants were aware, but the claimants were not, that there was a risk that the hotel would be compulsorily purchased and demolished within this period. When this eventuality occurred, the defendants contended that the contract was frustrated. The Court of Appeal held that the defendants were in breach of contract—the parties had impliedly agreed that the building would continue to exist whereas the possible compulsory acquisition of the hotel was within the contemplation of the defendants at the time of the contract. Accordingly, frustration was excluded.

Common assumption

There will be some cases where, although the particular event may or may not have been fore- **10–019** seen, performance of the contract is rendered impossible in a manner contemplated by only one of the parties. Frustration may be ousted here.

A classic illustration of this situation is the case of *Blackburn Bobbin Co Ltd v Allen & Sons Ltd*.[29] In this case there was an agreement by the defendants to supply the claimants with 70 standards of Finland birch timber at a certain price per standard. Owing to the outbreak of war, the defendants' source of Finnish timber was cut off. The claimants were unaware that such timber was normally imported and that stocks of it were not held in England. The Court of Appeal held that the contract was not frustrated as the source of supply was a matter of concern to one party only, i.e. the seller. As Pickford L.J. explained:

> "Why should a purchaser of goods, not specific goods, be deemed to concern himself with the way in which the seller is going to fulfil his contract by providing the goods he has agreed to sell? The sellers in this case agreed to deliver the timber free on rail at Hull and it was no concern of the buyers as to how the sellers intended to get the timber there. I can see no reason for saying . . . that the continuance of the normal mode of shipping the timber from Finland was a matter which both parties contemplated as necessary for the fulfilment of the contract."

Thus the lack of a common assumption between the parties may prevent frustration arising.

Event provided for

As has already been noted, a contract may contain an express provision dealing with the **10–020** possibility of a frustrating event which then in fact occurs. If this is the case, the doctrine of

---

[28] [1931] 1 Ch. 274.
[29] [1918] 2 K.B. 467.

frustration does not apply and the risks are allocated in accordance with the terms of the contract (illegality excepted).

It would seem that such provisions are construed quite narrowly by the courts. In *Jackson v Union Marine Insurance Co Ltd*[30] the ship *Spirit of the Dawn* was chartered to carry goods from Newport, Wales to San Francisco. It was a term of the charterparty that the vessel would proceed with all possible despatch "dangers and accidents of navigation excepted". The day after the ship left Liverpool in order to pick up the cargo from Newport, she ran aground in the Bay of Caernarvon. Six weeks later the charterers procured another ship and the *Spirit of the Dawn* was not fully repaired until a further five months had elapsed. The owners sued the defendant company on an insurance claim. The Court of Exchequer Chamber held that the contract was frustrated. The wording of the clause in question would have protected the owners from liability for delay but did not cover an interruption of such character and duration as occurred in this case. In *Metropolitan Water Board v Dick, Kerr & Co* (the facts are given at para.10–008) the clause provided that if the work were "unduly delayed or impeded" an extension of time would be granted. The House of Lords held that the clause did not apply to a delay of such a nature that it brought about a radical change in the obligation. The appellants' argument that the contract should remain on foot with an extension of time was rejected.

Legal effect of frustration

10–021   The legal effect of frustration at common law is to discharge the contract immediately and automatically as to the future from the moment of the frustrating event onwards.[31] The result is that the rights and liabilities of the parties existing before the frustrating event are preserved, whereas the rights and liabilities accruing after the frustrating event are extinguished. In this respect, frustration differs from an operative common mistake where the contract is void from the outset (see para.12–005) and it also differs from breach of contract where the innocent party may elect whether or not they wish to affirm the contract (see para.9–010).

The legal effect of frustration is sometimes described by saying that "the loss lies where it falls". There can be no doubt that it produced harsh consequences as illustrated by one of the "coronation cases", *Chandler v Webster*.[32] Here the claimant agreed to hire a room in Pall Mall from the defendant to watch the coronation procession. The contract price was £141. 15s and it was payable immediately. The claimant paid £100 on account, but before he paid the balance the procession was cancelled and the contract frustrated. The claimant sought to recover the £100 alleging a total failure of consideration[33] and the defendant counterclaimed for £41. 15s. The Court of Appeal held that not only could the claimant not recover the £100, he was also liable for the balance of £41. 15s as the obligation to pay the whole contract price had fallen due before frustration. In other words, the full amount was payable when the contract was still valid; the claimant had therefore paid a lot of money and got nothing in return. The law could not come to his assistance.

---

[30] L.R. 10 C.P. 125.
[31] *Hirji Mulji v Cheong Yue Steamship Co Ltd* [1926] A.C. 497.
[32] [1904] 1 K.B. 493.
[33] "Total failure of consideration" is discussed at para.17–019.

This rigid rule, which attracted widespread criticism, was modified by the House of Lords in *Fibrosa Spolka Akcyjna v Faibairn Lawson Combe Barbour Ltd.*[34] In this case, the respondents were an English company who agreed to sell some machinery to the appellants, a Polish firm. The goods were to be delivered to the appellant's factory in Gdynia, Poland with a deposit of one-third of the contract price of £4,800 being payable in advance. The sum of £1,000 had been paid by appellants when Poland was invaded by Germany in September 1939 and the contract was frustrated. The appellants, via their London agent, requested the recovery of the £1,000 but this was resisted on the ground that the respondents had already done considerable work on the machinery. It may be noticed at this point that if *Chandler v Webster* were applied, the deposit paid by the appellants would have been irrecoverable because it had been paid before frustration. Nevertheless the House of Lords held, overruling *Chandler v Webster*, that the appellants were entitled to recover the £1,000 as there had been a total failure of consideration—money had been paid to secure performance and there had been no performance. No machinery had been delivered.

The decision of the House of Lords in the *Fibrosa* case addressed the injustice of *Chandler v Webster* but the law was still unsatisfactory in two respects. First, it did not provide a remedy where the failure of consideration was only partial. So if the party seeking to recover a pre-payment had received some part of what they had contracted for (however minor), the failure of consideration would not be total and there could be no recovery. This would have been the case if the respondents had, before frustration, delivered some part of the machinery. Secondly, *Fibrosa* did not provide for the situation where the payee had incurred expenditure in reliance on the contract—as the respondents had done in *Fibrosa* but they received nothing by way of recompense.

10–022

Another consequence of the common rule that "the loss lies where it falls" is illustrated by the case of *Appleby v Myers*.[35] In that case, the claimants agreed to instal machinery in the defendants' factory for the sum of £459, payment on completion. When the work was nearly finished, an accidental fire destroyed the factory and all its contents. An action for £419 for work and materials failed—the contract was frustrated and no payment was due at the time of discharge. The defendants were not obliged to pay the claimants anything.

In an attempt to deal with these problems, the Law Reform (Frustrated Contracts) Act 1943 was passed.

Law Reform (Frustrated Contracts) Act 1943 (LR(FC)A)

The Act applies "where a contract governed by English law has become impossible of performance or been otherwise frustrated" (s.1(1)). The provisions of the Act may be excluded by the parties to a contract where the contract makes its own provisions as to the effect of frustration. In such a case, in the event of frustration, the contractual provisions will apply to the exclusion of the Act (s.2(3)). The Act essentially deals with two situations where it adjusts the rights and liabilities of the parties as established by the old common law. These are: (i) where money is paid or is payable before the frustrating event (s.1(2)); and (ii) where one party obtains a valuable benefit by reason of anything done by the other party in performance of the contract before the frustrating event (s.1(3)).

10–023

[34] [1943] A.C. 32.
[35] (1867) L.R. 2 C.P. 651.

Recovery of money paid – s.1(2)

10–024   LR(FC)A, s.1(2) provides as follows:

> "All sums paid or payable to any party in pursuance of a contract before the time when the parties were so discharged [ie by frustration] . . . shall, in the case of sums so paid, be recoverable from him as money received by him for the use of the party by whom the sums were paid, and, in the case of sums so payable, cease to be so payable:
>
> Provided that, if the party to whom the sums were so paid or payable incurred expenses before the time of discharge in, or for the purpose of, the performance of the contract, the court may, if it considers it just to do so having regard to all the circumstances of the case, allow him to retain or, as the case may be, recover the whole or any part of the sums so paid or payable, not being an amount in excess of the expenses so incurred."

The first part of the subsection repudiates *Chandler v Webster* and builds on the position established by *Fibrosa* in that it provides (to put it in simpler language) that money paid before the frustrating event is recoverable and money payable before frustration ceases to be payable, whether or not there has been a total failure of consideration.

The second part of the subsection fills a gap in *Fibrosa* by providing that if the party to whom such sums are paid or payable incurred expenses before discharge in performance of the contract, the court may *in its discretion* award them such expenses up to the limit of the money paid or payable before frustration as it considers just. For example, suppose that A contracts with B and, under the terms of the contract, £2,000 is payable by A to B on completion. Before frustration, A pays B a deposit of £500 but B incurs expenditure of £750. The maximum amount of expenditure that B can retain under s.1(2) is £500. The additional £250 cannot be recovered, unless s.1(3) (see below) can be invoked.

Further, the wording of the subsection makes it clear that if nothing was paid or payable before discharge, the relevant party will be unable to recover expenses under s.1(2), although, again, they may be able to rely on s.1(3).

10–025   The first reported case to consider the exercise of the court's discretion under s.1(2) was *Gamerco SA v ICM/Fair Warning (Agency) Ltd*.[36] The claimants, who were concert promoters, agreed with the defendants to promote a rock concert by the band "Guns N' Roses" at the Atletico Madrid stadium on a certain date. Owing to concerns about the structural safety of the stadium, the local authority closed it to the public just before the concert was due to be held. No other venue could be found at short notice and so the concert was cancelled. The contract was therefore frustrated. The claimants had paid $412,500 to the defendants in advance, with a balance of $362,500 to be paid later. The judge, Garland J., had difficulty in establishing the defendants' expenses but estimated them at $50,000. The claimants had also incurred expenses of some $450,000 prior to frustration. The judge held that justice would be served if the claimants recovered the advance payment of $412,500 under s.1(2) with the defendants not being allowed to set-off any expenditure incurred. In arriving at this decision the judge rejected the total retention of the deposit by the defendants or the equal division of the moneys between the parties. He said that there was:

[36] [1995] 1 W.L.R. 1126.

"... no indication in the [Act], the authorities or relevant literature that the court is obliged to incline towards total retention or equal division. Its task is to do justice in a situation which the parties had neither contemplated nor provided for, and to mitigate the possible harshness of allowing all loss to lie where it falls."

The judge therefore favoured an approach based on the court exercising a broad discretion under s.1(2) LR(FC)A.

Valuable benefit—s.1(3)

LR(FC)A, s.1(3) provides as follows: **10–026**

"Where any party to the contract has, by reason of anything done by any other party thereto in, or for the purpose of, the performance of the contract, obtained a valuable benefit (other than a payment of money to which the last forgoing subsection applies [ie s.1(2)]) before the time of discharge there shall be recoverable from him from by the said other party such sum (if any), not exceeding the value of the said benefit to the party obtaining it, as the court considers just, having regard to all the circumstances of the case and, in particular –
(a) the amount of any expenses incurred before the time of discharge by the benefited party in, or for the performance of the contract, including any sums paid or payable by him to any other party in pursuance of the contract and retained or recoverable by that party under the last foregoing subsection [ie s.1(2)], and
(b) the effect, in relation to the said benefit, of the circumstances giving rise to the frustration of the contract."

Cumbersomely drafted though the subsection is, the intention appears to be that either party to a frustrated contract may be awarded a just sum by way of compensation in respect of any non-monetary valuable benefit they have conferred on the other party in performance of the contract. The sum awarded must not exceed the value of the benefit. In arriving at the sum, the court must consider all the circumstances of the case, in particular whether the benefited party has incurred expenses in performance of the contract before discharge and the effect, in relation to the benefit of the circumstances giving rise to the frustration. Any sums retained or recovered by the other party under s.1(2) may also be taken into account. It should be noted, however, that there is no automatic right of recovery under s.1(3)—it is at the court's discretion having regard to the provisions of the subsection.

As an illustration of how s.1(3) of the Act could provide a different result to the common law, suppose that A, who owns rooms overlooking Pall Mall, agrees to hire the rooms to B for two consecutive days to watch processions related to a Royal event. It is the common assumption of the parties that the purpose of the hiring is to view the processions and payment by B is to be entirely on completion, there is no advance deposit. Suppose that the processions take place on the first of the two days and B watches them in accordance with the contract. Before the second day's processions can take place, intelligence reports of a terrorist bomb plot cause the processions to be cancelled and the contract is frustrated. Under the old common law the loss lay where it fell and A could recover nothing as his right to payment did not arise until after frustration.

However, under s.1(3) LR(FC)A, B has received a valuable benefit (i.e. one day watching the processions) and the court has a discretion to order B to pay a just sum in respect of it to A.

10–027   LR(FC)A was considered by Robert Goff J. in *BP Exploration Co (Libya) v Hunt (No 2)*[37] in a decision which was subsequently affirmed by the Court of Appeal and House of Lords. In this case, the defendant was a wealthy US citizen, Nelson Bunker Hunt, and he obtained a concession from the Libyan government to explore for and, ultimately extract, oil. The defendant later entered into an agreement with the claimant oil company, BP Exploration, whereby he assigned a half-share in the concession to the claimants. Under the terms of the contract, the claimants were to finance and carry out the exploration and exploitation from their own resources—thus the failure to find oil in commercial quantities was at the claimants' risk. If, however, there was a commercially viable find of oil, the agreement provided that the claimants' expenditure was to be repaid out of the defendants' share of the oil. A large oil field was discovered after the claimants had spent considerable sums in exploration and development. The Libyan government then expropriated the concession following a political revolution in the country and the contract was frustrated. At the time of frustration, the claimants had received only a proportion of the payments to which they were entitled. The claimants successfully brought a claim under s.1(3) LR(FC)A, the court holding that the claimants had conferred a valuable benefit on the defendant as they increased the value of his share of the concession. The claimants were awarded a just sum.

Robert Goff J. considered that the fundamental principle underlying the Act was the prevention of unjust enrichment of either party to the contract at the expense of the other — it was not concerned with the apportionment of losses. He said that making an award under s.1(3) involved two distinct stages, i.e. (i) the identification and valuation of the benefit; and (ii) the award of the just sum. He considered that, under the Act, the "valuable benefit" should, in appropriate cases, be the end product of the services and not just the services themselves, and he gave the following example:

> "Suppose that a contract for work on a building is frustrated by a fire which destroys the building and which, therefore, also destroys a substantial amount of work already done by the [claimant]. Although it might be thought just to award the [claimant] a sum assessed on a quantum meruit basis, probably a rateable part of the contract price, in respect of the work he has done, the effect of s.1(3)(b) will be to reduce the award to nil, because of the effect, in relation to the defendant's benefit, of the circumstances giving rise to the frustration of the contract . . . This will not be so in every case, since in some cases the services will have no end product; for example, where the services consist of doing such work as surveying, or transporting goods. In each case, it is necessary to ask the question: what benefit has the defendant obtained by reason of the [claimant's] contractual performance?"

10–028   By treating the valuable benefit as the end product in cases where there is an end product, it is likely that *Appleby v Myers* (the facts are given at para.10–022) would not be decided any differently under the Act than it was at common law, since the fire destroyed the factory and the machinery which the claimants had installed. This rather restrictive interpretation of s.1(3) is not inevitable since the subsection refers to the obtaining of a valuable benefit "before the time of discharge"—this arguably refers to the state of affairs immediately before frustration. Further, s.1(3)(b) [see above] was apparently regarded by the court in *BP Exploration v Hunt* as

---

[37] [1979] 1 W.L.R. 783, affirmed by the House of Lords 1983] 2 A.C. 352.

relevant to the identification of the valuable benefit whereas on the wording of the Act it appears to relate to the assessment of the just sum. The opportunity for what might be described as a more liberal interpretation of the provision, allowing for some recompense in cases such as *Appleby v Myers* was forgone.

In arriving at the "just sum", the Act provides that court must consider (under s.3(1)(a)) any expenses incurred by the benefited party and any sum received by the claimant under s.1(2); and (under s.1(3)(b)) the effect on the benefit of the circumstances giving rise to the frustration of the contract. The amount awarded must not be in excess of the valuable benefit that the court has identified. Where that benefit is negligible or even nil, the award will reflect that.

Contracts excluded from the Act

LR(FC)A, s.2(5) provides that the Act is not to apply to the following contracts: **10–029**

> "(a) any charterparty, except a time charterparty or a charterparty by way of demise, or to any contract (other than a charterparty) for the carriage of goods by sea; or
> (b) to any contract of insurance, save as is provided by [s.1(5) of the Act]; or
> (c) to any contract to which [section 7 of the Sale of Goods Act 1979] (which avoids contracts for the sale of specific goods which perish before the risk has passed to the buyer) applies, or to any other contract for the sale, or for the sale and delivery, of specific goods, where the contract is frustrated by reason of the fact that the goods have perished."

Frustration: conclusion

The Law Reform (Frustrated Contracts) Act has been criticised as being a badly drafted and   **10–030**
poorly designed piece of legislation. Whatever the difficulties with the measure may be, it should not be forgotten that it is open to the parties (under s.2(3) of the Act) to exclude the Act by agreement, although a clearly worded clause may be required in order to achieve this. Indeed, as we have seen, the law of frustration in general can be avoided by the use of force majeure clauses excusing the parties from performance of the contract in defined circumstances. Such provisions may allow for much more flexibility than the doctrine of frustration, which provides only for discharge.

Further reading

McElroy and Williams, *The Coronation Cases* (1941) 4 M.L.R. 241 and 5 M.L.R. 1.
McKendrick, *The Construction of Force Majeure Clauses and Self-Induced Frustration* [1990] L.M.C.L.Q. 153.
Haycroft and Waksman, *Frustration and Restitution* [1984] J.B.L. 207.
Stewart and Carter, *Frustrated Contracts and Statutory Adjustment: the Case for a Reappraisal* [1992] C.L.J. 66.
Ewan McKendrick, "The Consequences of Frustration – The Law Reform Frustrated Contracts Act 1943" in McEndrick (ed.) *Force Majeure and Frustration of Contract*, 2nd edn, (London: Lloyds of London, 1995).

Chapter 11

MISREPRESENTATION

The law of misrepresentation is concerned with the situation where a false statement is made   **11–001**
by one party A to another party B which induces B to enter into a contract with A.

We have seen from previous chapters that a statement made during the course of negotiations
may amount to a term of the contract. If it is not a term, the statement may form the basis of
a collateral contract or it may be a "mere representation". The statement may, however, amount
to no more than "mere puff"—a statement so vague that it cannot form the basis of any liability. The slogans and catch-phrases used by advertisers fall into this category.

The distinction between terms and representations was discussed above at para.6–008, and
collateral contracts were considered at para.6–015.

If a statement is a contractual term, or forms the basis of a collateral contract, the remedy
for non-compliance will be an action for breach of contract. If, on the other hand, a mere representation proves false and it induces a person to enter a contract, an action may be brought
for misrepresentation. The remedies, if misrepresentation is established, will be rescission
(setting aside the contract) and/or damages for misrepresentation.

An actionable misrepresentation will render the contract voidable, i.e. the contract is valid
unless and until the party who has been misled into entering the contract chooses to set it aside
and recover damages for any loss. The definition of actionable misrepresentation, the types of
misrepresentation, and the remedies available will be considered in this chapter.

ACTIONABLE MISREPRESENTATION

An actionable misrepresentation may be defined as a *false statement of fact*[1] made by one party   **11–002**
to the other which *induces* the other party to enter the contract. The two elements which have
been italicised in the previous sentence will now be considered.

False statement of fact

An actionable misrepresentation arises from a false statement of some specific existing fact or   **11–003**
past event.[2] Thus the vendor of a house who states, "there is no rising damp" or the seller of a

---

[1] Statements of law, as opposed to fact, may now also be actionable; see para.17–023.
[2] It seems that a statement may be false if not "substantially correct": *Avon Insurance Plc v Swire Fraser Ltd* [2000] 1
All E.R. (Comm) 573.

car who says, "the engine has been fully re-conditioned" would clearly be making a statement of fact which would be actionable if manifestly false. However, statements of future conduct or intention, and statements of opinion or belief, are not normally regarded as statements of fact.

Statements of future conduct or intention

11–004 A false statement by a person as to what they will do in the future is not misrepresentation; for example, the company prospectus that states that, over the next five years, the company intends to invest five million pounds. In *Inntrepreneur Pub Co (CPC) Ltd v Sweeney*[3] the tenant of a public house alleged that he had been induced to enter a new lease as a result of predictions by the landlord that the tenant would be released from a beer tie by March 31, 1998. Park J. considered that, if that was all the statements amounted to, they would be looking only at the future and there would be no present element in them at all; in the absence of dishonesty on the part of the maker of the statements "they would merely be predictions, and as such they could not give rise to liability [for misrepresentation]."[4]

If, however, the statement of intention is a wilful or reckless untruth, the position may be very different—there could be a fraudulent misrepresentation. In *Edgington v Fitzmaurice*[5] company directors issued a prospectus inviting subscriptions for debenture bonds. The prospectus stated that the money raised would be used to improve the company's buildings, to acquire their own fleet of horses and vans, and to further develop the arrangements for the direct supply of cheap fish. It transpired that the company was in financial difficulties at the time the debentures were issued and although a small part of the money raised was spent on improvements to the business, most was used in paying off the company's existing debtors. The Court of Appeal held that the company's statements amounted to a fraudulent misrepresentation of fact. The true objects of the company in raising the money were not those stated in the prospectus—the directors had therefore misrepresented their state of mind. In a well-known passage Bowen L.J. said:

> "There must be a misstatement of an existing fact: but the state of a man's mind is as much a fact as the state of his digestion. It is true that it is very difficult to prove what the state of a man's mind at a particular time is, but if it can be ascertained it is as much a fact as anything else. A misrepresentation as to the state of a man's mind is, therefore, a misstatement of fact."

Statements of opinion or belief

11–005 A person who honestly expresses an opinion or belief which turns out to be false does not make a misrepresentation of fact.

---

[3] [2002] EWHC 1060 (Ch).
[4] Even if the statements could be regarded as a statements of fact on the basis that the maker knew of facts which justified their prediction (see para.11–005) the statements were not actionable because they were not false—it was the landlord's policy at the time to release their public houses from the tie.
[5] (1884) 29 Ch. D. 459.

In *Bisset v Wilkinson*[6] during negotiations for the sale of land in New Zealand, the vendor stated that he believed it would support 2,000 sheep. Both vendor and purchaser were aware that the land had never before been used as a sheep farm. It was held that the purchaser was not justified in regarding what was said by the vendor as to the capacity of the land as anything more than an expression of opinion—the vendor was in no better position to know the true facts than the purchaser. There was, therefore, no actionable misrepresentation.

A statement of opinion may, however, involve an implied misrepresentation of fact. This may occur where the maker of the statement has special knowledge or skill in relation to the subject matter; or where the maker of the statement is in a better position to know the true facts. The principle is exemplified by the case of *Smith v Land and House Property Corporation*[7] where the claimant put up an hotel for sale, saying that it was let to "Mr Frederick Fleck (a most desirable tenant)." The defendants agreed to buy the hotel but before completion Mr Fleck was declared bankrupt. The defendants refused to complete the sale and the claimants sought specific performance. The claimants contended that their statement was a mere expression of opinion. Affirming the decision of Denman J., the Court of Appeal held that there was an actionable misrepresentation and rescinded the contract. Bowen L.J. said:

> "The vendors state that the property is let to a most desirable tenant. What does that mean? I agree that it is not a guarantee that that the tenant will go on paying his rent, but it is to my mind a guarantee of a different sort, and amounts at least to an assertion that nothing has occurred in the relations between the landlords and the tenant which can be considered to make the tenant an unsatisfactory one. That is an assertion of a specific fact."

Thus if the facts are not equally known to both parties, a statement of opinion by the party who knows the facts best may involve a statement of material fact, for (per Bowen L.J.), "he impliedly states that he knows facts which justify his opinion." By comparison, in *Bisset v Wilkinson* the vendor was not in a stronger position to know the facts—as both parties were aware—and the statement as to the capacity of the farm was both incapable of verification and made honestly. The position was quite different in *Smith v Land and House Property Corporation*—the desirability of the tenant was verifiable and the defendants' statement was not made honestly.   **11–006**

Some expressions of opinion may be so vague as to amount to no more than "mere puff"— they are devoid of any factual content. Statements made by advertisers and sales talk by tradesmen usually fall into this category.

Statements of law

The traditional rule was that a false statement of law could not amount to actionable misrepresentation.[8] One possible explanation for this is the notion that most statements of law amount   **11–007**

---

[6] [1927] A.C. 177. See also *Economides v Commercial Union Insurance Co Plc* [1997] 3 W.L.R. 1066.

[7] (1884) 28 Ch. D. 7. See also *Esso v Mardon* [1976] Q.B. 801 where the forecast of the potential throughput of a petrol station by an expert and experienced Esso representative was held to amount to a statement of fact that the forecast had been made with reasonable care and skill. *Bisset v Wilkinson* was distinguished on the basis that there the maker of the statement had no such knowledge and skill.

[8] For a discussion of the difference between statements of fact and law, see Treitel, *Law of Contract*, 12th edn, pp.365-6.

to no more than opinions as to what the law is, but it is probable the rule was based on the maxim "everyone is taken to know the law". Nevertheless even under this rule, if the statement of law was dishonest, liability could arise under the principle in *Edgington v Fitzmaurice*, discussed above.

It seems however, that the rule has not long survived the decision of the House of Lords in *Kleinwort Benson Ltd v Lincoln City Council*.[9] In that case their Lordships held that the rule precluding the recovery of money paid under a mistake of law could no longer be maintained. The implications for the rule regarding misrepresentations of law were obvious. The issue came before Rex Tedd Q.C., sitting as a Deputy Judge of the High Court, in *Pankhania v Hackney London Borough Council*.[10] Here the representation in question was a statement that the company, NCP, who occupied a car park, was a contractual licensee whose occupation was determinable on three months notice, whereas in fact NCP was a business tenant with security of tenure. Having reviewed the authorities the judge said:

"I have concluded that the 'misrepresentation of law' rule has not survived the decision in *Kleinwort Benson Ltd v Lincoln City Council* . . .[i]ts historical origin is an off-shoot of the 'mistake of law' rule, created by analogy with it, and the two are logically inter-dependent. Both are grounded in the maxim 'ignorantia juris non excusat',[ignorance of the law is no excuse] a tag whose dubious utility would have been enhanced had it gone on to explain who was not excused, and from what."

The judge therefore held that the representation in question was actionable as a misrepresentation of law and awarded damages accordingly.

The distinction between a statement of law and a statement of fact is not an easy one to draw in practice, as is illustrated by *Solle v Butcher*.[11] The parties mistakenly believed that a house to be leased to the claimant was a "new" dwellinghouse for the purpose of the Rent Acts and therefore could be let at a rental of £250. In fact £140 was the maximum permitted sum. The Court of Appeal held (Jenkins L.J. dissenting) that the mistake was a mistake as to the quality of the flat and not a mistake of law. The proposition of law which lay behind the statement was accurate. The mistake was factual as to whether the identity of the property had changed to such an extent that it was a new house. This type of mistake is sometimes described as a "mistake of private rights". The principle may also be applicable to misrepresentation—in this respect it is noteworthy that the misrepresentation in the *Pankhania* case might well have been regarded as one as to private rights.

Silence or non-disclosure

11–008   The general rule is that to remain silent does not amount to a misrepresentation—there is no duty to disclose facts which might influence the other party's decision to enter or not to enter the contract.[12] The rule is a corollary of the well-known maxim "caveat emptor" (let the buyer beware) and is rooted in classical contract theory. Thus a person who puts a car up for sale

---

[9] [1999] 2 A.C. 349.
[10] [2002] EWHC 2441 (Ch).
[11] [1950] 1 K.B. 671.
[12] See, for example, *Hands v Simpson Fawcett* (1928) 44 T.L.R. 295 where a commercial traveller who failed to disclose at a job interview that he had had serious motoring convictions made no misrepresentation.

privately may know, for example, that the shock absorbers need replacing, that there is rust in the floor pan and that the wheels are out of track. But they are under no duty to inform a potential purchaser of these facts. Of course, if they are asked directly about these matters they must give an honest and truthful response.[13]

Sykes v Taylor-Rose,[14] was a case of alleged non-disclosure which attracted national media coverage at the time. The defendants, who were aware that that a horrific murder had been committed in their house, put it up for sale. They had been previously advised by their solicitor that they would be under no obligation to disclose this fact when they came to sell it. As part of standard pre-contractual enquiries the defendants were asked: "Is there any other information which you think the buyer might have a right to know?" The defendants answered this question in the negative. The claimants purchased the property for £83,000 and moved in. Subsequently the claimants happened to watch a TV documentary which detailed the murder that had occurred at the property and inferred that human remains might still be present in the property. Horrified, the claimants decided to move house but felt obliged to inform the prospective purchasers of the murder. The house was sold for £75,000 although the market price, disregarding the history of the property, would have been in the region of £100,000. The claimants sought damages arguing that the non-disclosure amounted to misrepresentation or negligent misstatement.

The Court of Appeal held that the claimants action failed. The question was one intended to be answered by persons without legal expertise. It concerned information which the buyers had a right to know but there was nothing in the wording of the question that would suggest to the vendors that the answer would imply they had reasonable grounds for the answer. The court rejected the contention that the question extended to any information which would affect the enjoyment of the property. The question therefore only required an honest answer and the defendants honestly believed that the purchasers had no right to be informed. Moreover, the defendants had acted on advice from their solicitor and therefore they had not acted negligently.

Silence, in the context of the rule that "silence is not misrepresentation", means remaining completely silent because, although mere reticence does not amount to a legal wrong, " a single word or a nod or a wink or a shake of the head or a smile " from one party might constitute misrepresentation.[15] Such behaviour on the part of one party might create the impression in the mind of the other party that particular facts are being affirmed or denied.

11–009

A misrepresentation can take place by conduct. Thus the deliberate physical concealment of structural defects in buildings—so as to render them invisible on inspection—can amount to misrepresentation.[16] In *Spice Girls Ltd v Aprilia World Service BV*[17] the defendants agreed to sponsor a Spice Girls tour. The group appeared in promotional material, including a photoshoot, before the contract was concluded when they knew that one of their number, Geri Halliwell, was about to leave the group. It was held that there had been a misrepresentation by conduct—taking part in the photo-shoot amounted to a statement that the group did not know or believe that a group member would leave before the end of the contract.

---

[13] It should be noted however that the sale of an "unroadworthy" car may involve criminal liability under the Road Traffic Acts.

[14] [2004] All E.R. (D) 468 (Feb).

[15] *Walkers v Morgan* (1861) 3 D. F. & J. 718, per Lord Campbell L.C.

[16] *Gordon v Selico Co* (1986) 278 E.G. 53. In *R v Barnard* (1837) 7 C. & P. 784 the defendant donned academic dress in Oxford in order to persuade a shopkeeper to extend credit. Appearing so dressed was held to amount to a false pretence; although this was a criminal case, the same principle would apply in a civil context.

[17] [2002] E.M.L.R. 27.

The rule that silence is not misrepresentation is subject to some important exceptions:

Where the statement is a half-truth

11–010   A statement that is misleading in that it does not present the whole truth may be regarded as a misrepresentation.[18] Thus in *Nottingham Patent Brick and Tile Co v Butler*[19] on a sale of land the vendor's solicitor was asked by the purchaser whether the land was subject to any restrictive covenants. The solicitor replied that he was "not aware of any restrictions". However, he did not add that he had not read the relevant documents. Lord Esher M.R. said that the solicitor had led the other party to believe that he was stating ". . . facts within his own knowledge . . . his statements in fact misled them, so that what he said amounts to a mis-statement of fact". It was held that the purchaser was entitled to rescind.

Change of circumstances

11–011   A duty of disclosure may arise where a statement, although true when made, becomes false by the time it is acted upon. In *With v O'Flanagan*[20] the vendor of a medical practice truthfully stated that to a prospective purchaser that it was worth £2,000 per annum. The vendor then fell ill, so that, by the time the contract was signed four months later, the receipts had fallen to almost nothing. It was held that the failure of the vendor to disclose this state of affairs to the purchaser gave him the right to rescind.

There is authority that the principle in *With v O'Flanagan* does not apply to statements of future intention. It will be recalled that such statements, unless fraud is involved, do not normally amount to misrepresentation. Thus in the case of *Wales v Wadham*[21] the marriage of the claimant husband and the defendant wife had broken down. In the course of divorce proceedings the claimant offered the defendant the sum of £13,000 (which represented his share from the sale of the matrimonial home) in return for her undertaking not to seek an award of maintenance. The defendant had stated that it was not her intention to remarry—this statement was important to the claimant because maintenance payments cease on remarriage. After the statement was made the defendant decided that she would remarry but did not inform the claimant; the agreement was then signed. Tudor Evans J. refused to order rescission of the agreement— the defendant had made an honest statement of her intention which was not a misrepresentation of fact. The judge could find no basis for saying that she was under a duty to inform the husband of her change of mind.

Contracts of the utmost good faith (uberrimae fidei)

11–012   In this class of contracts, there is a duty to disclose material facts on the basis that one party is in a strong position to know the truth. The leading such example is the contract of insurance

---

[18] *Tapp v Lee* (1803) B. & P. 367.
[19] (1886) 16 Q.B.D. 778. See also *Dimmock v Hallett* (1866) L.R. 2 Ch. App. 21.
[20] [1936] Ch. 575.
[21] [1977] 1 W.L.R. 199. In the earlier case of *Traill v Baring* (1864) 4 D.J. & S. 318 the court made an apparently contrary decision, however the contract was one of insurance requiring the utmost good faith.

where there is a duty on the insured to disclose every circumstance which would influence the judgment of the prudent insurer in fixing the premium or deciding whether they will take the risk.[22] It makes no difference that the applicant for insurance has not been asked about such matters, although insurance companies often use detailed questionnaires which people taking out, e.g. life insurance, have to complete.

To succeed in a claim for non-disclosure, it seems that the insurer must show that they have been induced to enter the insurance policy by the non-disclosure of a material circumstance. In *Pan Atlantic Insurance Co Ltd v Pine Top Insurance Ltd*[23] a majority of the House of Lords held (Lords Lloyd and Templeman dissenting) that a material circumstance was one which would have an effect, not necessarily decisive, on the mind of a prudent insurer. The minority would have insisted that the effect be decisive. However their Lordships were unanimously of the view that an insurer who is not in fact induced by the non-disclosure, cannot rely on it in order to rescind the contract.

Fiduciary relationships

A fiduciary relationship is one where a person has placed confidence in another, such that the latter is bound to exercise their powers in good faith for the benefit of the former. Examples of such relationships include solicitor and client, trustee and beneficiary and partnership. Where such a relationship exists, a duty of full disclosure will arise.   **11–013**

The meaning of inducement

A misrepresentation will only be actionable if it has actually induced the misrepresentee to enter the contract. Whether or not a statement operates as an inducement depends upon a number of factors which are set out below.   **11–014**

The statement must be intended to be acted upon

In *Peek v Gurney*[24] a prospectus for an intended company was prepared by the directors and issued to the public. It was addressed to the public at large and its purpose was to invite applications for an allotment of shares. The document contained misrepresentations of fact. When the allotment had been completed, the claimants subsequently purchased shares in the market, claiming to have been induced to purchase by the statements in the prospectus. The House of Lords held that the claimants' action for misrepresentation must fail as the misrepresentation was intended to mislead a different class of purchaser from that to which the claimants belonged. Thus, once the statements had induced the public to become original allottees, the force of the prospectus was spent.   **11–015**

Nevertheless, if it can be shown that the maker of the statement knew that the statement

---

[22] See, e.g. *Lambert v Co-operative Insurance Society* [1975] 2 Lloyd's Rep. 485—a wife taking out insurance on valuables should have disclosed that her husband had been convicted of conspiracy to steal.
[23] [1995] 1 A.C. 501.
[24] (1873) L.R. 6 H.L. 377.

would be passed on the claimant, the maker of the statement may be liable. In *Pilmore v Hood*,[25] the defendant wished to sell his public house and informed A, a potential purchaser, that the income was £180 per annum. This statement was false but A did not proceed with the purchase for his own reasons. However, as the defendant was aware, A persuaded the claimant to purchase the pub by repeating the defendant's false statement to him. The defendant was held to be liable in damages for fraudulent misrepresentation. This principle was applied by the Court of Appeal in more modern times in *Clef Aquitaine SARL v Laporte Materials (Barrow) Ltd*.[26]

The statement must be the actual inducement

11–016   To amount to actionable misrepresentation, the false statement of fact must induce the misrepresentee to enter the contract. There will be no liability on the part of the misrepresentor if the other party relies on their own judgment—this is what happened in the case of *Attwood v Small*.[27] Attwood entered into negotiations with Small for the sale of certain mines and iron works. Attwood made representations as to the earning capacity of the mine and Small instructed a firm of expert mining surveyors to check the truth of the representations. The surveyors reported that Attwood's statements were accurate, on the basis of which Small entered into a contract of purchase. In fact the statements of Attwood as to earning capacity were shown to have been exaggerated and false. Small brought an action for rescission of the contract. The House of Lords held that the action failed—the purchaser had been induced to enter the contract by his own judgment consequent upon the surveyors' report and not by the statements of the vendor Attwood.

It seems that a party may rescind a contract on the grounds of misrepresentation where, in the course of negotiations, they were offered the means of verifying the truth of a statement but declined to take that offer up. In *Redgrave v Hurd*[28] the claimant, a solicitor, advertised his practice for sale. Having seen the advertisement, the defendant had an interview with the claimant, during the course of which the claimant stated that the business brought in about £300 per annum. The claimant produced paperwork which in fact showed only a trifling amount of business and the gross returns of the practice were only about £200 per annum. The defendant did not examine these documents and shortly afterwards entered into a contract to purchase the practice. On discovering that the practice was virtually worthless, the defendant refused to complete, whereupon the claimant sought specific performance. The Court of Appeal held the misrepresentation to be actionable and that the defendant was entitled to rescission. It was no defence to an action for rescission that the misrepresentee had the means of discovering the truth and might, with reasonable diligence have discovered it. Lord Jessel M.R. said:

> "Nothing can be plainer . . . on the authorities in equity than that the effect of a false representation is not got rid of on the ground that the person to whom it was made has been guilty of negligence. One of the most familiar instances . . . is where men issue a

---

[25] (1838) 5 Bing., N.C. 97.

[26] [2001] Q.B. 488.

[27] (1838) 6 Ch. & Fin. 232. See *S Pearson & Son Ltd v Dublin Corporation* [1907] A.C. 351, where it was stated (obiter) that even where the claimant relies on their own investigations, the original maker of the statement may be liable for misrepresentation where the statement was made fraudulently.

[28] (1881) 20 Ch. D. 1.

prospectus in which they make false statements of the contracts made before the formation of a company, and then say that the contracts themselves may be inspected at the offices of the solicitors. It has always been held that those who accepted those false statements as true were not deprived of their remedy merely because they neglected to go and look at the contracts."

Redgrave v Hurd involved an action for rescission brought at a time when damages could not be awarded for non-fraudulent misrepresentation. Now that damages are available for negligent misrepresentation[29] there is the possibility that, as held in *Gran Gelato Ltd v Richcliff (Group) Ltd,*[30] the damages awarded may be reduced on the basis of the claimant's contributory negligence. Thus a lack of care on the part of the misrepresentee, e.g. in failing to examine relevant documents, may affect the measure of damages awarded but it should not, per se, prevent rescission.   **11–017**

It is perhaps an obvious principle that if a party is unaware of a misrepresentation at the time of entering the contract, there can be no liability on the part of the misrepresentor. In *Horsfall v Thomas*[31] the claimant agreed to make a gun for the defendant. The gun that was delivered was defective in that it had a soft spot in the barrel which had been concealed by a metal plug. When it was fired by the defendant it blew up after several shots being fired. In an action by the claimant to recover the cost of the gun, the defendant's contention that he was entitled to rescind the contract for misrepresentation was dismissed. The defendant had never examined the gun and so his judgment could not have been affected by the state of the barrel.

A further possibility is that the innocent party is aware of a misrepresentation at the time of entering the contract, but it is proved that it cannot possibly have affected their judgment. In *Smith v Chadwick*[32] the claimant sought damages for fraudulent misrepresentation from the defendants as a result of buying shares in a company on faith of certain alleged misrepresentations in the company prospectus. One of the misrepresentations was a statement that a certain Mr J J Grieves MP was on the board of directors, whereas he had withdrawn the day before the prospectus was issued. However, the claimant had never heard of the MP in question and admitted that he had not been influenced by the name in the prospectus. The claimant had not therefore relied on the statement which could not therefore be the basis of a remedy for misrepresentation.

Must the misrepresentation be material?

Whether a person was actually induced to enter the contract as a result of the statement, i.e. whether they relied on it, is essentially subjective. This is well illustrated by the case of *Smith v Chadwick*, discussed above.   **11–018**

Is there a further requirement that the misrepresentation must be material? The traditional view of the courts has been that a misrepresentation must be material in the sense that it must be one that would affect the judgment of a reasonable person in deciding whether to enter the contract, or on what terms they wish to contract.[33] It seems that materiality is judged objectively so that the subjective view of the misrepresentor that the statement is not material would be of

---

[29] See para.11–037.
[30] [1992] Ch. 560.
[31] (1862) 1 H. & C. 90.
[32] (1884) 9 App. Cas. 187.
[33] This seems to have been assumed in *Edgington v Fitzmaurice* (1885) 29 Ch. D. 459. More recently, see *Pan Atlantic Insurance Co Ltd v Pine Top Insurance Co Ltd* [1995] 1 A.C. 501; and *Downs v Chappell* [1996] 3 All E.R. 344.

no relevance. It should be noted, however, that fraudulent misrepresentation is an exception in that the immateriality of the statement cannot be set up as a defence to an action for fraud.

In modern times the requirement of materiality has been questioned. The difficulty in this area is that the courts have not always treated inducement and materiality as distinct. The approach of the courts seems to be that if the representation is found to be material then the inference is that it must have induced the contract unless there is evidence to the contrary; conversely, if the representation is not material then the onus is on the innocent party to show that he was in fact induced to enter the contract by the statement. Thus in *Museprime Properties Ltd v Adhill Properties Ltd*[34] three properties were sold by auction. The auctioneers made representations to the effect that rent reviews on the properties had not been finalised but, in fact, new rents had already been fixed. The purchasers sought rescission for misrepresentation and the defendants argued, inter alia, that the misrepresentations were not material since no reasonable bidder would have allowed them to affect their bid. Scott J. granted rescission of the contract—if the misrepresentation would not have induced a reasonable person to enter the contract, the burden of proof was on the innocent party to show that they were in fact induced to enter the contract. If that can be established, they are entitled to rescission.

The misrepresentation does not have to be the sole inducing factor

11–019   Provided the misrepresentation induced the innocent party to enter the contract, it does not have to be the sole or main reason why the claimant entered the contract. Thus the claimant in *Edgington v Fitzmarice* (discussed at para.11–004) succeeded where he had been induced to buy debentures in the company partly by a fraudulent misrepresentation in the company prospectus and partly by his own erroneous belief that, as a debenture holder, he would have a charge over the company's assets.

There will however be no remedy where, despite the misrepresentation, the innocent party would have acted in the same way in any event. This is illustrated by the case of *JEB Fasteners Ltd v Marks Bloom & Co*[35] where the claimants, JEB Fasteners, decided to acquire the share capital of a company, BG Fasteners, for the purpose of acquiring the services of two directors of BG Fasteners. The claimants inspected the accounts of the company which had been prepared by the defendants, a firm of chartered accountants. Because of the negligence of the defendants, the audited accounts did not give a true and accurate picture of the state of the company. Nevertheless, the claimants, suspecting that the accounts were erroneous, decided to purchase the company in any event. The claimants brought an action against the defendants for negligence but Woolf J. found for the defendants as the claimants' real object was to obtain the services of the two directors. They had not therefore relied on the accounts; this decision was upheld by the Court of Appeal on the basis that the defendants had not caused the claimants' loss.

TYPES OF MISREPRESENTATION

11–020   Originally, the law only recognised two types of misrepresentation, fraudulent and innocent. Developments in the mid-1960s led to the introduction of damages for negligent

[34] (1991) 61 P. & C.R. 111.
[35] [1983] 1 All ER. 583.

misrepresentation with the result that there are now three broad types of misrepresentation, fraudulent, negligent and innocent. Negligent misrepresentation may take two forms, (a) negligent misstatement at common law and (b) negligent misrepresentation under the Misrepresentation Act 1967.

The type of misrepresentation is important because it determines the remedies available. Before examining the remedies, it is necessary to consider the different types of misrepresentation.

Fraudulent misrepresentation

Fraudulent misrepresentation is essentially an action in the tort of deceit. "Fraudulent" in this sense was defined by Lord Herschell in *Derry v Peek*[36] as a false statement that is "made (i) knowingly, or (ii) without belief in its truth, or (iii) recklessly, careless whether it be true or false." In *Derry v Peek*, a share prospectus falsely stated that the company had the right to use mechanical power to draw trams, without explaining that governmental consent was required for this. In fact, the directors honestly believed that the obtaining of consent was a pure formality, although it was ultimately refused. The House of Lords held that there had been no fraudulent misrepresentation.

11–021

The essence of fraud is the absence of honest belief and so even where a statement is made recklessly or carelessly the maker of the statement cannot be liable for fraud if they believed the statement to be true. In *Thomas Witter Ltd v TBP Industries Ltd*[37] the defendants, in selling their carpet manufacturing business, failed to disclose a change in their accounting policy and the claimants alleged that this was recklessness amounting to fraudulent misrepresentation. Jacob J. held that there had been no fraud as the defendants believed their statements to be true—the misrepresentation was properly categorised as negligent.

An allegation of fraud is a serious matter and a claimant basing their action on fraudulent misrepresentation has a heavy burden of proof to discharge—they may be penalised in costs if the allegation is not made out. For these reasons the innocent party may prefer to base their claim on negligent misrepresentation under the Misrepresentation Act 1967, which is discussed below.

Negligent misrepresentation

Under the modern law, a claim for damages for misrepresentation may take two forms, negligent misstatement at common law and a statutory claim for damages under s.2(1) of the Act of 1967.

11–022

Negligent misstatement at common law

Before 1963, all misrepresentations were classed as either fraudulent or innocent and damages could only be claimed as such for fraudulent misrepresentation. We saw in an earlier chapter (see para.6–015) the methods deployed by the courts to get round this rule, such as the development of the collateral contract or warranty. In a ground-breaking decision in 1963 the House

11–023

---

[36] (1889) 14 App. Cas. 337.
[37] [1996] 2 All ER. 573.

of Lords stated, obiter, that in certain circumstances damages may be recoverable in tort for negligent misstatement causing financial loss.

The case in question was *Hedley Byrne & Co Ltd v Heller & Partners Ltd*[38] where the claimant advertising agents asked their bank to make inquiries about the financial standing of a company, Easipower. The defendants, who were Easipower's bankers, replied that the company was "good for its ordinary business engagements"—this advice was given "without responsibility". Relying on the defendants' statement, the claimants placed advertisements on behalf of Easipower but the company went into liquidation and the claimants lost £17,000. The claimants sought damages on the basis that the defendants' statements were given negligently in breach of a duty to exercise reasonable care. The action was tortious as the claimants had no contract with the defendants. The House of Lords held that on the facts of the case the defendants' disclaimer was effective to exclude the assumption of a duty of care on their part. However, in the absence of such an exemption, the defendants would have owed a duty of care to the claimants on the basis of a special relationship between the parties. Such a special relationship was said to arise where a party possessing and professing to exercise a special skill undertook to apply their expertise for the assistance of another who relied on that skill.

In the years following the decision in *Hedley Byrne v Heller*, the courts sought to restrict considerably the circumstances in which the duty of care arose[39] although in more recent times there has been evidence of a reversion to a more liberal approach.[40] *Esso Petroleum Co Ltd v Mardon* was an important case[41] because it confirmed that the duty of care could arise between parties in a pre-contractual relationship. The case also showed that the duty could exist in an ordinary commercial transaction (the tenancy of a petrol filling station) where one party was possessed of superior skill and knowledge which was relied on by the other. Originally it had been thought that the duty of care only arose in relation to statements made by those whose profession it was to give expert advice, such as accountants, solicitors or surveyors.[42] This case established that the maker of the statement need not be in business to give advice.

Negligent misrepresentation under the Misrepresentation Act 1967, s.2(1)

11–024 The Misrepresentation Act 1967 introduced, for the first time, a statutory claim for damages for non-fraudulent misrepresentation. The provisions of s.2(1) are as follows:

> "Where a person has entered into a contract after a misrepresentation has been made to him by another party thereto and as a result thereof he has suffered loss, then, if the person making the misrepresentation would be liable in damages in respect thereof had the mis-representation been made fraudulently, that person shall be so liable notwithstanding that the misrepresentation was not made fraudulently, unless he proves that he had reasonable grounds to believe and did believe up to the time the contract was made that the facts represented were true."

The most striking difference between the form of liability created by s.2(1) and negligent misstatement at common law is that, under the sub-section, it is assumed that the statement is

---

[38] [1964] A.C. 465.
[39] See, e.g. *Caparo Industries Plc v Dickman* [1990] 2 A.C. 605.
[40] See, e.g. *Henderson v Merrett Syndicates Ltd* [1995] 2 A.C. 145.
[41] [1976] Q.B. 901. See para.6–017 above for a fuller discussion of the case.
[42] *Mutual Life and Citizens' Insurance Co Ltd v Evatt* [1971] A.C. 793.

made without reasonable grounds for believing in its truth. The burden of proof is therefore placed on the maker of the statement to prove that they had such reasonable grounds for believing its truth, i.e. that the misrepresentation was innocent. The burden of proof is therefore reversed.

It will be noticed also that s.2(1) only applies where the claimant has "entered into a contract". This is not a necessary requirement of the common law action at all, thus an action may be brought under *Hedley Byrne v Heller* where the misrepresentation was made by a third party to the contract. Indeed, it is not necessary, under the negligence claim, to prove that a misrepresentation as such has been made—the statement might well be a statement of opinion. On the other hand, under s.2(1) there is no need to establish a duty of care, all that needs to be shown is that A has made a false statement of fact to B that has induced B to enter into a contract with A.

In order to avoid liability under s.2(1), the maker of the statement must not merely disprove **11–025** negligence, they must establish positively that they had reasonable grounds for believing in the truth of the statement.

This is illustrated by the decision of the Court of Appeal in *Howard Marine & Dredging Co Ltd v A Ogden & Sons (Excavations) Ltd.*[43] Here, the defendants entered into negotiations with the claimants for the hire of two sea-going barges for transporting clay out to sea to be dumped. In negotiations, the claimants' manager stated that the capacity of the barges was 1,600 tonnes dead-weight. He relied on his recollection of an entry in Lloyd's Register (the "Bible" of shipping) which was in fact erroneous—the true capacity was 1,055 tonnes. The correct figure could have been ascertained from shipping documents in the claimants' possession. In reliance on this statement, the defendants entered into a contract of hire with the claimants. When the barges had been used for some time it became apparent that the barges were not of the stated capacity and the defendants refused to pay the hire charges. The claimants sued the defendants for the hire charges and the defendants counterclaimed, relying on s.2(1) of the Act of 1967 and negligent misstatement.

The Court of Appeal held (Lord Denning M.R. dissenting) that the claimants were liable for damages under s.2(1) on the ground that the claimants could not show they had reasonable grounds for believing the truth of their statement. However, by a majority, the claim based on negligent misstatement failed. At first sight it seems odd that a person induced to enter a contract as a result of a misrepresentation should have two possible actions for damages in respect of negligent statements. The reason for this is that the law developed in a piecemeal fashion; the Act of 1967 resulted from a report of the Law Reform Committee some five years earlier which proposed that damages should be awarded for non-fraudulent misrepresentation. Some time before this recommendation could be translated into legislation, the House of Lords, in 1963, arrived at their decision in *Hedley Byrne v Heller.*

Where a person has entered a contract as a result of a misrepresentation, s.2(1) is the normal **11–026** and more desirable remedy from the point of view of the innocent party. The burden of proof is reversed and, as the law stands at present, damages are awarded on a more favourable basis. (Damages for negligent misrepresentation are discussed below at para.11–041).

Innocent misrepresentation

Originally "innocent misrepresentation" was the term used to describe all misrepresentations **11–027** that were not fraudulent. As a result of the developments in the law that began with *Hedley Byrne v Heller* in 1963, followed by the Misrepresentation Act 1967, innocent misrepresentation

---

[43] [1978] Q.B. 574.

now refers to a statement made by a person who has reasonable grounds for believing its truth. "Wholly innocent" misrepresentation might be a better label for this kind of statement.

REMEDIES FOR MISREPRESENTATION

11–028   Once an actionable misrepresentation is established, it becomes necessary to consider the remedies available. It will be useful to recall at this point that misrepresentation renders a contract voidable, i.e. valid until avoided at the suit of the innocent party. This needs to be borne in mind when considering remedies. The two main remedies for misrepresentation are rescission and damages.

Rescission

11–029   Rescission, an equitable remedy, involves setting aside the contract and it is available for all types of misrepresentation. Where a contract is rescinded it is terminated ab initio; the object is to put the parties back in the position they would have been in had the contract never been made. Rescission, therefore, restores the status quo ante ("the state of things as they were").

Where the innocent party elects to rescind the contract, they may apply to the court for an order of rescission. Alternatively, rescission may be achieved by notifying the other party or, where appropriate, by repossessing property transferred. Where these are not possible, it seems that other acts indicating a wish to set aside the contract may suffice.

In *Car and Universal Finance Co Ltd v Caldwell*[44] N, a "rogue" (the traditional legal term for a fraudster) purchased a Jaguar car from C, the original owner, and paid by cheque. The cheque was dishonoured and when C sought to rescind the transaction it was found that N had absconded with the car. C immediately informed the police and the Automobile Association of the fraudulent transaction. Later, N sold the car to a firm of dealers, M, who had notice of the fraud. The car was eventually sold to innocent purchasers, CUF. At issue was whether CUF had acquired a good title—this turned on whether C had by his actions rescinded the contract with N, even though C had not communicated the rescission to N.

The Court of Appeal held that C's actions were sufficient to rescind the transaction. By absconding with the property the rogue had made it impossible for C to communicate rescission and C had done all that he could reasonably have done in the circumstances. The outcome favours the original owner at the expense of the innocent third party who purchases the goods. As such, the case is illustrative of a problem that will be discussed more fully in a later chapter (see para.12–027); i.e. which of two innocent parties should be made to suffer from the fraudulent dealings of a rogue.

11–030   The remedy of rescission may be accompanied by the court ordering an "indemnity". This is a money payment by the misrepresentor to restore the parties to their position as if the contract had never been made and is available for all types misrepresentation. An indemnity is a much more restricted remedy than the award of damages and is payable in respect of obligations necessarily created by the contract.

The distinction between indemnity and damages is illustrated by *Whittington v Seale-Hayne.*[45] The claimants bred prize poultry and took a lease of the defendant's premises, as a

[44]   [1965] 1 Q.B. 525.
[45]   (1900) 82 L.T. 49.

result of an innocent misrepresentation that the premises were sanitary. In fact, the water supply was poisoned and the defendant submitted to rescission. The claimants requested an indemnity to cover:

(i)   loss of profits;
(ii) value of stock lost;
(iii) removal costs;
(iv) medical expenses;
(v)   rent and rates; and
(vi) the cost of repairs ordered by the local authority.

Farwell J. held that an indemnity could be awarded in respect of items (v) and (vi) only, as these were obligations necessarily created by the lease. As the claimants were not obliged to run a poultry farm, or indeed any business, by the terms of the lease, items (i)–(iv), had they been awarded, would have amounted to an award of damages.

The power to award an indemnity is not affected by the Misrepresentation Act 1967, although it will not be necessary where damages are in fact awarded as these should include the expenses element. The remedy remains significant where a contract is rescinded for a wholly innocent misrepresentation.

Bars to rescission

In certain circumstances the innocent party's right to rescind the contract for misrepresentation may be barred and they are left to whatever claim they may have in damages. The bars to rescission are: **11–031**

(i)   affirmation;
(ii) lapse of time;
(iii) the impossibility of restitution; and
(iv) third party rights.

These will now be considered.

Affirmation

Once the innocent party becomes aware of the misrepresentation, they may elect to rescind or affirm the contract. They will be said to have affirmed the contract if, with full knowledge of the misrepresentation and of their right to rescind, they expressly state that they intend to continue with it, or if they do an act from which the intention may be implied.   **11–032**

In *Long v Lloyd*[46] the claimant, a haulage contractor, purchased a Dennis 12/14- ton lorry at the price of £750 from the defendant in reliance on a misrepresentation that it was in "exceptional condition". The defendant had also said that the lorry would do 11 miles per gallon. A few days after taking delivery of the vehicle, the claimant went on a local journey in the vehicle to pick up

---

[46] [1958] 1 W.L.R. 753.

a load and during that journey the dynamo ceased to work, there was an oil leak, there was a crack in one of the wheels and the petrol consumption was just five miles per gallon. The defendant then agreed to share the cost of a reconstructed dynamo and this was fitted. Shortly after, the lorry was driven on a long journey from Kent to Middlesbrough but it broke down. The claimant sought rescission. The Court of Appeal held that the claimant had by his actions affirmed the contract. Accepting the offer to pay half the cost of repair to the dynamo and despatching the lorry on a long business trip amounted to a final acceptance of the vehicle by the claimant. As the misrepresentation was held to be non-fraudulent, the claimant in this case recovered no damages; it seems likely that, were such an action brought today, the claimant would recover damages under s.2(1) of the Misrepresentation Act 1967. The defendant would have some difficulty in establishing that he had reasonable grounds for believing that the lorry was in excellent condition.

It seems that the right to rescind will be lost by affirmation where the innocent party not only knows the facts giving rise to their right to rescind but is aware of their legal right to rescind. In *Peyman v Lanjani*[47] the tenant of a restaurant, L, an Iranian who spoke no English, obtained the assignment of the lease from the landlord by a fraudulent misrepresentation, i.e. getting another person to impersonate him. This rendered L's title defective. L then agreed to sell the lease to P, obtaining the landlord's consent to the assignment once again by being impersonated by another. P became aware of the fraud but nevertheless paid a deposit and went into possession on his solicitor's advice. P then changed his solicitor and was informed that he had a right to rescind. The Court of Appeal held that P's right to rescind had not been lost by taking possession as he had acted in ignorance of the fact that he had a legal right to rescind.

Lapse of time

11–033   Lapse of time may be evidence of affirmation. Where the misrepresentation is fraudulent, the time which may be evidence of affirmation runs from the time when the fraud was, or with reasonable diligence, could have been discovered.

In the case of non-fraudulent misrepresentation (i.e. negligent or innocent misrepresentation) time runs from the date of the contract, not the date of the discovery of the misrepresentation. In these circumstances "lapse of time" is a separate bar to rescission. In *Leaf v International Galleries*[48] the claimant purchased a painting for £85 from the defendants which they had represented to have been painted by J. Constable. Five years later the claimant took the picture to the auction house, Christies, with the intention of selling it. He was informed that the painting was not a genuine Constable. The claimant sought rescission but the Court of Appeal held that rescission was barred by lapse of time. Jenkins L.J. said:

"... contracts such as this cannot be kept open and subject to the possibility of rescission indefinitely ... it behoves the purchaser either to verify or, as the case may be, disprove the representation within a reasonable time, or else stand or fall by it. If he is allowed to wait five, ten, or twenty years and then reopen the bargain, there can be no finality at all."

This seems to be a just outcome in the circumstances. The misrepresentation in this case was found to be innocent and therefore there had been no dishonesty on the part of the sellers. The

---

[47] [1984] 3 All E.R. 703.
[48] [1950] 2 K.B. 86. See also *Government of Zanzibar v British Aerospace (Lancaster House) Ltd* [2000] 1 W.L.R. 2333.

judge in the court below had suggested that the claimant's proper remedy was a claim in damages for breach of warranty and when asked by the judge if he wished to amend his claim, the claimant declined to do to so. That being the case, to expect that the transaction be rescinded some five years after the contract had been entered into was to expect too much.

Impossibility of restitution

The injured party will lose the right to rescind if the parties cannot be restored to the original position they were in before the contract. In *Vigers v Pike*[49] a lease of a mine which had been entered into as a result of a misrepresentation could not be rescinded as there had been extensive extraction of minerals since the date of the contract. The mine had been virtually worked out. In other words, it was not possible to restore the mine to the owners in its original condition—what is termed a restitutio in integrum was impossible.

11–034

It would be unreasonable if this rule was applied too strictly. Accordingly, the courts require substantial as opposed to precise restitution. Thus where there has been a mere deterioration in the value or condition of the property, rescission may be allowed with a cash adjustment. In *Erlanger v New Sombrero Phosphate Co*[50] the purchaser of a phosphate-bearing island partially extracted the phosphate. He sought rescission on the basis of a misrepresentation—this was allowed by the House of Lords subject to him accounting to the vendors for the profits he had made.

Since the object of rescission is to place the parties back into their original position, it is not possible to partly rescind a contract for misrepresentation. Unless the whole of the contract can be rescinded, the contract cannot be rescinded at all.[51]

Third party rights

Rescission cannot be ordered where third party rights have accrued, bona fide and for value, in the subject matter of the contract. Thus if A obtains goods from B by misrepresentation and sells them on to C, who takes in good faith, B cannot later rescind on learning of the misrepresentation. The rights of a third party have intervened. Suppose that in *Car and Universal Finance Co Ltd v Caldwell* (discussed at para.11–029) the rogue had sold the car to an innocent third party before C had informed the police and the Automobile Association. Rescission would have been barred and the innocent third party would have obtained a good title.

11–035

Misrepresentation Act 1967, s.1

Prior to the enactment of the Misrepresentation Act 1967, there existed two further bars to rescission, namely that the contract could not be rescinded (i) where the misrepresentation had become incorporated as a contractual term; and (ii) where, after a non-fraudulent misrepresentation, the contract had been executed. However these bars to rescission were abolished by s.1 (a) and (b) respectively of the Act of 1967. Given the passage of time that has elapsed since the Act of 1967, only (i) above requires further discussion.

11–036

---

[49] (1842) 8 E.R. 20.
[50] (1873) 3 App. Cas. 1218.
[51] *De Molestina v Ponton* [2002] EWHC 2413.

It is possible that a statement is made during the negotiations leading up to a contract and the same statement is repeated in the later written contract. The first statement is regarded as a representation and the second statement is incorporated into the contract as a term. In this situation, under the pre-1967 law the only remedy lay in an action for breach of contract based upon the term, no remedies were available for the misrepresentation. After 1967, the innocent party may rescind for misrepresentation notwithstanding that the statement has later become a term of the contract.

Damages for misrepresentation

11–037   Damages for misrepresentation may be claimed, or as the case may be, awarded, under the following heads.

Damages for fraudulent misrepresentation

11–038   The claim for damages for fraudulent misrepresentation is a claim in the tort of deceit. Such damages are awarded under what is traditionally known as the "out of pocket" rule. The object is to restore the claimant to the position they would have been in had the misrepresentation not been made, i.e. the amount by which they are out of pocket as a result of entering the contract. The principle was confirmed by Lord Collins M.R. in *McConnel v Wright*,[52] a case in which the claimant suffered loss as a result of entering a contract to buy shares in a company as a result of fraudulent misrepresentations in the company's prospectus. In explaining the basis of damages in the tort of deceit, his Lordship said:

> "[T]he common sense and principle of the thing is this . . .it is an action for a wrong done whereby the [claimant] was tricked out of certain money in his pocket; and therefore prima facie, the highest limit of his damages is the whole extent of his loss, and that loss is measured by the money which was in his pocket and is now in the pocket of the company."

In other words, the claimant is to be put in the position he would have been in had the tort of deceit not been committed.

There is a significant difference between damages for deceit and damages recoverable in the law of tort generally. The usual position in tort is that damages can only be recovered for loss that is reasonably foreseeable by the defendant—loss that is not reasonably foreseeable is said to be too "remote".[53] In deceit, however, the claimant can recover for all the direct loss incurred as a result of the fraudulent inducement, regardless of forseeability. This principle was laid down by the Court of Appeal in *Doyle v Olby (Ironmongers) Ltd*[54] where Lord Denning made it clear that all the loss suffered by the misrepresentee as a result of the fraud should be recovered, and "it does not lie in the mouth of the fraudulent person to say that they could not have been foreseen." This suggests a punitive element to the damages—it is unusual for civil damages to be unlimited in this way.

---

[52] [1903] 1 Ch. 546.
[53] The rules of remoteness are considered below in Chapter 16, at para.16–024.
[54] [1969] 2 Q.B. 158.

The ruling in *Doyle v Olby (Ironmongers) Ltd* was affirmed by the House of Lords in *Smith* **11–039**
New Court Securities Ltd v Scrimgeour Vickers (Asset Management) Ltd.[55] Here, the defendants, who owned shares in Ferranti Inc, offered them to the claimants and fraudulently stated
that in bidding for the shares, the claimants would be in competition with two other named
bidders. This misrepresentation led the claimants to increase their offer per share from 78p to
82.25p but before this fraud was discovered it was announced that Ferranti Inc had been the
victim of another unrelated fraud perpetrated by a third party. This news led the share price to
slump to not much more than 40p a share. The claimants eventually sold the shares at a considerable loss and the trial judge assessed the damages at £10,764,005. This figure was based on
the difference in the market value at the date of the contract and the value of the shares when
the claimants sold them for 44p a share. This decision was reversed by the Court of Appeal who
awarded the sum of £1,196,000 by way of damages—this was based the difference between
82.25p and 78p, i.e. the price paid and the real value of the shares.

The House of Lords reinstated the decision of the court at first instance. The claimants had
been induced to offer too high a price for the shares by the fraud and once they had bought the
shares, they were locked into the property. Applying *Doyle v Olby (Ironmongers) Ltd*, their
Lordships held that the claimants could recover their full consequential losses as a result of
entering the transaction.

It is necessary at this point to distinguish between the assessment of damages for misrepresentation and for breach of contract. Whereas damages for misrepresentation are awarded on the
basis of putting the parties back in the position they would have been in had there been no misrepresentation (essentially a tortious basis), the usual basis for the award of damages in contract
is expectation loss or "loss of bargain" (see para.16–002). This means that the innocent party
will be put in the position they would have been in had the contract been performed as agreed
between the parties. In the case of a false statement this means awarding damages on the basis
that the statement had been true. Thus in contract, the law strives to protect the innocent party's
expectations under the contract, that is, what they expected to gain from it. For this reason, loss
of prospective business profits will not be recoverable in an action for misrepresentation, unless
they fall into the category of consequential losses as in the case of *East v Maurer.*[56]

In this case, the claimants purchased one of the two hairdressing salon businesses in **11–040**
Bournemouth belonging to the defendant, who carried on business under the name of "Roger
de Paris". The defendant was a successful hair stylist with an international reputation and a
loyal clientele. In the course of negotiations, the defendant had misrepresented to the claimants
that he did not intend working in his other salon, unless in an emergency, and that he would
probably be opening a salon abroad in Switzerland. In fact he continued to work full-time at
his other salon. Despite the claimants' best efforts their salon was never profitable because of
the presence of the defendant in his salon. Eventually, the claimants sold the premises for £7,500
having paid the defendant £20,000 for the business. At first instance the claimants were awarded
damages for misrepresentation including the sum of £15,000 for loss of profits during the three
to four years in which the claimants attempted to run the business.

On appeal against that award, the Court of Appeal held that loss of profits could be recovered
in an action for fraudulent misrepresentation if (applying *Doyle v Olby (Ironmongers) Ltd*) it was
loss suffered as a direct consequence of the misrepresentation. Such damages had to be assessed on
tortious principles, i.e. putting the parties back in the position they would have been had the mis-

---

[55] [1997] A.C. 254.
[56] [1991] 1 W.L.R. 461. See Marks (1992) 108 L.Q.R. 386.

representation not been made. Accordingly, the claimants were awarded damages on the profit they might have made had they bought another hypothetical hairdressing salon. These profits would have been more modest than the profits that the claimants would have made had the defendant's statements been true, i.e. if damages had been awarded on the contractual basis. The court could not award damages on that basis because that would have amounted to treating the representation as a contractual term. The court reduced the award to £10,000. This type of award has been described as allowing recovery for the "opportunity cost" of relying on the misrepresentation.

Damages for negligent misrepresentation

11–041   Where damages are successfully claimed at common law for negligent misstatement under the principle in *Hedley Byrne v Heller* (see para.11–023) they will be awarded on the tortious measure but, unlike in the case of damages for deceit discussed in the previous section, the test of remoteness will be one of reasonable forseeability.

The precise basis upon which damages are to be awarded under s.2(1) on the Misrepresentation Act 1967 (see para.11–024) has proved to be a controversial issue. Some earlier cases under the Act indicated that the contractual "loss of bargain" measure was appropriate[57]. However, in *Sharneyford Supplies Ltd v Edge*[58] it was established by the Court of Appeal that the correct measure is tortious.

In *Royscot Trust Ltd v Rogerson*[59] the defendant car dealer agreed to sell a car on hire-purchase to a customer for £7,600 with a £1,200 deposit. In submitting a proposal to the claimant finance company, the defendant falsely stated the figures to be £8,000 and £1,600 respectively. The claimants, who had a policy of not entering into hire-purchase arrangements unless the deposit was at least 20 per cent of the purchase price, purchased the car from the dealer and let it on hire-purchase to the customer. The customer later stopped paying the instalments and dishonestly sold the car. The claimants sought damages from the defendants under s.2(1) of the Misrepresentation Act. The trial judge held that the defendants were liable for misrepresentation and assessed damages on a basis that neither party had asked for, involving a sale of the car at a hypothetical price. The defendants appealed, contending that the damages should be nil as the sale of the car by the customer was a *novus actus interveniens* breaking the chain of causation. The claimants argued that the correct figure was the difference between the sum paid by the claimants to the defendants for the car and the total sum received by the claimants from the customer, which was £3,625.

11–042   The Court of Appeal found for the claimants. The measure of damages under s.2(1) was tortious, and, because of the wording of s.2(1) was on the same basis as for fraudulent misrepresentation, the claimants could recover for all loss directly flowing from the misrepresentation regardless of forseeability. As it happened, the sale of the car was foreseeable in this case and did not break the chain of causation. The quantum of damages sought by the claimants was upheld.

Referring to the wording of s.2(1) of the Misrepresentation Act, Balcombe L.J. said:

> "In my judgment the wording of the subsection is clear: the person making the innocent misrepresentation shall be 'so liable', ie liable to damages as if the representation had been made fraudulently."

---

[57] See, eg *Watts v Spence* [1976] Ch. 165.
[58] [1976] Ch. 165.
[59] [1991] 2 Q.B. 297.

This interpretation of s.2(1) (the so-called "fiction of fraud") is at variance with most academic commentators who favour the view that, despite the wording of s.2(1), damages under the sub-section should be on the same basis as negligence.[60] The purpose of introducing s.2(1) was to provide a statutory action for negligent misrepresentation and it therefore seems illogical to interpret s.2(1) as providing a more generous measure of damages than negligent misstatement at common law. The deceit rule has a punitive element which takes account of dishonesty or recklessness on the part of the maker of the statement and should therefore be reserved for fraudulent misrepresentation. To equate innocent but negligent conduct with fraud in the award of damages seems rather draconian. It is suggested that the wording of the sub-section is wide enough to enable the courts to take a purposive approach should they wish to do so in future. Indeed, in *Smith New Court Securities Ltd v Scrimgeour Vickers (Asset Management) Ltd* (the case is discussed at para.11–039) Lord Steyn in the House of Lords did not think the wording of the statute, which he described as "rather loose" should compel the court to "treat a person who was morally innocent as if he was guilty of fraud when it comes to the measure of damages." However the fiction of fraud issue was not directly in issue and in the House no concluded view was expressed on the correct interpretation of s.2(1). Given the very generous level of damages which may be awarded under s.2(1) for what is essentially negligence not fraud, Rix J. in *Avon Insurance Plc v Swire Fraser Ltd*[61] was moved to suggest that the courts should not be too willing to find a negligent misrepresentation where there was room for the exercise of judgment.

In *Gran Gelato Ltd v Richcliff (Group) Ltd*[62] the Court of Appeal held that where there were concurrent claims against a party for negligent misrepresentation under s.2(1) of the Misrepresentation Act and for negligent misstatement at common law, damages awarded under both could be reduced on account of the injured party's contributory negligence (under the Law Reform (Contributory Negligence) Act 1945—see para.16–041). Damages were not, in fact, reduced in the case itself as the court did not consider it would have been just and equitable to do so, given the facts of the case. Sir Donald Nicholls observed that:

11–043

> "[L]iability under the Misrepresentation Act 1967 is essentially founded on negligence . . . This being so, it would be very odd if the defence of contributory negligence were not available to a claim under that Act. It would be very odd if contributory negligence were available as a defence to a claim for damages based on a breach of the duty to take care in and about the making of a particular representation, but not available as a claim for damages under the Act in respect of the same representation."

Logical as these sentiments are, they sit rather uneasily with the "fiction of fraud", particularly since, in *Alliance & Leicester Building Society v Edgestop*[63] it was held by Mummery J. that contributory negligence has no application to an action founded on deceit. If damages under s.2(1) of the Act of 1967 are to based on the fiction of fraud, then apportionment of damages for contributory negligence should not be applicable. The law in this area is in urgent need of clarification.

---

[60] See, for example Cheshire, Fifoot and Furmston, *Law of Contract*, 15th edn, pp. 366-367. See also Hooley (1991) 1 L.Q.R. 547.

[61] [2000] C.L.C. 665.

[62] [1992] 2 W.L.R. 867.

[63] [1993] 1 W.L.R. 1462. The principle was affirmed by the House of Lords in *Standard Chartered Bank v Pakistan National Shipping Corporation* (No 2) [2003] 1 A.C. 959.

Damages in lieu of rescission

11–044   It is clear that, under the scheme of the Act of 1967, damages may not be claimed as such for a wholly innocent misrepresentation, i.e. one that is neither fraudulent or negligent. The usual remedy for wholly innocent misrepresentation is rescission, which may be accompanied by an indemnity (see para.11–030). Nevertheless the Act does contain a discretionary power for the court to award damages for non-fraudulent misrepresentation as an alternative to rescinding the contract. Accordingly, the Misrepresentation Act 1967, s.2(2) provides as follows:

> "Where a person has entered into a contract after a misrepresentation has been made to him otherwise than fraudulently, and he would be entitled, by reason of the misrepresentation, to rescind the contract, then, if it is claimed, in any proceedings arising out of the contract, that the contract ought to be or has been rescinded, the court or arbitrator may declare the contract subsisting and award damages in lieu of rescission, if of opinion that it would be equitable to do so, having regard to the nature of the misrepresentation and the loss that would be caused by it if the contract were upheld, as well as the loss that rescission would cause to the other party."

It may be useful at this point to note s.2(3) of the Act, which provides:

> "Damages may be awarded against a person under subsection (2) of this section whether or not he is liable to damages under subsection (1) thereof, but where he is so liable any award under the said subsection (2) shall be taken into account in assessing his liability under the said subsection (1)."

On the basis of the wording of s.2(2) (it speaks of the entitlement to rescission) it had always been assumed that the loss of the right to rescind through one or more of the bars to rescission (see para.11–031) would remove the power to award damages under the sub-section. This analysis was not accepted by Jacob J. in *Thomas Witter Ltd v TBP Industries Ltd*[64] who found the argument "unattractive: rescission might or might not be available at the time of trial depending on a host of factors which have nothing to do with behaviour of either party."

Later cases have come to the opposite conclusion. In *Government of Zanzibar v British Aerospace Ltd*[65] Judge Raymond Jack Q.C. reviewed the legislative history of the provision and concluded:

> "[S]ection 2(2) gives the court a discretionary power to hold the contract to be subsisting and to award damages where it would otherwise be obliged to grant rescission . . . The court does not have that power, and does not need to have that power, where rescission is no longer available. In short, the power to award damages is an alternative to an order for rescission."

11–045   Thus the discretionary power to award damages is an alternative to rescission where this would afford an adequate remedy in lieu of the ordering or upholding of rescission. It might, for example, be more just and equitable to award damages where the loss suffered by the misrep-

---

[64]   [1996] 2 All E.R. 573.
[65]   [2000] 1 W.L.R. 2333.

resentee is minor compared with the effects of rescission. Since damages are, under s.2(2), an alternative to rescission, they cannot be awarded where there is no entitlement to rescission. Judge Humphrey Lloyd Q.C. came to the same conclusion in *Floods of Queensferry Ltd v Shand Construction Ltd.*[66]

Another issue which has exercised the courts is the measure of damages to be awarded in lieu of rescission under s.2(2). The issue was considered, obiter, in *William Sindall Plc v Cambridgeshire County Council.*[67] In this case, a firm of developers purchased a site from the county council in order to build on it. Planning permission for residential development was not obtained until some 18 months later by which time property values had fallen and the land was worth £3m less than the figure the purchasers had paid. At the time of the contract, the vendors had stated that they were unaware of any public rights or rights of easement affecting the land. Some time after planning permission was granted, it was discovered that, unknown to either party, a foul sewer was located under the site. The purchasers claimed that the existence of the sewer compromised the development of the site and sought rescission of the contract of sale on the grounds of common mistake (see para.12–005) and misrepresentation. The Court of Appeal held that there was neither an operative mistake nor an actionable misrepresentation, as the contract provided that the risk of the existence of any encumbrances affecting the use of the land fell on the purchaser. The vendors had truthfully stated, after making reasonable investigations, that they had no knowledge of the existence of any sewer and this did not therefore constitute an actionable misrepresentation. The court went on to consider, obiter, the position had the misrepresentation been actionable; the members of the court did not think it would have been equitable to rescind the contract since the sewer did not significantly inhibit the use of the land. Damages would therefore have been awarded in lieu of rescission under s.2(2) of the Act.

The court considered the measure of damages under s.2(2) which referred to "the loss caused by [the misrepresentation] . . . if the contract were upheld". Hoffmann L.J. thought that since s.2(3) (see above) contemplates that damages under s.2(2) may be less than under s.2(1) this means that the measure under s.2(2) must be different from the measure under s.2(1). He said: **11–046**

> "[S]ection 2(1) is concerned with the damage flowing from having entered into the contract, while section 2(2) is concerned with the damage caused by the property not being what it was represented to be."

Hoffmann L.J. considered that consequential losses (which are recoverable under s2(1)) should not be recoverable under s.2(2). Evans L.J. thought that in a case where the claimant cannot rescind the contract and retained the property which they have received, the measure should be, "the difference in value between what the [claimant] was misled into believing he was acquiring, and the value of what he has in fact received." He indicated, however, that if appropriate, consequential losses might be awarded under s.2(2). All the members of the court agreed in *William Sindall* that if the contract had been upheld, the considerable fall in the value of the land could not have been compensated under s.2(2) as that loss was not caused by the misrepresentation. Damages would have been confined to the relatively modest cost of remedying the defect by diverting the sewer.

---

[66] [2000] B.L.R. 81.
[67] [1994] 1 W.L.R. 1016.

Exclusion or restriction of liability for misrepresentation

11–047   The Misrepresentation Act 1967, s.3, as amended by s.8 of the Unfair Contract Terms Act 1977, provides that if a contract contains a term which would exclude or restrict:

> "(a) any liability to which a party to a contract may be subject by reason of any misrepresentation made by him before the contract was made; or
> (b) any remedy available to another party to the contract by reason of such misrepresentation, that term shall be of no effect except in so far as it satisfies the requirement of reasonableness as stated in s.11(1) of the Unfair Contract Terms Act 1977; and it is for those claiming that the term satisfies that requirement to show that it does."

Thus, terms which purport to exclude or restrict liability for misrepresentation, or a remedy, must satisfy the reasonableness requirement in s.11 UCTA (see para.7–054). At common law, although liability could be excluded for non-fraudulent misrepresentation (subject to the restrictions applicable to all such clauses at common law) there could be no exclusion of liability for fraudulent misrepresentation.[68]

Clauses in general use can be struck down by s.3. One of the first cases on the amended version of s.3 was *Walker v Boyle*[69] which concerned Condition 17 of the Law Society's Conditions of Sale (subsequently amended), as applicable to contracts for the sale of land. The provision sought to eliminate the right to rescind for "errors, misstatements or omissions in the preliminary answer concerning the property". The vendor of a dwellinghouse told the purchaser that there were no boundary disputes affecting the property. This was untrue, although the vendor was unaware of the fact. Dillon J. granted rescission, holding that the clause failed to satisfy the requirement of reasonableness.

The provisions of s.3 cannot be evaded by the contract term in question deeming that statements of fact are not representations. In *Cremdean Properties Ltd v Nash*[70] conditions of sale by tender contained a clause providing that statements in the particulars were statements of belief only and "any error, omission or misdescription shall not annul the sale or be grounds on which compensation may be claimed". By a further clause, any intending purchaser was advised to satisfy themselves, by inspection or otherwise, of the correctness of the statements. As Scarman L.J. observed:

> "[T]he case for the [defendants] . . . runs thus: a statement is not a representation unless it is also a statement that what is stated is true. If in context a statement contains no assertion, express or implied, that its content is accurate, there is no representation. *Ergo*, there can be no misrepresentation; *ergo*, the Misrepresentation Act 1967 cannot apply to it. Humpty Dumpty would have fallen for this argument. If we were to fall for it, the Misrepresentation Act would be dashed to pieces which not all the King's lawyers could put together again."

The Court of Appeal held that the provisions were caught by s.3.

11–048   In *Overbrooke Estates Ltd v Glencombe Properties Ltd*[71] particulars of an auction sale stated that: " . . . neither the auctioneers nor any person in the employ of the auctioneers has any

---

[68] *Pearson & Son Ltd v Dublin Corporation* [1907] A.C. 351.
[69] [1982] 1 W.L.R. 995.
[70] (1977) 244 E.G. 547.
[71] [1974] 1 W.L.R. 1335.

authority to make or give any representation or warranty." A few days before the property in question had been knocked down to the defendants and a memorandum of sale signed, the auctioneers as agents for the claimant vendors had told the defendants that there were no plans for the compulsory acquisition of the property. In fact, the property was in an area where a slum clearance programme was likely. The defendants, on discovering this, attempted to withdraw from the transaction. The claimants sought an order of specific performance. The defendants argued that the clause was an unreasonable limitation of liability under s.3.

Brightman J. held that the clause operated as a limitation on the apparent authority of the auctioneers and fell outside s.3—it was not a clause excluding or restricting liability for misrepresentation. The claimants were therefore entitled to specific performance. The court was of the view that s.3 of the Act did not qualify the right of the principal to limit the agent's authority (see para.8–024).

Contracts often nowadays contain "entire agreement" clauses (see para.6–004). Such clauses state that the written document is intended and agreed to contain the entire terms of the contract, and that neither party has relied on any representations or statements outside the written contract.

In the case of *Inntrepreneur Pub Co v East Crown Ltd*[72] Lightman J. explained the effect of **11–049** such clauses. In this case, the claimants leased a public house to the defendants containing a "beer tie", under which the defendants were obliged to purchase their beer from the claimants' nominated supplier. The claimants brought an action for an injunction retraining the defendants from breaching the terms of the tie and for damages. The defendants argued that in the course of various discussions the claimants had given a collateral warranty (see para.6–015) that the defendants would be released from the tie. The claimants denied that any such warranty had been given; alternatively, they relied on an entire agreement clause in the lease agreement. The clause in question, clause 14, was in two parts. Clause 14.1 stated that the agreement "constitutes the entire agreement between the parties" (i.e. an entire agreement clause). Clause 14.2 stated that the tenants, before entering the agreement, either took independent professional advice or chose on advice not to do so and "accordingly they have not relied upon any advice or statement of the Company or its solicitors." Lightman J. stated:

> "An entire agreement provision does not preclude a claim in misrepresentation, for the denial of contractual force to a statement cannot affect the status of the statement as a misrepresentation. The same clause in an agreement may contain both an entire agreement provision and a further provision designed to exclude liability, eg for misrepresentation or breach of duty."

In the present case, as the judge explained, clause 14.1 (an entire agreement clause) was followed by clause 14.2 which set out to exclude liability for misrepresentation and breach of duty. Whether this provision was valid was dependent upon its reasonableness as required by s.3 of the Misrepresentation Act,[73] but it had no application to an entire agreement clause defining where the contractual terms are to be found.[74] The court concluded that there was no such collateral warranty as alleged, but even if there were, the claimants could rely on clause 14.1 as a complete defence.

[72] [2000] 2 Lloyd's Rep. 611.
[73] See *Inntrepreneur Estates (CPC) v Worth* [1996] 1 E.G.L.R. 84.
[74] *McGrath v Shah* (1987) 57 P. & C.R. 452.

11–050   In *Watford Electronics Ltd v Sanderson CFL Ltd*[75] a contract for the supply of computer hardware and software contained an entire agreement clause which provided that "no statement or representations made by either party have been relied upon by the other in agreeing to enter into the contract". At first instance, Judge Thornton Q.C. considered that s.3 of the Misrepresentation Act applied to the clause as its effect was to exclude liability for misrepresentation. The Court of Appeal (the point was obiter) disagreed as to the application of s.3. Chadwick L.J. said:

> "Liability in damages under the Misrepresentation 1967 can arise only where the party who has suffered the damage has relied on the misrepresentation. Where both parties to the contract have acknowledged, in the document itself, that they have not relied on any pre-contract representation, it would be bizarre (unless compelled to do so by the words which they have used) to attribute to them an intention to exclude a liability which they must have thought could never arise."

This approach, which is based the notion that an acknowledgment of non-reliance may operate as an evidential estoppel, is difficult to reconcile with *Walker v Boyle* and *Cremdean Properties v Nash*.

Misrepresentation: conclusion

11–051   In addition to the remedies for misrepresentation discussed in this chapter, it should be noted that misrepresentation may raise an estoppel (an "estoppel by representation"). Thus a party who makes an unambiguous representation of existing fact may be prevented from denying the truth of the statement if the person to whom it was made was intended to act upon it and did act upon it.

Traditionally, the doctrine has not been regarded as giving rise to a cause of action, either to the representor, who may be the other party to a contract, or against some third party. It may, however, operate as a defence. Thus, suppose a landlord A agrees to let a property to a tenant B, falsely representing that the drains are in good working order. B may be able to sue A for damages for misrepresentation but he cannot found any claim for damages on estoppel. However, if after B executes the lease, A brings an action for beach of covenant to repair, B may raise the misrepresentation as a defence. It would seem to make no difference that he has affirmed rather than rescinded the contract.

Further reading

Beale, *Points on Misrepresentation* (1995) 111 L.Q.R. 385.
Hooley, *Damages and the Misrepresentation Act 1967* (1991) 107 L.Q.R. 547.
Marks, *Loss of Profits in Damages for Deceit* (1992) 108 L.Q.R. 386.

---

[75] [2001] 1 All E.R. (Comm) 696. (The case is also discussed at para.7–063).

Chapter 12

MISTAKE

In certain situations a contract may be void owing to the existence of some fundamental mistake on the part of one or both parties. Not all mistakes will have this effect; most will not—indeed the circumstances in which a contract is vitiated in this way have been very narrowly circumscribed by the courts. There are good reasons for this.

12–001

First, it is not the role of the law to protect a party from the consequences of a bad bargain and the maxim caveat emptor ("let the buyer beware") prevails. Thus, suppose A purchases an item from B for £1,000 and believes it to be worth that amount but in fact it is only worth £10. In the absence of misrepresentation or other legal wrong, the contract is perfectly valid—A must bear the loss. To the layperson, such an error of judgment may well be thought of as a "mistake", but it is not a mistake which is legally recognised in the law of contract. Similarly, a customer in a clothes store who, without consulting a shop assistant, mistakenly picks up and purchases the wrong size of garment has no legal right to return the goods and obtain a refund if they are not defective. Of course, many high street retailers have a "returns" policy whereby they are prepared to refund the purchase price of goods returned in saleable condition, but that is not the same thing as saying they are legally obliged to do so.[1]

Secondly, the courts are concerned to give effect to the intentions of the parties and enforce apparent agreements. It is in the interests of commercial certainty that a party should not be able easily to escape from a contract on the ground that they had made some minor mistake in entering it. This is particularly true of complex transactions such as construction projects where various components such as land acquisition, finance and sources of supply have to be assembled and planned in great detail. This gives rise to a related point—the courts are anxious not to disturb the rights of third parties to a contract.

We saw that where there is an actionable misrepresentation, the courts will not grant rescission where third parties have acquired rights in the subject matter of the contract (see para.11–035). Misrepresentation, of course, renders a contract voidable. Where a mistake vitiates a contract, it is said to be an "operative" mistake and an operative mistake renders a contract not voidable, but void. Under a void transaction, no contract comes into existence at all. Thus if a sale of goods contract is void for mistake, no title or ownership passes from seller to buyer and the buyer would be obliged to return the goods to the seller.

12–002

A particular difficulty arises where the "buyer" sells the goods on to a third party. The third

---

[1] Some contracts that are regulated by statute may contain brief "cooling-off" periods which allow a consumer to withdraw from a transaction after it has been entered into—examples include consumer credit arrangements (see para.5–004) and distance selling contracts (see para.5–005).

party will acquire no title to the goods because the person from whom they have bought the goods has no title to pass. The original seller will then be able to recover the goods from the third party who will have no contractual rights against the person they have bought the goods from. Further difficulties may arise if the goods are passed on to fourth and fifth parties and so on. The reluctance of the courts to disturb third party rights is another reason why the courts are reluctant to hold that a contract is void for mistake.

Mistake of law

12–003   Until quite recently, the law held that only fundamental mistakes of fact were operative. A mistake of law was not considered to be operative unless it could be said to amount to a mixed statement of fact and law.[2] In *Kleinwort Benson Ltd v Lincoln City Council*[3] (see para.17–023) the House of Lords held that the right to recover money under the law of restitution when paid under a mistake of fact also extends to a mistake of law. In *Brennan v Bolt Burdon*[4] the Court of Appeal accepted in principle that a mistake of law could render a contract void for mistake but refused to vitiate a compromise agreement where the law was merely in doubt. In this case, B was a local authority tenant who sought damages for personal injury as a result of being exposed to carbon monoxide poisoning as a result of a faulty boiler. B compromised her claim in the belief that proceedings had been brought out of time, and the claim was withdrawn. A relevant legal precedent was subsequently overruled by the Court of Appeal[5] and B argued that the compromise was void for mistake as the parties had been mistaken about proceedings being out of time. A majority of the Court of Appeal rejected the argument on the basis that the compromise was capable of being performed—a change in the law was a risk which the parties entering such an agreement must accept. However, the decision establishes that it is now possible for a contract to be void for a mistake of law.

Categories of mistake: common, mutual and unilateral mistake

12–004   There are three main types of factual situation which may give rise to a contract being void for mistake.

In the first, often referred to as a "common mistake", the parties have entered into the agreement on the basis of a false and fundamental assumption. For example, they may be unaware at the time of contracting that the subject matter of their agreement is no longer in existence or has never existed. Although the parties are apparently "in agreement" there may be no contract because the transaction is impossible of performance.[6] For this reason, this type of mistake is also referred to as "initial impossibility" and is the counterpart of frustration or "subsequent impossibility" (see Chapter 10) where events which take place after the formation of the contract may lead to the parties being excused further performance.

---

[2] See, e.g. *Solle v Butcher* [1950] 1 K.B. 671.
[3] [1998] 3 W.L.R. 1095.
[4] [2004] 3 W.L.R. 1321.
[5] In *Anderton v Clwyd County Council* [2002] EWCA Civ 933.
[6] In *Bell v Lever Brothers Ltd* [1932] A.C. 161, (the case is discussed at para.12–010) Lord Atkin in the House of Lords referred to this type of mistake as mistake "nullifying" consent.

In the second type of mistake, "mutual mistake",[7] the parties are at cross-purposes and are mistaken about each others' intentions so that they never reach agreement. It is essentially a failure of offer and acceptance. In the third category, "unilateral mistake" only one of the parties is mistaken but the other party knows or may be taken to know of the mistake. Once again, the parties cannot be said to be in agreement.[8] As a result, both mutual and unilateral mistake have been classified by some commentators as single category of "agreement mistake", as opposed to common mistake which is classified as "possibility mistake".

We shall now consider the various categories of mistake—common, mutual and unilateral. We will then deal with two specific remedies for mistake concerning documents which either contain an error or have been signed under a mistake, i.e. the equitable remedy of "rectification" and the plea of non est factum respectively.

COMMON MISTAKE

As we have seen, a common mistake occurs where the two parties have reached agreement but have both made the same mistake as to some fundamental fact concerning the contract. At common law, the contract is not necessarily void in these circumstances and, as we shall see, a fairly stringent test has to be passed for the contract to be void. We shall begin by looking at mistake as to the existence of the subject matter.   **12–005**

Mistake as to the existence of the subject matter

It would seem that if, unknown to the parties, the specific subject matter of the contract does   **12–006**
not exist or has ceased to exist, the contract will be void. This situation is traditionally referred to as *res extincta*. Thus in *Galloway v Galloway*[9] the parties, believing they were lawfully married, entered into a deed of separation. Later, it was discovered that the marriage was void. The claimant's action for arrears of an allowance due under the deed failed on the ground that the deed was void. It was based upon a non-existent marriage. Similarly, in *Scott v Coulson*[10] the claimant contracted to sell the defendant a life insurance policy on the life of a Mr Death. At the time of the contract, unknown to the parties, Mr Death was already dead. The court was prepared to set aside the transaction.[11]

The *res extincta* rule has been given statutory effect in relation to the sale of goods in s.6 of the Sale of Goods Act 1979 which provides:

> "Where there is a contract for the sale of specific goods, and the goods without the knowledge of the seller have perished at the time when the contract was made, the contract is void".

It should be noted that the section refers only to goods that have been in existence but have perished. There is no reference to goods which have never existed but it is difficult to see why

---

[7] Confusingly, the expression mutual mistake is sometimes used to refer to a common mistake; see, e.g. Fenton Atkinson L.J. in *Magee v Pennine Insurance Co Ltd* [1969] 2 QB 507, at p.513.
[8] Lord Atkin refers in *Bell v Lever Brothers Ltd* to mutual and unilateral mistakes as mistakes "negativing consent".
[9] (1914) 30 T.L.R. 531.
[10] [1903] 2 Ch. 249.
[11] See also *Strickland v Turner* (1852) 7 Ex. 208.

goods which have never existed should be treated in any way differently from goods which have perished.

A leading case on the sale of goods which have ceased to exist is *Couturier v Hastie*.[12] In this case, the appellants were corn merchants who had a cargo of Indian corn in transit by sea from Salonika to London. The master of the ship had to sell the corn at a port of call, Tunis, as it had overheated and had begun to ferment. A short time after this, the respondents, acting as the appellants' *del credere* agents,[13] agreed a sale of the cargo in London to C. The parties were unaware of the disposal of the corn in Tunis. When C discovered the fate of the corn he withdrew from the transaction and the appellants sought to recover the price of the cargo from the respondents in C's place. The appellants argued that the contract was based on the shipping documents and insurance and that the respondents had purchased, not a cargo but a "maritime adventure" and they therefore assumed the risks relating to shipment. The House of Lords did not accept this argument and held that the respondents were not liable under the contract. Lord Cranworth L.C. stated:

> "[T]he whole question turns on the construction of the contract which was entered into between the parties . . . The contract plainly imports that there was something which was to be sold at the time of the contract, and something to be purchased. No such thing existing, I think the [court below] has come to the only reasonable conclusion upon it, and consequently that there must be judgment [for the respondents]".

12–007 This case is sometimes quoted as an authority for the rule that a contract will be void for common mistake where, unknown to the parties, the subject matter of the contract has ceased to exist. It also seems that this interpretation was placed on it by the draftsman of Sale of Goods Act 1893, which has now become s.6 of the Act of 1979. But since the finding of the court was that the buyer was not liable for the price, the decision assumes that there was a contract rather than that the contract was void. It is clearly not a case of *res extincta*. Indeed there was no mention of mistake in the judgments and therefore a more likely basis for the decision was that there was a total failure of consideration (see para.17–019) where the validity of the contract is not an issue. This view is supported by a dictum of Denning L.J. in *Frederick E Rose v William H Pim, Junr & Co Ltd (London)*[14] where he said that *Couturier v Hastie* "was not a case where the contract was void for mistake". Nevertheless the facts of the case fall within what is now s.6 of the Sale of Goods Act and therefore it would be open to a court to treat the facts of the case today as giving rise to an operative common mistake.

In cases involving non-existent subject-matter, it may be possible to argue that one party has impliedly warranted the existence of the subject matter so that they may be liable in damages for breach of contract. This was the conclusion arrived at by the court in an Australian case, *McRae v The Commonwealth Disposals Commission*,[15] in relation to a situation where the goods had never existed. It may be that the courts are more likely to take this approach where there has been negligence by one party.

12–008 The facts of the case were that the defendants invited tenders for the purchase of an oil tanker, said to be lying on the "Jourmand Reef". The claimant submitted a tender, which was

---

[12] (1856) 5 H.L. Cas. 673.
[13] An agent who, for an extra commission, agrees to indemnify the principal for any losses arising out of a contract with a third party introduced by the agent.
[14] [1953] 2 Q.B. 450, at p.472.
[15] (1951) 84 C.L.R. 377.

accepted, and then went to considerable trouble in fitting out a salvage ship and engaging a crew. It turned out that there was no tanker anywhere near the map reference given by the defendants, nor indeed was there any such place as the Jourmand Reef. The claimant sought damages for breach of contract and the defendants argued that the transaction was void by reason of *res extincta*, relying on *Couturier v Hastie*. The High Court of Australia held that the claimants were entitled to damages for breach of contract because the defendants had warranted that the goods existed. This finding allowed the claimant to recover the substantial losses incurred in assembling the failed salvage expedition, losses they would have been unable to recover if the contract had been declared void for mistake. The court did not think that *Couturier v Hastie* had established a rule of law that the contract was automatically void whenever the goods are not in existence at the time of the contract.

The court stated:

> "The truth is that the question whether the contract was void, or the vendor excused from performance by reason of the non-existence of the supposed subject matter, did not arise in *Couturier v Hastie*. It would have arisen if the purchaser had suffered loss through non-delivery of the corn and had sued the vendor for damages. If it had so arisen, we think that the real question would have been whether the contract was subject to an implied condition precedent that the goods were in existence. Prima facie, one would think, there would be no such implied condition precedent, the position being simply that the vendor promised that the goods were in existence".

Further, the court rejected the notion that the local equivalent of s.6 of the Sale of Goods Act applied (Victorian Goods Act 1928, s.11) since the section had no application to the facts of *McRae*, where the goods had never existed and the seller ought to have known that they did not exist.

It is suggested that the construction of the contract approach in the *McRae* case is an entirely sensible and productive of a just result. It is unfortunate that on the wording of s.6 it cannot be applied to a case where the goods have perished since the contract is declared by the section to be void—this is an anomaly which should be resolved.

Mistake as to title

12–009

A contract may be void at common law for common mistake where a buyer contracts to purchase something which already belongs to them, but neither buyer nor seller is aware of the fact; this state of affairs is known as *res sua*.

The factual situation is illustrated by the case of *Cooper v Phibbs*,[16] although the case was one where the contract was apparently rescinded in equity as opposed to being declared void at common law (there are grounds for thinking, however, that the contract was void). In this case the appellant agreed to lease a salmon fishery near Sligo from the respondent for a term of three years. Neither party was aware that the appellant himself was the tenant for life of the property under a trust. The House of Lords was prepared to rescind the transaction on terms that the respondent should have a lien on the fishery for the money he had expended on its improvement.

---

[16] (1867) L.R. 2 H.L. 149. See also *Cochrane v Willis* (1865) 1 Ch. App..58.

There are limits to this principle—in many cases the seller will give a warranty as title and even when parties contract under a common mistake as to the title of the seller, the seller may be liable in damages for breach of contract. This is the case in sale of goods contracts where, under s.12(1) of the Sale of Goods Act 1979, there is an implied condition that the seller has a right to sell or will have a right to sell at the time the property is to pass (see para.6–030).

Common mistake as to quality

12–010   Moving beyond *res extincta* and *res sua* the question that arises is whether the common mistake will be operative where the parties are mistaken as to the *quality* of the subject matter of the contract. Suppose that A purchases a painting from B that both A and B believe to be the work of a famous artist and a price of £500,000 is paid. If it turns out to be a copy and worth only £50, is the contract to be treated as being void?

The starting point for examining this issue must be the decision of the House of Lords in *Bell v Lever Brothers Ltd*.[17] The appellant Bell was employed as chairman of the Niger company, whose business included cocoa trading in West Africa. The respondent company, Lever Bros, which had a controlling interest in the Niger Company, amalgamated the two companies and Bell was made redundant. On the termination of his contract of service, the respondent company agreed to pay the appellant the sum of £30,000 by way of compensation. The money was paid to the appellant and he resigned from the company. A few months later, it was discovered that the appellant had been engaged in secret cocoa transactions on his own account whilst a member of the company. This trading was a breach of the appellant's duties to his employers and as such would have entitled his employers to dismiss him without compensation. It was accepted that at the time the termination agreement was entered into the appellant had not remembered these dealings, nor did he realise that the respondents could have dismissed him. The respondents sought to set aside the £30,000 settlement on the grounds of a common mistake. Their case was that the parties thought they were dealing with a contract of service that was terminable with compensation when in fact they were dealing with a contract that could be brought to an end without compensation.

The House of Lords held, by a majority of 3:2, that there was no operative mistake and the agreement was a valid contract—the mistake was merely as to the quality of the contract of service. Lord Atkin said:

> "Mistake as to the quality of the thing contracted for . . . will not affect assent unless it is the mistake of both parties, and is as to the existence of some quality which makes the thing without the quality essentially different from the thing it was believed to be".

This statement appeared to allow the possibility that some common mistakes as to quality would be operative, if sufficiently fundamental. But this did not extend to the case where the parties believed, for example, that a painting that is in fact a fake is a genuine work, for his Lordship stated:

> "A buys a picture from B: both A and B believe it to be the work of an old master, and a high price is paid. It turns out to be a modern copy. A has no remedy in the absence of representation or warranty".

[17] [1932] A.C. 161.

Lord Atkin recognised that such a case involves an unjust hardship to A and a benefit to B but it could be supported because of the "paramount importance" that contracts should be observed. Turning to the facts of the case itself, he said: **12–011**

> "It would be wrong to decide that an agreement to terminate a definite specified contract is void if it turns out that the agreement had already been broken and could have been terminated otherwise. The contract released is the identical contract in both cases, and the party paying the release gets exactly what he bargains for. It seems immaterial that he could have got the same result in another way, or that if he had known the true facts he would not have entered into the bargain".

The precise ratio of *Bell v Lever Bros* is unclear but the decision and the speeches of the majority admit of two potential interpretations: (1) a mistake as to quality can be operative if the mistake as to quality is sufficiently fundamental (and it was not sufficiently fundamental on the facts of the case); or (2) that a mistake as to quality is never operative. On the subject of *Bell v Lever Bros* Treitel[18] has stated:

> "The mistake in this case gave rise to a belief that subject matter which was actually worthless had a value of [£30,000]. It might be though that if such a mistake is not fundamental, no mistake as to quality can ever have this effect; but once one accepts the principle that a mere mistake as to value is not fundamental, the size of that difference cannot be decisive".

In the years following the decision of the House of Lords in *Bell v Lever Bros*, the decisions of the courts inclined towards the second of the above-mentioned interpretations. The most well-known of these authorities is *Leaf v International Galleries*[19] which concerned the sale of a painting of Salisbury Cathedral for £85 which both seller and buyer believed to be a Constable. Denning L.J. observed, obiter, that:

> "There was a mistake about the quality of the subject matter, because both parties believed the picture to be a Constable; and that mistake was in one sense essential or fundamental. But such a mistake does not avoid the contract: there was no mistake at all about the subject matter of the sale. It was a specific picture, 'Salisbury Cathedral'. The parties were agreed in the same terms on the same subject matter, and that is sufficient to make a contract".

In the later case of *Harrison & Jones Ltd v Bunten & Lancaster Ltd*[20] there was a sale of kapok,   **12–012**
identified as "Sree Brand". Both parties mistakenly thought that "Sree" was pure kapok but in fact it was not. Pilcher J. held the contract to be valid—the parties had contracted on the basis of a known trade description and that fact that goods of that description lacked a particular quality was irrelevant. Similarly, in *Frederick E Rose (London) Ltd v William H Pim Jnr & Co Ltd*[21] the parties agreed a sale of horsebeans known in Egypt as "feveroles". Both

---

[18] Treitel, *The Law of Contract* (2007) 12th edn, Thomson, p. 320.
[19] [1950] 2 K.B. 86. The case is discussed in connection with rescission for misrepresentation at para.11–033. See also *Solle v Butcher* [1950] 1 K.B. 671; and *Harlington & Leinster Enterprises Ltd v Christopher Hill Fine Art Ltd* [1990] 3 W.L.R. 13.
[20] [1953] 1 Q.B. 646.
[21] [1953] 2 Q.B. 450.

parties believed at the time of the sale that "feveroles" was a synonym for horsebeans but in fact the beans delivered, though horsebeans, were not actually feveroles. The written contract referred to "horsebeans". The Court of Appeal held that the contract was not void even though the parties were under a fundamental mistake as to the nature of the subject matter. The court refused to rectify the written contract (see para.12–047).

The cases on common mistake as to quality were not quite all one way, however. Some cases appear to have recognised that mistakes of quality could be operative if sufficiently fundamental. In *Nicholson & Venn v Smith-Marriott*[22] a set of table linen was put up for auction and described as bearing "the crest and arms of Charles I and . . . the authentic property of that monarch". Relying on this description, the claimants successfully bid for the lot and it was knocked down at £787. It turned out that the linen was Georgian and only worth £105. The claimants recovered damages for breach of s.13 of the Sale of Goods Act (non-correspondence with description—see para.6–031) but Hallett J. considered (obiter) that the contract might well have been treated as being void for fundamental mistake. The judge thought that, applying to the dictum of Lord Atkin in *Bell v Lever Bros* (see above), a Carolean relic was an "essentially different" thing from a Georgian one and the contract was therefore not of table linen but of a Carolean relic. Hallett J. did, however, concede that the issue was one of great difficulty; indeed in *Solle v Butcher*[23] Denning L.J. did not think that the contract in *Nicholson & Venn v Smith-Marriott* was void from the beginning. There is also the point that an award of damages presupposes that a contract is valid and it is difficult to see how the same contract could at the same time be void for mistake. In a majority decision of the Supreme Court of Michigan in the United States, *Sherwood v Walker*,[24] a contract for the sale of a cow was held to be void for mistake. The parties believed the cow to be barren but the sellers later discovered that she was in calf at the time of the contract and refused to deliver her to the buyers. The value of a breeding cow was approximately ten times that of a barren one. The court considered that the mistake was not as to the mere quality of the animal but went to the very nature of the thing and was fundamental. The approach of the English courts as exemplified by such cases as *Bell v Lever Bros* and *Leaf v International Galleries* has been to reject difference in value as a basis for operative mistake.

In *Sheikh Brothers Ltd v Ochsner*[25] the appellants granted the respondents a licence to exploit sisal. Under the terms of the contract, the respondents were to cut the sisal and deliver to the appellants 50 tons of sisal fibre each month. The parties believed that the land was capable of producing this quantity. The Privy Council, applying the dicta in *Bell v Lever Brothers*, held that the contract was void for fundamental mistake because the estate was not capable of producing the specified quantity of sisal. Treitel[26] treats the case as falling into a class of its own, "physical impossibility"—it may be, however, that the case turns solely on the interpretation of the Indian Contract Act 1872.[27]

22 (1947) 177 L.T. 189.
23 [1950] 1 K.B. 671.
24 (1887) 33 N.W. 919.
25 [1957] A.C. 136. See also *Griffith v Brymer* (1903) 19 T.L.R. 434 where a contract to hire a room to view the coronation procession of Edward VII was held to be void for mistake where the decision to cancel the procession was taken earlier on the same day. Wright J. considered that the parties, who were unaware of the cancellation at the time of the contract, had based their agreement on a false premise which went to the whole root of the matter. See, in relation to frustration, the "coronation cases" at para.10–009.
26 Treitel, *The Law of Contract* (2007) 12th edn, p.317.
27 This is the view expressed by the author of Cheshire, Fifoot and Furmston's, *Law of Contract* (2007) 15th edn, p.293, fn.42.

The Associated Japanese Bank case

The scope of common mistake as to quality was revisited by Steyn J. in the case of *Associated*   **12–013**
Japanese Bank (International) Ltd v Credit du Nord SA.[28] In this case, B, wishing to raise money, agreed a sale and leaseback agreement with the claimants, Associated Japanese Bank. Under this arrangement, the claimants purchased four textile machines from B for £1,021,000 and leased them back to him on rental terms. B's obligations under the agreement were guaranteed by the defendants, Credit du Nord. B fell into arrears with the rental payments, and when B was found to be bankrupt, the claimants sought to enforce the guarantee against the defendants. At all times both the claimants and defendants believed that the machines existed. In fact, it was discovered that the machines did not exist and the sale and leaseback was a fraud perpetrated by B.

Steyn J. held that the defendants were not liable as the guarantee was subject to an express condition precedent that the machines existed; even if that construction was wrong, there was an implied condition precedent to the same effect. The learned judge went on to say that (obiter), even if he was wrong about the construction of the agreement, the contract would have been void for mistake at common law, applying the dictum of Lord Atkin in *Bell v Lever Bros*. It may be recalled that in that case his Lordship considered that mistake at common law was restricted to mistakes as to the existence of some quality which makes the thing without the quality "essentially different from the thing as it was believed to be". As Steyn J. explained:

"For both parties the guarantee of obligations under a lease with non-existent machines was essentially different from a guarantee of a lease with four machines which both parties at the time of the contract believed to exist. The guarantee is an accessory contract. The non-existence of the subject matter of the principal contract is therefore of fundamental importance. Indeed, the analogy of the classic *res extincta* cases . . . is fairly close. In my judgment the stringent test of common law mistake is satisfied: the guarantee is void *ab initio*".

The learned judge did not think the decision in *Bell v Lever Bros* precluded the court from considering whether a common mistake as to quality was operative on the facts before it. He considered that Lord Denning's view, expressed in several cases including *Solle v Butcher* (see para.12–016), that a common mistake as to quality, however fundamental, never renders a contract void at common law to be an "individual opinion" which did not do justice to the majority speeches in *Bell v Lever Bros*. The views expressed by the court in the *Japanese Bank* case are therefore in line with the first of the two interpretations of *Bell v Lever Bros* mentioned above at para.12–011.

The Great Peace Shipping case

In *Great Peace Shipping Ltd v Tsavliris Salvage (International) Ltd, The Great Peace*[29] the Court   **12–014**
of Appeal re-examined the issue of common mistake.

The facts of the case were that a ship, the *Cape Providence*, had suffered serious structural

[28] [1989] 1 W.L.R. 255.
[29] [2003] Q.B. 679.

damage and lay stricken in the South Indian Ocean. The defendants offered salvage services to her; that offer having been accepted, the defendants attempted to arrange for a tug through brokers in London, but the nearest such vessel was five or six days sailing time away. There was concern that the *Cape Providence* might founder and fearing for the safety of her crew, the defendants sought the assistance of a merchant vessel in the vicinity. They were given the name of the claimants' vessel, the *Great Peace*, which was believed to be about 35 miles away from the *Cape Providence*. The claimants and the defendants entered into hire contract for a minimum of five days to escort and stand by the stricken ship for the purpose of saving life. The contract gave the defendants a right to cancel on payment of five days hire. It was then discovered that the *Great Peace* was 410 miles away from *the Cape Providence*, however the defendants did not cancel the contract immediately but sought a vessel nearer to the damaged ship. Within a few hours, they found such a vessel and cancelled the contract with the claimants, refusing to pay for the hire of the *Great Peace*. The claimants sought the sum of US $82,500 representing five days hire or as damages for wrongful repudiation. The defendants argued that the contract had been concluded on the basis of a false and fundamental assumption of fact, namely that the two vessels were in close proximity when they were not. Accordingly, so the defendants contended, the contract was either void at common law for common mistake, or voidable in equity (this aspect of the case is considered at para.12–018). In the High Court, Toulson J. found for the claimants.

The Court of Appeal affirmed the decision of the trial judge and held that the contract was not void for common mistake. The mistake as to the distance between the two vessels was not such as to render the services supplied by the claimants (applying *Bell v Lever Bros*) essentially different from what the parties had agreed. The fact that the defendants did not cancel the agreement until they knew they could obtain the services of a nearer vessel showed that the mistake could not be operative under the common law test; as did the fact that the *Great Peace* would have arrived in time to give some days of assistance. The defendants would have wanted this were it not for the fortunate arrival of another vessel in the area prepared to render the same service. It was not therefore impossible to perform the contractual adventure and the claimants were entitled to their hire charges. The approach to common mistake as to quality as exemplified in the speeches of Lords Atkin and Thankerton in the House of Lords in *Bell v Lever Bros* was endorsed, as were the obiter statements of Steyn J. in the *Japanese Bank* case. Thus a common mistake as to quality may have the effect of rendering a contract void.

12–015   Consistent with these authorities, Lord Phillips adopted the following five principles as a correct statement of the law, i.e. these elements must be present if common mistake is to avoid a contract:

(i)   there must be a common assumption as to the existence of a state of affairs;

(ii)   there must be no warranty by either party that that state of affairs exists;

(iii)   the non-existence of the state of affairs must not be attributable to the fault of either party;

(iv)   the non-existence of the state of affairs must render performance of the contract impossible;

(v)   the "state of affairs" may be the existence, or a vital attribute, of the consideration to be provided or circumstances which must subsist if performance of the contractual adventure is to be possible.

Lord Phillips considered that the second and third of these elements referred to the decision in *McRae v Commonwealth Disposals Commission* (see para.12–007). At the same time, the third element taken together with the fourth align common mistake with the doctrine of frustration.

It may be recalled from the discussion in Chapter 10 that, under the doctrine of frustration, a contract may be discharged if further performance becomes impossible or something "radically different" from what the parties originally intended. As mentioned at the beginning of this chapter, the doctrine is sometimes referred to as "subsequent impossibility", whereas common mistake has been called "initial impossibility". The difference between the two can come down to a matter of timing as a comparison of two "coronation cases" shows: *Griffith v Brymer* (see para.12–012, fn 25) and *Krell v Henry* (see para.10–009). In *Bell v Lever Bros*, Lord Atkin had advanced the theory of an implied term as an alternative test for common mistake as to quality but Lord Phillips in *Great Peace Shipping* rejected this and felt that "consideration of the law of frustration assisted with the analysis of the law of common mistake."

Further, element (v) above confirms that operative common mistake extends beyond cases of *res extincta* although the circumstances in which it does so are likely to be rare indeed. This is borne out by post-*Great Peace Shipping* cases such as *Brennan v Bolt Burdon* (discussed at para.12–003)[30].

Common mistake in equity: before and after the Great Peace Shipping case

Until the Court of Appeal's decision in the *Great Peace Shipping* case decided that it was wrong in law, there existed for over 50 years a doctrine of common mistake in equity whereby a contract otherwise valid at law could be rescinded and terms imposed on the parties to do justice between them. This doctrine only really made sense if one accepted the proposition that a common mistake as to quality is never operative at common law—a proposition that recent cases, including *Great Peace Shipping* itself, have called into question. And even then it made only limited sense since it was difficult to reconcile the doctrine with the common law principle of caveat emptor—the doctrine seemed to protect a party from the consequences of a bad bargain. In order to understand the current position it is necessary to examine some of the decisions decided under this discredited doctrine.

12–016

The starting point is the decision of the Court of Appeal in *Solle v Butcher*.[31] Here the claimant agreed to lease a flat in Beckenham from the defendant for seven years at a rent of £250 per annum. Both parties believed that the lease was outside the Rent Restriction Acts. In fact that legislation did apply which meant that the maximum chargeable rent was no more than £140 per annum. Nevertheless, the defendant could have charged approximately £250 to take account of repairs and improvements had he served statutory notice on the claimant at the time the lease was executed. No such notice had been served by the defendant. After two years, the claimant realised the mistake and sued for the recovery of the overpaid rent and sought a declaration that he could remain in possession as a statutory tenant at a rental of £140. The defendant counterclaimed for rescission of the lease on the ground of mistake. It was held by a majority of the Court of Appeal (Jenkins L.J. dissenting) that the mistake was one of fact, not law. However, the common mistake was not one that rendered the contract void at common law as it was a mistake as to quality; nevertheless the lease was held to be voidable in equity. As such it could be rescinded by the court and the parties put on terms so as to achieve a just result.

Accordingly, the claimant was offered the choice of either surrendering the lease or remaining

---

[30] See also *Champion Investments Ltd v Ahmed* [2004] EWHC 1956 (QB). Cf *EIC Services Ltd v Phipps* [2005] 1 W.L.R. 1377.

[31] [1950] 1 K.B. 671.

in possession but paying the full allowable rent of £250 once the statutory notices had been served. Denning L.J. explained that, in his view, in *Bell v Lever Bros* the House of Lords had decided that a common mistake as to quality was not operative. In Denning L.J.'s analysis, that case was decided according to exclusively common law principles and ignored a broader doctrine of common mistake in equity where the contract could be rescinded in circumstances involving mistake as to quality. It seems odd that the equitable doctrine was not invoked by the House of Lords in *Bell* particularly since counsel cited equity authorities to the court. Denning L.J. stated:

> "A contract is also liable in equity to be set aside if the parties were under a common mis-apprehension either as to facts or as to their relative and respective rights, provided that the misapprehension was fundamental and that the party seeking to set it aside was not himself at fault . . . [in this case] there was clearly . . . a common misapprehension, which was fundamental and in no way due to any fault of the landlord, and . . . by reason of the common misapprehension, this lease can be set aside on terms that the court thinks fit".

12–017   Particular reliance was placed by Denning L.J. on the decision of the House of Lords in *Cooper v Phibbs* as authority for a doctrine of rescission in equity. The difficulty with this analysis is that the facts of that case seem to disclose a contract that is void by reason of *res sua*—if the contract was void there would be no contract to rescind in equity (see para.12–009).

The decision in *Solle v Butcher* was followed in a number of cases over the years. These cases included the decision of Goff J. in *Grist v Bailey* [32] and that of the Court of Appeal in *Magee v Pennine Insurance Co Ltd.* [33]

In *Grist v Bailey* a house was sold for £850, both vendor and purchaser believing that it was occupied by a statutorily protected tenant. In fact the protected tenant had died by the time of the sale—with vacant possession the house was worth £2,250. The court held that the mistake was not such as to render the contract void at common law—there was not an "essential difference" between the subject matter as it was believed to be and as it was. But the court considered that the contract could be set aside in equity as the mistake was fundamental. Terms were imposed that the vendor should give the purchaser the opportunity of buying the house at a full vacant possession price. This decision is open to several objections. First, can a mistake really be said to be "fundamental" of it fails the "essential difference" test of *Bell v Lever Bros*? If so, what precisely is meant by fundamental mistake in these circumstances? Secondly, and this point is related to the first, the facts of the case are very difficult to distinguish from the examples given by Lord Atkin in *Bell v Lever Bros* of contracts where there would be no operative mistake and the contract would be valid. Thirdly, the decision goes too far towards protecting the vendor who has made a bad bargain.

In *Magee v Pennine Insurance* the court rescinded the contract but no terms were imposed. The claimant bought a car for his 18-year-old son to drive and signed without reading properly an insurance proposal form to insure the car with the defendant company. The proposal form stated that the claimant held a provisional licence when in fact he held no licence. This information became the basis of the contract of insurance between the claimant and the defendant company, and the policy was issued and renewed each year. Four years later, the claimant's son was involved in a serious accident and a claim on the policy was brought. The claimant sought £600 under the policy, which was the value of the car, but was offered £385 by the defendants in settlement of the claim.

[32]   [1967] Ch. 532.
[33]   [1969] 2 Q.B. 507.

The claimant accepted this offer. However, the defendants later refused to pay the sum agreed when they discovered that the claimant's original proposal form had contained incorrect information (i.e. an innocent misrepresentation). The claimant sought to recover the sum of £385.

By a majority decision, the Court of Appeal held that in entering into the settlement agreement that parties were under a common mistake that the claimant had a valid claim under the insurance policy. Accordingly the agreement was set aside but the defendants were not required by the court to return the premiums even though they had been paid under an invalid policy. Lord Denning M.R. again observed that in his view, a common mistake, even on a fundamental matter did not make the contract invalid at law but made it voidable in equity, following *Solle v Butcher*. Fenton Atkinson L.J. agreed with Denning L.J. in the result but on different grounds; dissenting, Winn L.J. found it impossible to distinguish *Bell v Lever Bros* and considered that the agreement should stand. This is surely correct—there is plainly no material difference in the type of mistake in this case and the one in *Bell v Lever Bros*.

12–018

In the *Japanese Bank* case (discussed at para.12–013), Steyn J. explained the relationship between common law mistake and mistake in equity as follows:

> "Where common law mistake has been pleaded, the court must first consider this plea. If the contract is held to be void, no question of mistake in equity arises. But if the contract is held to be valid, a plea of mistake in equity may have to be considered".

In later cases, the courts struggled to formulate the precise circumstances in which a contract affected by a common mistake as to quality, although valid in law, could be rescinded in equity. [34] This equitable jurisdiction has now been denied by the Court of Appeal in the *Great Peace Shipping* case (the facts are given at para.12–014). In that case, the defendants had argued, in the alternative, that the contract was voidable in equity on the grounds of common mistake. In the High Court, Toulson J. doubted the very existence of the doctrine of rescission in equity of a contract on the grounds of mistake. The learned judge was at a loss to understand what was "the test for determining the nature of the 'fundamental mistake' necessary to give birth to the right to rescind."

The Court of Appeal agreed. The court examined the authorities and came to the conclusion that it was not possible to reconcile *Bell v Lever Bros* and *Solle v Butcher* and that therefore *Solle v Butcher* was of dubious authority. There is no power possessed by the courts to rescind a contract for common mistake other than that laid down in *Bell v Lever Bros*. Agreeing with the views of Steyn J. in the *Japanese Bank* case, the Court of Appeal confirmed that operative mistake at common law goes beyond cases of *res extincta* and *res sua* to include mistakes as to quality that are sufficiently fundamental under the test laid down by Lord Atkin in *Bell v Lever Bros*. In other words, the first of the two suggested interpretations of that case (see para.12–011 above) has been affirmed.

As for the reliance placed by Denning L.J. in *Solle v Butcher* upon the decision of the House of Lords in *Cooper v Phibbs*, Lord Phillips M.R. had this to say:

12–019

> "[T]he House of Lords in *Bell v Lever Bros* considered that the intervention of equity, as demonstrated in *Cooper v Phibbs*, took place in circumstances where the common law would have ruled the contract void for mistake. We do not find it conceivable that the House of Lords overlooked an equitable right in *Lever Bros* to rescind the agreement, not

---

[34] See, for example, *William Sindall Plc v Cambridgeshire County Council* [1994] 1 W.L.R. 1016, per Evans L.J. (obiter) at p.1042.

withstanding that the agreement was not void for mistake at common law. The jurisprudence established no such right".

The result is to simplify the law and answer questions that have fuelled academic debate for
many years. However, Lord Phillips M.R. envisaged that legislation might be desirable to introduce a measure of flexibility to the law:

> "We can understand why the decision in *Bell v Lever Bros Ltd* did not find favour with Lord
> Denning MR. An equitable jurisdiction to grant rescission on terms where a common
> fundamental mistake has induced a contract gives greater flexibility than a doctrine of
> common law which holds the contract void in such circumstances. Just as the Law Reform
> (Frustrated Contracts) Act 1943 was needed to temper the effect of the common law doc-
> trine of frustration, so there is scope for legislation to give greater flexibility to our law of
> mistake than the common law allows".

It should not be forgotten that the judgment in *Great Peace Shipping* is not a decision of the
House of Lords but of the Court of Appeal, as was *Solle v Butcher*. This being the case, it is
technically possible that a later Court of Appeal could choose between the two authorities.

MISTAKES AFFECTING AGREEMENT: MUTUAL AND UNILATERAL MISTAKE

12–020   As indicated at the beginning of this chapter, there are two categories of mistake which may
have the effect of negativing agreement between the parties—these are mutual mistake and
unilateral mistake. In the former, neither party is aware of the other's mistake; in the latter, one
party is aware of the other's mistake.

Mutual mistake

12–021   In a case of mutual mistake, the offer and acceptance do not coincide and the parties are mistaken about each other's intentions. They are at cross-purposes.

In *Raffles v Wichelhaus*[35] the defendants agreed to buy from the claimants "125 bales of Surat
cotton . . . to arrive *ex Peerless* from Bombay." In fact, there were two ships called Peerless and
both were due to leave Bombay. The defendants intended that the ship leaving in October was
the ship referred to in the agreement, but the claimants had in mind the other ship which was
not due to leave until December. The defendants refused to accept the goods sent on the
December ship but the claimants sought to enforce the contract, arguing that the defendants
were liable for refusing to accept them. The court did not actually decide that there was no
contract but found that the defendants were not liable. The transaction was ambiguous—it
contained a latent ambiguity and whether viewed subjectively or objectively it was impossible
to say which of the two ships was the subject matter of the intended contract. It is permissible,
therefore, to conclude that in the circumstances of the case there was no contract.

---

[35]   (1864) 2 H. & C. 906.

The approach of the courts to mutual mistake is objective. The court will try to ascertain the "sense of the promise", i.e. would a reasonable third party understand the sense of the agreement in the way one party, A, understood it to mean, or in the sense the other party, B, understood it to mean. It is only where the transaction is ambiguous under this test that the contract will be void for mistake. The objective approach is the same as taken for offer and acceptance (see para.2–002)—indeed an operative mutual mistake is really an instance of a contract which fails for defective offer and acceptance. The contract is void as much for the uncertainty as for the application of any specific doctrine of mistake.

In many cases of mutual mistake, however, the court may be able to uphold the contract in the sense as understood by one or other of the parties. In *Raffles v Wichelhaus* this was not possible, but it was achievable in *Wood v Scarth*. [36] The defendant offered to lease a public house to the claimant at a rent of £63 per annum and the claimant accepted this offer. The defendant had intended that a premium of £500 would be payable in addition to the rent and he had instructed his clerk to explain this to the claimant. The clerk failed to inform the claimant of this, so that when the claimant accepted, he believed that £63 a year would be the total sum payable under the lease. The claimant sought damages at common law for the refusal to grant a lease. The damages were awarded by the court as the contract as understood by the claimant should be enforced. A reasonable person would have understood the contract in the way that the claimant understood it—this was the sense of the promise. [37]

12–022

Cases concerning auction sales have given rise to disputes based on mutual mistake—this may be because the opportunity for misunderstandings to be corrected through negotiation is more limited than in other types of sale. Two cases afford an interesting comparison: *Scriven Bros & Co v Hindley & Co* [38] and *Tamplin v James*. [39]

In *Scriven Bros v Hindley* an auctioneer put up for sale bales of Russian hemp and bales of tow (an inferior commodity) belonging to the claimant, both of which had, unusually, arrived by the same ship and bore the same shipping marks. The auction catalogue did not mention that one lot was hemp and the other tow. The defendant's agent bid for a lot of tow and the bid was about the right amount for hemp but extravagant for tow. He believed that he was bidding for hemp and the lot was knocked down to him. The auctioneer was aware that the defendant's agent was labouring under a mistake but he thought that the bidder was unaware of the true value of tow rather than that he was mistaken as to the subject matter. The defendant refused to take delivery of the tow and was sued for breach of contract by the claimant. Lawrence J. held that there was no contract as the parties were not in agreement; they were genuinely at cross-purposes. Viewed objectively, one could not say whether the contract was for hemp or tow—the catalogue and samples were misleadingly described and marked and the ship which had brought the tow usually brought only hemp. It was, perhaps, significant that there had been no negligence on the part of the defendant's agent and that any reasonable person would have been misled into making the mistake which he had made. On the other hand, the learned judge considered that there had been negligence on the part of the auctioneer; he felt it had been the duty of the auctioneer to make clear to bidders which lots were hemp and which were tow. A contract could not arise where the party seeking to enforce it had "by his own negligence, or by that of those for whom he is respon-

---

[36] (1858) 1 F. & F. 293.

[37] This action was preceded by equity proceedings ((1855) 2 K. & J. 33) where the court concluded that there was no operative mistake but nevertheless refused specific performance on the grounds of hardship. Thus even where the sense of the promise can be ascertained, equity may grant relief and not compel performance.

[38] [1913] 3 K.B. 564.

[39] (1880) 15 Ch. D. 219.

sible, caused, or contributed to cause, the mistake." Thus in such cases the presence or absence of fault may be a factor in the court's decision as to whether to avoid the contract.

12–023   In *Tamplin v James* the argument that the parties were genuinely at cross-purposes failed. The defendant purchased a public house, "The Ship Inn", and adjoining saddler's shop at auction. The defendant, who had known the property all his life, assumed that two gardens which had been occupied with the pub were included in the sale. In fact, they were held under a separate title and were not part of the lot offered. The particulars of sale and plans, which were on display in the saleroom, contained no misdescription or ambiguity but the defendant did not look at these before bidding. The claimant vendor sued for specific performance and the defendant put forward a defence based on mistake. The argument did not impress the Court of Appeal. James L.J. said:

> "If a man will not take reasonable care to ascertain what he is buying, he must take the consequences. The defence on the ground of mistake cannot be sustained".

It was held that specific performance of the contract would be granted.

The circumstances in which a contract will be void on the ground of a unilateral mistake are extremely narrow. Equitable remedies are discretionary and specific performance was refused on similar facts to *Tamplin v James* in the case of *Malins v Freeman*.[40] Although the mistake in that case was due to the defendant's own carelessness, it would have been harsh to enforce the contract in the circumstances. The claimant was left to seek damages at common law.

Unilateral mistake

12–024   As already stated above, in a unilateral mistake, only one party is mistaken and the other party is aware of the mistake, or the circumstances are such that they must have been aware of it. If the other party is not aware of the mistake, the contract will be valid unless it falls into the category of a mutual mistake sufficiently serious so as to negative agreement as explained in the previous section.

The circumstances in which a contract will be void on the ground of a unilateral mistake are extremely narrow. The principal requirement, in addition to knowledge of the mistake by the non-mistaken party, is that the mistake must be *as to a term of the contract* rather than an error of judgment as to the quality or value of the subject matter. It must also be the case that the mistaken party is not at fault in any way. Operative unilateral mistake is illustrated by the case of *Hartog v Colin & Shields*.[41] The defendants offered to sell to the claimants a quantity of Argentinian hare skins at a certain price per pound. After the claimants had accepted this offer, the defendants failed to deliver the goods, as they had intended (as was the custom of the trade) to sell at the specified price per piece. The value of a piece was one-third that of a pound so that the defendants' offer was roughly one-third of the usual market price. The claimants sought damages for breach of contract. Singleton J. found for the defendants—the claimants must have realised that the defendants' offer contained a mistake. The contract was therefore void as the mistake concerned a term of the contract and it was a mistake of which the other party was aware. The principle in this case should not be taken too far; there will be cases where a low

---

[40]   (1837) 2 Ke. 25.
[41]   [1939] 3 All E.R. 566.

price is mistakenly offered but the offeree does not know, and could not reasonably be expected to have known of the mistake at the time of the contract.

In *Centrovincial Estates Plc v Merchant Investors Assurance Co Ltd* [42] the claimants leased office premises to the defendants at a rental of £68,320 per annum, subject to review from December 25, 1982. The lease provided that the rent could only be increased to the current market rental value as agreed between the parties or as determined by an independent assessor in default of agreement. The claimants, through their solicitors, wrote to the defendants asking them to agree a rent of £65,000 and the next day the defendants agreed to that figure. The claimants then realised that their letter contained a mistake and that they had intended to quote a figure of £126,000 for the annual rent. The claimants sought a declaration to the effect that there was no legally binding agreement. Slade L.J. considered that the case must be decided in accordance with the principle of objectivity:

> "It is a well-established principle of the English law of contract that an offer falls to be interpreted not subjectively by what has actually passed through the mind of the offeror, but objectively, by reference to the interpretation which a reasonable man in the shoes of the offeree would place on the offer. It is an equally well-established principle that ordinarily an offer, when unequivocally accepted according to its precise terms, will give rise to a legally binding agreement as soon as acceptance is communicated to the offeror in the manner contemplated by the offer, and cannot thereafter be revoked without the consent of the other party".

Refusing to grant the declaration, the Court of Appeal held that in the absence of evidence that the defendants knew, or ought reasonably to have known that the claimants had made an error, the contract would be upheld. It might be thought that, as the lease provided only for an increase in the rental, the defendants should have been aware of the mistake but this did not make any difference.

12–025

As has been stated above, an operative unilateral mistake must be based on a mistake as to the terms of the contract rather than an error of judgment by one party as to the quality of the subject matter. The distinction is demonstrated by the well-known case of *Smith v Hughes*,[43] where the claimant, a farmer, offered to sell oats to the defendant, a racehorse trainer, and showed him a sample. The defendant agreed to buy the whole quantity. When the oats were delivered, the defendant refused to pay for them as they were "new" oats and he only wanted "old " oats. The claimant, who knew that the oats were new (he had no old oats) refused to take them back and sued for the price. There was a conflict of evidence as to whether anything was said in preliminary negotiations about the oats being "old". The defendant's evidence was that he had said that he was always a buyer of good *old* oats; according to the claimant, the word "old" was never used. The judge left two questions to the jury: (i) had the word "old" been used? If so, the verdict would be for the defendant; (ii) if the word "old" was not used, did the claimant believe that the defendant believed that he was contracting for old oats? If so, the verdict would be for the defendant. The jury found for the defendant; the claimant appealed to the Court of the Queen's Bench. The court considered that question (ii) above was a misdirection and ordered a new trial.

Their Lordships considered that if the oats had been described as old oats in negotiations, the defendant would not be liable. They went on to consider the position if the jury found that there was no mention of the oats being old. Cockburn C.J. considered that there should be

[42] [1983] Com. Law. Rep. 158.
[43] (1871) L.R. 6 Q.B. 597.

judgment for the claimant—the question was whether "passive acquiescence [by the seller] in the self-deception of the buyer" would entitle the buyer to avoid the contract. His Lordship considered that it would not. He said:

> "[T]he defendant agreed to buy a specific parcel of oats. The oats were what they were sold as, namely good oats according to the sample. The buyer persuaded himself they were old oats, when they were not so; but the seller neither said nor did anything to contribute to his deception. He [the buyer] has himself to blame. The question is not what a man of scrupulous morality or nice honour would do under such circumstances".

12–026   Blackburn J. agreed that, even if the claimant knew of the defendant's mistake (i.e. if the mistake is unilateral), he came under no duty to disclose the true facts (see para.11–009 as to the principle regarding silence and misrepresentation). This was a mistake merely as to the quality of the subject matter; on the other hand, if the buyer mistakenly believed to the seller's knowledge that the seller had *warranted* that the oats were old, then the contract would be void. In other words, if the buyers's mistake had been as to the terms of the contract, and the seller was aware of the mistake, the mistake would have been operative.

As with mutual mistake, the courts, exercising their equitable jurisdiction may refuse specific performance of a contract affected by unilateral mistake. In *Webster v Cecil*[44] the defendant, having refused to sell several plots of land to the claimant for £2,000, wrote a letter offering to sell the plots to him for £1,250. This offer was accepted by the claimant. In fact, the defendant had made a mistake in adding up the prices of the plots and had intended to state a figure of £2,250. Given the previous refusal, the court considered that the claimant must be taken to have been aware that the defendant's offer contained a mistake. Specific performance was refused.[45]

Many cases of unilateral mistake are cases of mistaken identity and this issue will be considered in a separate section below.

MISTAKE AS TO IDENTITY

12–027   The circumstances in which a contract may be void because of a mistake by one party as to the indentity of the other party are, like the other forms of mistake already discussed, very narrowly circumscribed. As explained at the beginning of this chapter (see para.12–001), one of the reasons for this is the reluctance to disturb third party rights. This issue is raised in a particularly acute form in cases of mistake as to identity because these cases highlight the problem: which of two innocent parties is to suffer as a result of the dealings of another fraudulent person?

In a typical such case, "S", a person wishing to sell goods may be approached by a fraudster (a "rogue") "R" giving a false identity and whose objective is to acquire the goods without paying for them. A sale is agreed and R takes possession of the goods, giving S a cheque which is subsequently dishonoured as a forgery. As R is aware that S is contracting under a mistake, the mistake is unilateral. R immediately sells the goods to "P", an innocent purchaser, a person unaware of the circumstances in which R acquired the goods. R then usually absconds. When

---

[44] (1861) 54 E.R. 812.
[45] The claimant was left to whatever remedies at common law as might be available, but it would seem that on the facts the contract would be void: *Hartog v Colin & Shields* [1939] 3 All E.R. 566.

S discovers that they have been duped, they will wish to recover their property from P. S can only do this by showing that the contract between S and R is void on the grounds of mistaken identity. If that contract is void then no title will have passed to R who then has no title to pass to P so that S will be able to recover the goods. This outcome is, of course harsh on P.

However, if the contract between S and R is not void for mistake, it will be voidable on the grounds of a fraudulent misrepresentation. In this situation, S will be unable to recover the goods from P. R has dishonestly misrepresented his identity and a result the transaction between S and R is voidable, not void. This means that R acquires title to the goods which he can pass onto a third party. Because of the misrepresentation, S has the right to rescind, but that right will be barred where the third party P has acquired rights to the subject matter of the contract (see para.11–035). S also has a right to recover damages from R but R is a rogue who will usually have vanished. The position would be different if S could have avoided the contract with R *before* R sold to S—in such a case R would not acquire any title to pass on (see the discussion of *Car and Universal Finance Co Ltd v Caldwell* at para.11–029). However, where S is unable to rescind the result is harsh on S although it is possible to argue that as between S and P, S is less "innocent" as they have handed over possession of goods in return for a forged cheque, i.e. before clearing the cheque through the banking system.

The general attitude of the courts towards mistake as to identity has been to confine narrowly **12–028** the circumstances in which a contract will be void for this type of mistake—the effect has been to favour the innocent third party purchaser (see the discussion at para.12–035). In the great majority of contracts, identity will not be an issue—the parties' concerns will be focussed upon the subject matter of the contract and whether it is performed in accordance with contractual specification. However, when the issue of identity is raised, the general approach of the courts is to distinguish between a person's attributes and their identity. A mistake as to a person's attributes (for example, their creditworthiness) will not suffice—the claimant must show that they regarded the identity of the other party as a matter not only of importance, but of crucial importance. This is not an easy test to satisfy. The difficulty is further compounded by the fact that the courts are more ready to treat mistakes as to identity as operative where the parties are dealing at a distance (e.g. through the post) (*inter absentes*) rather than when they are dealing face to face in each other's presence (*inter praesentes*).

Identity must be of crucial importance

The obstacle for the claimant is to establish that identity is crucial. It seems that it may be more **12–029** easy to establish this where identity is crucial or fundamental to the basis on which the contract is made, as in *Boulton v Jones*. [46] This was a case where the parties were dealing *inter absentes*. The claimant had been foreman and manager in a business belonging to Brocklehurst, a manufacturer of pipe hose, with whom the defendants had had previous dealings. Brocklehurst sold the business to the claimant and later on the same day, the defendants submitted an order addressed to "Brocklehurst" for 50 feet of leather hose. The claimant supplied the goods but the defendants refused to pay for them. They intended to enforce a set-off against Brocklehurst as he owed them money from a previous transaction and they argued that they had no intention of contracting with the claimant. The court accepted that identity was in these circumstances a matter of crucial importance and the contract was held to be void.

[46] (1871) 27 L.J. Ex 117.

A similar conclusion was arrived at in *Hardman v Booth*[47] where the claimants were worsted manufacturers who intended to sell cloth to Thomas Gandell & Co. This company consisted of Thomas Gandell himself alone, although it was managed by his son Edward Gandell. The claimants' agent called at the company's offices and negotiated with Edward who fraudulently intended to buy the cloth on his own account. Edward told the claimant's agent that he was a member of "Gandell & Co" and a contract was concluded with "Edward Gandell & Co" Edward obtained possession of the cloth and sold it to the defendants. It was held that no contract was concluded between the claimants and Edward and the defendants were therefore liable in conversion. The claimants had never intended to deal with Edward but with the firm that employed him. Identity may therefore be crucial where it can be shown that the claimant approached and intended to contract with a particular firm or individual rather than someone purporting to be acting on behalf of them.[48] It may be, however, that the true nature of the mistake in this case is that it is a mistake as to capacity rather than identity.

The law on mistaken identity in contract law was reviewed by the House of Lords in *Shogun Finance Ltd v Hudson*[49] where it had been anticipated that their Lordships would take the opportunity to clarify the law and lay down more consistent principles. This did not exactly result from that decision but before considering the case (at para.12–034), it is necessary to examine some of the pre-existing case law. We will consider first cases where the parties are not dealing face to face and then discuss those where they are so dealing. The logical starting point for considering contracts *inter absentes* is the decision of the House of Lords in *Cundy v Lindsay*.[50]

Contracts made inter absentes

12–030   The facts of *Cundy v Lindsay* were that the claimants, Lindsay & Co, were linen manufacturers in Belfast and they received an order for linen handkerchiefs from a rogue called Alfred Blenkarn. The rogue gave his address as "37, Wood Street, Cheapside" (where he occupied a room in a house) and signed his name in such a way as to resemble "Blenkiron & Co". There was a respectable firm, W Blenkiron & Co, known by reputation to the claimants, carrying on business at 123, Wood Street, Cheapside, although the claimants were not aware of the street number from which they operated. The claimants sent the goods to No. 37 where the rogue Blenkarn took possession of them. He did not pay for them and later sold the goods to the defendants. It was held that the contract between the claimants and the rogue Blenkarn was void for mistake as the claimants did not intend to deal with him but with someone else. No title passed to the rogue and therefore none passed to the defendants who were liable in conversion. The decision therefore favoured the original seller over the innocent third party purchaser. Lord Cairns posed the question, "[H]ow is it possible to imagine that . . . any contract could have arisen between the [claimants] and Blenkarn, the dishonest man?" His Lordship answered thus:

> "Of him they knew nothing, and of him they never thought. With him they never intended to deal. Their minds never, even for an instant of time rested upon him, and as between

---

[47] (1863) 1 H. & C. 803.
[48] Cf *Citibank NA v Brown Shipley & Co Ltd* [1991] 2 All E.R. 690 where it was held that the identity of a person acting as a mere messenger (or "conduit pipe") between two companies was not crucial.
[49] [2004] 1 A.C. 919.
[50] (1878) 3 App. Cas. 459.

him and them there was no *consensus* of mind which could lead to any agreement or any contract whatsoever".

Identity, therefore, was regarded by the House as crucial. It may be that the decision was influenced by the *consensus as idem* theory that contract formation required an actual "meeting of the minds". The courts have latterly moved to an objective basis for determining the issue of offer and acceptance (see para.2–002). Clearly the claimants did not want to deal with a rogue but, it may be asked, was it really the actual identity of the firm that concerned them or merely the fact that as a reputable firm it could be expected to pay for goods on credit? Nevertheless, *Cundy v Lindsay* found favour with the majority of the House of Lords (but not the minority) in *Shogun Finance Ltd v Hudson*—see para.12–034 below.

Cundy v Lindsay may be contrasted with the decision in *King's Norton Metal Co Ltd v Edridge, Merrett & Co Ltd*.[51] The case shows that the mere fact that a rogue uses a false name in dealings with another party will not necessarily mean that there will be an operative mistake. In this case, the claimants, metal manufacturers in Worcestershire, received an order for a ton of brass rivet wire from a firm called "Hallam & Co, Soho Hackle Pin & Wire Works" in Sheffield. Hallam & Co appeared from the headed notepaper to be a substantial firm with a large factory and depots and agencies at places in Ireland, France and Belgium. In fact Hallam & Co was a rogue named Wallis. Relying on the description of the company in the letter, the claimants despatched the goods on credit to the fictitious firm. Wallis took possession of the goods and, having failed to pay for them, sold them on to the defendants, a metalworking company in Birmingham. In a reported judgment, Smith L.J. is quoted as saying:

> "With whom, upon this evidence, which was all one way, did the [claimants] contract to sell the goods? Clearly with the writer of the letters. If it could have been shown that there was a separate entity called Hallam & Co and another entity called Wallis then the case might have come within the decision in *Cundy v Lindsay* . . . there was a contract by the [claimants] with the person who wrote the letters, by which the property passed to him. There was only one entity, trading . . . under an alias".

Thus the Court of Appeal held that the claimants had intended to contract with the writer of the letter, whoever it was, and there was no operative mistake. The mistake was merely as to the creditworthiness of the other party. The defendants were therefore not liable in conversion as the property had passed to them.

Contracts made inter praesentes

There is a marked difference of approach where the parties are dealing face to face in each other's presence. Here there is a presumption that a person intends to deal with person physically before them so that any mistake will be as to that person's attributes rather than their identity. If, therefore, a person is induced by a fraudulent statement of identity to let a rogue have goods on credit, then unless they can prove otherwise, the mistake will be viewed as being as to that person's creditworthiness not their identity. Thus in *Phillips v Brooks Ltd*[52] a man   **12–031**

---

[51] (1897) 14 T.L.R. 98.
[52] [1919] 2 K.B. 243.

called North entered the claimant's jewellers shop and asked to see items of jewellery. He selected, inter alia, a ring worth £450 and then produced a chequebook, announcing that he was Sir George Bullough of St James's Square. The claimant, who had heard of this person, checked the address in a directory and then allowed North to take the ring in exchange for a cheque. The cheque was dishonoured and the rogue later pledged the ring with the defendant. Horridge J. held that the claimant had contracted to sell the ring to the person in the shop and therefore the defendant had a good title to it. There was no operative mistake as to identity.

Phillips v Brooks was followed by the Court of Appeal in *Lewis v Averay*[53] where the claimant advertised his car for sale for £450. The advertisement was seen by a rogue who introduced himself as Richard Greene, a well-known actor who had starred in the television series "Robin Hood". He was not Richard Greene. After testing the car, the rogue agreed to buy it for £450 and wrote a cheque for that amount, signing it "R A Green". As evidence of identity, the rogue produced an admission pass to Pinewood Studios with a photograph of the rogue on it and the name "Richard A Green". The claimant then allowed the rogue to take away the car and log book in return for a cheque which proved to be worthless, having come from a stolen cheque book. The rogue sold the car to the defendant for £200 who took it in all innocence. Lord Denning M.R. explained the principles applicable to such a case as follows:

> "When a dealing is had between a seller like the [claimant] and a person who is actually there present before him, then the presumption in law is that there is a contract, even though there is a fraudulent impersonation by the buyer representing himself as a different man than he is. There is a contract made with the very person there, who is present in person . . . In this case [the claimant] made a contract of sale with the very man, the rogue, who came to the flat. I say that he "made a contract" because in this regard we do not look into his intentions, or into his mind to know what he was thinking or into the mind of the rogue. We look to the outward appearances".

The court therefore adopted an objective approach and did not attempt to identify the claimant's intention. The action for the return of the car failed, the Court of Appeal holding that the contract between the claimant and the rogue, though voidable for fraud, was not void for mistake and the defendant obtained a good title.

12–032   Both *Phillips v Brooks* and *Lewis v Averay* are very difficult to reconcile with the decision of the Court of Appeal in the case of *Ingram v Little*.[54] Three ladies, the claimants, jointly owned a car and advertised it for sale. A rogue who called himself "Hutchinson" came to examine the car and go for a trial run. After some negotiation the rogue offered £717 for the car which the claimants were prepared to accept. The rogue then produced a chequebook but Elsie Ingram, who was conducting the negotiations on behalf of the claimants, said that in no circumstances would she take a cheque and that the proposed deal was off. It was then that the rogue informed them that he was P G M Hutchinson, a businessman living at Stanstead House, Stanstead Road, Caterham. One of the claimants, Elsie's sister Hilda, went to the post office to check in a directory that there was such a person living at such an address. Having confirmed that there was, the claimants accepted the cheque in return for the car. The rogue was not the real Hutchinson and had no connection with him. The rogue sold the car to the defendant, an innocent third party, from whom the claimants sought to recover it, or its value. Despite the minimal attempt

[53] [1972] 1 Q.B. 198.
[54] [1961] 1 Q.B. 31.

made by the claimants to verify the rogue's identity, a majority of the Court of Appeal in *Ingram v Little* held that the contract between the claimants and the rogue was void for mistake. The defendant, who was a car dealer, acquired no title.

The majority of the court (Sellers and Pearce L.JJ.) considered that the claimants had intended to contract with the real P G M Hutchinson and not the rogue. This was because no contract was concluded before the claimants refused to take a cheque; thereafter, identity became in the words of Pearce L.J., "of the utmost importance" and the rogue, as perpetrator of the fraud, was aware of this. In other words, the claimants were only prepared to contract on the basis that the man before them was the very man he said he was—the mistake was not as to attributes but as to identity. The majority seem to have taken a subjective approach similar to that taken by House of Lords in *Cundy v Lindsay*. Dissenting, Lord Devlin thought that the contract was voidable, not void, and the presumption that the claimants intended to deal with the person before them as identified by sight and hearing had not been rebutted. The decision has been explained on a "policy" ground in that, as the innocent third party was a dealer, the court sought to protect the interest of the claimants, who might been seen as vulnerable because they were elderly. But in reality, as Lord Denning M.R. said in *Lewis v Averay*, that case, *Phillips v Brooks* and *Ingram v Little* are indistinguishable. In *Shogun Finance Ltd v Hudson* (see para.12–034) both Lords Phillips and Walker supported the approach to face to face contracts established in *Phillips v Brooks* and both the majority and minority considered that *Ingram v Little* was wrongly decided.

Another questionable decision on mistake as to identity is the one arrived at by the House of Lords in an *inter praesentes* case, *Lake v Simmons*.[55] The facts of the case were that the claimant, who ran a jewellers' shop, was insured against loss or damage to jewels by theft, except where the theft was committed by any "customer" in respect of goods entrusted to them by the insured. A woman called Esme Ellison induced the claimant to let her have possession, on approval, of two valuable pearl necklets by fraudulently misrepresenting that she was the wife of a Mr Van der Borgh, a gentleman of some wealth. In fact she lived with Van der Borgh as his mistress. She claimed that she wanted one of the necklets to show her supposed husband and the other to show a certain Commander Digby, in both cases with a view to purchase. In fact, Van der Borgh knew nothing of the transaction regarding the necklets and Commander Digby did not exist. Ellison made away with the goods and disposed of them. The claimant sought to recover under the insurance policy but the defendant insurers pleaded the exception clause. It was held by the House of Lords that the loss was covered by the insurance policy. Viscount Haldane considered that the contract between the claimant and Ellison was void for mistake, and stated:

12–033

> "Ellison was a mere intermediary, little more than a porter . . . No doubt she got possession physically, but there was no mutual assent to any contract . . . The [claimant] thought he was dealing with a different person, the wife of Van der Borgh, and it was on that footing alone that he parted with the goods. He never intended to contract with the woman in question. . . . It was only on the footing and in the belief that she was Mrs Van der Borgh that he was willing to deal with her at all".

His Lordship concluded that there was no *consensus ad idem*. He distinguished *Phillips v Brooks* on the basis that the actual sale had been concluded before Sir George Bullough was mentioned

---

[55] [1927] A.C. 487.

so that the fraudulent identity influenced only the delivery of the goods—this interpretation of the facts was clearly not the basis on which Horridge J. decided that case. Moreover, it should be noted that, as acknowledged by Lord Phillips in *Shogun Finance Ltd v Hudson*, Viscount Haldane was the only member of the House to adopt this line of reasoning, reasoning which is extremely difficult to reconcile with other decided cases involving face to face transactions, such as *Phillips v Brooks* and *Lewis v Averay*.

Contracts made in writing: Shogun Finance Ltd v Hudson

12–034   In *Shogun Finance Ltd v Hudson*[56] the House of Lords reviewed the case law on mistake as to identity, including contracts made *inter absentes* and *inter praesentes*. The House of Lords decided that where a contract is made in writing, the parties to the contract are prima facie those described as such in the documentation.

The facts were that a rogue visited a car dealer and expressed interest in buying a Mitsubishi Shogun car on hire purchase terms. The rogue identified himself as, and produced the stolen driving licence of, a Mr Dulabh Patel. Having agreed a price of £22,500 with the rogue, the dealer checked the details with the claimant finance company by faxing them copies of the draft agreement and the driving licence. The agreement was signed by the rogue with the forged signature of Mr Patel. The claimants conducted a search against the name of Mr Dulabh Patel, and having satisfied themselves as to credit rating, approved the transaction. On payment of a 10 per cent deposit, the rogue was allowed to drive the vehicle away. The rogue then sold the vehicle to an innocent purchaser, the defendant Mr Hudson, for £17,000. The rogue disappeared and the claimants brought an action in conversion against the defendant. The defendant claimed that he had acquired a good title under s.27 of the Hire Purchase Act 1927. Under that provision, a private purchaser, acting in good faith without notice of the hire purchase agreement, who buys a car from a seller (a "debtor") who in turn holds the car under a hire purchase agreement, will obtain a good title. The Court of Appeal held (Sedley L.J. dissenting) that as the rogue was not the hirer named in the hire purchase agreement, he was not the "debtor" able to pass on a good title to the defendant under s.27. The person named in the agreement, Mr Patel, could not be liable on the agreement because his signature had been forged. The majority of the court also rejected the argument that the transaction was a fact to face one between the claimants and the rogue—the dealer had not acted as the finance company's agent so that the presumption applying to face to face transactions did not apply. The contract between the claimants and the rogue was therefore void for mistake.

The decision of the Court of Appeal was confirmed by the House of Lords (Lords Nicholls and Millett, dissenting, felt that the transaction in question was voidable not void). Lord Hobhouse, in the majority, considered that where parties are specifically named in a written agreement, oral evidence cannot be adduced to contradict the agreement (applying the parole evidence rule—see para.6–003). In this respect Lord Hobhouse approved of the reliance placed by the Court of Appeal on the case of *Hector v Lyons*.[57] In this case, the respondent L was negotiating with the appellant, H (Senior), for the sale of a property. L believed at all times that H (Senior) was the purchaser of the property. In fact, H was negotiating on behalf of his son H (Junior), who was below the age of majority. H (Senior) instructed solicitors who drew up a

---

[56] [2004] 1 A.C. 919.
[57] (1989) 58 P. & C.R. 156.

contract which named H (Junior) as the purchaser and H (Senior) signed in the son's name. When L defaulted on the contract, H (Senior) brought an action for specific performance. His action failed, the Court of Appeal holding that in a written contract, the identity of the parties is determined by their names as they appear in the written document. H (Senior) was not a party to the contract and could not enforce it. The principles applying to oral contracts made face to face have no application to a written contract. The court distinguished *King's Norton Metal Co Ltd v Edridge, Merrrett & Co Ltd* (a contract made in writing; see para.12–030) on the ground that in that case, there was no separate third party with whom the claimant could have intended to deal.

Lords Phillips and Walker emphasised the distinction between face to face contracts and those concluded in writing. The established approach of case law to face to face contracts (see para.12–031), i.e. the presumption that a party intends to deal with the person present as identified by sight and hearing, is to be preserved (with the exception of *Ingram v Little* which was considered to be wrongly decided). This is a welcome clarification of the position with regard to such contracts. In endorsing the approach to written contracts of *Hector v Lyons*, the majority confirmed the correctness of the decision of the House of Lords in *Cundy v Lindsay* (see para.12–030).

12–035

In the minority, Lords Nicholls and Millett thought that the distinction between face to face contracts and other transactions was unrealistic. They did not approve of the decision in *Cundy v Lindsay* and thought that it should be overruled. Their Lordships focussed on the issue of which of two innocent parties should suffer as the result of the actions of a rogue. There is no doubt that the outcome of the majority decision in *Shogun Finance v Hudson* operated very harshly on the defendant Mr Hudson. Although innocent of any wrongdoing, he was liable to the claimant finance company for the value of the car. Lord Nicholls was of the view that the loss would be more appropriately borne by the party who takes the risks inherent in parting with his goods without receiving payment.

The question of which party should bear the loss had been addressed in previous cases. In *Ingram v Little*, Devlin L.J. (dissenting) considered that the contract between the claimants and the rogue was voidable for fraud, not void for mistake. He explained:

> "The true spirit of the common law is to override theoretical distinctions when they stand in the way of doing practical justice . . . the relevant question in this sort of case is not whether the contract was void or voidable, but which of two innocent parties shall suffer for the fraud of a third. The plain answer is that the loss should be divided between them in such proportion as is just in all the circumstances. If it be pure misfortune, the loss should be borne equally; if the fault or imprudence of either party has caused or contributed to the loss, it should be borne by that party in the whole or greater part".

Devlin L.J. considered that the solution might lie in parliamentary reform of the law such as that achieved in relation to frustrated contracts in the Law Reform (Frustrated Contracts) Act 1943 (see para.10–023). This suggestion was considered by the Law Reform Committee in its 12th Report, *Transfer of Title to Chattels*, in 1966,[58] but it was rejected as likely to give rise to practical and procedural difficulties. But the Committee did recommend that where goods are sold under a unilateral mistake as to the identity of the buyer, the contract should be voidable and not void, thus protecting the interest of the innocent third party. In *Lewis v Averay*, Lord

12–036

---

[58] Cmnd. 2958, 1966.

Denning M.R. came to the same conclusion. He felt that it was wrong that the innocent purchaser should have his title depend on such fine distinctions as to whether the contract between the claimant and the rogue was affected by a mistake as to attributes or identity. Lord Denning M.R. did not accept that a mistake as to identity rendered a contract void. He thought that the true rule was as follows:

> "When two parties have come to a contract—or rather what appears, on the face of it, to be a contract – the fact that one party is mistaken as to the identity of the other does not mean that there is no contract, or that the contract is a nullity and void from the beginning. It only means that the contract is voidable".

This was Lord Denning's solution to the problem of which party should bear the loss. The minority in *Shogun Finance v Hudson* did not go as far as Lord Denning in *Lewis v Averay* but they did think that the presumption that a person intends to contract with the person with whom they are dealing should apply to all contracts, whether they be made face to face or in writing. In practical terms this would mean that most such transactions would be voidable for fraud but not void for mistake. In other words, the policy of the law should be to protect the innocent third party purchaser. This is, in some respects, a better solution than that favoured by the majority of the House with its rather arbitrary distinction between face to face contracts and contracts made in writing. It is difficult to escape the conclusion that in *Shogun Finance Ltd v Hudson* an opportunity to clarify and rationalise the law on mistake as to identity has been postponed.

MISTAKE RELATING TO DOCUMENTS

12–037   Two specific remedies are available where a written contract has been executed under a mistake: the plea of non est factum and the equitable remedy of rectification.

Non est factum

12–038   We have seen that, as a general rule, a person is bound by their signature on a document and this is so whether or not they have read the document, or, having read it, whether or not they have understood it (see *L'Estrange v Graucob* at para.7–004).[59] At the end of the sixteenth century, a limited exception to this rule was introduced to protect illiterate or blind persons who executed a deed after the contents had been falsely read over to them—they could plead non est factum ("it is not my deed") and avoid liability.[60] The basis of the plea is that "the mind of the signer did not accompany the signature"[61] so that they have signed something they never intended to sign.

In the nineteenth century, the doctrine developed so as to include not just deeds but any written contract. The scope of the plea was also widened to embrace not only persons who

---

[59] See also *Galbraith v Mitchenall Estates Ltd* [1965] 2 Q.B. 473 (discussed at para.2–003) for an example of the signature rule operating harshly in the absence of fraud or other unconscionable conduct.

[60] *Thoroughgood's Case* (1584) 2 Co. Rep. 9a.

[61] *Foster v Mackinnon* (1869) L.R. 4 C.P. 704, per Byles J. at p.711.

could not read but any person who, without negligence and usually as a result of fraud, signed a contract believing it to be something fundamentally different from what it actually was; the basis for this expansion was said to be the lack of *consensus ad idem*. Thus in *Lewis v Clay*[62] Lord Nevill covered a document with a piece of blotting paper that had four holes cut in it. The defendant Clay was asked to sign his name in these apertures for the purpose, he was told, of witnessing Lord Nevill's own signature on a document relating to a private matter. In fact, the defendant had signed promissory notes in the claimant's favour to the value of £11,113. It was held that the defendant could raise the plea of non est factum as a defence when sued by the claimant Lewis on the notes. The defendant had no knowledge of the promissory notes and had been deceived into signing them in the belief that he was signing a document of an entirely different nature.

The courts, however, sought to place restrictions on the availability of the plea. If it were too widely available, it would have brought about commercial uncertainty—third parties should be able to assume that a signed document will normally be valid. Two limitations emerged.

First, only a certain type of mistake about the document would suffice; and secondly, the plea was not available if the signer had been negligent. With regard to the first of these limitations, before the decision of the House of Lords in *Saunders v Anglia Building Society*[63] in 1969, the type of mistake required to raise successfully non est factum was a mistake as to the nature, class or character of the document rather than merely as to its contents. This distinction may be illustrated by comparing two cases, *Foster v Mackinnon*[64] and *Howatson v Webb*.[65] In *Foster v Mackinnon* the defendant was a gentleman of advanced years who had feeble eyesight. He was fraudulently induced to sign his name on the reverse of a document that he was told was a guarantee. In fact it was a bill of exchange upon which the defendant ultimately became prima facie liable to the claimant in the sum of £3,000. It was held that the defence of non est factum was available to the defendant. The defendant in this case had without any negligence signed a document of an entirely different nature from the one he had intended to sign. In *Howatson v Webb* the defendant was a solicitor who was asked to execute a deed which he was told was a conveyance. He did so but in fact it was a mortgage. The Court of Appeal held that the defendant was bound as the misrepresentation related to the contents rather than the character of the deed. Farwell L.J. (with whom the other members of the court agreed) observed that the deed that the defendant had signed was not of a character so wholly different from that which it was represented to be as to support a plea of non est factum.

The second limitation, the need for no negligence on the part of the signer, was recognised long before *Saunders v Anglia Building Society*. At one stage, there was doubt as to whether a person could be barred from pleading non est factum by their negligence. The uncertainty arose from a decision of the Court of Appeal, *Carlisle and Cumberland Banking Co v Bragg*,[66] where although the signer had been found to be negligent, he was able to raise the plea of non est factum. The court confined the principle that negligence defeats non est factum to where the document signed was a negotiable instrument. This was based upon a very restrictive interpretation of the case of *Foster v Mackinnon*, where, as we have seen, the document signed was a negotiable instrument.

12–039

[62] (1897) 67 L.J. Q.B. 224.
[63] [1971] A.C. 1004. In the lower courts, the case was referred to as *Gallie v Lee*.
[64] (1869) L.R. 4 C.P. 704. This decision was approved by the House of Lords in *Saunders v Anglia Building Society*.
[65] [1908] 1 Ch. 1.
[66] [1911] 1 K.B. 489.

The scope of non est factum: Saunders v Anglia Building Society

12–040   The scope of the plea of non est factum was reappraised by House of Lords in *Saunders v Anglia Building Society*.[67]

The facts of the case were that Mrs Gallie, an elderly widow, wished to transfer the title of her house by way of gift to her trusted nephew, Parkin, of whom she was very fond. The object of this proposed transaction was to ease Parkin's financial position and to enable him to raise moneys on the property. However, Parkin and a business associate, Lee, drew up a document replacing the nephew's name with that of Lee; the document was a transfer of title by way of sale for a price not intended to be paid, rather than a gift. This was done without Mrs Gallie's knowledge. On the day of the signing, Mrs Gallie had broken her glasses and was unable to read. Lee dishonestly informed her that the document was a deed of gift in favour of her nephew and, in view of Parkin's presence, she was content to sign the document placed before her without further explanation. Her assumption was that she would be able to continue to live in the house during her lifetime, whilst her nephew would be able to raise money on the security of the property. However, in fraud of the nephew Parkin, Lee mortgaged the property to the Anglia Building Society and defaulted on the repayments. He disposed of the money for his own use and paid nothing to either Mrs Gallie or Parkin. In order to prevent the building society from taking possession of the house, Mrs Gallie sought a declaration that the transfer of the property to Lee was void by reason of non est factum. Stamp J. found for the claimant and upheld the plea, but a unanimous Court of Appeal reversed this decision. The decision of that court was upheld by the House of Lords. By the time that the case came before the Lords, Mrs Gallie had died and the action was brought by her executrix.

The House held that the transaction that Mrs Gallie had entered was not fundamentally or radically different from that which she had intended to enable her nephew to raise money by using the house as security. Although at first sight the two documents appeared very different, regard should be had to the "object of the exercise". In this case the object of the exercise was to enable the nephew to raise money and the document that Mrs Gallie signed would have achieved this—her misunderstanding of the details of it was not sufficiently fundamental. Their Lordships further found that she had been careless in signing the document. If the decision seems harsh it should not be forgotten that Mrs Gallie had a remedy against the Lee for fraud but once the house had been mortgaged to the building society third party rights intervened so as to prevent rescission. The building society, who saw only the documents, had no reason to suspect that there was anything amiss in the way that Lee had acquired the property. In other words, it is the same problem as discussed above in relation to unilateral mistake as to identity—which of two innocent parties should suffer for the fraud of a third.

12–041   Their Lordships considered that a party seeking to invoke the plea has a heavy burden of proof to discharge. As to the type of mistake required to support the plea, their Lordships considered that the previous distinction between class or character on the one hand and contents on the other was neither sensible nor logical. It prevented the plea from being raised where the signer had signed a document making them liable to pay a much greater sum than they believed, but where the class of document was no different. On the other hand, the plea could be successfully raised where the amount of money involved was no different but it happened to be payable on a document of a different character. On the issue of the type of mistake, Lord Reid said:

[67] [1971] A.C. 1004.

"There must I think be a radical difference between what he signed and what he thought he was signing - or one could use the words "fundamental" or "serious" or "very substantial". But what amounts to a radical difference will depend on all the circumstances. If he thinks he is giving property to A whereas the document gives it to B the difference may often be of vital importance, but in the circumstances of the present case I do not think that it is. I think that it must be left to the courts to determine in each case in light of all the facts whether there was or was not a sufficiently great difference".

Lord Hodson thought that the difference to support the plea "must be in a particular which goes to the substance of the whole consideration or to the root of the matter." Thus where a mistake as to contents is as fundamental as one as to class or character the plea may be raised.

On the question of whether carelessness on the part of the signer operated to defeat the plea, the House of Lords held that it did and overruled the case of *Carlisle and Cumberland Banking v Bragg*. In *Saunders v Anglia Building Society* it was said by the House of Lords that Mrs Gallie had been careless in signing the document—she could not be expected to follow the intricacies of conveyancing but she could at least have made sure that the transfer of the property was to the person intended by her. Lord Wilberforce made it clear that the burden of proof lies upon the signer to prove that they acted carefully and Viscount Dilhorne considered that in every case the person who signs the document must exercise reasonable care, and what amounts to reasonable care "will depend on the circumstances of the case and the nature of the document which it is thought is being signed."

In *United Dominions Trust Ltd v Western*[68] the defendant agreed to buy, on hire- purchase, a **12–042** secondhand Ford Corsair for £550 from a firm of car dealers. He paid a deposit of £34 and signed the claimant finance company's form in blank, leaving the dealers to fill in the figures. The dealers sent a form to the claimants which was in fact a loan agreement and the figures inserted were £730 for the purchase price and £185 for the deposit. The claimants accepted this as constituting the contract between the defendant and the dealers. When the defendant received a copy of the document he did nothing to rectify the mistake and paid no instalments under it. The claimants sought to recover the sum of £750 and the defendant raised the plea of non est factum by way of defence. The Court of Appeal upheld the decision of the trial judge that a person who signs a contractual document in blank knowing that someone else would complete it could not successfully argue that they did not consent to whatever had been inserted. The court rejected a contention that there was any distinction between the careless signing of a completed document and a document in blank. Applying *Saunders v Anglia Building Society* it was held that in permitting the dealer to complete the document, the defendant had the burden of showing that he had acted carefully and he had failed to discharge that burden. It was further held that the document which the defendant had signed related to a transaction that was not fundamentally different in substance or in kind from that intended. The contract was therefore not void by reason of non est factum.

Non est factum after Saunders v Anglia Building Society

The effect of the *Saunders* case was to restrict considerably the circumstances in which the non **12–043** est factum plea can be raised. Leaving aside the possibility of the signer being the victim of

[68] [1976] Q.B. 513. See also *Mercantile Credit Co v Hamblin* [1965] 2 Q.B. 242.

some elaborate trickery, literate persons of full capacity will find it difficult to discharge the burden imposed on them to prove that they were not careless in signing.

In *Saunders* Lord Reid examined the origins of the plea and noted that originally the plea was available to those who were unable to read owing to blindness or illiteracy and had to trust someone to read the document over to them. His Lordship added:

> "I think it must also apply in favour of those who are permanently or temporarily unable through no fault of their own to have without explanation any real understanding of the purport of a particular document, whether that be from defective education, illness or innate incapacity. But that does not excuse them from taking such precautions as they reasonably can".

It would seem, therefore, that in addition to blindness or illiteracy, other forms of disability may (where consent is lacking) fall within the protection of the plea, such as senility or abnormally low intelligence. However, as both Lords Reid and Wilberforce emphasised, signers falling into this category must act carefully and responsibly according to their circumstances when appending a signature to a document.

Cases decided subsequent to *Saunders v Anglia Building Society* show that the availability of the plea has been curtailed. In *Avon Finance Co v Bridger*[69] a son arranged the purchase of a house for his elderly parents' retirement. The parents—the defendants in the case—borrowed £5,000 from a building society to assist in financing the purchase. The son promised to invest £2,500 in the property but, without telling the parents, obtained a loan of £3,500 from the claimant finance company at a high interest rate, secured by a charge on the home. The son deceived the parents into signing the charge by saying the document related to an earlier matter in connection with their building society mortgage. The son later defaulted on payments to the claimants and they commenced proceedings against the defendants to enforce their security. In the Court of Appeal, the argument that the transaction was void by reason of non est factum received short shrift. The defendants had not acted with reasonable care in signing the document and the defence of non est factum could not be relied on. The transaction was nevertheless held to be voidable in equity on the grounds of undue influence (see para.13–037). A similar reluctance to invoke the plea of non est factum is to be seen in the case of *Norwich & Peterborough Building Society v Steed (No 2)*.[70]

12–044   The case of *Lloyds Bank Plc v Waterhouse*[71] provides a rare example of the plea being successfully raised in a modern case. Here the defendant, a farmer, was illiterate. His son wanted to buy a farm so the defendant signed a guarantee of a loan from the claimant bank. Before the signing, the bank's official had informed the defendant that the guarantee covered only the loan but in fact it was an "all monies guarantee" covering all the son's liabilities. Eventually, the bank sought to recover £193,000 from the defendant, the amount of the son's indebtedness. The Court of Appeal held, on several grounds, that the defendant was not liable on the guarantee. Purchas L.J. was in no doubt that the plea of non est factum applied; the father was under a disability, illiteracy, and the document he had signed was fundamentally different from that which he had thought he had signed. It exposed the guarantor to considerably broader liability. Moreover, the defendant had not been careless in signing. Purchas L.J. further held that the defendant could raise the defence of a negligent misrepresentation by the claimant bank. They

[69] [1985] 2 All E.R. 281.
[70] [1993] Ch. 116.
[71] [1990] Fam. Law. 23.

had misled the defendant when they failed to give him an accurate answer to a question concerning the nature of the guarantee. Woolf L.J. expressed doubts concerning the applicability of non est factum and preferred to base his decision on negligent misrepresentation. The third member of the court, Sir Edward Eveleigh, held that the guarantee should be set aside on the basis of an operative unilateral mistake—the bank must have known that the father was acting under a mistake and that he would never have agreed to guarantee such extensive liabilities.

Rectification

Where the parties are orally agreed on the terms of the contract but by mistake record them incorrectly in a subsequent written document, the equitable remedy of rectification may be available. The court may rectify the error in the document and order specific performance of the contract as rectified. Thus in *Craddock Brothers v Hunt*[72] there was an oral agreement for the sale of a dwellinghouse exclusive of an adjoining piece of land. The written agreement and later conveyance included the land in question. Specific performance was ordered of both documents as rectified by the court. The type of mistake in this case is a common mistake (see para.12–005), i.e. both parties mistakenly believe that the document accurately records their transaction. **12–045**

The remedy of rectification forms an exception to the parole evidence rule (see para.6–003) in that oral evidence is admissible to show that the written document is in error. Decisions of the courts have established that certain criteria must be established before the remedy of rectification may be granted. These are:

(i)   the parties must have reached agreement;
(ii) the written document must fail to express what the parties had agreed;
(iii) the written document must, as a general rule, fail to record the common intentions of the parties; and
(iv) it must be equitable to grant the remedy.

The parties must have reached agreement

It was traditionally thought that there had to be a "concluded antecedent agreement" on all the terms of the contract before rectification could be ordered. But in *Joscelyne v Nissen*[73] the Court of Appeal held that it was sufficient if there was common continuing intention with regard to a particular provision or aspect of the agreement. **12–046**

The facts of the case were that the claimant, J, sought rectification of a written document under which he had agreed to hand over his car-hire business to his daughter, the defendant, N. It had been agreed between the parties that, in consideration for the transfer of the business, N would pay certain household expenses of J, but this understanding was not expressly included in the written contract. N failed to pay these expenses and J claimed that the written document should be rectified to include payment of the expenses. The trial judge found that there had been no complete antecedent agreement between the parties but nevertheless ordered rectification. N appealed on the basis that the judge had misdirected himself. The Court of Appeal held that it

---

[72] [1923] 2 Ch. 136.
[73] [1970] 2 Q.B. 86.

was not necessary that a concluded binding contract existed before rectification could be ordered of a written document. It was sufficient to find some outward expression of accord with regard to the term in question, however, convincing proof of such agreement would be required.[74]

The document must fail to express what the parties have agreed

12–047   In *Frederick E Rose (London) Ltd v William Pim Jnr & Co Ltd* (the case is discussed in relation to common mistake at para.12–005), the claimants were asked by a third party to supply them with "Moroccan horsebeans described as 'feveroles'." The claimants entered into a contract with the defendants whereby the defendants agreed to supply them with "horsebeans". Both parties mistakenly believed that "feveroles" was just another word for horsebeans but the goods supplied, though horsebeans, were not feveroles. The claimants wanted to have the contract rectified to refer to "feveroles", so that they could claim damages from the defendants for the delivery of the wrong type of goods. Denning L.J. said:

> "[The] agreement, as outwardly expressed, both orally and in writing was for "horse-beans". That is all the defendants ever committed themselves to supply; and that is all they should be bound to. There was, no doubt, an erroneous assumption underlying the contract—an assumption for which it might have been set aside on the grounds of misrepresentation or mistake—but that is very different from an erroneous expression of the contract, such as to give rise to rectification".

Thus the remedy was refused because the written agreement correctly recorded what the parties had agreed. It is not sufficient that the parties intended something different. The case should be compared with *Craddock Brothers v Hunt* (discussed above) where the written document failed to record what the parties had agreed.

The common intention of the parties

12–048   Rectification will usually only be ordered where the document fails to express the *common* intention of the parties; in other words, it is a remedy for a common mistake. It seems that rectification is not a remedy where the parties are at cross-purposes, i.e. where the mistake is mutual.

In *Riverlate Properties Ltd v Paul*[75] the claimants granted a lease of a self- contained maisonette to the defendant for a term 99 years. The defendant and her solicitors believed that the claimants were to be responsible for exterior and structural repairs and that she would not be liable for these expenses. It was the claimants' intention that the defendant should pay half of these costs but, owing to a drafting error, the lease that was forwarded to the claimants' solicitors omitted this obligation. The lease, which placed the full exterior repairing obligation on the claimants, was duly executed but neither the defendant nor her solicitors were aware of the mistake. It had always been the defendant's understanding that she would not be responsible for these repairs. Upholding the objective principle, the Court of Appeal refused to rectify the

---

[74] In *Munt v Beasley* [2006] EWCA Civ 370 the Court of Appeal considered that "out ward expression of accord" was not a strict legal requirement for rectification and was more in the nature of an evidential factor in establishing a continuing common intention.

[75] (1974) 28 P. & C. R. 220.

lease so as to make the defendant responsible for half the repairs. The defendant was not only not guilty of any sharp practice, but, in allowing the transaction to proceed in the form that it did, was unaware of the mistake. Of course, if a mutual mistake is sufficiently fundamental according to the test discussed earlier in this chapter (see para.12–021) the contract may be void at common law; but in cases where the mistake is not operative, rectification will not be ordered.

Where one party does know of the mistake (that is to say where the mistake is unilateral) rectification may be ordered where the party aware of the mistake remains silent and derives some unfair advantage or benefit. By the expression "aware of the mistake" we mean that the party conscious of the error knows that the written document does not reflect what the parties have agreed. Authority for this principle is to be found in the well-known case of *A Roberts & Co Ltd v Leicestershire County Council.*[76] This decision was applied in *Thomas Bates & Son Ltd v Wyndham's (Lingerie) Ltd.*[77] Here the claimant landlords and defendant tenants executed a new lease which did not contain a clause providing for arbitration in the event of failure to agree a rent upon renewal. The lease was drawn up by the landlords. On the two previous occasions when the tenants had taken a lease from the claimants, the lease had contained such a clause. When the lease was executed, the defendants' representative noticed that the rent review clause was defective but did not draw it to the attention of the claimants. An order of rectification was granted by Judge Michael Wheeler Q.C. The defendants appealed to the Court of Appeal. In considering the knowledge that the defendant must have in such cases before rectification will be ordered Buckley L.J. did not think that sharp practice as such was necessary. His Lordship said:

> "In any such case the conduct of the defendant must be such as to make it inequitable that he should be allowed to object to the rectification of the document. If this necessarily implies some measure of "sharp practice", so be it; but for my part I think I think that the doctrine is one which depends more upon the equity of the position. The graver the character of the conduct involved, no doubt the heavier the burden of proof may be . . . the conduct must be such as to affect the conscience of the party who has suppressed the fact that that he has recognised the presence of a mistake".

His Lordship considered that there must be a further element, that is, that the mistake must be one calculated to benefit the party conscious of the mistake. Eveleigh L.J. thought that the mistake must be one which is "detrimental" to the mistaken party. The order of the trial judge was accordingly upheld by the Court of Appeal.   **12–049**

In *Commission for the New Towns v Cooper (Great Britain) Ltd*[78] Stuart-Smith L.J. in the Court of Appeal suggested that the equity in such cases rested upon evidence of unconscionable behaviour. His Lordship considered that "shutting one's eyes to the obvious" was dishonest conduct which fell into this category[79] and that the suspicion that the other party may be mistaken would amount in law to actual knowledge of the mistake. He was also of the view that where one party intends the other to be mistaken as to the construction of the contract and makes misleading statements to divert the other's attention away from discovering the mistake, and the other makes the intended mistake, the written agreement may be rectified. This will be

---

[76] [1961] Ch. 555.
[77] [1981] 1 W.L.R. 505.
[78] [1995] Ch. 259.
[79] Relying on the categorisation of the various forms of knowledge made by Peter Gibson J. in *Baden v Societe Generale pour Favoriser le Developpement du Commerce et de l'Industrie en France SA* [1993] 1 W.L.R. 509, at pp.575–6.

so even where it cannot be shown that the agreement has been induced by misrepresentation and the non-mistaken party does not actually know but merely suspects that the other is mistaken. Rectification for unilateral mistake does, however, rest upon clear evidence that the non-mistaken party has been guilty of unconscionable behaviour.[80]

It must be equitable to grant the remedy

12–050   As the remedy is equitable, it may be lost where third parties have acquired rights on the faith of the written contract or where there has been a lapse of time. In such cases the parties will be left to any possible remedy for mistake at common law. It seems that the impossibility of restitution will not in general operate as a bar to rectification.

Mistake: conclusion

12–051   In our examination of the circumstances in which a contract will be void for mistake, we have seen a close interrelationship with the law of misrepresentation, particularly where mistake as to identity is concerned. Where the contract in such cases is not void for mistake, it is likely to be voidable on the grounds of fraudulent misrepresentation.

There are also close links between common mistake and the law of frustration (see Chapter 10). In both cases the contract is rendered incapable of performance; in the case of common mistake the contract is impossible of performance owing to factors unknown to the parties at the time of the contract, whereas frustration occurs *after* the parties have entered into the contract—some supervening event occurs which renders further performance impossible, illegal or something radically different from that which the parties originally undertook. The close parallel between the two areas of law was recognised by Lord Phillips M.R. in the Court of Appeal the *Great Peace Shipping* case (the case is discussed at para.12–014). His Lordship considered that the two doctrines had developed in tandem so that consideration of the development of frustration assisted with the analysis of common mistake. This comment was made in the context of the "implied term" theory which he considered to be as unrealistic when dealing with common mistake as with frustration (see para 10–003).

An interesting case which lies at the interface of common mistake and frustration is the decision of the Court of Appeal in *Amalgamated Investment & Property Co Ltd v John Walker & Sons Ltd.*[81] In this case the claimants agreed to purchase a warehouse in East London from the defendants for £1,710,000. The property had been advertised as being suitable for redevelopment. During negotiations, the claimants enquired whether the property had been listed as a building of special archictectural or historic interest (under s.54 of the Town and Country Planning Act 1971). Contracts were exchanged on September 25, 1973. The following day, the defendants were informed by the Department of the Environment that the building had been selected for listing as a building of special interest and on September 27 the listing became official. As a listed building, planning permission for redevelopment would be much harder to obtain and the value of the building fell to approximately £200,000. The claimants sought to

---

[80] See further *Templiss Properties Ltd v Dean Hyams* [1999] E.G.C.S. 60; *Hurst Stores and Interiors Ltd v ML Europe Property Ltd* [2004] EWCA Civ 490; and *George Wimpey UK Ltd v VI Components Ltd* [2005] EWCA Civ 77.
[81] [1976] 3 All E.R. 509.

avoid completion of the contract and the defendants counter-claimed for a decree of specific performance. It was contended by the claimants that the contract was either entered into under a mistake or discharged by frustration.

The Court of Appeal held that the contract was not void for common mistake since the build-   **12–052**
ing was not listed until two days after the contract had been entered into. It was further held that the contract was not frustrated and the risk of listing fell on the claimants as purchasers. The claimants had been well aware of the risk of listing and could have stipulated in the contract that it was conditional on obtaining planning permission for redevelopment but had not done so. The claimants were therefore saddled with a property worth in the region of £1.5 million less than they had paid for it. Whether the contract was governed by the law of mistake or of frustration was simply a matter of timing. In fact the decision to list the building had been taken on August 22, well before the date of the contract, but the court held that this was merely an administrative act and the property did not acquire listed status until the list was signed on behalf of the Secretary of State on September 27. Had mistake applied, the contract would have been voidable in equity under the rule in *Solle v Butcher* (see para.12–016) and the contract could, at the court's discretion, have been rescinded on terms. This would have been a better outcome for the claimants than the finding that there was no frustration. Since the time of the case, of course, the Court of Appeal has ruled in the *Great Peace Shipping* case that *Solle v Butcher* cannot stand with the decision of the House of Lords in *Bell v Lever Bros* (para.12–018).

Further reading

Atiyah, *Couturier v Hastie* and the Sale of Non-existent Goods (1957) 73 L.Q.R. 340.
Macmillan, How Temptation Led to Mistake: an Explanation of *Bell v Lever Bros* (2003) 119 L.Q.R. 625.
Yeo, *Great Peace: A Distant Disturbance* (2005) 121 L.Q.R. 393.
Brownsword, *New Note on the Old Oats* (1987) 131 S.J. 284.
Macmillan, *Mistake as to Identity Clarified?* (2004) 120 L.Q.R. 369.
Macmillan, *Rogues, Swindlers and Cheats: the Development of Mistake as to Identity in English Contract Law* (2005) C.L.J. 711.
Stone, *Non Est Factum after Gallie v Lee* (1972) 88 L.Q.R. 190.

Chapter 13

DURESS AND UNDUE INFLUENCE

The agreement which the parties have reached may be the result of some improper pressure exerted by one party over the other. The problem is dealt with by the common law doctrine of duress and the equitable doctrine of undue influence.

13–001

DURESS

Duress is a common law concept under which contracts (and gifts) may be avoided. It is gener-ally said to render a contract voidable.[1] Traditionally, duress was confined to duress to the person, but more recently the courts confirmed that it extends to duress of goods. In the past 30 years or so, it has also become recognised by the courts that certain types of economic pres-sure can amount to duress. We will consider first the scope of duress as traditionally defined and then examine "economic duress".

13–002

Duress: to the person and of goods

Duress was originally confined to actual or threatened physical violence to, or unlawful con-straint of, the person of the other contracting party—"duress to the person". In *Cumming v Ince*[2] an elderly lady was induced to enter into a settlement of her property by the threat of unlawful confinement in an asylum. The settlement was set aside on the grounds of duress; it amounted to a threat of false imprisonment. In another, more recent case, the defendants entered the claimant's flat when she was alone and forced her to sign a receipt for some of her valuables, which they then took away. After they had gone, the claimant found that the defend-ants had left a cheque for £90. The transaction was set aside on the grounds of duress.[3]

Traditional doctrine ruled that the threat had to be unlawful to constitute duress (in the sense of a threat to commit a crime or a tort), although latterly the courts have recognised that certain types of lawful threat may suffice (see para.13–011). For many years, it was uncertain whether a contract could be invalidated by "duress of goods" so that, for example, a promise to pay money

13–003

---

[1] *Pao On v Lau Yiu Long* [1980] A.C. 614.
[2] (1847) 11 Q.B. 112.
[3] *Friedeberg-Seeley v Klass* [1957] C.L.Y. 1482.

for the release of goods unlawfully detained or seized, was in one case held to be valid.[4] At the same time, it was also decided that money which had actually been paid for such a purpose could be recovered.[5] It is now acknowledged that the doctrine applies to the actual or threatened violence to, or unlawful seizure of, goods; in *Occidental Worldwide Investment Corporation v Skibs A/S Avanti, The Siboen and the Sibotre,*[6] Kerr J. said, obiter, that a person coerced into a contract by the threat of having his house burnt down or a picture slashed could plead duress.

In the case of duress to the person, it seems that the threats need not be the only or even the main reason why the innocent party entered the contract, as illustrated by the decision of the Privy Council in *Barton v Armstrong.*[7] A was the chairman and B the managing director of a company and B executed a deed selling his interest in the company to A. Later B sought to avoid the deed on the grounds of duress, on the basis that death threats and other improper pressure had been brought to bear. Statements made by A included the following: "The city is not as safe as you think between office and home. You will see what I can do against you and you will regret the day when you decided not to work with me", and "I will show you what I can do against you and you had better watch out." The deed was in B's commercial interests and A argued that B would have entered the contract had there been no threats. Rejecting that argument, the Privy Council held that the deed was void (sic). A similar rule operated as in the case of fraudulent misrepresentation (see para.11–019), i.e. that if A's threats were a reason for B entering the contract, he was entitled to relief even though he might well have entered the contract if there had been no threats. Moreover, it was for A to prove that the threats and unlawful pressure did not contribute to B's decision to enter the contract; although B might have executed the deed in the absence of threats, the threats and unlawful pressure did contribute to B's decision to sign the agreement.

Duress: economic duress

13–004   In the past 30 years or so, the courts have extended the concept of duress to economic duress— this may be said to occur where a party is subject to improper economic pressure such that, in entering a contract, they cannot be said to have done so under their own free will. Typically, this may occur where one party threatens to breach an existing contract (an unlawful act) unless the other party agrees to renegotiate it on terms that are favourable to the party issuing the threat. Two well-known cases illustrate this situation: *North Ocean Shipping Co Ltd v Hyundai Construction Ltd, The Atlantic Baron;*[8] and *Atlas Express Ltd v Kafco (Importers and Distributors) Ltd.*[9]

The *Atlantic Baron* was one of the first decisions to propound the doctrine of economic duress. In this case, the defendants entered into a contract to build an oil tanker for the claimants for an agreed price, payable in five instalments. A letter of credit was opened by the defendants to provide security in case of a default in performance. The claimants paid the first instalment but then the US dollar was devalued by 10 per cent, so the defendants refused to complete the

---

[4] *Skeate v Beale* (1841) 11 A. & D. 983. Cf *Astley v Reynolds* (1731) 2 Str 915.
[5] *Maskell v Horner* [1915] 3 K.B. 106.
[6] [1976] 1 Lloyd's Rep. 293. See also *Vantage Navigation Corporation v Suhail & Saud Bahwan Building Materials Llc, The Alev* [1989] 1 Lloyd's Rep. 138.
[7] [1976] A.C. 104.
[8] [1978] Q.B. 705.
[9] [1989] Q.B. 833.

contract unless a further 10 per cent on the remaining instalments was paid. As the claimants required the ship urgently to fulfil a lucrative charter, they agreed to pay a further 10 per cent and asked the defendants to make a similar increase in the letter of credit, which they did. The defendants delivered the tanker and the claimants accepted it without protest but eight months later the claimants sought the return of the additional 10 per cent they had paid.

Mocatta J. considered whether any consideration had been given for the claimants' promise to pay the additional money. It was argued for the owners that the agreement to pay the extra 10 per cent was void for lack of consideration under the principle in *Stilk v Myrick* (the facts are given at para.4–022) in that the shipyard were under an existing contractual duty to build the ship. The judge reluctantly found a technical consideration in that the shipyard had increased the letter of credit. Of course, since this case was decided, the Court of Appeal has held in *Williams v Roffey Bros* (see para.00–024) that the performance of an existing contractual duty can constitute fresh consideration where there are practical or factual benefits to the promisor (or the avoidance of disbenefits) in the performance of the duty.

However, Mocatta J. considered that the payment could, in principle, have been recovered on the ground of economic duress. He said: **13–005**

> "First, I do not take the view that the recovery of money paid under duress other than to the person is necessarily limited to duress to goods falling within one of the categories established by the English cases . . . Secondly, from this it follows that the compulsion may take the form of "economic duress" if the necessary facts are proved. A threat to break a contract may amount to such economic duress. Thirdly, if there has been such a form of duress leading to a contract for consideration, I think that contract is a voidable one which can be avoided and the excess money paid under it recovered."

The judge considered that the agreement to increase the price was caused by economic duress; the shipyard had insisted on an increase in price without any legal justification for doing so and therefore the agreement could truly be said to have been reached under compulsion. Nevertheless, the court considered that the claimants had lost their right to rescind as they had affirmed the contract (the principles are the same as misrepresentation; see para.11–032). They had paid the money without protest and made no further complaint until some eight months after taking delivery of the ship—thus the voidable contract had been affirmed.

In *Atlas Express v Kafco* the defendants secured a contract to supply basketware to a major retail chain store, Woolworths. The defendants then agreed with the claimants, a firm of carriers, that the claimants would deliver the basketware to branches of Woolworths on the basis of a certain carriage rate per carton. This figure resulted from an erroneous calculation by the claimants. The claimants then refused to deliver the goods to the retailers unless the defendants paid a higher price. The defendants agreed to this, though expressing the sentiment that they were "over a barrel". In the circumstances, they reasonably believed that it would be impossible to find another carrier and that a breach of the contract with Woolworths would be commercially ruinous for them. The claimants sued for the additional carriage cost but Tucker J. held that the agreement was vitiated by economic duress. The court accepted that the defendants had no real alternative but to submit to the revised terms—an action against the claimants for compensation for breach of the original contract would not have been an adequate remedy given the likely consequences of breaching the Woolworths contract.

In *Atlas Express v Kafco*, the threat to break the contract was explicit and direct. In other cases, the threat may be indirect—a veiled threat—but it may nevertheless amount to economic   **13–006** duress. This is illustrated by the earlier case of *B & S Contracts and Design Ltd v Victor Green Publications Ltd*[10] where the claimants agreed to erect exhibition stands for the defendants at the venue Olympia. The stands were to be used for a trade exhibition and the claimants intended to use workers employed by an insolvent subsidiary company. On arriving at Olympia, these workers, who had been given redundancy notices, refused to work. They claimed to be entitled to £9,000 severance pay and rejected the claimants' offer of £4,500. The claimants then informed the defendants that the contract would be cancelled unless the defendants paid an additional £4,500 over the contract price to meet the workers' demands. The defendants paid the money and the contract was performed. Later, the defendants deducted £4,500 from the price they paid for the contract. The claimants sued to recover this sum but the Court of Appeal held that the money had been paid under duress. It was argued on behalf of the claimants that there had been no overt demand; as to this Griffiths L.J. said:

> "[I]t was implicit in negotiations between the parties that the [claimants] were putting the defendants into a corner and it was quite apparent to the defendants, by reason of the [claimants'] conduct, that unless they handed over the £4,500 the [claimants] would walk off the job. This is, in my view, a situation in which the judge was fully entitled to find in the circumstances of this case that there was duress."

The court therefore concluded that the defendants had no choice but to pay the sum of money in question—cancellation of the contract would have seriously damaged their interests.

There is another group of cases involving economic duress and these involve a threat by the defendant to induce a third party to breach a contract with the claimant. This situation often arises in the context of industrial disputes. For example, in *Universe Tankships Inc of Monrovia v International Transport Workers' Federation, The Universe Sentinel*[11] the claimant's ship was "blacked" by a trade union, i.e. the harbour operatives who were members of the union were told to have nothing to do with it, and it could not therefore set sail from Milford Haven. The Union was attempting to secure better conditions for the crew of the ship. This industrial action was a breach of the harbour operatives' contract with their employers, the Harbour Authority. In order to secure its release from blacking, the claimants, inter alia, paid a "contribution" of $6,480 into the union's welfare fund. There would have been serious financial consequences for the claimants had they not done so as the ship was under charter. The claimants sought to recover the money they had paid. It was conceded by the defendants that there had been economic duress but they argued that their actions were taken in furtherance of a trade dispute under the Trade Union and Labour Relations Act 1974—this would have provided them with immunity in tort so as to legitimise their actions. The House of Lords held, by a majority, that the payment to the Union welfare fund was recoverable on the ground of duress as the immunity granted by the Act did not apply on the facts.

The test for duress

13–007   Earlier cases decided under the doctrine of economic duress appeared to lay down a test that duress, "whatever form it takes, involves coercion of the will so as to vitiate consent". So said

---

[10] [1984] I.C.R. 419.
[11] [1983] 1 A.C. 366. See also *Dimskal Shipping Co SA v International Transport Workers Federation, The Evia Luck* [1992] 2 A.C. 152.

Lord Scarman in the decision of the Privy Council in *Pao On v Lau Yiu Long*.[12] His Lordship continued:

> "In determining whether there was coercion of the will such that there was no true consent, it is material to enquire whether the person alleged to have been coerced did or did not protest; whether, at the time he was allegedly coerced into making the contract he did or did not have an alternative course open to him such as an adequate legal remedy; whether he was independently advised; and whether after entering the contract he took steps to avoid it."

All these were matters, in the view of Lord Scarman, relevant in determining whether there was true consent or not. This theory, which has been referred to as "the theory of the overborne will" has attracted criticism in that it uses language suggesting that the innocent party is acting in an involuntary fashion when they enter the contract—they have no choice as there is no true consent. In fact, the party pressed into a contract as a result of duress does exercise a choice—it is between choosing the least worst of two undesirable alternatives.[13] They are fully and, no doubt, painfully aware of the nature of the transaction they have entered into. As a result, in establishing whether a party is under duress, the courts seem to have moved away from asking whether innocent party acted voluntarily or not to considering whether in the circumstances in which the contract was made the pressure *caused* the innocent party to enter the contract.

Under this approach, it seems that in considering whether a threat to break a contract amounts to duress, the courts are concerned with two matters: (i) the illegitimacy of the threat; and (ii) whether the threat amounts to a significant cause in inducing the threatened party to enter the contract.

Illegitimate threat

The threat must be to do something illegitimate, such as to breach an existing contract, and **13–008** therefore as a general rule (but see the possible exception at para.13–011) a threat to do something legitimate will not suffice. This is illustrated by *Huyton SA v Peter Cremer GmbH Ltd*[14] where H agreed to buy a consignment of Romanian grain from C. Under the terms of the contract, freight was to be arranged by H and paid for by C against shipping documents. A dispute arose over "demurrage" payments, i.e. sums payable under the charterparty for the detention of the ship in port beyond a number of days. The goods were delivered but H refused to pay for the consignment unless further documents in proper form were presented and unless C agreed to pay demurrage without going to arbitration. C reluctantly agreed to do this although then commenced arbitration proceedings. In an action brought by H to restrain the arbitration proceedings, C argued that he was not bound by the agreement on the ground of economic duress in that H's threat amounted to illegitimate pressure. Mance J. held that H's threat to withhold payment was not illegitimate as H was not bound to pay the price until he had received shipping documents in proper form from C.

---

[12] [1980] A.C. 614; agreeing with Kerr J. in *The Siboen and the Sibotre* [1976] 1 Lloyd's Rep. 293, at p. 336. See also *Barton v Armstrong* [1976] A.C. 104, at p. 121; and *The Atlantic Baron* [1978] Q.B. 705, at pp. 717, 719.
[13] See Atiyah (1982) 98 L.Q.R. 197.
[14] [1999] 1 Lloyd's Rep. 620.

It might be thought that any threat to breach a contract would constitute illegitimate pressure but there is some authority that this is not necessarily always the case. There may be a requirement that the threat must be made in circumstances involving bad faith, as for example, in *Atlas Express v Kafco* (the facts are given above) where the conduct of the haulage company was clearly oppressive. The requirement of "bad faith" is supported by the decision of Dyson J. in *DSND Subsea Ltd v Petroleum Geo Services ASA*[15] where the threat to breach the contract was held to be justified in the circumstances as a reasonable attempt to clarify insurance arrangements in connection with North Sea oil development. On the other hand, Mance J. in *Huyton v Peter Cremer* expressed doubts as to the proposition that a threat to breach a contract would only be illegitimate if made in bad faith. The judge found it difficult to accept that "illegitimate pressure applied by a party who believes bona fide in his case could never give relief against an apparent [agreement]." It is suggested that the test of bad faith introduces an unnecessary complication and that all threats to breach a contract should be regarded as affording grounds for economic duress, subject to the causation requirements discussed below.

Causation

13–009   Once it has been established that illegitimate pressure has been brought to bear, it must be shown that such pressure actually caused the threatened party to enter the contract; in *Dimskal Shipping Co SA v International Transport Workers' Federation, The Evia Luck*[16] Lord Goff stated that the economic pressure must constitute a "significant cause inducing the [claimant] to enter the relevant contract". And in *Huyton v Peter Cremer* Mance J. considered that the pressure must be "decisive and clinching" in the sense that the innocent party would not have entered the contract at all or would have done so on different terms.[17] Indeed, the judge thought that there may well be a third requirement; i.e. that the innocent party must show that they had no reasonable alternative to making the contract they did. Mance J. explained:

> "It is not necessary to go so far as to say that it is an inflexible third essential ingredient of economic duress that there should be no or no practical alternative course open to the innocent party. But it seems . . . self-evident that relief may not be appropriate, if an innocent party decides, as a matter of choice, not to pursue an alternative remedy which any and possibly some other reasonable persons in his circumstances would have pursued."

It seems, therefore, that this third requirement is to be judged objectively.

It was explained above that the theory of duress depending on "coercion of the will" has fallen out of favour and more recent cases have stressed the test of causation. It is clear, however, that the same factors will be relevant in establishing economic duress under the new test as under the old. These were identified by Lord Scarman in *Pao On v Lau Yiu Long* (see para 13–007). To recap, the factors are: whether the innocent party (i) did or did not protest; (ii) whether at the time they did or did not have an alternative course open to them such as an adequate legal remedy; (iii) whether they were independently advised; and (iv) whether after entering the contract they took steps to avoid it. We have seen some of these factors to be

[15] [2000] B.L.R. 530.
[16] [1992] 2 A.C. 152.
[17] Duress to the person is different—see *Barton v Armstrong*, discussed at para.13–003.

present to a greater or lesser degree in the cases discussed above, thus in *Atlas Express v Kafco* an action for breach of contract against the haulage company would not have been an adequate legal remedy (under (ii) above) given the consequences of the loss of the Woolworths contract. The basketware suppliers had no reasonable alternative but to submit to the illegitimate pressure. However, of the four factors, (ii) is the one which is likely to be given the most weight and which may, in many cases, be decisive.

From an early stage in the development of the doctrine of economic duress, the courts have drawn a distinction between actionable duress and "mere commercial pressure". Such pressure is legitimate and extremely common in business dealings.

Thus in *Pao On v Lau Yiu Long*[18] the Privy Council found that there had been commercial **13–010** pressure but no duress. Here one party threatened to break an existing contract unless the other party gave an indemnity against loss resulting from the performance of that contract. It was held that the transaction was not vitiated by duress—the decision to enter the renegotiated contract was a commercial decision taken after due consideration; upon legal advice; and without protest. A similar conclusion was arrived at in *Alec Lobb (Garages) Ltd v Total Oil Great Britain Ltd*[19] concerning a "solus" tie[20] in the petrol trade (the facts are given at para.15–017). Although the defendants had driven a hard bargain, the claimant did not enter into the transaction under any compulsion and his financial difficulties were of his own making. Such pressure as there was came from other creditors and not the defendants. The court considered that even if the existence of the tie did constitute coercive pressure, the claimant neither protested at the time nor took prompt action to repudiate the agreement once the pressure was lifted and had, indeed, affirmed the transaction. Sir Peter Millett Q.C., sitting as deputy judge, concluded that "to set the transaction aside in those circumstances on the ground of economic duress is out of the question."

Lawful act duress

In *CTN Cash and Carry Ltd v Gallaher*[21] it was suggested that, in appropriate circumstances, a **13–011** threat to commit a lawful act could amount to duress.

In this case, the claimant company, a cash and carry business, purchased a consignment of cigarettes from the defendants. In error, the defendants sent the consignment to the wrong warehouse for the claimants; before they could redirect it to the correct warehouse, the consignment was stolen. The defendants genuinely (but mistakenly) believed that the goods were at the claimants' risk at the time of the theft and therefore sent them an invoice for the goods. The claimants initially refused to pay for them, whereupon the defendants threatened not to supply the claimants with goods on credit unless they paid for the stolen cigarettes. This was a lawful threat. The claimants paid in order to keep their credit facilities but then sought recovery of the sum paid on the grounds of economic duress. The Court of Appeal held that the defendants' conduct did not involve economic duress. A threat to perform a lawful act might amount to economic duress in certain circumstances but this could not be the case in a commercial transaction between two companies dealing at arm's length where the party issuing the threat

---

[18] [1980] A.C. 614.
[19] [1983] 1 W.L.R. 87.
[20] Solus agreements under the restraint of trade doctrine are discussed at para.15–016.
[21] (1994) 4 All E.R. 714.

genuinely believed that the demand was valid. The commercial pressure was exerted by the defendants to recover a sum which they bona fide believed to be due to them. Steyn L.J. added, however, that the fact that the defendants used lawful means did not necessarily remove the case from the ambit of economic duress. The court relied on the views of a leading academic, Professor Birks, where he said:[22]

> "Can lawful pressures also count? This is a difficult question, because, if the answer is that they can, the only viable basis for discriminating between acceptable and unacceptable pressures is not positive law but social morality. In other words, the judges must say what pressures . . . are improper or contrary to prevailing standards. . . .On the other hand, if the answer is that lawful pressures are always exempt, those who devise outrageous but technically lawful means of compulsion must always escape restitution until the legislature declares the abuse unlawful."

13–012   The court recognised (obiter) that, in appropriate circumstances, a threat to commit a lawful act could constitute duress, although it was conceded that in a purely commercial context, it might be relatively rare that such liability could be established. Would it have made any difference if, in *CTN Cash and Carry v Gallaher* the defendants had acted in bad faith in that they had no honest belief in the validity of their demand? The court placed particular emphasis on the fact that the defendants had acted in good faith when making the demand, thus, had the defendants' belief not been genuine, liability for economic duress might possibly have been established as arising from their lawful threat.

Support for the notion of duress arising from a lawful act comes also from the decision of the Privy Council in the case of *R v Her Majesty's Attorney-General for England and Wales*.[23] Following involvement in military action during the Gulf War of 1991, members of the SAS had published books detailing their experiences. The Ministry of Defence (MOD) were concerned that such publications would undermine the traditions and ethos of the SAS which demanded total secrecy. Wishing to prevent any such revelations in the future, the MOD drew up confidentiality agreements forbidding any unauthorised disclosures relating to the work of the Special Forces. The defendant, R, was a soldier who had been involved in military action but had not written about his experiences in the Gulf War. Along with his fellow soldiers, R was informed by his commanding officer that if he wished to remain in the SAS he would have to sign a confidentiality agreement. If he did not sign, he would be "returned to unit" (RTU), i.e. sent back to his regiment and no longer be a member of the SAS. This would involve a reduction in pay and a dimunition in status and was reserved for those who were guilty of misconduct or regarded as unsuitable for the SAS. From the point of view of the MOD, any person who was unwilling to sign such an agreement was unsuitable for service in the SAS.

R signed the agreement without taking legal advice and in circumstances whereby he felt that he had no alternative but to sign. In due course, R left the army and moved to New Zealand where he took up civilian employment. R later entered into a contract with a publisher to write a book of his military experiences whereupon the Attorney- General commenced proceedings in the New Zealand courts for the breach of the confidentiality agreement. At first instance, the judge held that R had been ordered to sign as a result of a military order which was unlawful as it attempted to restrict the civil rights to which he was entitled after leaving the service. The

---

[22] Birks, *An Introduction to the Law of Restitution* (1989), p. 177.
[23] [2003] UKPC 22.

unlawful order combined with the threat of RTU vitiated the contract on the ground of duress. The Court of Appeal disagreed—there had been no military order to sign as R had been given a choice; a choice which placed him under pressure, but it was not unlawful. The court, however, exercised its discretion to refuse an injunction but ordered instead an account for profits and an assessment of damages. R appealed to the Privy Council against this decision. The appeal was dismissed. The Board conceded that there had been overwhelming pressure and the threat of RTU meant that the defendant had no practical choice but to sign the agreement; but their Lordships agreed with the Court of Appeal that there had been no unlawful threat. Lord Hoffmann discussed the nature of the "illegitimate pressure" which is required as one of the elements in establishing duress.[24] His Lordship said:

> "The legitimacy of the pressure must be examined from two aspects: first, the nature of the pressure and secondly, the nature of the demand which the pressure is applied to support: see Lord Scarman in [*Universe Tankships Inc of Monrovia v International Transport Workers Federation, The Universe Sentinel* [1983] 1 AC 366, at p. 401]. Generally speaking, the threat of any form of unlawful action will be regarded as illegitimate. On the other hand, *the fact that the threat is lawful does not necessarily make the pressure legitimate* [author's italics]. As Lord Atkin said in *Thorne v Motor Trade Association* [1937] AC 797, 806: 'The ordinary blackmailer normally threatens to do what he has a perfect right to do – namely, communicate some compromising conduct to a person whose knowledge is likely to affect the person threatened . . . What he has to justify is not the threat, but the demand of money.'"

The court applied this reasoning to the case and concluded that the demand arising from the lawful threat was justifiable. The MOD had been acting lawfully as it was entirely within their discretion to transfer servicemen—it was not unreasonable for them to do this where they considered that a person was unsuitable for the SAS. Moreover, the concerns which prompted the MOD to introduce confidentiality agreements were perfectly legitimate. The judicial statements in this case are only of persuasive authority but may be a pointer as to the way the doctrine of duress may develop in the future—if so, it represents a potentially difficult extension of the doctrine. It is difficult enough as things stand to distinguish between legitmate pressure and duress. Those problems are likely to be compounded by an extension of duress to embrace unlawful demands arising from lawful threats.

13–013

Remedies for duress

As mentioned at the beginning of this chapter, duress renders a contract voidable and therefore the available remedy is rescission. As with misrepresentation (see para.11–032), rescission may be barred by affirmation (see the discussion of *The Atlantic Baron* at para.13–004); lapse of time; and the intervention of third party rights. It seems that rescission for duress, as for misrepresentation and undue influence, may be barred by the impossibility of effecting a restitutio in integrum ("counter-restitution").[25] It is generally understood that damages cannot be recovered for duress, whether or not the contract is rescinded.

13–014

---

[24] The other is "compulsion of the will" but there was no doubt on the facts that there was such compulsion.

[25] *Halpern v Halpern* [2006] EWHC 1728 (Comm) (High Court); on appeal in the Court of Appeal it was held that a definitive response to the issue was not possible or appropriate until the facts were known; [2007] EWCA Civ 291, at para.75.

UNDUE INFLUENCE

13–015   We have seen that before the development of economic duress, the common law doctrine of duress was very narrow in scope, embracing duress to the person and of goods. The very limited extent of the common law led to the development of the equitable doctrine of undue influence. Under this doctrine, where undue influence is found, the contract is voidable at the instance of the victim of the influence. Gifts, as well as contracts, may be avoided under the doctrine.

Undue influence cannot be precisely defined, indeed the courts have deprecated attempts to do so, thus in *National Westminster Bank Plc v Morgan*[26] Lord Scarman observed, " . . . there is no precisely defined law setting limits to the equitable jurisdiction of a court to relieve against undue influence"; and in *Royal Bank of Scotland Plc v Etridge (No 2)*[27] Lord Clyde observed that undue influence "is something which can more easily be recognised when found than when exhaustively examined in the abstract." Unlike duress, cases of undue influence are based on some *relationship* between the parties existing *before* the particular transaction that is challenged. Typically, it is a relationship where one party places trust and confidence in the other such that the other party is able to abuse that trust by entering into a transaction advantageous to themselves. The "weaker" or more vulnerable party in the relationship may have had their judgment undermined in relation to the relevant transaction because of the faith they have in the "stronger" party. The influence exercised in these circumstances may be quite subtle but nevertheless amount to "undue" influence in law. We saw with duress that the difficulty for the courts lies in deciding what type of pressure should be categorised as illegitimate (see para.13–008). A similar problem arises with undue influence—when does influence become undue influence? After all, influence in a relationship may be perfectly benign, just as commercial pressure may be an acceptable and legitimate element in successful business dealings.

Some of the older cases on undue influence were decided before the development of economic duress and might well now be treated as falling more appropriately under the heading of duress, since they involve pressure rather than influence. It may be recalled that, until recently, it was thought that a lawful threat could never give rise to a claim of duress (see para.13–011). A case of undue influence involving pressure is *Williams v Bayley*[28] where a young man, who was the son of a colliery owner, forged his father's signature on some promissory notes and presented them to his bank. There took place a meeting between the young man's father (the claimant in the case), the young man himself and officials of the defendant bank. The defendants' representatives made it clear that, unless some satisfactory arrangement was arrived at, the son would be prosecuted. It was mentioned by the bank that the case was one attracting the penalty of transportation for life. No doubt fearing for his son, the father entered into an agreement to mortgage the colliery to the bank in return for handing back the forged promissory notes. This agreement was set aside by the House of Lords on the grounds of undue influence. The case would seem now to fit more neatly into the category of duress.[29]

13–016   Our understanding of the modern law of undue influence owes much to the speeches of the House of Lords in *Barclays Bank Plc v O'Brien*[30] where their Lordships examined the doctrine.

---

[26] [1985] A.C. 686.
[27] [2002] 2 A.C. 773.
[28] (1866) L.R. 1 H.L. 200.
[29] See Birks and Chin, 'On the Nature of Undue Influence' in *Good Faith and Fault in Contract Law*, Beatson and Friedmann (eds), (Oxford: Clarendon Press, 1995).
[30] [1994] 1 A.C. 180.

Essentially, Lord Browne-Wilkinson adopted a classification of undue influence whereby there were two main categories of undue influence, Class 1 and Class 2.

Class 1 comprised actual undue influence and Class 2 comprised presumed undue influence. Class 2 was divided into two sub-categories, Class 2(A) and Class 2(B). Class 2 (A) covered relationships which by their very nature always raised a presumption of undue influence and Class 2(B) applied to cases where the particular relationship between the parties, usually one of trust and confidence, gave rise to a presumption of undue influence. *Barclays Bank v O'Brien* itself was concerned with the effect of undue influence exercised by a third party and that aspect of the doctrine will be considered later in this chapter (see para.13–034). The classification of undue influence put forward by Lord Browne-Wilkinson in the *O'Brien* case was followed in a number of subsequent cases but came up for re-appraisal in a later House of Lords decision, *Royal Bank of Scotland v Etridge (No 2)*.[31] Although the three categories remain, presumed undue influence has been clarified as involving a presumption that there was influence rather than that the influence was undue. The evidential presumption of undue influence will only arise if there is something about the transaction which is suspicious or which calls for an explanation. These matters are more fully discussed below at para.13–019.

Actual undue influence

A claim of actual undue influence will be substantiated if the claimant can establish that the defendant used undue influence in relation to a particular transaction. There does not need to be any previous history of such influence but there will normally be some relationship between the parties, since it is really only from a relationship that influence can arise. This is perhaps what distinguishes actual undue influence from duress, to which it bears close similarities. In *Bank of Credit and Commerce International SA v Aboody*[32] Slade L.J. explained what must be established:

13–017

> "A person relying on a plea of actual undue influence must show that (a) the other party to the transaction (or someone who induced the transaction for his own benefit) had the capacity to influence the complainant; (b) the influence was exercised; (c) its exercise was undue; (d) its exercise brought about the transaction."

In the *Aboody* case Mrs A came from a traditional in background in Iraq and at a young age had entered into an arranged marriage with Mr A, a man 20 years her senior. Mr A later formed a textile company and Mrs A became a nominal director of the business, although she did not understand the business and came from a world where business was an exclusively male province. At her husband's request, she would sign documents relating to the business without reading them, although she would read other documents presented by a stranger. Mr A wanted his wife to sign various guarantees and charges in favour of the claimant bank, and in relation to one of these transactions the claimant bank tried to ensure that Mrs A received independent advice. When the solicitor was in the process of advising Mrs A at the bank's premises, her husband burst into the room in an agitated state and shouted, "Why the hell don't you get on with what you are paid to do and witness her signature?" There then followed a scene which reduced Mrs A to tears. Mr A had told her, prior to the interview that the solicitor was there

[31] [2002] A.C. 773.
[32] [1990] 1 Q.B. 923.

merely to witness her signature. It was the solicitor's impression that Mrs A was resolved to sign regardless of the advice. She signed as she wanted peace.

13–018   The Court of Appeal found that there had been actual undue influence even though Mr A had not acted from any improper motive or intention to injure his wife. However, his overbearing manner and concealment of information meant that she was prevented from giving a proper detached consideration to her independent interests in transactions which involved substantial risks to her.[33] But the court did not set aside the transactions because it concluded that they were not to Mrs A's "manifest disadvantage" because the transactions she had guaranteed gave the company a reasonable prospect of survival which would have been to her substantial advantage. In so holding, the Court of Appeal was following the decision of the House of Lords in *National Westminster Bank Plc v Morgan*.[34] However, a House of Lords' decision of the early 1990s, *CIBC Mortgages Plc v Pitt*,[35] indicated that manifest disadvantage was not a requirement in cases of actual undue influence. This position regarding actual undue influence has been preserved by the House of Lords in *Royal Bank of Scotland v Etridge* (see para.13–024). It seems likely that cases on facts similar to *Aboody* would therefore be decided differently today, although in *Etridge* Lord Nicholls introduced a cautionary note that it may be more difficult to establish actual undue influence in cases involving husbands and wives than previously thought. In relation to whether a wife's guarantee of her husband's bank overdraft has been procured by undue influence, his Lordship said this:

> "Undue influence has a connotation of impropriety. In the eye of the law, undue influence means that influence has been misused. Statements or conduct by a husband which do not pass beyond the bounds of what may reasonably be expected of a reasonable husband in the circumstances should not, without more, be castigated as undue influence."

It seems that, as with fraudulent misrepresentation, a finding of actual undue influence does not depend on the claimant proving that they would not have entered the transaction but for the influence. Providing the influence is one of the factors inducing the claimant to enter the transaction, that will suffice.[36]

Presumed undue influence

13–019   Presumed undue influence falls into two categories, those where there is a special relationship between the parties and those where there is no such relationship.

Special relationship: Class 2(A)

13–020   This is the category of undue influence designated as Class 2(A) in *Barclays Bank v O'Brien*. Under this category certain specified relationships gave rise to a presumption of undue influence. In *Etridge*, the House of Lords clarified the position: the relationship gives rise to a presumption of influence only, but not of undue influence. Another factor must be present for

---

[33] For a case involving actual undue influence, see also *Drew v Daniel* [2005] 2 P. & C.R. D.G.14.
[34] [1985] A.C. 686.
[35] [1994] A.C. 200.
[36] *UCB Corporate Services Ltd v Williams* [2002] EWCA Civ 555.

there to arise a second evidential presumption. This is that there is a transaction which "calls for an explanation" or which is not "readily explicable by the relationship of the parties". In other words, it is a suspicious transaction. This second evidential presumption, unlike the first presumption, is rebuttable. The ascendant party will be presumed to have exercised undue influence in relation to the transaction in question unless they can adduce evidence to the contrary. The circumstances in which the transaction may be voidable under this test will be considered more fully below (at para.13–027).

The relationships include—parent and child, guardian and ward, trustee and beneficiary, solicitor and client, medical advisor and patient, and religious advisor and disciple. The relationship of husband and wife is not included. The relationships subject to the presumption of influence are those traditionally termed as "fiduciary" in which one party has trust and confidence in the other party so that they will act on the other's guidance without question and without seeking independent advice. All that the vulnerable party needs to prove in such cases is that one of the special relationships exists—they do not need to establish affirmatively that they actually reposed trust and confidence in the stronger party. The presumption of influence is not rebuttable.

The well-known case of *Allcard v Skinner*[37] is an illustration of the type of relationship that falls under this category. The claimant joined a protestant religious sisterhood, St Mary at the Cross, taking vows of poverty, chastity and obedience. The latter rule required interns to regard the voice of the lady superior, the defendant in the case, as the voice of God. There was also a rule that no sister should seek the advice of any extern without the superior's permission. Over the years that she was a member of the sisterhood, the claimant transferred considerable property to the defendant. Eventually, the claimant left the sisterhood and was received into the Roman Catholic Church. Some six years later the claimant sought the return of her property and commenced an action against the defendant. The Court of Appeal held that the gifts of property were voidable on the grounds of undue influence. The presumption of undue influence had not been rebutted. Although direct pressure had not been brought to bear on the claimant, the influence was nevertheless undue. As Cotton L.J. explained:

13–021

> "At the time of the gift the [claimant] was a professed sister, and, as such, bound to make absolute submission to the defendant as superior of the sisterhood. She had no power to obtain independent advice, she was in such a position that she could not freely exercise her own will as to the disposal of her property, and she must be considered as being . . . 'not in the largest and amplest sense of the term, not in mind as well as person, an entirely free agent'."[38]

Despite the finding of undue influence, however, the claimant's recovery of her property was barred by delay as six years had elapsed from when she left the sisterhood to when she initiated the action. The claimant had affirmed the transaction.

No special relationship: the old Class 2(B)

We are concerned here with cases where there is no special relationship falling under Class 2(A). This was the old *Barclays Bank v O'Brien* Class 2(B). Under this category, a presumption of

13–022

---

[37] [1887] L.R. 36 Ch. D. 145. See also *Morley v Loughnan* [1893] 1 Ch. 736
[38] Per Knight Bruce L.J. in *Wright v Vanderplank* (1856) 8 De G.M. & G. 133.

undue influence arose where, although the relationship between the parties did not fall within one of the categories discussed in the previous section, the relationship was nevertheless one of trust and confidence where one party was in a position to exert undue influence over the other. Following the *Etridge* case, there is no longer any presumption of undue influence in such cases. It will be for the claimant to show that they placed trust and confidence in the defendant in the handling of their affairs. Once that is established, then where there is a transaction which "calls for an explanation", an evidential presumption that undue influence has been exerted arises. It will be for the defendant to prove that no such influence was exercised. It should be noted that doubts were expressed (obiter) in *Etridge* as to whether Class 2(B) should continue to be recognised. Lord Hobhouse considered that the Class 2(B) presumption was a "limited forensic tool".

Many of the cases decided under the old Class 2(B) continue to be illustrative of the type of relationship which will be subject to the doctrine and depending upon a relationship of trust and confidence being established. In *Lloyds Bank Ltd v Bundy*[39] the defendant was an elderly farmer who had a son who ran a plant hire company. The father, son and his company all banked at the same branch of the claimant bank. The company got into financial difficulties and ran up an overdraft which was secured by a guarantee of £6,500 by the father and a charge on the farm of £7,500. When the overdraft reached £10,000 the bank requested further security. The son told the bank that his father would provide this, and the son and the bank's assistant manager visited the father. The evidence was that the assistant manager knew that the defendant implicitly relied on him as "the bank manager" to advise him and that he knew that the house was the defendant's only asset. Without seeking any independent advice, the defendant signed a guarantee increasing the company's overdraft and a further charge on the house of £3,500 bringing the total charge to £11,000, a sum greater than the house was worth. Some months later, the bank stopped the company's overdraft facilities and sought the money due from the defendant. The claimant bank, not having been paid, sought possession of the farm.

13–023   The Court of Appeal held that the transaction should be set aside. The Court of Appeal considered that the defendant's reliance on the bank to advise him on the wisdom of the transaction raised (under the pre-*Etridge* law) a presumption of undue influence. It was a relationship of trust and confidence. The nature of the relationship was explained by Sir Eric Sachs who said that the signing of the documents by the defendant had to be assessed in the light of the general background of the long- standing relations between the Bundy family and the bank. As he stated:

> "It not infrequently occurs in provincial and country branches of great banks that a relationship is built up over the years, and in due course the senior officials may become trusted counsellors of customers of whose affairs they have an intimate knowledge. Confidential trust is placed in them because of a combination of status, goodwill and knowledge."

It did not make any difference that the defendant had not met the particular assistant manager who called with the documents for signing. Although there was a conflict of interest between the bank and the defendant, the bank did not advise the defendant to seek independent advice. The transaction was one where the defendant, if the company's troubles continued, could be left penniless in his old age—the bank had therefore failed in their duty to advise him properly. The presumption of undue influence had not been rebutted and the transaction was set aside.

[39] [1975] Q.B. 326.

Post-*Etridge*, the court would be likely to arrive at the same conclusion on the facts, but on the basis that the transaction was one calling for an explanation and it would be for the bank to prove that no undue influence had been exercised.

The decision of the House of Lords in *National Westminster Bank Plc v Morgan*[40] affords an instructive comparison with *Lloyds Bank Ltd v Bundy*.

The facts of the *Morgan* case were that a husband and wife were in danger of losing their **13–024** home as the building society had begun proceedings for repossession for non-payment of the mortgage. The husband wished to make an arrangement with the claimant bank whereby they would refinance the building society loan, and for this purpose, the claimants required a charge on the property for the loan. The bank manager called at the house to obtain the wife's signature on the document executing the legal charge. The wife informed the manager that she did not want the charge to cover her husband's business liabilities and in good faith the manager assured her that it would not do so. This was incorrect as the document was widely enough worded to cover such liabilities although the manager was not aware of this. Before signing the document, the wife did not receive independent legal advice. When the husband died, the claimants sought possession of the house. The defendant argued that the charge was voidable on the grounds of undue influence. It was held by the House of Lords that the claimants were entitled to succeed.

No presumption of undue influence arose on the facts because the relationship between the bank and the wife had never got beyond the ordinary business relationship between banker and customer—it had never "crossed the line". The bank was not therefore under any duty to ensure that she received independent legal advice. As to the relationship between banker and customer, Lord Scarman (who gave the main speech and with whom the other Lords agreed) explained the position:

> "It was . . . conceded by counsel for the [wife] that the relationship between banker and customer is not one which ordinarily gives rise to a presumption of undue influence: and that in the ordinary course of banking business a banker can explain the nature of the proposed transaction without laying himself open to a charge of undue influence. This proposition has never been in doubt, though some, it would appear, have thought that the Court of Appeal held otherwise in *Lloyds Bank Ltd v Bundy*. If any such view has gained currency, let it be destroyed now once and for all time."

An additional ground for the decision in *National Westminster Bank v Morgan* was that the **13–025** transaction was not to the wife's disadvantage, indeed she had benefited from it because it would have prevented repossession of the matrimonial home. When the case was decided, transactions were only regarded as voidable on the grounds of undue influence if they were to the "manifest disadvantage" of the complainant. However, this requirement has now been redefined and clarified by the House of Lords in the *Etridge* case (see para.13–028).

It seems that a relationship of trust and confidence does not necessarily require that the stronger party exercises a dominating influence over the weaker, as had been suggested by Lord Scarman in *National Westminster Bank v Morgan*. Thus, in *Goldsworthy v Brickell*[41] the claimant G was an 85–year–old farmer who came to trust and depend on a neighbouring farmer B, a younger man, for help and advice. In a short period of time, the relationship developed to the

---

[40] [1985] A.C. 686.
[41] [1987] 1 All E.R. 853.

point where B was effectively running G's farm. G granted B a tenancy and option to purchase his farm on terms very disadvantageous to G himself. The Court of Appeal set aside the transaction. Although the relationship between the two men was not characterised by the domination of the one over the other, it was nevertheless one of trust and confidence.

Lloyds Bank Ltd v Bundy, which was discussed above, is something of an exceptional case. The majority of cases decided under the old Class 2(B) involved husband and wife relationships, where the former was dominant and the latter subservient. It will be recalled from the previous section that husband and wife is not one of the "special relationships" falling under Class 2(A). It seems that the reason for this is a recognition that even where a wife does everything she is told by her husband, her motives in conferring substantial financial benefits on him may stem from love and affection or some other natural reason.[42] It follows that the wife will have to establish a relationship and trust and confidence under Class 2(B) for the evidential presumption of undue influence to apply to transactions that are not readily explicable. Alternatively, a wife may be able to demonstrate actual under influence under Class 1 if she has been induced into a transaction by an overbearing husband as in the *Aboody* case (see para.13–017).

13–026   A relationship between a couple may be regarded as one of trust and confidence even if they are not married—a long term loving relationship may suffice. In *Leeder v Stevens*[43] the claimant, a married man, had had a relationship with a lady, the defendant, for 10 years and they were "very fond of each other". The claimant entered into a transaction with the defendant in which she transferred to him a half-share in her house (worth £70,000) in return for him paying of the outstanding £5,000 on her mortgage. Under the terms of the deed of transfer, if the claimant wished, the defendant could be forced to sell the house immediately unless she bought him out. The defendant did not obtain her own legal advice. The Court of Appeal held that a relationship of trust and confidence had been established on the facts. Jacob L.J. said that the transaction "cried out" for an explanation and nothing had been put forward to rebut the evidential presumption of undue influence. The transaction was set aside.

Transactions calling for an explanation

13–027   Under what circumstances will a transaction be one that "calls for an explanation" and is "not readily explicable by the relationship of the parties"? In order to consider this question, we need to examine the development of the doctrine prior to the *Royal Bank of Scotland v Etridge* case.

We have seen that in *National Westminster Bank Plc v Morgan* the House of Lords confirmed that "manifest disadvantage" was seen as a prerequisite for setting aside a contract on the grounds of presumed undue influence. The requirement that manifest disadvantage be proved can be traced to the judgment of Lindley L.J. in *Allcard v Skinner* (the facts are discussed at para.13–021) in which his Lordship was speaking of gifts but the principles apply equally to contracts:

> "Where a gift is made to a person standing in a confidential relation to the donor, the Court will not set aside the gift if of a small amount simply on the ground that the donor had no independent advice. In such a case, some proof of the exercise of the influence of the donee

---

[42]   *Yerkey v Jones* (1939) 93 C.L.R. 649, per Dixon J. at p. 675.
[43]   [2005] EWCA Civ 50.

must be given. The mere existence of such influence is not enough in such a case . . . But if the gift is so large as not to be reasonably accounted for on the ground of friendship, relationship, charity, or other ordinary motives on which ordinary men act, the burden is upon the donee to support the gift."

Following the House of Lords' decision in *CIBC Mortgages Plc v Pitt* it seemed to be confirmed that manifest disadvantage was necessary requirement to vitiate transactions of presumed undue influence, either under class 2(A) or 2(B), but it was not a requirement in cases of actual undue influence. But doubts were expressed by Lord Browne-Wilkinson in the *CIBC Mortgages v Pitt* case as to whether manifest disadvantage was an absolute requirement even in cases of presumed undue influence, but these statements were obiter. Similar obiter assertions were made by Nourse L.J. in the Court of Appeal in *Barclays Bank Plc v Coleman*.[44] The concept of manifest disadvantage caused little difficulty in straightforward transactions such as the sale of a property at a substantial undervalue. The main problem arose in cases where wives acted as surety for the payment of their husband's business debts. The question that exercised the courts was whether such a transaction, usually where the wife guaranteed the husband's overdraft and executed a charge on her share of the family home, was to the wife's manifest disadvantage. As Lord Nicholls observed in the *Etridge* case, in a narrow sense such transactions are disadvantageous to the wife because she undertakes a serious financial obligation and personally receives nothing. But this is to ignore the wider picture that a married couple's fortunes are bound up together and that if funds were made available to support her husband's business then she may indirectly benefit.

Given the difficulties surrounding the requirement of manifest disadvantage, the House of Lords in *Etridge* favoured a return to an analysis more closely based on the judgment of Lindley L.J. in *Allcard v Skinner* (to which reference was made above), as adopted by Lord Scarman in *National Westminster Bank Plc v Morgan*. Henceforth any disadvantage to the claimant from the transaction should be no more than *evidence* that the influence was undue and the transaction needs to be explained. The House ruled that manifest disadvantage was no longer a requirement and that the claimant did not have to prove it in order to establish undue influence. The label "manifest disadvantage" should be discarded. The nature of the transaction is relevant only in so far as it shows that the transaction "calls for an explanation" or is "not readily explicable by the relationship of the parties". It will then be for the defendant to prove that no undue influence was exercised over the complainant in the transaction in question. **13–028**

On the issue of those cases where a wife guarantees her husband's business debts, Lord Nicholls had this to say:

"I do not think that, *in the ordinary course*, a guarantee of the character I have mentioned is to be regarded as a transaction which, failing proof to the contrary, is explicable only on the basis that it has been procured by the exercise of undue influence by the husband. Wives frequently enter into such transactions. There are good and sufficient reasons why they are willing to do so, despite the risks involved for them and their families. They may be enthusiastic. They may not. They may be less optimistic than their husbands about the prospects of the husband's businesses. They may be anxious, perhaps exceedingly so. But this is a far cry from saying that such transactions as a class are to be regarded as prima facie evidence of the exercise of undue influence by their husbands. I have emphasised the phrase 'in the

---

[44] [2000] 3 W.L.R. 405.

ordinary course'. There will be cases where a wife's signature of a guarantee or a charge of her share of the matrimonial home does call for an explanation. Nothing I have said above is directed at such a case."

The main hurdle to surmount, therefore, in husband and wife surety cases, is not establishing a relationship of trust and confidence, this should be relatively easy, but in showing that the transaction is of a nature sufficiently suspicious as to raise the evidential presumption of undue influence, i.e. that the transaction is outside "the ordinary course".

13–029   Despite the ruling of the House of Lords that the expression "manifest disadvantage" should not be used, the phrase was used by Jacob L.J. in speaking of the transaction in the post-*Etridge* case of *Leeder v Stevens*[45] (the case is discussed in the previous section). However, the context indicates that his Lordship considered that the fact that the transaction was manifestly to the disadvantage of the defendant was the sort of matter that called for an explanation. In other words, the court considered the degree of disadvantage to the defendant to be evidence that the agreement was a suspicious one not readily explicable by the relationship of the parties. However, if the requirement of manifest disadvantage is not to creep in by the back door, as it were, it would perhaps be best if the expression was avoided altogether in the exposition of the law.

Rebutting the presumption

13–030   Once the evidential presumption of undue influence is raised, how may the alleged undue influencer rebut it?

This may be done if the party benefiting from the transaction is able to show that the decision of the other party to enter the transaction was the free exercise of independent will. This may be proved by establishing that the complainant received competent independent advice from a suitably qualified person in which the nature of the transaction was fully explained so that the complainant fully appreciated what they were doing.[46] However, the mere existence of independent advice may not be enough; in the case of *Inche Noriah v Shaik Allie bin Omar*[47] an aged widow gave away almost the whole of her property to her nephew. The widow had consulted a solicitor, but the solicitor was unaware of the full circumstances and did not advise her that she could equally well have benefited her nephew by will. Thus the advice must be competent and appropriate in the circumstances.

In *Royal Bank of Scotland v Etridge* the House of Lords indicated that the existence of independent advice may not be conclusive. Lord Nicholls suggested that a person may well understand fully the implications of a proposed transaction, e.g. a substantial gift, but still nevertheless be acting under the undue influence of another. His Lordship said:

"Proof of outside advice does not, of itself, necessarily show that the subsequent completion of the transaction was free from the exercise of undue influence. Whether it will be proper to infer that outside advice had an emancipating effect, so that the transaction was not brought about by the exercise of undue influence, is a question of fact to be decided having regard to all the evidence in the case."

[45] [2005] EWCA Civ 50, at para.14.
[46] *Inche Noriah v Shaik Allie bin Omar* [1929] A.C. 127, at p. 135.
[47] [1929] A.C. 127.

Thus the weight, or importance, to be attached to the advice will depend upon an assessment of all the circumstances of the case. Lord Nicholls acknowledged, however, that in the "normal course", advice from a solicitor or other independent advisor should give the complainant a proper appreciation of the implications of the proposed transaction.

Remedies for undue influence

Undue influence, if established, renders a transaction voidable and the normal remedy will be rescission. There are certain bars to rescission similar to those which apply to mirepresentation (see para.11–031).

13–031

First, it must be possible to restore the parties substantially to their original positions and the claimant must restore any benefits received. The court attempts to achieve a solution that is practically just and thus where the value of the property that the claimant has been induced to invest in has fallen the claimant may be expected to share that loss.[48] Secondly, the right to rescind may be lost through delay and affirmation but only after the influence has ceased or the relationship giving rise to the influence has terminated. This was the case in *Allcard v Skinner* (the facts are given at para.13–021) where the claimant waited for a period of almost six years after leaving the religious order before seeking rescission. Thirdly, rescission may be barred where a third party acquires rights in the subject matter of the transaction, bona fide and for value.

Damages as such are not awarded in cases of undue influence but, where rescission is barred, the court has an equitable jurisdiction to award a sum in the nature of damages to take account of what the claimant received for the subject matter and what it was worth at the time of the transaction.[49] In some cases, undue influence is effectively raised as a defence, such as where a third party attempts to enforce an agreement tainted by undue influence against the influenced party. Here, the "remedy" is that the victim of the undue influence is not liable under the contract.[50]

Unconscionable bargains

Is the law on duress and undue influence part of a wider principle of fairness in contract bargaining under which the courts will not enforce transactions that are very unfair or "unconscionable"?

13–032

, Lord Denning M.R. considered this to be the position in his judgment in the case of *Lloyds Bank v Bundy* (the case is discussed at para.13–022). In that case, his Lordship famously asserted that all the instances where the courts intervene to set aside transactions where the parties have not met on equal terms are united by a "single thread"—inequality of bargaining power.[51] He said:

---

[48] See *Cheese v Thomas* [1994] W.L.R. 129. The flexibility that the court has in achieving a just result is illustrated by *O'Sullivan v Management Agency and Music Ltd* [1985] 1 Q.B. 428.

[49] *Mahoney v Purnell* [1996] 3 All E.R. 61.

[50] See the cases discussed at para.13–034.

[51] The transactions embraced by this principle are, according to Lord Denning, duress of goods; unconscionable bargains; undue influence; undue pressure; and salvage agreements. In later cases Lord Denning M.R. was to apply the principle to other transactions, including an exclusion clause in a standard form contract: *Levison v Patent Steam Carpet Cleaning Co Ltd* [1978] Q.B. 69. See also *Credit Lyonnais Bank Nederland NV v Burch* [1997] 1 All E.R. 144, discussed at para.13–039.

"By virtue of it [inequality of bargaining power] English law gives relief to one who, without independent advice, enters into a contract on terms which are very unfair or transfers property for a consideration which is grossly inadequate, when his bargaining power is grievously impaired by reason of his own needs and desires, or by his own ignorance or infirmity, coupled with undue influences or pressures brought to bear on him by or for the benefit of others."

This radical approach, however, did not find favour with the House of Lords. In *National Westminster Bank Plc v Morgan*,[52] Lord Scarman was unable to accept that such a sweeping principle should be introduced by the courts when Parliament had intervened in specific cases, such as the Consumer Credit Act 1974 (as now amended by the Consumer Credit Act 2006). The principle has not been followed by the courts, although some have argued that the equitable jurisdiction to set aside "unconscionable bargains" might form the basis of a general doctrine.

13–033   The doctrine of unconscionable bargains derives from *Fry v Lane*[53] where it was held that the court has an equitable jurisdiction to set a contract aside if the transaction is unconscionable where three elements are satisfied. A purchase must have been made from (i) a "poor and ignorant person"; (ii) at a considerable undervalue; and (iii) the vendor must not have had any independent advice. In *Cresswell v Potter*[54] Megarry J. applied the doctrine to a post office telephonist who was held to be "poor and ignorant" as she was a member of the lower income group and less highly educated. The claimant had conveyed her share in the matrimonial home to her husband, whom she had left, in exchange for being released from her liability under the mortgage. The sale was at an undervalue because the house was worth substantially more than the amount of the mortgage. Although the courts have shown some flexibility in interpreting the concept of "poor and ignorant", the equity is difficult to establish as there must be evidence of impropriety going beyond mere unfairness. The doctrine has not expanded and it appears to be destined for a limited role. The courts have other powers to strike at unfair bargains in limited situations. Thus a "penalty" clause is invalid (see para.16–045) and at common law the courts have the power to hold that agreements that are an unreasonable restraint of trade are unenforceable—a good example is *Schroeder Music Publishing Co v Macaulay*.[55] Given the absence of a general doctrine of unconscionability in English law,[56] Parliament has intervened in a piecemeal fashion, most notably with the Unfair Contract Terms Act 1977 (see para.7–038) which regulates clauses excluding or restricting liability and the Unfair Terms in Consumer Contracts Regulations 1999 (see para.7–064) which regulate unfair terms by imposing a requirement of good faith. But the regulations apply only to consumer transactions and do not control the fairness of the contract as a whole or the adequacy of the price or remuneration as against the goods or services supplied. This is precisely the area where a transaction may be unconscionable.

UNDUE INFLUENCE AND THIRD PARTIES

13–034   Suppose that X enters into a contract with Y where X is under the undue influence of Z. As Z is not a party to the transaction, under the privity rule, the transaction between X and Y would

---

[52] [1985] A.C. 686. The case is discussed at para.13–024.
[53] (1888) 40 Ch. D. 312.
[54] [1978] 1 W.L.R. 225. See also *Watkin v Watson-Smith* (1986) The Times, July 3.
[55] [1974] 1 W.L.R. 1308. The case is discussed at para.15–018.
[56] This is in contrast to other common law jurisdictions, such as the United States and Australia; as to the latter, see *Commercial Bank of Australia Ltd v Amadio* (1983) 151 C.L.R. 447.

not be affected. This may be unsatisfactory where Y is aware of the possibility of undue influence, actual or presumed, exercised by Z, or of some other legal wrong, e.g. misrepresentation.

We have already seen in this chapter that many cases of undue influence coming before the courts involve wives who guarantee their husband's business debts with a lending institution such as a bank. In *National Westminster Bank Plc v Morgan* (see para.13–024) the action was brought by the bank against Mrs Morgan and she argued, unsuccessfully, that the transaction whereby she guaranteed her husband's business debts was voidable on the grounds of undue influence exercised by the bank manager over herself. The type of case we are now concerned with is one where the husband may be exerting undue influence over the wife to sign the guarantee. The question is, how far should this affect the rights of the bank to enforce the transaction? If the bank is aware of the influence, or may be deemed from the circumstances to be aware of it, should the wife be able to set the transaction aside so that it is unenforceable against her? Of course, this problem does not just arise in husband and wife cases nor is it confined to contracts of guarantee, but it has proved difficult for the courts because it involves a delicate balancing exercise. On the one side there is the need to protect a wife against undue influence exerted by her husband; on the other, there is the need for the bank to be able to secure its lending with reasonable confidence. If banks are unwilling to lend money in such circumstances, this would have an adverse effects on small businesses and on the economy as a whole.

Prior to the decision of the House of Lords in *Barclays Bank Plc v O'Brien*[57] there was considerable uncertainty as to how the law should deal with the technical problem of privity mentioned above. The *O'Brien* case arrived at a novel solution based on the doctrine of notice and sought to lay down some guidelines as to how such cases should be approached by the courts. However, the conflicting approaches in subsequent cases as to how this guidance should be applied meant that it was not too long before the issue was before the House of Lords once more, in the case of *Royal Bank of Scotland Plc v Etridge (No 2)*.[58] We have already considered in this chapter the impact of that case on the doctrine of undue influence generally and must now consider the way in which *Etridge* has restated the law relating to third party undue influence cases. Before considering that ruling a useful starting point will be the case of *O'Brien*.

Barclays Bank Plc v O'Brien

The facts of the case were that Mr O'Brien, a chartered accountant with an interest in a   **13–035** company, persuaded his wife to sign a guarantee relating to the company's bank overdraft, using the matrimonial home as security. Mr O'Brien had falsely represented to his wife that the security was limited to £60,000 but in fact the amount was £130,000. In breach of the instructions of a superior official, the bank representative who dealt with the matter failed to explain the transaction to Mrs O'Brien or suggest that she took independent legal advice. When the papers were presented to Mrs O'Brien for signature, she did not read them, and signed them where she was asked. She was not given a copy of the documents. Unfortunately, the company did not prosper and fell further into debt. When the bank sought to enforce the security, Mrs O'Brien argued that she had signed under the undue influence of her husband, and because of his

[57] [1994] 1 A.C. 180.
[58] [2002] 2 A.C. 773.

misrepresentation, her liability should not exceed the sum of £60,000. The Court of Appeal held that the husband had not exercised undue influence—Mrs O'Brien was an intelligent and independent-minded woman—but the court found for her on the ground of misrepresentation and held that the guarantee was not enforceable beyond £60,000. On appeal to the House of Lords, it was accepted that although the case turned on misrepresentation, the principles involved would apply equally to undue influence had it been found.

The House of Lords held that Mrs O'Brien was entitled to set aside the legal charge on the matrimonial home. She had been misled by Mr O'Brien and had signed the documents without receiving proper advice from the bank about the risks of the transaction or being recommended to take independent legal advice. The basis of the Lords' decision depended upon an application of the doctrine of notice. Before considering that decision it will be useful to consider how this type of case had been dealt with by the courts prior to *O'Brien*.

Agency and special equity

13–036   There were two approaches pre-*O'Brien*; agency, and the so-called "special equity" of wives.

Under the agency device, the husband was treated as agent for the creditor bank in obtaining the signature of the wife.[59] This meant that the creditor, as principal, by entrusting the husband as agent to obtain the wife's signature could be in no better than the husband himself when it came to enforcing the guarantee against the wife. Thus the principal would be tainted by any legal wrongs (such as the exercise of undue influence) committed by its agent. This analysis allows the doctrine of privity to be neatly side-stepped but ultimately it smacks of an artificial device without reference to whether there really was an intention to appoint the debtor as agent.[60]

Under the special equity doctrine, wives who provided security for their husbands' debts fell into a protected class of guarantor and the transaction could be set aside even if the bank was unaware of any undue influence (or misrepresentation) committed by the husband in procuring the signature of the wife. The equity placed an obligation on the creditor, who was taken to be aware of the risk of undue influence, to ensure that the wife understood the nature of the transaction and was advised to seek independent advice. This was the basis upon which the Court of Appeal found in favour of Mrs O'Brien. The doctrine applied by the Court of Appeal was based on an acknowledgment that, even in modern society, many wives place confidence and trust in their husbands when it comes to business matters. There was a limitation on this principle in that it applied only to married women. What of other cohabiting couples, e.g. an unmarried heterosexual couple or same sex partners?

The doctrine of notice

13–037   As mentioned above, the decision of the House of Lords in *O'Brien* rested upon the doctrine of notice. Giving the main speech of the House in a unanimous decision Lord Browne-Wilkinson considered that in certain circumstances creditors should be put on inquiry where a wife offers to stand surety for her husband's debts. This was where:

---

[59] *King's North Trust v Bell Ltd* [1986] 1 W.L.R. 119. See also *Coldunell Ltd v Gallon* [1986] Q.B. 1184.
[60] As recognised by Scott L.J. in the Court of Appeal in *O'Brien*.

(a)   The transaction on its face is not to the financial advantage of the wife; and
(b)   There is a substantial risk in transactions of that kind that, in procuring the wife to act as surety, the husband has committed a legal or equitable wrong that entitles the wife to set aside the transaction.

His Lordship considered that the creditor who is put in inquiry in this way must take reasonable steps to ensure that the wife's agreement to stand surety has been properly obtained—if they fail to do this, they will have constructive notice of the wife's rights to set aside the transaction on the basis of misrepresentation or undue influence. Lord Browne-Wilkinson considered that the same principles should apply to all other cases where there is an emotional relationship between cohabitees. He said:

> "The 'tenderness' shown by the law to married women is not based on the marriage ceremony but reflects the underlying risk of one cohabitee exploiting the emotional involvement and trust of the other. Now that unmarried cohabitation, whether heterosexual or homosexual, is widespread in our society, the law should recognise this. Legal wives are not the only group which are now exposed to the emotional pressure of cohabitation."

His Lordship therefore considered that if (but only if) the creditor is aware that the guarantor is cohabiting with the debtor, the same principles should apply as apply to married couples. Indeed, in any case where the creditor is aware that the guarantor reposes trust and confidence in the debtor in relation to their financial affairs, the creditor is put on inquiry—his Lordship cited with approval the case of *Avon Finance Co Ltd v Bridger*[61] where a son persuaded his elderly parent to stand surety for his debts by means of a misrepresentation. As we shall see, the relationships covered by the doctrine of notice were further widened by the House of Lords in *Etridge* (see para.13–040).

According to the House of Lords in *O'Brien* it seems that to avoid being fixed with constructive notice, the creditor must take reasonable steps to be satisfied that the guarantor entered the transaction freely and with knowledge of the true facts. They may do this by: **13–038**

(i)   Warning the surety (not in the presence of the debtor) of the amount of the potential liability, and the risks involved; and
(ii) Advising the surety to take independent legal advice.

(In *Etridge*, further and more detailed guidance was provided by the House of Lords as to how lenders may avoid being fixed by constructive notice: this is discussed at para.13–041. It supersedes the *O'Brien* guidance in cases decided after the judgment in *Etridge* was handed down).

Barclays Bank Plc v O'Brien may be contrasted with another House of Lords' decision, decided at the same time, involving actual undue influence exercised by a husband over his wife; *CIBC Mortgages Plc v Pitt*.[62] Mr and Mrs Pitt obtained a loan of £150,000 secured by a charge on the matrimonial home, having told the claimant lenders on the application form that the money was required to buy a holiday home. Mrs Pitt did not read the documents, was unaware of the sum being borrowed and received no independent advice about the nature of the transaction. In fact, Mr Pitt used the money to speculate on the stock market but he later found himself unable to repay the mortgage and the claimants sought possession of the matrimonial home.

---

[61] [1985] 2 All E.R. 281. The facts are given at para.12–043.
[62] [1994] 1 A.C. 200. See also *Chater v Mortgage Agency Services Number Two Ltd* [2003] EWCA Civ 490.

Taking an approach based on notice, the House held that they could enforce the charge against the defendant Mrs Pitt. Although her husband had exercised actual undue influence over Mrs Pitt, the claimants were not affected by this as they had no actual knowledge of the undue influence. The claimants were not regarded as having constructive notice as to the creditor it would appear straightforward—simply a "normal advance to a husband and wife for their joint benefit". Thus they were not required to make further inquiries and could rely on what was stated on the loan application form. A joint advance by way of loan could be distinguished from a guarantee because, on its face, the latter is not to the wife's benefit and there is not only the possibility, but an increased risk, of undue influence having been exercised.

The House of Lords in *O'Brien* laid down clear guidance on the procedures that the lending institution should take in order to avoid being fixed with constructive notice in surety cases where there is a risk of undue influence. In fact, such procedures were not uncommon in the banking industry before the case was decided. It may be recalled that, had the bank in the *O'Brien* case followed their own recommended practice the outcome of the case might well have been different. But in some of the cases which followed *O'Brien* there was some weakening of the guidelines laid down by Lord Browne-Wilkinson in that case. Indications were given at the level of the Court of Appeal that the *O'Brien* guidelines did not need to be applied mechanically and the advice given need not be exhaustive. Moreover, it was held that banks need not be concerned with the independence of solicitors and could assume that they would give proper advice.[63] The effect of these decisions was to shift the responsibility onto solicitors, particularly since the banks themselves were reluctant to give advice for fear of liability for misrepresentation. There was also uncertainty brought about by conflicting decisions.[64]

13–039   In general it became more difficult for guarantors to establish that surety transactions were affected by undue influence. However, in a case where the undue influence was exercised by an employer over an employee, *Credit Lyonnais Bank Nederland NV v Burch*,[65] the court leaned the other way. In this case a young employee agreed, at her employer's request, to put up her own flat, worth £100,000, as security for the unlimited liabilities of the employer's company. The employee was advised by the bank on several occasions to obtain independent legal advice but did not do so. The Court of Appeal, however, considered that the transaction was so unconscionable that the bank could not claim to have taken reasonable steps to avoid being fixed with constructive notice, and the transaction was set aside. The bank knew of a relationship from which undue influence could be inferred—it should therefore have ensured the employee obtained legal advice and explained to her the full extent of the transaction.

Royal Bank of Scotland Plc v Etridge (No 2)

13–040   The *Etridge* case[66] involved eight conjoined appeals raising issues relating to undue influence and constructive notice in the context of loans secured on matrimonial homes. The House of Lords provided practical guidance as to the approach to be taken by lenders and legal advisors in such cases. In the ensuing discussion we will refer to "wives", "husbands" and "banks" (as did their Lordships in referring to the typical type of transaction) but the law applies equally to other parties in like position.

---

[63]   *Massey v Midland Bank Plc* [1995] 1 All E.R. 929; and *Banco Exterior Internacional v Mann* [1995] 1 All E.R. 936.
[64]   Cf *Barclays Bank Plc v Thomson* [1997] 4 All E.R. 816; and *Royal Bank of Scotland Plc v Etridge* [1997] 3 All E.R. 628.
[65]   [1997] 1 All E.R. 144.
[66]   [2002] 2 A.C. 773.

Balancing the interests of the parties

Lord Bingham began his speech by observing that the transactions giving rise to the appeals **13–041**
were "commonplace but of great social and economic importance". It was important that wives
should not place at risk their interest in the family home by securing their husbands' debts
without fully appreciating the nature and effect of the proposed transaction. It was a decision
for the wife alone. It was also important that lenders should feel able to advance money, in the
normal type of case, on the security offered by the wife with reasonable confidence that the
transaction will be enforceable should the need arise. Both parties should be afforded a measure
of protection by the law. The law could indicate minimum requirements which should, if met,
reduce the risk of error, misunderstanding or mishap. His Lordship added that the "paramount
need in this field is that these minimum requirements should be clear, simple and practicably
operable". The first issue was to establish when the bank would be put on inquiry.

Non-commercial relationships

Lord Nicholls made it clear that the bank is put on inquiry whenever a wife stands as surety for **13–042**
her husband's debts. The position is the same in the case of other couples, of whatever sexual
orientation, assuming that the bank is aware of the relationship. But his Lordship observed that
the types of relationships in which undue influence could arise were infinitely various and went
beyond sexual or family relationships to include, e.g. employment relationships as in *Credit
Lyonnais Bank v Burch* (to which reference was made above). Lord Nicholls therefore put
forward a "wider principle" whereby the bank would be put on inquiry in all cases where the
relationship between the surety and the debtor is "non-commercial".[67] He did not think there
could be a rational cut-off point with some relationships subject to the *O'Brien* principle and
others not. He felt that the so-called wider principle was the only way forward and he thought
that it was a modest burden for the lending institutions.

The steps to be taken by the lender when put on inquiry

Lord Nicholls considered that the furthest a bank could be expected to go when put on inquiry **13–043**
is to take *reasonable steps* to satisfy itself that the wife has had brought home to her the practical implications of the proposed transaction. His Lordship recognised that this did not wholly
eliminate the risk of undue influence or misrepresentation but it did mean that the wife would
enter the transaction with her "eyes open" as far as the basic elements of the transaction were
concerned. The suggestion of Lord Browne-Wikinson in *O'Brien* that the bank's officials
should have a private meeting with the guarantor to explain the transaction and its implications
was not followed in *Etridge*. This was in deference to the reasonable concerns of the banking
industry that lengthy litigation might arise if there were disputes as to what was actually said at
such a meeting. However, a suitable alternative means of communicating the information to the
wife had to be used and Lord Nicholls identified four stages in the process:

First, the bank should take steps to check directly the name of the solicitor who is to act for
her, by communicating directly with the wife and informing her that, for its own protection, it

---

[67] The principle was applied in *First National Bank Plc v Achampong* [2003] EWCA Civ 487.

will need confirmation by the solicitor that the transaction and its implications have been fully explained to her. The wife should also be informed that the solicitor may be the same solicitor as is acting for the husband in the transaction. The bank should not proceed unless the wife has responded appropriately to this initial communication from the bank. Secondly, the bank must provide the nominated solicitor with the financial information necessary to advise the wife. As this information is confidential, the husband's consent will be required to disclose it and without that consent, the transaction must not proceed. Thirdly, if the bank believes or suspects that the wife has been misled by her husband or is not acting under her own free will, it must inform the wife's solicitor. Fourthly, the bank must obtain from the solicitor a written confirmation that the wife has been advised accordingly.

13–044   *The content of the legal advice*

The solicitor's discussion with the wife should take place face-to-face and in the absence of the husband. The solicitor will need to explain the purpose for which he or she has become involved, that is, that the bank will rely on the solicitor's involvement to counter suggestions of impropriety. The solicitor will need to confirm that the wife wishes him or her to act for her and to receive advice on the legal and practical implications. Concern at the poor quality of advice given to such clients in past transactions led the House to prescribe a "core minimum" of such advice. Lord Nicholls summarised this in four points:

(1) The solicitor will need to explain to the wife the nature of the documents and the practical consequences, such as the loss of her home or bankruptcy, if she signs.

(2) The solicitor will need to point out the seriousness of the risks involved. This should cover: the purpose of the facility; its extent and principal terms; the bank's ability to vary the terms without reference to the wife; and whether the married couple has other assets from which repayment might be made.

(3) The solicitor should make it clear that the wife has a choice and the decision to sign the guarantee is hers and hers alone.

(4) The solicitor should check whether the wife wishes to proceed, for example by asking her whether further negotiation on her behalf is necessary, or by writing to the bank to confirm that the advice has been given. The solicitor should not give any confirmation to the bank without the wife's authority.

It should be noted, however, that as a general rule it is not for the solicitor to veto the transaction except in an exceptional case "where it is glaringly obvious that the wife is being grievously wronged".[68] Thus ordinarily the bank may rely upon confirmation by a solicitor that the wife has been given appropriate advice. Of course, if the bank knows that the solicitor has not properly advised the wife it would not be reasonable for the bank to rely on that confirmation. As a general rule, if there are deficiencies in the advice given by the solicitor that will be a matter between the wife and the solicitor—the solicitor is not to be regarded as acting as an agent for the bank. The guidance contained in the *Etridge* decision as to how lenders may avoid constructive notice arising apply to transactions carried out after the date of the House of

---

[68] The employer-employee case of *Credit Lyonnais Bank v Burch* (discussed at para.13–039) is such an example of an exceptional case.

Lords' decision in the case. Transactions entered into prior to *Etridge* are subject to the *O'Brien* rules.

Duress and undue influence: conclusion

There is no doubt that duress and undue influence is an area of the law of contract that has seen **13–045** considerable development in recent times, principally with the expansion of economic duress and the efforts of the House of Lords to grapple with the problems of husband and wife surety cases where the family home is put up as security. It remains to be seen whether *Etridge* has struck the right balance in this type of case. In fact, the *Etridge* solution is to shift the burden from the bank to the solicitor who is instructed to advise the wife—the balance has therefore been struck in the creditor's favour. The bank has only to take "reasonable steps" and can ordinarily rely on the solicitor's confirmation regarding the advice. Moreover, the solicitor does not need to be wholly independent and can be acting for both husband and wife. Lord Nicholls considered that the advantages of the wife having her own solicitor would be outweighed by the expense involved in a couple instructing two solicitors. Solicitors concerned about a conflict of interest could withdraw from the transaction.

Further reading

Atiyah, *Economic Duress and the Overborne Will* (1982) 98 L.Q.R. 197.
Birks and Chin, 'On the Nature of Undue Influence', in *Good Faith and Fault in Contract Law* (Oxford: Clarendon Press, 1995).
O'Sullivan, Developing *O'Brien* (2002) 118 L.Q.R. 337.
Thompson, *Wives, Sureties and Banks* (2002) Conv. 174.

Chapter 14

ILLEGALITY

It will perhaps not come as too much of a surprise to learn that the courts, as a general propo- **14–001** sition, will not enforce contracts of which the purpose is illegal. The concept of illegality in this context embraces not only agreements that are criminal in intent but those that are, in a wider sense, injurious to society.

In this chapter we shall begin by considering those contracts that are illegal by statute; we shall then consider those that are illegal as being contrary to public policy; and conclude by considering the effects of illegality. Contracts in restraint of trade, which are considered to be prima facie void as being contrary to public policy are, for ease of exposition, considered in the next chapter. We consider first contracts illegal by statute.

STATUTORY ILLEGALITY

A contract may be expressly forbidden by statutory provision—"statute" here includes both **14–002** primary and secondary legislation.[1] Such illegality may be express or implied.

Express illegality

Express illegality is illustrated by *Re Mahmoud and Ispahani*[2] where by delegated legislation **14–003** (the Defence of the Realm regulations) it was forbidden to buy or sell linseed without obtaining a licence. The claimant agreed to sell a consignment of linseed to the defendant who lied and said that he, like the claimant, had the necessary licence. Later, the defendant refused to take delivery and, when sued by the claimant, pleaded that the contract was illegal. The Court of Appeal held that the contract was unenforceable on the grounds of illegality—it made no difference that the claimant was innocent and that he had been deceived by the defendant. The policy of the legislation was to prevent unlicensed trading. Whether the claimant might have proceeded against the defendant on the basis of a fraudulent misrepresentation was left open by the court.

---

[1] *Mohamed v Alaga & Co (A Firm)* [2000] 1 W.L.R. 1815.
[2] [1921] 2 K.B. 716.

Implied illegality

14–004   Where it is alleged that the prohibition is implied, the court has to construe the statute; the question is—was it the object of the legislature to forbid the contract? If it appears that the object of the statute was to protect the public in some way, then it may render the contract impliedly illegal. In *Cope v Rowlands*[3] a statute required that a person who wished to act as stockbroker in the City of London must obtain a licence, or forfeit £25. The claimant did brokerage work for the defendant without a licence. In the absence of an express prohibition in the statute, the contract was held to be impliedly illegal since the object of the licences was to protect the public by excluding undesirable persons from practice. It was a "necessary inference" that contracts concluded by unlicensed brokers were unenforceable on the grounds of illegality.

On the other hand, if the wording of the statute indicates that it was introduced for some administrative purpose and one not directly related to the making of the contract itself, the contract in question may be valid. Thus in the case of *Smith v Mawhood*[4] tobacconists were required by statute to take out a licence and paint their name over their place of business or pay a fine of £200. The claimant, who had not complied with these legal requirements, agreed to sell tobacco products to the defendant who refused to pay for them. When sued for the price, the defendant argued that the contract was illegal. The Court of Exchequer rejected this contention holding that the purpose of the statute was not to invalidate contracts made in such circumstances but to impose a penalty for revenue purposes. The contract was therefore valid and enforceable.

In a later case, *St John Shipping Corporation v Joseph Rank Ltd*,[5] Devlin J. laid down a more precise test for determining the issue of statutory illegality. He said:

> "Two questions are involved. The first – and the one which hitherto has usually settled the matter – is: does the statute mean to prohibit contracts at all? But if this be answered in the affirmative, then one must ask: does this contract belong to the class which the statute intends to prohibit?"

These principles were applied by the Court of Appeal in *Hughes v Asset Managers Plc*[6] where the appellant investors entered into five discretionary management agreements with the respondents, a company dealing in securities. Under these agreements, the sum of £3,000,000 was remitted to the respondents, who invested the money on behalf of the appellants. Four weeks later, on the appellants' instructions, the respondents remitted the proceeds and the uninvested portion to the appellants. In the meantime the market had fallen and the shares were sold at a loss of £1,000,000. The appellants brought summary proceedings under rules of court claiming that the management agreements were void under the Prevention of Fraud (Investments) Act 1958, s.1 in that the persons who executed the agreements on behalf of the respondents did not hold representatives' licences as required by s.1(1)(b) of the Act. It was contended that the agreements were void. The Court of Appeal held that the agreements were not void—the purpose of the Act was to impose sanctions on those who engaged in securities dealings without a licence. It did not forbid contracts made by unlicensed persons and was not directed at these transactions; the public interest was met by the imposition of sanctions on unlicensed dealers.

14–005   A further and instructive illustration is afforded by the case of *Archbolds (Freightage) Ltd v*

[3] (1862) 2 M. & W. 149.
[4] (1845) 1 M. & W. 452.
[5] [1957] 1 Q.B. 267.
[6] [1995] 3 All E.R. 669.

Spanglett Ltd.[7] The Road and Rail Traffic Act 1933 provided that "no person shall use a goods vehicle on a road for the carriage of goods" unless they first obtained a licence entitling them to carry other peoples' goods for reward (an "A" licence); or a licence entitling them to carry their own goods (a "C" licence). The Act further provided that "any person who fails to comply with a condition of a licence held by him shall be guilty of an offence". The defendants, who held only a C licence, agreed with the claimants to carry a consignment of whisky belonging to a third party from London to Leeds, although the claimants were unaware that the defendants did not have an A licence. During the journey the goods were stolen and the claimants sued for damages; the defendants argued, inter alia, that the contract was prohibited by law and therefore unenforceable.

The Court of Appeal held that the claimants could enforce the contract. The contract was neither expressly nor impliedly forbidden by the Act as the legislation was not concerned with contracts to carry goods but with the use of unlicensed vehicles on the road. This could be achieved through criminal sanctions without invalidating the contracts of carriage themselves.

Illegality in performance

Infringement of a statutory provision may render a contract either illegal as formed, i.e. unlawful in its inception, or illegal as performed. In the first case the formation of the contract is forbidden. An example is *Re Mahmoud and Ispahani* (discussed above) where the defendant failed to take out a licence to deal in linseed as required by statute. Such a contract is void and unenforceable, and as we have seen, neither party acquires rights under it. In the second case, the contract is carried out in a way that is prohibited by statute although the formation of the contract is perfectly lawful.   **14-006**

In *Anderson v Daniel*[8] the claimants sold 10 tons of artificial fertiliser to the defendants. It was a statutory requirement that the seller should give the buyer an invoice stating the chemical contents of the fertiliser, but on this occasion the claimants did not give the invoice. When the claimants sued for the price, the defendants argued that as the statute had not been complied with, the contract was illegal. The Court of Appeal agreed. The purpose of the legislation was to protect the purchasers of fertiliser but in this case the claimants had failed to perform the contract in the only way the law allowed it to be performed. Thus where a contract is lawful in its inception but performed illegally the party at fault cannot sue to enforce the contract. Atkin L.J. said:

> "The question of illegality in a contract generally arises in connection with its formation, but it may also arise, as it does here, in connection with its performance. In the former case, where the parties have agreed to do something which is prohibited by Act of Parliament, it is indisputable that the contract is unenforceable by either party. And I think it is equally unenforceable by the offending party where the illegality arises from the fact that the mode of performance adopted by the party performing it is in violation of some statute even though the contract as agreed upon by the parties was capable of being performed in a perfectly legal manner."

There is evidence that the courts take a more benign stance where the innocent party is unaware of the illegality.[9] In *Archbolds (Freightage) Ltd v Spanglett Ltd* (discussed above) the contract   **14-007**

[7] [1961] 1 Q.B. 374.
[8] [1924] 1 K.B. 138.
[9] See further *Wheeler v Quality Deep Trading Ltd* [2005] I.C.R. 265.

was held to be neither expressly nor impliedly illegal by statute but in any event the claimant was unaware that the contract had been performed illegally by the defendants. As Pearce L.J. explained:

> "[N]o case has been cited to us establishing the proposition that where a contract is on the face of it legal and is not forbidden by statute, but must in fact produce illegality by reason of a circumstance known to one party only, it should be held illegal so as to bar the innocent party from relief."

Pearce L.J. felt that such a conclusion would "put a premium on deceit". Nevertheless, his Lordship recognised that the position might differ where both parties knew that the contract could not be carried out without a violation of the law.

In *Ashmore, Benson, Pease & Co Ltd v A V Dawson Ltd*[10] the defendants, road hauliers, agreed to carry two 25 ton tube banks for the claimant company. The claimants' transport manager and his assistant were present when one of the tube banks was loaded onto one of the defendant's lorries to a laden weight of 35 tons. The maximum permitted weight under the Road Traffic Acts was 30 tons. On the journey, the lorry toppled over and the load was damaged. The claimant company sought damages for negligence. The Court of Appeal held that the contract, although lawful in its inception, had been carried out in an unlawful manner to the knowledge of the claimants' servants. Applying *Anderson v Daniel*, the Court of Appeal held that damages were not recoverable.

It is possible that the illegality in the course of performance may be viewed by the court as merely incidental to the contract. This is perhaps another way of formulating the principle discussed above, i.e. that the contract as performed was not one which the statute was intended to prohibit. In *St John Shipping v Joseph Rank Ltd*[11] the master of the claimants' ship took on cargo which caused the vessel's load line to be submerged. This was an offence under the Merchant Shipping (Safety and Load Lines Conventions) Act 1932 and as a result the master of the ship was convicted and fined. The maximum fine under the statute—which had been fixed when the Act was passed in 1932—was by 1955 less than the profit that a ship owner could make by carrying an excess load. The defendants refused to pay part of the freight on their goods which had been carried on the ground that the contract was unenforceable owing to the illegal manner in which it had been performed. Devlin J. held that the payment could be recovered as the contract of carriage was not rendered illegal by the loading infringement. This approach was applied by the Court of Appeal in *Shaw v Groom*[12] where an action by a landlord for arrears of rent did not fail merely because the rent book did not contain all the details required by statute. The court was undoubtedly influenced by the fact that arrears of rent could greatly exceed the maximum fine of £50 for omitting details from the rent book.

Gaming and wagering contracts

14–008   Certain statutes may declare particular types of contract to be "void"—this is not quite the same thing as the statutory prohibitions of contracts discussed above. One of the most notable examples and one which gave rise to some difficult litigation over the years is the recently repealed Gaming Act 1845.

[10]   [1973] 1 W.L.R. 828.
[11]   [1957] 1 Q.B. 267.
[12]   [1970] 2 Q.B. 504.

Under the first limb of s.18 of this statute it was enacted that "all contracts or agreements . . . by way of gaming and wagering, shall be null and void". This meant that a simple wager, or bet, was void ab initio although not strictly illegal. Thus the winner could not sue for the winnings from the loser and if the loser did pay the bet, the money was irrecoverable. But the contracts were not without all legal consequences, thus if the winner cheated, the loser could probably recover back his losses on the ground of fraud; and where bookmakers made overpayments, or payments to the wrong person, the moneys were irrecoverable but the recipient could be guilty of theft if they retained the money with knowledge of the error.

The second limb of s.18 further provided that no suit could be brought or maintained "in any court of law or equity for recovering any sum of money or valuable thing alleged to be won on any wager". It was originally held that this merely repeated the first limb and therefore the loser could be sued if he made a fresh promise supported by fresh consideration to pay the amount of the debt but this was overruled by the House of Lords in *Hill v William Hill (Park Lane) Ltd*[13]. Under the third limb, no action to recover any money "deposited in the hands of any person to abide the event on which any wager shall have been made" could be brought. This was construed by the courts as meaning that there could be no recovery by the winner of the money deposited with a stakeholder—the words did not apparently prevent a party from recovering their own stake before it had been paid over to the winner.[14]

The final limb of s.18 was a provision to ensure that where lawful games or sports were played, the winner would be entitled to any prize even though it consisted of money deposited by the competitors.

14–009 As part of the reform of the regulation gambling, the Gambling Act 2005 repealed s.18 of the Gaming Act 1845, as from September 1, 2007. Under s.335 of the Act, "the fact that a contract relates to gambling shall not prevent its enforcement" (s.335 (1)). This is without prejudice "to any rule of law preventing the enforcement of a contract on the grounds of unlawfulness (other than a rule of law relating specifically to gambling)" (s.335(2)). Thus there is no reason why a gambling contract could not be unenforceable on other grounds, such as wager on the outcome of some illegal act. Powers are given to a Gambling Commission by s.336 to make an order that any contract in relation to a bet is void and "any money paid in relation to the bet . . . shall be repaid to the person who paid it, and repayment may be enforced as a debt due to that person."

CONTRACTS CONTRARY TO PUBLIC POLICY

14–010 Certain contracts are regarded as illegal and void at common law on the grounds that they are contrary to public policy, in the sense of being "injurious to society". It has been recognised for quite some time that this is a controversial proposition since one person's view of what is inimical to social relations may not accord with that of another. And, of course, even assuming that there are commonly accepted norms of public morality, they are likely to change markedly over the course of time.

It is not open to a judge to strike down a contract merely because they personally think that it is not in the public interest. What is or is not in the public interest is primarily a matter for

[13] [1949] A.C. 580.
[14] *Diggle v Higgs* (1877) 2 Ex. D. 422.

Parliament rather than the judiciary. However, the court can interfere where the contract falls under one of the judicially established heads of public policy and, to that extent, the doctrine of public policy is limited by precedent. The traditional view is that, although it is not open to the courts to invent new heads of public policy, the existing categories can be extended to meet new situations. But this proposition has been doubted—there does not seem to be any compelling reason why new categories could not be established to meet new and possibly unforeseeable threats to society.

In any event, many of the existing heads of public policy involve criminal or fraudulent conspiracies of one form or another. Such contracts would not be tolerated in any rational legal system. The various heads of public policy will now be considered.

Contracts to commit a legal wrong

14–011   A contract will be illegal if its object, whether direct or indirect, is the commission of an act that is criminal, tortious or involves a fraud upon a third party. Such contracts may also, of course, amount to a criminal conspiracy.

So far as a criminal objective is concerned, the old case of *Everet v Williams*[15] is particularly instructive. Two highwaymen agreed to ambush a coach and share their ill-gotten gains equally. When one of them refused to honour this obligation, the other sued—the court held that the contract was unenforceable. Not only were counsel who signed the pleading required to pay costs, but the solicitors were fined and the parties to the action suffered the death penalty. An agreement to publish a libel (a tortious act) was held to be illegal in *Apthorp v Neville & Co*[16] and was therefore unenforceable, as was a contract defraud third parties by "rigging the market"; i.e. offering inflated prices for shares in a particular company.[17]

There is a rule of public policy that no person, or their estate, should benefit from committing a crime. Thus in *Beresford v Royal Insurance Co*[18] a man who had taken out life insurance policies but could not keep up the payments shot himself. Although the contract contained no clause invalidating the policy on the grounds of suicide, the executors' action to recover the sum insured failed. As suicide was at the time a criminal offence,[19] the Court of Appeal declined to uphold a contract allowing a criminal or his relatives to benefit from an illegal act. Interestingly, it seems that as the contract of insurance was not itself illegal, thus if the deceased had in his lifetime assigned the policy and then committed suicide, his assignees would have been entitled to the benefit of the policy.

14–012   Similarly, in *Gray v Barr*[20] B shot and involuntarily killed his wife's lover in the course of a violent assault with a loaded weapon. He had been acquitted of manslaughter by the criminal court, but in civil proceedings he was held liable to pay damages to the victim's widow. B admitted liability and claimed an indemnity under an insurance policy covering liability to pay damages for personal injury. In the view of the Court of Appeal, B's actions effectively amounted to manslaughter and therefore his claim failed on public policy grounds. There is a clear exception to this rule in the law of motor insurance—in *Tinline v White Cross Insurance*

---

[15] (1725) Unreported. See also *Allen v Rescous* (1676) 2 Lev. 174; and *Dann v Curzon* [1911] 104 L.T. 66.
[16] (1907) 23 T.L.R. 575.
[17] *Scott v Brown, Doering, McNab & Co* [1892] 2 Q.B. 724.
[18] [1937] 2 K.B. 197.
[19] It ceased to be so by virtue of s.1 of the Suicide Act 1961.
[20] [1970] 2 Q.B. 626, affirmed [1971] 2 Q.B. 554.

Association Ltd[21] a driver killed a pedestrian when driving with criminal negligence and was convicted of manslaughter. He was insured against liability for accidental personal injury and successfully recovered from the insurers the compensation he had to pay the deceased. It seems that the motorist only has this right where the offence is committed negligently rather than deliberately.[22]

Any agreement intended by the parties, or either of them, to defraud the national or local revenue will be contrary to public policy. Thus in *Napier v National Business Agency Ltd*[23] the defendants employed the claimant to work as a secretary at a wage of £13 per week plus expenses of £6 per week. Both parties knew that the claimant's expenses would never amount to £6 per week and they never in fact exceeded £1 per week. The £13 per week sum had tax deducted which was remitted to the revenue, but the expenses were reimbursed without deduction of tax. The claimant was summarily dismissed and sought payment of £13 in lieu of notice. It was held that the claim failed—the agreement was illegal as being contrary to public policy.

Similarly, in *Alexander v Rayson*[24] R agreed to rent an apartment in Piccadilly from A at a rent of £1,200. The contract was drawn up in two documents—in the first, R agreed to pay £450 for the flat and certain services; in the second, she agreed to pay £750 for the same services plus the use of a refrigerator. A's objective in having two documents was to defraud the local rating authority by showing them the first document only and misleading them as to the rental value. This came to light when a dispute arose between R and A and A sued for money due under the agreement. R, who had originally been unaware of the alleged fraud, argued that the agreement was illegal and unenforceable. The Court of Appeal agreed, holding that unless A could disprove the allegation, he could recover nothing. It should be noted that there was nothing objectionable about the two documents in themselves, and had the claimant not intended to exploit them for an illegal purpose, the transaction would have been perfectly valid.

Contracts prejudicial to justice

Contracts may be illegal where, for example, they involve a criminal conspiracy such as where a person offers another money to give perjured testimony at a trial; or where an agreement has the effect of stifling a prosecution for a public offence.   **14–013**

However, if the offence in question is both a crime and a tort (such as, e.g. assault) and the claimant may choose between a criminal and civil remedy, any compromise agreement will be valid.[25] But this may not be the case where the offence in question is of public concern.

In *Keir v Leeman*[26] the claimant intended to prosecute seven defendants for riot and assault on a constable who was levying execution on the claimant's behalf. The claimant told them he would drop the charges if they would pay off the debt the subject matter of the writ of execution.

[21] [1921] 3 K.B. 327.
[22] *Gardner v Moore* [1984] A.C. 548.
[23] 1951] 2 All E.R. 264. See also *Miller v Karlinski* (1945) 62 T.L.R. 85.
[24] [1936] 1 K.B. 169. See *21st Century Logistic Solutions Ltd (in Liquidation) v Madysen Ltd* [2004] 2 Lloyd's Rep. 92 where a contract for the sale of goods was held to be valid even though the seller was a company formed to evade Value Added Tax. The seller's fraudulent intention was too remote from the contract—the fraud would only be committed at the end of the accounting period when the seller failed to account for VAT.
[25] *Fisher & Co v Apollinaris Co* (1875) 10 Ch. App. 297 (trade mark offence).
[26] (1846) 9 Q.B. 371.

The defendants agreed and since no evidence was given against them, they were acquitted. They did not honour their promise and so the claimant sued to recover the money. The action failed and the contract was held to be illegal—the offence here was not confined to personal injury and involved riot, a matter of public concern.

Cases such as *Keir v Leeman* should now be read in the light of the Criminal Law Act 1967 which introduced a new offence of concealing an arrestable offence. This offence is not committed where the only consideration for withholding the information which may lead to the conviction of the offender is the making good of the loss or injury caused by the offence (s.5(1)). It is possible that such contracts are enforceable.

14–014　　A contract may be contrary to public policy and void if it purports to deprive the courts of a jurisdiction which they otherwise would have. This means that the parties cannot make some body other than the courts the final arbiter on points of law. As Denning L.J. stated in *Lee v Showmen's Guild of Great Britain*:[27]

> "If the parties should seek, by agreement, to take the law out of the hands of the courts and put it into the hands of a private individual, without any recourse to the courts in cases of error of law, then the agreement is to that extent contrary to public policy and void."

The principle that the parties cannot by contract oust the jurisdiction of the courts is illustrated by the case of *Baker v Jones*.[28] An amateur weightlifters association was formed to promote the sport and control its affairs. Under the rules of the association, the governance of the organisation was vested in a central council which had the sole power to interpret the rules of the association. The decisions of the council, under the rules, were final, and the rules formed a contract between association members. A dispute arose between the members which gave rise to libel actions against certain council members. The council authorised payments to solicitors out of association funds to finance legal costs. The claimant sought a declaration that the use of the funds for this particular purpose was improper. The court granted the declaration. Placing reliance on the dictum of Denning L.J. in *Lee v Showmen's Guild*, the court held that, first, giving the association's central council the sole power to interpret the rules was contrary to public policy and void as it ousted the jurisdiction of the courts. Only the court had the power to assess the legal validity of the council's interpretation of the rules, to see whether it was correct in law. Secondly, the rules of the association did not authorise the council to use association funds in the manner the council proposed.

Contracts purporting to oust the jurisdiction of the courts must be distinguished from those transactions expressed to be binding in honour only—the so-called "gentleman's agreement" which provides that the contract in question shall not be enforced in any court. The leading case on such agreements is *Rose & Frank Co v J R Crompton & Brothers Ltd* discussed at para.3–020. Whereas the parties to a contract would appear to be at liberty to specify that their contract shall not be subjected to the jurisdiction of the courts, if they do intend legal relations they cannot substitute some body other than the courts to test the legality of the transaction.

14–015　　Clauses providing that the parties to a contract shall resort to arbitration before going to court are valid and were upheld by the House of Lords in *Scott v Averay*.[29] Here an insurance policy provided that the insured should not be entitled to maintain any action on the contract

---

[27] [1952] 2 Q.B. 329.
[28] [1954] 1 W.L.R. 1005.
[29] (1855) 5 H.L. Cas. 811.

"until the matters in dispute shall have been referred to and decided by arbitrators". The clause was held to be valid—obtaining the arbitrator's decision was a condition precedent of the right of the insured to bring an action in the courts. It did not oust the jurisdiction of the courts. A party who disregards such a clause and commences a court action without first going to arbitration will be liable at common law in damages to the other party[30] and the court can stay the action.[31]

Arbitration proceedings are now regulated by the Arbitration Act 1996. The Act provides for an appeal to the courts in order to challenge an arbitral award on the grounds of some serious illegality affecting the tribunal, the proceedings or the award (s.68(1) and (2)). An appeal may also be made to the court on a point of law arising out of arbtitration proceedings but only with the agreement of all parties or with the leave of the court (s.69(2)) on restrictive criteria set out in s.69(3) of the Act.

A further exception to the general rule at common law regarding the ousting of the jurisdiction of the courts is the maintenance agreement. A husband may promise to pay his wife an allowance in return for the wife undertaking not to apply to the courts for maintenance. In *Hyman v Hyman*[32] the House of Lords held that such an agreement was void as being contrary to public policy and there was nothing to prevent the wife going to court for maintenance. Whereas that continues to be the case, the wife can now (under the Matrimonial Causes Act 1973, s.34) sue the husband for the promised allowance.

Sexually immoral contracts

At common law a contract promoting sexual immorality is contrary to public policy. In *Benyon v Nettlefold*[33] a gentleman executed a deed in favour of a Miss Nettlefold to pay her the sum of £200 per annum if she would co-habit with him as his wife without marrying. The deed was to be held unenforceable on her part as a contract promoting immorality and offending against public policy.

14–016

The rule extends to contracts indirectly promoting sexual immorality. In *Pearce v Brooks*[34] the claimants entered into a contract to supply the defendant, whom they knew to be a prostitute, with a new carriage "of intriguing design". The defendant intended to use the carriage in the course of her vocation and the court was satisfied that the claimants understood this. The claimants' action to recover payment failed—the contract was held to be illegal. This case was applied in *Upfill v Wright*[35] where a flat was let to the defendant for the purposes of enabling her to be visited by a man whose mistress she was and to engage in sexual intercourse with him there. Darling J. held that the landlord, who knew of the circumstances, could not recover the rent. The judge was in no doubt "that fornication is sinful and immoral" and the contract was therefore illegal.

Attitudes to sexual morality have changed since the Edwardian era (when *Upfill v Wright* was decided), particularly so in the late twentieth and early twenty-first centuries. This shift in public

---

[30] *Doleman & Sons v Ossett Corpn* [1912] 3 K.B. 257.
[31] *Channel Tunnel Group Ltd v Balfour Beatty Construction Ltd* [1993] A.C. 334.
[32] [1929] A.C. 601.
[33] (1850) 3 Mac. & G. 94.
[34] (1866) L.R. 1 Ex. 213.
[35] [1911] 1 K.B. 506.

attitudes is reflected in the decision of the Court of Appeal in *Armhouse Lee Ltd v Chappell*[36] where the defendants were providers of three types of service: pre-recorded erotic stories played to customers over the telephone; live sex chat with girls over the telephone; and the arrangement of sex dating. The defendants placed advertisements in the claimants' pornographic magazines but, owing to changes in the code of practice for telephonic services, the defendants' business became less profitable and they discontinued paying the claimants. The claimants sought to recover payment. The defendants argued that the services they provided were so immoral or illegal that they were not liable to pay, as the contract was unenforceable as being contrary to public policy.

14–017   The Court of Appeal held that the contract was enforceable and considered that the defendants' case was "hypocrisy writ large". A contract for the advertising of such services is not contrary to public policy—the women involved were not prostitutes nor could the advertisements be said to be obscene, nor was there any conspiracy to corrupt public morality. There was "no generally accepted moral code" that condemned such services, indeed they were not only condoned by society but a regulatory body (ICSTS) had been set up to regulate them. The court indicated that it was not for judges exercising civil jurisdiction to "impose their own moral attitudes" given that the area was the province of the criminal law. Thus, unless a criminal offence is involved, it may be that sexually immoral contracts are no longer unenforceable.

It should also be noted that another modern tendency is for the courts to look benignly on agreements which contemplate stable extra-marital relations. Thus in *Somma v Hazlehurst*[37] an unmarried couple occupied a room under a licence agreement but the agreement was not struck down on public policy grounds.

Contracts prejudicial to marriage

14–018   The preservation of the status of marriage has long been regarded by the courts as a matter of public policy.

Agreements in restraint of marriage

14–019   Generally, agreements which have the effect of restraining a person's freedom to marry whomsoever they wish will be void. In *Lowe v Peers*[38] Catherine Lowe was a widow and the defendant executed a deed in her favour promising to pay her £1,000 if he married anyone besides Catherine. Some years later he did marry another woman but Catherine's action to recover the £1,000 failed. The contract was in restraint of marriage and therefore void.

It might have been different if the contract had imposed a similar restriction on the claimant. In any event an engagement to marry is no longer a binding contract—the action of breach of promise to marry was abolished by s.1 of the Law Reform (Miscellaneous Provisions) Act 1970. The arrangement in *Lowe v Peers*, unlike an engagement, was not reciprocal.

---

[36] (1996) *The Times*, August 7.
[37] [1979] 1 W.L.R. 1014.
[38] (1786) 4 Burr. 2225.

Marriage brokage contracts

A marriage brokage contract is one by which a person promises in return for consideration to   **14–020**
procure the marriage of another. Thus A may agree with B to procure the marriage of B to C;
or A may agree to find a spouse, any spouse, for B.

In *Hermann v Charlesworth*[39] the defendant advertised in his newspaper ("The Matrimonial
Post and Fashionable Marriage Advertiser") that he would arrange introductions with a view
to marriage. The claimant, who was looking for a husband, signed a contract under which
she paid £52, £47 being returnable if an engagement or marriage took place within nine
months. She was to pay a further £250 if a marriage took place following the introductions.
After nine months had elapsed, and after being introduced to several gentlemen, no marriage
had taken place and so the claimant sought the return of her money. The Court of Appeal
held that the transaction was void as being contrary to public policy. Mathew L.J. explained
that the reason for the court discountenancing such contracts was "to prevent reckless and
unsuitable marriages". It was held that the claimant was able to recover the money she had
paid on the basis of a total failure of consideration (see para.17–019) as no marriage had
taken place.

Contracts entered into by dating and introductions agencies are not caught by the above rule
providing there is no obligation to procure a marriage. But is this really a valid distinction? The
rationale for invalidating marriage brokage contracts alluded to by Mathew J. in *Hermann v
Charlesworth* looks rather obsolete in modern conditions. It is difficult to see what harm would
be caused to the public if such transactions were valid.

Agreements between spouses for future separation

Public policy seeks to preserve the sanctity of marriage. Thus, a contract providing for a pos-   **14–021**
sible future separation will be contrary to public policy and void since it may induce the parties
to be less than fully committed to the marriage.[40] A contract providing for the immediate separation of spouses is valid and enforceable if an immediate separation takes place,[41] except where
the parties have been separated and then resume cohabitation. In such a case, an agreement
relating to a renewed separation will be valid.[42]

Contracts prejudicial to the security of the state   14–022

Unsurprisingly, at common law (and also by virtue of the Trading with the Enemy Act 1939)
contracts involving commercial intercourse with a person voluntarily residing in enemy terri-
tory in time of war are illegal unless made with licence of the Crown.[43] If the contract is executory at the time of outbreak of war, it is generally terminated automatically.[44] Where the
contract is partly performed at the time of outbreak of war, accrued rights of an enemy are kept

---

[39] [1905] 2 K.B. 123.
[40] *Brodie v Brodie* [1917] P. 271.
[41] *Wilson v Wilson* (1848) 1 H.L. Cas. 538.
[42] *Harrison v Harrison* [1910] 1 K.B. 35.
[43] *Potts v Bell* (1800) 8 Term. R. 548.
[44] *Ertel Bieber & Co v Rio Tinto Co* [1918] A.C. 260.

in suspense and entrusted to an administrator of enemy property until the war is over; thus the effect of war is not to expropriate enemy property.

An agreement to perform in a friendly foreign country an act that is illegal in that country is illegal in English law.

The case of *Foster v Driscoll*[45] affords a good illustration of the principle. During the period of "prohibition" in the United States, several persons in the United Kingdom, including a financier, a distiller, and a firm of shipbrokers, formed a partnership (or syndicate) and entered into a contract to equip a steamer and load her with a cargo of 7,500 cases of Scotch whisky. The real purpose of the venture was disguised by the parties, but in essence, the ship was to sail to the United States where the goods were to be sold either inside that country or on its borders to persons who would sell it on inside that country. These sales would involve a violation of United States' prohibition laws. Before the venture could get fully under way, a dispute arose over the bills of exchange which had been issued to finance the venture. The Court of Appeal held that the contract was illegal and void as a breach of international comity and therefore contrary to public policy under the law of the United Kingdom. No action could therefore be brought in relation to any issue arising out of the agreement.

14–023   A similar conclusion was arrived at by the House of Lords in *Regazzoni v K C Sethia Ltd*[46] where the defendants agreed to sell to the claimants a consignment of jute bags, both parties intending that they should be shipped from India to Genoa and then on to South Africa. However, India had banned the export of goods to South Africa in condemnation of the "apartheid" system and the contract was an attempt to evade the ban. The defendants failed to deliver the goods and the claimants brought an action for damages. The contract was governed by English law. The House of Lords held that it was unenforceable as being contrary to public policy.

In another case, a loan to support an armed revolt in a friendly foreign country was held to be illegal.[47]

Contracts furthering corruption in public life

14–024   Contracts for the sale of public offices are illegal as having a tendency to further corruption in public life.

In a case that has echoes in modern British society, it was held that a contract to procure a title in return for a monetary consideration was illegal and void. In *Parkinson v College of Ambulance Ltd*[48] the secretary of the defendant charity told Colonel Parkinson that if he made a generous enough donation to the charity he would receive a knighthood. This was a fraudulent misrepresentation. Relying on this statement, the Colonel donated the sum of £3,000 but he did not receive a knighthood. He brought an action against the charity and its secretary to recover the £3,000. Lush J. held that the action must fail. Although Parkinson had been the victim of a fraud, he knew that the contract was improper and illegal and therefore he could neither recover the donation nor claim damages.

It should be noted that the Honours (Prevention of Abuses) Act 1925 provides that the parties to such transaction are guilty of an offence.

---

[45] [1921] 1 K.B. 490.
[46] [1958] A.C. 301. See also *Lemenda Trading Co v African Middle East Petroleum Co Ltd* [1988] Q.B. 448.
[47] *De Wutz v Hendricks* (1824) 2 Bing. 314.
[48] [1925] 2 K.B. 1.

Contracts in restraint of trade

Certain contracts which impose a restriction on a person's right to carry on a trade or profession fall within the restraint of trade doctrine. All contracts falling within the doctrine are prima facie contrary to public policy and void. These contracts are considered in the following chapter, Chapter 15.

14–025

EFFECTS OF ILLEGALITY

The first matter to be considered here is the state of mind of the parties. At common law, if the contract is illegal as formed (such as a contract to commit a crime or a contract expressly prohibited by statute), neither party will be able to sue or acquire rights under the contract. This is so even where the contract on the face of it (ex facie) appears to be legal but there is a common intention to achieve an illegal purpose. Where the contract is *legal* as formed but one party (and not the other) intends to exploit the contract for an illegal purpose, the innocent party may be able to sue on the contract and exercise other remedies.[49]

14–026

Thus effects of illegality differ according to whether the contract is illegal as formed or illegal as performed.

Contract illegal as formed

The consequences of illegality where a contract is illegal as formed may be summarised as follows.

14–027

Contract void

The contract is null and void and neither party can secure any rights or obtain any remedy under it. This is based on the famous maxim, *ex turpi causa non oritur actio* ("no right of action arises from a base cause"). The position will be the same whether the contract is one where the formation is prohibited by statute or where it is illegal at common law on the grounds of public policy. Thus in *Re Mahmoud & Ispahani* (discussed at para.14–003) neither party acquired any rights under the contract; and in *Alexander v Rayson* (see para.14–012) the landlord could not recover rent or damages for breach of covenant under the lease. Similarly, an employee will not be able to recover any arrears of salary under an illegal contract of employment.[50]

14–028

---

[49] *Oom v Bruce* (1810) 12 East. 225—an insurance policy was illegal and void as it was taken out in ignorance of the fact that war had broken out the previous day (trading with the enemy) but the agent of the insured recovered premium on the basis that it was paid under a mistake of fact.

[50] *Miller v Karlinski* [1945] 62 T. L. R. 85. But see *Hall v Woolston Hall Leisure Ltd* [2001] 4 All E.R. 787 where an employee was held to be entitled to recover compensation for loss of earnings on the grounds of unlawful sex discrimination in circumstances where her employer was defrauding the revenue—the employee did not actively participate in the illegality. The court seems to have regarded the rights granted by the anti-discrimination legislation to be independent of the validity of the contract of employment.

Money paid or property transferred are irrecoverable

14–029   The basic rule is that there can be no recovery of money or property transferred under the contract. Thus in *Taylor v Chester*[51] at the request of the defendant, the claimant delivered to her half a £50 note as a pledge or security for the payment of £20. The money was due in respect of wine and food supplied to the claimant and various prostitutes for the purposes of a debauch in the defendant's brothel. The claimant brought an action to recover the half-note; the Court of Queen's Bench division held that the claim failed. The maxim, *in pari delicto potior est conditio possidentis* ("where both parties are equally in the wrong, the position of the possessor is the stronger") applied. The claimant was unable to recover without revealing the true character of the deposit and as it was an illegal consideration to which he himself was a party, there could be no recovery. The loss lies where it falls. This was the case in *Everet v Williams* (see para.14–011) and also *Parkinson v College of Ambulance* (see para.14–024) where the claimant was unable to recover money paid under an illegal contract to procure a title. The charity to which the money was paid was allowed to keep the donation.

There are certain exceptions to this rule where recovery of property may be possible: (a) where the claimant can recover without pleading the illegal contract; (b) where the parties are not equally in the wrong (*in pari delicto*); or (c) where the claimant resiles from the contract before the illegal purpose has been fully performed. These will now be considered in turn.

(a) Recovery without pleading the illegal contract. Where ownership has not been transferred under the contract, the claimant may be able to recover their property without pleading the illegal contract.

14–030   In *Bowmakers Ltd v Barnet Instruments Ltd*[52] the claimants transferred machine tools to the defendants under hire-purchase contracts which were illegal under war-time regulations. The defendants failed to keep up the instalments and sold some of the tools and refused to return the remainder to the claimants. The claimants sued, not on the illegal contracts, but in the tort of conversion, on the basis that the machine tools belonged to them. The defendants contended that such a claim could not be established without resort to the illegal contracts. The Court of Appeal held that the defendants were liable; the wrongful sale had terminated the hire-purchase contracts which meant that the claimants could lawfully base their claim on ownership. As Du Parcq L.J. explained:

> "A man's right to possess his own chattels will as a general rule be enforced against one who, without any claim of right, is detaining them, or has converted them to his own use, even though . . . the chattels in question came into the defendant's possession by reason of an illegal contract between himself and the [claimant], provided that the [claimant] does not seek, and is not forced, either to found his claim on the illegal contract or to plead its illegality in order to support his claim."

It seems that this principle applies to a claim arising out of the contract under the law of trusts. In *Tinsley v Millgan*[53] T and M, both single women, were lovers and they jointly contributed to the purchase of a house in which they lived. The house was purchased in the sole name of T to enable them to make false benefit claims on social security. After some time M repented and

---

[51] (1869) L. R. 4 Q. B. 309.
[52] [1945] K.B. 65. For a critical analysis of the case, see Coote 35 M.L.R. 38.
[53] [1994] A.C. 340.

disclosed the fraud to the Department of Social Security. Later T and M fell out and T brought an action for sole possession of the house; M contended that the house was held on trust for both of them in equal shares. T argued that as the purchase of the house in the sole name of T had been to further an illegal purpose, M had no equitable rights under the transaction. By a majority of 3:2 (Lords Goff and Keith dissenting) the House of Lords found for M. She had shown there was a resulting trust by contributing to the purchase of the house and there was a shared understanding that they jointly owned the house. M's rights to her share in the house could be asserted independently of any illegal contract and she did not have to rely on any illegality to establish her claim. The illegality had been raised by T as a defence to M's claim.

(b) Parties not equally in the wrong. Where the parties have both participated in the illegal transaction but are not *in pari delicto*, the less guilty party may be allowed to recover. However, it must be shown that the claimant was the victim of duress, oppressive conduct or fraud at the hands of the defendant. In *Atkinson v Denby*[54] the claimant, who was in financial difficulties, offered his creditors 25 per cent of his debts as a composition (see para.4–032). All the creditors agreed to this, except the defendant who secretly told the claimant that he would only agree if the claimant gave him £50. The claimant paid, but then brought an action to recover the money. It was held that the claimant could recover as he had been co-erced into entering the illegal transaction by oppressive conduct on the part of the defendant.

In the case of statutory illegality, it may be that the purpose of the statute in question is to **14–031** protect a class of persons from certain types of conduct. If the claimant falls within that class, they may be allowed to recover money or property transferred under the contract. An illustration is afforded by the Privy Council decision in *Kiriri Cotton Co Ltd v Dewani*[55] where, in order to get possession of an apartment in Kampala, Uganda, the tenant paid a premium to the landlord. Under the Uganda Rent Restriction Ordinance, it was an offence for a person to ask for a premium in consideration of letting residential premises. Neither the landlord nor the tenant were aware that the taking of a premium was illegal and the Ordinance contained no provision allowing for the recovery of the premium. It was held that the premium was recoverable as the object of the legislation was to protect tenants. As the duty of observing the law rested on the shoulders of the landlord, the parties could not be said to be *in pari delicto*.

In some cases, the particular statute will contain an express provision allowing for recovery of the payment. Under s.125 of the Rent Act 1977, it is provided that where a premium cannot lawfully be required, the tenant may recover from the landlord any premium paid to secure a lease. The fact that the tenant may be to some extent a participant in the illegal payment will not prevent recovery.

(c) Where the claimant resiles from the contract. There is authority that the claimant may be able to recover where they repent before the illegal purpose has been fully performed. Thus the claimant is granted a *locus poenitentiae* despite the illegal circumstances.

In *Taylor v Bowers*[56] the claimant, who was financially embarrassed, wished to prevent his creditors getting their hands on his stock-in-trade, including a steam engine. Accordingly, he made a fictitious sale of the property to one Alcock and bogus bills of exchange were given in the claimant's favour as a pretended consideration. Alcock took possession of the property. He then mortgaged the property to the defendant without the claimant's knowledge, although the defendant was aware of the unlawful transaction between the claimant and Alcock. Two

[54] (1862) 7 H. & N. 934.
[55] [1960] A.C. 192.
[56] (1876) 1 Q.B.D. 291.

meetings of the claimant's creditors were held but no composition was arrived at. The claimant brought an action to recover back the property—the Court of Appeal held that he must succeed. When the claimant repented, nothing beyond the removal of the property from the claimant's premises had been done to further the illegal design. Accordingly, he could recover the property from the defendant. More recently, in *Tribe v Tribe*[57] the Court of Appeal indicated that "repentance" as such may not be necessary and it may be sufficient that the party merely withdraws from the illegal transaction.

14–032   In *Taylor v Bowers* recovery was allowed after a partial performance; it seems that a person may not resile after a substantial performance of the illegal transaction. In *Kearley v Thomson*[58] the claimant had a friend who was bankrupt and the defendants were solicitors acting for the petitioning creditor. The defendants' expenses were to be paid out of the bankrupt's estate and the claimant offered to pay those costs if the defendants promised to stay away from the public examination and not oppose the discharge from bankruptcy. The defendants accepted the offer and in return for the payment, stayed away from the proceedings. Before the discharge, the claimant brought an action to recover the money that he had paid on the basis that it had been paid under an illegal contract. It was held that the action failed; the illegal design had been substantially effected.

It may be that the claimant, in order to recover, will have to show that their repentance was voluntary, rather than it being a case of being thwarted in an illegal venture. In *Bigos v Bousted*[59] the parties entered into an illegal currency transaction whereby the claimant was to pay the defendant a sum of money in England if the defendant would supply the defendant's wife with Italian currency in Italy. As security, the defendant handed over a share certificate to the claimant. The claimant did not honour her part of the agreement but sued for payment, and the defendant counterclaimed for the return of the security. The court held that the reason why the defendant had not fully performed the contract was that he had been frustrated by the claimant, rather than by any repentance on his part. This rather harsh decision was doubted by the Court of Appeal in the above-mentioned case of *Tribe v Tribe*; as Millett L.J. observed:

> "Suppose, for example that in *Bigos v Bousted* . . . exchange control had been abolished before the foreign currency was made available: it is absurd to suppose that the [claimant] should have been denied restitution."

Of course, if, as the Court of Appeal held in *Tribe v Tribe*, genuine repentance is not necessary, then all that is required is that the claimant withdraws from the transaction before any part of the illegal purpose has been carried out.

Collateral transactions may be void

14–033   The consequences of illegality cannot be evaded by setting up a collateral contract between the parties to the illegal design. In *Fisher v Bridges*[60] the defendant agreed to purchase from the claimant a plot of land which the defendant intended to put up as the prize in a lottery, a purpose illegal by statute. The claimant was aware of this intention. The purchase price was

---

[57] [1996] 71 P. & C.R. 503.
[58] (1890) 24 Q.B.D. 742.
[59] [1951] 1 All E.R. 92.
[60] (1854) 3 E. & B. 642. See also *Cannan v Bryce* (1819) 3 B. & Ald. 179; and *Spector v Ageda* [1971] 3 All E.R. 417.

paid for the land, save for the sum of £630, and title conveyed. In a separate deed executed between the parties, the defendant covenanted to pay the claimant £630. When the claimant sued on the deed it was held that no action lay. Jervis C.J. said that the covenant "springs from and is the creature of the illegal agreement."

Contract illegal as performed

We are concerned with the situation here where the contract is lawful as formed but one party only intends to exploit it for an illegal purpose.   **14–034**

In these circumstances, the guilty party cannot recover back money or property transferred, nor may they maintain an action on the contract to recover damages. In *Cowan v Milburn*[61] the defendant hired assembly rooms to the claimant whose purpose it was to deliver blasphemous lectures there (an illegal purpose). When the defendant learned of this, he refused the claimant possession. An action for damages for breach of contract by the claimant failed on the grounds of illegality. The court recognised, however, that if the defendant, after hearing of the illegal purpose, had then let the claimant into possession, he could not have recovered. No rights can be exercised by a party who is aware of the illegal purpose, or to whom the guilty knowledge can be imputed. We saw this earlier in the chapter in the discussion of the case of *Ashmore, Benson, Pease & Co Ltd v A V Dawson Ltd* (see para.14–007 above).

The innocent party, in a contract which the other intends to exploit for an illegal purpose, is in a much better position.

First, they may sue on a quantum meruit (see para.17–024) and recover reasonable remuneration for work done and materials provided. In *Clay v Yates*[62] the claimant, a printer, entered into an agreement with the defendant whereby he was to print for him 500 copies of a book entitled "Military Tactics". A dedication, as yet unwritten at the time of the contract, was to be prefixed to the book. The claimant began printing but when he saw the dedication for the first time, he realised it was defamatory (i.e. illegal) and omitted it from the book. The defendant refused to pay for the book without the dedication and the claimant sought to recover a reasonable sum for labour and materials. It was held that the claimant was entitled to payment for the lawful part of his work.

Secondly, the innocent party may be able to maintain an action on a collateral or preliminary promise that the work would be carried out legally. In *Strongman v Sincock*[63] the claimants, a firm of builders, provisionally agreed to modernise some houses belonging to the defendant, who was an architect. At the time, such work required a licence under the Defence (General) Regulations 1939. The defendant orally promised to obtain the necessary licences and on the strength of that undertaking, the contract was concluded. The claimants did work to the value of £6,359. However, licences to the value of only £2,150 had been obtained. The defendant at this point had paid the claimants £2,090; he informed them that the contract was illegally performed and refused to pay the balance. The claimants' action for the balance was successful in the Court of Appeal. The claimants relied not on the illegal building contract but on the defendant's collateral promise that he would obtain the necessary licences—the defendants had contracted on this basis.   **14–035**

---

[61] (1867) L.R. 2 Ex. 230. See also *Archbolds (Freightage) Ltd v S Spanglett Ltd* [1961] 1 Q.B. 374, discussed at para.14–005.
[62] (1856) 1 H. & B. 73.
[63] [1955] 2 Q.B. 525.

Denning L.J. considered that the law was as follows:

"Although a man may have been guilty of an offence which is absolutely prohibited so that he is answerable in a criminal court, nevertheless if he has been led to commit that offence by the representation or promise of another, then in those circumstances he can recover damages for fraud if there is fraud, or for breach of promise or warranty if he proves such to have been given, provided always that he himself has not been guilty of culpable negligence on his part disabling him from that remedy."

On the facts of the case, the claimants justifiably believed that the obligation to ensure that the contract was lawfully performed was no longer theirs, since the court accepted that it was the "universal practice" for the architect and not the builder to get the licences. The court found that there was no fault or negligence on the builders' part. The remedy is likely to be invoked only rarely; indeed the case is difficult to distinguish on the facts from that in *Re Mahmoud & Ispahani* (see para.14–003). Denning L.J. distinguished it on the basis that in *Re Mahmoud & Ispahani* the court only decided that no action lay on the contract for the purchase of the goods—it did not decide whether an action for fraud or breach of warranty might lie.[64] *Strongman v Sincock* should also be distinguished from *Fisher v Bridges* (see para.14–033) which established that a collateral contract will be tainted by illegality where claimant and defendant are party to an illegal purpose in the main contract.

14–036   Thirdly, the innocent party should be able to recover damages for breach of contract—the guilty defendant cannot rely on their own illegal performance to resist such a claim. This was indicated, obiter, by the Court of Appeal in *Anderson v Daniel* (see para.14–006) and confirmed in *Marles v Philip Trant & Sons Ltd (No 2)*.

In this case the defendants purchased wheat which they thought was spring wheat known as "Fylgia", but in fact the sellers had knowingly delivered "Vilmorin", a winter wheat. In good faith, the defendants sold the wheat as spring wheat to the claimants. This contract was illegal as performed because the defendants did not comply with s.1 of the Seeds Act 1920 which required that an invoice had to be given to the buyer giving certain information about the seeds. When they discovered that the wheat was winter wheat, the claimants sued the defendants. The Court of Appeal held that the claimant could, as the innocent party, recover damages from the defendants. The court held further that since the defendants' statutory offence was one of inadvertence and no damage resulted from it, they were entitled to recover from their suppliers the loss arising from the contract with the claimants.

Finally, the innocent party (who, of course, is not in *pari delicto*) may recover money paid or property transferred to the guilty party.

Severance

14–037   In some cases, the court will permit "severance", that is the removal of an illegal or void provision from a contract so as to permit the enforcement of the remainder.[65]

Most instances of severance arise in relation to contracts in restraint of trade, which will be

---

[64] See *Shelley v Paddock* [1980] Q.B. 348 where damages for fraud were awarded to a wholly innocent claimant who was induced to pay over money to the defendants for an illegal currency transaction.
[65] *Carney v Herbert* [1985] A.C. 301.

discussed in the following chapter, but it can occur in other types of illegal contract. An example is the case of *Ailion v Spiekermann*[66] where the claimant occupied a flat under a statutorily protected tenancy. He entered into an agreement with the defendants to assign to them the remainder of his lease on payment by them of a £3,750 for certain chattels. Both the claimant and the defendants were aware that the goods in question were not worth that sum and that the claimant could not lawfully demand or require such a payment as it was an illegal premium under the Rent Act 1968. The defendants went into possession but refused to pay the premium; they then offered to pay a reasonable sum representing what the chattels were actually worth. The claimant sought rescission of the contract and the defendants counterclaimed for specific performance. In the High Court, Templeman J. granted that remedy. Even though the defendants were aware of the illegality, the legal and illegal elements of the contract were capable of being severed; the Act did not render the assignment itself illegal but only the receipt by the assignor of the premium; and in any event the Act existed for the protection of tenants.

Illegality: conclusion

The overriding public interest in the refusal of the law to countenance illegal contracts means that the court may raise the issue of illegality of its own motion and is not dependent on one or other of the parties pleading the matter.[67]   **14–038**

There is no doubt that the unenforceability of illegal contracts can lead to unjust results as between the parties to the contract themselves. This is particularly true of contracts which are illegal in their inception where the wrongdoer may make an undeserved windfall gain and the other party, who could be quite innocent of the illegal purpose, may be left without a remedy (see, for example, *Re Mahmoud v Ispahani*, discussed at para.14–003). In other cases, if the court can find an alternative means of recovery or if one party resiles from the contract, the courts are prepared to recognise exceptions in order to allow the innocent party a remedy. The result is that, like any area of law that has developed in a piecemeal fashion over time, the rules are technically complex and confusing. Indeed, the Law Commission[68] has put forward proposals for reform of the law, based on what it refers to as a "structured discretion" to replace the existing rules of public policy. Under these proposals, in deciding whether illegality should be a defence to an action for recovery of property transferred under the contract, the court should have regard to the seriousness of the illegality; the state of mind of the party wishing to enforce the transaction; and whether refusing the normal contractual remedies would deter illegality, further the purpose of the illegality rule or be proportionate to the illegality in the case in question. These proposals have attracted some criticism on the ground that they may be productive of uncertainty and unpredictability, but in reality, as the preceding discussion has shown, the courts have always exercised a measure of discretion in dealing with cases of illegality.

Illegality is a topic that defies precise categorisation. It must be pointed out that some of the contracts categorised above as being illegal on the grounds of public policy are classified by some commentators as being merely void, on the ground that they are less reprehensible.[69] These contracts are: contracts to oust the jurisdiction of the court (see para.14–014); contracts

---

[66] [1976] Ch. 158.
[67] *Northwestern Salt Co Ltd v Electrolytic Akali Co Ltd* [1914] A.C. 461.
[68] Law Com No 154 (1999) *Illegal Transactions: the Effect of Illegality on Contracts and Trusts*. See paras. 1.18 and 1.19.
[69] See, e.g. Cheshire, Fifoot and Furmston, *Law of Contract*, 15th edn, p.470.

prejudicial to marriage (see para.14–018); and contracts in restraint of trade (see Chapter 15). It is said that the consequences differ in the case of contracts which are merely void as opposed to illegal; thus, the contract is only void in so far as it contravenes public policy;[70] money paid and property transferred is recoverable;[71] and subsequent or collateral transactions are not necessarily void. Severance is possible and there is a greater readiness to sever void provisions than is the case with "illegal" contracts, particularly in restraint of trade cases.

Contracts in restraint of trade are considered in the following chapter.

Further reading

Buckley, *Illegal Transactions: Chaos or Discretion?* (2000) 20 Legal Studies 155.
Coote, *Another Look at Bowmakers* (1972) 35 M.L.R. 38.
Grodecki, *In Pari Delicto* (1955) 71 L.Q.R. 254.
Enonchong, *Illegal Transactions: The Future?* [2000] R.L.R. 82.

---

[70] See *Wallis v Day* (1837) 2 M. & W. 273.
[71] There is a dearth of authority, but *Hermann v Charlesworth* [1905] 2 K.B. 123 (see para.14–020) is usually cited.

Chapter 15

CONTRACTS IN RESTRAINT OF TRADE

A contract in restraint of trade may be defined as an agreement imposing a restriction on the **15–001** right of one or both parties to pursue a trade, business or profession.

All contracts falling within the restraint of trade doctrine are contrary to public policy and prima facie void, unless they can be regarded as being reasonable as between the parties and as regards the public interest. The burden of proving that, as between the parties, the restraint is reasonable lies on the promisee; the burden of proving that, as far as the public interest is concerned, the restraint is unreasonable, lies on the promisor. These principles were established in a case that is the foundation of the modern doctrine of restraint of trade—the decision of the House of Lords in *Nordenfelt v Maxim Nordenfelt Guns and Ammunition Co Ltd*.[1]

The facts of the case were that the appellant, who owned a business manufacturing machine-guns, sold the business to the respondents who had a worldwide armaments business. The agreement contained a covenant that the appellant would not engage in the business of manu-facturing guns, gun mountings, explosives or ammunition for a period of 25 years, except on the respondents' behalf. Later, the appellant entered into a contract with another gun manufac-turer and the respondents sought an injunction to restrain the alleged breach. The House of Lords upheld the restraint as being reasonable and valid—although it was without geographical limit, the covenant was necessary to protect the respondent's commercial interests as their busi-ness connection was worldwide. In a famous judicial statement, Lord Macnaghten said:

> "The public have an interest in every person's carrying on his trade freely: so has the indi-vidual. All interference with individual liberty of action in trading, and all restraints of trade of themselves, if there is nothing more, are contrary to public policy, and therefore void. That is the general rule. But there are exceptions: restraints of trade and interference with individual liberty of action may be justified by the special circumstances of a particu-lar case. It is a sufficient justification, and indeed it is the only justification, if the restriction is reasonable – reasonable, that is, in reference to the interests of the parties concerned and reasonable in reference to the interests of the public, so framed and so guarded as to afford adequate protection to the party in whose favour it is imposed, while at the same time it is in no way injurious to the public."

It is only contracts that fall within the restraint of trade doctrine that are treated in the manner **15–002** indicated by Lord Macnaghten. Not all contracts that restrict a person's freedom to trade will

[1] [1894] A.C. 535.

fall within the doctrine, as explained by Lord Wilberforce in the House of Lords in *Esso Petroleum Co Ltd v Harper's Garage (Stourport) Ltd* :[2]

> "It is not to be supposed, or encouraged, that a bare allegation that a contract limits a trader's freedom of action exposes a party suing on it to the burden of justification. There will always be certain general categories of contract to which it can be said, with some degree of certainty that the "doctrine" does or does not apply to them. Positively, there are likely to be certain sensitive areas as to which the law will require in every case the test of reasonableness to be passed . . . Negatively . . . there will be types of contract as to which the law should be prepared to say with some confidence that they do not enter into the field of restraint at all."

Currently, there are, broadly speaking, four classes of contract that fall within the restraint of trade doctrine. First, there are covenants imposed by an employer upon an employee whereby the former imposes a restriction upon the latter after leaving employment; for example, that the employee shall not work in a similar capacity for a specified period within a defined geographical area. Secondly, as we have seen in the *Nordenfelt* case above, a covenant may be imposed upon the seller of a business by the buyer whereby the former agrees to a restriction as to where they carry on business. Clearly, the purchaser of, for example, a corner shop that is a going concern will want safeguards that the vendor will not set up shop across the road and entice away all the established custom. Thirdly, there may be contracts where a group of manufacturers or traders combine to restrict output or fix prices of certain commodities. Such agreements fall within the common law doctrine of restraint but it should be noted that they are also regulated by statute; the provisions are currently contained in the Competition Act 1998. (These statutory rules are beyond the scope of this book—readers are referred to specialist works on competition law[3]). Finally, there are exclusive dealing contracts such as "solus" agreements in the petrol trade where a garage proprietor agrees to sell only the products of a particular oil company. It must be stressed again that all these agreements are prima facie void and their validity depends upon it being established that they are reasonable.

We shall first examine covenants in employment contracts and those imposed upon the sale of a business.

COVENANTS RELATING TO EMPLOYMENT OR THE SALE OF A BUSINESS

Agreements between employer and employee relating to the subsequent occupation of the employee

Proprietary interest meriting protection

15–003   An agreement imposing a restriction on the employee after leaving an employer will only be reasonable as between the parties if the employer has some proprietary interest meriting protection. The restriction must be no wider than reasonably necessary to protect such interest. What this means in practice is that the employer is entitled to protect: (i) trade secrets; and (ii) business

---

[2] [1968] A.C. 269.
[3] See Whish, *Competition Law* 5th edn, (London; Lexis Nexis, Butterworths, 2003).

connection. The employer cannot impose a restraint merely because the employee has acquired skill and expertise which might be useful to some future rival employer. But where the employee has learned trade secrets in the course of employment, it is a different matter. It seems that the employer must establish that the employee has acquired substantial knowledge or understanding of some form of secret or confidential process.

In *Forster & Sons Ltd v Suggett*[4] the defendant was employed as works engineer in the claimants' glass works. Under his contract of employment he agreed that, for five years after termination of employment with the claimants, he would not divulge any secret manufacturing process learnt during employment, nor would he work in the glass industry in the United Kingdom. Sargant J. held that an injunction would be granted to protect the claimants' legitimate interest in protecting their trade secrets. Neither the duration nor the geographical area of the restriction was unreasonable in the circumstances. But a restraint will not be upheld if its effect is merely to restrain competition as such.

In *Herbert Morris Ltd v Saxelby*[5] the respondent was employed by the appellants, the leading manufacturers of lifting machinery in the country, as a draughtsman. A clause in his contract of employment provided that for seven years after leaving, he would not be engaged anywhere in the UK in any business carrying on work similar to that of the appellants. After leaving the employ of the appellants, he went to work for a rival firm which made lifting machinery and the appellants sought an injunction. The action failed. The House of Lords held that the clause was wider than necessary to protect the appellants' interest—they were merely trying to reduce competition rather than safeguard a process in which they had a proprietary right. Lord Atkinson said that the clause would:

> " ... deprive him for a lengthened period of employing, in any part of the United Kingdom, that mechanical and technical skill and knowledge which, as I have said, his own industry, observation, and intelligence have enabled him to acquire in the very specialised business of the appellants, thus forcing him to begin life afresh, as it were, and depriving himself of the means of supporting himself and his family."

15–004 Similarly, where the employee is in a position whereby they may subsequently be able to exploit their employer's business connection, a restraint that is no wider than reasonably necessary to protect that interest may be upheld. It is not every employee who can be validly restrained in this way. They must not only be in contact with customers or clients, they must be in a position to have some influence over them. Restraints of this type have been upheld against a solicitors' clerk,[6] a milk roundsman,[7] and a hairdresser.[8]

Other interests meriting protection

15–005 Occasionally, the courts are prepared to recognise other interests as meriting protection. In *Eastham v Newcastle United Football Club Ltd*[9] the claimant played professional football for

---

[4] (1918) 35 T.L.R. 87.

[5] [1916] 1 A.C. 688.

[6] *Fitch v Dewes* [1921] 2 A.C. 158.

[7] *Home Counties Dairies Ltd v Skilton* [1970] 1 W.L.R. 526.

[8] *Marion White Ltd v Francis* [1972] 1 W.L.R. 1423.

[9] [1964] Ch. 413. It should be noted that in *Union Royale Belge des Societes de Football Association v Bosman* [1996] All E.R. (EC) 97 (the "Bosman case") the ECJ held that football association rule preventing a player transferring to a club in another country of the EU without the payment of a transfer fee was in breach of Treaty provisions on the free movement of workers.

the defendant football club. He sought a transfer to a different club, but Newcastle United were unwilling to release him, so they put him on their list of "retained" players. Under the rules of the governing bodies of the sport, this meant that the claimant could not play for any other club provided the defendants paid him a "reasonable" wage. The player sought a declaration that the system of retention was an unreasonable restraint of trade. It was held that the declaration would be granted—the rules of the governing bodies were not justifiable by an interest capable of protection; they did not protect either of the two traditional interests. Nevertheless, Wilberforce J. recognised that the ruling bodies, the Football Association and the Football League, did have an interest in the organisation of football in the UK. This approach was endorsed in relation to the game of cricket in the case of *Greig v Insole*[10] where a professional cricketer sought to challenge a ban on cricketers who had joined a commercial "World Series". Slade J. recognised that the governing bodies of cricket had a legitimate interest in ensuring that the game was properly administered; however, in the circumstances the ban was held to be unreasonable.

Reasonableness with regard to area, duration and activity restrained

15–006 The restriction must be reasonable as regards the geographical area covered and the length of time that the restriction is to last. In *Mason v Provident Clothing & Supply Co Ltd*[11] a restriction on a canvasser who was employed in the district of Islington not to work within 25 miles of London was held void as the area of restraint was a thousand times larger than the area of employment. With regard to duration, it will depend on the circumstances. In *Fitch v Dewes*[12] the claimant was a solicitor's managing clerk who agreed with his employer, the defendant, a Tamworth solicitor, not to "be engaged or manage or concerned in the office, profession, or business of a solicitor, within a radius of seven miles of the Town Hall of Tamworth". The House of Lords held that although the restraint was effectively a lifetime one, this did not exceed what was reasonably required to protect the claimant's interest. The area contained no more than approximately 20,000 people and the covenant was not against the public interest. As Lord Parmoor explained:

> "The limitation of time, having regard to the business of solicitor, is not too wide in its application. It is no more than adequate protection for a solicitor who desires to protect his professional secrets and to protect his clients from being enticed away by a former clerk who has access to all his papers and has been in direct personal relation with a number of his clients."

On the other hand, in *Eastes v Russ*[13] the defendant was a laboratory assistant who worked for the claimant, a pathologist whose work involved a new method of medical research. A restraint to the effect that the defendant could not engage in a similar work within ten miles of the claimant's laboratory in Queen Ann Street, London, was held to be void by the Court of Appeal. The restriction lasted for the whole of the defendant's life and was wider than reasonably necessary in the circumstances.

---

[10] [1978] 1 W.L.R. 302. See further *Leeds Rugby Ltd v Harris* [2005] EWHC 1591 (Civ).
[11] [1913] A.C. 724.
[12] [1921] 2 A.C. 158.
[13] [1914] 1 Ch. 468.

The covenant must also not be too wide in terms of the activity which is sought to be restrained. This principle is illustrated by the case of *Commercial Plastics Ltd v Vincent*.[14] The claimants manufactured thin PVC calendered sheeting used, amongst other things, in the manufacture of adhesive tape. The defendant was employed by the claimants in a research and development role in connection with the production of adhesive tape. A covenant in the defendant's contract of service provided that he would not seek employment with any of the claimants' competitors in the PVC calendering field for at least one year after leaving employment. When the claimant left to work for one of the claimants' rivals, the claimants sought to enforce the restrictive covenant in the contract of service. The Court of Appeal held that the action failed as the clause exceeded what was reasonably required to protect the claimants' interest. It extended to the claimants' competitors in the whole PVC calendering field whereas the claimants only required protection in the adhesive tape sector of that market. But in any event the covenant was world-wide and the claimants only required protection in the United Kingdom.

Some covenants seek to prevent the employee from soliciting the clients or customers of the former employer ("non-solicitation covenants").[15] No problem arises with the area of operation such clauses; indeed, they may be upheld in circumstances where an area covenant would amount to a pure restraint on competition. The duration, however, must be reasonable.   **15–007**

Restraints linked to pension rights

In *Bull v Pitney-Bowes Ltd*[16] the claimant was employed by the defendant and it was a condition of the contract of employment that employees should belong to a compulsory non-contributory pension scheme. Rule 16 of the scheme provided that any retired member who took employment in any activity in competition with the defendants would forfeit their pension. On retirement, the claimant took up paid employment with one of the defendants' competitors. The defendants requested him to discontinue this activity but he declined to do so; he then sought a declaration that the rules of the scheme were an unreasonable restraint of trade. Thesiger J. granted the declaration—the employer had no proprietary rights meriting protection and the rule in question was unlimited as to area and duration; it was not confined to the particular activity with which the claimant had been concerned. The claimant recovered his pension rights.   **15–008**

Restraints in agreements between employers

A restraint can arise from an agreement between employers as in *Kores Manufacturing Co Ltd v Kolok Manufacturing Co Ltd*.[17] Here, two companies, who manufactured carbon papers and other typewriting products, agreed that neither would employ any person who had in the previous five years been employed by the other, unless the other company consented. The purpose of the agreement was the protection of trade secrets. The claimants' chief chemist sought employment with the defendants. The claimants, who were unwilling to consent to this, claimed   **15–009**

---

[14] [1964] 1 W.L.R. 820.
[15] See *G W Plowman & Son Ltd v Ash* [1964] 2 All E.R. 10.
[16] [1967] 1 W.L.R. 273.
[17] [1959] Ch. 108.

an injunction to enforce the agreement. Giving the judgment of the court Jenkins L.J. explained that the restraint was too wide to protect the relevant interest:

> "The defendants . . . placed it out of their power to take into their service any person who had during the preceding five years been in the service of the claimants for any period, however short, and in any capacity, however humble. The five-year ban was equally applicable to an unskilled manual labourer who had been for a single day in the employment of the [claimants], and to a chief chemist with many years' service. . . The agreement . . . is in terms applicable to all employees possessed of trade secrets and confidential information and employees not so possessed, and not in the remotest degree likely to be so possessed."

The Court of Appeal refused to grant the relief—the agreement was held to involve an unreasonable restraint of trade. The fact that the parties were two companies dealing on equal terms made no difference if in substance it amounted to an unreasonable restraint.

Construction of restraint clauses

15–010   The traditional approach is that the court will not rewrite the clause for the parties—it is given a literal interpretation and if it is too wide it will be void even though it is possible to see what the parties had in mind.[18] In some cases, however, the courts have been prepared to uphold a clause which, on its literal wording, *is* wider than reasonably necessary. Thus, in *Home Counties Dairies Ltd v Skilton*[19] a milkman covenanted not to sell milk or dairy produce. Although this literally would have prevented him from "selling cheese as a grocer's assistant", the court refused to invalidate the covenant on the basis that the parties clearly did not intend it to have such a meaning. More recently, in *Clarke v Newland*[20] a similar approach was taken in respect of a restraint upon a medical practitioner. The court considered that covenants should be judged in their context and in the light of the "factual matrix" at the time the agreement was entered into.

The leading case on the non-literal or "flexible" approach to construction is the decision of the Court of Appeal in *Littlewoods Organisation Ltd v Harris*.[21] The facts were that Paul Harris was a young executive (in the words of Lord Denning M.R.) of "outstanding ability" who was employed by the mail-order firm of Littlewoods. He entered into a covenant with his employers whereby, if he left them, he would not go to work for a rival firm, Great Universal Stores (GUS) for a period of 12 months. Mr Harris was the executive director in charge of the mail-order business—he was privy to the policy decisions of the company and had an important part to play in preparing the catalogue which was the foundation of the business. In the mail-order business, GUS was Littlewoods' main competitor; however GUS had a world-wide business and their business interests were very broad and not limited to mail-order. Littlewoods, on the other hand, operated only in the UK. It was held by a majority of the Court of Appeal (Browne L.J. dissenting) that although on its literal wording the clause was too wide to protect the relevant interest, it would be construed so as to apply only

---

[18]   See, for example, *Gledhow Autoparts Ltd v Delaney* [1965] 3 All E.R. 288.
[19]   [1970] 1 W.L.R. 526.
[20]   [1991] 1 All E.R. 397.
[21]   [1977] 1 W.L.R. 1472.

to the mail-order business in the United Kingdom. This was the interest which the parties had clearly intended to protect. The decision appears to be quite contrary to that arrived at by the same court in *Commercial Plastics v Vincent* (discussed above) but Lord Denning felt that the court should have upheld the clause in that case because it was "a just and honest agreement made in good faith". The defendant, Mr Vincent, had sought to break both the wording and the spirit of the agreement. The majority of the court in *Littlewoods v Harris* felt that such clauses should not be rendered ineffective by unskilful drafting. In a powerful dissenting judgment, Browne L.J. said that construing the clause in the way that the other members of the court had done was:

> "[R]ewriting the clause, and re-writing it so as to make enforceable that which would otherwise be unenforceable . . . I think that this is something which this court cannot do."

On the facts of the case itself Mr Harris had a great deal of confidential information which, in the view of the court, his former employers were entitled to protect. Lord Denning did not consider that it was enough simply to have a covenant against disclosing confidential information as the information was of such a character that the employee could carry it away "in his head". In these circumstances his Lordship considered that a covenant preventing the employee going to work for a rival for a limited period would be reasonable. Perhaps, therefore, the real basis of the decision is that it falls into a special category of cases where the employee is prevented by the terms of the covenant from working for a specified competitor.

15–011

In fact, the freedom to construe the covenant which the Court of Appeal afforded itself in *Littlewoods v Harris* has not subsequently gone unquestioned. Shortly after *Littlewoods v Harris* was decided, it was distinguished by the Court of Appeal in the case of *Greer v Sketchley Ltd*[22] where the court applied the traditional approach to an "area" covenant that was worded too widely. Some years later, in *J A Mont (UK) Ltd v Mills*[23] the Court of Appeal took a very much more restrictive view of its powers of construction than that demonstrated in *Littlewoods v Harris*. In *Mont v Mills*, the defendant was employed for some years by a firm as managing director in their paper tissue business; the firm later merged with the claimant company and he became redundant. In his severance agreement with the claimants, he agreed that, for 12 months after leaving the employ of the claimants, he would not go to work for another company in the paper tissue industry. The claimants sought an injunction to prevent a breach of covenant. This was granted at first instance as the judge considered that the defendant could have exploited confidential information in working for another firm. The Court of Appeal, however, considered the clause to be drafted too widely as it had not been worded in terms which restrained the defendant from using confidential information. As a matter of policy, the court did not consider that it should investigate whether there was some implicit limitation in the clause which rendered it less wide than its literal wording so that it could be enforced by an injunction. Nevertheless, *Littlewoods v Harris* was followed in relation to interlocutory proceedings in *Hanover Insurance Brokers Ltd v Schapiro*[24] where a differently constituted Court of Appeal expressed the view that *Littlewoods v Harris* and *Mont v Mills* required reconciliation in a full hearing. The circumstances, if any, in which the non-literal approach may be followed require clarification.

---

[22] [1979] F.S.R. 197.
[23] [1993] I.R.L.R. 173.
[24] [1994] I.R.L.R. 82.

Another means of achieving the same objective as in *Littlewoods v Harris* may be arrived by the court applying the doctrine of severance. This is discussed at the end of this chapter (at para.15–020).

The public interest element

15–012   In the *Nordenfelt* case (see para.15–001), the House of Lords considered that a restraint clause, in order to be reasonable, had not only to be reasonable between the parties but also not unreasonable as regards the public interest. The public interest principle was applied in *Wyatt v Kreglinger & Fernau*[25] where the employers of a wool broker promised him a pension on retirement provided he did not re-enter the wool trade. The Court of Appeal held that the stipulation against competition was void as it was contrary to the public interest, irrespective of whether it might or might not be reasonable as between the parties. The ruling has attracted some criticism on the basis that a restriction imposed on an elderly wool worker is unlikely to injure the public, nevertheless, it was followed in *Bull v Pitney-Bowes* (the facts are given at para.15–008). Lord Denning M.R. supported the principle in relation to a restraint imposed on a solicitor in *Oswald, Hickson and Collier & Co v Carter Ruck*.[26]

In recent cases the courts have shown a reluctance to apply the principle although its existence has not been called into question. It is conceivable that the principle might apply to a leading person in a particular field whose talents and skills were of great value to the public, e.g. a research scientist, composer or artist.

Agreements between the buyer and seller of a business

15–013   Restraints in contracts for the sale of a business are more readily upheld than in employment contracts because there is likely to be greater equality of bargaining power in the former. There must, of course, be a proprietary interest meriting protection and this is usually business connection, or "goodwill" as it is sometimes called. Generally speaking, the greater the amount paid for the goodwill the more extensive the restraint the purchaser can validly impose.

As with covenants in contracts of employment, any restraint must be no wider than reasonably necessary to protect the relevant interest. For this reason, it is only the actual business sold that is entitled to protection; and a restriction which purports to restrain a business not actually carried on will be void. Two cases illustrate these principles.

In *British Reinforced Concrete Engineering Co Ltd v Schelff*[27] the claimants made and sold "BRC" road reinforcements. The defendants sold but did not make "Loop" road reinforcements. The claimants bought the defendants business, the defendants covenanting not to compete in the manufacture and sale of road reinforcements in the United Kingdom for a specified period. It was held that the restraint was unreasonably wide as it extended to manufacture instead of being confined to sale. It amounted to a pure restraint upon competition.

In *Vancouver Malt and Sake Brewing Co Ltd v Vancouver Breweries Ltd*[28] a company that had a licence to brew beer but did not in fact brew any agreed to sell its goodwill and to refrain from

---

[25] [1933] 1 K.B. 793.
[26] [1984] A.C. 720. But see *Deacons v Bridge* [1984] A.C. 705.
[27] [1921] 2 Ch. 563.
[28] [1934] A.C. 181.

brewing beer for 15 years. The Privy Council held that the restraint amounted only to a covenant not to compete and was illegal and void.

AGREEMENTS BETWEEN SUPPLIERS TO RESTRICT OUTPUT AND FIX PRICES

Agreements whereby suppliers or manufacturers combine to regulate competition between themselves are subject to the restraint of trade doctrine at common law. They are also extensively regulated by European and also domestic legislation (under the Competition Act 1998).

15–014

Agreements of this nature are prima facie void but there is perhaps a greater readiness to enforce them than in some of the other examples we have looked at so far. Nevertheless, the restriction must be reasonable between the parties and not contrary to the public interest. In *English Hop Growers Ltd v Dering*[29] the defendant was a member of the claimant society, English Hop Growers, which had been formed to organise the marketing of hops. The defendant undertook to sell to the claimants all the hops grown on his 63 acre plot in 1926 and if he failed to do this he would pay liquidated damages of £100 per acre. He failed to deliver the hops and the claimants sued to recover £6,300. The defendant argued that the agreement was a void restraint of trade. The Court of Appeal upheld the restriction—the defendant was of equal bargaining strength and had joined the society of his own free will. Moreover, the rules of the society were to the mutual advantage of its members as they were designed to minimise the consequences of a glut of hops on the market and to spread the losses evenly between members.

The opposite conclusion was arrived at in another case, *McEllistrim v Ballymacelligott Co-operative Agricultural and Diary Society Ltd*,[30] where the society had been formed for the manufacture and sale of diary products supplied by its members, local farmers. The society promised to buy all the milk produced by its members, who in turn promised not to sell the milk to anyone else. The rules further provided that no member could withdraw from the organisation without the consent of the committee of the society—this consent could be withheld without reason. Because of this latter stipulation, the House of Lords ruled that the agreement was unreasonable between the parties and therefore void. It enabled the society, should it wish to do so, to impose a lifetime restriction on the members' freedom to trade. It seems that, without this provision, the agreement may have been valid.

It must be stressed that these cases deal only with the common law position. For the full picture regarding anti-competitive trading agreements, reference should be made to Articles 81 and 82 of the Treaty of Rome, the Competition Act 1998 and the Enterprise Act 2002.

EXCLUSIVE DEALING AGREEMENTS

Certain exclusive dealing agreements fall within the restraint of trade doctrine. These include so-called "solus" agreements where a party agrees to obtain their supplies of a commodity from

15–015

---

[29] [1928] 2 K.B. 174.
[30] [1919] A.C. 548.

one source; and exclusive service agreements such as those entered into by songwriters with music publishing companies. Such contracts must be reasonable between the parties and not contrary to the public interest.

Solus agreements

15–016   Such agreements are common in the petrol industry whereby the operator of a garage agrees to buy their petroleum products from only one oil company. In *Petrofina (Great Britain) Ltd v Martin*[31] the Court of Appeal confirmed that the restraint of trade doctrine applied to solus agreements. The leading case is the decision of the House of Lords in *Esso Petroleum Co Ltd v Harper's Garage (Stourport) Ltd.*[32]

The facts of the case were that the respondents owned two garages, Mustow Green and Corner, and entered into solus agreements with the respondents, a major oil company. In relation to Mustow Green the agreement was to last for almost four and a half years and it provided that the respondents should buy only the respondents' petrol which was supplied at a small discount. With regard to Corner, the appellants loaned the respondents the sum of £7,000 who then mortgaged the garage premises to the appellants; repayment was to be over a period of 21 years. A contract containing a solus tie on terms to similar Mustow Green was entered into and was also to last for 21 years. The respondents began to sell petrol supplied by another manufacturer and the appellants sought to enforce the two agreements. The House of Lords confirmed that the agreements in question were within the doctrine of restraint of trade. In relation to the Mustow Green garage, the period of under five years was reasonable as being no longer than necessary to protect the legitimate interest of the appellant, which was identified as the maintenance of a stable system of distribution. It was not contrary to the public interest. With regard to Corner garage the tie of 21 years went beyond what was reasonable—developments over such a period were not reasonably foreseeable and in the absence of evidence justifying such a duration, the tie was struck down.

The House of Lords drew a distinction between (a) an operator of a garage who is already in possession of land before they tie themselves to an oil company; and (b) a party who is out of possession and let into it by the company, for example, under a lease. The transaction in (a) is within the restraint of trade doctrine; (b), however, is not, as the party going into possession surrenders no freedom they had previously enjoyed. Lord Reid said:

> "Restraint of trade appears to me to imply that a man contracts to give up some freedom which otherwise he would have had. A person buying or leasing land had no previous right to be there at all, let alone to trade there, and when he takes possession of that land subject to a negative restrictive covenant he gives up no right or freedom which otherwise he would have had."

15–017   The distinction was applied by the Court of Appeal in the case of *Cleveland Petroleum Co Ltd v Dartstone Ltd*[33] and affirmed by the Privy Council in *Amoco (Australia) Pty Ltd v Rocca Bros Motor Bros Motor Engineering Pty Ltd.*[34] It had been thought for some time that, as a result of

---

[31] [1966] Ch. 146.
[32] [1968] A.C. 269.
[33] [1969] 1 W.L.R. 116.
[34] [1975] 1 All E.R. 968.

the House of Lords decision in the *Harper's* garage case, solus ties for more than five years would be unreasonable. That this is not so is illustrated by *Alec Lobb (Garages) Ltd v Total Oil GB Ltd*.[35] The claimants, whilst in financial difficulties, leased their garage to the defendants for a period of 51 years at a premium of £35,000. The defendants sub-leased it back to the claimants for 21 years at an annual rent of £2,250, with a mutual right to break at seven or 14 years, The sub-lease contained a solus tie whereby the claimants agreed only to sell the defendants' petrol.

The Court of Appeal held that the lease and lease-back were subject to the restraint of trade doctrine but the tie was valid as being reasonable in the circumstances. The agreement was essentially a financial rescue operation designed to benefit the defendants—they received ample consideration for the lease and they could exercise the break clause after 7 or 14 years.

It should be noted that the common law relating to petrol solus agreements is overlaid by statutory regulation under European and domestic law Unlike the common law, the scope of the relevant statutory regulation is based on a test of market share.

Exclusive service agreements

Exclusive service agreements, such as where, for example, a songwriter agrees to provide his services solely for a record company or firm of music publishers for a period of time are within the restraint doctrine.   **15–018**

The validity of such an agreement came before the House of Lords in *Schroeder Music Publishing Co Ltd v Macaulay*.[36] In this case, a young and unknown songwriter, Tony Macaulay, entered into a standard form contract with a firm of music publishers for a period of five years. Under the terms of the agreement, the songwriter assigned to the publishers the full copyright for the whole world in all his musical compositions during the term. If the total royalties received during the term exceeded £5,000, the agreement would be automatically extended for a further five years. The publishers could determine the agreement at anytime by one month's written notice. No such right was given to the songwriter. Although the publishers had the right to assign the agreement, the songwriter could not assign his rights under the agreement without the publisher's consent. The publishers were under no obligation to publish any of the songwriter's compositions. The songwriter brought an action claiming a declaration that the agreement was contrary to public policy and void.

Affirming the decision of the Court of Appeal, the House of Lords granted the declaration sought. Given the likely duration of the agreement and the publisher's right to assign, the agreement was on its face unduly restrictive. It was contrary to the public interest that the publishers could choose for whatever reason not to publish the songwriter's compositions so that he would earn nothing and his work would be sterilised. There was no provision allowing the songwriter to terminate the agreement; and given that it had not been arrived at as result of negotiation between parties of equal bargaining power, the publishers had failed to show that this one-sided agreement was not an unreasonable restraint of trade. In the words of Lord Reid:

> "The public interest requires the interests both of the public and the individual that everyone should be free so far as practicable to earn a livelihood and to give to the public the

---

[35] [1985] 1 W.L.R. 173.
[36] [1974] 1 W.L.R. 1308.

fruits of his particular abilities. The main question to be considered is whether and how far the operation of the terms of this agreement is likely to conflict with this objective. The respondent is bound to assign to the appellants during a long period the fruits of his musical talent. But what are the appellants bound to do with those fruits? Under the contract nothing. If they do use the songs which the respondent composes they must pay in terms of the contract. But they need not do so. As has been said they may put them in a drawer and leave them there."

15–019 The approach of the House of Lords to exclusive service agreements established by *Schroeder v Macaulay* was followed by the Court of Appeal in relation to the group Fleetwood Mac in the case of *Clifford Davis Management Ltd v W E A Records Ltd*.[37] In two later cases, *Zang Tumb Tuum Records Ltd v Johnson*[38] (the group Frankie Goes to Hollywood) and *Silvertone Records Ltd v Mountfield*[39] (the Stone Roses), the contracts were held to be void as being one-sided and unfair. On the other hand, *Schroeder v Macaulay* was distinguished in the case of *Panayiotou v Sony Music International (UK) Ltd*,[40] where the singer George Michael sought to challenge a recording contract which had been renegotiated after he had become an established star. The claimant, who was aware of the restraint doctrine, had received expert advice and the contract was highly favourable for the performer in terms of remuneration. In addition, the renegotiated contract had arisen from the settlement of an earlier dispute—the court considered that it would be unconscionable to allow the singer to rely on the restraint doctrine to avoid the provisions of the settlement.

SEVERANCE

15–020 Severance is the power of the court to strike out a provision which offends the restraint doctrine so as to be able to enforce the remaining valid part of the contract. Where the whole of the restraint covenant is void as being contrary to public policy, whether the rest of the contract is enforceable may depend upon whether there is any consideration other than the covenant. Thus in *Wyatt v Kreglinger & Fernau* (the facts are given at para.15–012) there was no other consideration moving from the claimant apart from the covenant not to compete – the transaction was therefore void. On the other hand, in *Bull v Pitney-Bowes* (the facts are given at para.15–008) the covenant not to compete was severable as the claimant had given other consideration, apart from the clause, in the contract. As a result the claimant recovered his right to a pension.

Severance may be applied in another sense, that is, cutting out part of a covenant which represents a void restriction so that what is left is valid and enforceable. The court applies the so-called "blue pencil" test to this situation—the offending words are struck out and what is left must make sense without any further additions or deletions. The court will not rewrite the clause in any way.

In *Putsman v Taylor*[41] the defendant was manager and cutter in the claimant's tailoring business in Birmingham. The defendant entered into an agreement with the claimant which

[37] [1975] 1 All E.R. 237.
[38] [1993] E.M.L.R. 61.
[39] [1993] E.M.L.R. 152.
[40] [1994] Ch. 142.
[41] [1927] 1 K.B. 637.

provided that after the determination of the agreement the manger should not for a period of five years "carry on any business similar to that of the employer in Snow Hill, Birmingham, or within a half-mile radius of Aston Cross or Bristol Road, Birmingham." After some 15 months working for the claimant, the defendant went to work for a tailor in Snow Hill. The claimant sought an injunction. The court found that the restriction as to Snow Hill was valid, whereas the other restrictions were void. It was possible to strike out the references to these other areas which were "independent and severable" without altering the nature and meaning of the original agreement which was intended to protect the claimant's legitimate interests. Thus the effect of severance was to limit the scope of operation of the covenant.

A similar case, but one concerning the sale of a business, is *Goldsoll v Goldman*.[42] In this case, **15–021** the defendant sold his business to the claimant—the business consisted of the sale of imitation jewellery. The defendant covenanted that he would not for a period of 10 years carry on the business of vendor or dealer in "real or imitation jewellery in the county of London or any part of the United Kingdom of Great Britain and Ireland and the Isle of Man or in France, the United States. Russia or Spain, or within 25 miles of the Potsdamerstrasse, Berlin, or St Stephans Kirche, Vienna." The defendant, in breach of covenant, became involved in a business in the same street as the claimant. The claimant sought an injunction. The Court of Appeal found that because custom was obtained through national advertising, the restraint as to the United Kingdom or the Isle of Man was no wider than reasonably necessary to protect the claimant's interest. However, the restraint as to places outside the United Kingdom was too wide, as was the reference to real jewellery since the defendant only dealt in imitation jewellery. Applying the blue pencil test, the court was able to simply delete the void restrictions and an injunction to enforce the modified covenant was granted. The clause as severed still made sense.

It seems that severance will not be possible where the clause is a single indivisble covenant for the protection of the claimant's entire business. This was the conclusion of the Court of Appeal in *Attwood v Lamont*.[43]

The facts of the case were that the claimant, a general outfitter in Kidderminster, employed the defendant as cutter and head of the tailoring department. There were several departments in the store, each with a manager. The defendant's contract of employment contained a covenant that he would not engage in the trade or business of a "tailor, dressmaker, general draper, milliner, hatter, haberdasher, gentleman's, ladies' or children's outfitter at any place within a radius of ten miles" of Kidderminster. The defendant subsequently obtained and carried out tailoring orders in Kidderminster. The claimant sought an injunction; this was granted by the Divisional Court which held that the clause was too wide to protect the claimant's interest, but it could be severed by striking out the various trades except that of tailor. The Court of Appeal disagreed, holding that severance was not possible as the clause was not a series of covenants for the protection of each department. The whole covenant was therefore void. (Atkin and Younger L.JJ. held also that even if the covenant could be severed, it would still be void as being in restraint of competition.) On the issue of severance Younger L.J. said:

> "The learned judges of the Divisional Court . . . took the view that such severance always was permissible when it could be effectively accomplished by the action of a blue pencil. I do not agree. The doctrine of severance has not, I think, gone further than to make

[42] [1915] 1 Ch. 292.
[43] [1920] 3 K.B. 571.

[severance] permissible in a case where the covenant is not really a single covenant but is in effect a combination of several distinct covenants. In that case and where the severance can be carried out without the addition or alteration of a word, it is permissible. But in that case only . . . here, I think, there is in truth but one covenant for the protection of the respondent's entire business, and not several covenants for the protection of his several businesses. The respondent is, on the evidence, not carrying on several businesses but one business, and, in my opinion, the covenant must stand or fall in its unaltered form."

15–022   It is not easy to reconcile *Attwood v Lamont* and *Goldsoll v Goldman*. One distinction is that the latter case involved the sale of a business and, as has already been observed (see para.15–013), the courts are more ready to uphold such restraints because of greater equality of bargaining power. It may be that the courts are less likely to sever the clause in employment cases,[44] although in *Putsman v Taylor*, discussed above, severance was allowed on the basis that it did not alter the nature of the agreement. This approach was approved recently by the Court of Appeal in relation to an employment contract in *Beckett Investment Management Group Ltd v Hall*.[45]

Restraint of trade: conclusion

15–023   As a final observation, it should noted that there is an alternative to severance and that is the flexible or non-literal approach to construction (see para.15–010). The approach achieves the same objective by rendering enforceable a clause that would otherwise be struck down because of its width, providing it is reasonable as between the parties and in the public interest. It may be recalled that in *Littlewoods v Harris*, the court did not feel itself bound by the literal meaning of the words used and felt able to interpret the clause according to the factual matrix at the time of the agreement. The difficulty at the moment with this approach is that the law is in a state of uncertainty as to whether, and in what circumstances, this approach is permissible.

Further reading

Smith, *Reconstructing Restraint of Trade* (1995) 15 O.J.L.S. 565.
Wynn-Evans, *Restrictive Covenants and Confidential Information – Some Recent Cases* (1997) 18 B.L.R. 247.
Whish, *Competition Law* 5th edn, (London: LexisNexis/Butterworth, 2003).

---

[44] But see *T Lucas & Co Ltd v Mitchell* [1974] Ch. 129.
[45] [2007] EWCA Civ 613.

Chapter 16

REMEDIES I: DAMAGES FOR BREACH OF CONTRACT

Where a party to a contract suffers loss as a result of the other party's breach, they are entitled **16–001** at common law to an award of damages. In some cases, as we have seen from earlier chapters, the injured party will, in addition, be entitled to repudiate the contract (see para.9–010). Even where the innocent party has suffered no loss, nominal damages may be awarded, i.e. a token sum to recognise that a legal right has been infringed. The normal purpose of damages in contract is to compensate rather than punish the victim and, as we shall see, they are usually designed to place the injured party in the same financial position as they would have been in had the contract been properly performed.

The award of damages in contract raises two main issues: first, the "measure" of damages—how is the court to quantify the claimant's loss? Secondly, "remoteness of damage"—for what types of loss is the claimant entitled to recover damages; what is the extent of the defendant's liability? These issues will be considered in this chapter.

The award of damages is not the only remedy for breach of contract. In some cases, the claimant will not be seeking damages but the right to receive an agreed price for goods delivered or an agreed sum under the contract. In other cases the claimant is looking for reasonable remuneration on a quantum meruit, for example, where they are wrongly prevented by the other party from completing performance. There are also restitutionary remedies arising from what historically has been referred to as "quasi-contract". In exceptional cases, the court may be prepared to order the defendant to perform the contract or alternatively, to restrain them from breaching of contract. The former is achieved by a decree of specific performance and the latter by the granting of an injunction. These are equitable remedies and available at the discretion of the court. All these other remedies, together with the statutory rules regarding the limitation of actions, will be discussed in the following chapter, Chapter 17.

We begin our discussion of the law of damages with the issue of the measure of damages.

MEASURE OF DAMAGES

Basis of the award

16–002   The fundamental principle with regard to the measure of damages to be awarded for breach of contract was stated by Parke B. in *Robinson v Harman*:[1]

> "The rule of common law is, that where a party sustains a loss by reason of the breach of contract, he is, so far as money can do it, to be placed in the same situation, with respect to damages as if the contract had been performed."

Expectation loss

16–003   The above-mentioned statement of Parke B. closely represents what is the normal basis for the recovery of damages for breach of contract, that is "expectation loss" or "loss of bargain".[2] In other words, the injured party has lost, as a result of the breach, what they *expected* to gain if the contract had been properly performed. So far as money can do it, they are to be placed in that position. If the claimant was expecting to make a profit out of the transaction, then, subject to the rule of remoteness to be discussed later in this chapter (see para.16–024), their loss of profit will be reflected in the damages awarded including any consequential loss arising from the breach.

Reliance loss

16–004   Exceptionally, damages are awarded to compensate the claimant for expenses incurred in reliance on the contract which have been wasted as a result of the defendant's breach. This is referred to as "reliance loss"—the object of damages for reliance loss is to place the claimant in the position they would have been in had the contract never been made. In this respect, damages protecting reliance are similar to damages awarded on a tortious basis.

Where damages are awarded on the reliance basis, it seems that pre-contractual expenses may be included. In *Anglia Television Ltd v Reed*[3] the claimant television company wished to make a television play about an American having an adventure in an English wood, to be called "The Man in the Wood". The claimants incurred expenditure of £2,750 in advance, in finding a place to film the play and employing a director, a designer and a stage manager. They then looked for a suitable leading man and found the American actor, the defendant Robert Reed. The claimants hired the defendant who agreed to play the leading role. Unfortunately, the defendant had double booked himself and he therefore repudiated the contract. The claimants were unable to find a suitable replacement so they accepted the repudiation and abandoned the play. The claimants sued for damages but, as they could not estimate what their loss of profit would have been, they claimed instead their wasted expenditure.

Lord Denning M.R., in the Court of Appeal, said that the claimants were entitled to elect to claim wasted expenditure rather than loss of profits and continued:

---

[1]   (1848) 1 Ex. 850.
[2]   For an analysis, see Fuller and Perdue (1936) 46 Yale L.J. 52.
[3]   [1972] 1 Q.B. 60.

"If the [claimant] claims the wasted expenditure, he is not limited to the expenditure incurred *after* the contract was concluded. He can claim also the expenditure incurred *before* the contract, provided that it was such as would reasonably be in the contemplation of the parties as likely to be wasted if the contract was broken [ie the loss must not be too remote]. Applying that principle here, it is plain that, when Mr Reed entered into this contract, he must have known perfectly well that much expenditure had already been incurred . . . he must pay damages for all the expenditure so wasted and thrown away."

Lord Denning also stated that the claimant in cases such may elect to claim either loss of profits or wasted expenditure, but he must elect between them—he cannot claim both. Although correct in the context of *Reed v Anglia Television* it is submitted that this statement is probably not of general application.[4] The concern is that a claimant might be doubly compensated for the same loss, but this would only occur where the claimant was awarded gross profits as well as wasted expenditure. There seems to be no reason why a claim for net profits and wasted expense could not be combined.

Although the claimant can generally choose either a claim based on expectation or reliance losses, the court may deny a claim based on reliance where they feel the claimant is trying to salvage something from a "bad bargain", i.e. the transaction is so unprofitable so as to not even cover the claimant's expenses. In *C & P Haulage v Middleton*[5] the Court of Appeal held that reliance damages should not be awarded so as to place the injured party in a better financial position than if the contract had been properly performed. In the case itself, the claimant sought compensation for improvements he had carried out to garage premises. He occupied the premises under a licence from the defendant but, before the end of the term, the defendant wrongfully ejected him. The contract provided that the fixtures installed by the claimant became the property of the defendant on the expiry of the licence—the claimant recovered only nominal damages as the wasted expenditure resulted from the terms of the contract rather than from the breach. Indeed the claimant's costs were reduced as a result of the breach since the local authority had allowed the claimant to occupy his own premises and therefore he did not have to pay rent.

In *Anglia Television v Reed*, it seems to have been assumed that the film, if made, would have made enough money to at least cover the claimants' expenditure. In *CCC Films (London) Ltd v Impact Quadrant Films Ltd*,[6] however, it was held that on the facts the burden lay on the defendant to show that the claimant had made a bad bargain. The defendants granted the claimants a licence for US $12,000 to exploit, distribute and exhibit three films of which the rights were owned by the defendants. In breach of contract, the defendants sent uninsured tapes which were lost and so the claimants could not exploit the licence. The claimants sought to recover the US $12,000 as reliance expenditure but the defendants argued that the burden of proof was on the claimants to show that they had not made a bad bargain—if so, the expenditure would have been incurred whether or not the defendants were in breach of contract. Hutchinson J. held that the burden of proof was on the defendants to show that the expenditure would have been lost even if the claimants could have exploited the licence. As the defendants submitted no such evidence, the claimants action succeeded.

16–005

---

[4] Lord Denning M.R. relied on *Cullinane v British "Rema" Manufacturing Co Ltd* [1954] 1 Q.B. 292 where a claim for capital expenditure on defective plant was allowed and loss of profits was disallowed.

[5] [1983] 1 W.L.R. 1461.

[6] [1985] Q.B. 16.

The restitutionary interest

16–006   There is a third basis on which damages for breach of contract are awarded, and that is the restitutionary interest. Generally in the law "restitution" refers to the recovery of money or property from another person where that person is not entitled to it, so as to prevent unjust enrichment (see para.17–017).

In relation to damages for breach of contract, where there is a repudiatory breach of contract which has been accepted, the innocent party will be able to recover any benefits which have been transferred to the contracting breaking party. Thus suppose that in a sale of goods contract, A gives B an advance payment of £500 for goods which B ultimately fails to deliver; the court will order B to restore the advance payment to A. The position will be the same where the goods prove to be defective—A will return the goods and receive a refund of the money from B. We have seen that, in an appropriate case, a claim for reliance loss may be combined with a claim for expectation loss. Similarly, there is no reason why a restitutionary claim could not be joined with one for reliance or expectation loss. Indeed, there is nothing to prevent all three interests being recovered. Thus, suppose A sells B a piece of machinery for use in B's factory. B pays A for the machine and it is delivered and installed; the machine, however, turns out to be defective and is rejected by B. B will have incurred costs in installing the machine (reliance loss) and will have lost profits as a result of not having the use of it (expectation loss). He will also, of course, wish to recover the price (restitution). He may recover all three but the loss of profits awarded will be net profits.[7]

Account for profits

16–007   Historically, awards of damages for breach of contract have been limited to what the claimant has lost as a result of the breach of contract, as in the examples given above. Where the effect of the breach of contract was that the defendant made a *profit*, the courts would not allow the claimant to recover.

This approach is illustrated by the case of *Surrey County Council v Bredero Homes Ltd*[8] where the county council had sold land to the defendants, a firm of developers. Under the terms of the contract, the defendants were required to build 72 houses in accordance with planning permission already granted by the local planning authority. After the sale had been completed, the defendants were granted planning consent to build a further five homes on site. In a deliberate breach of contract, the defendants put up the additional properties and made a profit therefrom. The claimant county council sought damages based on the amount the defendants would have had to pay the council in order to obtain a relaxation from the contract. In other words, the council was asking the developers to hand over part of their profit. The Court of Appeal held that the claimant could recover nominal damages only since it had suffered no loss from the breach of contract—the 72 houses had been built and the claimant was in the position it would have been in had the contract not been breached.

However, the Court of Appeal had taken an apparently different approach in an earlier case, *Wrotham Park Estate Co Ltd v Parkside Homes Ltd*.[9] Here the defendant developers, in 1971, bought land burdened by a restrictive covenant which prohibited building, to the benefit of

---

[7] See *Millar's Machinery Co Ltd v David Way & Son* (1935) 40 Com. Cas. 204.
[8] [1993] 1 W.L.R. 1361.
[9] [1974] 1 W.L.R. 798.

the claimants' adjoining property. In breach of covenant, the defendants started to build on the land and the claimants sought an injunction to prevent further building and to require the demolition of the properties already built. By 1973, when the case came to trial, 14 houses had been built. Brightman J. refused to countenance the destruction of such a valuable social and economic resource as housing, but he did award damages in lieu of an injunction under Lord Cairns' Act.[10] Although the claimants had not suffered any financial loss as a result of the construction of the houses, the court awarded the sum which might reasonably have been demanded by them as a quid pro quo for relaxing the restrictive covenant. This was estimated as at five per cent of the profit which the defendants made as a result of the breach of contract. The decision appears at first sight to be quite contrary to that arrived at in *Surrey CC v Brodero Homes* but it can be distinguished on the basis that it was concerned with the power to award damages in lieu of an injunction—in the *Surrey* case, no injunction was sought as there was no danger of any future breach. This was the view of Dillon and Rose L.JJ. in the *Surrey* case.[11] Alternatively, the damages awarded in *Wrotham Park* could be seen as compensatory rather than restitutionary—the claimants were being compensated for losing an opportunity to negotiate a release from the restrictive covenant.

In *Attorney-General v Blake*[12] the House of Lords took matters a stage further and required the defendant, exceptionally, to give a full account for profits. The facts of the case were most unusual. George Blake, a British intelligence officer, had spied for the Soviet Union and in 1961 he was convicted and sentenced to 42 years for treason. In 1966 he escaped from prison and defected to the USSR. Whilst in Moscow, Blake wrote an autobiography which was published in England by Jonathan Cape Ltd. When the book was published in 1990, the information it contained was neither confidential nor damaging to the public interest. Nevertheless, the publication of the information was a breach of Blake's contract of employment and an offence under the Official Secrets Act. When the matter came to the Government's notice, Blake was still to receive about £90,000 in payments from the publisher and an action was launched by the Attorney-General to prevent the moneys from being paid to Blake.

16–008

The Court of Appeal[13] held that the Crown was entitled to nominal damages only since it could not establish that it had suffered any loss as a result of the breach of contract. The court did, however, recognise two situations where a restitutionary claim for profits might succeed. The first is so-called "skimped performance" where the defendant has failed to provide the full extent of the services which he has contracted to provide and for which the claimant has been charged. The second is where the profit is obtained by the defendant doing the very thing which he has contractually promised not to do. The House of Lords (Lord Hobhouse dissenting) allowed the claim. Preferring the *Wrotham Park* case (a "solitary beacon") over the decision in *Surrey CC v Bredero Homes*, the majority found that, in exceptional cases, damages for breach of contract could be measured "by the benefit gained by the wrongdoer from the breach." Lord Nicholls felt that "no fixed rules could be prescribed" for when to order an account of profits and added:

"A useful general guide, although not exhaustive, is whether the [claimant] had a legitimate interest in preventing the claimant's profit-making activity, and, hence, depriving him of his profits."

[10] The Chancery Amendment Act 1858, s.2. The power is now the conferred by the Supreme Court Act 1981, s.50.
[11] But see *Jaggard v Sawyer* [1995] 1 W.L.R. 269.
[12] [2001] A.C. 268.
[13] [1998] Ch. 439.

The majority of the House considered that the Crown had such an interest in preventing Blake profiting from the disclosure of official information. Lord Nicholls said that normally, the remedies of damages, specific performance and injunction would provide an adequate remedy for a breach of contract. An account for profits would only arise in exceptional cases where the court, having regard to all the circumstances, felt that those traditional remedies would be inadequate.

In his speech dissenting from the majority in *Attorney-General v Blake,* Lord Hobhouse sounded a note of warning that:

> "[I]f some more extensive principle of awarding non-compensatory damages for breach of contract is to be introduced into our commercial law the consequences will be very far reaching and disruptive. I do not believe that such is the intention of [the majority of the House] . . . but if others are tempted to try to extend the decision of the present exceptional case to commercial situations so as to introduce restitutionary rights beyond those presently recognised by the law of restitution, such a step will require very careful consideration before it is acceded to."

16–009   The danger of too liberal an interpretation of the "exceptional" nature of the remedy granted in *Attorney-General v Blake* is perhaps to be seen in the subsequent case of *Esso Petroleum Co Ltd v Niad Ltd*.[14] In this case, N owned a petrol filling station and entered into an agreement with the petrol company E whereby, in return for a discount on the petrol supplied, N would report the prices charged by competitors in the locality. N would then charge the price recommended by E—the purpose was to enable E to remain competitive. N deliberately broke this agreement by not passing the discounts on to its customers. Morritt V.C. considered that an account for profits under *Attorney-General v Blake* would be an available remedy in a case such as this as the circumstances were "exceptional". Damages were not an adequate remedy, the judge said, because E could not establish the extent to which lost sales were attributable to N's breach and therefore any damages awarded would be nominal; moreover, E had a legitimate interest in preventing N from profiting from its breach. It may be questioned why the circumstances of this case were adjudged to be so exceptional. The difficulty is that the "legitimate interest" of E in the performance of the contract in this case is difficult to distinguish from that of many, if not most, commercial parties.

The potential application of *Attorney-General v Blake* arose in a subsequent decision of the Court of Appeal, *Experience Hendrix LCC v PPX Enterprises Inc*.[15]

In 1965 the guitarist Jimi Hendrix entered into a recording contract with the defendants. Two years later Hendrix was sued by them for breach of that contract and the action was eventually settled in 1973, although Hendrix had died in 1970. Under the terms of a settlement agreement, the defendants agreed with the deceased's estate that some 19 master recordings were to be handed over and destroyed. The defendants, owners of the copyright to the recordings, failed to hand over all the recordings and subsequently exploited them commercially. At first instance, Buckley J. granted an injunction against the defendants but did not award damages. The Court of Appeal distinguished *Attorney-General v Blake*—the *Hendrix* case was not an exceptional case within the terms of the *Blake* decision and the defendants were not required to account for profits. As Mance L.J. explained:

[14] [2001] EWHC 458 (Ch).
[15] [2003] E.M.L.R. 25.

"[T]here are . . . obvious distinctions from Blake's case. First, we are not concerned with a subject anything like as special or sensitive as national security. The State's special interest in preventing a spy benefiting by breaches of his contractual duty of secrecy, and so removing at least part of the financial attraction of such beaches, has no parallel in this case. Secondly, the notoriety which accounted for the magnitude of Blake's royalty earning capacity derived from his prior breaches of security, and that too has no present parallel. Thirdly, there is no direct analogy between PPX's position and that of a fiduciary."

Nevertheless the court applied the *Wrotham Park* case and awarded the claimant such sum as might reasonably have been demanded as a quid pro quo for allowing the defendants to exploit the recordings.

The *Wrotham Park* basis was also applied by Clarke J. in *Lane v O'Brien Homes Ltd*[16] which **16–010** involved a sale of land for housing which was subject, not to a restrictive covenant, but to a collateral contract limiting the number of houses to be built on site to three. In breach of contract, the defendant built four houses and the county court judge awarded the claimant the sum of £150,000 on the footing that she had lost the chance of negotiating a release from the restriction in the contract. On appeal, Clarke J. refused to upset the award. The judge did not think that the cases decided under the *Wrotham Park* principle laid down any general rule that damages must be limited to a small percentage of the purchaser's potential profit arising from the breach of contract, although this was the case in the *Wrotham Park* case itself. The judge considered that the relevant time for assessing damages was the time at which planning permission for the four houses had been granted,[17] i.e. the time at which the defendants would have sought to be released from their contractual obligation to build no more than three houses. He said:

"At that time, with the certainty rather than merely the remote prospect of planning permission being granted, the stakes had become very much higher. What the claimant had, namely the benefit of a contractual term prohibiting development to the full extent which the defendant now had planning permission to carry out, would have been very much more valuable to her than it was before. Conversely, the defendants would . . . have been prepared to pay a substantially higher price for it."

Thus the whole exercise is based on hypotheticals.

There is no doubt that the law has moved away from awarding damages purely on the basis of compensation for loss. The difficulty for the courts will be to keep the lid on things but in that respect the *Hendrix* case is a welcome development and it is to be preferred to the decision in *Esso Petroleum v Niad*.

Quantification of expectation loss

We started the discussion of the basis on which damages for breach of contract are awarded by **16–011** noting that the normal basis for the award of damages is expectation loss. Damages awarded on the reliance or restitutionary bases alone are something of an exception and we have looked

---

[16] [2004] EWHC 203. See also *WWF World Wide Fund for Nature v World Wrestling Federation Entertainment* [2006] EWHC 184.
[17] The judge considered that the planning application for four houses amounted to an anticipatory breach.

at cases where such damages are awarded and the principles upon which they were assessed. We now turn to an examination of expectation loss.

Available market

16–012   There are no specific rules for the quantification of damages for expectation loss in contract—quantification is a matter for the court. An exception concerns contracts for the sale of goods where damages are assessed on the basis of the market price. The Sale of Goods Act 1979, s.51(3) provides that where the seller fails to deliver the goods and the buyer brings an action for non-delivery, where there is an "available market" for the goods, the measure of damages should be prima facie the difference between the contract price and the current market price at the time the goods ought to have been delivered. Similarly, where the buyer refuses to accept or pay for the goods, s.50(3) of the Act of 1979 provides that where there is an available market, the measure of damages should be prima facie the difference between the contract price and the current market price at the time when the goods ought to have been accepted.

It follows that there will be many cases where the damages will be nominal since there will be no difference between the market price and the contract price. Where the seller is a dealer, the loss arising in the usual course of things is the loss of profit that would have been made had the goods been sold to that particular buyer. If they have been able to find another buyer at the same or a higher price, the damages will be nominal.[18] Where supply exceeds demand, full loss of profits may be awarded as the dealer will have sold one less item than they otherwise would.

In *W L Thompson v Robinson (Gunmakers) Ltd*[19] the defendants contracted to purchase a new Standard Vanguard car from the claimant car dealers. The retail price of the car was fixed by the manufacturers which the dealer could not vary. The defendants wrongfully repudiated the contract and refused to accept the car but the claimants managed to persuade their whole-sale suppliers to take the car back. The claimants then sought to recover from the defendants the loss of profit on the sale which would have been £61. The defendants argued that the claimants were entitled only to nominal damages, as there was no difference between the market price of the car and the contract price. They contended that s.50(3) of the Sale of Goods Act applied because there was an available market for the goods in question, and that market the price of Vanguards was fixed. As the claimants had mitigated their loss the damages should be nil.

Upjohn J. rejected this contention and explained the position as follows:

> "[A]n "available market" merely means that the situation in the particular trade in the particular area was such that the particular goods could be freely sold, and that there was a demand sufficient to absorb readily all the goods that were thrust on it, so that if a particular purchaser defaulted, the goods in question could readily be disposed of. Indeed, such was the situation in the motor trade until very recently. It was, of course, notorious that dealers all over the country had long waiting lists for new motor cars . . . if any purchaser fell out there were many waiting to take his place, and it was conceded that if those circumstances were still applicable to the Vanguard motor car the claim for damages must have necessarily been nominal. But . . . circumstances had changed in relation to Vanguard motor cars, and . . . there was not a demand in the [locality] which could readily absorb all

---

[18]   *Charter v Sullivan* [1957] 2 W.L.R. 528.
[19]   [1955] Ch. 177.

the Vanguards available for sale. If a purchaser defaults, the sale is lost and there is no means of readily disposing of the Vanguard contracted to be sold so that there is not even on the extended definition an available market."

Upjohn J. held that s.50(3) of the Sale of Goods Act was merely a prima facie rule that could be displaced by evidence that supply exceeded demand. The claimants were therefore awarded the £61 profit they would have made on the sale—they had sold one fewer car than they otherwise would. By contrast, in *Charter v Sullivan*[20] the facts were similar but the car in question was a Hillman Minx. The buyer repudiated the contract and the dealers sold the car to another customer. The dealers admitted that they could sell all the Hillman Minxes they could get—as demand exceeded supply the dealers were entitled only to nominal damages.

These two cases involved new cars—what is the position with regard to second-hand cars? The issue arose in *Lazenby Garages Ltd v Wright*[21] where the defendant W purchased a secondhand BMW 2002 from the claimants L, a firm of dealers. W agreed to pay £1, 670 for the car but he repudiated the contract the next day. Two months later, L resold the vehicle for £1,770. Nevertheless L sought damages from W. They argued that since they had bought the car for £1, 325 five days before W agreed to buy, they had lost £345 which they claimed as damages. W contended that L's loss was nil since they had resold the car for a higher price. L claimed that they had sold one fewer car than they otherwise would. In the Court of Appeal Lord Denning M.R. said:

16–013

> "The cases show that if there are a number of new cars, all exactly of the same kind, available for sale, and the dealers can prove they sold one less car than they otherwise would have done, they would be entitled to damages amounting to their loss of profit on the one car . . . But it is entirely different in the case of a secondhand car. Each secondhand car is different from the next, even though it is the same make . . . some secondhand cars, of the same make, even of the same year, may sell better than others of the same year."

It followed that there was no "available market" for such cars under s.50(3) of the Sale of Goods Act since a secondhand car was effectively a unique item. Instead the court based the measure of damages on s.50(2) of the Act which provides that the measure is the loss directly and naturally resulting in the ordinary course of events from the buyer's breach of contract.[22] Lord Denning continued;

> "The buyer in this case could not have contemplated that the dealer would sell one car less. At most he would contemplate that, if they resold this very car at a lower price, they would suffer by reason of that lower price and recover the difference. But if they resold this very car at a higher price, they would suffer no loss. Seeing that these [claimants] resold this car this car for £100 more than the sale to [W], they clearly suffered no damage at all."

Interestingly, the trial judge did not think that L had proved that they had sold one car fewer, but there was a 50:50 chance they would have sold an extra car, so he had reduced the damages to half of the sum claimed.

---

[20] [1957] 2 W.L.R. 528.
[21] [1976] 1 W.L.R. 459.
[22] This is a statutory expression of the rule of remoteness of damage in contract generally for normal or usual loss (see para.16–025).

Damages for lost opportunity

16–014 Generally, substantial damages for loss of expectation will not be awarded where the claim is based on too much speculation. In such a case the successful claimant may be awarded reliance losses or receive only nominal damages. In *McRae v Commonwealth Disposals Commission*[23] the Commission invited tenders for the salvage rights to an oil tanker, said to be wrecked at a particular location. The claimants tender was successful and they fitted out a ship and set sail but could not find the wreck—it was non-existent. The claimants sought damages based on the profit they would have made in salvaging the ship. The High Court of Australia rejected the claim—it was impossible to assess the value of a non-existent ship. The court did, however, award reliance damages for the wasted expenditure as a result of the salvage expedition.

The difficulty of assessing damages and the fact that the award contains an element of speculation will not necessarily bar a claim. This can be seen in cases where the courts are prepared to award damages where the breach of contract causes the claimant to lose an opportunity, such as *Chaplin v Hicks*.[24]

The facts were that the defendant, a theatrical manager, advertised a competition in a newspaper, for young ladies to submit their photograph. Over 6,000 people around the country entered—50 girls were to be auditioned and 12 would be offered remunerative employment in a theatrical production. The claimant was shortlisted but, in breach of contract, the defendant failed to give her sufficient notice of the interview and so she lost her chance of selection. The claimant sued but the defendant argued for nominal damages since the claimant only stood a one in four chance of selection. The jury awarded her £100 and this award was upheld by the Court of Appeal. Fletcher Moulton L.J. said:

> "Where by contract a man has a right to belong to a limited class of competitors, he is possessed of something of value and it is the duty of the jury to estimate the pecuniary vale of that advantage if it is taken from him."

In other words, the loss of an opportunity should be compensated despite the fact that it may be difficult to place a pecuniary value on the loss and, of course, despite the fact that the claimant may be made better off than if she had attended the audition and failed to be selected. Later cases have stressed that there needs to be a substantial, that is, a real and measurable chance of the opportunity being fulfilled for such damages to be awarded.[25]

Difference in value and cost of reinstatement

16–015 In certain types of contract, and especially building and construction contracts, there are two principal measures of damages; these are (i) difference in value; and (ii) cost of reinstatement or "cost of cure". The latter has traditionally been regarded as the normal measure of damages in building contracts but the difficulty is that it may involve, if awarded, disproportionate expense. Suppose that A contracts with a builder B that B will build a house for A. A specifies that a particular brand of insulation material should be placed in the cavity walls. In breach of

---

[23] (1951) 84 C.L.R. 377. The case is discussed at para.12–007 on the issue of mistake.
[24] [1911] 2 K.B. 786. See also *Simpson v London and North Western Railway Co* (1876) 1 Q.B.D. 274.
[25] *Davies v Taylor* [1974] A.C. 207; *Allied Maples Group Ltd v Simmons & Simmons* [1995] 1 W.L.R. 1602.

contract, B uses a different make, although it is perfectly suitable for the purpose. If A could insist on the reinstatement of what he originally stipulated for, it would probably involve the reconstruction of the entire house. The cost would be prohibitive and out of all proportion to the breach which has occurred, so that such an award would be totally unreasonable. An award of damages on the alternative basis, i.e. difference in value, would probably yield only nominal damages since the difference in the value of the house as specified and, as built, is likely to be nil.[26]

The problem arose in *Ruxley Electronics and Construction Ltd v Forsyth*[27] where the defendant employed the claimants to build a swimming pool and it was agreed that it was to have a maximum depth of 7ft 6in. When the pool was completed, it was discovered that the depth of the pool was only 6ft 9in. The claimant sought to recover the balance of the contract price and the defendant counterclaimed for the cost of deepening the pool to the original contract specification. This would have required the demolition and reconstruction of the pool and would have cost over £20,000. The pool was perfectly safe for diving and the judge at first instance found that there was no diminution in the value of the pool as a result of the way in which the works had been carried out. Damages could not therefore be based on difference in value as this was nil. The judge further found that it would have been unreasonable and wholly disproportionate to the cost to require the reconstruction of the pool. Nevertheless, the court held that the defendant was entitled to damages of £2,500 based on "loss of amenity". The claimant appealed to the Court of Appeal which, by a majority, held that damages should be based on the cost of reconstruction of the pool which was assessed at £21,560. The court felt that this was the only way the defendant could have his expectations under the contract met. The claimant appealed to the House of Lords.

Their Lordships restored the decision of the trial judge. Demolition and reconstruction of **16–016** the swimming pool would have been unreasonable and so damages could not be assessed on the cost of reinstatement—even though the breach of contract did not result in a diminution in value, the court could award damages based on the loss of amenity suffered by the defendant. The judge's assessment of this at £2,500 was allowed to stand. This award is the most interesting aspect of the case. As Lord Mustill explained:

> "[T]here would be something wrong if, on the hypothesis that cost of reinstatement and the depreciation in value were the only available measures of recovery, the rejection of the former necessarily entailed the adoption of the latter; and the court might be driven to opt for the cost of reinstatement, absurd as the consequence might often be . . . . But these remedies are not exhaustive, for the law must cater for those occasions where the value of the promise to the promisee exceeds the financial enhancement of his position which full performance will secure. The excess, often referred to in the literature as the "consumer surplus" . . . is usually incapable of precise valuation in terms of money, exactly because it represents a personal, subjective and non-monetary gain. Nevertheless, where it exists the law should recognise it and compensate the promisee if the misperformance takes it away."

The House indicated that awards under the loss of amenity head would usually be modest. The amount to be awarded will be at the discretion of the judge—there are not as yet any principles

[26] See the USA decision of *Jacob & Youngs v Kent* (1921) 230 N.Y. 239.
[27] [1996] A.C. 344.

upon which such compensation is assessed but given the non-monetary basis of the damages this is perhaps inevitable, as Lord Mustill acknowledged. It is an imperfect solution to the problem raised by cost of cure in certain types of contract.

The issue will be considered further in the next section where we will consider the extent to which damages for expectation loss can cover non-pecuniary losses, such as mental distress and disappointment.

Damages for mental distress

16–017   Although damages in contract may be recovered for physical inconvenience and pain and suffering caused by *personal injury*, it was the traditional rule that damages could not be awarded for purely mental distress and suffering.

A useful starting point is the decision of the House of Lords in *Addis v Gramophone Co*[28] where the claimant was employed by the defendants as a manager and could be dismissed on six months notice. The defendants sacked the claimant on six months notice but appointed another person in his place and prevented him from doing his job. At trial the jury awarded damages for wrongful dismissal including a sum that reflected the harsh and humiliating way that the claimant had been dismissed and "the pain he experienced by reason . . . of the imputation upon him conveyed by the manner of his dismissal." The House of Lords held that such damages were not recoverable. The claimant's entitlement to damages extended only to lost salary and commission, i.e. the economic losses arising from the breach of contract.

In more recent times the courts have shown a readiness to award damages for breach of contract where the whole purpose of the transaction is to provide a pleasurable experience or greater peace of mind, such as a holiday. In *Jarvis v Swans Tours Ltd*[29] the claimant was a solicitor who booked a fortnight's skiing holiday with the defendant company. The cost of the holiday was just under £64. The brochure described the holiday as a "house party" and referred to afternoon tea parties, a bar, a yodeller evening and ski-packs. The holiday turned out to be very disappointing for the claimant. In the first week there were only 13 people present and in the second week the claimant was the only guest, so that there were no parties and the hotel manager did not speak English. The yodeller was a gentleman in working clothes who came and sang a few songs on his way home from work. The bar was only open on one evening in the second week and full-size skis were only available for two days. The claimant sought damages for loss of enjoyment. In the county court, the claimant was awarded £32 and he appealed to the Court of Appeal. As Lord Denning M.R. explained:

"In a proper case damages for mental distress can be recovered in contract, just as damages for shock can be recovered in tort. One such case is a contract for a holiday, or any other contract to provide entertainment and enjoyment. If the contracting party breaks his contract, damages can be given for the disappointment, the distress, the upset and frustration caused by the breach. I know that it is difficult to assess in terms of money, but it is no more difficult than the assessment which the courts have to make every day in personal injury cases for loss of amenities . . . Here, Mr Jarvis's fortnight winter holiday has been a grave disappointment. It is true that he was conveyed to Switzerland and back and had

---

[28] [1909] A.C. 488.
[29] [1973] Q.B. 233.

meals and a bed in the hotel. But that is not what he went for. He went to enjoy himself with all the facilities which the defendants said he would have."

The court awarded the claimant damages of £125. The decision was affirmed in a later, very similar case, *Jackson v Horizon Holidays Ltd*[30] (the decision is discussed at para.8–016 above in the context of privity of contract). The case of *Heywood v Wellers*[31] provides a different example of a contract the purpose of which was to provide freedom from distress. Here a woman was being stalked by a man with whom she had previously had an affair. The claimant instructed the defendants, a firm of solicitors, to obtain relief from the situation. The defendants negligently handled the case so that the injunction they sought was ineffective and the claimant suffered further harassment. The Court of Appeal held that the claimant could be compensated for the consequent mental distress.   **16–018**

It should also be noted that mental upset caused by *physical inconvenience* and discomfort is compensatable in contract. Thus in *Bailey v Bullock*[32] the claimant recovered damages for discomfort as a result of being forced to live for two years in the small house belonging to his wife's parents. The claimant's solicitor had negligently mishandled proceedings for the recovery of the claimant's own house from a third party.

It was not long before the scope of damages for purely mental distress was extended to the employment situation and in *Cox v Phillips Industries Ltd*[33] an employee who had been wrongfully demoted by his employers recovered damages for distress and anxiety. This decision was difficult to reconcile with *Addis v Gramophone Co* and in the case of *Bliss v South East Thames Area Health Authority*[34] the Court of Appeal overruled *Cox v Phillips Industries*.

In the *Bliss* case, the claimant was a consultant surgeon who was required by his employers, the defendant health authority, to undergo a psychiatric examination. The claimant refused and, having been suspended by the defendants, sought damages for breach of contract. The trial judge's award included an element of damages for mental distress and anxiety. The Court of Appeal disallowed it. As Dillon L.J. explained: **16–019**

> "Modern thinking tends to be that the amount of damages recoverable for a wrong should be the same whether the cause of action is laid in contract or in tort. But in the *Addis* case, Lord Loreburn regarded the rule that damages for injured feelings cannot be recovered in contract for wrongful dismissal as too inveterate to be altered."

Citing *Jarvis v Swans Tours* and *Heywood v Wellers* Dillon L.J. recognised an exception where the contract "was itself a contract to provide peace of mind and freedom from distress." In *Hayes v James and Charles Dodd*[35] Staughton L.J. in the Court of Appeal affirmed the approach of Dillon L.J. in the *Bliss* case and stated:

> "It may be that the class is somewhat wider than that. But it should not, in my judgment, include any case where the object of the contract was not comfort or pleasure, or the relief of discomfort, but simply carrying on a commercial activity with a view to profit."

---

[30] [1975] 1 W.L.R. 1468.
[31] [1976] Q.B. 446.
[32] [1950] 2 All E.R. 1157. See also *Perry v Sidney Phillips & Son* [1982] 3 All E.R. 705.
[33] [1976] 1 W.L.R. 638.
[34] [1987] I.C.R. 700.
[35] [1990] 2 All E.R. 815.

Following this approach, the Court of Appeal in *Alexander v Rolls Royce Motor Cars*[36] refused to award damages for disappointment and loss of enjoyment where a garage had breached an agreement to repair a car. The contract did not fall within the special exception and was not analogous to a contract for a holiday—it was a contract to repair a car rather than to provide a pleasurable experience.

16–020　　In *Watts v Morrow*[37] Bingham L.J. took to opportunity to clarify the scope of the exceptions to the general rule. In the case itself, the claimants had purchased a farmhouse in the country as a weekend retreat from their stressful city jobs. In purchasing the house, they had relied on a surveyor's report provided by the defendant. In breach of contract, the defendant's report was carried out negligently and wrongly concluded that there were no major defects. In fact, the claimants had to spend almost £34,000 on repairs to the house; the property at the time of purchase was worth about £15,000 less than they had paid for it; and for the eight months while the repairs were being carried out the claimants had to endure discomfort and inconvenience of staying at the house over the weekends. The Court of Appeal awarded the claimants damages for dimunition in the value of the house but not for the cost of the repairs. The trial judge had awarded the claimants £4,000 each for mental distress generally but this was disallowed by the court. Instead the claimants recovered damages for distress arising from the physical inconvenience they had suffered which was assessed at £750 each. Bingham L.J. laid down some authoritative guidance and confirmed that contract breaker is not in general liable "for any distress, frustration, anxiety, displeasure, vexation, tension or aggravation which his breach of contract may cause to the innocent party." Bingham L.J. continued:

> "But the rule is not absolute. Where the very object of the contract is to provide pleasure, relaxation, peace of mind or freedom from molestation, damages will be awarded if the fruit of the contract is not provided or if the contrary result is procured instead . . . A contract to survey a house for a prospective purchaser does not fall within this exceptional category. In cases not falling within this exceptional category, damages are in my view recoverable for physical inconvenience and discomfort caused by the breach and mental suffering directly related to that inconvenience and discomfort."

Thus according to Bingham L.J., damages for non-pecuniary loss are recoverable (i) where the "very object" of the contract is to provide a pleasurable experience or (ii) where the breach of contract causes physical inconvenience. Such was the state of the law when the matter came before the House of Lords in *Farley v Skinner (No 2)*.[38]

16–021　　The facts were that the claimant, who wished to acquire a peaceful country residence, became interested in a property called Riverside House in Sussex. It was situated some 15 miles from Gatwick Airport and the claimant wanted to be sure that it was not seriously affected by aircraft noise. The claimant instructed the defendant, a surveyor, to carry out the usual structural survey but in addition to investigate whether the house would be affected by aircraft noise. The defendant reported that it was unlikely that the property would suffer greatly from such noise. The claimant purchased the property for £420,000 and then spent in the region of £125,000 on modernisation and refurbishment. A few months later the claimant moved in and soon discovered that

---

[36] [1996] R.T.R. 95.
[37] [1991] 1 W.L.R. 1421.
[38] [2002] A.C. 732.

the property was indeed affected by aircraft noise. The property was situated near a navigation beacon where aircraft waiting to land would be "stacked" by air traffic control in a spiralling queue until runway space became available. The claimant's enjoyment of the property was diminished—he decided not sell it but to pursue a claim for damages. The trial judge held that the surveyor had been negligent and that if he had carried out his instruction properly, the claimant would not have bought the house. The judge found that there had been no dimunition in the value of the property after taking into account the aircraft noise and so that part of the claim was dismissed. The court, however, awarded the claimant the sum of £10,000 for distress consequent upon physical discomfort, i.e. the second of Bingham L.J.'s two exceptions in *Watts v Morrow*.

The defendant's appeal to the Court of Appeal was allowed by a majority decision. The court felt that the facts fell outside both exceptions stated by Lord Bingham in *Watts v Morrow*—there was no physical inconvenience as such and the "very object" of the contract was not to provide pleasurable experience, etc. The claimant successfully appealed to the House of Lords who restored the decision of the trial judge. Their Lordships drew a significant distinction between the present case and *Watts v Morrow*. In *Farley v Skinner* the surveyor had undertaken to carry out a distinct and important contractual obligation, i.e. to confirm the presence or absence of aircraft noise, before the buyer committed himself to purchase the property. This was essential to the purchaser's peace of mind. *Watts v Morrow*, on the other hand, was a case where the surveyor had been charged with carrying out a general inspection of the property and had negligently failed to discover defects; in other words, it was an ordinary surveyor's contract. In such contracts, there is no promise by the surveyor to endow the purchaser with peace of mind and freedom from mental distress. The general observations of Bingham L.J. *Watts v Morrow* should therefore be viewed in this light. Their Lordships went on to hold that as far as Bingham L.J.'s first exception in *Watts v Morrow* was concerned (that pleasure, etc. should be the "very object" of the contract) it was not necessary that the contract as a whole should be concerned with the provision of pleasure. As Lord Steyn put it:

> "There is no reason in principle or policy why the scope of recovery in the exceptional category should depend on the object of the contract as ascertained from all its constituent parts. It is sufficient if a major or important object of the contract is to give pleasure, relaxation or peace of mind."

The obligation placed on the defendant specifically to investigate aircraft noise and report on it showed that the presence or absence of such noise was a major or important part of the contract. This conclusion therefore represents a significant re-interpretation of Bingham L.J.'s first category.   **16–022**

There was a second and alternative ground on which the defendant could have been held liable—that is under the second of Bingham L.J.'s exceptional cases. The claimant had suffered physical inconvenience and discomfort as a result of the breach of contract and his distress was consequent upon that. Once again, the House of Lords introduced some qualification to the principle as expressed by Bingham L.J. in *Watts v Morrow*. As Lord Scott explained:

> "[T]he adjective "physical", in the phrase "physical inconvenience and discomfort", requires . . . some explanation or defintion. The distinction between the "physical" and "non-physical" is not always clear and may depend on the context. Is being awoke at night by aircraft noise "physical"? If it is, is being unable to sleep because of worry and anxiety

"physical"? . . . [T]he critical distinction to be drawn is not a distinction between the different types of inconvenience or discomfort of which complaint may be made but a distinction based on the cause of the inconvenience or discomfort. If the cause is no more than disappointment that the contractual obligation has been broken, damages are not recoverable even if the disappointment has led to a complete mental breakdown. But, if the cause of the inconvenience or discomfort is a sensory (sight, touch, hearing, smell etc) experience, damages can, subject to the remoteness rules, be recovered."

Thus the aircraft noise suffered by the claimant was held to be physical inconvenience entitling him to damages.

The House upheld the award of £10,000 made by the judge at first instance, however it was thought to be "at the very top end" of the permissible range of awards under this head—it was felt that such awards should normally be modest. The award therefore resembles the £2,500 damages for "loss of amenity" that was awarded to the claimant in *Ruxley Electronics v Forsyth* (see para.16–015). In *Farley v Skinner* there was some difference of judicial opinion in the House of Lords as to the precise basis of loss of amenity damages. It is submitted that Lord Steyn's interpretation is preferable, i.e. they represent the loss of a pleasurable amenity, so that the claimant may recover damages for the resulting disappointment.

16–023   The principles expounded in *Farley v Skinner* were applied by Neuberger J. in *Hamilton-Jones v David Snape*.[39] In this case, the claimant was concerned that her husband, from whom she was separated, would take their children to Tunisia. Accordingly, she instructed the defendants, a law firm, to ensure that the husband could not take the children out of the country. The defendants obtained court orders to this effect and notified the Passport Agency accordingly but failed to renew the notification after 12 months, as they were advised to do. As a result, the claimant's husband was able to remove the children to Tunisia. The claimant sought damages for breach of contract including an element of compensation for mental distress. In the Chancery Division, Neuberger J. said:

"In light of the reasoning of Lord Steyn in *Farley v Skinner* . . . it appears to me unrealistic to suggest that a significant part of the purpose of the claimants instructing the defendants . . . was not to protect the claimant's peace of mind in respect of the very event which happened, namely the removal of the twins from this country."

The court held that damages for mental distress of £20,000 should be awarded. The case is similar to *Heywood v Wellers* (discussed at para.16–018) although in that case the instruction given to the claimant's solicitors to protect their client from molestation was perhaps more explicit than in the present case. Nevertheless the court was satisfied that both parties in the present case would have been aware that a significant reason for instructing the defendants was that the mother wished to retain custody of her children for her own peace of mind.

REMOTENESS OF LOSS

16–024   The claimant may not be able to recover damages for all the loss they have suffered as some of the loss may be adjudged by the court to be "too remote" a consequence of the breach to be

[39] [2004] 1 W.L.R. 924.

compensatable by the defendant. The rule of remoteness constitutes a major potential limitation on the award of damages. Two further such limitations, mitigation and contributory negligence, will be considered after we have examined remoteness of loss.

Remoteness: the rule in Hadley v Baxendale

The fundamental rule of remoteness of loss in contract derives from the case of *Hadley v Baxendale*.[40] Here, the claimants were millers in Gloucester who contracted with the defendant carriers to take a broken mill shaft to the repairers in Greenwich, as a pattern for a new shaft. The claimants had no spare shaft. Although the defendants had promised to deliver within a day, they in fact delayed, and the shaft was not delivered until a week later. The claimants sued the defendants for damages for loss of profits arising from the fact that the mill was out of action for longer than anticipated, owing to the delay.   **16–025**

Alderson B. said that damages for breach of contract should be such as may:

(i)   " . . . fairly and reasonably be considered as either arising naturally, ie according to the usual course of things, from such breach of contract itself"; or be
(ii) " . . . such as may reasonably be supposed to have been in the contemplation of both parties, at the time they made the contract as the probable result of the breach of it."

It was held that a claim for damages falling outside these two heads would be adjudged to be too remote. The rule as originally laid down was perceived as being in two parts, (i) dealing with normal or usual loss; and (ii) dealing with special, abnormal or unusual loss. Later cases (discussed below) have telescoped the two limbs into a single principle since the contract-breaker will be presumed to be aware of normal loss in any event, and recovery for the special loss will depend on such loss being within their reasonable contemplation at the time of the contract. That the time of the contract is the relevant time for ascertaining whether the loss is too remote was confirmed by the House of Lords in *Jackson v Royal Bank of Scotland*[41]—the case is discussed at para.16–031 below.

Returning to the facts of *Hadley v Baxendale*, and applying the above-stated principles, the court held that the claimant's loss did not arise "naturally" because the claimants might well have possessed a spare shaft; neither was it "in the contemplation of the parties" as the defendants were unaware that the shaft entrusted to them was the only one which the claimants possessed. It would have been different if, at the time of the contract, the claimants had informed them of the position. Accordingly, loss of profits was too remote a head of damage.

The principle laid down in *Hadley v Baxendale* was restated by the Court of Appeal in the case of *Victoria Laundry (Windsor) Ltd v Newman Industries Ltd*[42] where the defendants agreed to sell to the claimant launderers a boiler, which, as the defendants were aware, was required for immediate use. In breach of contract, the defendants delayed delivery by five months. The claimants sought damages for loss of profits of (a) £16 a week that they could have earned by taking on extra business with their new, larger boiler; (b) £262 a week that they could have earned from certain lucrative dyeing contracts with the Ministry of Supply. It was held by the Court of   **16–026**

---

[40] (1854) 9 Ex. 341.
[41] [2005] UKHL 3.
[42] [1949] 2 K.B. 528.

Appeal that the defendants were not liable for item (b), the loss was too remote. The defendants did not actually know of the lucrative dyeing contracts and could not therefore be liable for their loss. However, knowing what the claimants business was, they would have been aware that if the boiler was delayed the claimants would suffer a loss on their ordinary day-to-day business.

A similar approach was taken in *Balfour Beatty Construction (Scotland) Ltd v Scottish Power Plc*[43] where it was held by the House of Lords that there was no general principle that parties were presumed to have knowledge of each other's business practices, particularly where complex construction or manufacturing processes were involved. In the case itself, the defendants agreed to supply the claimants with a supply of electricity to a site where they were constructing a concrete aqueduct. The defendants were not aware that the works required a "continuous pour" of concrete. In breach of contract, the defendants caused a power cut and the works were interrupted. As a result, the work that had been done had to be demolished and the installation rebuilt. This loss was held not to be in the reasonable contemplation of the defenders and too remote. As the Lord Ordinary at first instance had put it:

"The defenders could certainly contemplate that if the supply failed the plant would not operate and that if it was operating at the time the manufacture of concrete would be interrupted. What they did not know was the necessity of preserving a continuous pour for the purposes of the particular operation . . . nor were they asked for any specially secure supply of electricity. Furthermore they did not know that a construction joint [ie remedial works] would not be an acceptable solution if the power was terminated so that demolition would follow."

The case of *Kemp v Intasun Holidays Ltd*[44] affords an interesting comparison. A holidaymaker verbally informed his travel agent that he was prone to asthma attacks. Whilst on holiday, the defendants, in breach of contract, required the claimant to relocate his hotel accommodation which triggered off an asthma attack. On a claim for additional damages, the Court of Appeal held that the mention of asthma was merely conversational and not part of the booking as the claimant had left blank a box on the booking form headed "Special Requests". The injury to the claimant was therefore outside the defendants' reasonable contemplation.

Contemplation and foreseeability

16–027 In giving judgment in the case of *Victoria Laundry v Newman* (the facts are given at para.16–026), Asquith L.J. stated:

"In cases of breach of contract the aggrieved party is only entitled to recover such part of the loss actually resulting as was at the time of the contract *reasonably foreseeable* as liable to result from the breach [Author's italics]."

Although the decision in the case itself cannot be impugned, the use of the words "reasonably foreseeable" by Asquith L.J. might suggest that the test of remoteness is the same in contract as it is in tort, since reasonable foreseeability is the test in tort.[45]

---

[43] 1994 S.C. 20.
[44] [1987] F.T.L.R. 234.
[45] See *Overseas Tankship (UK) Ltd v Mort Dock & Engineering Co, The Wagon Mound* [1961] A.C. 388.

The issue was clarified by the House of Lords in *Koufos v Czarnikow, The Heron II*[46] where the appellants, shipowners, contracted to carry a cargo of sugar belonging to the respondents from Constanza to Basrah. In breach of contract, the ship deviated to Berbera to load a cargo of livestock for the owners, and, as a result, she arrived in Basrah nine days later than would otherwise have been the case. As the appellants knew, the respondents were sugar merchants and there was a sugar market at Basrah. What the appellants did not know was that the respondents intended to sell the sugar immediately on arrival at that port. In the meantime, there had been a sharp fall in the price of sugar on the Basrah market and the respondents sold the sugar at a lower price than if the ship had arrived on time. The respondents sought damages for the difference in price, about £4,000. The House of Lords held that the difference in price could be recovered by way of damages—the loss was not too remote. The appellants should reasonably have contemplated that the respondents would be intending to sell the cargo on arrival at Basrah. As Lord Reid explained:

> "[The shipowner] did not know what the charterers intended to do with the sugar. But he knew there was a market in sugar at Basrah, and it appears to me that, if he had thought about the matter, he must have realised that at least it was *not unlikely* that the sugar would be sold in the market at market price on arrival. He must also be held to have known that in any ordinary market prices are apt to fluctuate from day to day [Author's italics]."

Lord Reid stated that he used the words "not unlikely" as denoting "a degree of probability considerably less than an even chance but nevertheless not very unusual." Lords Reid and Morris rejected the notion that reasonable forseeability is the test in contract—the contractual test is reasonable contemplation. Referring to *Victoria Laundry v Newman* Lord Reid said:

> "To bring in reasonable foreseeability appears to me to be confusing measure of damages in contract with measure of damages in tort. A great many extremely unlikely results are reasonably foreseeable: it is true that Lord Asquith may have meant foreseeable as a likely result, and if that is all he meant I would not object further other than to say that I think the phrase is liable to be misunderstood."

Thus the difference between contemplation and foresight seems to lie in the degree of probability: something may be foreseeable even if it is only a slight possibility. Contemplation, on the other hand, is a rather narrower formulation—a thing will only be in contemplation if, according to the House of Lords, it is "not unlikely", or a "serious possibility" or a "real danger".

16–028

The reason for the distinction was explained by Lord Reid as follows:

> "The modern rule of tort is quite different and it imposes a much wider liability [than contract]. The defendant will be liable for any type of damage which is reasonably foreseeable as liable to happen even in the most unusual case, unless the risk is so small that a reasonable man would in the whole circumstances feel justified in neglecting it. And there is good reason for the difference. In contract, if one party wishes to protect himself against a risk which to the other party would appear unusual, he can direct the other party's attention to it before the contract is made . . . But in tort there is no opportunity for the injured party to protect himself in that way, and the tortfeasor cannot reasonably complain if he

---

[46] [1969] 1 A.C. 350.

has to pay for some unusual but nevertheless foreseeable damage which results from his wrongdoing."

Type of loss and extent of loss

16–029   It seems that, for the loss not to be too remote, all the contract-breaker needs to contemplate is the particular *type* of loss in question rather than its actual extent. This is a qualification upon the principles as expressed by Alderson B in *Hadley v Baxendale*.

The rule is illustrated by the case of *Parsons (H) (Livestock) Ltd v Uttley Ingham & Co Ltd*.[47] The claimants were pig farmers and they contracted with the defendants for the supply and installation of a bulk feed storage hopper. This was a device for storing and feeding the herd with pig nuts. When the hopper was delivered a ventilator at the top of the hopper (28 feet above the ground) was taped shut—the delivery man should have removed the tape and opened the ventilator. When pig nuts were put into the hopper, they went mouldy. Because of eating the mouldy food, the pigs initially developed diarrhoea and then became ill with a serious (and at the time rare) condition, E Coli. As a result 254 pigs died out of the claimants' total stock of 700. The defendants were held liable under s.14 of the Sale of Goods Act for the sale of goods not fit for the purpose. The Court of Appeal held that the defendants were liable for the loss of the pigs—their demise was not too remote a consequence of the breach. Even though the death of the pigs through eating the mouldy feed may not reasonably have been contemplated by the parties, *some physical injury* to the pigs could have been contemplated as a serious possibility as a result of the breach. Thus for the purposes of the reasonable contemplation test, it is sufficient if the type of injury is within the contemplation of the parties. The judges agreed in the result but arrived at it by different routes.

Lord Denning M.R. considered that where a breach of contract resulted in loss of profit or economic loss generally, the test of "reasonable contemplation" and "serious possibility" were applicable. Such cases were covered by the line of authorities, *Hadley v Baxendale*; *Victoria Laundry v Newman*; and *Koufos v Czarnikow, The Heron II* (these cases are discussed above). On the other hand, where the breach caused physical injury (as in the death of the pigs) the contract breaker is liable for the loss they ought reasonably to have foreseen at the time of the breach, even if it was only a slight possibility. In other words, the test of remoteness in such cases, in the view of Lord Denning, is similar to the test in tort. This is a radical approach which appears to have little real support in the authorities but the reason for it Lord Denning explained as follows:

> "Coming to the present case, we were told that in some cases the makers of these hoppers supply them direct to the farmer under contract with him, but in other cases they supply them through an intermediate dealer – who buys from the manufacturer and resells to the pig farmer on the self-same terms – in which the manufacturer delivers direct to the pig farmer. In the one case the pig farmer can sue the manufacturer in contract. In the other in tort. The test of remoteness should be the same. It should be the test in tort."

16–030   Lord Denning concluded that under the test of reasonable foreseeability, the claimant could recover for the loss of the pigs. An additional claim for loss of profits on future sales was too remote on the reasonable contemplation test.

---

[47] [1978] 1 Q.B. 791.

Scarman and Orr L.JJ. rejected the distinction in law between loss of profit and physical damage favoured by Lord Denning and found for the claimant on the issue of the loss of the pigs on the reasonable contemplation test (but Scarman L.J. disallowed the claim for loss of profits). He suggested that there was little substantive difference between reasonable foreseeability in tort and reasonable contemplation in contract. This approach is difficult to reconcile with the views of Lord Reid in the House of Lords in *The Heron II*, i.e. that the remoteness rule is stricter in contract than in tort.

The difficulty with the *Parsons Livestock v Uttley Ingham* principle is in identifying precisely what is meant by a "type" of loss. For example, in *Victoria Laundry v Newman* (the facts are given above), the particular type of loss in question was loss of profits. Was there any difference between the loss of the "ordinary" business profits and the lucrative dyeing contracts? Are they not both the same type of loss, albeit that one is greater in extent than could have been contemplated? An endeavour to draw the line was made in *Brown v KMR Services Ltd*[48] where the Court of Appeal held that "Lloyd's names"[49] could recover their losses against those who had encouraged them to take on excessive liabilities. The extent of the losses went well beyond what might arise in the usual course of things but all that was required was that the particular type of loss, i.e. financial, should have been contemplated.

There is a lack of clarity on this aspect of the remoteness rule in contract which requires resolution by a precise ruling of the House of Lords.

Reasonable contemplation at the time of the contract

The principle under the rule in *Hadley v Baxendale*, i.e. that the time of the contract is the relevant time for deciding what losses could be reasonably contemplated, was confirmed by the House of Lords in *Jackson v Royal Bank of Scotland*.[50]   **16–031**

The facts were that the appellants Jackson were importers and they supplied a business called Economy Bag with cheap dog chews manufactured in Thailand. The transactions between the appellants and Economy Bag were carried out by the issue of letters of credit issued by the respondents, the Royal Bank of Scotland to Economy Bag. Although Economy Bag knew the identity of the supplier in Thailand, it did not realise how cheaply the dog food was being supplied to the appellants, i.e. the mark-up on each transaction. The respondents, in error, revealed this information to Economy Bag when they sent them documents showing a mark-up of some 19 per cent. On receiving this information, Economy Bag decided to source the goods directly from Thailand and ceased to purchase them from the appellants. This was a disaster for the appellants because it deprived them of their principal source of business and they had to cease trading. The appellants brought proceedings against the respondents for breach of their contractual duty of confidence and claiming damages for the loss of the opportunity to make profits from repeat business with Economy Bag. At first instance the judge held that the respondents were in breach of contract with the appellants and awarded damages on the basis that the trading relationship with Economy Bag would have continued for four more years on a decreasing scale—beyond that the losses were too speculative. On appeal, the Court of Appeal held that such losses were too remote and based the award on a one year period only.

---

[48] [1995] 4 All E.R. 598.
[49] That is, those at Lloyds who provided financial backing for certain insurance policies but who suffered losses when major claims were made under those policies.
[50] [2005] UKHL 3.

The House of Lords restored the award made by the trial judge. The loss of repeat orders was not too remote—once the test of remoteness in *Hadley v Baxendale* was satisfied, as it was, there could be no arbitrary cut-off point after which damages could not be awarded since the respondents' contractual obligation was open-ended. They had not limited their liability under the contract to any particular period. The Court of Appeal had fallen into the error of considering the state of the parties' knowledge at the time of the breach—it is the knowledge at the time of the contract that is the relevant time for the purposes of the remoteness rule.

MITIGATON AND CONTRIBUTORY NEGLIGENCE

16–032   In addition to the rule about remoteness of loss, there are two further limitations on the award of damages for breach of contract; these are mitigation and contributory negligence.

Mitigation

16–033   Once a breach of contract has occurred, the claimant comes under an expectation to take all reasonable steps to mitigate the loss caused by the breach of contract. Recovery cannot be made for any part of the loss which the defendant can prove to have resulted from a failure to mitigate.

Mitigation: the general rule

16–034   The classic statement of the mitigation principle was made by Viscount Haldane L.C. in *British Westinghouse Electric and Manufacturing Co v Underground Electric Railways Co of London*[51] where he said:

> "The fundamental basis is thus compensation for pecuniary loss naturally flowing from the breach; but this first principle is qualified by a second, which imposes on the [claimant] the duty of taking all reasonable steps to mitigate the loss consequent on the breach, and debars him from claiming any part of the damage which is due to his neglect to take such steps."

In the case itself, the appellants agreed to supply the respondents with turbines meeting the respondents' specification. When the turbines were delivered, it was discovered that, in breach of contract, they did not meet that specification. In due course, the respondents replaced these with turbines manufactured by a different firm which were much more efficient, and these new turbines soon paid for themselves. The respondents sought damages to cover the cost of replacing the original turbines with the new ones but the House of Lords disallowed the claim. The respondents had successfully mitigated their losses and could recover damages only for the period when the original turbines had been operating inefficiently. As Viscount Haldane L.C. explained:

[51]   [1912] A.C. 673.

"[W]hen in the course of his business [the claimant] has taken action arising out of the transaction, which action has diminished his loss, the effect in actual dimunition of the loss he has suffered may be taken into account even though there was no duty on him to act."

Two further illustrations of mitigation may be given, one from the field of employment, the other from the sale of goods:

In *Brace v Calder*[52] the defendants were a four-member partnership who agreed to employ the claimant as manager for two years. Shortly afterwards, the partnership was dissolved which amounted to a wrongful dismissal of the claimant. However, two of the former partners offered to employ the claimant on the same terms but he refused the offer. The claimant brought an action to recover the salary he would have received had he served the full two years. The Court of Appeal held that he was entitled only to nominal damages as it was unreasonable to have rejected the offer of continued employment.

In *Payzu v Saunders*[53] the defendants agreed to sell to the claimants 200 pieces of silk. The goods were to be delivered as required and payment was to be made monthly following delivery. The first consignment was delivered; the claimants wrote a cheque for it which the defendants did not receive, and so the claimants sent another cheque. This delay caused the defendants to form the mistaken impression that the claimants were in financial difficulties and so the defendants refused to make any further deliveries unless the claimants paid in cash. The claimants refused to accept this offer and sued for damages for breach of contract, claiming the difference between the contract price and the current market price, the price of the goods having risen. Although the defendants had wrongfully repudiated the contract, the Court of Appeal refused to award damages for difference in price. This loss arose, not from the breach of contract, but from the failure to accept the defendants' offer to supply the goods in return for a cash payment. The claimants should have mitigated their loss and were confined to damages based on the loss they would have incurred had they accepted the defendants' offer.

16–035

The important point to grasp in connection with mitigation is that the claimant is only required to act *reasonably*; as Viscount Haldane L.C. observed in the *British Westinghouse* case, the principle "does not impose on the [claimant] an obligation to take any step which a reasonable and prudent man would not ordinarily take in the course of his business." The point is illustrated by the case of *Pilkington v Wood*[54] where the claimant purchased a house after the solicitor acting for him failed to inform him that the vendor did not have a good title. Because of the defective title, the property was unsaleable, and so the claimant sued the defendant solicitor. The claimant recovered by way of damages the difference between what he paid for the house and its actual worth. Harman J. rejected an argument that the claimant should have mitigated his loss by suing the vendor under s.76 of the Law of Property Act 1925. The judge said:

"I do not propose to decide whether an action against . . . [the vendor] would lie or be fruitful. I can see it would be one attended with no little difficulty. I am of opinion that the so-called duty to mitigate does not go so far as to oblige the innocent party . . . to embark on a complicated and difficult piece of legislation against a third party. The damage to the [claimant] was . . . the direct result of negligent advice tendered by his solicitor . . . it is no

---

[52] [1895] 2 Q.B. 253.
[53] [1919] 2 K.B. 581.
[54] [1953] Ch. 770.

part of the [claimant's] duty to embark on the proposed litigation in order to protect his solicitor from the consequences of his own carelessness."

16–036   There is a further point in relation to mitigation—although Viscount Haldane in the *British Westinghouse* case spoke of a "duty" to mitigate, it is not in fact a duty as such. This was made clear by Sir John Donaldson M.R. in the case of *Sotiros Shipping Inc v Sameiet Soholt, The Soholt*[55] where he said:

"The [claimant] is under no duty to mitigate his loss, despite the habitual use by lawyers of the phrase "duty to mitigate". He is completely free to act as he judges to be in his best interests. On the other hand, a defendant is not liable for all loss suffered by the [claimant] in consequence of his so acting. A defendant is only liable for such part of the [claimant's] loss as is properly regarded to be caused by the defendant's breach of duty."

Mitigation and anticipatory breach

16–037   Anticipatory breach can give rise to difficulties in relation to mitigation. It may be recalled that an anticipatory breach is a breach occurring before the date due for performance (see para.9–011). In such circumstances, the claimant may either accept the breach and sue for damages immediately or they may refuse to accept the breach and await the date due for performance of the contract. If the innocent party accepts the breach then they may not be able to recover losses attributable to a failure to mitigate. If they do not accept the breach, the issue of mitigation does not arise as the contract remains on foot. This state of affairs can have unusual results, as is evidenced by the decision of the House of Lords in *White and Carter (Councils) Ltd v McGregor*.[56]

The facts of the case were that the appellants agreed to advertise the respondents' garage business on litter bins for three years for an agreed price.[57] The respondents' sales manager had not been authorised to make this contract and when his employer heard of it later the same day he wrote to the appellants to cancel the contract. The appellants chose to ignore this repudiation and proceeded to display the advertisements for three years, eventually claiming the full amount due under the contract. They had made no effort to sell the advertising space to anyone else. Before the House of Lords, the respondents argued that, as they had repudiated the contract before anything had been done under it, the respondents were not entitled to carry out the contract and sue for the price.

By a majority of 3:2 (Lords Morton and Keith dissenting) the House held that the appellants could recover the full contract price—the appellants were under no obligation in these circumstances to mitigate their losses. The result is the logical consequence of the innocent party's right to affirm the contract rather than to accept the other party's repudiation as discharging the contract and claim damages. Moreover, the appellants were entitled to act as they did even though they did not benefit particularly, and despite the fact that the respondents suffered greater loss than they would have done if sued for damages. The decision appears to sanction capricious and wasteful conduct on the part of the innocent party and bears down too heavily

[55] [1983] Com. L.R. 114.
[56] [1962] A.C. 413.
[57] It was an action for an agreed sum (see para.16–050) rather than a claim for damages.

on the contract-breaker—it is not surprising that it has attracted some criticism.[58] As Lord Hodson (in the majority) explained:

"It may be unfortunate that the appellants have saddled themselves with an unwanted contract, causing an apparent waste of time and money. No doubt this aspect impressed [the court below, which found for the respondents] but there is no equity that can assist the respondents. It is trite that equity will not rewrite an improvident contract where there is no disability on either side. There is no duty laid upon a party to a subsisting contract to vary it at the behest of the other party so as to deprive himself of the benefit given to him by the contract."

Lord Reid, who delivered the leading speech for the majority, was prepared to allow two limita-   **16–038**
tions to the *White and Carter* principle. Thus it may not apply, first, where the contract requires the co-operation of the other party; and secondly, where the claimant has no "legitimate interest" in performing the contract rather than pursuing a damages claim.

The first limitation was applied in *Hounslow London Borough Council v Twickenham Garden Developments Ltd*[59] where contractors were instructed by the borough council to carry out works on a site owned by the council. Relying on a clause in the contract, the council purported to cancel the contract but the contractors refused to accept this and proceeded with the work on the site. The council sought an injunction on the basis that the contractors were committing a trespass and should be restrained from so doing. Relying on *White and Carter*, the contractors contended that they were entitled to carry out the works and complete the contract. Megarry J. disagreed and held that they were not so entitled. The contract was clearly one which could not be performed without the co-operation of the council and it required their active co-operation. As the judge pointed out, the entire mechanism of the contract was geared to "acts by the architect and quantity surveyor, and it is a contract that is to be performed on the borough's land." Megarry J. went further. He found it difficult to believe that Lord Reid in *White and Carter* intended to limit the concept "of co-operation" to active co-operation— passive co-operation would suffice. Thus it seems the limitation would apply even if the contract was such that there was no requirement for architects, surveyors, building inspectors and so forth to go on the land. This means that there will not be many contracts which do not require some degree of co-operation from the other party. In this respect *White and Carter* was an atypical case on its facts. This therefore represents a very significant practical limitation on the operation of the principle.

The second limitation is that the *White and Carter* principle will not apply where the claimant has no legitimate financial or other interest in performing the contract rather than claiming damages. In such a case, Lord Reid felt that the innocent party "ought not to be allowed to saddle the other party with an additional burden with no benefit to himself." One example of such an interest would be where the innocent party would be in breach of obligations owed to third parties if the contract were not performed.[60]

The issue of whether there was a legitimate interest arose in *Clea Shipping Corpn v Bulk*   **16–039**
Oil International Ltd, The Alaskan Trader.[61] Here, the defendants chartered a ship from the

---

[58] See Goodhart (1962) 78 L.Q.R. 263.
[59] [1971] Ch. 233.
[60] As in the decision of Kerr J. in *Gator Shipping Corpn v Trans-Asiatic Oil Ltd SA, The Odenfeld* [1978] 2 Lloyd's Rep. 357.
[61] [1984] 1 All E.R. 129.

claimants for a period of two years with the hire charge being paid in advance. Approximately twelve months into the charter period, the vessel suffered a major engine breakdown and at this point the defendants indicated that they would no longer require the ship. Nevertheless the claimants proceeded with the repair of the ship which took three months and cost over £800,000. The defendants then repudiated the contract but the claimants refused to accept the repudiation. They maintained the vessel fully crewed and ready to sail until the expiration of the charter period. It was held that the claimants could not recover the hire charge for that period. They had no legitimate interest in so doing rather than accepting the repudiation and recovering damages. Although there is a general and unfettered right to elect to affirm the contract after a breach, Lloyd J. considered that there must come a point at which the court "will cease, on general equitable principles, to allow the innocent party to enforce his contract according to its strict legal terms." The election to affirm must be shown to be "wholly unreasonable" in the circumstances. It seems that the onus is on the contract-breaker to demonstrate that the innocent party has no legitimate interest in fulfilling the contract rather than seeking damages; the burden is not discharged simply by showing that the innocent party's benefit is small in relation to the loss to the contract-breaker.[62]

In *Attica Sea Carriers Corporation v Ferrostaal Poseidon Bulk Reederei GmbH, The Puerto Buitrago*[63] Lord Denning M.R. stressed the adequacy of damages to the claimant. He spoke of the *White and Carter* decision in the following terms:

> "Even though [*White and Carter*] was a Scots case, it would appear that the House of Lords . . . would expect us to follow it in any case that is precisely on all fours with it. But I would not follow it otherwise. It has no application whatever in a case where the [claimant] ought, in all reason, to accept the repudiation and sue for damages—provided that damages would provide an adequate remedy for any loss suffered by him. The reason is because, by suing for the money, the [claimant] is seeking to enforce specific performance of the contract—and he should not be allowed to do so where damages would be an adequate remedy."

16–040   It may be asked, what legitimate interest did the appellants have in the *White and Carter* case itself? This seems to have been assumed as the respondents advanced no evidence to the contrary, e.g. that no alternative advertising contracts were available. It is quite possible, of course, that this was because they were not aware that it was necessary to do this.[64]

Contributory negligence

16–041   It is clear that contractual liability may be removed altogether by the claimant's fault as shown by the case of *Quinn v Burch Bros (Builders) Ltd*.[65] The claimant was a plasterer employed as a sub-contractor by the defendants in carrying out building work. The defendants were contractually obliged to supply any equipment reasonably required for the job within a reasonable time of being requested. In breach of that obligation, the defendants failed to supply

---

[62]   *Ocean Marine Navigation Ltd v Koch Carbon Inc, The Dynamic* [2003] 2 Lloyd's Rep. 693.
[63]   [1976] 1 Lloyd's Rep. 250.
[64]   See further *Ministry of Sound (Ireland) Ltd v World Online Ltd* [2003] EWHC 2178 (Ch); and *Reichman v Beveridge* [2006] EWCA Civ 1659.
[65]   [1966] 2 Q.B. 370.

the claimant with a step-ladder that he had requested. Instead, and to save time, the claimant stood on a trestle which he knew to be unsecure as it was not steadied by a workmate. The trestle collapsed and the claimant suffered injury. It was held that the defendants were not liable in contractual damages. The cause of the claimant's injury was his own negligence which had broken the chain of causation.

The law has been less clear on whether damages for breach of contract can be apportioned by the court on the ground of the claimant's contributory negligence under the Law Reform (Contributory Negligence) Act 1945. In actions in tort, such as negligence claims, it is well-established that the Act applies where the claimant is contributorily negligent, that is, they have contributed to their own harm. The 1945 Act, s.1(1) provides:

"Where any person suffers damage as the result partly of his own fault and partly of the fault of any other person or persons, a claim in respect of that damage shall not be defeated by reason of the fault of the person suffering the damage, but the damages recoverable in respect thereof shall be reduced to such extent as the court thinks just and equitable having regard to the claimant's share in the responsibility for the damage."

The operation of the Act in a simple negligence action is demonstrated by *Capps v Miller*[66] where the defendant motorist negligently collided with a motorcyclist who suffered a head injury. Although the claimant was wearing a helmet, the strap was not secured properly, and the helmet came off in the accident, thus aggravating his injury. The damages awarded to the claimant were reduced by 10 per cent—the court considered this to be just and equitable having regard to the claimant's share in the responsibility for his injury. As the case illustrates, the claimant's lack of care need not have been a factor in causing the accident itself; it is sufficient that it is a factor in causing the claimant's injury.

The Act of 1945, s.4 provides that "fault" means negligence, breach of statutory duty, or **16–042** "other act or omission which gives rise to liability in tort or would, apart from this Act, give rise to the defence of contributory negligence." Do ss.1(1) and 4 of the Act apply to actions for breach of contract, so that the court may apportion damages in such cases? The law on this issue was considered by the Court of Appeal in *Forsikringsaktieselskapet Vesta v Butcher*[67] where the court approved a categorisation of the cases put forward by Hobhouse J. at first instance.[68] The judge said:

"The question whether the 1945 Act applies to claims brought in contract can arise in a number of classes of case. Three categories can conveniently be identified.
(1) Where the defendant's liability arises from some contractual provision which does not depend on negligence on the part of the defendant.
(2) Where the defendant's liability arises from a contractual obligation which is expressed in terms of taking care (or its equivalent) but does not correspond to a common law duty to take care which would exist in the given case independently of contract.
(3) Where the defendant's liability in contract is the same as his liability in the tort of negligence independently of the existence of any contract."

---

[66] [1989] 2 All E.R. 333.
[67] [1989] A.C. 852.
[68] [1986] 2 All E.R. 488, at p.508. The case went on appeal to the House of Lords but on other grounds: [1989] A.C. 582.

Hobhouse J. confirmed that the Act of 1945 applied to category (3). The courts have not, as yet, unequivocally extended it to category (2) and the wording of the statute would seem to rule out category (1). Hobhouse J. gave as an example of category (3) the well-known decision in *Sayers v Harlow Urban District Council*.[69] In this case, the claimant paid to use a public lavatory operated by the defendant council (i.e. she was a contractual visitor) and entered a cubicle. She was unable to exit as there was no handle on the inside of the door and so she tried to see if there was a way of climbing out. To do this she placed one foot on a toilet roll holder. She was climbing down when the holder rotated with the result that she slipped and was injured. The Court of Appeal held that the council was liable in negligence but the damages recovered by the claimant were reduced by 25 per cent in view of the claimant's share in the responsibility for the injury. The court said it made no difference whether the action was brought in tort or contract.

The position established by *Vesta v Butcher* was subsequently affirmed by the Court of Appeal in *Barclays Bank Plc v Fairclough Building Ltd*[70] where the court held that the 1945 Act did not apply to category (1). The Law Commission has recommended that apportionment under the 1945 Act should apply to category (2) as well as (3).[71] There does not seem to be any compelling reason why this should not be so.

LIQUIDATED DAMAGES AND PENALTIES

16–043   We now turn to cases where the contract itself makes provision for payment to be paid by the contract-breaker to the innocent party in the eventuality of a breach or breaches of contract.

Liquidated damages clauses

16–044   Contracts commonly contain clauses providing for the payment of a fixed sum on breach. In view of the issues we have encountered in this chapter thus far regarding such matters as measure of damages, remoteness, mitigation and so forth, it is not surprising that commercial parties in particular will seek to use the contract itself to fix the level of compensation on breach. If the sum specified in the contract represents a genuine pre-estimate of the loss, the court will allow the claimant, on breach, to recover this sum without proof of actual loss. This is so whether the actual loss is greater or smaller than the sum stipulated in the contract. Such provisions are usually referred to as "liquidated damages" or "agreed damages" clauses.[72]

Penalty clauses

16–045   Where the sum stipulated for in the contract is not a genuine pre-estimate of the loss, but is more in the nature of a threat held over the head of the other party (*in terrorem*) to compel performance, it is referred to as a "penalty". A penalty cannot be enforced and a claimant who attempts to enforce a penalty may recover compensation only for their actual loss. The

---

[69] [1958] 2 All E.R. 342.
[70] [1995] Q.B. 214. See also *Platform Home Loans Ltd v Oyston Shipways Ltd* [2000] 2 A.C. 190.
[71] Law Com Report No 219 (1993). See the first instance decision in *De Meza v Apple* [1978] 1 Lloyd's Rep. 508.
[72] Damages that are "unliquidated" are those where the amount is fixed by the court.

antipathy of the courts towards such penal provisions in contracts has its roots in equity—the notion that it is unconscionable for a contracting party to demand an extortionate sum on breach even though the payment has been specifically agreed between the parties.

Distinguishing between liquidated damages and penalties

As Lord Dunedin observed in the leading case on the distinction between the two types of provision, whether a clause is a liquidated damages clause or a penalty is a question of construction depending upon the intention of the parties judged as at the time the contract was made. The case in question is *Dunlop Pneumatic Tyre Co v New Garage & Motor Co Ltd*[73] where the House of Lords laid down some authoritative principles. The first point is that the expression used by the parties to describe the clause is a relevant, but not a conclusive factor; e.g. the term may be described as "agreed damages" but in fact be a penalty, and vice versa.[74] As Lord Dunedin observed:

16–046

> "Though the parties to a contract who use the words "penalty" or "liquidated damages" may prima facie be supposed to mean what they say, yet the expression used is not conclusive. The Court must find out whether the payment stipulated is in truth a penalty or liquidated damages."

Lord Dunedin then proceeded to lay down various tests to assist the task of construction:

(a) If the sum stipulated for is "extravagant and unconscionable" in relation to the greatest loss which could conceivably follow the breach, it will be held to be a penalty.

(b) Where the breach consists of the non-payment of a sum of money and the sum to be paid on breach is greater than the sum which ought to have been paid, the sum will be held to be a penalty.

(c) There is a presumption (but no more) that where a single lump sum is to be paid on the occurrence of one or more or all of several events, some seriously harmful and others trivial, the lump sum is a penalty. On the other hand:

(d) A sum is not prevented from being liquidated damages by the fact that *precise* pre-estimation of the loss is impossible; indeed Lord Dunedin considered that this is "just the situation when it is probable that pre-estimated damage was the true bargain between the parties." Although (c) and (d) are not exactly contradictory, there is some tension between them and therefore the courts tend to approach the issue with some pragmatism.

In the *Dunlop Pneumatic Tyre v New Garage* case itself, the claimants supplied tyres to the defendants subject to an agreement that the defendants would not, inter alia, resell them below list price. The defendants had to pay £5 "by way of liquidated damages and not as a penalty" for every tyre sold in breach of the agreement. The House of Lords held that the provision was not penal and was in the nature of liquidated damages. Price undercutting would have damaged the claimant's business, and although precise pre-estimation of the loss was impossible, the sum stipulated for was reasonable in the circumstances. As Lord Dunedin explained:

---

[73] [1915] A.C. 79.
[74] *Cellulose Acetate Silk Ltd v Widnes Foundry Ltd* [1933] A.C. 20.

"Damage as a whole from . . . [breach of the agreement] would be certain, yet damage from any one sale would be impossible to forecast. It is just, therefore, one of those cases where it seems quite reasonable for parties to contract that they should estimate the damage at a certain figure, and provided that figure is not extravagant there would seem no reason to suspect that it is not truly a bargain to assess damages, but rather a penalty to be held *in terrorem*."

16–047   The decision of the Court of Appeal in *Ford Motor Co Ltd v Armstrong*[75] provides an instructive comparison with the *Dunlop Pneumatic Tyre v New Garage* case. In the *Ford Motor* case the defendant car dealer agreed to sell cars manufactured by the claimants. The contract provided that the defendant should pay the sum of £250 if he sold any car or parts below list prices, "such sum being the agreed damages which the manufacturer will sustain." The claimants sued for £250 when the defendant sold goods below list prices but the court held that the sum stipulated for in the contract was a penalty, not liquidated damages. It was not a reasonable pre-estimate of the damage—it was an arbitrary sum fixed *in terrorem*.

The party who is liable to pay the sum has the burden of proving that it is a penalty as opposed to liquidated damages;[76] and the fact that the parties expressly agree that the sum *is* a reasonable pre-estimate of the loss will make no difference if in fact it is found to be a penalty.[77]

The decision of the Privy Council in *Philips Hong Kong Ltd v Attorney-General of Hong Kong*[78] signalled a more flexible approach than that laid down by Lord Dunedin in *Dunlop Pneumatic Tyre v New Garage*. The Board urged a general pre-disposition against finding that clauses were penalties, particularly in commercial transactions where parties were of not unequal bargaining strength and where there is a need for certainty. The deployment in argument of unlikely hypothetical illustrations was said not to assist a court in determining the issue of whether the clause was penal or an agreed damages provision. Lord Woolf said:

"The fact that the issue has to be determined objectively, judged at the date the contract was made, does not mean that what actually happens subsequently is irrelevant. On the contrary, it can provide valuable evidence as to what could reasonably be expected to be the loss at the time the contract was made. Likewise the fact that two parties who should be well capable of protecting their respective commercial interests agreed the allegedly penal provision suggests that the formula for calculating liquidated damages is unlikely to be oppressive."

Sometimes a contract may stipulate for a sum of money to be paid upon the occurrence of an event that is not a breach—the House of Lords confirmed in *Export Credit Guarantee Department v Universal Oil Products Co*[79] that the penalty rules only apply to sums of money payable on breach.

16–048   A case where the stipulated sum was payable on an event that was not a breach is *Alder v Moore*.[80] In this case, the defendant Brian Moore was a professional footballer who played for West Ham FC. He suffered an injury to his right eye which was believed to be permanent. As a result, the claimant insurer paid him the sum of £500 under a policy which provided that if he

---

[75] (1915) 31 T.L.R. 267.
[76] *Robophone Facilities Ltd v Blank* [1966] 1 W.L.R. 1428.
[77] *Duffen v Fra Bo SpA* [2000] 1 Lloyd's Rep. 180.
[78] (1993) 61 B.L.R. 41.
[79] [1983] 1 W.L.R. 339.
[80] [1961] 2 Q.B. 57.

played professional football in the future he would be liable to a "penalty" of the amount paid to him in settlement of the claim, i.e. £500. A year after the injury he began to play professional football for Cambridge United FC. The claimant sought payment of the £500. A majority of the Court of Appeal held that the sum was recoverable by the claimant as the resumption of professional football was not a breach of contract—the penalty rules were inapplicable. It is therefore possible for a party to evade the penalty rules by stipulating that a sum is payable on some event that is not a breach.

Hire-purchase companies have in the past not been slow to exploit this state of affairs. In *Bridge v Campbell Discount Co Ltd*[81] the defendant entered into a hire purchase agreement with the claimants to hire a used Bedford camper van for a price of £482. There was an initial payment of £105 and the balance was payable by 36 monthly instalments of £10. 9s. Clause 6 of the agreement provided that that: "The hirer may at any time terminate the hiring by giving notice of termination in writing to the owners, and thereupon the provisions of clause 9 shall . . . apply." Clause 9 provided that if the agreement was terminated for any reason before the vehicle became the property of the hirer the hirer must deliver up the vehicle and pay to the owners ". . . by way of agreed compensation for depreciation of the vehicle such further sums as may be necessary to make the rentals paid and payable equal to two-thirds of the hire-purchase price." After paying the initial rental and the first monthly instalment, the defendant informed the claimants apologetically that he would be unable to meet any further instalments and returned the vehicle. Relying on clause 9, the claimants sought the sum of £206, i.e. two-thirds of the price less the sums the defendant had already paid.

The Court of Appeal reversed the decision of the judge at first instance that the sum payable was a penalty. The appellate court took the view that the defendant had not breached the contract but had simply exercised his right of termination—as a result the penalty rules did not come into play and the defendant was bound to pay the sum stipulated in the contract. The House of Lords, by a majority (4:1) restored the decision of the trial judge who had assessed the damages at £30. Their Lordships were satisfied that the defendant had breached the contract and that the clause was a penalty—it was not a genuine pre-estimate of the loss. Although with the passage of time the depreciation in the value of the car would increase, the payment under clause 9 would decrease. The real purpose of the provision, therefore, was to discourage early termination by the hirer; Lord Radcliffe described it as a sliding scale of compensation, but one that slides "in the wrong direction, if the measure of anticipated depreciation is supposed to be the basis for the compensation." Lord Denning pointed to the fact that the hirer would be worse off if he exercised his contractual rights of termination than if he breached the agreement. His Lordship memorably observed:

> "Let no one mistake the injustice of this. It means that equity commits itself to this absurd paradox: it will grant relief to a man who breaks his contract but will penalise the man who keeps it."

Despite the ruling of the House of Lords in the *Export Credit Guarantee Department v Universal Oil Products Co* case, that the penalty rules only apply to a sum of money payable on breach, in *Jobson v Johnson*[82] the Court of Appeal held that the equitable rules against penalty clauses applied where the penalty involved the transfer of property whose value exceeded the actual

16–049

---

[81] [1962] A.C. 600.
[82] [1989] 1 All E.R. 621.

loss of the innocent party, as well as where it involved the payment of an excessive sum of money.

There is an abundance of judicial authority to the effect that penalty clauses are a "bad thing" but is this necessarily so? Where the parties are businesspeople bargaining on terms of equality, is a penalty any more objectionable than an exclusion or limitation clause? It may be recalled from Chapter 7 that it is extremely difficult to strike down such exempting clauses on the ground that they fail to satisfy the reasonableness requirement (under UCTA 1977) where the parties are dealing on an equal footing in the course of business (see para.7–062). So far as consumers are concerned, the law has moved on in that protection against penalties would seem to be afforded by the Unfair Terms in Consumer Contracts Regulations 1999 (UTCCR—see para.7–064). Thus Sch.2, para.1(e) of the regulations (the indicative list of terms regarded as unfair) refers to a term "requiring any consumer who fails to fulfil his obligations to pay a disproportionately high sum in compensation". It is at least arguable that the special rules applicable to penalties discussed above are no longer necessary.

Damages for breach of contract: conclusion

16–050   The law relating to damages for breach of contract is in a state of flux. The rules relating to remoteness of loss are in need of clarification by means of an authoritative ruling by the House of Lords (see para.16–024 above); paradoxically, the position regarding damages for mental distress has been made, for the time being, less certain by the decision of the House in *Farley v Skinner* (see para.16–017). And as the ruling in the case of *Attorney-General v Blake* has shown, damages in contract may not be confined merely to what the claimant has lost—profits accruing to the contract- breaker may be recoverable (see para.16–007 above).

Before leaving the law of damages, we should note that an action for damages must be distinguished from "an action for an agreed sum", such as an agreed price for work and materials or the price of goods sold. Such a claim is more straightforward than a claim for damages, since issues of remoteness and measure do not arise. The action may not be available where damages are an adequate remedy although there is an exception, and that is where the principle in *White and Carter (Councils) v McGregor* applies (see para.16–037 above). As we saw, however, where the co-operation of the other party is required, or the innocent party has no legitimate interest in completing performance, the action for the price will not be available.

A recent ruling of the House of Lords has introduced a further development; the case concerns the question of what is the proper date for assessing damages for the repudiation of a long term charterparty. In *Golden Strait Corporation v Nippon Yusen Kubishka Kaisha, The Golden Victory*[83] by a charter dated July 10, 1998, shipowners G chartered *The Golden Victory* to the charterers N for a period of seven years. Clause 33 of the charter provided that both parties should have the right to cancel if war broke out between certain countries. On December 14, 2001, N repudiated the charter and on December 17, G accepted the repudiation. On March 20, 2003, a war broke out in the Gulf region which would have given N a right to cancel as it fell within the terms of Clause 33. The issue that arose was: where a repudiation has been accepted (see para.9–010 for the principles involved), can the party in breach rely on subsequent events to show that they could have cancelled the charter and probably would have done so. The normal rule in such cases has been that damages are assessed as at the date of the contract of

[83] [2007] UKHL 12.

the acceptance of repudiation so that the award of damages would reflect the whole contract period.

A bare majority of the House of Lords (Lords Bingham and Walker dissenting) held that the assessment of damages should allow for the fact that war had broken out in 2003. The majority felt that this result better reflected the basic principle that damages should compensate the victim for loss of their contractual bargain. The party suffering the loss was entitled to be placed in the position they would have been in had the contract been properly performed—the "breach date" rule usually achieved that result but not always. The minority placed emphasis on the need for certainty and predictability in commercial contracts since at the date of acceptance of the breach the outbreak of war was no more than a possibility. In the view of the minority the value of the charter was not affected by this possibility and therefore damages should have been awarded on the basis of the full term. Thus adherence to basic principle has prevailed over considerations of certainty.

16–051

Further reading

Fuller and Perdue, *The Reliance Interest in Contract Damages* (1936) 46 Yale L.J. 52.

Coote, Contract Damages, *Ruxley* and the Performance Interest (1997) 56 C.L.J. 537.

Phang, *The Crumbling Edifice? The award of Contractual Damages for Mental Distress* (2003) J.B.L. 341.

Goodhart, *Measure of Damages When a Contract is Repudiated* (1962) 78 L.Q.R. 263.

Chapter 17

REMEDIES II: EQUITABLE REMEDIES, RESTITUTION AND LIMITATION OF ACTIONS

In this chapter, we are concerned with the equitable remedies of specific performance and injunction and with certain remedies that strictly speaking fall outside the law of contract and are part of the law of restitution, traditionally referred to as "quasi-contract".

17–001

We will conclude by examining the operation of the Limitation Act 1980 as it affects causes of action in contract.

EQUITABLE REMEDIES

We have already encountered the equitable remedies of rescission and rectification in dealing with misrepresentation and mistake—see paras.11–029 and 12–045 respectively. We will now examine the equitable remedies of specific performance and injunction which are available, not as of right, but at the discretion of the court. They will only be granted where it is equitable to do so, and may be refused on the ground of hardship. As with all equitable remedies, they may also be denied where the claimant has behaved unconscionably, in accordance with the maxim— "he who comes to equity must come with clean hands." By contrast, the common law remedy of damages for breach of contract discussed in the previous chapter, is a remedy available as of right.

17–002

Specific performance

Specific performance is an order of the court compelling the party in breach to perform their part of the contract. If the contract-breaker fails to comply with the order, they may be liable to criminal proceedings for contempt of court.

17–003

The fact that the remedy may be refused on the grounds of hardship is illustrated by the case of *Patel v Ali*.[1] The defendant and her husband as co-owners entered into a contract for the sale of their house to the claimants but completion was delayed owing to the defendant's husband being adjudicated bankrupt. At the time of the contract, the defendant, who spoke almost no

---

[1] [1984] Ch. 283.

397

English, was in her early 20s and had one child. She then developed bone cancer and had to have her right leg amputated; she later had a second child and then a third. Although fitted with an artificial leg, the defendant needed help with household chores and in looking after the children and she was reliant for this on relatives and friends who lived close by in the neighbourhood. It was accepted that enforced removal from the home, such as would be necessitated by an order of specific performance, would have caused the defendant great hardship. In the Chancery Division, Goulding J. refused to grant the order. Although on a sale of land, the remedy of specific performance would be normally be granted as a matter of course, in a proper case the remedy could be refused by the court on grounds of hardship. The discretion of the court was wide enough to take into account matters arising subsequent to the contract and problems not caused by the claimants. The claimants in this case were left to their right to recover damages at common law.

The remedy of specific performance is subject to a number of limitations. Thus it will not be granted: (i) where damages are an adequate remedy; (ii) where the contract is one requiring constant supervision; (iii) where the contract involves personal services; and (iv) where there is a lack of mutuality. These limitations will be considered below.

Damages an adequate remedy

17–004   The principle that specific performance will not be granted where damages are an adequate remedy received early recognition by the courts in *Flint v Brandon*.[2] The defendant granted the claimant a lease of 21 years of some land where there were gravel pits, the defendant covenanting to keep the property in repair and make good the land affected by quarrying. The defendant breached these obligations and at the end of the lease the claimant sought specific performance. The action failed—damages would provide a sufficient remedy for the wrongs suffered by he claimant. Sir William Grant M.R. said:

> "This court does not, I apprehend, profess to decree a specific performance of contracts of every description. It is only where the legal remedy is inadequate or defective, that it becomes necessary for the Courts of Equity to interfere."

As a result of this principle, specific performance will not, in general, be awarded for a contract for the sale of goods because the buyer will be able to go into the market and buy similar goods. If they have to buy goods at a higher price than that stipulated for under the contract, they will be adequately compensated by an award of damages. The remedy may be granted where the goods in question are unique, such as a valuable work of art by a famous artist. There must, however, be some element of uniqueness. In *Cohen v Roche*[3] the claimant sued the defendant, an auctioneer, requesting specific performance of a contract for the sale of eight Hepplewhite chairs to which the claimant alleged he was entitled after a sale. McArdie J. awarded only damages and refused specific performance—the chairs were "ordinary article[s] of commerce and of no special value or interest." In *Falcke v Gray*,[4] however, it was accepted in principle by the court that specific performance could be obtained to enforce a contract for the sale of

---

[2] (1803) 8 Ves. 159.
[3] [1927] 1 K.B. 169. By s.52(1) of the Sale of Goods Act 1979, the court is given the discretionary power to order specific performance in an action for breach of contract to deliver specific or ascertained goods.
[4] (1859) 4 Drew. 651.

articles of "unusual beauty, rarity and distinction" so that damages would be an inadequate recompense. (The articles in question were antique oriental jars.) Heirlooms are included in this category and in the case of *Pusey v Pusey*[5] specific performance was ordered of a contract for the sale of the famous Pusey horn, now displayed in the Victoria and Albert Museum, London.

It seems the courts are also prepared to recognise "commercial" uniqueness in the case of **17–005** capital goods such as industrial plant or ships, where such goods cannot be readily obtained from another source.[6] An unusual case that perhaps falls into this category is *Sky Petroleum Ltd v VIP Petroleum Ltd*[7] where the defendants had agreed to supply the claimants with petrol for their filling stations for a period of 10 years. During the energy crisis of the early 1970s, when there was a worldwide shortage of petroleum and diesel products, the defendants purported to terminate the contract leaving the claimants without a source of supply. The claimants sought an interlocutory injunction restraining the defendants from withholding supplies, which would have been tantamount to a temporary order of specific performance. Goulding J. accepted that oil-based products could hardly be described as unique, but said:

> "[I]t is common knowledge that the petroleum market is in an unusual state in which a would-be buyer cannot go out into the market and contract with another seller, possibly at some sacrifice as to price. Here, the defendants appear for practical purposes to be the [claimants'] sole means of keeping their business going, and I am prepared so far to depart from the general rule as to try to preserve the position under the contract until a later date."

Accordingly the judge granted an injunction.

Specific performance is most commonly ordered in contracts for the sale of land since, as the courts regard each piece of land as unique, damages would not be adequate compensation.

In *Beswick v Beswick* (the facts are discussed at para.8–004) specific performance was granted to enforce a contractual obligation to pay a sum of money. Damages would not have been an adequate remedy because they would have been purely nominal, as the promisee's estate had suffered no loss. The breach of a contract to pay a sum of money is normally considered to be adequately compensated by an award of damages, but in this case specific performance was considered to be appropriate in order to compel the promisor to honour his obligation to the third party.

Contracts requiring constant supervision

Specific performance will be refused where the constant supervision of the court is required. In **17–006** *Ryan v Mutual Tontine Westminster Chambers Association*[8] the defendants leased an apartment in a residential block to the claimant, and it was an obligation of the lease that the defendants should provide a resident porter to be constantly in attendance to perform certain duties for the residents. It seems that the defendants appointed as porter a person whose true calling was that

[5] (1864) 1 Vern. 273.
[6] See *Behnke v Bede Shipping Co* [1927] 1 K.B. 648; Cf *Societie des Industries Metallurgiques SA v Bronx Engineering Co Ltd* [1975] 1 Lloyd's Rep. 465.
[7] [1974] 1 W.L.R. 576.
[8] (1893) 1 Ch. 116.

of a chef and he absented himself for many hours each day to act as chef in a neighbouring club. He delegated his portering duties to charwomen and boys. The defendants never managed to engage a competent porter and the claimant sought a decree of specific performance. The Court of Appeal ruled that damages would be an adequate remedy—the contract was one requiring the constant superintendence of the court. Lord Esher M.R. confirmed that this is one of the grounds upon which equity had always refused specific performance. In *Posner v Scott-Lewis*[9] the *Ryan* case was distinguished and specific performance was ordered for the breach of a landlord's obligation to *appoint* a resident porter. Mervyn Davies J. did not consider that such an order would involve any protracted supervision by the court and the contract clearly defined what it was the landlords were required to do. Thus the wording of the contract may be the crucial element in such cases.

Because of the problems with constant supervision, the courts are generally reluctant to order specific performance of building contracts. In many cases, the wording of such contracts will be too vague—the works may not be described with sufficient precision; and in any event, damages will be an adequate remedy for breach. An exception was established in the case of *Wolverhampton Corporation v Emmons*[10] where, under an improvement scheme the corporation acquired land and sold a part of it to a builder who agreed to redevelop the site. Romer J. ordered specific performance of the covenant to build houses on the site. He said that there were three things that the claimant must establish in such cases:

> "The first is that the building work, of which he seeks to enforce the performance, is defined by the contract, that is to say, that the particulars of the work are so far definitely ascertained that the court can sufficiently see what is the exact nature of the work of which it is asked to order the performance. The second is that the [claimant] has a substantial interest in having the contract performed, which is of such a nature that he cannot be adequately compensated for breach of the contract by damages. The third is that the defendant has by the contract obtained possession of the land on which the work is contracted to be done."

The three criteria were established in the case itself. The plans precisely defined the builder's obligations under the contract; damages would not have been an adequate remedy as the corporation had an interest as a local authority in ensuring that a town centre site did not remain undeveloped; and since the defendant had possession of the site the corporation could not get the works completed by any other builder.

17–007   There is a settled practice of the courts not to order the specific performance of a contract requiring persons to carry on a business. The issue arose in the case of *Co-operative Insurance Society Ltd v Argyll Stores (Holdings) Ltd*.[11] In this case, the claimants had in 1979 granted the defendants a lease for a term of 35 years of a retail unit in the Hillsborough Shopping Centre, Sheffield. The defendants operated a Safeway supermarket which was the largest retail store and the greatest attraction in the complex. It was to act as an "anchor" which would be to the commercial benefit of the smaller shops in the centre and the centre as a whole. The lease contained a covenant that the defendants should keep the supermarket open for retail trade during the usual hours of business in the locality. By 1995, the store was losing money and the defendants

[9] [1986] 3 W.L.R. 531.
[10] [1901] 1 Q.B. 515.
[11] [1998] A.C. 1.

closed it down and stripped out the internal fittings. The claimants sought an order of specific performance. The judge at first instance refused to grant the order. The Court of Appeal, however, reversed that decision and ordered that the covenant should be specifically enforced. The court ordered the defendants to carry on trading on the premises until the end of the term or until an earlier sub-letting or assignment.

An appeal against the decision of the Court of Appeal was allowed by the House of Lords. Lord Hoffmann explained the basis of the "settled practice" of not ordering the defendant to carry on a business by a decree of specific performance:

> "[I]t cannot be in the public interest for the courts to require someone to carry on a business at a loss if there is any plausible alternative by which the other party can be given compensation. It is not only a waste of resources but yokes the parties together in a continuing hostile relationship. The order for specific performance prolongs the battle. If the defendant is ordered to run a business, its conduct becomes the subject of a flow of complaints, solicitors' letters and affidavits. This is wasteful for both parties and the legal system. An award of damages, on the other hand, brings the litigation to an end."

Lord Hoffmann (with whom the other members of the House agreed) found various reasons for upholding the settled practice of the courts, although none was decisive in itself. Performance of the contract would have required constant superintendence by the courts—this would possibly have necessitated an indefinite series of rulings in order to ensure the execution of the order. Failure to abide by such rulings would involve proceedings for contempt of court—this quasi-criminal procedure was a heavy-handed weapon not appropriate for the circumstances. There was also the difficulty of drawing up an order with a sufficient degree of precision so as to enable it to be specifically enforced; in *Wolverhampton Corporation v Emmons* Romer J. had emphasised the importance of defining with precision the exact nature of the works. There was a further objection to specific enforcement which was that injustice may be caused by allowing the claimant to enrich himself at the defendant's expense. The loss which the defendant might suffer through having to comply with the order could be far greater than the claimant might suffer through the contract being broken. On this point Lord Hoffmann said:

> "It is true that the defendant has, by his own breach of contract, put himself in such an unfortunate position. But the purpose of the law of contract is not to punish wrongdoing but to satisfy the expectations of the party entitled to performance. A remedy which enables him to secure, in money terms, more than the performance due to him is unjust."

The decision has been criticised as taking an over-restrictive attitude to specific enforcement **17–008** and as paying excessive regard to the interests of the contract-breaking party.

Contracts for personal services

Specific performance will not be granted where the contract involves personal services, such as **17–009** in contracts of employment, partnership and agency. It is considered undesirable to force one person to work with or for another in a personal capacity (especially when they are clearly already in dispute). As Lord Jessell M.R. explained[12]:

---

[12] *Rigby v Connol* (1880) 14 C.H. D. 482, at p.487.

"The courts have never dreamt of enforcing agreements strictly personal in their nature, whether they are agreements of hiring or service, being the common relation of master and servant, or whether they are agreements for the purpose of pleasure, or for the purpose of scientific pursuits, or for the purpose of charity or philanthropy."

The issue most commonly arises with the remedy of injunction and will be considered more fully below (see para.17–011).

Lack of mutuality

17–010   Specific performance will not, in general, be ordered against a defendant unless the remedy could have been ordered against the claimant, that is, there must be mutuality of remedy between the parties. This means that, for example, a minor will not be awarded an order of specific performance since it cannot be decreed against them.[13] In *Lumley v Ravenscroft*[14] a defendant minor granted the claimant a lease but then breached the agreement. The claimant's action for specific performance failed—there was a want of mutuality between the parties.

It seems that the relevant time for testing mutuality is the time of the trial rather than the time of the contract. In *Price v Strange*[15] the defendant promised to grant the claimant a sub-lease in return for the claimant undertaking to carry out repairs to the interior and exterior of the property. The claimant completed the repairs to the interior but before he could carry out the exterior repairs, the defendant repudiated the agreement and had the work done at her own expense. The claimant sought an order of specific performance but the judge at first instance dismissed the action on the ground that the parties were not mutual at the date of the contract, as the defendant could not have compelled the claimant to carry out the repairs. The Court of Appeal reversed that decision. Want of mutuality is to be judged on all the circumstances prevailing at the date of the hearing and not at the time of the contract; in the absence of any disqualifying circumstances the court would grant specific performance if it can be done without injustice or unfairness to the defendant.

Injunction

17–011   An injunction is an order of the court instructing a person to desist from committing a legal wrong. Injunctions may be either "mandatory" or "prohibitory".

A mandatory injunction is an order to the defendant to do some positive act to right the wrong that has been caused by a breach of contract, such as an order to demolish a building erected in breach of restrictive covenant. It is a drastic remedy and will only be ordered where absolutely necessary and only where the breach has been committed deliberately and with full knowledge of the claimant's rights.[16]

A prohibitory injunction is granted by the court in order to enforce a negative stipulation in a contract and its effect will be to restrain a party from committing a breach of contract. There is a general principle that such an injunction will not be granted if its effect would be to compel

---

[13] *Flight v Bolland* (1828) 4 Russ. 298.
[14] [1895] 1 Q.B. 683.
[15] [1978] Ch. 337.
[16] See, e.g. *Wakeham v Wood* (1982) 43 P. & C. R. 40.

the defendant to so something they could not have been ordered to do by a decree of specific performance, for example to perform a contract for personal services.

In *Lumley v Wagner*[17] the defendant agreed to sing at the claimant's theatre in Drury Lane for two nights a week for three months. During that time, she promised not to sing at any other theatre without the claimant's written consent. The defendant abandoned that contract and agreed to sing for Gye at Covent Garden for greater remuneration. The claimant sought an injunction to prevent the defendant working for Gye. The court granted the injunction. Although specific performance could not be granted of a contract for personal services, an injunction could be granted because it did not actually compel the defendant to sing for the claimant. She could have chosen not to sing at all. Lord St. Leonards, giving judgment, considered that such an injunction was entirely within the powers of the court—he recognised that he did not have the means of compelling the defendant to sing, but felt that she would have no cause to complain "if I compel her to abstain from the commission of an act which she has bound herself not to do, and thus possibly cause her to fulfil her engagement [with the claimant]."[18]

It would seem then that an injunction may be granted if its effect is to encourage and not to compel the defendant to perform a positive service. This was the conclusion of Branson J. in *Warner Bros Pictures Inc v Nelson*.[19]   **17–012**

In this case, the film actress Bette Davis agreed to act for the claimants for a period of one year, during which she undertook not to undertake other acting work for a third party without the claimants' written consent. The defendant came to England and entered into another contract with a third party to make a film. The claimants sought an injunction to restrain her breach of contract. The court granted the injunction—this would not compel her to act for the claimants because she could make a living doing other work. Endorsing the judgment of Lord St. Leonards in *Lumley v Gye*, Branson J. justified the decision in the following terms:

> "It was . . . urged that the difference between what the defendant can earn as a film artiste and what she might expect to earn by any other form of activity is so great that she will in effect be driven to perform her contract . . . The defendant is stated to be a person of intelligence, capacity and means, and no evidence was adduced to show that, if enjoined from doing the specified acts otherwise than for the [claimants], she will not be able to employ herself both usefully and remuneratively in other spheres of activity, though not as remuneratively as her special line. She will not be driven, although she may be tempted, to perform the contract."

Thus in the view of the court the defendant was not faced with the alternative of destitution or   **17–013** of service with the claimants. The injunction was to last for three years or for the continuance of the contract, whichever the shorter. Both *Lumley v Gye* and *Warner Bros v Nelson* have been criticised for coming as close to specifically enforcing contracts for personal service as makes no difference.

If the courts are to grant such injunctions as encourage rather than compel performance of personal services, the defendant must have entered into a clear negative stipulation expressly

---

[17] (1852) 1 De. G. M. & G. 604.
[18] For the sequel, see *Lumley v Gye* (1853) 2 El. & Bl. 216; there is an interesting account by Waddams (2001) L.Q.R. 431.
[19] [1937] 1 K.B. 209.

precluding the defendant from acting inconsistently with their express contract. Thus in *Whitwood Chemical Co v Hardman*[20] the defendant obtained employment from the claimants and agreed to give "the whole of his time" to his employers. From time to time, the defendant worked for others and the claimant sought to enforce the provision in his contract of service by means of an injunction. The court held that no injunction could be granted because there was no express negative stipulation—the court would not imply a negative stipulation from a positive one. The position may, however, be different in contracts other than those for personal services, thus in *Metropolitan Electric Supply Co v Ginder*,[21] which concerned a contract to supply electricity, a negative stipulation was inferred from a positive one.

17–014   In *Page One Records Ltd v Britton*,[22] Stamp J. took a different approach to that indicated above in *Lumley v Gye* and *Warner Bros v Nelson*.

The claimant was the manager of the defendants, the pop group The Troggs. The agreement between the claimant and the defendants was a standard music industry contract which was to last for five years and provided that the claimant was to receive 20 per cent of all moneys earned. The contract stipulated that the defendants were not to engage any person other than the claimant as manager or agent. The Troggs became successful and, some 14 months after entering it, repudiated the agreement. The claimant brought an action for damages and an interlocutory injunction to restrain the defendants from appointing another manager until the trial. The court refused the injunction as it would be tantamount to ordering specific performance of a contract for personal services. It was found that the defendants, being "simple persons" with no business experience, were wholly dependent on their manager for their success. They could not possibly have continued their career without a manager. Stamp J. said that the parties were tied together in a relationship of mutual confidence, trust and reciprocal obligations—on this basis *Lumley v Gye* and *Warner Bros v Nelson* could be distinguished. The relationship between the parties in those cases gave rise to no such obligations.

Page One Records v Britton was preferred by the Court of Appeal in *Warren v Mendy*[23] where an injunction was refused to compel the boxer Nigel Benn to continue to employ the exclusive services of a particular manager, Nigel Warren. The action was unusual in that it was brought not against the boxer but against a third party, Mendy, to restrain him from inducing a breach of contract by the boxer. Once again the decision was based on the nature of the relationship which was one of mutual trust and confidence. It would have been wrong to compel the performance of such a contract when the boxer had lost confidence in the manager.[24]

17–015   It seems that in very exceptional cases the courts will grant an injunction so as to compel the performance of a contract for personal services. In *Hill v C A Parsons & Co Ltd*[25] the defendant company had succumbed to the pressure of a trade union, DATA, that their employees should belong to that union. The claimant, an employee with 35 years service with the company, refused to join the union and his employers gave notice to dismiss him, although they had no

---

[20] [1891] 2 Ch. 416.
[21] [1901] 2 Ch. 799.
[22] [1968] 1 W.L.R. 157.
[23] [1989] 1 W.L.R. 853.
[24] *Warren v Mendy* was distinguished by the Court of Appeal in *Lauritzencool AB v Lady Navigation Inc* [2005] 2 Lloyd's Rep. 63 where the court granted a prohibitory injunction to prevent shipowners from using their ships inconsistently with a time charter—the case was not one involving especially personal skills or talents and the relief sought was considered to be juristically different from a decree of specific performance.
[25] [1972] Ch. 305.

wish to do so, i.e. confidence between the parties continued to exist. The Court of Appeal (Stamp J. dissenting) granted an injunction to prevent dismissal as damages would be an inadequate remedy. The majority of the court (Lord Denning M.R. and Sachs L.J.) were partly influenced by the fact that, at the time of the case, Part II of the Industrial Relations Act 1971 would shortly be in force so that the claimant could, under the Act, have sought an order allowing him to remain at work, or alternatively, claim compensation in excess of common law damages.

Damages in lieu of specific performance and injunction

Under Lord Cairns's Act (Chancery Amendment Act 1858) the Court of Chancery was given   **17–016**
the power to award damages in addition to, or in lieu of specific performance or injunction. Originally, only the common law courts could award damages. The power granted by the 1858 Act is now contained in the Supreme Court Act 1981, s.50, which provides:

> "Where the Court of Appeal or High Court has jurisdiction to entertain an application for an injunction or specific performance, it may award damages in addition to, or in substitution for, an injunction or specific performance."

Where such damages are awarded, they are assessed in the same way as common law damages for breach of contract.[26] There is, however, nothing to prevent an injured party being awarded common law damages as well as specific performance or an injunction since both remedies can be granted by the same court (Supreme Court Act 1981, s.49).

RESTITUTION

"Restitution" may be described as a legal process whereby property or money is restored to the   **17–017**
owner or the person entitled to possession of it. The underlying basis of restitution is that the property or money should be returned to the rightful owner in order to prevent "unjust enrichment". The basis upon which the courts will grant a remedy for unjust enrichment has been identified as involving three elements: (i) that the defendant has been enriched by some benefit given to him; (ii) that the enrichment has been acquired at the expense of the claimant; and (iii) that the retention of the benefit by the defendant would be unfair or unjust (Goff and Jones, *The Law of Restitution*, 6th edn, (London; Sweet & Maxwell, 2002)).

We are concerned here with that part of the law of restitution traditionally referred to as "quasi-contract". It is not strictly part of the law of contract itself because it deals with situations where there has been unjust enrichment but where there is no contract as such, for example, because the contract is void for mistake or where it has been discharged by frustration or breach; or because the parties never finally reached agreement. We shall deal with two situations—first, where a person is seeking to recover money paid to another; and secondly, where a person is seeking reasonable remuneration on a quantum meruit for a benefit provided to another.

---

[26] *Johnson v Agnew* [1980] A.C. 367.

Recovery of money paid

17–018   An action in restitution to recover money paid can be implemented in certain situations, including the following:

Total failure of consideration

17–019   "Total failure of consideration" has already been mentioned in Chapter 10 when dealing with effects of frustration. In *Fibrosa Spolka Ackyjna v Fairbairn Lawson Combe Barbour Ltd* (the facts are given at para.10–021) the Polish company, who had paid a deposit but had received nothing in return, was entitled to recover the money on the grounds of a total failure of consideration. Money had been paid to secure performance but there had been no performance; had the English company been allowed to retain the monies paid they would have been injustly enriched. One of the difficulties was that the remedy did not provide for the situation where the payee had incurred expenses in reliance on the contract (as had the English company in *Fibrosa*) and it was partly to deal with this problem that the Law Reform (Frustrated Contracts) Act 1943 was passed.

The use of the word "consideration" in this context is potentially confusing since, as we saw when considering the doctrine of consideration in Chapter 4, the promise to perform an act is just as good a consideration as the performance of the act itself. But we were concerned there with the formation of a contract. As Lord Simon explained in the *Fibrosa* case:

> "In English law, an enforceable contract may be formed by an exchange of a promise for a promise, or by the exchange of a promise for an act . . . and thus, in the law relating to the formation of a contract, the promise to do a thing may often be the consideration, but when one is considering the law of failure of consideration and of the quasi-contractual right to recover money on that ground, it is, generally speaking, not the promise that is referred to as the consideration, but the performance of the promise. The money was paid to secure performance and, if the performance fails, the inducement which brought about the payment is not fulfilled."

In dealing with frustrated contracts, another difficulty acknowledged by the House of Lords in the *Fibrosa* case was that no remedy would be available if the failure of consideration was incomplete. This is a long established principle—no claim will lie for a total failure of consideration where the failure is only partial. In *Whincup v Hughes*[27] the claimant apprenticed his son to a watchmaker and jeweller for a period of six years and paid the master a premium of £25. After one year's instruction, the master died and the claimant sought to recover the premium from the master's executrix on a failure of consideration. It was held that the action failed, the failure of consideration being only partial. As the contract was frustrated, this is the type of case where a remedy would now lie under the Law Reform (Frustrated Contracts) Act 1943 (see para.10–023).

17–020   In certain circumstances, a partial failure of consideration can be converted into a total failure of consideration—this may happen where the claimant is able to return any benefit they have received as a result of the other party's defective performance. Suppose that in a contract

[27] (1871) L.R. 6 C.P. 78.

for the sale of goods, the buyer pays the seller the purchase price in advance but the seller delivers goods which, on delivery, are found to be defective in breach of the term implied by s.14(2) of the Sale of Goods Act 1979 (see para.6–033). The purchaser has the right to repudiate the contract and recover the purchase price on the basis of a total failure of consideration. Of course, if the claimant is unable to return the benefit, the remedy will not lie, as the failure of consideration will remain partial. This may occur, for example, in the case of a partially completed building contract. Similarly, the remedy may not be obtainable where the claimant has had the use of the benefit, even if only for a short time. Thus in *Hunt v Silk*[28] under a contract for a lease the tenant paid the landlord the sum of £10 in return for a promise by the landlord to give immediate possession; to carry out repairs; and to execute a formal lease within 10 days. The tenant went into possession but the landlord failed to honour his promise and the tenant vacated the premises shortly afterwards. The tenant's action to recover the £10 failed as he had gone into occupation of the premises. The rule seems strict but it should not be forgotten that the claimant in such circumstances may well be able to recover damages for breach of contract.

In contracts for the sale of goods, failure by the seller to convey a good title to the goods to the buyer (in breach of s.12 of the Sale of Goods Act) may constitute a total failure of consideration. In *Rowland v Divall*[29] the claimant, a dealer, purchased a car from the defendant for £334. The car was delivered to the claimant and he used it for a period of four months before selling it on. It was then discovered that the defendant did not have a good title to the car and so the police repossessed it and returned it to the owner. The claimant repudiated the contract and sought to recover the £334 he had paid for the car. The Court of Appeal held that he could recover the sum on a total failure of consideration—it made no difference that he had had some use out of the vehicle. Atkin L.J. said:

> "There has been a total failure of consideration, that is to say the buyer has not got any part of that for which he paid the purchase money. He paid the money in order that he might get the property and he has not got it."

The decision in *Rowland v Divall* was applied in controversial circumstances in the case of *Butterworth v Kingsway Motors Ltd.*[30] Here the claimant bought a car from the defendant for £1,275 and used it for 12 months before it was discovered that it belonged to a finance company (since a previous keeper of the vehicle had sold the car before all the hire purchase instalments had been paid). The finance company offered to convey title to the claimant if he would pay the outstanding arrears of £125, otherwise he would have to return the car. At this point, owing to a slump in used car values, the car was now only worth £800. Nevertheless, the claimant sought to recover the sum of £1,275. Pearson J. allowed recovery of this sum even though the judge conceded that the claim lacked merit. The decision was especially regrettable since shortly after the claimant had sought the recovery of the purchase price, the original hirer had paid off the arrears so that the claimant could have acquired a good title. In *Rowland v Divall*, the purchaser was a dealer who purchased in order to resell and therefore required an immediate good title. Where the buyer is a consumer who acquires the goods in order to use them, and does use them, the remedy of total failure of consideration is less easy to justify where damages would be an

17–021

[28] (1804) 5 East. 449.
[29] [1923] 2 K.B. 500.
[30] [1954] 1 W.L.R. 1286.

adequate remedy. An award of damages would take into account the use that the buyer has had of the goods.

Mistake of fact

17–022   Money paid under a mistake of fact is recoverable if the mistake is such that the fact, if true, would have entitled the payee to payment.

In *Norwich Union Fire Insurance Society Ltd v William Price Ltd*[31] an insurance company paid the insured the full value of a cargo of citrus fruit in the mistaken belief that the goods had been sold because they had been damaged. In truth, they had been sold because the fruit had ripened too quickly; a risk for which the insured was not covered under the terms of the policy. The Privy Council held that the company was entitled to recover the payment as it had been made under a mistake of fact. It does not seem to make any difference that the party making payment should have been aware of the mistake. In *Kelly v Solari*[32] the claimant insurance company made a large payment to the defendant on her husband's death. In fact, the life assurance policy had lapsed as not all the premiums had been paid but the company had apparently forgotten this at the time of payment. It was held that the claimants were entitled to recover the amount which they had paid. The obligation to repay money paid under a mistake of fact can extend to cases where the fact, if true, would have imposed a moral (but not necessarily legal) obligation to pay.[33]

Another type of case where money will be recoverable under this heading is where money is paid under a contract that is void on the grounds of an operative common mistake of fact (see para.12–005).

Mistake of law

17–023   The traditional rule was that money paid under a mistake of law was not recoverable.[34] The rule was based on the old maxim, *ignorantia juris non excusat* ("ignorance of the law is no excuse") but it had come under increasing criticism in modern times. Why should a person be unjustly enriched by such a payment when they would not have been allowed to retain it were it made under a mistake of fact? In any event, the dividing line between law and fact is notoriously difficult for the courts to draw and in 1994 the Law Commission recommended that the rule should be abolished.[35]

The rule was overturned by the House of Lords in *Kleinwort Benson Ltd v Lincoln City Council*.[36] The appellant bank sought recovery of money advanced to local authorities under so-called "interest rate swap" agreements which were believed at the time to be valid. These transactions were subsequently held to be void by the Court of Appeal in *Hazell v London Borough of Hammersmith & Fulham*[37] on the basis that they were ultra vires the authorities

[31] [1934] A.C. 544.
[32] (1841) 9 M. & W. 54.
[33] *Larner v London County Council* [1949] 2 K.B. 683.
[34] *Bilbie v Lumley* (1802) 2 East. 469.
[35] (1994) Law. Com. No. 227.
[36] [1999] 2 A.C. 349.
[37] [1992] 2 A.C. 1.

concerned. The appellants argued in each case (there were four consolidated appeals) that they had paid the money on advice as to "settled law" that the money was paid under a binding contract. The money had therefore been paid under a mistake of law.

The House of Lords held (Lords Browne-Wilkinson and Lloyd dissenting) first, that the mistake of law rule could no longer be maintained in English law; there was no principle of that law that payments made under a settled understanding of the law which was subsequently departed from by the courts could not be recovered. Secondly, it was no defence to a claim for restitution for money or property transferred under a mistake of law that the defendant honestly believed when he learned of the transaction that he was entitled to retain the money or property. Thirdly, the fact that the contract had been fully performed did not prevent recovery on the grounds of a mistake of law. Fourthly, s.32(1)(c) of the Limitation Act 1980 (see para.17–031) applied to a cause of action for the recovery of money paid under a mistake of law, thus time does not begin to run until the claimant has discovered the mistake.

The principle enunciated by the House of Lords in the *Kleinwort Benson* v *Lincoln City Council* case was applied by Neuberger J. in *Nurdin & Peacock Plc* v *D B Ramsden & Co Ltd*[38] so as to enable an overpayment under a lease to be recovered on the basis that it had been made under a mistake of law.

Claims on a quantum meruit

A quantum meruit ("as much as he deserves") is a claim for reasonable remuneration for services performed or goods supplied. Such a claim may arise: (a) independently of a contract, for example, where the contract is void, discharged by breach or where the contract fails to materialise; or (b) it may arise within the contract itself. Only in the first situation is the remedy truly restitutionary.   **17–024**

Restitutionary claims

Recovery on a quantum meruit may be made where there is performance under a contract   **17–025** which, unknown to both parties, is void. In *Craven-Ellis* v *Canons Ltd*[39] the claimant was employed as managing director by a company under a deed under seal which provided for remuneration for his services. The articles of association of the company required that each director must obtain qualification shares within two months of appointment. Neither the claimant nor his fellow directors obtained the required number of shares with the result that the deed was invalid. The claimant had rendered services for the company and sought remuneration on a quantum meruit. The Court of Appeal held that the claimant had no contractual claim to the money but he succeeded on a quantum meruit in respect of the services he had rendered. Greer L.J. (with whom the other member of the court, Greene L.J., agreed) rejected the notion that the obligation to pay for the services rested upon an implied contract:

> "In my judgment, the obligation to pay reasonable remuneration for work done when there is no binding contract between the parties is imposed by a rule of law, and not by an inference of fact arising from the acceptance of services or goods."

[38] [1999] 1 W.L.R. 1249.
[39] [1936] 2 K.B. 403.

A claim on a quantum meruit may also arise on a breach of contract in the circumstances that arose in the case of *Planche v Colburn* (the facts are given at para.9–006). Let us suppose that A enters into a contract with B whereby A agrees to do some work for B and B agrees to pay A a sum of money on completion. When A has done only part of the work, B repudiates the contract and A accepts the repudiation as discharging the contract. A cannot maintain an action for an agreed sum because the work to be performed under the contract has not been completed. It seems that he will, however, be able to claim reasonable remuneration for the work actually done, on a quantum meruit. This principle would be consistent with the other examples of restitution that we have looked at if it could be shown that the work done by A was to the benefit of B. In *Planche v Colburn*, however, the work done by the claimant was a half completed book for a series that had been abandoned. It is difficult to see in what respect this benefited the defendant. The case is perhaps therefore best seen as an anomalous one where there can be recovery in the absence of unjust enrichment. It seems just that the claimant should recover something for his fruitless labours—after all, it was the defendant who was at fault for breaching the contract.

In addition, there will be occasions when a party carries out work in contemplation of a contract which fails to materialise. Such a situation may arise in building and construction contracts where work is begun in the expectation that a formal contract will be drawn up at a later time. This was the situation in the case of *British Steel Corporation v Cleveland Bridge & Engineering Co Ltd* (the facts are given at para.3–009) and in that case the claimant was able to recover on a quantum meruit for the value of what had been delivered to the defendants. It seems that for recovery to be possible the claimant will have to establish two things: (i) the work must have been done at the defendant's request; and (ii) the work must have been freely accepted by the defendant. It should be noted, however, that the more relaxed approach to contract formation evinced by the Court of Appeal in *G Percy Trentham Ltd v Archital Luxfer Ltd* (the case is discussed at para.2–005) may mean that the court would nowadays be more inclined to find a contract in such circumstances.

Quantum meruit as a contractual remedy

17–026   In the cases discussed in the preceding section, recovery was allowed on a quantum meruit where either no contract came into being or the contract had been discharged. In certain circumstances, recovery on a quantum meruit may be permitted where the contract continues to subsist.

One such situation is where a party breaches the contract by only partly performing their obligations under the contract. If the partial performance is voluntarily accepted by the other party (as in *Christy v Row*, discussed at para.9–005) then the party in default will be able to recover reasonable remuneration for the benefit conferred. But if the innocent party has no option but to accept the partial performance, as in *Sumpter v Hedges* (see para.9–005), quantum meruit will not apply.

Another situation where a quantum meruit may be recovered in a subsisting contract is where the contract does not include provision as to payment. In such cases the law implies an obligation to pay a reasonable sum on a quantum meruit basis. In contracts for the sale of goods this rests on a statutory footing—see Sale of Goods Act 1979, s.8(2) (discussed at para.3–010). In relation to contracts for the supply of goods and services, a similiar provision is contained in s.15 of the Supply of Goods and Services Act 1982.

LIMITATION OF ACTIONS

Rights of action for breach of contract may be extinguished: (i) by an express release by way of deed; (ii) by accord and satisfaction (see para.9–020); and (iii) by the passage of time under the provisions of the Limitation Act 1980. This Act contains time limits within which actions for breach of contract must be brought. Once the specified time limit has passed, the action becomes "statute-barred".

17–027

Simple contracts

Actions founded on a simple contract (s.5) or on a tort (s.2) shall not be brought after the expiration of six years from the date on which the cause of action accrued. The period is three years if damages are claimed for personal injuries caused by negligence, nuisance or breach of duty, whether the duty arises contractually or not (s.11) although there are provisions permitting an extension of time (s.33). In a contract action, the cause of action accrues on breach of contract, from which date time starts to run against the claimant. This is so even where the actual damage suffered by the claimant did not occur until some later date. By contrast, a cause of action in the tort of negligence accrues from when the damage occurs—it follows that where the cause of action can be formulated in either contract or tort, or both of them, there will be an advantage in bringing a tortious claim.[40]

17–028

Deeds

Where the action is founded upon a deed, the action cannot be brought after the expiration of a period of 12 years from when the cause of action accrued (s.8(1)).

17–029

Action for an account

An action for an account shall not be brought after the expiration of any time limit which is applicable to the claim which is the basis of the duty to account.

17–030

Effect of fraud or mistake

In cases of fraud or mistake, the Act of 1980, s.32(1) provides as follows:

17–031

"[W]here in the case of any action for which a period of limitation is prescribed by this Act, either –
(a) the action is based on the fraud of the defendant; or
(b) any fact relevant to the plaintiff's right of action has been deliberately concealed from him by the defendant; or

---

[40] *Midland Bank Trust Co Ltd v Hett, Stubbs and Kemp* [1979] Ch. 384.

(c) the action is for relief from the consequences of a mistake;
the period of limitation shall not begin to run until the plaintiff has discovered the fraud, concealment or mistake (as the case may be) or could with reasonable diligence have discovered it."

The application of what is now s.32(1)(b) (formerly contained in s.26 of the Limitation Act 1939) can be seen in the case of *Applegate v Moss*.[41] In 1957 the claimants purchased two houses from the defendant, an estate developer. It was agreed that the houses would be built on a type of foundation known as a "raft". The houses were completed in late 1957 and the claimants took possession of the homes. In 1965 it was discovered that the foundations had not been constructed according to specification, i.e. with a raft, and the properties were irreparably damaged and would have to be demolished. The Court of Appeal held that the claimant's right of action had been concealed by the builder (who was agent of the developer) as he had not followed the contract specification. He had installed inadequate foundations and then covered them up. The claimant's action was therefore not statute-barred—they only discovered their cause of action in 1965. In the similar case of *King v Victor Parsons & Co*[42]—where in breach of contract a house had been built on a rubbish tip without adequate foundations—it was held that the claimant's action was not statute-barred. Referring to the defendant builders' concealment, Lord Denning M.R. said:

"It may be that [the defendant] has no dishonest motive; but that does not matter. He has kept [the claimant] out of the knowledge of his right of action; and that is enough."

The meaning of the words "reasonable diligence" in s.32(1)(c) of the Act arose in the case of *Peco Arts Inc v Hazlitt Gallery Ltd*.[43] The claimants purchased a drawing from the defendants in 1970 for $18,000, relying on the recommendation of a specialist. Both parties believed the work to be an original by Ingres. When the piece was revalued for the second time in 1981 it was discovered that it was a copy and worth virtually nil. The defendants admitted liability but argued that the claim was statute-barred. Webster J. held that there had been no lack of diligence on the part of the claimants and they were therefore protected by s.32(1)(c)—they were granted rescission of the contract and recovered the purchase price. The judge explained that:

"[R]easonable diligence means not the doing of everything possible, not necessarily the using of any means at the [claimant's] disposal, not necessarily the doing of anything at all, but that it means the doing of that which an ordinary prudent buyer and possessor of a valuable work of art would do having regard to all the circumstances, including the circumstances of the purchase."

17–032   In this case, the claimants had relied on the recommendations of an expert; had bought from a reputable dealer; and on the fact that the first revaluation had apparently authenticated the drawing. They had acted with reasonable diligence.

---

[41] [1971] 1 Q.B. 406.
[42] [1973] 1 W.L.R. 29.
[43] [1983] 1 W.L.R. 1315.

Effect of disability

For the purposes of the Act, a person shall be treated as being under a disability while they are a minor or where they lack capacity (within the meaning of the Mental Capacity Act 2005) to conduct legal proceedings (s.38).

17–033

Where the claimant is under such disability when the cause of action accrues, the period of limitation does not start to run until their contractual disability ends, or until their death, whichever event occurs first (s.28(1)). There is no extension of time unless the disability exists when the cause of action accrues. Thus, when time has begun to run, it is not stopped by the subsequent occurrence of some disability—for example, if the claimant becomes mentally unsound after the cause of action accrues (s.28(2)).

Effect of acknowledgment or part payment

The Limitation Act 1980, s.29(5) provides:

17–034

> "[W]here any right of action has accrued to recover –
> (a) any debt or other liquidated pecuniary claim . . .
> and the person liable or accountable for the claim acknowledges the claim or makes any payment in respect of it the right shall be treated as having accrued on and not before the date of the acknowledgment or payment."

Thus if, in the period of limitation commencing with the accrual of a cause of action for a debt, the debtor acknowledges the debt or makes a part payment in respect of it, time begins to run afresh. In s.30 of the Act it is further provided:

> "(1) To be effective for the purposes of section 29 of this Act, an acknowledgment must be in writing and signed by the person making it.
> (2) For the purposes of s.29, any acknowledgment or payment –
> (a) may be made by the agent of the person by whom it is required to be made under that section; and
> (b) shall be made to the person, or to an agent of the person, whose title or claim is being acknowledged or, as the case may be, in respect of whose claim the payment is being made."

Providing it indicates that a debt is due, an acknowledgment need not specify the amount nor even have been written for the purpose. In *Dungate v Dungate*[44] a debtor wrote to his creditor saying, "Keep a check on totals and amounts I owe you and we will have account now and then." These words were held in the circumstances to be a sufficient acknowledgment of the debt even though no amount was stated—the court held that time ran afresh from the date of the letter and the claim was not statute-barred. That a person cannot be compelled to acknowledge a debt is illustrated by *Lovell v Lovell*[45] where, in pre-trial civil proceedings the claimant served interrogatories on the alleged debtor asking whether on a certain date he had owed money to the claimant, and if so, to specify the amount. The Court of Appeal held that the

---

[44] [1965] 1 W.L.R. 1477.
[45] [1970] 1 W.L.R. 1451.

questions need not be answered—to force a debtor to acknowledge a debt in this way would mean that no person could ever rely on the Limitation Act. The acknowledgment must be voluntary even though, of course, it might be given unwittingly by the debtor.

Effect of the statute

17–035   When a claim is statute-barred, the claimant's legal liability is not extinguished; rather, the claimant's suit is not actionable (nor is he entitled to a set-off). Thus the statute is essentially procedural rather than substantive—it follows that if the claimant has other means of obtaining satisfaction he may exploit them. For example, if the creditor has a lien and obtains possession of the debtor's goods, he may retain them until the debtor satisfies the debt even if it is statute-barred.

Equity

17–036   The Limitation Act, s.36(1) provides that the statutory limitation provisions do not apply to specific performance, injunction or any other equitable relief. However, this proposition requires further elaboration.

First, where a suit in equity corresponds to an action in law (e.g. proceedings in the Chancery Division involving the recovery of a simple contract debt) then equity acts on the analogy of the statute and applies the same limitation periods as the statute.

Secondly, in the case of purely equitable claims (e.g. rescission for misrepresentation) the court applies the doctrine of laches—delay. Thus the equitable remedy will be denied where there has been delay in bringing proceedings on the part of the claimant; see, for example, *Leaf v International Galleries* (discussed at para.11–033).

Further remedies and limitation of actions: conclusion

17–037   As a final observation we should note that "restitition" in the sense that it has been used in this chapter should be distinguished from "restitutionary damages" discussed in the previous chapter (see para.16–007). In the latter case, a party has made a profit as a result of committing a breach of contract but the innocent party has suffered no measurable loss. The question that arises is whether the contract-breaking party should account for the profits they have made. This is quite distinct from the forms of quasi-contractual restitution examined earlier in this chapter which arise from situations where there has been unjust enrichment but recovery is not on the basis of the existence of a contract.

Further reading

Jones, *Specific Performance: A Lessee's Covenant to Keep Open a Retail Store* [1997] C.L.J. 488.
Kronman, *Specific Performance* (1978) University of Chicago Law Review 351.
Virgo, *Recent Developments in Restitution of Mistaken Payments* [1999] C.L.J. 479.
Birks, *An Introduction to the Law of Restitution* (Oxford: Oxford University Press, 1985).
Goff and Jones, *The Law of Restitution*, 6th edn (London: Sweet and Maxwell, 2002).

INDEX

LEGAL TAXONOMY
FROM SWEET & MAXWELL

This index has been prepared using Sweet and Maxwell's Legal Taxonomy. Main index entries conform to keywords provided by the Legal Taxonomy except where references to specific documents or non-standard terms (denoted by quotation marks) have been included. These keywords provide a means of identifying similar concepts in other Sweet & Maxwell publications and online services to which keywords from the Legal Taxonomy have been applied. Readers may find some minor differences between terms used in the text and those which appear in the index. Suggestions to sweetandmaxwell.taxonomy@thomson.com.

(All references are to paragraph number)

Acceptance
  "battle of the forms", 2–027—2–030
  communication
    conduct of offeror, 2–036
    generally, 2–033
    Internet, 2–051
    post, 2–035—2–048
    telephone, 2–049—2–050
    telex, 2–049—2–050
    unilateral contracts, 2–034
  conditional upon events, 2–031—2–032
  conduct, by, 2–037
  counter-offer, 2–025
  generally, 2–023
  ignorance of offer, in, 2–052
  Internet, 2–051
  "mirror image rule", 2–024
  post, by
    circumstances in which not apply,
      2–044—2–046
    exclusion by offeror, 2–046
    generally, 2–042—2–043
    improperly posted letter, 2–044
    introduction, 2–035
    misaddressed letter, 2–045
    reasonable method, and, 2–047
    retraction, 2–048
  prescribed method, by, 2–040—2–041
  request for information, 2–026
  requirements
    unconditional, 2–031—2–032
    unqualified, 2–024—2–030
  silence, by, 2–038—2–039
  standard terms, 2–027
  telephone, 2–049—2–050

  telex, 2–049—2–050
Account of profits
  damages, and, 16–007—16–010
Actual undue influence
  generally, 13–017—13–018
  introduction, 13–016
Advertisements
  intention to create legal relations, 3–024—3–035
  invitation to treat, and, 2–010—2–011
Affirmation
  duress, and, 13–014
  misrepresentation, and, 11–032
  undue influence, and, 13–031
Agency
  breach of warranty of authority, 8–029
  generally, 8–024—8–025
  ratification, 8–026
  undisclosed principal, 8–027—8–028
  undue influence, and, 13–036
Agreement
  discharge, and
    bilateral discharge, 9–019
    consideration, 9–017—9–020
    formalities, 9–021
    introduction, 9–017
    unilateral discharge, 9–020
    variation of terms, and, 9–022
    waiver, 9–022
  introduction, 2–001
  judicial approaches, 2–004—2–006
  objective test, 2–002—2–003
Assignment
  privity of contract, 8–030
Auctions
  invitation to treat, and, 2–015—2–016